THE OXFORD HANDBOOK OF

EGYPTIAN EPIGRAPHY AND PALAEOGRAPHY

THE OXFORD HANDBOOK OF

EGYPTIAN EPIGRAPHY AND PALAEOGRAPHY

Edited by

VANESSA DAVIES

and

DIMITRI LABOURY

OXFORD
UNIVERSITY PRESS

OXFORD
UNIVERSITY PRESS

Oxford University Press is a department of the University of Oxford. It furthers
the University's objective of excellence in research, scholarship, and education
by publishing worldwide. Oxford is a registered trade mark of Oxford University
Press in the UK and certain other countries.

Published in the United States of America by Oxford University Press
198 Madison Avenue, New York, NY 10016, United States of America.

Library of Congress Control Number: 2020930581

ISBN 978–0–19–060465–3

1 3 5 7 9 8 6 4 2

Printed by Sheridan Books, Inc., United States of America

Contents

III. TRADITIONAL AND NEW TECHNIQUES OF EPIGRAPHY

IV. ISSUES IN PALAEOGRAPHY

Acknowledgments

First, we would like to express our deepest gratitude to Stefan Vranka, our editor at Oxford University Press and a figure ubiquitous in the field of the ancient Mediterranean world, for his constant support as we worked on this Handbook. His enthusiasm for the project and his realization of the great need for it was clear from our very first meeting. Sarah Svendsen, John Veranes, and Alexia Sereti, also of Oxford University Press, provided us with much assistance along the way. At the beginning of the project, Georgia Irby generously shared her expertise after having recently edited a large collected volume. We dodged a few issues that we would not have foreseen except for her advice. A number of people helped us in our early stages, including Terry Wilfong, Betsy Bryan, Glenn Godenho, Joyce Tyldesley, Ray Johnson, Violaine Chauvet, Simon Connor, Hughes Tavier, and Stéphane Polis. Many of the authors in this Handbook shared their time with us, discussing issues related to the web side of this project, including Ginger Emery, Chiara Salvador, Hanane Gaber, and Jan Moje. On a sad note, one of our intended authors, Brian Curran, died after a long illness. In terms of scholarship, he has left a great legacy in art history, Classics, and Egyptology, and his passing is a great loss for all three fields. At the Egypt Exploration Society, Carl Graves and Brigitte Balanda were so helpful when Vanessa visited there to research her chapter. Other colleagues who assisted us during this process include JJ Shirley, Carol Redmount, Ben Porter, Ron Hendel, and Michael Nylan. Warm thanks are due also to Serge Rosmorduc for allowing free access to JSesh, his invaluable word processor for hieroglyphic texts. Finally, we gratefully acknowledge the assistance of the American Research Center in Egypt. Generous support from their Antiquities Endowment Fund enabled us to include in this publication color images, which are vital to illustrate the points made by the authors.

List of Contributors

Mohamed Sherif Ali is Lecturer Professor, Department of Egyptology, Rheinische Friedrich-Wilhelms-Universität Bonn, Associate Professor of Egyptology, Cairo University

Niv Allon is Associate Curator in the Department of Egyptian Art at The Metropolitan Museum of Art

Tamás A. Bács is Associate Professor of Egyptology at Eötvös Loránd University

Andrew Bednarski is Affiliated Scholar, McDonald Institute for Archaeological Research, University of Cambridge

Anne Boud'hors is Directrice de recherche at CNRS, Institut de recherche et d'histoire des textes, section Grecque et de l'Orient chrétien, Paris

Peter J. Brand is Professor of History, University of Memphis, and Director, Karnak Hypostyle Hall Project, University of Memphis

Vanessa Davies is Associate Director of Institutional Grants and Research Grants Compliance Manager, Bryn Mawr College

Peter Der Manuelian is Barbara Bell Professor of Egyptology and Director, Harvard Semitic Museum, Harvard University

Andrés Diego Espinel is Senior Scientist, Instituto de Lenguas y Culturas-CSIC, Madrid

Koenraad Donker van Heel is Lecturer in Demotic, Papyrologisch Instituut Leiden

Hans-Werner Fischer-Elfert is Professor of Egyptology, Ägyptologisches Institut & Ägyptisches Museum-Georg Steindorff-der Universität Leipzig

Virginia L. Emery is Program Manager of the Center for Adult and Returning Students, University of Wisconsin – Parkside

Hanane Gaber is Membre associé, UMR 5140, Université Paul-Valéry Montpellier 3, France and Chercheur associé, Chaire de la Civilisation pharaonique, Collège de France, Paris, France

Éric Gady is an independent researcher and teacher at Education Nationale in France

Svenja A. Gülden is project coordinator and scientific researcher of the project Altägyptische Kursivschriften (Akademie der Wissenschaften und der Literatur | Mainz) at the Johannes Gutenberg-Universität | Mainz and the Technische Universität Darmstadt

Lucie Jirásková is a PhD candidate at the Czech Institute of Egyptology, Charles University

Jannik Korte works on the Demotic Palaeographical Database Project at the Ägyptologisches Institut at the Universität Heidelberg

Celia Krause is a scientific librarian in the field of digital humanities at Darmstadt Technical University Library

Dieter Kurth is Director of the Edfu-Projekt and Professor Emeritus of Egyptology at the University of Hamburg

Dimitri Laboury is Research Director of the Belgian National Fund for Scientific Research (FRS-FNRS) and Associate Professor of ancient Egyptian art history and archaeology at the University of Liège

Christian E. Loeben is Keeper of Egyptian and Islamic Art, Museum August Kestner, Hanover

Rita Lucarelli is Associate Professor of Egyptology, University of California, Berkeley

Claudia Maderna-Sieben works on The Demotic Palaeographical Database Project at the Ägyptologisches Institut at the Universität Heidelberg

Lise Manniche is formerly Assistant Professor at the University of Copenhagen

J. Brett McClain is Assistant Director, Epigraphic Survey, Oriental Institute, University of Chicago

Dimitri Meeks is Directeur de recherche honoraire, CNRS, and Collaborateur scientifique de l'UMR 8546, Archéologie et Philologie d'Orient et d'Occident, École Normale Supérieure-CNRS-EPHE-PSL

Jan Moje is Wissenschaftlicher Angestellter at the Ägyptisches Museum und Papyrussammlung Staatliche Museen zu Berlin, ERC Project ELEPHANTINE, and Privatdozent at Freie Universität Berlin, Ägyptologisches Seminar

Ludwig Morenz is Professor in Egyptology, Rheinische Friedrich-Wilhelms-Universität Bonn, and Director of Ägyptisches Museum Bonn

Hana Navratilova is Research Associate, Department of Classics, University of Reading, and Visiting Scholar, Wolfson College, University of Oxford

Boyo G. Ockinga is Associate Professor of Ancient History, Macquarie University, Sydney, Australia

Laure Pantalacci is Professor Emerita of Egyptology at Université Lumière Lyon 2, HiSoMA (CNRS-UMR 5189)

Gabriele Pieke is Curator and Head of the Egyptian Department, Reiss-Engelhorn-Museen, Mannheim

Stéphane Polis is Research Associate of the Belgian National Fund for Scientific Research (FRS-FNRS)

Joachim Quack is Director of the Ägyptologisches Institut at the Universität Heidelberg

Ilona Regulski is Curator, Egyptian Written Culture, Department of Egypt and Sudan, The British Museum

Jean Revez is Professor in History, Université du Québec à Montréal, and Co-Director of the Karnak Hypostyle Hall Project

Chiara Salvador is Co-Director of the Ptah Graffiti Project at Karnak

William Schenck is a freelance archaeological illustrator

Frédéric Servajean is Professor of Egyptology at the Université Paul-Valéry Montpellier 3, UMR 5140

Andréas Stauder is Professor of Egyptology at the École Pratique des Hautes Études, Université Paris Sciences et Lettres (EPHE, PSL)

Julie Stauder-Porchet is Swiss National Science Foundation–Professor at the University of Geneva

Denys A. Stocks, Litt.D. is an Experimental Archaeologist

Annette Sundermeyer is a PhD candidate at the Institut für Archäologie, Humboldt-Universität zu Berlin

Christophe Thiers is Directeur de recherche au CNRS, UMR 5140-Archéologie des sociétes méditerranéennes, Montpellier

Claude Traunecker is Professor Emeritus of Egyptology, Université de Strasbourg, and Director of the TT 33 project, the Tomb of Padiamenope

Gemma Tully is Research Associate, McDonald Institute for Archaeological Research, University of Cambridge

Ursula Verhoeven is Professor of Egyptology, Johannes Gutenberg-Universität, Mainz

Pascal Vernus is Directeur d'Études émérite, École Pratique des Hautes Études IVème Section, En Sorbonne, Paris

Krisztián Vértes is Egyptologist, Senior Artist at the Epigraphic Survey of the Oriental Institute, University of Chicago

Willeke Wendrich is Professor of Egyptian Archaeology and Digital Humanities, Joan Silsbee Chair of African Cultural Archaeology, and Director of the Cotsen Institute of Archaeology, UCLA

Fabian Wespi works on the Demotic Palaeographical Database Project at the Ägyptologisches Institut at the Universität Heidelberg

Jean Winand is First Vice Rector and Professor of Egyptology at the University of Liège

INTRODUCTION

VANESSA DAVIES AND DIMITRI LABOURY

"Whereas pure scholarship dates rapidly, faithful copies grow in value according as destruction exacts its relentless toll."

Alan H. Gardiner, quoted as an incipit (Caminos 1976, 1).

ANCIENT DECORATION

THE unique relationship between word and image in Egyptian epigraphy is a defining feature of that ancient culture's records. A discussion of the written word in ancient Egypt is almost inevitably accompanied by a consideration of images, and the study of Egyptian images always implies an acknowledgment of the written word. The connection between word and image in the ancient Egyptian way of thinking and expressing oneself is probably best exemplified in hieroglyphic writing, whose various signs represent sounds (phonograms), as an alphabet does, but also ideas or objects (ideograms) and subject-matter clues or semantic categories (determinatives or classifiers). Regardless of the type of hieroglyph—phonogram, ideogram, or determinative—the hieroglyph itself is fundamentally a picture, an image of something from the natural or imagined worlds of ancient Egypt. Thus, all hieroglyphic texts are composed of images. Much of the large-scale depictions of humans, deities, and scenes from the natural world that appear on the walls of Egyptian temples and tombs are accompanied by texts that add information to the large depictions, which themselves might be thought of, at least in some cases, as hieroglyphs or hieroglyphic compositions (Vernus 1987).

Other Egyptian scripts move further away from the close connection between text and image that can be found in hieroglyphic writing and in the images that often accompany hieroglyphs. Hieratic, the cursive form of hieroglyphs, often retains a clear association with hieroglyphic images. Demotic and abnormal hieratic are even more cursive, and the connection between image-hieroglyph and written sign in those scripts is much less clear to modern readers and may have also been so for ancient readers.

With Coptic, the Egyptian language was written in a modified Greek alphabet, thus losing any connection with the hieroglyphic writing system (despite a few signs, borrowed from Demotic, that derived from the hieroglyphic system).

In the strictest sense of the words, epigraphy and palaeography are two distinct, but closely related, ways of analyzing and understanding ancient texts and images. In Egyptology, recording decoration becomes intimately associated with both practices. Thus, for Egyptologists, epigraphy and palaeography have value in both a heuristic and hermeneutic sense, that is, in the observation and recording of material and also in the analysis and interpretation of that material. In this Handbook, we stress the technical, or heuristic, issue of how to record text and art and the hermeneutical questions of what we do with those records and why we do it.

Epigraphy refers to carved and painted decoration, which comprises small- and large-scale figural depictions, divided by modern Egyptological convention into text and art although perhaps not so distinct to an ancient viewer (Fischer 1986). The decorations found on the walls of temples and tombs are common subjects of epigraphic study, as are those found on statues and stelae and the graffiti found carved and painted in places up and down the Nile River Valley and in many locales in the Eastern and Western deserts. The concerns of the epigrapher include the recording and translation of decoration, its social and cultural history, and its interpretations. Content, context, and form, such as hieroglyph, hieratic writing, or large image, contribute to the interpretation of ancient decoration.

Palaeography refers to the study of the change over time and space in the form of the writing. This can include the study of individual signs, sign groupings, whole words, and other combinations. Outside of Egyptology, palaeography typically refers to script, but again, because of the pictorial nature of the hieroglyphic and hieratic writing systems, palaeography might also refer to the images that go along with word (Laboury 2012, 203). The palaeographer often works with texts written on papyri or ostraca, but monumental texts, such as those written in hieroglyphs, are increasingly being studied palaeographically. With palaeography, form, the methodology of the ancient carver/painter/writer, and regional and local variations are crucial factors to consider. Decoration that contains multiple hands, that is to say, was executed by multiple individuals, might, of course, also raise questions of content and context.

THE LINK BETWEEN IMAGE AND TEXT

In Egyptian epigraphy, there can be no real separation between image and text (Fischer 1986). Figural and textual decoration are linked in the ancient Egyptian culture in two key ways. The hieroglyphic writing system, and by extension the hieratic as well, uses images as the very building blocks of words. Through their complex work, hieroglyphic and hieratic images unite vision, sound, and meaning (Vernus 1990; see chapter by Vernus, in this volume). A second link between image and text occurs when written words accompany the figural depiction, typically enhancing, expanding on, or specifying the image's meaning. In these cases, the decoration conveys information to the reader/viewer on two distinct levels: as the figural depiction and as the associated written text.

Image and text in Egypt may be approached on two levels: the object represented and the meaning communicated. In other words, the analysis of epigraphic content on separate levels allows one to consider, in Saussurian terms, the signifier and the signified. The pictorial nature of the Egyptian hieroglyphic writing system provides a connection between the original linguistic approach of Saussure ([1916] 1971) and subsequent understandings of his terms in twentieth-century art historical discourse. Egyptian hieroglyphs provide visual clues to the reader in the form of the determinative placed after the word, to dictate or reinforce what may be called the signified (Goldwasser and Grinevald 2012). Rebuses and other alternative writings suggest more visually than what is said on a purely linguistic level (Vernus 1982). One may even take the analysis a step further to the level of individual hieroglyph. Each sign that represents a sound or group of sounds (or phoneme) in a word can be examined both separately from and in relation to the concept that the word might have evoked in the mind of the viewer. For example, the word *is*, "tomb," is discussed in terms of the depictions and uses of some of its component hieroglyphic parts, specifically, the biliteral hieroglyph *is* (Gardiner M40), the house determinative (O1), and the coffin determinative (Q6), as well as concrete realities of burial in a reed mat, as known from archaeological and artistic examples (Régen 2008). A similar process can be applied to larger-scale depictions. The interplay between the depiction and the accompanying text becomes evident when image and text communicate different messages and when the image functions not only as a figural depiction but also as a determinative to words or concepts expressed in the text (Fischer 1986; Parkinson 1999, 114).

As the study of inscribed decoration, epigraphy necessarily focuses on records carved in or painted on stone. For this reason, the preponderance of material analyzed in this volume is monumental, that is, texts intended to serve as permanent records. Epigraphy, however, is closely connected to the study of palaeography, which is the study of the actual strokes of chisel or paintbrush of artists, draftsmen, and scribes, their so-called handwriting. For this reason, Part IV of this volume addresses a variety of concerns related to the study of the palaeography of both monumental and documentary texts, such as those found on papyri and ostraca.

Monumental records operate within particular codes, that is, the linguistic and cultural milieux specific to the text/art (Jakobson 1960). For example, the hierarchy of scale that is applied to Egyptian renderings of human and divine figures is a particular code that communicates information about the social and ideological positions of the individuals represented. Unless the viewer is familiar with the Egyptian convention of scale—that the relative size of the individual's representation reflected the individual's social status or importance—one will not understand the visual message communicated. Such a code applied to writing, as well, and influenced word choice, topics of texts, and types of representation (Assmann 1987; Baines 1990). Thus, images and text communicated multivalent messages to the viewing and reading audiences.

Importance of Epigraphy and Palaeography in Egyptology

The scientific research of Egyptology has been greatly enhanced by the linguistic understanding of the ancient writing systems. The decipherment of hieroglyphs was famously achieved after the discovery of the Rosetta Stone in 1799. Other scholars studied and continue to study the intricacies of the cursive scripts of hieratic and Demotic, as well as Meroitic, a related African writing system. Although the recording of epigraphic decoration long predates the discovery of the Rosetta Stone, the subdisciplines of epigraphy and palaeography, as we practice them today, owe much to the discovery of that famous tablet and were forever changed because of the knowledge of the ancient writing systems that were derived from it.

Before the Rosetta Stone's decipherment, which provided access to large numbers of ancient texts, the ancient culture of Egypt was accessed primarily through its large built structures decorated with silent images that could be seen but not "heard" by a modern audience who had lost the knowledge of the ancient language. The translation of hieroglyphic texts into modern languages brought to life not just writing, but also the large-scale figurative images that had for so long stood silently on the walls of the ancient monuments. The interplay of text and image, so critical to the ancient monuments and likewise to epigraphic work, are a hallmark of Egyptian decoration.

Approach of This Volume

This Handbook aims to

- discuss current theories with regard to the cultural setting and material realities in which Egyptian epigraphy was produced;
- familiarize the reader with epigraphic techniques and practices; and
- outline and review traditional and emerging techniques and challenges as a guide for future research.

Taken as a whole, the chapters offer: a diachronic perspective, covering all ancient Egyptian scripts from the fourth millennium BCE through the first half of the first millennium CE, that is, from prehistoric Egypt through the Coptic era, a perspective on recording techniques that considers the past, present, and future, and a focus on the experiences of colleagues.

By focusing on all scripts, the Handbook addresses a range of techniques used to record different phases of writing in different media. Readers can compare and contrast methods and approaches across time frame and language groups. By including all phases of ancient

Egyptian history in this volume, we aim to unite the writings of those time periods within the disciplines of epigraphy and palaeography.

The current, historical, and future methodologies and technologies that are addressed in these chapters allow readers to consider how and why we preserve and interpret ancient art and text, as well as how, and where possible why, previous generations of people have preserved and interpreted them with an eye toward the approaches we see in our futures. Readers can understand and assess why epigraphy and palaeography are or were done in a particular manner by stressing the essential and inextricable link between the aims of an epigraphic or palaeographic effort and the technique chosen to reach those aims. Authors address the present, as well as the beginning of the previous century that is, in a way, still part of the present, and future, or what we may imagine about the future. We stress that the choice of epigraphic techniques is always a matter of goals (e.g., whether the epigrapher is primarily interested in content, form, style, materiality, etc.) and of the work circumstances of the records. This is an inevitable consequence of the fact that epigraphy is a double projection: a geometrical projection, transcribing in two dimensions an object that is always physically in three dimensions (including paintings); but also a mental projection, that is, an interpretation, with an inevitable selection among the characteristics that actually define the recorded object.

The experiences of colleagues provide a range of approaches to particular challenges, techniques of recording, and ways of reading and interpreting text and image. We focus on practicalities in order to allow the book to fulfill its goal as a true handbook, a guide for beginners, whether students or confirmed scholars who face new and challenging situations, through possible choices that will have to be made in order to meet their documentary and interpretative objectives. Many of the chapters in Parts III (Traditional and New Techniques of Epigraphy) and IV (Issues in Palaeography) contain first-person narratives about experiences in epigraphy and palaeography (e.g., Kurth, Schenck, Salvador). The practice of these two fields is very much dependent on assessing the particular situation of the epigrapher or palaeographer—among many factors, there is the nature of the ancient material, the medium, the natural and built environment around it, the purpose for recording—and then adapting one's techniques to infinitely varying situations and to unforeseen circumstances that inevitably arise. It is hoped that this book's historiographical approach to the past and the present and its glimpse into the future will ensure its longevity as a useful resource.

It is important to note that for the past few years, the Ministry of Antiquities in Egypt has forbidden tracing on plastic film. This method of copying decoration was used by many epigraphers, both historically and in contemporary times. The Ministry's ban occurred while this Handbook was in production, so some authors may discuss tracing as a recording technique, but that is because those chapters were written before the ban was put into place. Epigraphic missions that had employed tracing as a copying technique are now turning to digital epigraphy.

Part I, "Cultural and Material Setting," presents issues relevant to the epigraphic and palaeographic study of decoration and discusses current theories with regard to the cultural setting and the material realities in which Egyptian carved and painted texts and images were produced. This section begins with an in-depth discussion of the relationship between the figurative hieroglyphic writing system and figurative images (Vernus). Two fundamental questions concerning Egyptian epigraphic decoration are how to interpret those texts, for example, literally or figuratively (Allon), and how the idea of permanence relates to those texts (Ockinga). The study of epigraphic decoration usually spans multiple disciplines that are separate in a traditional university context. To bridge those divides, chapters discuss epigraphic decoration in relation to how we reconstruct Egyptian history (Brand) and in relation to other ancient texts, such as literary, religio-magical, and administrative texts (Stauder-Porchet and Stauder). To explain how and why the ancient carved and painted decoration was made, chapters address the questions of who created the decoration (Laboury), who read and saw the decoration (Navratilova), and how stone and other materials were worked (Stocks). This part concludes with a discussion of Egyptian decoration from the perspective of art history and as compared with the demands of epigraphy and palaeography (Pieke).

Part II, "Historical Efforts at Epigraphy," treats a variety of past attempts to record ancient epigraphic decoration in order to familiarize the reader with receptions, records, and interpretations of Egyptian texts and art. The purpose(s) behind recording and ana-lyzing ancient decoration may determine the technique(s) used to make records. For example, a drawing on an ostracon might indicate either an artist's informal sketch or an apprentice's formal, though perhaps inexpert, attempt to practice rendering Egyptian art (see chapter by Bács, in this volume). Beginning with the ancient Egyptians themselves (Bács), who showed an interest in studying, copying, and modifying their own decoration, the section moves chronologically through Classical and Late Antiquity (Winand), the period after the Islamic conquest of Egypt (Sundermeyer), Medieval and Renaissance Europe (Jirásková), and the scientific expedition that accompanied the French military campaign in Egypt of 1798–1801 (Gady). These are historical moments when knowledge of the ancient writing system was lost, but there was nevertheless a strong interest in copying and trying to understand the decoration. The chapter on the Rosetta Stone (Regulski) ushers in the era when epigraphers could actually read the ancient texts. Many examples of ancient decoration that are now lost to us due to theft, natural wear, and intentional damage were preserved in copies made by adventurous travelers to Egypt and the Sudan (Manniche), a large expedition funded by the king of Prussia and headed by Karl Richard Lepsius (Loeben), and the work of subsequent epigraphers, first many who worked without the benefit of institutional or governmental backing (Emery) and later, those who worked under the auspices of research societies and academic institutions (Davies).

The age of epigraphic missions funded by academic institutions and scholarly foundations begins in Part III, "Traditional and New Techniques of Epigraphy," which outlines traditional and emerging techniques and challenges in the recording and inter-preting of ancient decoration in the modern era. The section moves through various site-specific and technique-specific reviews, such as a general discussion of publishing temples (Traunecker), a narrative focusing particularly on experiences at Edfu Temple (Kurth), the techniques developed by and named for the French mission to Karnak

Temple (Thiers) and the American mission based at Chicago House in Luxor (McClain), and a retrospective of the career of an epigrapher who participated in many significant projects (Schenck). Various digital techniques are outlined (Wendrich, Vértes, Revez), and an overview of issues related to digital epigraphy, past and present, is given by one of the earliest Egyptological innovators in this area (Manuelian). Specific challenges are addressed with regard to work in temples versus in tombs (Gaber), on recording graffiti and informal decoration (Salvador), and in reference to the study and restoration/restitution of ancient decoration that had been severely damaged (Diego Espinel). When methodological or analytical issues arise in relation to the particular type of script being recorded, the epigrapher/palaeographer must be prepared to adapt to changing circumstances. Such issues are addressed with regard to archaic decoration (Morenz), Ptolemaic hieroglyphs (Pantalacci), and Demotic (Moje). Mindful of the fact that the ancient decoration does not exist in a vacuum, but shares the landscape with contemporary inhabitants of the Nile River Valley, one chapter explores the complexities of ancient and contemporary lives when scientific and academic pursuits overlap or interfere with political, economic, and social considerations (Bednarski and Tully).

Part IV, "Issues in Palaeography," reviews methodologies and challenges in the study of the palaeographies of various ancient Egyptian scripts. The first chapter bridges the fields of epigraphy and palaeography in a discussion of the significance of medium in the two subfields (Meeks). Issues and methodologies are laid out in the study of various scripts, such as hieroglyphs (Servajean), hieratic (Polis), carved hybrid scripts (Ali), the so-called *Totenbuch kursiv* (Lucarelli), abnormal hieratic (Donker van Heel), Demotic (Quack, Korte, Wespi, and Maderna-Sieben), and Coptic (Boud'hors). Other issues discussed are techniques for palaeographic study in relation to a new digital initiative (Gülden, Krause, and Verhoeven) and the workmen's community at Deir el-Medina (Fischer-Elfert), where an unusually high rate of literacy and much background information about the people who lived in that community contribute to rich discussions about script and handwriting.

PAST, PRESENT, AND FUTURE OF EPIGRAPHIC AND PALAEOGRAPHIC EFFORTS

Techniques of analyzing epigraphic and palaeographic texts and images are changing quickly, not only because of changes in the technology that epigraphers and palaeographers often use but also because of the creativity and ingenuity of the epigraphers and palaeographers who study ancient texts and images and because of the changing nature of historical questions posed by researchers. New approaches to recording information and new challenges encountered in the field and in the museum have led and will continue to lead to groundbreaking ways of documenting and thinking about the carved and painted records of ancient Egypt. The recording techniques described in this volume will stand as a historical record of how work has been done in our discipline and why it had or has to be done in that way at a particular moment in time, that is, how the purposes and techniques of recording changed over time to meet different ends. The types of information derived from epigraphic and palaeographic sources, such as constructing chronologies, providing information on social and cultural history, making connections between and among texts or images, and adding to an understanding of the linguistic, writing, and artistic systems, will change and grow over time, spurred on by the questions that we ask of and through the ancient records and informed by the theoretical contributions of other fields and the discovery of new archaeological and epigraphic finds in our own field.

This Handbook is as much about epigraphers and palaeographers as it is about epigraphy and palaeography. All Egyptologists who work in these subdisciplines will have their own perspectives and opinions about issues such as methodology and techniques of recording and ways of reading and interpreting text and image. The variety of approaches to epigraphy and palaeography enriches our field of study and allows for a lively debate and exchange of information and perspectives. For that reason, this Handbook records the individual experiences of the practitioners of epigraphy and palaeography: the particular difficulties and trials, the puzzles and conundrums, the creative solutions, temporary work-arounds, and paths for future work development that constitute the interesting and instructive stories of human innovation. In these chapters, the recorders briefly become the recorded. As editors, we care as much for the people doing this work—their scientific aims and their hopes for future research—as we do for the critical service they do in preserving, recording, deciphering, interpreting, and disseminating the ancient monumental and nonmonumental text and image of the African land on which we have focused our careers.

BIBLIOGRAPHY

Assmann, J. 1987. "Hierotaxis: Textkonstitution und Bildkomposition in der altägyptischen Kunst und Literatur." In *Form und Mass: Beiträge zur Literatur, Sprache und Kunst des alten Ägypten. Festschrift für Gerhard Fecht zum 65. Geburtstag am 6. Februar 1987*, edited by J. Osing and G. Dreyer, 18–42. ÄAT 12. Wiesbaden.

Baines, J. 1990. "Restricted Knowledge, Hierarchy, and Decorum: Modern Perceptions and Ancient Institutions." *JARCE* 27:1–23.

Caminos, R. A. 1976. "The Recording of Inscriptions and Scenes in Tombs and Temples." In *Ancient Egyptian Epigraphy and Palaeography*. New York.

Fischer, H. G. 1986. *L'écriture et l'art de l'Égypte ancienne: Quatre leçons sur la paléographie et l'épigraphie pharaoniques*. Essais et conférences. Paris.

Goldwasser, O., and C. Grinevald. 2012. "What Are 'Determinatives' Good For?" In *Lexical Semantics in Ancient Egyptian*, edited by E. Grossman, S. Polis, and J. Winand, 17–53. LingAeg-StudMon 9. Hamburg.

Jakobson, R. 1960. "Closing Statements: Linguistics and Poetics." In *Style in Language*, edited by T. A. Sebeok, 350–377. New York.

Laboury, D. 2012. "Tracking Ancient Egyptian Artists, a Problem of Methodology: The Case of the Painters of Private Tombs in the Theban Necropolis during the Eighteenth Dynasty." In *Art and Society: Ancient and Modern Contexts of Egyptian Art: Proceedings of the International Conference Held at the Museum of Fine Arts, Budapest, 13–15 May 2010*, edited by K. A. Kóthay, 199–208. Budapest.

Parkinson, R. 1999. *Cracking Codes: The Rosetta Stone and Decipherment*. London.

Régen, I. 2008. "Tomb and Mat: Palaeographical and Archaeological Approach of a Burial Practice through the Case of the Word *js*." In *Egypt at Its Origins 2: Proceedings of the International Conference "Origin of the State. Predynastic and Early Dynastic Egypt," Toulouse (France), 5th–8th September 2005*, edited by B. Midant-Reynes and Y. Tristant, 975–984. OLA 172. Leuven.

Saussure. F. de. (1916) 1971. *Cours de linguistique générale*. Paris.

Vernus, P. 1982. "Les jeux d'écriture." In *Naissance de l'écriture: Cunéiformes et hiéroglyphes. Galeries Nationales du Grand Palais, 7 mai–9 août 1982*, edited by C. Ziegler, 130–133. Paris.

Vernus, P. 1987. "L'ambivalence du signe graphique dans l'écriture hiéroglyphique." In *Espaces de la lecture: Actes du Colloque de la Bibliothèque publique d'information et du Centre d'étude de l'écriture, Université Paris VII*, edited by A.-M. Christin, 60–65. Paris.

Vernus, P. 1990. "Les espaces de l'écrit dans l'Égypte pharaonique." *BSFE* 119:35–56.

PART I

CULTURAL AND MATERIAL SETTING

FORM, LAYOUT, AND SPECIFIC POTENTIALITIES OF THE ANCIENT EGYPTIAN HIEROGLYPHIC SCRIPT

PASCAL VERNUS

THE BASIC FIGURATIVITY OF THE EGYPTIAN HIEROGLYPHIC SCRIPT

THE most salient characteristic of the Egyptian hieroglyphic script is its "figurativity," a concept derived from art history ("*arts figuratifs*"). Several scholars use the more ambiguous term "pictography." To speak of "iconicity" would be too vague. A script is commonly labeled "figurative" when the signs it uses, or some of them, are figural depictions that can be more or less identified as *realia*, even by someone foreign to the culture to which the script belongs. A glance at the following inscription (Figure I.1.1) suffices for one to understand that Egyptian hieroglyphs meet with such a definition:

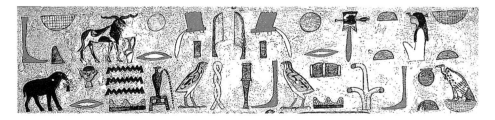

FIGURE I.1.1. From the tomb of Sarenput II/Nubkaurenakht, Aswan, necropolis of Qubbet el-Hawa, no. 31. Photography: Pascal Vernus.

Most of the hieroglyphs from this text are easily identifiable by anyone, even those unfamiliar with Egyptian culture.

Artistic Conventions

This rough definition, however, may be questioned on the grounds of the subjectivity it implies. For instance, Chinese-literate people are culturally inclined to consider that the signs of their script depict *realia*, while foreigners might not. Egyptian hieroglyphs can be characterized as figurative in a less subjective sense because they depict the *realia* of the pharaonic universe *in the same manner as do the figurative arts*. Let us consider this example (Figure I.1.2):

FIGURE I.1.2. Block 180N from Hatshepsut, Chapelle Rouge, Karnak. Photography: IFAO.

On the right, the kneeling king is offering a basket on which lies a dummy foreleg of an ox.

Between him and the god Amun, sitting on the left, there is a column of text (Table I.1.1A). At the end of the column, the two signs depicting an ox leg and a cup (Gardiner F24, W10) obviously represent the same object, the basket with the dummy foreleg, as the image does.

Clearly, the same basic artistic conventions—the so-called Egyptian canon—hold whether depicting the physical object in the figural representation or depicting it as a script sign in the caption. The basket and the foreleg are in profile view. The latter is graphically superimposed on the former, although we are meant to understand that it would be inside it.

Table I.1.1. Hieroglyphic Text in Typography

Pascal Vernus working with JSesh software, Serge Rosmorduc

1 Water

2 Flame and smoke

3 Neck

4 Hill

5 Locust, fly, deity

6 Sleeping man, stool, owl

7 Structural relationships

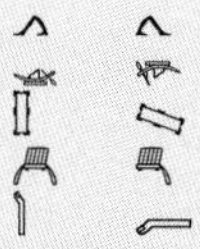

8 Primary hieroglyphs–simple

9 Primary hieroglyphs–complex

10 Composite hieroglyphs

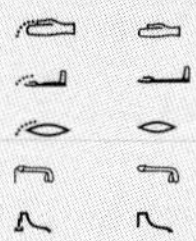

11 Remaining phonetic feature and plays on standard forms

12 Superimposition

13 Juxtaposition

14 Overlapping

15 Inclusion

16 Horse

(continued)

Table I.1.1. Continued

17 "Egypt" in a straight row

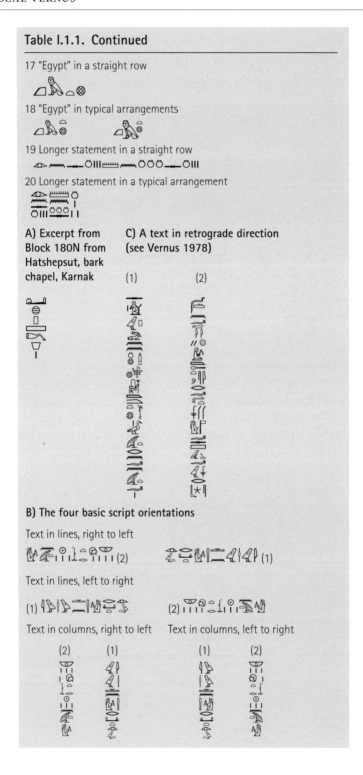

18 "Egypt" in typical arrangements

19 Longer statement in a straight row

20 Longer statement in a typical arrangement

A) Excerpt from Block 180N from Hatshepsut, bark chapel, Karnak

C) A text in retrograde direction (see Vernus 1978)

(1)   (2)

B) The four basic script orientations

Text in lines, right to left

(2)   (1)

Text in lines, left to right

(1)   (2)

Text in columns, right to left   Text in columns, left to right

(2)   (1)   (1)   (2)

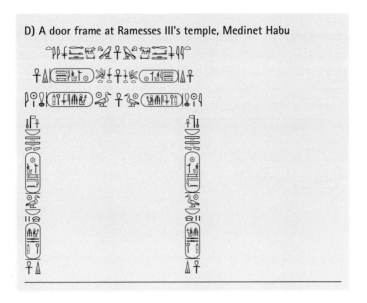

D) A door frame at Ramesses III's temple, Medinet Habu

Stylization

More generally, hieroglyphs are highly stylized, according to specific conventions. For instance, water is depicted as a zigzag in the sign Gardiner N35, and also in hieroglyphs involving it, such as a man swimming, or a man receiving purification (Table I.1.1.1). Flame and smoke are sketched in a very conventional manner in a hieroglyph depicting a brazier (Q7) and in a hieroglyph depicting a bowl with burning incense (R7) (Table I.1.1.2). In certain hieroglyphs, the neck is excessively lengthened because it is the salient part that accounts for their meanings (Table I.1.1.3).

A hieroglyph is not intended to depict its referent as a particular observer would see it from a particular viewpoint, in a particular place, or at a particular moment. Rather, it is supposed to show it so as to highlight its main stable and essential characteristics (Hornung 2001); it is conceptual rather than realistic. That accounts for the fact that some hieroglyphs, far from depicting a concrete object, are mere "mental images." For instance, Gardiner N29 schematically sketches the idea of a hill rather than presenting a detailed image of a hill (Table I.1.1.4).

The depicted objects are reduced to their mere outlines. (For their drawing, see Fischer 1983.) They are often in the profile view, but they can also be in the frontal view, or viewed from above; compare respectively a locust, a fly, and a deity whose face is particularly frightening (Table I.1.1.5). One hieroglyph can combine different viewpoints, as is conspicuous, for example, in those depicting humans (Pierrat-Bonnefois 2013). Inter alia, in the hieroglyph depicting the sleeping man, he lies on his back, viewed from above, but the headrest and his head are in profile view (Table I.1.1.6). The same holds for the stool: the seat is seen from above, but the legs are in profile view (Brovarski 1996, 140). In the hieroglyph depicting an owl, its body is in the profile view, but its head is in the frontal view, which was deemed the most characteristic in that particular case.

Some hieroglyphs may be rendered with an extraordinary profusion of details so as to enhance their original figurative value (see later, "Details"), or through a nonstandard individualizing treatment so as to suggest "realistic notations" (Fischer 1969), escaping thus to the "*stratégie d'épure*" to fall under the less common "*stratégie d'appogiature*," as do the figural representations (Vernus 2012b).

A particular style of hieroglyphs, referred to as "linear hieroglyphs," "semi-cursive hieroglyphs," or "book-writing hieroglyphs," was used for small objects and portable writing surfaces (Fischer 1976a, 40–42; Goelet 2010, 125 and n27). They were not bound to right-left orientation of reading and thus should be carefully distinguished from tachygraphies (hieratic and demotic).

Color

Theoretically, hieroglyphs should be colored, a requirement that was not systematically met for reasons of investment. Nevertheless, they are often monochrome, being painted in blue, in green, less frequently in yellow (Fischer 1976a, 32; Delange 1998), or even sometimes in black so as to suggest that the text, while being written on an object or a monument, refers to a manuscript.

In elaborate inscriptions, each hieroglyph possesses its specific colors (Gander 2005). Assigning colors relies on two approaches. According to one of them, which might be called the "naturalist" trend, the colors should reflect the visual perception that the Egyptian had of the hieroglyph's referent. This trend is illustrated by the quail chick in Figure I.1.1. The body is ocher, with black on the back suggesting the top feathers; the belly is white, and the legs are red. Another approach might be called "symbolic," since the colors of a hieroglyph depend on the symbolic values of its referent. For instance, the green color of the hieroglyph depicting a swallow or a swift (G36), does not relate to the perceived appearance of these birds, but arises rather from the fact that they are closely bound to the morning, a time of regeneration and growth that is closely associated with the color green (Vernus 2005, 65).

INVENTORY OF SIGNS

The signs inventory encompasses an overwhelming number of hieroglyphs that are figural depictions of the concrete and imaginary *realia* of the ancient Egyptian universe. According to Egyptological tradition (Gardiner 1957, 438–548), they are classified in twenty-six categories, including humans, deities, parts of the human body, animals and parts of animals, trees and plants, natural phenomena, and many sections encompassing buildings, objects, and artifacts of different kinds. Abstract and geometrical signs are few in number. Some are cursive forms of hieroglyphs, having reentered the hieroglyphic inventory from the hieratic tachygraphy according to a phenomenon of "feedback" or back formation.

Structure

Within the inventory, embryonic microsystems show up here and there, involving structural relationships between the position, the orientation, or the morphology of the signs (e.g., Table I.1.1.7).

Moreover, three categories of hieroglyphs should be distinguished according to their constituency.

A. Primary hieroglyphs cannot be analyzed into autonomous, meaningful components. They are often very simple (Table I.1.1.8), but they may be rather complex (Table I.1.1.9).

B. Composite hieroglyphs involve self-sufficient, full-fledged signs to which are added an element that is not a full-fledged sign. For instance, the human hand from which water flows (D46a), has a different use from the full-fledged sign (D46). It is the same for other signs as well (Table I.1.1.10).

Particularly interesting is the tethering rope (V14, V13). The diacritic tick on the former indicates a remaining phonetic feature that vanished elsewhere. The constituency of other hieroglyphs (e.g., Table I.1.1.11; Beaux 2009) involves a play on the standard form, where an original part is substituted with a phonetic sign. This illustrates how the signs inventory can be enlarged by standardizations of scribal devices and, more generally, how the hieroglyphic system involves its own metadiscourse.

C. Monograms are built from particular arrangements of two or more self-sufficient and full-fledged hieroglyphs. These are common (Lacau 1954, 103–105; Fischer 1977a; Van Essche 1997c) and are composed in four main types of arrangements.

1. Superimposition (Table I.1.1.12)
2. Juxtaposition (Table I.1.1.13)
3. Overlapping (Table I.1.1.14)
4. Inclusion (Table I.1.1.15)

Innovations

Needless to say, the inventory of signs evolved over time. Some signs disappeared. Many others were created to fit a new Egyptian universe. For instance, the introduction of the horse led to the introduction of hieroglyphs taking it as a referent (Table I.1.1.16). The creation of signs may also be triggered by scribal speculations, including individual innovations that were never standardized (Fischer 1976b, 55–58; Laboury 2013, 39; see also earlier, "Stylization," and later, "Details"). During the Pharaonic Period, the inventory of signs could have encompassed between fifteen hundred and two thousand items (Collombert 2007). Their number increased theoretically ad libitum during the Greco-Roman Period.

Specific Constraints on Hieroglyphs

That the hieroglyphs are to be characterized as "figurative" in the strongest sense of the term does not mean that they are exactly on the same plain as the full-fledged figural representations or that there is not any distinction between them. While a hieroglyph is basically an image, it has to undergo three specific constraints to function as a script sign, that is to say, an element of a writing system:

1. Constraints of size ruling the conventions of scale.
2. Constraints of arrangement in occupying the space devoted to the text.
3. Constraints of orientation ruling the hieroglyphs and the direction of reading.

Constraints of Calibration Ruling the Conventions of Scale

A particular convention of scale governs an image when it assumes the status of script sign. Constraints of sizing imply that the respective dimensions of the hieroglyphs are not proportional to the respective sizes of their referents (i.e., of the reality they represent). For instance, in the inscription in Figure I.1.1, the elephant (E26) appears to be in the same size as the ram (E10); the mountains (N25) occupy the same space as the human mouth (D21); the sandy hill slope (N29) the same space as the human face (D2). Without such constraints of scale, signs with small referents would have been hardly readable, and conversely, others with large referents would have been unreasonably huge, and too much space would have been left blank.

In figural depictions, the relative sizes of the elements depend on another set of rules, involving, for instance, not only the relative physical sizes, but also the relative hierarchical positions of their referents.

Constraints of Arrangement in Occupying the Space Devoted to the Text

In European scripts, signs often follow each other in a straight row, lying on the same level. In hieroglyphic script, the signs are subject to particular rules of arrangement. Far from lying all on the same level, they are laid out at different heights, in virtual quadrangular frames—square or rectangular—that divide the space devoted to the text. These virtual frames are called "cadrats" or quadrats. The hieroglyphs have to fill these cadrats in such a manner that they could meet with two requirements:

- Density: the space left blank between each hieroglyph is reduced to the necessary minimum so as to avoid contact or overlap. Moreover, there is no separation between the words, the phrases, the clauses, and the sentences. A hieroglyphic text, as long as it might be, runs continuously from the beginning to the end without any punctuation or blank space. This is true chiefly for texts on objects or monuments. On portable writing surfaces, such as ostraca, writing boards, and papyri, and all the more when tachygraphies are used, the uniform succession of signs can be broken by specific marks of punctuation, by rubrications, and by blanks. Only exceptional devices, such as the "cartouche" (Gardiner 1957, 74), can delimit discrete units within the unbroken succession of signs.
- Harmony: the hieroglyphs occupy a whole cadrat or a regular subdivision— vertical or horizontal—(half, third, quarter, etc.) according to its morphology (Lacau 1954, 10).

Examples of Arrangements

Let us consider the hieroglyphs implemented in a spelling of the word "Egypt," in Egyptian "the Black one," referring to the soil of the Nile Valley. In a straight row, they would run as seen in Table I.1.1.17. In Egyptian practice, they are laid out in an arrangement that is half a cadrat plus one cadrat or even sometimes in an arrangement that is one cadrat (Table I.1.1.18).

Let us now consider the hieroglyphic arrangement of a longer statement that can be translated "after they have made their monuments." In straight row, the sequence would be as shown in Table I.1.1.19. According to the principles that rule layout, the sequence might be arranged as shown in Table I.1.1.20.

Other arrangements are possible. Contrary to Mayan script, a cadrat does not necessarily match a linguistic unity. Except for the two basic requirements of harmony and density, there are no strict rules in laying out the cadrats, but rather traditions depending on the period and regarding the nature of the writing surface, local style, and scribal mastership, among other factors. For instance, beginning with the Amarna Period, there is a trend to arrangement in rectangular cadrats rather than in square ones (Klotz 2014–2015, 99).

Constraints of Orientation Governing the Hieroglyphs and the Direction of Reading

Many hieroglyphs have a symmetrical morphology. Consider the jar (N24), water (N35), door bolt (O34), and game board (Y5) in Table I.1.1.19–20. They can be divided in two wholly identical halves, mirroring each other, by a vertical axis cutting them in the middle. But many others have an asymmetrical morphology. For instance, returning to Table I.1.1.A, it is clear that the sign depicting the arm holding a jar (D39) shows no symmetrical morphology. It has a front and a rear. One would be prone to take the hand holding a globular bowl as the front, and the right angle of the elbow as the rear. Be that as it may, the sign has a prevailing orientation.

The orientation is particularly conspicuous for the signs representing animates, when their heads are in profile view, which is most frequently the case. Asymmetrical signs cannot be displayed without regard to their prevailing orientation. Basically, they should look toward the beginning of the text, thus fronting the direction in which the text is to be read (Gracia Zamacona 2015, 12). When they look toward the left, the text is to be read from left to right. When they look toward the right, the text is to be read from right to left.

Consider Figure I.1.1: The seated woman with a vulture-shaped headdress and the vulture standing on a basket are facing left, which means that the section of text to which they belong reads left to right. The elephant and ram are facing right, which means that the section of text to which they belong reads right to left. As for the hieroglyph representing a quail chick, it faces right in the section of text reading right to left, and it faces left in the section of text reading left to right.

The rule holds for texts in lines as well as for texts in columns. Thus, hieroglyphic texts can be displayed in four basic directions, corresponding to four basic textual formats.

- From right to left in a row
- From right to left and downward in a column
- From left to right in a row
- From left to right and downward in a column

Table I.1.1.B shows the same text displayed in the four basic directions. However, the right-to-left direction of reading remained dominant (Fischer 1977b), as the tachygraphies (the so-called cursives), hieratic and demotic, show, as they are always to be read right to left.

Row Versus Column

In Table I.1.1.B, one can see that sometimes the arrangements in cadrats of the same group of hieroglyphs may be different in a line and in a column. For instance, the head in profile and the stroke are more susceptible to be laid out in a vertical half cadrat in a line and in a horizontal half cadrat in a column, although this is not a strict rule.

Image and Word Orientation

In a caption pertaining to the representation of a man or a god, the signs with asymmetrical morphology should face the same direction as the representation. If the representations look to the right, the hieroglyphs should look to the right, and the text is to be read right to left. The reverse is also true.

Let us return to Figure I.1.2. One can see that above the kneeling king, who is looking to the left, the asymmetrical hieroglyphs of the caption are oriented to the left: the duck, ibis, and cobra (G39, G26, I10) for the animates, the flag (R8) for the inanimates. Conversely, above the sitting god Amun, who is looking to the right, the asymmetrical hieroglyphs of the caption are oriented to the right: the horned viper and leg and foot (I9, D58) for the animates (or part of animates), the scepter and reed leaf (S40, M17) for the inanimates.

Retrograde Texts

Now, this rule may raise a semiotic difficulty: when a caption expresses what a depicted individual is saying to another one facing him or her, according to the standard rule, the text runs toward the speaker, and backward to the addressee. When the text is very long, this may appear contradictory. So, there is a fifth possible direction, the "retrograde" direction, mainly used in texts displayed in columns. In this textual format, originally limited to religious compositions (Goelet 2010; Gracia Zamacona 2015, 10–11), the text is to be read in the same direction in which the asymmetrical hieroglyphs are facing, so that they face away from the beginning. Table I.1.1.C shows this retrograde arrangement.

- The columns are to be read from left to right (column 1, then column 2).
- However, the asymmetrical signs are looking toward the right, facing away from the beginning of the text, thus in contradiction to the basic rule (e.g., the seated humans, animals, and body parts for the animates (and parts of them) and the flag and staff, among others, for the inanimates).
- Within the cadrats that involve several signs, these signs are to be read from right to left: for instance in the word *jstw*, the reed leaf (M17) should be read first, then the folded cloth (S29), then the group bread loaf+curl (X1, Z7).

Exploiting the Specific Potentialities of Hieroglyphic Script

The basic function of a script is to render language visible. In so doing, there is unavoidably both deficit and excess. There is deficit in that the script hardly renders suprasegmental features (intonation, accent, etc.). There is excess in that it brings specific connotations to the information conveyed by these productions due to the adaptation from the phonic to the visual. The importance of the connotations depends on the specific expressive capacities of the script. They are extremely rich in the hieroglyphic script due to its flexible manner of investing its writing surfaces, its figurativity, and its complex system of encoding the linguistic data. They have been developed accordingly to produce semiotic effects (Vernus 1987; 2012a, 68–70).

Reversals

A specific connotation may arise when the succession of some script signs does not match the linguistic unity they encode. This is often illustrated by the so-called honorific anticipation or honorific transposition. In Egyptian, a phrase such as "like Re" involves first the preposition *mj* (= "like") (W19) and then *r* (= Re) (N5, Z1), that is to say, *mj r*. Now, the linearity of the utterance is not transposed in its graphic rendering, which shows the sun disk and stroke in the first position in the rightward direction of reading and the sun disk and stroke in the second position in the leftward one. The group for Re (N5, Z1) should precede the hieroglyph for "like" (W19) as a mark of respect for the god.

Many semiotic effects are available from the use of different textual formats in the same unity. Play on the orientation of hieroglyphs is not uncommon, particularly the "reversal" device, which consists in giving to a sign, or a group of signs, an orientation contrary to the dominant one. Sometimes it merely suggests graphically what is expressed linguistically. Such is the case in the group "worshipping Osiris," where the sign "worshipping" (A30) is in reversed orientation vis-à-vis the sign "Osiris" (Clère 1987, 11; for other examples, Kurth 2007, 97–98). The different cases of reversals, often with demarcative or vocative meaning, were thoroughly studied by Fischer (1977b).

Orientation with Regard to Architecture

Through their different textual formats, hieroglyphic inscriptions, far from using a monument as a mere surface of display, can be influenced by the structure of the monument. Let us consider, for instance, how the texts are laid out on a temple doorframe (Table I.1.1.D).

On the lintel, there are three lines each divided into two sections with the same text in opposite orientations. In the left part, the asymmetrical hieroglyphs are oriented to the right and the text is to be read from right to left. On the right side, the asymmetrical hieroglyphs are oriented to the left and the text is to be read left to right. Thus, each text mirrors the other. Moreover, the *ankh* signs are common to them in each line, and their superimposition in the middle axis divides the gate into two symmetrical halves.

On each jamb, there is a column of text. On the left jamb, the asymmetrical hieroglyphs are rightward oriented and the virtual cadrats are to be read right to left. On the right jamb, it is the other way around. Once again, each text mirrors the other.

Thus, the layout of the inscription highlights the basic symmetrical structure of the gate, consisting of two mirroring halves divided by a central vertical axis. This would have been clearly impossible with European scripts.

Hieroglyph-Image Link

The original link between hieroglyph and image remains always present and is susceptible to be reactivated. Sometimes, the standard form of a hieroglyph in a caption is modified because of the representation to which it is attached. In a scene from the temple of Seti I at Abydos, the king is depicted lassoing a galloping wild bull. In the caption, the hieroglyph of the bull, far from showing the usual form (E2), is depicted galloping!

An element of a representation can function as a script sign. It is well established, for instance, that mainly in the Old Kingdom (Fischer 1973, 1977b, 3–4), but also sometimes later (Schenkel 2011, 131; Van Essche 1997a, 204–205), an element of the representation substitutes for an expected but absent hieroglyph in the spelling of a word belonging to the caption.

Decalibration

As much as a representation can fulfill the role of a sign from a text, a sign from a text can be transferred to the status of representation. Often, this particular status is marked by decalibration, when the enlarged hieroglyph is no longer subject to the constraints that governed its proportions. The enlarged ideogram of Anubis in Old Kingdom inscriptions is a classic instance (Fischer 1976b, 35–36; Harpur 1987, 47n42), as is the decalibration of the falcon hieroglyph (G5 or G5 wearing S5) introducing the so-called Horus name of the pharaoh (Van Essche 1997b). Not infrequently, the determinatives or classifiers of a god's name (El Hawary 2010, Bild 17, col. 48) or of a private name (Silverman 1997, 278–279, no 95) are enlarged and close a column, sometimes after a blank, so as to underscore their status as image.

Details

Reactivating and enhancing the original image value of a hieroglyph can rely not only on decalibration but also on providing it with an outstanding richness of detail that makes it break out of its standard form. For instance, on a sarcophagus, the *qrs.t* ideogram, meaning "burial," exceptionally encompasses a picture of a burying scene (Goldwasser 2009, 349). In some Ramesses II's architraves, the different occurrences of the ideogram for *wˁf* "subjugate" are each given a very particular detailed treatment involving a definite ethnic type (Van Essche 1997a, 211). Moreover, sometimes the pictorial promotion of the sign is highlighted by its encapsulating its own caption, according to a very sophisticated device, implemented elsewhere in temple inscriptions (Vernus 1987, 64–65 and fig. 5).

Developing original figurativity may involve not only a single hieroglyph but also long sequences of hieroglyphs, according to a trend more or less restricted during the Pharaonic Period and illustrated by some productions of the so-called sportive or enigmatic writing (Darnell 2004, 14–34), also clumsily labeled "cryptography."

The trend dramatically developed during the Greco-Roman Period. In particular parts of the temple, certain texts were composed in hieroglyphs deliberately chosen to build a purely pictorial discourse that is parallel to the linguistic discourse they convey as script signs (basically Sauneron 1982). This trend reached its climax in hymns to ram and crocodile deities that overwhelmingly implement hieroglyphs depicting rams or crocodiles to signify things other than rams and crocodiles (Leitz 2001)!

A Script Adapted to Object and Monuments

Due to its interplay with figural representations and to its multidirectionality, hieroglyphic script is prone to "decorative" uses on objects or monuments (Fischer 1986). Its birth in the proto-Thinite period, around 3150 BCE, was triggered, at least partly, by the need to actualize the name of the sovereign, and secondarily other names, in the iconic apparatus, thus, claiming his domination (Vernus 2011). At the beginning of the First Dynasty, the writing system appears fully constituted (Kahl 2001). It already functioned by implementing two major categories of signs: consonantal phonograms and semograms. The latter are subdivided between logograms/radicograms/ideograms, or signs possessing both phonetic and semantic components, and determinatives or classifiers, or signs that are purely semantic and devoid of phonetic content. (For the functional classifications in the writing system, see Polis and Rosmorduc 2015 with a thorough bibliography.)

However complete the writing system appeared in the late fourth millennium, four centuries after its birth the hieroglyphic script still remained restricted to "label statements," that is, phrases that do not involve a complete predication. Their partial meanings either find their completions in the object which they have for support, for instance, a proper name of an object indicating the person to which it belongs, to which it is consecrated, by which it is offered, its date with respect to ideological events in the case of tags, etc., or their partial meanings are complemented by representations for which they serve as captions.

Uses

From the end of the Second Dynasty onward (Morenz 2002), the script began to encode self-contained texts, including complete sentences, whose meanings were intended to be completed by the objects or monuments on which they are written or by the representations to which they are annexed. Not taking into account its derived tachygraphies, the hieratic and, later, the demotic, hieroglyphic script became more and more extensively implemented in three main domains that unavoidably overlapped.

1. Monumental expressions of religion: temple cults and rituals, mortuary religion, and everyday religious practices, including magic.

2. Monumental expression of the king's ideological activity: building inscriptions, military records, annals, royal commands, etc.

3. Self-presentations of nonroyal individuals: tomb inscriptions, autobiographies, inscriptions on votive monuments.

If hieroglyphic script was used overwhelmingly in these kinds of texts, it is because it was supposed to possess a performative power, being originally "divine words" (*mdw nṯr*). Thus, the script was particularly appropriate to "sacralize" the texts, that is to say, to associate them with creation (Vernus 2017).

Post-Third Century BCE

The end of the Pharaonic Period in the mid-fourth century BCE did not bring about the disappearance of hieroglyphic script. To the contrary, the script was deemed the ultimate expression of the Egyptian *Weltanschauung* and the instrument through which one could access the secret principles that rule the world. Its enormous potentialities were systematically developed. The number of hieroglyphs and the number of values attributed to each of them dramatically increased (Kurth 2007) as a result of an intense sacerdotal work for which Sauneron (1982) coined the felicitous expression "*philologie sacrée.*" (See also earlier, "Details.")

The Roman emperors' conversion to Christianity in 392 CE forced the closure of pagan temples and thus of the places where hieroglyphic script was mastered. The last known hieroglyphic text is dated from 394 CE, while demotic survived until the first half of the fifth century CE (Dijkstra 2011, 61–62).

Meroitic

Although the standard Meroitic script, which was used in the Sudan since the end of the third century BCE, borrows its inventory of signs from Demotic, there is a hieroglyphic Meroitic script, restricted to monumental uses, that implements many Egyptian hieroglyphs. Both involve the same basic syllabic system (Rilly 2007).

Of paramount importance is the borrowing of many hieroglyphs by the so-called Proto-Sinaitic script, an alphabetic script that was used by Semitic people serving the Egyptians from the end of the nineteenth century BCE onward (Darnell et al. 2005). Each of these hieroglyphs was given, as a phonetic value, the first consonant of the Semitic word naming what the hieroglyph depicted (Goldwasser 2012; Vernus 2015). For instance, the Egyptian hieroglyph of the ox head (F1) was given the value ʿ (*aleph*) since it depicts an ox, which is *ʾlp* in West Semitic languages. Proto-Sinaitic script was the source of the Hebrew and Phoenician alphabets and then, via the Greeks, of the European alphabet. Thus, many modern characters are ultimately rooted in Egyptian hieroglyphs!

Bibliography

Beaux, N. 2009. "Le signe figuratif égyptien: Types de (sur)motivation." In *Image et conception du monde dans les écritures figuratives. Actes du Colloque Collège de France-Académie des Inscriptions et Belles-Lettres, Paris, 24–25 janvier 2008*, edited by N. Beaux, B. Pottier, and N. Grimal, 364–371. EdE 10. Paris.

Brovarski, E. 1996. "An Inventory List from 'Covington's Tomb' and Nomenclature for Furniture in the Old Kingdom." In *Studies in Honor of William Kelly Simpson*, Vol. 1, edited by P. Der Manuelian, 117–155. Boston.

Clère, J. J. 1987. *Le papyrus de Nesmin: Un Livre des Morts hiéroglyphique de l'époque ptolémaïque.* BG X. Cairo.

Collombert, P. 2007. "Combien y avait-il de hiéroglyphes?" *EAO* 46:15–28.

Darnell, J. D. 2004. *The Enigmatic Netherworld Books of the Solar-Osirian Unity: Cryptographic Compositions in the Tombs of Tutankhamun, Ramesses VI and Ramesses IX.* OBO 198. Fribourg.

Darnell, J. D., F. W. Dobbs-Allsopp, M. J. Lundberg, P. K. McCarter, and B. Zuckerman. 2005. *Two Early Alphabetic Inscriptions from the Wadi el-Hôl: New Evidence for the Origin of the Alphabet from the Western Desert of Egypt.* AASOR 59. Boston.

Delange, É. 1998. "Couleur vraie." In *La couleur dans la peinture et l'émaillage de l'Égypte ancienne*, edited by S. Colinart and M. Menu, 17–30. CUEBC. Scienze e Materiali del Patrimonio Culturale 4. Bari.

Dijkstra, J. H. F. 2011. "Les derniers prêtres de Philae: Un mystère?" *EAO* 60:57–66.

Fischer, H. G. 1969. "Varia Aegyptiaca." *JARCE* 2:17–51.

Fischer, H. G. 1973. "Redundant Determinatives in the Old Kingdom." *MMJ* 8:7–25.

Fischer, H. G. 1976a. "Archaeological Aspects of Epigraphy and Palaeography." In *Ancient Egyptian Epigraphy and Palaeography*, 27–55. New York.

Fischer, H. G. 1976b. *Varia*. Egyptian Studies I. New York.

Fischer, H. G. 1977a. "The Evolution of Composite Hieroglyphs in Ancient Egypt." *MMJ* 12:5–19.

Fischer, H. G. 1977b. *The Orientation of Hieroglyphs: Part 1. Reversals*. Egyptian Studies 2. New York.

Fischer, H. G. 1983. *Ancient Egyptian Calligraphy: A Beginner's Guide to Writing Hieroglyphs.* 2nd ed. New York.

Fischer, H. G. 1986. *L'écriture et l'art de l'Égypte ancienne: Quatre leçons sur la paléographie et l'épigraphie pharaoniques.* Paris.

Gander, M. 2005. "Die Farbigkeit der Schrift: Zur Verwendung und Bedeutung monochromer und polychromer Inschriften auf Särgen de Mittleren Reiches." *SAK* 33:91–115.

Gardiner, A. H. 1957. *Egyptian Grammar: Being an Introduction to the Study of Hieroglyphs.* 3rd ed., rev. Oxford.

Goelet, O., Jr. 2010. "Observations on Copying and the Hieroglyphic Tradition in the Production of the *Book of the Dead*." In *Offerings to the Discerning Eye: An Egyptological Medley in Honor of Jack A. Josephson*, edited by S. H. D'Auria, 121–132. CHANE 38. Leiden.

Goldwasser, O. 2009. "La force de l'icône: Le signifié élu." In *Image et conception du monde dans les écritures figuratives. Actes du Colloque Collège de France-Académie des Inscriptions et Belles-Lettres, Paris, 24–25 janvier 2008*, edited by N. Beaux, B. Pottier, and N. Grimal, 336–362. EdE 10. Paris.

Goldwasser, O. 2012. "How the Alphabet Was Born from Hieroglyphs." *BAR* 36:40–53.

Gracia Zamacona, C. 2015. "The Two Inner Directions of the Ancient Egyptian Script." *BEJ* 3:9–23.

Harpur, Y. 1987. *Decoration in Egyptian Tombs of the Old Kingdom: Studies in Orientation and Scene Content*. London.

Hawary, A. El. 2010. *Wortschöpfung: Die Memphitische Theologie und die Siegesstele des Pije–zwei Zeugen kultureller Repräsentation in der 25. Dynastie*. OBO 243. Friburg.

Hornung, E. 2001. "'Hieroglyphisch Denken.' Bild und Schrift im alten Ägypten." In *Homo Pictor Colloquium Rauricum 7*, edited by G. Boehm, 76–86. Colloquia Raurica 7. Leipzig.

Kahl, J. 2001. "Hieroglyphic Writing during the Fourth Millennium BC: An Analysis of Systems." *Archéo-Nil* 11:101–134.

Klotz, D. 2014–2015. "Two Hymns to Isis from Philae Revisited (Žabkar, Hymns 1–2)." *BSEG* 30:75–107.

Kurth, D. 2007. *Einführung ins Ptolemäische: Eine Grammatik mit Zeichenliste und Übungsstücken*, Teil 1. Hützel.

Laboury, D. 2013. "De l'individualité de l'artiste dans l'art égyptien." In *L'art du contour: Le dessin dans l'Égypte ancienne*, edited by G. Andreu-Lanoë, 36–41. Paris.

Lacau, P. 1954. *Sur le système hiéroglyphique*. BdE 25. Cairo.

Leitz, C. 2001. "Die beiden kryptographischen Inschriften aus Esna mit den Widdern und Krokodilen." *SAK* 29:251–276.

Morenz, L. 2002. "Die Götter und ihr Redetext: Die ältest-belegte Sakral-Monumentalisierung von Textlichkeit auf Fragmenten der Zeit des Djoser aus Heliopolis." In *5. Ägyptologische Tempeltagung Würzburg, 23.–26. September 1999*, edited by H. Beinlich, J. Hallof, H. Hussy, and C. von Pfeil, 137–158. Wiesbaden.

Pierrat-Bonnefois, G. 2013. "Les principes du dessin égyptien." In *L'art du contour: Le dessin dans l'Égypte ancienne*, edited by G. Andreu-Lanoë, 52–57. Paris.

Polis, S., and S. Rosmorduc. 2015. "The Hieroglyphic Sign Functions: Suggestions for a Revised Taxonomy." In *Fuzzy Boundaries: Festschrift für Antonio Loprieno 1*, edited by H. Amstutz, A. Dorn, M. Müller, M. Ronsdorf, and S. Uljas, 149–174. Hamburg.

Rilly, C. 2007. *La langue du royaume de Méroé: Un panorama de la plus ancienne culture écrite d'Afrique subsaharienne*. BEHE SHP 344. Paris.

Sauneron, S. 1982. *L'écriture figurative dans les textes d'Esna*. Esna VIII. Le Caire.

Schenkel, W. 2011. "Wie ikonisch ist die altäyptische Schrift?" *LingAeg* 19:125–153.

Silverman, D., ed. 1997. *Searching for Ancient Egypt: Art, Architecture, and Artifacts from the University of Pennsylvania Museum of Archaeology and Anthropology*. Ithaca.

Van Essche, E. 1997a. "À propos d'une figure-monogramme d'Abou Simbel." *GM* 158:81–90.

Van Essche, E. 1997b. "Dieux et rois face à face dans les inscriptions monumentales ramessides." *BSEG* 21:63–79.

Van Essche, E. 1997c. "La valeur ajoutée du signe déterminatif dans l'écriture figurative ramesside." *RdE* 48:207–211.

Vernus, P. 1978. "Littérature et autobiographie. Les inscriptions de *sꜣ-mwt* surnommé *kyky*." *RdE* 30:115–146.

Vernus, P. 1987. "L'ambivalence du signe graphique dans l'écriture hiéroglyphique." In *Espaces de la lecture: Actes du Colloque de la Bibliothèque publique d'information et du Centre d'étude de l'écriture, Université Paris VII*, edited by A.-M. Christin, 60–65. Paris.

Vernus, P. 2005. "Les animaux dans l'écriture égyptienne." In *Bestiaire des Pharaons*, edited by P. Vernus and J. Yoyotte, 62–75. Paris.

Vernus, P. 2011. "Naissance des hiéroglyphes et affirmation iconique du pouvoir: L'emblème du palais dans la genèse de l'écriture." In *Les premières cités et la naissance de l'écriture: Actes du colloque du 26 septembre 2009 Musée Archéologique de Nice-Cemenelum*, edited by P. Vernus, 27–58. Arles.

Vernus, P. 2012a. "Les écritures de l'Égypte ancienne." In *Histoire de l'écriture de l'idéogramme au multimedia*, edited by A.-M. Christin, 53–73. Paris.

Vernus, P. 2012b. "Stratégie d'épure et stratégie d'appogiature dans les productions dites 'artistiques' à l'usage des dominants: Le papyrus dit 'érotique' de Turin et la mise à distance des dominés." In *Art and Society: Ancient and Modern Contexts of Egyptian Art; Proceedings of the International Conference Held at the Museum of Fine Arts, Budapest, 13–15 May 2010*, edited by K. A. Kóthay, 109–121. Budapest.

Vernus, P. 2015. "Écriture hiéroglyphique égyptienne et écriture protosinaïtique: Une typologie comparée; Acrophonie 'forte' et acrophonie 'faible.'" In *Origins of the Alphabet: Proceedings of the First Polis Institute Interdisciplinary Conference*, edited by C. Rico and C. Attucci, 142–175. Newcastle.

Vernus, P. 2017. "Modeling the relationship between reproduction and production of 'sacralized' texts in Pharaonic Egypt." In *(Re)productive Traditions in Ancient Egypt*, edited by T. Gillen, 475–509. AegLeo 10. Liège.

....

THE CONTENT OF EGYPTIAN WALL DECORATION

....

NIV ALLON

THE title of this chapter poses a seemingly unassuming question, asking what the content of an inscription or an image is, or in other words—what it is about. Years ago, I posed an equally simple question to a group of sophomore high-school students, asking them to define what was wrong with a black-and-white photograph with which I presented them. The subject of the class was history, and my students did their best at offering a probable answer. Some pointed out the lack of women in the crowd or the infrequent salutes, but as creative as they were, they stood little chance in providing the answer I was expecting, unless they had prior knowledge of the Russian Revolution and of Trotsky, whose image was removed from the side of Lenin, where he once stood. In class that day, we discussed history as written by victors, but this exercise provided another fundamental lesson: texts and images do not readily reveal their histories and their content.

Trotsky's removal from the image was key to the picture's significance that day, but even without it, the students were not entirely at loss. They could still identify it as a reproduction of an old photograph, showing a large group of men looking at the camera, the likes of which they had seen many times before. In fact, some recognized Lenin as its leader thanks to his central position in the photo, even though they could not specify his name. This information did not suffice in providing an answer to my question, but the students could nevertheless aptly describe the content of this picture in almost every other way.

If only we were as well informed as these teenagers when approaching ancient Egyptian texts and images. Undeniably, the image of the well-off ancient Egyptian man in his tomb seems to resemble portraits hung in museums today, and ancient Egyptian royal inscriptions fit quite comfortably into our understanding of propaganda. We may similarly recognize hymns singing praise to a deity or autobiographical texts reiterating an official's career, but did the ancient Egyptian elite understand the essence of the text to be the same as we do? Removed from this ancient culture by millennia, we should reflect on how adequate our categories and ways of understanding are when applied to ancient Egyptian sources. So much, in fact, in the understanding of content and its interpretation is culturally specific that we can often only securely say what these texts and images mean to us.

We can follow, nevertheless, a number of paths into the material that allow us to approximate what these texts and images might have meant to their ancient patrons and viewers. These include (1) consideration of context, where the inscription or scene was placed; (2) attention to the multimodality that abounds in ancient Egyptian epigraphy, considering relationships between text and image; and (3) study of the repertoire of texts and images, their variations, and the patterns that arise from them.

This chapter focuses on these three elements—context, multimodality, and repertoire—laying out each of these paths by employing sources from various periods of Egyptian history: an inscription from an Old Kingdom necropolis and scenes from tomb chapels of the Middle and the New Kingdoms; Ramesside royal inscriptions; and texts inscribed on scribal statues of various eras. This chapter does not attempt to be comprehensive in any way, nor does it try to establish a typology of scenes and inscriptions and their contents. Instead, it considers the assumptions of these three paths, their methodologies, their advantages, and their limitations.

Neither are these lines of inquiry limited to epigraphy nor is the investigation of content restricted to these approaches alone. These three sets of examples allow us, nevertheless, to touch on important questions of intention, agency, and audience, thereby establishing common ground in our investigation, from which further explorations may proceed.

Context

Paper, for the most part, mediates nowadays our encounters with ancient Egyptian texts and images through translations, editions, commentaries, and compilations. These books and articles allow us to establish a broad knowledge of a culture whose remnants are dispersed in Egypt and throughout the world, at archaeological sites and in museums. When we are fortunate, however, to encounter the object of study in its original context, its surroundings—its appearance, its dimensions, the surface on which it appears, and what is in its vicinity—inform us about its content even before we approach its first sign.

Consider, for example, the texts inscribed on the walls of the temple of Medinet Habu (Epigraphic Survey 1930, pls. 35–37; see Figure I.2.1) and the stela of Hetepi (MMA 26.3.351; see Figure I.2.2 and Hayes 1959, I:334). Both hieroglyphic inscriptions were carved into a stone surface, but the impression they give to their viewers and the expectations they set as for their content are markedly different. One is a monumental text inscribed on a temple wall, and the other is an inscription written on a stela that was found within a tomb in Deir el-Bahri. While the former is beautifully carved and decorated with images of chariots and galloping horses, the latter was clearly not executed by the most skillful hands. It is of little surprise, then, that one speaks of the victories of the king beyond the borders of Egypt and the other is a private (nonroyal) funerary text.

FIGURE I.2.1. Photograph of the external wall of Medinet Habu by Felix Teynard. Purchase, Lila Acheson Wallace Gift, 1976 (MMA 1976.607.36).

Context, however, does more than evoke impressions and set expectations. It also suggests a framework through which to interpret the image or the text (Tefnin 1991). Another hieroglyphic inscription may help further explicate this point. The text was found in Qubbet el-Hawa—an important Old Kingdom necropolis at the southern border of Egypt (Vischak 2015)—and it records the emphatic words of King Neferkare Pepi II (2278–2184 BCE):

> When he descends with you to the boat,
>   appoint excellent men to be around him on the two sides of the boat
>   lest he fall in the water!
> When he sleeps at night,
>   appoint excellent men to sleep around him in his tent.[1]
> Inspect ten times a night!
> More than the tribute of Sinai and Punt,
>   (My) Majesty desires to see this dwarf.
>
> (*Urk.* I 130.6–14)

[1] The text writes the word here with a cloth hieroglyph at the end, suggesting it is the word *ẖnw*, "abode," which is made of textiles, hence "tent."

FIGURE I.2.2. Stela of Hetepi. Limestone, Rogers Fund, 1926 (MMA 26.3.351).

The king is addressing Harkhuf, an official who led at least four expeditions to the south of Egypt's border and lived to serve three kings (Strudwick 2005, 328–333). In his last campaign, he sent a missive notifying the king of a dwarf he was bringing north with him for his sovereign's entertainment. Pepi II responds with enthusiasm, showing concern for the dwarf's well-being insofar as he is not hurt and does not escape.

Despite the royal character of the inscription, it was not the king who inscribed it, but rather Harkhuf himself. He placed this text along with other inscriptions on his tomb chapel's walls. This part of Harkhuf's inscriptions opens with the words, "Missive of the king, which he himself wrote," stating that Harkhuf copied a royal letter penned by the king himself. Nevertheless, though the title presents what follows as a royal text, it is hardly a royal inscription. It is a text inscribed on the wall of an elite tomb, and its context is critical to the understanding of this inscription and how it might have been appreciated in ancient times.

What might have motivated Harkhuf to include this royal missive on the walls of his tomb chapel? The context of the tomb chapel is revealing, and the adjacent scenes and inscriptions point at a possible answer. These inscriptions were laid out with contemporary and future viewers (and readers) in mind, as stated in the texts themselves:

> O those who are living upon the earth, [who will pass upon this tomb] sailing upstream and downstream, who will say "thousands (of) breads and beer for the owner of this tomb;" I will argue for them in god's land.   (*Urk.* I 122.9–12)

Visitors to the tomb chapel are thus invited to recite offering formulae for the deceased and are promised his assistance from the afterlife. His deeds and character may indeed persuade them to remember him, act for him, and believe that he will be able to act on their behalf in the afterlife. (The literature on autobiographical texts is extensive; see, for example, Frood [2007].) By including the royal missive in his tomb, Harkhuf then presents an important aspect of his life that probably not many others could claim—a direct line of communication to the king. A select few included such missives in their tomb, as only two other examples are known to us from the entire history of ancient Egypt: Senedjemib-Inti of the Fifth Dynasty and Usersatet of the Eighteenth Dynasty (Eyre 2013). A letter written by the king himself thus might have been quite an attraction, drawing visitors to Harkhuf's tomb, not to mention the provisions the letter itself promises the tomb owner, which—as the appeal to living indicates—was a real concern.

Since the tomb serves as meeting point for living and the dead, it functions also as a site in which values are negotiated across generations (Assmann 1983). Through art and text, elite men could highlight values that they held high before their contemporaneous and future viewers, while visitors entering the tomb could meet and reinterpret the past. Self-representation is pertinent here to this negotiation of values, as it operates on multiple levels: memorializing the protagonist, highlighting his values, as well as negotiating them (Greenblatt 1980, 3; Allon 2013).

Context proves to be similarly critical when dealing with images. An oft-occurring image in elite tombs of the New Kingdom depicts the tomb owner fishing and fowling in the marshes. One such scene appears in the tomb of Nakht (TT 52; Davies 1917; Shedid and Seidel 1996), where he is shown standing on a skiff, his wife and children by him, while he is hunting birds and fish around him (MMA 15.5.19e, l–m). This and other images in the tomb were often regarded in Egyptological literature as scenes of everyday life—aspects of life that the owner enjoyed on earth and hoped to replicate in his afterlife. Along with this scene of fishing and fowling, others represent desert hunting, agriculture, and administration, all of which were taken as close to accurate testimonies to daily life in ancient Egypt.

An important detail in Nakht's image, however, raises doubts regarding this interpretation. Nakht and his family are all dressed in white clothes and fine adornments, hardly the equipment one would expect on a day in the watery and murky marshes. This incongruity points to the highly idealized nature of this imagery and suggests a more multilayered meaning of the scene. Scholars have associated, for example, the tomb owner's activities in the marshes to the conquering of chaos or to icons that relate to creation and rebirth (Laboury 1997, 70–71; Hartwig 2004, 103–106). This similarity suggests that the tomb owner wished to show himself actively participating in maintaining order. This interpretation fits well into the context of the tomb, which could be described as a mechanism that is aimed toward the tomb owner's continued existence in the afterlife.

Questions of audience (see chapter by Navratilova) further complicate our understanding of content, even when it is the very same text appearing in different copies. The "poem" on the battle of Qadesh speaks, for example, of a battle in modern-day Syria that took place between the Egyptian military and the Hittites around 1274 BCE. The military campaign ended in great victory, but on the way there, the Egyptian king found himself deserted in the battlefield, cut from his division, and saved only through divine grace. The text appears both on temple walls throughout the land as well as on papyri, the most complete of which is now in the British Museum (Spalinger 2002).

Though each of these copies relates the battle of Qadesh, their content is not exactly the same (see chapter by Brand). When Ramesses II inscribed this account on religious monuments like Karnak and Abu Simbel, he memorialized his achievements and especially his personal deliverance through the god Amun before a select few who had the privilege of entering the temple, but most importantly, the deities themselves (see chapter by Ockinga). When Pentaweret inscribed his version on papyrus, he must have intended it for very different eyes, who would appreciate it as a literary narrative rather than as a royal inscription (Spalinger 2002; Manassa 2013) (see chapter by Stauder-Porchet and Stauder). The king's victory seems quite different, therefore, when carved on temple walls or when inscribed with ink on sheets of papyrus.

Content is thus closely linked to context, which aids in setting our expectations regarding an image or a text. As well informed as we might be regarding the context, our expectations remain subjective and based on our own views of the ancient Egyptian material. Context may point at other frames of reference in which the inscription or the scene was placed in the past, but for these to be fully appreciated, they need to be studied with comparable material in mind. Beyond questions of repertoire and variation, which will be dealt with in the third section, another line of inquiry involves text and image relationships that abound in Egyptian art. To this, the next section is dedicated.

MULTIMODALITY: TEXT AND IMAGE

As script that retains much of its pictographic dimension, hieroglyphs show a close relationship between image and text (Goldwasser 1995; see chapter by Vernus). This intimate link is evident in the ancient Egyptian lexicon, in which the word for "writing" and "to write" (zḫꜣ) can also mean "drawing" and "to draw" (Wb. 3.475–476). These blurred lines between text and image continue throughout the history of ancient Egypt in sportive writings (Fischer 1977), for example, or in the role of classifiers (Goldwasser 1995). These close relationships between text and image often offer us a view via one medium into how the content of the other was understood.

The most common example of these close relationships between the visual and the written involves cases of naming and identifying. Titles and names identify, for example, in an unfinished stela to Amun-Re the men carrying the divine barque in the upper register and those showing adoration below (MMA 21.2.6). In a scene from the tomb of Raemkai from centuries earlier, a scene of hunting takes places in the desert (MMA.

o8.201.1g). Above the wildlife to the right, the hieroglyphs read *gsh*, "antelope," and the animal biting one of them by the leg is labeled "dog." Below, a scene shows an ibex and a hunter, above whom a longer inscription reads "lassoing the ibex by the hunter." The inscription thus describes not only the individual components but also the action taking place in the scene, serving as its caption.

While seemingly straightforward, the relationships between texts and images are often quite difficult to assess. Naming and defining are quite different activities, and we cannot always ascertain that the label refers to the species itself or perhaps to the kind of object depicted. In certain cases, the word might actually refer to a wider class of which the antelope above is only a prime example (Weeks 1979).

Similarly, texts that accompany images as captions are not as straightforward as they may seem. Two inscriptions accompany, for example, the aforementioned scene of fishing and fowling from the tomb of Nakht. Written above the figures of the tomb owner, they read, "Crossing the ponds, traversing the marshes, enjoying piercing fish by. . . . Nakht," and "Enjoying seeing the goodness, spending pastime (at) the work of the (goddess) Sekhet by. . . . Nakht." Sekhet was the deity of the fields and of the marshes, as indicated by her name, which literally means "marshland" (Guglielmi 1974; Laboury 1997, 70). Since activities in these areas were associated with her, the two captions seem to closely follow what is depicted in the scene.

Other inscriptions on this wall show similar relationships between text and image. A scene to the left represents provisions being brought before the tomb owner and his wife. The inscription above them describes them as "enjoying inspecting the goodness of the Delta marshes' tribute." Another scene below shows the couple sitting in a pavilion in front of numerous food offerings, while the inscription above them reads, "Sitting in a booth in order to enjoy inspecting the goodness of the Delta." The intimate relationship between text and image seemingly offers us here an understanding of the scene's content, summarized into a few words: the first two describe a marsh scene, and the other two, inspecting provisions.

None of these inscriptions perfectly match, however, what is described in the scene. Understandably, they omit many components when providing a verbal interpretation to the scene. In the fishing and fowling scene, for example, the family is represented but not mentioned at all in the text. In fact, while the birds are depicted being hunted, the inscriptions only allude directly to the fish.

This might suggest that certain details were deemed more significant, and therefore, only they were included, but the captions also add new information to the scene. All scenes, for example, are bound by a common theme: a sense of entertainment that appears in all inscriptions. Admittedly, were it not for the inscriptions, this joy would have been hard to detect in the images themselves, that is, at least for a modern eye. In addition, one of the inscriptions in the marsh scene speaks of movement: crossing and traversing, both of which are classified with the walking legs hieroglyph (Gardiner D54). The scene is indeed very dynamic, but does it really convey the progress through the marshes that the inscription suggests?

This complexity can sometimes be manipulated to explore multiple levels of meaning within a scene. An image in the tomb of Khnumhotep in Beni Hasan depicts foreigners

FIGURE I.2.3. Facsimile of scene depicting leaders of the *Aamu* bringing tribute, in the tomb of Khnumhotep in Beni Hasan; painted by Norman de Garis Davies, ca. 1931; Rogers Fund, 1933 (MMA 33.8.17).

bringing desert animals and tribute before the tomb owner (Figure I.2.3). This specific scene is especially famous as it describes the foremost Asiatic as *ḥqꜣ ḫꜣs.wt*—literally "ruler of foreign lands"—a term that was later employed to describe the Asiatic dynasty ruling in the north of Egypt in the Second Intermediate Period, and from which the later name Hyksos most probably derives. For our purposes, the interesting detail lies in the inscription above the scene. While the image represents a peaceful row of merchants and tribute bearers, the inscription defines them as enemies, using the hieroglyph of a bound captive with his hands tied behind his back. (For an image and a text with reversed relationship, see Davies 2012.)

In fact, the desert animals depicted with these men may signal a subtle symbolic meaning as well. Vanquishing foreigners and hunting desert animals in art symbolized the overcoming of chaos by order (Kamrin 2015). The depiction of the civil foreigner and the tamed desert animal may thus hint at this concept.

Finally, it is noteworthy that similar relationships appear also in three-dimensional art, and also there they often prove to be productive and complex. Scribal statues, for example—statues that depict their patrons seated on the ground unrolling a papyrus—place an inscription on the scroll that beginning from the Middle Kingdom describes the literate activity the statue represents. The inscriptions vary, but during the Middle and the early New Kingdoms, they often emphasize legal procedures. These inscriptions seemingly serve as captions, explicating what kind of writing is carried out, but the image has important implications for the text as well. By visualizing law as writing, they suggest laws had a textual substance (Allon and Navrátilová 2017, 86). This representation thus contributes to the modern discussion on ancient laws and whether they were written down. Writing down laws may be still interpreted in different ways—composing, copying, enacting—but however it is to be understood, these statues certainly point at a textual aspect of law.

Thus, though seemingly simple, caution is necessary when using one medium to interpret another. Nevertheless, whether naming, identifying, complementing, or contradicting, text and image relationships present a productive method of inquiring about meaning. Often exploring a wider corpus of similar images and texts allows us to recognize patterns and employ them in our analysis. This exploration invites the question of repertoire and variation, to which the next and final section of this chapter is dedicated.

Repertoire and Variation

"The Egyptian could not give written expression even to his aesthetic emotions without a complete surrender to the conventional phraseology," remarks Sir Alan H.Gardiner—one of the most prominent Egyptologists of the twentieth century—when recording ancient Egyptian graffiti (Gardiner 1920). These inscriptions were left in tombs and monuments, scribbled by ancient visitors who wrote on the wall their name, titles, and at times a remark expressing their admiration to the visited monument. Even when prompted to write on the spur of the moment, Gardiner laments, these graffiti lacked any personal or spontaneous tone, employing instead the same stock phrases time and again.

We might not ascribe to Gardiner's sentiment nowadays, but his remark is not entirely off the mark. Even a brief survey of ancient Egyptian epigraphic texts and images reveals a rather restricted repertoire of phrases and motifs. Autobiographical texts, for example, describe their protagonists in very similar terms throughout Egyptian history. All men of the elite are just, loyal, impartial, and attentive to the weak. Even the phrases that characterize them are often the same: they dress the naked, feed the hungry, and care for the widow and the orphan (Doxey 1998). Similarly, certain motifs, such as agriculture and administration, occur in tombs of various periods, and in the Eighteenth Dynasty, even in the same part of the tomb.

Despite the general sense of conformity, a closer inspection reveals variations within the system. As noted before, Harkhuf and only a few others inscribed a letter from the king on the walls of their tomb chapels. In another tomb from a later period, a military official by the name of Amenemhab (also called Mahu) wrote an autobiographical text in his time following all the customary phrases. Like others before him, he too was just and loyal. As the text carries on, however, the reader suddenly finds themselves in very different terrain, when Amenemheb speaks of a gruesome act:

> Then this ruler of Qadesh let a female horse come forth, which was quick on its feet and it entered within the military. I ran after it on my feet bearing my knife and I opened its belly, having cut off its tail. Just as I gave it to the king, so did one praise god upon it.   (*Urk.* IV, 894.5–13)

With the majority of tombs having suffered damage and decay to their wall decoration or only partially published, it is rather difficult to ascertain whether Amenemheb's anecdote and Harkhuf's royal letter are as singular as they seem. We can, nevertheless, at least suggest that they are not common motifs based on the material available to us.

Similar variations are to be found also in the most seemingly conventionalized imagery. Several men of the Eighteenth Dynasty, for example, represented the king in their tombs, thereby differentiating themselves from most of the Egyptian elite through-out history (Radwan 1969; Hartwig 2004, 54–73). Others, emphasized the military in their tombs, like Horemheb—a high official who later ruled Egypt—who depicted a rare scene of the inspection of captives in the wake of war (Martin 1989).

Appreciation of repertoire and variations allows us to recognize patterns within the material. During the Amarna period, for example, we begin to see men who emphasize modest background—the reality of which is to be questioned at times—indicating that their rise to power was thanks to the king who recognized them for their extraordinary character. Similarly, with the beginning of the Ramesside period, one notices a shift in decoration in the Theban necropolis, with a decline in scenes of administration, agriculture, and such, and a growing emphasis on interactions with the divine (Fitzgerald 2013). In certain cases, we can identify intertextuality and intericonicity, intentional borrowing of elements and even whole scene compositions from one source to another (Laboury 2017). These variations, furthermore, indicate a certain flexibility in the system that defies assumptions of strict governing rules.

These variations invite us to consider what they could tell us about those who employed them, whether kings, scribes, artists, or elite patrons. Most often, ancient Egyptian sources ascribe agency to the patron or the king. By describing patron or king as the one who made the monument or stela, the text obliterates the myriad other actors who took part in the process: administrators, stonemasons, artists, and so forth (see chapters by Stocks, Laboury). In reality, rarely do sources discuss the processes through which objects were made, and we might assume a more varied and nuanced set of relationships between the different actors, from direct involvement of the patron in the choice of motifs and content to the approval of a completed product.

On the other hand, variations require us to consider how selective texts and images often are. Thus, for example, textual sources celebrate the successful career of their commissioners, and their images, whether in statuary or in tomb art, are always unblemished and healthy. For the most part, illnesses, failures, and old age are nowhere to be seen, and the imagery that one sees is often idealized, if not purely symbolic (Weeks 1970). Much remains, therefore, beyond representations.

In some cases, new elements that appear in representations might be newcomers to ancient Egyptian culture and society, but in others they might have been always present but not deemed important enough to represent. In this context, it is important to consider the term "decorum," which is often evoked for this purpose (compare Gillen forthcoming). Most recently, John Baines who introduced the term into Egyptology defined it as follows:

> The decorum found on monuments, which can be traced from late predynastic times, is a set of rules and practices defining what may be represented pictorially with captions, displayed, and possibly written down, in which context and in what form. It can be related to other constraints on action and reports on action....and was probably based ultimately on rules of conduct and etiquette, of spatial separation and religious avoidance.   (Baines 1990, 20)

Decorum thus reminds us of that which remains outside the scope of representation and invites us to consider what is absent.

With decorum, we return full circle to the question of expectations, the starting point of this chapter. By definition, identifying absence is a product of an expectation, the assumption that a certain element should have been there. It is difficult and perhaps impossible not to apply our own subjective expectations when dealing with ancient materials. It is exactly here that the repertoire and its variations allow us to observe our expectations critically and base them on evidence.

Concluding Remarks

In this short chapter, I tried to highlight three paths to *enter a text or an image*, to borrow an Egyptian idiom. Context, multimodality, and repertoire and variations set, I suggest, certain expectations when approaching an image or a text. Each of these could be further developed, and other paths could be explored. In certain cases, secondary inscriptions, such as textual and figurative graffiti, allow us at least a glimpse into how later generations related to their past (Doncker 2012; Ragazzoli et al. 2017). One could also add questions of materiality, script, and quality as well as other issues that were tangentially touched on in previous pages.

In these few concluding lines, I would like to consider two final elements that further complicate our investigation of content and its understanding in ancient times. As indicated earlier, the understanding of content is very much reliant on audience and reception. Considerations of literacy are therefore highly significant in this context, asking who could have deciphered and understood the inscriptions we discuss. On the one hand, even with the highest estimates of literacy, the majority of the population could neither read nor write (Baines and Eyre 2007). On the other, certain inscriptions indicate that visitors might have been able to listen to their words if accompanied by a literate person.

While literacy regarding texts is often discussed, there is frequently an underlying assumption that no such considerations should be taken regarding imagery. These are assumed to be open to all, who could easily decipher and enjoy their multiple layers of meaning. As we assume that ancient Egyptian iconography is imbued with symbolism and has multiple layers of meaning, we should acknowledge that these were not open to all viewers (Doncker, 2010, 2017). As scholars invested in the study of ancient Egypt, we can access worlds of knowledge through editions, dictionaries, and compilations. We often, therefore, run the risk of assuming that our comprehensive knowledge of the system and its multiple possibilities and variations was shared by all ancient viewers and readers.

Our understanding of ancient Egyptian ways of representation is still very limited, affected by the arbitrary state of preservation and our distance from that ancient culture. The context of the text or the image, the surrounding signals in other media, and even the conformity, which Gardiner finds understandably disappointing, are all helpful in developing our interpretations and in the challenging task of assessing our expectations. They provide us with a framework through which to recognize the common and the rare, the probable and the improbable. Yet, in the end, we are still not very much better off than the ninth-grade student encountering an altered image of Trotsky and Lenin for the first time.

BIBLIOGRAPHY

Allon, N. 2013. "The Writing Hand and the Seated Baboon: Tension and Balance in Statue MMA 29.2.16." *JARCE* 49:93–112.

Allon, N., and H. Navrátilová. 2017. *Ancient Egyptian Scribes: A Cultural Exploration*. Bloomsbury Egyptology. London.

Assmann, J. 1983. "Schrift, Tod und Identität: Das Grab als Vorschule der Literatur im alten Ägypten." In *Schrift und Gedächtnis: Beiträge zur Archäologie der literarischen Kommunikation*, edited by A. Assmann, J. Assmann, and C. Hardmeier, 64–93. Munich.

Baines, J. 1990. "Restricted Knowledge, Hierarchy, and Decorum: Modern Perception and Ancient Institutions." *JARCE* 27:1–23.

Baines, J., and C. J. Eyre. 2007. "Four Notes on Literacy." In *Visual and Written Culture in Ancient Egypt*, 63–94. New York.

Davies, N. de G. 1917. *The Tomb of Nakht at Thebes*. Robb de Peyster Tytus Memorial Series 1. New York.

Davies, V. 2012. "The Treatment of Foreigners in Seti's Battle Reliefs." *JEA* 98:73–85.

Doncker, A. Den. 2010. "Prélude à une étude de la réception de l'image égyptienne par les anciens Égyptiens." In *Thèbes aux 101 portes: Mélanges à la mémoire de Roland Tefnin*, edited by E. Warmenbol and V. Angenot, 79–89. MonAeg 12. Turnhout.

Doncker, A. Den. 2012. "Theban Tomb Graffiti during the New Kingdom: Research on the Reception of Ancient Egyptian Images by Ancient Egyptians." In *Art and Society: Ancient and Modern Contexts of Egyptian Art: Proceedings of the International Conference Held at the Museum of Fine Arts, Budapest, 13–15 May 2010*, edited by K. A. Kóthay, 23–34. Budapest.

Doncker, A. Den. 2017. "Identifying-Copies in the Private Theban Necropolis: Tradition as Reception under the Influence of Self-Fashioning Processes." In *(Re)productive Traditions in Ancient Egypt*, edited by T. Gillen, 333–370. AegLeo 10. Liège.

Doxey, D. M. 1998. *Egyptian Non-Royal Epithets in the Middle Kingdom: A Social and Historical Analysis*. PdÄ 12. Leiden.

The Epigraphic Survey. 1930. *Medinet Habu I: Earlier Historical Records of Ramses III*. OIP 8. Chicago.

Eyre, C. 2013. *The Use of Documents in Pharaonic Egypt*. Oxford.

Fischer, H. G. 1977. "The Evolution of Composite Hieroglyphs in Ancient Egypt." *MMJ* 12:5–19.

Fitzgerald, C. 2013. "Traditional Mechanisms and New Applications: Identity Construction and Definition of Space through Image in Post-Amarna and Nineteenth Dynasty Elite Tombs at Thebes." PhD diss., Emory University.

Frood, E. 2007. *Biographical Texts from Ramessid Egypt*. WA 26. Atlanta.

Gardiner, A. H. 1920. "Graffiti." In *The Tomb of Antefoker, Vizier of Sesostris I, and of His Wife, Senet* (No. 60), by N. de G. Davies and A. H. Gardiner, and N. de Garis. TTS 2. London.

Gillen, T. J. Forthcoming. "Besides Decorum: Notes on Formality." In *Filtering Decorum—Facing Reality*, edited by A. Dorn. AegLeo. Liège.

Goldwasser, O. 1995. *From Icon to Metaphor: Studies in the Semiotics of the Hieroglyphs*. OBO 142. Fribourg.

Greenblatt, S. 1980. *Renaissance Self-Fashioning: From More to Shakespeare*. Chicago.

Guglielmi, W. 1974. "Die Feldgöttin *Sx.T*." *WDO* 7 (2):206–227.

Hartwig, M. K. 2004. *Tomb Painting and Identity in Ancient Thebes, 1419–1372 BCE*. MonAeg 10(2). [Brussels].

Hayes, W. C. 1959. *The Scepter of Egypt: A Background for the Study of the Egyptian Antiquities in the Metropolitan Museum of Art*. 2 vols. Cambridge.

Kamrin, J. 2015. "Facsimile of a Tomb Painting Depicting the Leaders of the Aamu of Shu." In *Ancient Egypt Transformed: The Middle Kingdom*, edited by Di. Arnold, Do. Arnold, K. Yamamoto, and A. Oppenheim, 176–177. New Haven.

Laboury, D. 1997. "Une relecture de la tombe de Nakht (TT52, Cheikh 'Abd el-Gourna)." In *La peinture égyptienne ancienne: Un monde de signes à préserver; Actes du Colloque international de Bruxelles, avril 1994*, edited by R. Tefnin, 49–81. MonAeg 7. Brussels.

Laboury, D. 2017. "Tradition and Creativity: Toward a Study of Intericonicity in Ancient Egyptian Art." In *(Re)productive Traditions in Ancient Egypt*, edited by Todd Gillen, 229–258. AegLeo 10. Liège.

Manassa, C. 2013. *Imagining the Past: Historical Fiction in New Kingdom Egypt*. New York.

Martin, G. T. 1989. *The Memphite Tomb of Ḥoremheb, Commander-in-Chief of Tutʿankhamūn: The Reliefs, Inscriptions, and Commentary*. Vol. 1. EM 55. London.

Radwan, A. 1969. *Die Darstellungen des Regierenden Königs und seiner Familienangehörigen in den Privatgräbern der 18. Dynastie*. MÄS 21. Berlin.

Ragazzoli, C., Ö. Harmanşah, C. Salvador, and E. Frood, eds. 2017. *Scribbling through History: Graffiti, Places and People from Antiquity to Modernity*. London.

Shedid, A. G., and M. Seidel. 1996. *The Tomb of Nakht: The Art and History of an Eighteenth Dynasty Official's Tomb at Western Thebes*. Translated by Marianne Eaton-Krauss. Mainz.

Spalinger, A. J. 2002. *The Transformation of an Ancient Egyptian Narrative: P. Sallier III and the Battle of Kadesh*. Wiesbaden.

Strudwick, N., ed. 2005. *Texts from the Pyramid Age*. WA 16. Atlanta.

Tefnin, R. 1991. "Éléments pour une Sémiologie de l'image Égyptienne." *CdE* 66 (131–132):60–88.

Vischak, D. 2015. *Community and Identity in Ancient Egypt: The Old Kingdom Cemetery at Qubbet El-Hawa*. New York.

Weeks, K. R. 1970. "The Anatomical Knowledge of the Ancient Egyptians and the Representation of the Human Figure in Egyptian Art." PhD diss., Yale University.

Weeks, K. R. 1979. "Art, Word, and the Egyptian World View." In *Egyptology and the Social Sciences: Five Studies*, edited by K. R. Weeks, 59–81. Cairo.

THE EGYPTIAN THEORY OF MONUMENTAL WRITING AS RELATED TO PERMANENCE OR ENDURANCE

BOYO G. OCKINGA

THE MONUMENT AS A MEANS TO OVERCOME TRANSIENCE

ONE of the primary factors motivating the ancient Egyptians to construct monuments, in particular those of a funerary nature, was the desire to overcome the transience of human existence. The two possible concepts of an existence beyond death, living on in the memory of the group and continuing to live independent of society as an immaterial being, an "immortal soul" (Assmann 1988, 97), were realized in their funerary monuments: the rituals conducted there and in many instances inscribed on the walls were for the benefit of the *ka*, *ba*, and *akh* of the deceased; the biographical inscriptions and addresses to the living, indeed the very recording of the name and title(s) of the tomb's owner, were intended to ensure that they would be remembered by succeeding generations and continue to live in the social context. In the case of temples, although they were constructed for the benefit of the deity as part of the symbiotic relationship between the gods and humankind, building inscriptions (Grallert 2001) provided the kings who commissioned them an avenue for preserving their memory among future generations. Temple statues, both royal and nonroyal, were intended not only to ensure that their owners would not be forgotten, as the inscriptions on nonroyal statues clearly indicate, but also to serve their immaterial form, their *ka*, as the recipient of the offerings they hoped to share in.

The permanence of existence in the memory of society that ancient Egyptian monumental inscriptions were intended to give was of course dependent on the durability of the monuments on which they were carved; the inscription and the monument that bears it were attempts at overcoming the transience of time and memory. Probably the most dramatic and universally recognized statement from ancient Egypt expressing the desire to prevail over time through the durability of a monument is made not in words but in stone: the massive pyramids of Giza. This message in stone is summed up in the Arab proverb "Man fears time but time fears the pyramids."[1] In ancient Egypt, the intimate association between a monument and the striving for permanence lies at the very heart of the Egyptian word for "monument," *mnw*. It designates all types of structures from a massive pyramid or temple to a statue or stela and encapsulates the concept of endurance and stability for it is derived from the verbal root *mn* "to remain, to endure;" thus a monument is "that which endures," a term that captures the very essence of the object it designates and points to its purpose, which was to enable its builder or owner to overcome transience (Assmann 1988, 92).

Durability of Material

It is not the size alone of monumental structures such as the pyramids and temples but also their material that gives them this quality. Stone was for the ancient Egyptians the epitome of permanence and indestructibility: When, in the course of the embalming ritual, the priest wished to emphasize the durability of the deceased's body he stated: "Your corpse is eternally enduring, like the stone of the two mountains" (pBoulaq 3, x+8, 3–4; Töpfer 2017; Assmann 1983, 11). Anhurmose (Nineteenth Dynasty) expresses the wish that his "name might remain (*mn*) like the mountain of Behedet (el-Mashayikh)" (Ockinga and Al-Masri 1988, 45). On the colossal statue of Amenemope (Twentieth Dynasty) carved out of the living rock in his Theban tomb (TT 148) he addresses his statue with the words, "My statue of the rock of my city, may I last (*rwḏ*)... my name being remembered upon your surface" (Ockinga 2009, 56). Although the ancient Egyptians did build in less permanent materials, in particular mudbrick, this was generally only used for houses and palaces, structures that were not built for eternity; where permanence was desired, as was the case with temples and tombs, stone was the preferred medium. This apparent excessive investment in the tombs of the dead at the expense of the dwellings of the living is a phenomenon that intrigued ancient Greek visitors to Egypt. Diodorus Siculus (first century BCE), drawing on Hecataeus of Abdera (fourth century BCE), states: "For the Egyptians regard the time spent in this life as completely worthless; but to be remembered for virtue after one's demise they hold to be of the highest value. Indeed they refer to the houses of the living as "inns," since we dwell

---

[1] It is attributed to an unidentified "learned Arab of the Twelfth Century" (Speake 2008, 321–322), but the sentiment is doubtless one that many have shared.

in them but a short time, while the tombs of the dead they call "everlasting homes,"[2] since in Hades we remain for an endless span. For this reason, they trouble themselves little about the furnishings of their houses, but betray an excess of ostentation concerning their places of burial" (*Bibliotheca Historica* I, 51; trans. Murphy 1990, 65–66). J. Assmann (1983, 11) sees reflected in this statement a concept that could be defined as an Egyptian "philosophy of stone" to which Egyptian art and monumental architecture owes its existence and its permanence.

The superiority of stone over mudbrick is expressed in New Kingdom inscriptions recording the replacement of a temple built of mudbrick with one constructed of stone, a deed considered to be laudable and worthy of commemoration: At Semna, it is said of Thutmose III, "through his monument he has acted for his father Dedwen, foremost of Nubia, and for the King of Upper and Lower Egypt Khakaure (Senwosret III), constructing for them a temple of good white stone (*inr ḥḏ nfr*) of Nubia (i.e., sandstone)—His Majesty having found (it) of brick, very ruined—being what a son does with a loving heart for his father" (*Urk.* IV 197.13–198.2; also, 169.4–14).

It is clear that what motivated replacing a mudbrick structure with one of stone was the desire that the monument would be enduring. In an inscription on a stela from the temple of Ptah at Karnak, Thutmose III says, "My Majesty commands the construction of the temple of Ptah South of his Wall in Thebes.... Now, my Majesty found this temple built of mudbrick, its columns and gates of wood, fallen to ruin. My Majesty commands the stretching of the cord for this temple anew, it being erected of sandstone (*inr ḥḏ nfr n.y rwḏ.t*)" (*Urk.* IV 765. 7, 12–15). In this text, the Egyptian expression designating "sandstone" captures the desired quality of endurance: *inr ḥḏ nfr n.y rwḏ.t* literally means "good bright stone of hard stone." The word *rwḏ.t* is the operative term; it is derived from the verbal root *rwḏ* "to be firm, strong, enduring" and designates hard stone in general, including sandstone (Faulkner 1962, 148).

Written Statements of the Desire for Permanence

Not only does the Egyptian word for "monument" in and of itself contain the concept of permanence, the desire and intention that a monument endure for eternity (*nḥḥ, ḏ.t*) is also explicitly stated in both royal and nonroyal inscriptions.

A classic formulation that clearly emphasizes this is found in the biographical inscription of Khnumhotep II at Beni Hasan. In his description of the construction of his own funerary monument Khnumhotep tells us that he emulated his father, who built himself a *ka*-chapel "of good stone of limestone (*ʿnw*) to make firm (*srwḏ*) his name for eternity (*nḥḥ*), so that he might make it effective forever (*ḏ.t*), his name living in the mouth of the *pat*-people, enduring in the mouth of the living, in his tomb of the

---

[2] Rather than seeing this as a translation of a specific ancient Egyptian term, Burton (1972, 159) suggests that Diodorus is translating a concept.

necropolis, in his effective house of eternity (*nḥḥ*), the place of his house of everlastingness (*ḏ.t*)" (*Urk.* VII 33.11–18).

Building for eternity is also stressed in royal inscriptions: "Year 47 under the Majesty of the King of Upper and Lower Egypt Menkheperre, Son of Re, Thutmose III (who lives) eternally: His Majesty ordered that this temple be surrounded by a massive wall in enduring work for [his father] Re-Horakhty for the length of eternity (*ḏ.t*)" (*Urk.* IV 832.12–14). In the hypostyle hall at Karnak, Seti I (usurped by Ramesses II) is described as "One who makes monuments for his father Amun-Re, who enlarged his house for eternity (*ḏ.t*) in enduring (*rwḏ.t*) work of eternity (*nḥḥ*)." (*KRI* I 205.6; also, V 322.8–9).

It is not only buildings that one desires to endure and remain for eternity, the same applies to other monuments, such as statues: In an inscription of Thutmose III from Karnak recording the endowment of an offering cult for his statue, he recounts his building works in Karnak, stating, "That [I] did this for my father, Amun, Lord of [the Thrones of the Two Lands], was in return for the statues of my Majesty, which are in his temple, being enduring (*rwḏ*)" (*Urk.* IV 175.7–9).

One encounters similar statements in the inscriptions of nonroyal persons: On his Karnak statue, the vizier Khay asks, "May my statue endure (*rwḏ*) in the temple of Amun, receiving offerings that come from the presence" (*KRI* III 38.13–14; also, IV 129.4–5, 131.12, 132.5).

Desire for Permanence of Identity: Preservation of the Name

However, monuments were not an end in themselves, the quality of durability and permanence one wished for them had a specific purpose, namely, to ensure that the person who made them would also share in this attribute. The identity of monument and person already finds expression in the Pyramid Texts: "O Great Ennead that is in Heliopolis! May you let NN endure; may you let this pyramid of NN endure, this work of his forever and ever, as the name of Atum, foremost of the Great Ennead, endures" (PT Spell 368; Sethe 1908–1922, §§669–670).

Preserving the identity of a monument's owner over an extended length of time, forever and ever as the texts express it, could obviously only be assured through the written word, inscribed on the monument itself or an object, typically a stela, associated with it. Thus, we find that the identity of the owners of the earliest monuments, the tombs of the Early Dynastic Period, which are otherwise devoid of inscriptions, is established through stone stelae that were set up at the place where offerings were brought to the deceased and that were inscribed with the owner's name. The name encapsulates the essence of the identity of the individual, and the preservation of the name is the central objective of a monument. The close connection between the preservation of the name and the monument finds regular expression in texts from the time of the Pyramid Texts onward, on both royal as well as nonroyal monuments. In the pyramid of Merenre, we read, "(As) the name of Shu, Lord of the Upper Menset in Heliopolis endures (*rwḏ*), the name of Merenre will endure (*rwḏ*), this pyramid will endure (*rwḏ*) likewise forever and ever (*ḏ.t ḏ.t*)" (PT Spell 368; Sethe 1908–1922, §§1660a–1661a; also, Cairo CG 42185, *KRI* IV 130. 9–10, 13–14; DZA 25.868.150).

As Jan Assmann (1988, 97) has observed, in the context of the tradition of building monuments, the concept of a person's continuing, enduring existence after death is located in a social context, in the person being remembered and spoken about, expressed as being "in the mouth" of succeeding generations. This is particularly graphically illustrated by inscriptions from the reign of Amenhotep III in which a monument is personified. In an inscription in room XVII of the temple of Luxor, the building is attributed with having a "mouth": Amun says to the king, "Your name will be enduring (*ḏdi.w*) in the 'mouth' of your monument, it being permanent (*rwḏ*) like the horizon of heaven" (DZA 25.868.020; Brunner 1977, pl. 86).

A text attested on several nonroyal monuments personifies the statue or stela, identifying it with the owner's heir, entrusted with the task of ensuring that the owner continues to be remembered: "O you living ones upon earth, scribes, lector priests, *wab*-priests, *ka*-servants, those who will see this statue/stela, my 'imitator,' my heir on earth, my remembrance in the necropolis" (*Urk.* IV 1032.2–6; also, 1034, 1036, 412, 1641; James 1974, pl. 51a,b).

The whole concept is encapsulated in a widely attested phrase found on monuments that were made not by their owners but for them by another person, usually a son or other family member: "It is his son who lets his name live" (*Wb.* IV 47.1–7), and this is achieved by inscribing the owner's name on the monument. Thus, inscribed monuments are entrusted with the task of ensuring that their owners will not be forgotten, but rather that their names will be remembered and that following generations will speak about them.

MEASURES TAKEN TO ENSURE THE PRESERVATION OF MONUMENTS AND INSCRIPTIONS

Committing a name or event to writing did not in and of itself provide a guarantee of permanence and durability. Experience would soon have revealed that inscriptions were threatened both by the natural degradation of the material on which they were inscribed as well as the deliberate actions of others, that is, erasure or usurpation. Various measures were undertaken in an attempt to mitigate these threats.

Measures against "Wear and Tear/Natural Attrition"

The desire to ensure that the monument and its inscription would endure through time will also have influenced the choice of the medium on which a text was written.

A preference for stone has already been mentioned. The selection of a particularly hard stone like quartzite for the annals of Senwosret I at Heliopolis surely reflects both the importance placed on the text and the intention that it should survive (Baines 2008, 21).

The wish for permanence is also illustrated by cases where a text that was recorded on a less durable medium was subsequently copied and inscribed onto a stone surface. A well-known example is the annals of Thutmose III, which he ordered to be inscribed (using the causative of the verb *mn*, "to remain," from which "monument," *mn.w* ["that which remains"] is also derived) in stone on the walls of the inner chambers of the temple of Karnak. This was done even though the information provided by the text carved in stone was already stored in the temple in other documents written not on the more usual papyrus, but on another relatively durable medium, leather (*Urk.* IV 662.5; Lichtheim 1976, 33).

Another text that was subsequently inscribed onto a more durable surface is the Memphite Theology (Ockinga 2010); its introduction states that King Shabaka of the Twenty-fifth Dynasty commanded that the text, which we are informed was found in the temple of Ptah written on a worm-eaten papyrus, be copied and inscribed on stone. The type of stone chosen, granodiorite, is also telling; it is particularly hard and durable and was doubtless chosen to ensure that the theological text would be preserved for posterity, but also, as the introduction explicitly states, to ensure that the king's "name might endure and his monument last in the House of his father . . . throughout eternity" (Lichtheim 1973, 52).

Certain inscribed architectural elements that were located in areas of higher traffic and therefore subject to more wear and tear were often made of more durable materials; for example, the doorways of temples were often built of granite, basalt, or granodiorite; these parts of the temple were those most often seen by the people who frequented them. Apart from the desire to use only the best for the deity's dwelling, another factor that probably influenced the choice of material will have been the wish that their texts, which included the name of the king who commissioned them, would survive (Figure I.3.1).

An early and unique attempt at ensuring the durability of reliefs and inscriptions is found in the tomb chapels of the official Nefermaat and his wife Atet at Meidum (Figure I.3.2). Apart from a few figures down the edge of the entrance to Nefermaat's chapel, which are in relief, the representations as well as hieroglyphs of the tomb decoration are deeply incised into the stone in sunken relief and the depressions then filled with colored pastes, level with the stone surface (Petrie 1892, 24–25; Bagh 2011). The rationale behind this unusual and inventive form of decoration is given in an inscription in the chapel of Atet that states explicitly that its images (referred to as *nt̲r.w* "gods") are made in writing that cannot be erased (*Urk.* I 7.11; Petrie 1892. 39; Simpson 1982). The method did not prove to be particularly effective and was not widely used (Wildung 1982; see also Harpur 2001, 56 with n1).

The repetition of names and titles in tomb decoration, as well as their positioning on hidden elements of the tomb, can also be plausibly linked to the desire for permanence. Since the preservation of the name, which ensured the individual's continued existence in social memory into the future and eternity, was one of the central functions of a

FIGURE I.3.1. Gate of Thutmose III, Karnak. © Boyo Ockinga.

funerary monument, the more frequently the name was recorded, the greater was the chance that it would survive. The function of funerary cones has been variously interpreted (Eggebrecht 1977; Manniche 2001), but one, and probably the original, purpose will have been to contribute to the perpetuation of the owner's name (Figure I.3.3). This is certainly the role that such cones have frequently fulfilled; the owners of many Theban tombs are only known because their cones have survived, the tomb decoration having been lost or the owners' names systematically erased.

Similarly, the friezes that were introduced in the Ramesside Period as an element that ran across the top of the wall decoration of tomb chapels will have had a similar purpose, since each element of the frieze included the owner's name and main title, sometimes also accompanied by a representation (Figure I.3.4).

Measures against Possible Deliberate Destruction

The choice of durable materials for the bearer of a text and the multiplication of the name of a monument's builder were attempts to counter one of the forces threatening the durability of a monument and its inscriptions, namely, wear and tear and natural deterioration, but this was not the only threat faced. Inscriptions and the monuments that bore them were also subject to the deliberate destructive activity of other people.

FIGURE I.3.2. Image of Atet, Meidum. © Boyo Ockinga.

This issue was addressed both by practical measures that were taken to make it more difficult for someone to do this, and by texts addressed to potential perpetrators that tried to persuade them to desist from doing so.

Practical Measures against Deliberate Damage

Among the practical measures undertaken to thwart the possible activity of those who might attempt to obliterate an inscription, some of the examples mentioned earlier that were primarily aimed at countering natural wear and tear, such as the repetition of names and titles, were likely also thought to be possible ways of escaping the results of deliberate attacks.

There are other interesting examples that are more likely to have been measures taken to counter deliberate erasure than natural attrition. To these belong the inscribing of the name of the king who built a monument on surfaces that were expected to remain hidden from sight. A notable case is the cartouches with the throne name of Hatshepsut that were carved into the ends of the blocks of quartzite from which the walls of her Red Chapel at Karnak were constructed. The blocks abutted one another when the structure was standing, and the names would have been out of sight and unreachable. It was only when the chapel was dismantled and the blocks stored in a heap for future reuse that

FIGURE I.3.3. Cone collection from the tomb of Neferrenpet (TT 147). © Boyo Ockinga and Leonie Donovan.

FIGURE I.3.4. Frieze in the tomb of Anhurmose, el-Mashayikh. From Ockinga and Al-Masri, 1988. © Boyo Ockinga.

some of them, depending on how they were placed, became visible and were erased (Dorman 1988, 52–55; Van Siclen 1989; Burgos and Larché 2006, 312).

Mudbricks stamped with the owner's name are known from both royal and nonroyal constructions (MMA 11.215.455). The sheer number of these would have contributed to the preservation of the owner's name, but their location hidden inside the structure would also have helped ensure their protection from possible deliberate damage.

The same applies to another hidden building element used in monumental constructions that is sometimes inscribed with the builder's name: clamps of stone or wood that were used to hold together stone wall constructions (Brussels E.8055).

In Hatshepsut's temple at Deir el-Bahri, the representations and accompanying inscriptions of Senenmut, the architect of the building, are an interesting case. On the reveals of almost every one of the over sixty doorways in the temple, Senenmut had himself represented, accompanied by inscriptions in which he praises a deity on behalf of the king. These compositions are positioned such that when opened inward, the leaves of the doors would cover and hide them from view. The workmanship of the figures give the impression of having been hastily executed and are distinctly inferior in craftsmanship to those of the neighboring temple reliefs (Hayes, 1957, 80–82). Although first impressions may suggest that the work was done secretly because it went against the rules of decorum for a nonroyal to represent himself in such a way in a temple, this was in fact not the case. Another contemporary official, the viceroy Nehi, depicts himself in a similar way in the temple of Buhen (Hayes 1957, 84n5; Caminos 1974, pls. 2, 88, 92; Dorman 1988, 173) and Hayes (1957, 82–85) has published a text inscribed on the reveals of the door leading into the Northwest Hall of Offerings at Deir el-Bahri which clearly indicates that Senenmut had been granted permission by Hatshepsut to represent himself in that temple, as well as in other temples in the land. Although the hidden locations of the representations do not point to an illicit act, the motivation behind making them so unobtrusive, as well as their number, can best be explained as being the desire to ensure the permanence of at least some. The appearance of hasty execution also fits this scenario. It so happened that this plan was successful because, although most were erased, four of the representations escaped the attentions of those who set about defacing Senenmut's images and texts (Hayes 1957, pl. XI).

In the preceding examples, where the name is hidden, the aim to achieve continued existence beyond death through being remembered in the social context may seem not as convincing; the mere existence of the name is often thought to magically ensure the person's survival. Yet even here, in the event that the structure was dismantled, its true owner would be revealed even if their name had been removed from the visible record.

A well-known and widely attested phenomenon, particularly in the Ramesside Period, that can probably also be seen as a practical measure to ensure an inscription's permanence are royal inscriptions that are carved in sunken relief that is noticeably very deep. It is difficult not to see this as a reaction to the practice of usurpation, that is, as an attempt to make it more challenging for subsequent kings to inscribe their names over one's own (see Brand chapter). The reign of Ramesses III provides particularly good examples of deeply carved hieroglyphs, such as the bandeau inscriptions on the outer walls of the king's memorial temple, his "House of millions of years," at Medinet

FIGURE I.3.5. Ramesses III, Medinet Habu, north wall. © Boyo Ockinga.

Habu, which are carved in hieroglyphs that in some cases have a depth of up to twenty centimeters (Figure I.3.5).

Warnings against Willful Damage

Already in the tomb inscriptions of the Old Kingdom, we encounter statements addressed to visitors to the tomb that broach the subject of willful damage to the monument as a whole; some attempt to encourage the desired behavior through positive sanctions, urging the reader to treat the tomb with respect and not damage or destroy (*sšn/shn*) it. Thus, we read in the tomb of Remenuka at Giza, "He who does not demolish (*sšn*) the stone of this tomb is one whom the king and Anubis, who is upon his mountain, love amongst all the people who come to the West to this tomb." The tomb owner then goes on to say that he did not bring stolen property to the tomb and that he paid the workers who built it (Hassan 1936), emphasizing that he himself was not guilty of the behavior he reprimands. More often, a threat is made against anyone who might damage the monument, as in the tomb of Tjetu at Giza: "I know every excellent magic that is effective in the necropolis. As for any man who will take or demolish (*sšn*) the stone (or) brick in this tomb, I will take legal action in the court of the Great God" (Simpson 1980, 8, fig. 14; see also Morschauser 1987).

In the early Middle Kingdom tomb of Djefai-Hapi near Asyut, a more specific warning is given to any who would damage his inscriptions:

> As for any persons, any scribe, any learned man, any commoner, any poor man who
> will cause a disturbance in this tomb, destroy its writings, do damage to its statues,

they will fall to the wrath of Thoth, the effective one who is among the gods. They are destined for the slaughter of the magistrates, the servants of the king who are in the court. Their gods will not accept their bread offerings. As for any persons, any scribe, any learned man, any commoner, any poor man who will enter this tomb, who will see what is in it, who will protect its writings, honor its statues, and speak an offering prayer for the *ka* of the owner of this tomb, the Mayor Djefai-Hapi, he will become an old man of his city, a revered one of his province.   (*Urk.* VII 53.9–54.4)

Interestingly, the same text is found in the New Kingdom tomb of Puyemre (TT 39; Davies 1922, pl. 20), indicating that, not surprisingly, the problem still existed at that time. (See also Anthes 1928, Graffiti 33 and 42; 19, 35, and 52; Malinine, Posener, and Vercoutter 1968, 48, No. 52.)

Assurances That Damage Was Not Done to Previous Works

As well as statements warning against damaging a monument, one text explicitly assures that this was not done: in an inscription in the temple of Montu at Karnak, Amenhotep III states that he built a temple for Amun anew, "of good bright sandstone, in an effective place of Thebes, without damaging that which had been made previously (*nn ḥḏi.t iri. yt ḏr-bȝḥ*), it being established as a work of eternity" (Helck 1955–1958, 1667.17–19). Presumably, Amenhotep assures that in the course of his own building works he did not damage earlier structures. This was clearly not always practicable. One structure that can plausibly be explained to be a measure taken to compensate earlier kings for the removal of their monuments is the "Chamber of Ancestors" built by Thutmose III at Karnak. It has been suggested that the extensive building program carried out by Thutmose in that temple necessitated the clearance of earlier buildings and monuments to make room for his new structures, and by way of recompense, the kings whose monuments were affected were represented and their names inscribed in the chamber built by Thutmose (Wildung 1974). This interpretation of the purpose of the chamber has been questioned on the basis that such an act does not really accord with the Pharaonic way of thinking (Delange 2015, 51), but the well-attested injunctions against damaging the monuments of others, and the assurance by Amenhotep III that he did not do so in the course of his building activity, suggest otherwise. Nor do other explanations proffered to account for the construction of the "Chamber of Ancestors" provide a convincing reason for the unusual selection of kings who appear there, in particular the absence of the immediate New Kingdom predecessors of Thutmose III.

THE RESTORATION OF
DAMAGED MONUMENTS

The positive contrast to doing injury to earlier monuments is the act of restoring them when they have fallen into decay or have been deliberately damaged by others.

Royal building inscriptions that record this activity have been referred to earlier. In the post-Amarna period, an extensive program of restoration of monuments that had been damaged under Akhenaten was undertaken. The best-known figure connected with this activity was prince Khaemwaset, the son of Ramesses II, whose activities went beyond making good Amarna Period damage and included doing repairs to the pyramids of a number of early kings and restoring their names (Gomaà 1973, 1975). There is a precedence to this activity from the nonroyal sphere that illuminates the rationale behind the restoration carried out by the post-Amarna kings. In the Twelfth Dynasty, Khnumhotep II of Beni Hasan twice records that he renewed the inscriptions and tombs of his fore-bears: "Then I embellished (*smnḫ*) it (his province), its wealth growing in everything. I made to endure (*srwḏ*) the name(s) of my father(s), I made effective (*smnḫ*) their *ka*-chapels" (*Urk.* VII 29.8–11). Further on, he states, "I made the name(s) of my fathers live (*sꜥnḫ*), which I found destroyed on the doorways, they being recognizable in (written) signs, precise/exact as that which is read, without placing another in the company of another (i.e., without confusing one with another), for it is an effective (*mnḫ*) son who causes the name(s) of his forebears to endure (*srwḏ*)" (*Urk.* VII 32.20–33.3). The restorations of the post-Amarna pharaohs can be understood in the context of the last statement of Khnumhotep II: by undertaking their program of restoration, the new dynasty was claiming to be the true successors, the "effective sons," of their predecessors.

There is little doubt that, with regard to permanence, the overwhelming opinion in ancient Egypt was that encapsulated in what Assmann (1983) has dubbed "the philosophy of stone," namely, that the most effective means of ensuring that one would be remembered for eternity was to have one's name inscribed on an enduring monument; the countless stone monuments from ancient Egypt with inscriptions commemorating individuals is eloquent testimony to this. However, in the New Kingdom school literature, we encounter a dissenting opinion: Papyrus Chester Beatty IV vs. 2.11–3.5 states, regarding the learned scribes of the past, the authors of the books used in scribal schools,

> Their ka-servants are [gone], their tombstones covered with dirt, their chambers forgotten. (But) their names are pronounced because of these books of theirs which they made, because they are good, and the memory of him who made them(?) is forever and ever.... More profitable is a book than an inscribed tombstone, than a firmly established chapel-wall(?). This serves as chapels and pyramids for the sake of pronouncing their name. For sure, a name in the mouth(s) of people is useful in the afterlife!... it is writings that will cause that he will be remembered in the mouth of the one who speaks.   (Gardiner 1935, vol. I, 39, vol. II, pls.18–19)

The text then lists sages of the past whose names are remembered because of their books. Here, the written word is still seen as providing the vehicle for permanence of memory, but it is not the physical durability of the medium bearing the words that will achieve this, but rather the quality of the composition. Nevertheless, the traditional view held sway for it is also from this period that we have a unique limestone relief from the lost Saqqara tomb of someone who doubtless came from this scribal milieu that includes some of these sages in a series of famous men (Simpson 2003, xvii, fig. 6). The monuments of the later phase of pharaonic history also clearly attest to the enduring nature of Egypt's "philosophy of stone."

Bibliography

Anthes R. 1928. *Die Felsinschriften von Hatnub*. UGAÄ 9. Leipzig.

Assmann, J. 1983. "Die Gestalt der Zeit in der ägyptischen Kunst." In *5000 Jahre Ägypten: Genese und Permanenz Pharaonischer Kunst*, edited by J. Assmann and G. Burkard, 11–32. Nussloch.

Assmann, J. 1988. "Stein und Zeit. Das 'monumentale' Gedächtnis der altägyptischen Kultur." In *Kultur und Gedächtnis*, edited by J. Assmann and T. Hölscher, 87–114. Frankfurt.

Bagh, T. 2011. *Finds from W.M.F. Petrie's Excavations in Egypt in the Ny Carlsberg Glyptotek*. Meddelelser fra Ny Carlsberg Glyptotek N.S. 13. Copenhagen.

Baines, J. 2008. "On the Evolution, Purpose, and Forms of Egyptian Annals." In *Zeichen aus dem Sand: Streiflichter aus Ägyptens Geschichte zu Ehren von Günter Dreyer*, edited by E.-M. Engel, V. Müller, and U. Hartung, 19–40. Wiesbaden.

Brunner, H. 1977. *Die südlichen Räume des Tempels von Luxor*. AVDAIK 18. Mainz.

Burgos, F., and F. Larché. 2006. *La chapelle rouge: Le sanctuaire de barque d'Hatshepsout*. Paris.

Burton, A. 1972. *Diodorus Siculus. Book I: A Commentary*. Leiden.

Caminos, R. 1974. *The New Kingdom Temples of Buhen*. 2 vols. ASE 33–34. London.

Davies, N. de G. 1922. *The Tomb of Puyemrê at Thebes*. Vol. 1. PMMA 2. New York.

Delange, É. 2015. *Monuments égyptiens du Nouvel Empire: Chambre des Ancêtres—Annales de Thoutmosis III—Décor de palais de Séti Ier*. Paris.

Dorman, P. 1988. *The Monuments of Senenmut: Problems in Historical Methodology*. London.

Digitales Zettelarchiv der Berliner-Brandenburgischen Akademie der Wissenschaften (DZA). Retrieved from http://aaew.bbaw.de/tla/.

Eggebrecht, A. 1977. "Grabkegel." In 1975–1992 *Lexikon der Ägyptologie*, 7 vols, edited by W. Helck, E. Otto, and W. Westendorf. Vol 2. Wiesbaden, 857–859.

Faulkner, R. O. 1962. *A Concise Dictionary of Middle Egyptian*. Oxford.

Gardiner, A. H. 1935. *Hieratic Papyri in the British Museum. Third Series: Chester Beatty Gift*. 2 vols. London.

Gomaà, F. 1973. *Chaemwese, Sohn Ramses' II. und Hoherpriester von Memphis*. ÄA 27. Wiesbaden.

Gomaà, F. 1975. "Chaemwese." In 1975–1992 *Lexikon der Ägyptologie*, 7 vols, edited by W. Helck, E. Otto, and W. Westendorf. Vol 1. Wiesbaden, 897–898.

Grallert, S. 2001. *Bauen—Stiften—Weihen: Ägyptische Bau—und Restaurierungsinschriften von den Anfängen bis zur 30. Dynastie*. ADAIK 18. Berlin.

Harpur, Y. 2001. *The Tombs of Nefermaat and Rahotep at Maidum: Discovery, Destruction and Reconstruction*. Oxford.

Hassan, S. 1936. *Excavations at Gîza 1930–1931*. Vol. 2. Cairo.

Hayes, W. C. 1957. "Varia from the Time of Hatshepsut." *MDAIK* 15:78–90.

James, T. G. H. 1974. *Corpus of Hieroglyphic Inscriptions in the Brooklyn Museum*. Vol. 1. New York.

Lichtheim, M. 1973. *Ancient Egyptian Literature, Vol. I: The Old and Middle Kingdoms*. Berkeley.

Lichtheim, M. 1976. *Ancient Egyptian Literature, Vol. II: The New Kingdom.* Berkeley.

Manniche, L. 2001. "Funerary Cone." In *Oxford Encyclopedia of Ancient Egypt*, vol. 1, edited by D. Redford, 565–567. Oxford.

Morschauser, S. 1987. "Threat Formulae in Ancient Egypt." PhD diss., Johns Hopkins University.

Malinine M., G. Posener, and J. Vercoutter. 1968. *Catalogue des stèles du Sérapéum de Memphis.* Vol. 1. Paris.

Murphy, E. 1990. *The Antiquities of Egypt: A Translation with Notes of Book I of the* Library of History *of Diodorus Siculus.* Rev. ed. New Brunswick.

Ockinga, B. 2009. *The Tomb of Amenemope (TT 148), Vol. 1: Architecture, Texts and Decoration.* ACE Reports 27. Oxford.

Ockinga, B. 2010. "The Memphite Theology—Its Purpose and Date." In *Egyptian Culture and Society: Studies in Honour of Naguib Kanawati*, edited by A. Woods, A. McFarlane, and S. Binder, 2:99–117. CASAE 38. Cairo.

Ockinga, B., and Y. Al-Masri. 1988. *Two Ramesside Tombs at El Mashayikh, Part 1.* Sydney.

Petrie, W. M. F. 1892. *Medum.* London.

Sethe, K. 1908–1922. *Die altägyptischen Pyramidentexte nach den Papierabdrücken und Photographien des Berliner Museums.* 4 vols. Leipzig.

Simpson, W. K. 1980. *Mastabas of the Western Cemetery, Part I.* GMas 4. Boston.

Simpson, W. K. 1982. "Nefermaat." In 1975–1992 *Lexikon der Ägyptologie*, 7 vols, edited by W. Helck, E. Otto, and W. Westendorf. Vol 4. Wiesbaden, 376–377.

Simpson, W. K., ed. 2003. *The Literature of Ancient Egypt.* 3rd ed. New Haven.

Speake, J., ed. 2008. *The Oxford Dictionary of Proverbs.* 5th ed. Oxford.

Töpfer, S. 2017. "Papyrus Boulaq 3 (Theben West). Balsamierungsritual x+8, 3–4." In *Thesaurus Linguae Aegyptiae.* Retrieved from http://aaew.bbaw.de/tla/index.html.

Van Siclen III, C. 1989. "New Data on the Date of the Defacement of Hatshepsut's Name and Image on the Chapelle Rouge." *GM* 107:85–86.

Wildung, D. 1974. "Aufbau und Zweckbestimmung der Königsliste von Karnak." *GM* 9:41–48.

Wildung, D. 1982. "Pastenfüllung." In 1975–1992 *Lexikon der Ägyptologie*, 7 vols, edited by W. Helck, E. Otto, and W. Westendorf. Vol 4. Wiesbaden, 913.

CHAPTER I.4

···

THE HISTORICAL
RECORD

···

PETER J. BRAND

Introduction

A large portion of the preserved textual and iconographic evidence for ancient Egyptian history and culture takes the form of monumental inscriptions and decorations. While records in more fragile mediums, especially documents written in ink on papyrus and ostraca, were produced in vastly larger quantities than monumental inscriptions, the fragile nature of the former has robbed us of most of them, while reliefs and inscriptions, often carved literally in stone, have proven much more durable. As a result, important historical questions in Egyptology often turn on the analysis of monumental records. Alongside philology and art history, historians of ancient Egypt make use of epigraphy as a method for recording and interpreting the monumental historical record. Whole categories of historical sources are largely or wholly subsumed within the category of epigraphic sources, including king lists, royal annals, self-laudatory biographies of officials, royal decrees, pious graffiti, dedicatory inscriptions, war scenes, and their caption texts. Monumental relief carvings and paintings decorate the walls of tombs and temples. Rock inscriptions, from formal royal texts to humble visitors' graffiti, were carved or etched in various remote locations throughout the Levant, the eastern and western deserts of Egypt, and in Nubia. Inscribed monumental objects include sarcophagi, stelae, sculptures ranging from miniature statuettes to huge royal colossi, offering tables, naoi, and the like—all of them grist for the historian's mill.

Whether in the field or in museum galleries and storerooms, epigraphy is a vital tool for making sense of monumental records, which are often fragmentary and which frequently reveal evidence of a second hand, which has altered, erased, or adapted them. Erasures and defacement of hieroglyphic texts and artistic imagery—even intentional dismantling of buildings and smashing of statues—are often rooted in historical events we are trying to understand. Likewise, modification and augmentation of monumental records can provide vital chronological, ideological, and historical data. The epigrapher turned historian should bring a forensic sensibility to analyzing damaged, fragmentary, and altered inscriptions. A healthy respect for the limits of sources, as well as a methodical and dispassionate mien, is also more likely to produce historical conclusions that are sound and enduring. As with other subdisciplines in Egyptology—archaeology, art history, philology, and so forth—overly passionate and subjective epigraphic analysis has often produced dubious historical conclusions. We can gain a better appreciation of both the promise and the pitfalls of epigraphic methods applied to the study of history by examining a handful of case studies dating to the New Kingdom period: so-called usurpations and erasures of monumental inscriptions by Ramesside-era pharaohs, and monumental epigraphic evidence for the question of coregencies during the late Eighteenth and early Nineteenth Dynasties.

Epigraphy and Historical Methodology

An important caveat for using epigraphic data to support historical interpretation is the danger of misconstruing the motives or purposes of the ancient Egyptians in cases of erasures, iconoclasm, reworking, or other instances in which they altered monumental reliefs and inscriptions (see chapter by Allon). In the modern history of Egyptology, scholars have often assigned visceral, personally antagonistic motives to cases such as Thutmose III's systematic effacement of Hatshepsut's royal monuments, which was often seen as arising from his supposed deep hatred of her. A more cautious approach to the evidence admits that our epigraphic sources are limited in what they can tell us about historical events. So, while an epigraphic approach may involve reconstructing Egyptian history as the record of "who did what to whose monuments," it rarely can tell us unequivocally *why* they did it.

When used in conjunction with other types of source material—textual, iconographic, and archaeological—epigraphic data can augment the historical record. There is also considerable overlap between these methodologies. So, erased or altered hieroglyphic texts can be approached epigraphically, philologically (to reveal what the text says and what has been changed or removed), and paleographically. Likewise, defaced or altered wall scenes have art historical and iconographic dimensions (e.g., McClymont 2016) on Amarna erasures as archaeological artifacts).

Naguib Kanawati's investigation (2003) of political upheaval in the early Sixth Dynasty through his work in the Teti pyramid cemetery at Saqqara offers an excellent example of such a holistic approach. From Manetho, we have the historical statement that Teti was assassinated by his "eunuchs," a claim that could never be proved or disproved. In addition, a handful of sources indicate that a shadowy king named Userkare seems to have reigned between Teti and Pepi I. Through his systematic excavations and epigraphic analysis of officials' tombs in the Teti pyramid cemetery, Kanawati showed that Userkare was likely a usurper who displaced Pepi I as Teti's rightful successor and that after the former's fall from power, various officials, including the *ḥnty-š*, who served as royal bodyguards, were subject to defacement of their names and images in inscriptions from their funerary monuments. Kanawati's study is an excellent example of epigraphic analysis applied to historical research.

Problems of Terminology

At times, the terminology Egyptologists have used in identifying and analyzing epigraphic phenomena in ancient sources has introduced bias, anachronisms, or culturally inappropriate implications that cast doubt on the historical conclusions that they have attempted to draw from them. Neutral terms are better (e.g., "memory sanctions" instead of the modern phrase *damnatio memoriae*, Flower 2006; "erasure" rather than "destruction," "hacking," or "defacement," McClymont 2016). Vincent Rondot (1997) called into question the term "usurpation" as applied to Ramesses II's practice of erasing the names of his predecessors on monuments and replacing them with his own. The term usurpation normally conveys a sense of illegitimacy and personal malice (Capart 1932; Brand 2010). Although Ramesses II may have frequently "usurped" the names and images of his predecessors—even of his own father and grandfather—no one today would describe him as a "usurper" in the political or legal sense. Still, Breasted argued a century ago that Ramesses had indeed assassinated and replaced an alleged older brother as Seti I's heir, based on his misinterpretation of palimpsest figures of an official named Mehy, together with some fanciful historical speculation (Breasted 1899). While The Epigraphic Survey (1986) proved that there was no older prince, only a troop commander, *ṭs pḏwt*, named Mehy, this did not prevent scholars like Helck (1988) and Murnane (1990, 1995) from suggesting that Mehy may have played a role in royal succession at the transition from the Eighteenth to the early Nineteenth Dynasties. These scholars' views suffer from the temptation to overinterpret epigraphic data to answer historical questions that are not appropriate to its purview. However desperately we wish to understand royal succession in the early Ramesside Period, a few palimpsest images from Seti I's Karnak war reliefs are unlikely to shed much light on the issue. Such evidence is often hopelessly inadequate to our historical inquiries.

Monumental Appropriation of Cartouches and Erasure of Royal Inscriptions in the Ramesside Period

A common epigraphic phenomenon among Ramesside-era royal inscriptions is the deliberate erasure or appropriation of cartouche names and other distinctive elements of royal titulary, over which the names and epithets of one or more later kings have been carved in succession (Brand 2009, 2010). The practice already occurs in earnest in the middle of the Eighteenth Dynasty, when Thutmose III systematically erased the names of Hatshepsut on her monuments at Karnak and often replaced them with those of his forbearers Thutmose I and II (Edgerton 1933; Dorman 2005; Laboury, 1998). At the end of the dynasty, Horemheb frequently erased the cartouches of his immediate predecessors, Tutankhamun and Ay, and replaced them with his own (Hari 1965; The Epigraphic Survey 1998). In all these cases, Thutmose III and Horemheb appropriated their predecessors' cartouches as part of memory sanctions against these pharaohs (Laboury 1998).

By contrast with such Eighteenth Dynasty appropriations and erasures of royal names on monuments, during the Nineteenth Dynasty, Ramesses II frequently erased and reinscribed the cartouches of his royal ancestors on a variety of monuments, including those of his own father, Seti I, and grandfather, Ramesses I, at Karnak (Seele 1940; Murnane 1975, 1997). In no case does Ramesses II employ this practice as an act of memory sanctions against his royal predecessors. Thus, we cannot find examples where Ramesses reinscribed the cartouches of pharaohs who suffered memory sanctions after their reigns like Hatshepsut and the Amarna Period kings. This situation makes it difficult for modern observers to understand the motivations behind Ramesses II's widespread reinscription and appropriation of earlier royal statuary (Magen 2011). and other monuments. Too often, modern viewers have resorted to a simplistic and pejorative explanation, namely that Ramesses was a "thief" who "stole credit" for the work of others by placing his names on their monuments.

In fact, Ramesses II's surcharging of royal names on existing monuments was part of his larger program to redecorate of royal monuments, including his own, which often involved additions to existing monuments that do not, in fact, obscure the names of earlier pharaohs (Brand 2006). Much of this decoration may be termed marginal inscriptions, that is, bandeau-style inscriptions and friezes of royal cartouches added at the undecorated margins of existing monuments and their original decoration.

Returning to Ramesses II's actual surcharging of earlier royal names with his own, we can see that these are usually part of a larger and discrete program of such reinscriptions of cartouches (Brand, Feleg, and Murnane 2018). At Karnak, we can date most of these replacements of cartouche names by the form of Ramesses II's nomen, R^c-ms-sw, which in Upper Egypt is mostly found from his year 21 and later. By plotting the positions of these replacements, we find also that they are concentrated along the main East-West processional axis of Karnak from the façade of the Second Pylon to the passageway of the Third Pylon including the columns, architraves, and clerestory roof adjoining the main processional route inside the Great Hypostyle Hall (Revez and Brand 2015). Yet aside from some inscriptions in the south wing of the Great Hypostyle Hall, we do not find that Ramesses surcharged the names of his predecessors on other structures at Karnak. Nor do we find such surcharged cartouches in architectural inscriptions at Luxor Temple or on other Theban monuments. Instead, his replacements of earlier kings' cartouches are confined largely to royal statuary of kings like Amenhotep III and pharaohs of the Twelfth Dynasty (Magen 2011).

At the end of the Nineteenth Dynasty, disputes over royal succession and the reign of the apparent usurper Amenmesse led to a renewed round of memory sanctions by Amenmesse against Merenptah and by Seti II against Amenmesse himself (Brand 2009; Dodson 2010; Hopper 2010). Occasionally, as with a marginal text of Merenptah at the Ramesseum, Amenmesse surcharged the cartouches of his predecessor and replaced them with his own (Brand 2009). More frequently, however, he preferred simply to erase Merenptah's cartouches and occasionally whole texts, but without placing his own name in their stead. After Amenmesse's demise, Merenptah's rightful successor Seti II replaced his father's erased cartouches with his own on reliefs from the *Cour de la Cachette* at Karnak temple. He also thoroughly erased Amenmesse's cartouches on a gateway from central Karnak near the Sixth Pylon. Similar erasures and surcharges targeted the last two Nineteenth Dynasty rulers, Siptah and Tawosret (Johnson 2010).

THE QUESTION OF LATE EIGHTEENTH- AND EARLY NINETEENTH-DYNASTY COREGENCIES

In the annals of Egyptian history and modern Egyptological scholarship, among the two best attested—and most debated—cases of possible coregency between two pharaohs are the alleged joint rule of Amenhotep III with Amenhotep IV/Akhenaten (Redford 1967; Murnane 1977) and later between Seti I and Ramesses II (Seele 1940; Murnane 1975; Brand 2000). Both have been highly controversial in scholarly literature for decades. In point of fact, however, the most secure case of a coregency during the New Kingdom and, indeed, all of Egyptian history is the undoubted joint rule of Thutmose III and Hatshepsut. That debate has centered on the date of Hatshepsut's assumption of formal royal style and the relative prominence of the female pharaoh with her younger coregent (Dorman 2006). By contrast, in the cases of Amenhotep III/Amenhotep IV and Seti I/ Ramesses II, the very existence of any genuine overlap in the exercise of kingship between these two pairs of individuals is hotly contested and the evidence is often ambiguous and of a secondary or even tertiary nature to the issue at hand (Murnane 1975, 1977). From a historiographical viewpoint, debate about the Amarna coregency has been especially heated, and the issue has carried forward over the years by new generations of "true believers" who have often applied curious logic, dubious analysis, and the tendency to view skeptics as heretics, often boiling down the argument to something along the lines of "it must be so because I say it is so" (Redford 1967; Giles and Knapp 1997; Giles 2001; Forbes 2014).

There is little in the way of actual epigraphic data that might indicate a coregency of Amenhotep III with Amenhotep IV/Akhenaten, and it is highly tenuous (Murnane 1977). In the Soleb royal cult temple of Amenhotep III, for example, are several scenes of a king worshiping deities, including the deified Amenhotep III as Nebmaatre-Lord-of-Nubia (Murnane 2000). It is clear in these cases that the cartouche names have been tampered with, but the question of who did what to whose names has led proponents of the coregency theory to speculate that the original names of the royal officiant were those of Amenhotep III and that they were then changed to Amenhotep IV once he became coregent. Careful examination led Murnane (2000, 2013) to conclude, rather, that Amenhotep IV reinscribed his father's cartouches with his own names (see also Laboury 2010, 381n99).

We are indebted to Murnane's meticulous epigraphic fieldwork for dispelling another shibboleth of the coregency debate, the identity of a pair of erased royal figures on the east face of the north tower of the Third Pylon at Karnak (Murnane 1979). These royal images were inserted at a smaller scale behind larger figures of Amenhotep III standing on the deck of Amun-Re's river barge. These smaller royal figures were subsequently erased, while the larger figures of Amenhotep III were left untouched. While it is universally agreed that these smaller, erased figures were secondary to the original decorative program of Amenhotep III, the identity of the two erased royal figures has been hotly debated. For coregency proponents, they were certainly Amenhotep IV, carved in an "early Amarna style" (Giles 2001; Forbes 2014). Murnane's exacting on-site epigraphic analysis casts grave doubt on this theory, revealing them to be post-Amarna in date, and probably the work of Tutankhamun (Murnane 1979). The erasure of the two royal figures was, then, likely the work of Horemheb. My own analysis of secondary restorations of the divine figures on the hull of the barge further corroborates Murnane's findings (Brand 1999).

More recently, a team of Spanish archaeologists excavating the tomb of the vizier Amenhotep-Huy offered what they termed to be "proof" of the hypothetical coregency after finding decorated fragments of column inscriptions from the vizier's tomb chapel that name both kings (Valentin and Bedman 2015). It is quite clear that construction and decoration of this tomb, like those of the Vizier Ramose and of the Royal Steward Kheruef, was underway at the very end of Amenhotep III's reign and in the earliest phase of Amenhotep IV's (Dorman 2009). None of these tomb inscriptions, including the new ones from Amenhotep-Huy's tomb, however, offer up definitive proof that there was an overlap in rulership between these pharaohs. It is equally, if not more, plausible that Amenhotep-Huy chose to honor both the recently deceased Amenhotep III and his new sovereign Amenhotep IV in the column decoration without the need to resort to coregency as an explanation (see also Dorman 2009).

The most unambiguous evidence for the hypothetical Seti I/Ramesses II coregency is a statement in Ramesses II's dedicatory inscription from the Seti I temple at Abydos wherein the king gives an account of his earliest career during his father's lifetime. Here Ramesses claims that Seti declared to courtiers: "place the crowns on his head that I might see his perfection while I am alive" (*KRI* II 328.1). Scholars have often taken this claim at face value as virtual proof of a coregency without considering the possibility that the whole episode described here might be fictive, comparable to Hatshepsut's ahistorical claim of a coregency with her father Thutmose I (Murnane 1977). Epigraphic data for a coregency consists largely of temple decoration dating to the earliest phase of Ramesses II's reign that, coregency proponents argue, reflects a period of joint rule during which Seti I allegedly permitted his son and co-ruler to decorate monuments like the Karnak Hypostyle Hall and Seti's royal cult temple at Qurna jointly with his father (Seele 1940; Murnane 1977; Spalinger 1979).

Seele, followed by Murnane and others, identified three phases in Ramesses II's early monumental relief decoration (Brand, Feleg, and Murnane 2018). At the outset of his reign, the king used raised relief for interior temple wall decoration, where his prenomen appears simply as Wsr-$m3^ct$-R^c, without the epithet stp-n-R^c, which he adopted later. Within a few months, however, Ramesses began to carve only in sunk relief while maintaining the short prenomen, marking a second identifiable phase in his work in Upper Egyptian monuments, such as the Karnak Hypostyle Hall. Finally, at the end of his first regnal year or early in his second, he adopted the definitive prenomen Wsr-$m3^ct$-R^c-stp-n-R^c while continuing to employ sunk relief for his decoration during the rest of his reign. According to Seele (1940), Murnane (1977), and Spalinger (1979), the first two phases of decoration occurred during a coregency when Seti I, they claim, was still alive, while the long form of the prenomen marked Ramesses's accession as sole king.

Confirmation of this theory seemed to come in the form of various reliefs at Karnak, Qurna, and Abydos that seemed to show the two kings jointly participating in the decoration of these monuments (Seele 1940; Murnane 1975). On the south wall of the Great Hypostyle Hall, Seti and Ramesses appear together in several scenes. Likewise, at Seti I's Qurna Temple, the two kings appear in alternating scenes in the hypostyle hall and together in the same scene a number of times in the vestibule to the cult rooms of Ramesses I. Further cases of alleged "joint decoration" occur in the Gallery of Kings and the Corridor of the Bull in Seti I's Abydos temple. At Qurna, friezes of cartouches along the tops of walls often alternate between Seti and Ramesses. For Seele and Murnane, one of the most telling indications of joint rule is the way that the prenomens of these kings appear to be blended together in rebus decoration inscribed on the cabin-shrine of Amun-Re's sacred barque in a scene on the south wall of the Karnak Hypostyle Hall (Murnane 1975). Closer epigraphic examination of this barque scene revealed that in every case, elements of Seti I's prenomen Mn-$m3^ct$-R^c were actually suppressed to create new rebuses of Ramesses prenomen Wsr-$m3^ct$-R^c (Brand, Feleg, and Murnane 2018).

From such evidence, proponents of the coregency theory argue that toward the end of his reign, Seti I allowed his son to become co-ruler and then permitted him to participate jointly in the decoration of newly constructed monuments at Karnak, Qurna, and Abydos. Moreover, during this time, Ramesses II undertook the construction and decoration of his own shrines at Beit el-Wali and a smaller temple next to Seti's own at Abydos (Spalinger 1979).

The epigraphic evidence for such a coregency is highly ambiguous and often dubious (Brand 2000). Comparison with other cases where two kings appear in the same scene or separately in adjoining scenes is instructive. During the coregency of Hatshepsut and Thutmose III, for instance, most of the decoration on the walls and obelisks of Karnak and at the queen's Deir el-Bahri cult temple features either: (1) Hatshepsut alone; (2) less commonly Thutmose III alone; or (3) both rulers acting in concert within the same scene with Hatshepsut appearing in the first position as in scenes from the Chapelle

Rouge barque sanctuary at Karnak (Burgos and Larché 2006–2008). Moreover, in all these scenes, both rulers take an active role in the ritual presented to deities (Davies 2004). There are no scenes in which one ruler is the active officiant and the other the passive recipient of the cultic act, as is typical with scenes at Karnak and Qurna showing Seti I and Ramesses II. Thus, despite the superiority of Hatshepsut's position vis-à-vis Thutmose III, reliefs explicitly indicate that both rulers were alive and active at the same time.

Cases where the names of two rulers appear in alternating scenes or inscriptions on the same monument include reliefs from the Colonnade Hall of Luxor Temple. Built late in the reign of Amenhotep III but with its decorative program scarcely begun when the project was abandoned upon the accession of Akhenaten, it languished in an unfinished state until decoration of the interior walls and fourteen great columns was laid out and carved mostly by Tutankhamun (The Epigraphic Survey 1998). Yet two other kings also appear on the columns: Amenhotep III and Seti I. To postulate hypothetical coregencies between any two of these monarchs stretches credulity to the breaking point. Instead, Tutankhamun sought to associate himself with the memory of his deceased grandfather, Amenhotep III, for ideological ends. The proximity of Seti I on the two southernmost pairs of columns to Tutankhamun's work farther north stems from the fact that Tutankhamun died before he completed decorating the south end of the Colonnade Hall.

Returning to the case of Seti I and Ramesses II, although coregency advocates can point to dozens of epigraphs on several monuments carved at the outset of Ramesses II's reign, a comparison with the Hatshepsut/Thutmose III coregency and the example of the Colonnade Hall at Luxor do not inspire confidence that these reliefs signal a genuine, early Nineteenth Dynasty coregency. Thus, while Seti and Ramesses appear together in several ritual episodes on the south wall of the Karnak hypostyle hall and in the vestibule to the Ramesses I cult chambers at Qurna, in each case Seti appears as a deified cult image receiving offerings, suggesting that he was dead when the reliefs were carved. In the vestibule chamber at Qurna, the certainly deceased Ramesses I also appears in scenes with his grandson. Likewise, friezes of cartouches along the tops of its walls present the names of all three kings side by side (Brand 2000).

Examining these epigraphic phenomena with the assumption that they were made early in Ramesses II's reign only after the death of Seti clears up these anomalies. Late in his reign, Seti I highlighted his son's role as "heir apparent and king's eldest son," *iry-pʿt, sꜣ-nsw smsw* (Murnane 1975; Spalinger 1979; Brand 2000). Father and son appear on a number of royal and private monuments, including scenes from the Gallery of Kings at Seti's Abydos Temple, where they participate jointly in the ritual before deities and royal ancestors in a fashion similar to reliefs of Hatshepsut and Thutmose III. A common feature of these reliefs is that Ramesses appears always as an adolescent prince wearing the sidelock and lacking the royal cartouche names.[1] Elsewhere, scenes juxtaposing the two

---

[1]   In one scene from the Gallery of Kings, Crown Prince Ramesses is entitled as a prince, but he wears a pendant on his kilt sash that gives his early prenomen as king, *Wsr-Mꜣʿt-Rʿ*. Murnane (1975) and others have taken this as evidence for coregency. I now suspect that sculptors completed this relief in the earliest days of Ramesses II's reign, just after his father died, at which point the decorative cartouche was inserted.

kings' names and images occur on monuments of Seti I that Ramesses was completing early in his reign, after Seti had died. It is crucial, moreover, that in scenes featuring Seti I and Ramesses II where both have the full royal style and iconography, the former king is the passive recipient of offerings made by his son (Brand 2000).

In contrast to the appearance of his father in Ramesses II's earliest decoration of monuments built originally for Seti I, the senior king is largely absent from the decoration of Ramesses's own earliest temples (one appearance in his Abydos temple and none at Beit el-Wali). This prompts the question: If Seti I was the senior partner in the coregency, why would he allow Ramesses so much latitude in decorating his own monuments while accepting that his son did not feature his father in his Beit el-Wali and Abydos shrines? As junior partner, why would Ramesses choose—or be allowed—to strike out on his own, so to speak? Such problems evaporate if one assumes that all the decoration carried out by Ramesses II as a king, with cartouches and other trappings of royal style, were made only after Seti I had died.

As with figures of kings in wall scenes, mere proximity of their royal names and titles in monumental decoration does not prove they ruled jointly. Such cartouche friezes at Qurna Temple are clearly designed to associate Ramesses II with his deceased father and grandfather as an act of filial piety. Far from proving a case of coregency, epigraphic data from Karnak, Abydos, Qurna, and Beit el-Wali indicate that Ramesses II ascended the throne only after his father's death, having remained crown prince, *iry-pʿt sꜣ-nsw smsw*, until that event. From a historical context, as young scion of a new royal house scarcely a decade old when he became king, Ramesses II chose to stress his filial piety to his father and grandfather in completing Seti's monuments at Qurna, Karnak, and Abydos. Nor should the political fiction contained in Ramesses's Abydos dedicatory inscription's imagined scene of his "coronation" during Seti's lifetime be given much weight as a valid historical source. Like other royal "autobiographies," including Hatshepsut's Coronation Inscription, the Abydos text is highly ideological. It is not "historical." Viewed as acts of filial piety after Seti I's death, and as part of an effort to legitimize his own reign, all of the scenes of Ramesses worshipping his deified father and of stereotyped friezes of cartouches juxtaposing their names make excellent sense.

Conclusions: Epigraphy as a Tool for History

Epigraphy, like other categories of data, can and must serve as a crucial tool for reconstructing ancient Egyptian history. In employing this evidence, the historian must be careful to understand fully the original chronological and ideological contexts in which epigraphic sources were created or altered. In using epigraphic data to answer difficult or complex historical questions, we must always be cognizant of the limitations of the evidence, including the fact that very often the preserved sources are woefully inappropriate for answering the questions that we demand of them. A sound approach to epigraphic data rests firmly on the need to accept and interpret the data on its own terms.

Failure to take this more cautious approach can lead to results that soon become dated and, in retrospect, may appear bizarre to later generations of scholars, as when Sethe became gripped by the so-called Hatshepsut Problem (Sethe 1896, 1932). The tendency for the queen's image to be defaced and for her cartouches to be erased and replaced by the names of Thutmose I and II led Sethe to postulate a complex chronology in which the queen and the first three Thutmoside kings successively seized and relinquished the throne until only Thutmose III remained. Others were skeptical, and Edgerton (1933) set the matter to rest when he demonstrated that, without question, the cartouche names of Thutmose I and II were never replaced in favor of Hatshepsut's—only the reverse. He concluded, therefore, that all this was done after Hatshepsut's death by Thutmose III, and this view, based on careful epigraphic analysis, has withstood the test of time.

However, one question remained: *When* were Hatshepsut's names and images defaced or replaced? In clearing up one misconception, Edgerton and his followers laid down a new one, namely, that the proscription of the queen's memory was a visceral act of personal animosity by Thutmose III, an act of revenge for having been sidelined by the queen for the first twenty years of his reign. By the 1940s and 1950s, it was taken largely for granted that Thutmose III acted with "vindictive fury" (Wilson 1951) against his former coregent's "usurpation" of the throne. The king, in Breasted's words, "was not chivalrous in his treatment of her when she was gone. He had suffered too much" (Breasted 1912). With her death, Thutmose III "wreaked with full fury his vengeance on the departed ones who in life had thwarted his ambitions. He was resolved that their memory should perish from the earth" (Steindorff and Seele 1942). Such florid prose makes for colorful reading but poor historical analysis.

More recently, rigorous epigraphic analysis of the monuments led scholars such as Dorman (1988, 2005), Van Siclen (1984, 1989), and Laboury (1998) to conclude that the earliest datable defacement of her image on the Chapelle Rouge at Karnak, took place only after the building was dismantled to make way for Thutmose III's new barque chapel. Since Thutmose's chapel, according to an inscription carved on it, was only completed some two decades after Hatshepsut's death, this would seem far too long for a powerful king to hold a grudge without acting on it, thereby calling into doubt the emotional explanation for Hatshepsut's proscription. Alternative explanations taking these epigraphic facts into consideration will no doubt be more cautious and, perhaps, even disappointing, but the alternative is to invent our own histories and project them on to whatever data lies conveniently at hand. This would be historical fiction, not history. We must accept the limitations of our sources.

BIBLIOGRAPHY

Brand, P. J. 1999. "Secondary Restorations in the Post-Amarna Period." *JARCE* 36:113–134.
Brand, P. J. 2000. *The Monuments of Seti I: Epigraphic, Historical and Art Historical Analysis.* PdÄ 16. Leiden.

Brand, P. J. 2006. "Veils, Votives, and Marginalia: The Use of Sacred Space at Karnak and Luxor." In *Sacred Space and Sacred Function in Ancient Thebes*, edited by P. F. Dorman and B. M. Bryan, 51–83. SAOC 61. Chicago.

Brand, P. J. 2009. "Usurped Cartouches of Merenptah at Karnak and Luxor. In *Causing His Name to Live: Studies in Egyptian Epigraphy and History in Memory of William J. Murnane*, edited by P. J. Brand and L. Cooper, 28–48. CHANE 37. Leiden.

Brand, P. J. 2010. "Usurpation of Monuments." In *UCLA Encyclopedia of Egyptology*. https://escholarship.org/uc/item/5gj996k5.

Brand, P. J., Feleg, R. E., and Murnane†, W. J. 2018. *The Great Hypostyle Hall at Karnak, Volume I, Part 2. Translations and Commentary* and *Part 3. Figures and Plates*. OIP 142. Chicago.

Breasted, J. H. 1912. *A History of Egypt from the Earliest Times to the Persian Conquest*. 2nd rev. ed. New York.

Breasted, J. H. 1899. "Ramses II and the Princes in the Karnak Reliefs of Seti I." *ZÄS* 37:130–139.

Burgos, F., and F. Larché. 2006–2008. *La chapelle rouge: Le sanctuaire de barque d'Hatshepsout*. 2 vols. Paris.

Capart, J. 1932. "L'usurpation des monuments dans l'antiquité égyptienne." In *Mélanges de philologie orientale publiés à l'occasion du Xe anniversaire de la création de l'Institut supérieur d'histoire et de littératures orientales de l'Université de Liège*, 57–66. Louvain.

Davies, V. 2004. "Hatshepsut's use of Tuthmosis III in her Program of Legitimation." *JARCE* 41:55–66.

Dodson, A. 2010. *Poisoned Legacy: The Decline and Fall of the Nineteenth Egyptian Dynasty*. Cairo.

Dorman, P. F. 1988. *The Monuments of Senenmut: Problems in Historical Methodology*. London.

Dorman, P. F. 2005. "The Proscription of Hatshepsut." In *Hatshepsut: From Queen to Pharaoh*, edited by C. H. Roehrig, R. Dreyfus, and C. A. Keller, 267–269. New York.

Dorman, P. F. 2006. "The Early Reign of Thutmose III: An Unorthodox Mantle of Coregency." In *Thutmose III: A New Biography*, edited by E. H. Cline and D. O'Connor, 39–68. Ann Arbor.

Dorman, P. F. 2009. "The Long Coregency Revisited: Architectural and Iconographic Conundra in the Tomb of Kheruef." In *Causing His Name to Live: Studies in Egyptian Epigraphy and History in Memory of William J. Murnane*, edited by P. J. Brand and L. Cooper, 65–82. Leiden.

Edgerton, W. 1933. *The Thutmosid Succession*. SAOC 8. Chicago.

The Epigraphic Survey. 1986. *Reliefs and Inscriptions at Karnak* IV: *The Battle Reliefs of King Sety I*. OIP 107. Chicago.

The Epigraphic Survey. 1998. *Reliefs and Inscriptions at Luxor Temple* II: *The Facade, Portals, Upper Register Scenes, Columns, Marginalia, and Statuary in the Colonnade Hall*. OIP 116. Chicago.

Forbes, D. C. 2014. "Circumstantial Evidence for an Amenhotep III/IV Coregency." *KMT* 25:36–49.

Flower, H. I. 2006. *The Art of Forgetting: Disgrace and Oblivion in Roman Political Culture*. Chapel Hill.

Giles, F. J. 2001. *The Amarna Age: Egypt*. ACE Studies 6. Warminster.

Giles, F. J., and Knapp, A. B. 1997. *The Amarna Age: Western Asia*. ACE Studies 5. Warminster.

Hari, R. 1965. *Horemheb et la reine Moutnedjemet ou la fin d'une dynastie*. Geneva.

Helck, W. 1988. "Der 'geheimnisvolle' Mehy." *SAK* 15:143–148.

Hopper, R. W. 2010. "The Monuments of Amenmesse and Seti II: A Historical Inquiry." PhD diss., University of Memphis.

Kanawati, N. 2003. *Conspiracies in the Egyptian Palace: Unis to Pepy I.* London.

Johnson, K. L. 2010. "Transition and Legitimation in Egypt's Late Nineteenth and Early Twentieth Dynasties: A Study of the Reigns of Siptah, Tausret, and Sethnakht." PhD diss., University of Memphis.

Laboury, D. 2010. *Akhénaton.* Les grands pharaons. Paris.

Laboury, D. 1998. *La statuaire de Thoutmosis III: Essai d'interprétation d'un portrait royal dans son contexte historique.* AegLeo 5. Liège.

Magen, B. 2011. *Steinerne Palimpseste: Zur Wiederverwendung von Statuen durch Ramses II. und seine Nachfolger.* Wiesbaden.

McClymont, A. 2016. "Reconstructing Destruction: Amarna Period Erasures in Tombs of the Theban Necropolis." PhD diss., MacQuarie University.

Murnane, W. J. 1975. "The Earlier Reign of Ramesses II and His Coregency with Seti I." *JNES* 34:153–190.

Murnane, W. J. 1977. *Ancient Egyptian Coregencies.* SAOC 40. Chicago.

Murnane, W. J. 1979. "The Bark of Amun on the Third Pylon at Karnak." *JARCE* 16:11–27.

Murnane, W. J. 1990. *The Road to Kadesh: A Historical Interpretation of the Battle Reliefs of King Sety I at Karnak.* 2nd rev. ed. SAOC 42. Chicago.

Murnane, W. J. 1995. "The Kingship of the Nineteenth Dynasty: A Study in the Resilience of an Institution." In *Ancient Egyptian Kingship*, edited by D. O'Connor and D. P. Silverman, 185–217. PdÄ 9. Leiden.

Murnane, W. J. 1997. "Ramesses I and the Building of the Great Hypostyle Hall at Karnak Revisited." *VA* 10:163–168.

Murnane, W. J. 2000. "Soleb Renaissance: Reconsidering the Temple of Nebmaatre in Nubia." *Amarna Letters* 4:6–19.

Murnane, W. J. 2013. "Amenhotep III and Akhenaten at Soleb." In *Soleb VI: Hommages à Michela Schiff Giorgini*, edited by N. Beaux and N. Grimal, 103–124. Cairo.

Redford, D. B. 1967. *History and Chronology of the Eighteenth Dynasty of Egypt: Seven Studies.* Toronto.

Revez, J., and Brand, P. J. 2015. "The Notion of Prime Space in the Layout of the Column Decoration in the Great Hypostyle Hall at Karnak." *KARNAK* 15:253–310.

Rondot, V. 1997. *La Grande Salle Hypostyle de Karnak: Les architraves.* 2 vols. Paris.

Seele, K. C. 1940. *The Coregency of Ramses II with Seti I and the Date of the Great Hypostyle Hall at Karnak.* SAOC 19. Chicago.

Sethe, K. 1896. *Die Thronwirren unter den Nachfolgern Königs Thutmosis' I., ihr Verlauf und ihre Bedeutung: Die Prinzenliste von Medinet Habu und die Reihenfolge der ersten Könige der zwanzigsten Dynastie.* UGAÄ 1. Leipzig.

Sethe, K. 1932. *Das Hatschepsut-problem: Noch einmal untersucht.* APAW 4. Berlin.

Spalinger, A. J. 1979. "Traces of the Early Career of Ramesses II." *JNES* 38:271–286.

Steindorff, G., and Seele, K. C. 1942. *When Egypt Ruled the East.* Chicago.

Valentin, F. M., and Bedman, T. 2015. "Proof for an Amenhotep III/Amenhotep IV Coregency." *Amarna Letters* 5:66–79.

Van Siclen, C. C., III. 1984. "The Date of the Granite Bark Shrine of Thutmosis III." *GM* 79:53.

Van Siclen, C. C., III. 1989. "New Data on the Date of the Defacement of Hatshepsut's Name and Image on the Chapelle Rouge." *GM* 107:85–86.

Wilson, John A. 1951. *The Culture of Ancient Egypt.* Chicago.

EGYPTIAN EPIGRAPHIC GENRES AND THEIR RELATION WITH NONEPIGRAPHIC ONES

JULIE STAUDER-PORCHET
AND ANDRÉAS STAUDER

GENERAL FEATURES OF EGYPTIAN INSCRIPTIONS

REFLECTING the digraphic nature of Egyptian written culture, written performance in the inscriptional—or lapidary—sphere differs fundamentally from writing on portable writing surfaces. With few exceptions, the lapidary sphere is associated with the more iconic hieroglyphic variety of the script (see chapter by Vernus), contrasting with the non-lapidary sphere, which is associated with the more cursive varieties, linear hieroglyphs, hieratic, and Demotic on portable writing surfaces. Hieroglyphic writing in the lapidary sphere, moreover, is often closely associated with pictorial representations of various sorts. In royal stelae of the New Kingdom and later, for example, the lunette often shows a pictorial representation of the king in ritual action with the gods, while the body of the stela consists of an amply developed textual inscription that often culminates in benefactions of the king for the gods. The textually expressed contents, which are specific as to royal name, and often time, place, or events, are thus inserted into the more generic order pictorially expressed in the topmost position of the monument (see chapters by Allon, Pieke).

Lapidary inscriptions are defined by their resultative aspect, sacralizing function, and performative force. Inscriptions establish a lasting situation, projecting a specific time-space—or chronotope—that is extracted from the regular flow of time and unbounded to the future (see chapter by Ockinga). Actions are recounted insofar as they result in such "from now on instituted" (i.e., resultative) situations (such as the benefactions given to a temple or cult resulting from royal action or the lasting tableau of the speaker's self in autobiographies). Lapidary inscriptions sacralize the contents they inscribe, inserting these permanently into the created world and ritual order that sustains it (Vernus 1990), and often have performative force, bringing about what they inscribe by the very fact of inscribing it. Beyond placement (in distinguished spaces, often ritual in nature: temples, funerary chapels), sacralizing and performative force are established through various features characteristic of ritual language, broadly understood (Silverstein, forthcoming; Stauder-Porchet, forthcoming b):

- an out-of-the-ordinary register defined by a high degree of material investment and semiotic density (hieroglyphic writing, associated pictorial representations, typically more formal varieties of language, aesthetic investment);
- a high degree of internal patterning (of language, of writing, and of representations: e.g., Stauder-Porchet 2015) and a general stability of formulations (including much formulaic language);
- and a series of licensing lines of authority (such as the prominent inscription of the royal name, date, and/or pictorial representation of the king in ritual action).

Lapidary inscriptions are authoritative: in their proper places, they outcompete any conceivable challenging discourses decidedly through their high investment of material and semiotic resources (Gillen 2014). In being performative, lapidary inscriptions define, or bring about, their own domain of truth. In the realm of lapidary inscriptions, Ramesses II at Qadesh did truly defeat the Hittite army in a heroic feat regardless of actual events on the ground, which belong to a different realm. Such authoritativeness notwithstanding, an awareness of the possible divorce with actuality is occasionally expressed in the lapidary sphere itself in metadiscursive assertions of the truthfulness of the inscription (first in nonroyal inscriptions from the First Intermediate Period on, then in royal ones as well from the Middle Kingdom on: Coulon 1997).

Inscriptions, more generally, tend to display a high degree of reflexivity, for example Old Kingdom inscriptions establishing the ritual integrity of the funerary chapel in which they are inscribed or building or restoration inscriptions inscribed in the very places they concern. Reflexivity can also concern the inscription itself. Mid-Fifth Dynasty inscriptions, such as Werre or Niankhsekhmet, thus abound in metatextual statements regarding their own making under royal authorization, pointing to these being, in fact, royal inscriptions inserted into nonroyal funerary chapels (Stauder-Porchet 2017, 35–73). From the Old Kingdom on, threats and curses are inscribed against whoever would contravene what the inscription brings about, or attempt at the inscription itself.

While some inscriptions did not imply any human viewer (e.g., "funerary literature" inscribed in sealed-off funerary apartments), other ones are strongly addressive, even though only few people had (full) competence in the hieroglyphic script versus relatively more widespread literacy in hieratic (see chapter by Navratilova). The addressive orientation of such inscriptions can be both social (as a matter of display, including competitive emulation: van Walsem 2013) and ritual (calling on the viewer to act ritually on behalf of who speaks in the inscription). It is variously manifest in placement (for example, on the outer facade of a funerary chapel), in aesthetic investment and epigraphic quality, and in rare or unique features that attract the viewer's attention. Instances of graphic playfulness thus display scribal prowess and entice the viewer to make him pause and recite an invocation offering (e.g., Diego Espinel 2014). Addressivity is made linguistically explicit in threat formulae (see earlier) and in appeals to the living (from the Old Kingdom on) that frame the ritual roles of the speaker and viewer, with effect over the set of texts inscribed next to them. A concern for future audiences and posterity becomes more linguistically explicit from the early New Kingdom on in nonroyal and royal inscriptions alike (Popko 2006).

The Early Development of Primary Epigraphic Genres

Ancient Egypt did not develop a descriptive or normative theory of genres. There are very few labels that could refer to type of text (e.g., in New Kingdom royal inscriptions, *sḏd nḫtw*, "Recital of victories," or *ḥ3ti-ʿ m nḫtw*, "Beginning of victories"). For example, there is no native designation for the main genre of nonroyal inscriptions: autobiographies. As practice, however, demonstrates, genres were clearly recognized as such, as schemes for composing and interpreting texts, marked by framing indexicals, and associated with specific cultural settings, discourses, and significations (general introduction to genre in a Bakhtinian perspective, e.g., Foley 1997, 359–378). By definition, genres are historically transmitted, and, therefore, intertextual—or dialogic—objects. Genres, accordingly, allow for deviations, fluidity, mixing, and change over time.

In lapidary inscriptions, a basic distinction is between primary and secondary epigraphic genres. The former have (a significant part of) their genealogy in the lapidary realm itself, to which they remained bound throughout their subsequent history. The latter, by contrast, originated outside the epigraphic realm and continued to exist there even after entering the epigraphic realm. Primary epigraphic genres include pictorial scenes with inscriptions (in royal funerary complexes, temples, and nonroyal funerary chapels), the autobiography, royal *wḏ* ("decree"; these include not only decrees in the narrow sense but also the many royal inscriptions that culminate in a *wḏ*), and various types of rock inscriptions along expeditions roads. Examples of secondary epigraphic genres are ritual and funerary texts, hymns and prayers, and monumentalized documents. Among the major primary epigraphic genres, the autobiography is exclusively nonroyal. By definition, an Egyptian autobiography's most basic purpose is to insert the speaker into the ritual, social, and political order articulated by the principle of *maat* and/or the figure of the king that upholds it. Conversely, the *wḏ* is typically royal, also by definition: a *wḏ* is an authoritative, or even performative, pronouncement, which is typically the king's (Vernus 2013).

In lapidary inscriptions, a major focus is the name (royal and/or nonroyal). Royal and nonroyal stelae of the early First Dynasty inscribe the name in spatial conjunction with the offering place. Nonroyal names are expanded into extended titularies on stelae from the late First Dynasty, then in built spaces (funerary chapels) from the Third Dynasty. The (expanded) name would remain a major element in both royal and nonroyal inscriptions, emphasized through prominent placement and/or iteration on the monument. (Self-)eulogy, which would become a major element in royal inscriptions and in autobiographical ones from the Middle Kingdom, can be viewed as further extensions of the expanded name.

Considering format, two interrelated parameters help define a typology of Old Kingdom inscriptions. One is the degree of integration of linguistic elements with pictorial representations, or, conversely, their relative autonomy. The other concerns the integration of the linguistic elements themselves: additive and visual (in lists and tabular formats) or through linguistic means (in continuous text, defined by factors such as referential cohesion, temporal organization, and hierarchies of foreground and background). In general, linguistically more tightly integrated inscriptions tended to be relatively more autonomous from pictorial representations, but a whole set of diverse configurations was explored. Consisting of pictorial representations with short nonpredicative inscriptions (names, entities, and "labeling infinitives," for which see later), royal ritual scenes originally developed on mobile artifacts (late proto-historical palettes, then ceremonial tags in the First Dynasty). Monumentalized, they are found in Old Kingdom royal funerary complexes, where they diversify considerably in themes and realization, and in divine temples as these were gradually developing architecturally (more prominently from the Middle, and especially New Kingdom). From the Fourth Dynasty, pictorial scenes including short nonpredicative inscriptions develop in nonroyal funerary chapels as well, to become a major focus of elite display and competition in the Old Kingdom. The list and tabular format is illustrated by the titulary (from the late First Dynasty, e.g., the stelae of Merka and Sabef), the offering list (from the Second Dynasty: Morales 2015), names of domains associated with pictorial representations of such domains (from the Fourth Dynasty), lists of participants and items in expedition inscriptions, and annals (attested from the Old Kingdom: Baines 2008). Later annalistic inscriptions would retain a distinctively additive patterning, manifest in long lists of gifts to temples and, further, in the use of the "labeling infinitive" presenting the event in its bare form outside linguistic connectivity. Beginning with the late Eleventh Dynasty Wadi Hammamat inscriptions, this "labeling infinitive" would be extended to narrative royal inscriptions as a more general index of royal action.

Isolated, or additively patterned, predicative sentences are first inscribed in association with pictorial representations in the "*Gott-König Rede*" expressing reciprocal action of the king and the gods (Netjerikhet's Heliopolis sanctuary; slightly earlier instances are on late Second Dynasty seals); this would remain a core element of ritual scenes until Roman times. In nonroyal funerary chapels from the Old Kingdom, so-called *Reden und Rufe* (from the late Fourth Dynasty) are short segments of speech associated with representations of lowly people busily working for the tomb owner. Continuous text proper consists of linguistically integrated multipropositional discourse. Beginning in the Fourth Dynasty, it is found in inscriptions establishing the rightful construction and ritual integrity of the tomb, in funerary texts of various sorts (the offering formula, ritual self-characterizations of the speaker, appeals to the living), in stipulations regarding the funerary cult (Goedicke 1970), then also in autobiographies (see later). In the royal sphere, early continuous texts are decrees (from the late Fourth Dynasty: Goedicke 1967) and texts that stage royal speech and action in relation to pictorial representations (in the Fifth Dynasty: e.g., el-Awady 2009, pls. XIII–XIV). Related to these are solely textual inscriptions that stage the king's speech in a narrative setting involving an official into whose funerary chapel these inscriptions are inserted (e.g., Werre, Niankhsekhmet, then Kaiemtjenenet: Stauder-Porchet 2017, 35–73, 121–135; forthcoming a). In the reign of Izezi, royal letters that praise the official in the king's own words (Senedjemib-Inti, Chepsesre: Stauder-Porchet 2017, 135–147) represent a further development of this tradition of inscribing royal speech in an official's funerary chapel. Overall, speech is prominent in the early development of continuous text in the lapidary sphere.

Autobiographies emerged out of this context. Old Kingdom autobiographies comprise two genres with distinctive formats and phraseology, the so-called ideal autobiography and the so-called event autobiography (Stauder-Porchet 2017; Kloth 2002). Both emerge by the reign of Izezi in the later Fifth Dynasty, at a time when the funerary chapel, including its facade, was developing into a major space for inscription and display. The "ideal autobiography" is often associated spatially with other funerary texts and inserts the speaker into *maat*, into an order, therefore, that is as much ritual as social. The ritual nature of the genre is demonstrated further by its strongly parallelistic patterning, stable phraseology, and set format. This consists of a single sequence with an opening formula ("When I came from my town, I descended from my nome, I had performed *maat*, I had said *maat*…") developed into generic types of action ("…I had given bread to the hungry, clothes to the naked, etc."). The "event autobiography," by contrast, tends to be separate spatially from other inscriptions and serves to provide a textual configuration of the speaker with the king, who could not be represented pictorially in nonroyal spaces in the Old Kingdom. In a recurrent format, the speaker's actions on the king's command are presented as culminating in the king's "praise" (*ḥzi*) of the speaker's unique qualities in the eyes of the king. The prehistory of the "event autobiography" is in the aforementioned royal inscriptions in the official's funerary chapel (royal speech in ceremonialized settings and royal letters). In these, the "praise" of the official had been associated with, then directly expressed in, royal speech directed at the official. In the "event autobiography," phrased in the first person, the voice is now the official's own, while royal speech has given way to generic mentions of the king's "praise."

Inscriptions on natural rock draw on multiple genres. Along with mobile artifacts in the Valley, proto-historic tableaus in the wadis adjacent to Upper Egypt had been a major locus for the development of proto-royal iconography, including signs of writing (e.g., Darnell 2015). Old Kingdom royal inscriptions, for example, in the Sinai, focus prominently on the ritual scene of smiting enemies. Nonroyal inscriptions (e.g., at the Hatnub quarries and in the Wadi Hammamat) include summary statements of mission, dates, and lists of people and items. The ritual dimensions of rock inscriptions are demonstrated in the late Old Kingdom notably by an inscription that includes an appeal to the living (Shemai) and one that is phrased in formulations similar to the "ideal auto-biography" (Anusu) (Eichler 1994).

THE DIVERSIFICATION OF GENRES

The regionalization of, and relatively more widespread access to, written culture during the First Intermediate Period prompted innovations that were instrumental in the subsequent evolution and diversification of lapidary genres. The fading of the royal, and ensuing increasingly local, reference in late Old Kingdom autobiographies led to an interpenetration, and eventually fusing, of the "ideal" and "event" autobiographies and thereby to a redefinition of the autobiography itself (Moreno-García 1998; Stauder-Porchet 2017, 294–310). Self-reliance and care for the welfare of the local community (including the famine topos) became new foci of autobiographical inscriptions in the First Intermediate Period (Moreno García 1997). Along with a thematization of the dis-cursive status of inscriptions (Coulon 1997), an exploration of rhetoric and poetic figures, and increasingly parallelistic modes of patterning inscribed language, these develop-ments would form the background for the development of royal discourse and the rise of literature in the Middle Kingdom (see what follows and the final section).

Middle Kingdom autobiography (Lichtheim 1988; for a survey of the history of the genre, Gnirs 1996) was internally diverse, with more narrative inscriptions (e.g., as expressions of "nomarchal" identity at places such as Beni Hasan or Deir el-Bersheh) and other texts that centered on the self-eulogizing characterization of the speaker in terms of his ethical and rhetorical qualities and composure in a court society in which etiquette and face-to-face interaction were paramount. Eighteenth Dynasty autobiogra-phies often emphasized the speaker's loyalism to, and action for, the king, for which the subject earned the king's praise and rewards (Guksch 1994). Ramesside autobiographies demonstrate an increasing textualization of personal piety and religious experience, and could include hymns and prayers (Frood 2007). Continuing often age-old phraseology, autobiographies would be composed until early Roman times, accommodating new themes and motifs, such as elegy (e.g., Isenkhebe and Taimhotep) or euergetism (in Tanite autobiographies: Zivie-Coche 2004), at the very end of the history of the genre.

In the Old Kingdom, textual narrative in the royal sphere had been limited to inscrip-tions that served the function of framing royal speech as the central element, while non-narrative royal inscriptions had consisted mainly in decrees for temples. Inscriptions, such as Senwosret I's Tod and Elephantine inscriptions or Senwosret III's Semna bound-ary stelae, witness to a broadening of the scope of royal inscriptions from the Middle Kingdom, leading to the rise of a rich variety of royal inscriptions in the New Kingdom in particular (for Thutmoside times, Beylage 2002). Originating in nonroyal contexts in the First Intermediate Period (e.g., Ankhtifi #2, Intef, son of Myt), restoration inscriptions would thus become a major royal genre from the Middle Kingdom (Tod Inscription; in the Eighteenth Dynasty, e.g., Ahmose's Tempest Stela, Hatshepsut's Speos Artemidos Inscription, Tutankhamun's Restoration Stela). Semantically allied to restoration inscriptions are building and dedicatory inscriptions (Grallert 2001), as well as inscriptions recounting exceptionally high Nile floods inasmuch as these, like restoration inscriptions, imply a return of the land to its pristine state (e.g., Sobekhotep VIII's Inundation Stela, Taharqa's Kawa V Inscription).

As far as current evidence goes, royal inscriptions centering on military matters (Spalinger 1982) are an innovation of the early New Kingdom (e.g., Thutmose I's Tombos Stela, Amenhotep II's Syrian Campaigns), arguably related to the increased social and ideological importance of the military observed already during the Second Intermediate Period. In the Kamose inscriptions, at the eve of the New Kingdom, a claim of innovation in format and subject matter was thus indexed by deliberately innovative expressions in language. In Thutmose III's "Annals," the first campaign is highlighted through its narrative development and partial framing as a *Königsnovelle* (see what follows), but the overall inscription is additively patterned, ultimately as a list of bounty given to the Karnak temple in which it was inscribed. A distinctive, although short-lived, development was the extension of a highly metrical patterning to narrative itself in Ramesses II's Qadesh "Poème" and Merneptah's Israel Stela, in both cases alongside a less tightly patterned and differently focused presentation of related materials elsewhere (in the Qadesh "Bulletin" and Merneptah's Great Karnak Inscription, respectively). Just as the development of pictorial tableaus of royal battles (first documented for Ahmose and Thutmose II, culminating in the battlefield reliefs of Seti I, Ramesses II, and Ramesses III) can be viewed as an expansion of the icon of the king smiting his enemies, such "epic poetry" (Lichtheim 1976, 58–59) can be seen as a narrative development of the eulogy. Taking different forms, narrative developments in the Medinet Habu inscriptions are also analyzed as expansions of the eulogies with which they alternate, the eulogies being themselves celebrative extensions of the royal name (Gillen 2014). In post-Ramesside times, military matters become much less a focus of inscription (see, however, Piye's Victory Stela and Psammetichus II's Shellal Inscription, for example).

Narrative forms are also adopted by inscriptions that concern the accession of the king to the throne (e.g., Thutmose IV's and Amenhotep II's Sphinx stelae; or, in altogether different contexts, Aspelta's Election Stela). Integrating pictorial representations, Hatshepsut's Cycle (Divine Birth, Youth, Proclamation) foregrounds divine election. Illustrating a variety of content, other major narrative compositions include, for example, Ramses II's First and Second Marriage Stelae or the Chronicles of Prince Osorkon. As in autobiographies, religions dimensions and personal piety become more prominent during the Ramesside period (e.g., Ramses II's Inscription Dédicatoire, Ramses III's Great Double Stela, or Ramses IV's Abydos Inscription). In the Third Intermediate Period, inscribed oracular decrees reflect aspects of the public staging of decision-making in the Theban polity. The Late Period witnesses an increased focus on sacerdotal matters (e.g., the Naucratis Stela or the Ptolemaic multilingual Sacerdotal Decrees; also the Bentresh Stela and the Sehel Famine Stela, both pseudepigrapha).

The two most basic elements in royal inscriptions are the opening royal titulary (which can be expanded into a eulogy) and, very commonly, the culminating royal wḏ or "decree," often consisting of benefactions to the gods or their temples. In inscriptions such as the ones referred to in the preceding paragraph, these elements are integrated with narrative parts. In Ahmose's Karnak Eulogy (CG 34001), the main part of the inscription consists of just such an extended eulogy, followed by loyalist appeals to the king and his queen mother, all culminating in a wḏ for the temple of Karnak, the place in which the text was inscribed. Among other formats, Thutmose III's Poetical Stela consists of a long speech of the god eulogizing the king in hymnic form. Sequences of divine speech, and the king's, are central in Ramses III's Great Double Stela.

Including both the eulogy and the wḏ, an important format of royal inscriptions is what has somewhat misleadingly become known as the "*Königsnovelle*" or "King's Tale," the definition of which is complicated by how inclusive or not a set of texts is considered. In a broad interpretation, the *Königsnovelle* has been taken to refer not to a genre, but to a general textual modality by which the king could feature in an episodic setting, not as "mediator" of history in an atemporal constellation, but as an "actor" of history (Loprieno 1996, 284). Under this definition, most royal inscriptions that comprise a narrative development could qualify as *Königsnovellen*. Alternatively, the *Königsnovelle* can be defined more restrictively as a genre consisting of a ceremonialized occasion of the king's performative speech, followed by its resulting effects presented as an wḏ, the occasion of the lapidary inscription itself (Stauder, forthcoming). Under this definition, the *Königsnovelle* has a deep genealogy in inscriptions of ceremonialized occasions of the king's speech in the Fifth Dynasty, well prior to its first securely dated instance in Neferhotep I's Abydos Inscription. In its classical forms, in the Second Intermediate Period and Thutmoside and early Ramesside times, the *Königsnovelle* centers around speech: the king's and often also the courtiers'. The latter serves to eulogize the king's action, foresight, and particularly speech itself, regularly including metapragmatic characterizations of such royal speech as performative. Third Intermediate Period and particularly Kushite inscriptions retain, or revive, certain features of this classic format, but with much less emphasis on speech.

RELATIONS BETWEEN LAPIDARY GENRES AND WITH NONLAPIDARY ONES

While royal and nonroyal inscriptions represent two fundamentally different realms of lapidary discourse, this did not prevent influences in either direction. In the Old Kingdom, scenes integrating pictorial representations and writing in nonroyal funerary chapels were in part adopted from royal models. Fifth Dynasty royal texts staging royal speech were inserted into nonroyal funerary chapels where they provided an early locus for the development of the "praise" (ḥzi) of the official by the king, leading to the rise of the "event" autobiography in the late Fifth Dynasty. Conversely, innovations in nonroyal inscriptions of the First Intermediate Period were instrumental in the rise of a more thoroughly textualized royal sphere developing from the Middle Kingdom. Shortly before the ideological apparatus of kingship was restored in its full forms, Wahankh Intef II's stela CG 20512 is uniquely inscribed with an autobiography—the quintessentially nonroyal genre—providing a link in the process. Features indexical of the royal sphere were in turn occasionally accommodated into nonroyal inscriptions as powerful expressions of an official's distinction. These include various occasions of royal speech, for example in Ikhernofret's autobiography (Twelfth Dynasty) where motifs of the contemporary autobiography are spoken by the king addressing the official (Stauder-Porchet, forthcoming a). In a similar vein, the *Königsnovelle*, a quintessentially royal genre that prominently features royal speech, was adapted to a nonroyal context in three tombs of high Thutmoside officials at Qurna (User, Senneferi, and Qenamun: Stauder, forthcoming, §3.3).

While the lapidary and the nonlapidary sphere represent two fundamentally different realms of written performance, major epigraphic genres have their origins in nonlapidary contexts. Among such secondarily epigraphic genres is "funerary literature," notably the Pyramid Texts (Hays 2012; Baines 2004; Allen 1993, 6–7) and so-called Netherworld Books inscribed mostly in royal tombs of the New Kingdom, then also in nonroyal tombs and on sarcophagi in the first millennium BCE. Rituals inscribed in tombs and temples similarly derive from originally nonlapidary contexts. Hymns to the gods are inscribed in lapidary form first in the late First Intermediate Period (Wahankh Intef II's stela MMA 13.182.3) and become more common from the early New Kingdom on (e.g., Paheri, Amenmose (Louvre C 286), Suty and Hor, the Hymns to Aton). From Ramesside times through the Late Period, hymns and prayers are an important element in self-presentations and autobiographies, in some royal inscriptions, and, closer to their original contexts, in temples. Considering their tabular format, lapidary annals also derive from and had counterparts in nonlapidary forms (Baines 2008). Administrative or judicial texts published in monumentalized format include dispositions for the funerary cult (e.g., Nikaiankh of Tehna in the Fifth Dynasty, Djefai-Hapi in the early Twelfth), judicial and administrative texts from the Second Intermediate Period on, and, prominently in the Third Intermediate Period, oracular decrees and donation texts, the latter often in hieratic. Monumentalization here was not just a matter of public display of content, but fundamentally, of sacralizing these hieroglyphically inscribed contents (Vernus 1990).

Transpositions of supports from the nonlapidary to the lapidary sphere are demonstrated in rare metatextual mentions that describe inscriptional texts as "copies" (miti) of nonlapidary originals (e.g., Amenhotep II's letter to Usersatet, Merneptah's Hermopolis Stela, Ramesses III's Gold Tablet Prayer). Absent such mentions, individual lapidary inscriptions may or may not derive from nonlapidary originals (e.g., the Duties of the Vizier, sometimes considered a monumentalization of an original document, but arguably a composition with primary inscriptional destination, part and parcel of the Thutmoside Vizieral Cycle). Conversely, inscriptions could circulate and thereby have a secondary reception in nonlapidary form. Clear cases are copies of the Kamose inscriptions on a writing board (T. Carnarvon I) and of the Qadesh inscriptions on papyrus (P. Sallier III) (Vernus 2010–2011; Spalinger 2002). Both of these compositions display literary features, which may have helped their reception and circulation on portable writing surfaces in conjunction with literary compositions. Harper's Songs are inscribed in funerary chapels in the New Kingdom, but were also transmitted on papyri alongside love poetry. Inscriptions, finally, could become the object of textual archaeology, in order to be transferred on other much later monuments or to be excerpted for model phraseology (Kahl 1999).

While inscriptions and literature (the latter written in cursive varieties on writing surfaces) belong to two fundamentally different realms of written performance, productive interactions between the two are observed as well. In retrospect, the thematic, poetic, rhetoric, and formal innovations of the First Intermediate Period inscriptions can be seen as a prologue to the rise of written literature shortly afterward. Middle Kingdom literature and inscriptions are allied by their linguistic register, a similarly high degree of patterning. Regarding cultural themes and formulations, the autobiography finds multiple echoes in literary teachings (e.g., Montuhotep of Armant's autobiography, UC 14333, early Twelfth Dynasty: Vernus 2010, 455–458). Loyalism, which receives a first developed textual expression in early Sixth Dynasty autobiographies (e.g., Kagemni, Merefnebef: Stauder-Porchet 2017, 218–224, 238–240), finds a paradigmatic expression in a "Teaching" (sb3yt) inscribed on a later Twelfth Dynasty stela alongside an autobiography (Sehetepibre, CGC 20538). This "Loyalist Teaching" would subsequently be expanded into a longer version documented in the New Kingdom in manuscript forms that circulated alongside other Middle Egyptian literary compositions (on the primacy of the short version, Stauder 2013, 293–301). In early narrative literature, Sinuhe is framed as an autobiography, re-entextualization on writing surfaces with fictionalizing effect to probe the normative cultural values associated with the underlying quintessentially lapidary genre. Expedition inscriptions are intertextually evoked in Sinuhe and the Shipwrecked Sailor. So are the autobiography in the apology spoken by the assassinated king in the Teaching of Amenemhat, restoration inscriptions in Neferti (which is about the return of kingship after disruption), and the *Königsnovelle* in Cheops's Court and the prologue of Neferti (which stages language and its authorization by the king). Such intertextual connections are less productive in Late Egyptian literature, possibly as a function of an increased linguistic distance between inscriptions and literature. Some are observed nonetheless, for example, the *Königsnovelle* in Apophis and Seqenenre with much ironic effect or extended curse formulae, such as those documented in Third Intermediate Period donation stelae as hypotexts for the speaker's utter loss of social bond, hence identity, in the Letter of Wermai (Fischer-Elfert 2005, 215–232).

Conversely, literary elements are found in inscriptions. Literary framing indexicals in inscriptions include the incipits ḏd.in … "And said …" (compare Shipwrecked Sailor) in Khnumhotep III's highly narrative inscription on the facade of his mastaba (late Twelfth

Dynasty: Allen 2008) or *s pw wn*… "There was a man…" (compare Eloquent Peasant, Neferpesedjet) in Samut son of Kyky's also otherwise literarizing biography (Ramesside: Vernus 1978). In the Second Intermediate Period, an inscription in lapidary hieratic in the Theban Westen Desert begins with *ḥȝtỉ-ᶜ* [*m*…] "Beginning [of…]," then presents various literary motifs and formulations, some possibly alluding to specific Middle Egyptian literary compositions (Wadi el-Ḥôl #8, Darnell 2002, 107–119). In the early-mid Eighteenth Dynasty, two inscriptions are framed as "teachings" (*sbȝyt*). While Aametju's Teaching (inscribed in columns of painted hieroglyphs in the tomb of his son Useramon: Dziobek 1998, 23–43; Vernus 2010, 59–63, 70–73), is a true *sbȝyt* in the full Middle Egyptian tradition, the High Priest of Amun Amenemhat's "Teaching" (*Urk.* IV 1408–1411) is, in fact, an autobiography framed as a *sbȝyt* so as to highlight the exemplary nature of the speaker's life.

Beyond such framing indexicals, the study of intertextual connections between inscriptional and literary texts poses a recurrent methodological problem. While there may be cases of a direct influence in one direction or the other, the relation more often is arguably better seen as involving common "clusters of language and imagery" on which both the inscription(s) and literature would have drawn (Parkinson 2012, 13). Illustrations are, for example, Ameny's graffito (WG 3042, with formulations in common with Ptahhotep: Vernus 1995), the Semna Stela (with related formulations in the el-Lahun Hymns to Senwosret III and Sinuhe's encomium to Senwosret I), a self-characterization of Bebi of el-Kab's in the Second Intermediate Period (also in Teaching of Amenemhat: Stauder 2013, 437–438), or the self-presentation of the Thutmoside great royal herald Intef (Louvre C 26, with motifs in common with Eloquent Peasant notably). Clear instances of allusions to literature are identified only occasionally, thus, to Sinuhe, in Dedusobek's graffito (Wadi el-Ḥôl #5, late Twelfth Dynasty; Darnell 2002, 97–101), arguably in Ineni's autobiography (Thutmoside, in relation to royal succession), or in echoes of the Sinuhean question ("Why have you come here?") in early Thutmoside compositions (as a learned *clin-d'œil*: Stauder 2013, 260–264). In the same period, the Vizieral Cycle (Appointment of the Vizier, Aametju's teaching, Installation of the Vizier, and Duties of the Vizier, including the associated pictorial compositions) is replete with references to Ptahhotep (as the prototypical model for a father–son transmission of the vizier's office as a realization of *maat*) and, further, to Merikare (thus analogizing the second "efficient office," the vizier's, with the first, the king's).

On an altogether different level, mention may be made, finally, of a group of hieratic graffiti consisting of excerpts, mostly incipits, of Middle Egyptian literary compositions that were inscribed—thereby inserted—into the much older hieroglyphically and pictorially preinscribed ritual space of a late First Intermediate Period funerary chapel in Asyut (Verhoeven 2013).

BIBLIOGRAPHY

Allen, J. 1993. "Reading a Pyramid." In *Hommages à Jean Leclant, Volume 1: Études pharaoniques*, edited by C. Berger, G. Clerc, and N. Grimal, 5–28. BdE 106. Cairo.

Allen, J. 2008. "The Historical Inscription of Khnumhotep at Dahshur: Preliminary Report." *BASOR* 352:29–39.

Awady, T. el-. 2009. *Abusir XIV: Sahure. The Pyramid Causeway. History and Decoration Program in the Old Kingdom*. Prague.

Baines, J. 2004. "Modelling Sources, Processes and Locations of Early Mortuary Texts." In *D'un monde à l'autre: Textes des Pyramides et Textes des Sarcophages*, edited by S. Bickel and B. Mathieu, 15–42. BdE 139. Cairo.

Baines, J. 2008. "On the Evolution, Purpose, and Forms of Egyptian Annals." In *Zeichen aus dem Sand: Streiflichter aus Ägyptens Geschichte zu Ehren von Günter Dreyer*, edited by E.-M. Engel, V. Müller, and U. Hartung, 19–40. Wiesbaden.

Beylage, P. 2002. *Aufbau der königlichen Stelentexte vom Beginn der 18. Dynastie bis zur Amarnazeit*. 2 vols. ÄAT 54. Wiesbaden.

Coulon, L. 1997. "Véracité et rhétorique dans les autobiographies égyptiennes de la Première Période Intermédiaire." *BIFAO* 97:109–138.

Darnell, J. 2015. "The Early Hieroglyphic Annotation in the Nag el-Hamdulab Rock Art Tableaux, and the Following of Horus in the Northwest Hinterland of Aswan." *ArchéoNil* 25:19–44.

Darnell, J. C. 2002. *Theban Desert Road Survey in the Egyptian Western Desert. Volume 1: Gebek Tjauti Rock Inscriptions 1–45 and Wadi el-Ḥôl Rock Inscriptions 1–45*. With the assistance of D. Darnell and contributions by D. Darnell, R. Friedman, and S. Hendrickx. OIP 119. Chicago.

Dziobek, E. 1998. *Die Denkmäler des Vezirs User-Amun*. SAGA 18. Heidelberg.

Eichler, E. 1994. "Zur kultischen Bedeutung von Expeditionsinschriften." In *Essays in Egyptology in Honor of Hans Goedicke*, edited by B. Bryan and D. Lorton, 69–80. San Antonio.

Diego Espinel, A. 2014. "Play and Display in Egyptian High Culture: The Cryptographic Texts of Djehuty (TT 11) and Their Sociocultural Contexts." In *Creativity and Innovation in the Reign of Hatshepsut: Papers from the Theban Workshop 2010*, edited by J. M. Galán, B. M. Bryan, and P. F. Dorman, 297–335. SAOC 69. Chicago.

Foley, W. 1997. *Anthropological Linguistics: An Introduction*. Malden.

Fischer-Elfert, H.-W. 2005. *Abseits von Maʾat: Fallstudien zu Aussenseitern im alten Ägypten*. Würzburg.

Frood, E. 2007. *Biographical Texts from Ramessid Egypt*. WA 26. Atlanta.

Gillen, T. 2014. "Ramesside Registers of Égyptien de Tradition: The Medinet Habu Inscriptions." In *On Forms and Functions: Studies in Ancient Egyptian Grammar*, edited by E. Grossman, S. Polis, A. Stauder, and J. Winand, 41–86. LinAeg-StudMon 15. Hamburg.

Gnirs, A. 1996. "Die ägyptische Autobiographie." In *Ancient Egyptian Literature: History and Forms*, edited by A. Loprieno, 191–241. PdÄ 10. Leiden.

Goedicke, H. 1967. *Königliche Dokumente aus dem alten Reich*. ÄA 14. Wiesbaden.

Goedicke, H. 1970. *Die privaten Rechtsinschriften aus dem alten Reich*. Vienna.

Grallert, S. 2001. *Bauen-Stiften-Weihen: ägyptische Bau—und Restaurierungsinschriften von den Anfängen bis zur 30. Dynastie*. ADAIK 18. Berlin.

Guksch, H. 1994. *Königsdienst: zur Selbstdarstellung der Beamten in der 18. Dynastie*. SAGA 11. Heidelberg.

Hays, H. M. 2012. *The Organization of the Pyramid Texts*. 2 vols. PdÄ 31. Leiden.

Kahl, J. 1999. *Siut-Theben: zur Wertschätzung von Traditionen im alten Ägypten*. PdÄ 13. Leiden.

Kloth, N. 2002. *Die (auto-)biographischen Inschriften des ägyptischen Alten Reiches: Untersuchung zur Phraseologie und Entwicklung.* SAK Bh 8. Hamburg.

Lichtheim, M. 1976. *Ancient Egyptian Literature, Volume II: The New Kingdom.* Los Angeles.

Lichtheim, M. 1988. *Ancient Egyptian Autobiographies Chiefly of the Middle Kingdom: A Study and an Anthology.* OBO 84. Fribourg.

Loprieno, A. 1996. "The 'King's Novel.'" In *Ancient Egyptian Literature: History and Forms*, edited by A. Loprieno, 277–295. PdÄ 10. Leiden.

Morales, A. 2015. "Iteration, Innovation und Dekorum in Opferlisten des Alten Reichs: zur Vorgeschichte der Pyramidentexte." *ZÄS* 142:55–69.

Moreno-García, J. C. 1997. *Études sur l'administration, le pouvoir et l'idéologie en Égypte, de l'Ancien au Moyen Empire.* AegLeo 4. Liège.

Moreno-García, J. C. 1998. "De l'Ancien Empire à la Première Période Intermédiaire: L'autobiographie de Q3r d'Edfou, entre tradition et innovation." *RdÉ* 49:151–160.

Parkinson, R. 2012. *The Tale of the Eloquent Peasant: A Reader's Commentary.* LingAeg-StudMon 10. Hamburg.

Popko, L. 2006. *Untersuchungen zur Geschichtsschreibung der Ahmosiden—und Thutmosidenzeit.* WSA 2. Würzburg.

Silverstein, M. Forthcoming. "Anthropological Views on Earlier Egyptian Inscriptions." In *Earlier Egyptian Inscriptions: Materiality, Locality, Landscape*, edited by J. Stauder-Porchet.

Spalinger, A. 1982. *Aspects of the Military Documents of the Ancient Egyptians.* New Haven.

Spalinger, A. 2002. *The Transformation of an Ancient Egyptian Narrative: P. Sallier III and the Battle of Kadesh.* GOF 40. Göttingen.

Stauder, A. 2013. *Linguistic Dating of Middle Egyptian Literary Texts.* LingAeg-StudMon 12. Hamburg.

Stauder, A. Forthcoming. "La *Königsnovelle*: Indices génériques, significations, écarts intertextuels." In *Questionner le sphinx. Festschrift in honorem a distinguished colleague*, edited by P. Collombert, L. Coulon, I. Guermeur, C. Thiers. Cairo.

Stauder-Porchet, J. 2015. "Hezi's Autobiographical Inscription: Philological Study and Interpretation." *ZÄS* 142:191–204.

Stauder-Porchet, J. 2017. *Les autobiographies de l'Ancien Empire égyptien.* OLA 255. Leuven.

Stauder-Porchet, J. Forthcoming a. "L'inscription de la parole royale chez les particuliers à la Vème dynastie." In *Questionner le sphinx. Festschrift in honorem a distinguished colleague*, edited by P. Collombert, L. Coulon, I. Guermeur, and C. Thiers. Cairo.

Stauder-Porchet, J. Forthcoming b. "Old Kingdom Monumental Discourse as Localized Ritual Inscription." In *Earlier Egyptian Inscriptions. Materiality, Locality, Landscape*, edited by J. Stauder-Porchet. OLA. Leuven.

Verhoeven, U. 2013. "Literatur im Grab—der Sonderfall Assiut." In *Dating Egyptian Literary Texts*, edited by G. Moers, K. Widmaier, A. Giewekemeyer, A. Lümers, and R. Ernst, 139–158. LingAeg-StudMon 11. Hamburg.

Vernus, P. 1978. "Litérature et autobiographie: Les inscriptions de *S3-mwt* surnommé *Kyky*." *RdÉ* 30:115–146.

Vernus, P. 1990. "Les espaces de l'écrit dans l'Égypte pharaonique." *BSFÉ* 119:35–56.

Vernus, P. 1995. "L'intertextualité dans la culture pharaonique: L'enseignement de Ptahhotep et le graffito d'*Jmny* (Ouâdi Hammâmât n. 3042)." *GM* 147:103–109.

Vernus, P. 2010. *Sagesses de l'Égypte ancienne.* Paris.

Vernus, P. 2010–2011. "'Littérature,' 'littéraire' et supports d'écriture: Contribution à une théorie de la littérature dans l'Égypte pharaonique." *EEDAL* 2:19–146.

Vernus, P. 2013. "The Royal Command (*wḏ-nsw*): A Basic Deed of Executive Power." In *Ancient Egyptian Administration*, edited by J. C. Moreno García, 259–340. HdO 104. Leiden.

Walsem, R. van. 2013. "Diversification and Variation in Old Kingdom Funerary Iconography as the Expression of a Need for 'Individuality.'" *JEOL* 44:117–139.

Zivie-Coche, C. 2004. *Statues et autobiographies de dignitaires: Tanis à l'époque ptolémaïque.* Travaux récents sur le tell Sân el-Hagar 3. Paris.

....

DESIGNERS AND MAKERS OF ANCIENT EGYPTIAN MONUMENTAL EPIGRAPHY

....

DIMITRI LABOURY

THIRTY years before the writing of this contribution, in an article aiming at a systematization of the procedures of excavating and recording a Theban tomb, Daniel Polz emphasized how the way of looking at a decorated monument strongly filters out "the elements which are not directly connected with the 'intended picture'" (Polz 1987, 135). To illustrate this unavoidable epigraphic—as well as epistemological and cognitive—reality, he juxtaposed his line-drawing recording of a scene in the entrance doorway of the tomb of Huy with a drawing made of exactly the same scene a few decades earlier by Norman de Garis Davies (Figure I.6.1). Whereas "the best archaeological draughtsman of his generation" (Reeves 2001, 22), indeed, one of the most famous and productive epigraphers Egyptology has ever known (see chapter by Davies), created a beautiful and very legible image, cleared from any element that could compromise its hieroglyphic readability, in keeping with the purposes of the Egyptological epigraphic practice of his time, the German archaeologist sought to record the material state of the archaeological object he had to document, just like any piece of ceramic or funerary furniture, integrating "additional information such as the remains of the grid, the sketch lines for the hieroglyphic inscriptions and more or less all the mutilations on the wall" (Polz 1987, 135; for further comments, see Laboury 2012, 203). An archaeological look, such as the one Polz advocated, considering all the marks of the work's history (from its genesis to its decline), allows one to detect—and document—the material traces of the making of the monument, and hence of its maker(s). In this sense, Egyptian epigraphy and palaeography may significantly contribute to the study of the artists and craftsmen responsible for the creation of ancient Egyptian monumental decoration. But, of course, in return, this double discipline can only greatly benefit from a better knowledge of those essential actors in the production of its own object of research.

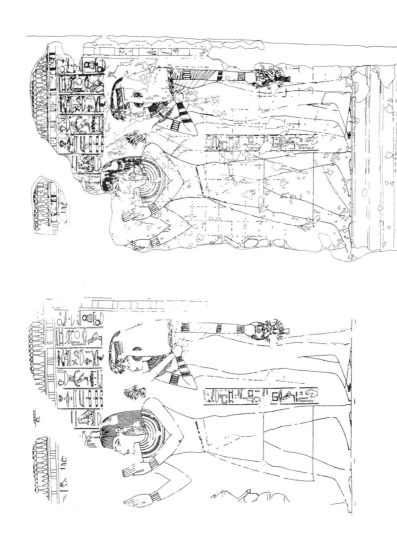

FIGURE 1.6.1. A scene in the tomb of Huy as represented in a photograph, a line drawing by N. de Garis Davies, and a line drawing by D. Polz. © DAI Kairo; photo D. Johannes © University of Uppsala; drawing by N. de G. Davies © DAI Kairo; drawing D. Polz.

So, in this context of mutually profitable interaction, what do we know about the designers and makers of ancient Egyptian monumental epigraphy? How did they work? And what kind of traces did they leave?

Social Identities, Education, and Training

Contrary to a widespread belief about ancient Egyptian art, artists in Pharaonic society could sign their work, and this was far from being as exceptional as has often been assumed (on this phenomenon, see Laboury 2016). Edith W. Ware (1927) gathered a first, nonexhaustive, but yet rather impressive list of such signatures almost a century ago. These self-promoting inscriptions, in addition to bespeaking a clear sense of authorship, and along with other kinds of visual and textual references to the creators of monumental epigraphy, reveal a diversified, specialized, and structured profession or—better—set of trades.

From an emic vantage point, ancient Egyptian vocabulary makes a distinction between various technical specialists involved in the production of monumental epigraphy, such as the plasterer, the sculptor, or the painter. But as in any other cultural context studied by art history, many overlaps are nonetheless well attested, with sculptors practicing the art of painting or painters engraving reliefs and inscriptions (e.g., Habachi 1957, 100, fig. 6; Ward 1977; Stefanovic 2012, 187, 189–190). Besides, if the sculptor is often referred to by the very technical designation of "chisel-holder" (ṯ3y-mḏ3.t; also ḳs.ty, probably a *nisbe* meaning "the one of the spike"), the expression traditionally translated as painter (or also draftsman), zš ḳd(.w), literally "scribe of forms," actually seems to refer to a specialty in image making, on any kind of two-dimensional media (what could be called graphic arts, i.e., the range of epigraphy), and of course closely connected to the production of writing in the hieroglyphic culture of ancient Egypt (for the semantic scope of the verbal root zš, meaning to write as well as to draw, paint, decorate, and even conceive the decoration of a monument, see *Wb.* III 475–476; Laboury 2016, 379–381). Furthermore, other reference frames, not exclusively based on techniques, might also be used, as is shown by the most frequently attested title to designate sculptors (especially when they (re)present themselves), sꜥnḫ, literally, "the one who causes to live (or gives life to)," alluding to the magical abilities of the statue or relief maker to convert an inert shaped object into an animated and living being.

Any ancient Egyptian image maker, whether a sculptor, a painter, a goldsmith, or any other, belonged to a category designated as ḥmw.w, that is, "practitioners of ḥmw.t." According to ancient Egyptian vocabulary, again, there were two ways to produce artificial things: they could just be "made" (iri) or created through a process called ḥmw.t. So, for instance, the professional manufacturer of arrows is an "arrow-maker" (iri-ꜥḥ3.w), whereas his neighbor in workshop scenes who builds chariots is a "ḥmw(.w) of chariot" (*ḥmw(.w)-wrry.t*). The *ḥmw(.w)* par excellence is the sculptor, but there were also *ḥmw.w* of certain specific prestigious goods (such as a chariot or an oar) or materials (the *ḥmw(.w)* of gold, i.e., the goldsmith, or the *ḥmw(.w)* of precious stones, i.e., the jeweler); and, interestingly enough, on a more metaphorical level, the excellent scribe or author is often portrayed as *ḥmw(.w)* of his fingers or of his words or excellent in his *ḥmw(.t)*, just like his artistic colleagues. The ancient Egyptian concept of *ḥmw(.t)* is always associated with a special mastery of the actor and an aesthetic added value attached to his product; and the divide between what belongs to *ḥmw(.t)* and what does not is plainly a cultural construct, just as it is for the current notion of art, which undoubtedly appears as the best translation or modern equivalent for the ancient Egyptian concept of *ḥmw(.t)* (Laboury 2016, 374–376). So even if every actor in the production of ancient Egyptian monumental epigraphy was certainly not a true artist, at least some of them could clearly be considered and valued by Pharaonic society as artists, experts, and master creators of objects endowed with a special aesthetic added value.

In temple administration and royal productions, those various actors were placed under the supervision of chief artists (*ḥry ḥmw(.w)*; but also chief sculptors (*ḥry ḳs. tyw/ṯꜣy.w mḏ.t*), goldsmiths (*ḥry nby.w*), plasterers (*ḥry ḳd.w*), etc.) and on top of the pecking order (with supervisors, commanders, chiefs of divisions, etc., at least in the Old and Middle Kingdom), a director of all arts (or artists) (*imy-r ḥmw(.wt) nb(.t)*), a function very significantly attributed to a high-ranking royal official, such as the vizier or the first or second high priest of Amun during the New Kingdom (Eichler 2000, 141–161; Laboury 2015). Those titles refer to a hierarchy of skills and responsibilities, but also of education. The majority of the wealthy artists who had access to commemoration—and were thus able to leave us a trace of themselves—displayed clear signs of literacy as well as priestly titles, often very distinguished ones, such as "lector priest" (*ḥry-ḥb*) or "scribe of the divine writings" (*zš mḏꜣ.t nṯr*) (e.g., Newberry [1895], 3, 20, pls. 12, 15; Junker 1959; Stefanovic 2012, 186–187, 189–190; Kahl 2016, 18, pl. 41), associated with the mastery of hieroglyphs and a sacerdotal expertise, obviously needed to devise an effective decoration from a religious point of view. It is certainly no coincidence that the authors of signed decorative programs almost always belonged to one of those two categories of scholar priests (Vernus 1990, 39). The creation of—or in the ancient Egyptian perspective, the "giving birth" (*msi*) or "life" (*sꜥnḫ*) to—an effective image also required ritual competences on behalf of chief or master artists (Fischer-Elfert 1998; Traunecker 1972; Derchain 1990), who could be initiated, that is, instructed, in a distinctly sacred knowledge, restricted to the highest categories of priests (Kruchten 1992).

But once again, such was clearly not the case for every specialist involved in the production of monumental epigraphy. The site of Deir el-Medina, where the community of artists and craftsmen responsible for the making of the tombs in the Valley of the Kings was settled during most of the New Kingdom, provides us with an exceptional clue in this respect. Unlike almost every other member of the crew in the Eighteenth Dynasty, the "servant" (*sḏm-ꜥš*, literally, "the call listener") Amenemhat managed to have a small decorated burial chamber in the local cemetery (Cherpion 1999), thanks to the talents developed by his son, Sennefer, who depicted himself as someone "who writes correctly

FIGURE 1.6.2. Self-portrait *in assistenza* of Sennefer, painted in the tomb of his father, Amenemhat, in Deir el-Medina (TT 340), as recorded in Cherpion 1999, pl. 8 © IFAO.

and causes his (i.e., his father's) name to live" (Figure I.6.2). Despite such a boastful (self-)assertion, the decorative program of this tiny tomb is surprisingly simple, directly derived from the iconography of funerary stelae, which were plainly part of the visual culture of the son of Amenemhat; moreover, the careful analysis of its inscriptions allowed the late Jean-Marie Kruchten to demonstrate that Sennefer clumsily reproduced learned-by-heart formulae that he tried to adapt or emend almost exclusively with uniliteral signs—what could be described as the basic alphabet of hieroglyphic writing system (see chapter by Vernus)—thus making many mistakes that betray his actual—and rather low—level of literacy (Kruchten 1999). So even if our genius, self-taught, novice scribe Sennefer was patently a professional painter working for Pharaoh's projects, he proved to be practically incapable of designing an original iconographic program and a fortiori texts to complement it. As a matter of fact, he belonged to a category of people who were not meant to have access to written or monumental death and are thus normally below the Egyptological radar, that is, practically undetectable in the usual Egyptological material, though they most probably constituted the majority of the artistic force in ancient Egypt (Laboury et al., forthcoming). His exceptional will to go beyond the limitations of his art and hieroglyphic abilities affords us a rare but telling insight into the diversity of skills and education of the actors of artistic and epigraphic production in Pharaonic society.

As in many other professions in ancient Egypt—and in most preindustrial societies— artistic education and knowledge transmission was based on apprenticeship (Lazaridis 2010; Cooney 2012; on contracts attested in Greco-Roman times, see Cannata 2012, 601–602). Thus, a substantial part of the training was performed on the site of monuments in the making, as is evidenced by graphic material found in situ (exercises and models on ostraca or pedagogic sketches on the walls, [regularly neglected in previous epigraphic efforts]), as well as stylistic—and palaeographic—analysis of monumental epigraphy (see what follows). Masters also took their pupils—often their own sons—on artistic and educational excursions in standing monuments, that were clearly used as models and sources of inspiration (notably through an ancient Egyptian practice of epigraphy and palaeography) (see chapter by Bács). Drawings on ostraca (for a synthesis on the subject, see Dorn 2013) and copying grids painted on the walls (e.g., Kanawati 2011) show the Egyptian artists' strong interest in compositions and iconography, with—quite expectedly—a special focus on uncommon or challenging details, and notably on human faces, which are usually diagnostic of the style of the time—and hence essential to master. Besides, plaster casts of older reliefs (Borchardt 1910, 104–105), as exact three-dimensional duplications of their models, also plainly reveal a very careful attention to morphological details and style proper, whereas outline copies of painted elements directly on the murals demonstrate a technical concern as well, for they aimed at reproducing the *ductus* of the brush strokes and the line sequence that created the image (e.g., Ragazzoli 2013, 284, fig. 10; Gervers 2013). As always in art history, art was acquired through imitation and practice.

Archives of previous works were also created and sometimes kept over long periods of time (for temple archives in Greco-Roman times, see the case of the provincial center of Tebtunis (Ryholt 2005), in which two-thousand-year-old texts were preserved (Osing and Rosati 1998, pls. 6–7, 10); for possible fragments of archival copies of iconographic material on papyrus, see Quack 2014; for evidence of personal artistic archives, see Laboury 2017, 241–247); and they most probably were used as well to train artists' apprentices and develop their iconographic and hieroglyphic skills. The discovery of trial pieces in domestic contexts also shows that junior artists, furthermore, practiced at home, in their spare time (e.g., on the urban site of Amarna (Phillips 1991); or in the so-called workmen's huts in the Valley of the Kings (Dorn 2011)). Every drawing board— made of a portable wooden tablet wrapped in linen and plastered with stucco—that came down to us combines drawing *and* writing exercises, thus strongly suggesting that, at least in some cases, maybe for those expected to become master artists, training in graphic arts was complemented by the study of hieroglyphic (Russmann 2001, 66) as well as hieratic writing (Hagen 2013; Galán 2007), and the acquisition of literary abilities and other artistic skills, such as designing statues (Galán 2007). The case of the painter of Amun Pahery, who was also "confidant of the treasurer and scribe accountant of grains in the southern district," and eventually became governor of his home town of el-Kab (Laboury 2017, 241–247; Allon and Navratilova 2017, 13–24; Ptolemaic parallel in

Klotz 2015), clearly shows that, in terms of education, artists in ancient Egypt could receive much more than just an exclusively artistic training and thus enjoy social mobility, some of them becoming members of the royal court (e.g., Kruchten 1992; Stauder 2018).

PRACTICALITIES

The mobility of ancient Egyptian artists was not only social, but also—and primarily—geographical. Textual sources indeed refer to artists and craftsmen commissioned by the king to work in different locations throughout the country, and even beyond (Laboury 2016, 377–378). So, for instance, it is no surprise to encounter Theban sculptors from the domain of Amun active in Ombos (Petrie and Quibell 1896, pl. 78) or Abydos (*Urk.* IV 2112) during the Eighteenth Dynasty (for parallels in the Middle Kingdom, see Connor 2018, 21–22; for late period evidence and contracts, see Clarysse and Luft 2012), or later colleagues of theirs dispatched on a mission at the court of Ugarit, in the northern Levant, by Merenptah (Lackenbacher 2001). This was actually part of a broader system developed since the dawn of Pharaonic state that consisted in raising teams of well-trained experts who could be moved and used according to the ruler's projects (e.g., for navigation and long-distance transportation in the reign of Khufu: Tallet 2017; on the continuation of this system nowadays, notably in the modern archaeological practices of Egyptology, see Georg 2018). They were organized in teams by their specialties and coordinated together, those teams being referred to as "sections" or "divisions" (*wʿr.t*) in Middle Kingdom administration (Quirke 1988) or, more generally and in other periods, as *is.(w)t*, which etymologically means "crew(s) (of a ship)." This highly centralized system, which actually characterizes Pharaonic society as a whole (on large-scale [re]settling of communities according to the state's aims, see Moeller 2016, 378–379; on the control of workers' whereabouts, see Gabolde 2008), is probably one of the main reasons why no free agent or independent artist has ever been attested in Egyptological sources; on the contrary, whenever an affiliation is mentioned, it is always to the king (or his residence) or to a temple, that is, to a royal institution. In other words, all artistic resources in ancient Egypt were institutionally monopolized by Pharaoh, the main producer, consumer, and patron of arts. "Yet," as Marianne Eaton-Krauss (2001, 136–137) underlined, "some freelance work was possible within that framework in all periods. Sculptors and painters might be sent from one place to another by the king, with a specific commission, or delegated to work temporarily for a favored official, but they did not travel on their own from place to place in search of work" (for evidence of informal workshop practices, see Cooney 2006; Phillips 1991).

Work conditions could, of course, vary a lot from royal to private projects. If Pharaoh had divisions, a real army of artists, craftsmen, and workers at hand to carry out his monumental policy on a national scale with the support of his elite (Andrassy 2007), such was clearly not the case for private customers. When the privileged of the regime were granted monuments as a favor of the king, they might enjoy royal logistics, at least partly, like, for instance, the governor of Elephantine Sarenput I, who received on his island at the southern border of Egypt on Senwosret I's orders no less than one hundred artisans from the royal residence to renew the sanctuary of a local saint, and also very likely to work in his own tomb (Franke 1994, 106–107; Quirke 2009, 117–118); in many respects, this was a royal work, since it was commissioned by the king. But in most cases (and increasingly from the Old Kingdom on), private self-thematizing patrons had to raise their own team and rely on their own resources. Obviously, it was far from unusual for high-ranking dignitaries to use the administration under their responsibility for their personal projects (Eyre 1987, 198–199)—in the context of the time, it was apparently not considered as some sort of corruption—but regarding the epigraphy of their monuments, they needed specially trained experts. The main issue was to be able to engage the best ones, because the more artistically qualified, polyvalent, and autonomous they would be, the smaller the group of specialists to divert from their usual professional commitments. This explains why most of the signatures or self-portraits *in assistenza* (on this concept, see Laboury 2015; 2016, 388–389), that is, textual or pictorial signatures, mention master, literate, and highly educated artists, often assisted by one (or two) colleague(s) or disciple(s) (e.g., where painters are identified by name in Keller 2001 and Bács 2011). But limited teams (for administrative evidence, see Laboury 2012, 202) and moreover, the limited access of nonroyal commissioning patrons to master artists, usually busy with state duties, sometimes—and actually quite often—engendered logistic and trades coordination difficulties, as well as disruptions of work in the making of large private monuments, such as tombs (e.g., Owen and Kemp 1994; on those ergonomic conflicts, as I suggest they be called, see Laboury 2012, 204–205). Furthermore, as always in art history, next to social and political importance, personal connections could also constitute an alternative means to gain access to art and epigraphy experts, and thus to monumental commemoration. This is well substantiated by stelae, statues, statuettes, and even tombs, usually rather small in size but of the highest quality, made for less prominent people by artists who revealed themselves as members of the owner's family or circle of friends (e.g., Davies 2009; Hill 2007). Lastly, for lower-ranking individuals who did not have exceptional social opportunities to come into contact with expert artists, it was obviously still possible to afford—rather—humble commemorative or devotional monuments through local workshops (for a functional definition of the concept of workshop in this context, see Connor 2018), usually linked to sacred places, that is, places where there was a private or consumer demand for such monuments. The classic case in this respect is provided by Middle Kingdom private stelae, usually—but not always—of a lesser quality than the ones of the coeval elite, often with epigraphic idiosyncrasies corresponding to workshops' habits or usages (notably Freed 1996; Marée 2009), but also, in some cases, with orthographic mistakes, that might reveal a lower level of literacy or hieroglyphic mastery on behalf of both the makers and the consumers.

The work procedure was, of course, also adapted according to those varying circumstances, royal production representing, as always in ancient Egypt, the ideal—or reference—case. In order to proceed from ideation to execution, the artist in charge of the work—whether a stela or a complete architectural monument, an inscription or a depiction—had to follow a set of compositional rules inherited from the tradition (and formalized for monumental decoration at the latest in Greco-Roman times: Derchain 1970; on this tradition, see Davis 1989) and to produce a visual plan of his—future—creation. Whatever its initial form and materiality, this design was intended to match the surface to be decorated, so that the first task of the artist on the spot, just as any artist in the history of art, was to set and lay out the composition on this surface (notably with the help of guidelines or proportion grids in order to secure scale consistency), looking for the best interaction between epigraphy and its carrier (prepared in advance), an essential characteristic of ancient Egyptian art. As can be seen on many unfinished works (Hornung 1971; Baines 1989), this first sketch (almost always drafted in red ochre, the most frequent and available basic pigment) could then be adjusted, corrected, or detailed, that is, finalized (normally in black), and later on used to guide the operations of carving or painting (Figure I.6.3; for early efforts to record in watercolors the materialization of those successive steps, see Davis 1912, pls. 48–49, 55), the monument becoming, in the end, as is described in the famous royal tomb papyrus of Turin, "drawn with forms, graven with the chisel, filled with colors, and completed" (Carter and Gardiner 1917, 139–140).

When used on a large scale, with an appropriately large workforce, as Pharaoh could plainly afford, this very well attested procedure allowed efficient and relatively rapid execution through a rather intense fragmentation of the sequence of operations in order to distribute the work among various teams of specialists dispatched in their own work zones, as well as between masters and artists still in training or apprentices (e.g., Baines 1989, 25–27; Keller 1991, 2003; for examples of repetitive motifs abbreviated or only suggested by one or two samples, to be completed by younger artists, see Baines 1989, 18, 25; Hornung 1971, pls. 25–27, 33, 48–49, 51–52).

As one would expect, once again, such an ideal, well-organized royal model of work—almost a production-line work—required some adjustments when applied to privately funded monuments. It was often necessary—or desired—to reduce the number of actors and, consequently, the variety of specialists in the production process. So for instance, hard stone sculpture (i.e., in granite, diorite, quartzite, etc.) was obviously a specialty of its own, less accessible to nonroyal consumers than its soft stone counterpart (e.g., Wittmann 1998, 178–181), hence the many painted replicas of granite false doors or architectural elements. Besides, converging indications, such as more free-hand drafting with a less systematic use of grids and guidelines (e.g., Robins 2001) or sketched designs on ostraca found—and thus very likely made—in situ (e.g., Hayes 1942, pl. 1.6, [compared with Dorman 1991, pl. 9]; Davies 1923, 15, pls. 72, 79), evidence a clear will to shorten or simplify the procedure. An exemplary case in this respect is provided by the private tombs of the Theban necropolis, especially during the Eighteenth Dynasty, most of them featuring an imitation solely in paint of (royal) painted reliefs at a lower cost (compare Laboury and Tavier 2016 with Baines 1989), but usually of the highest quality. Interestingly enough—and this is, in fact, a fundamental driving force throughout art

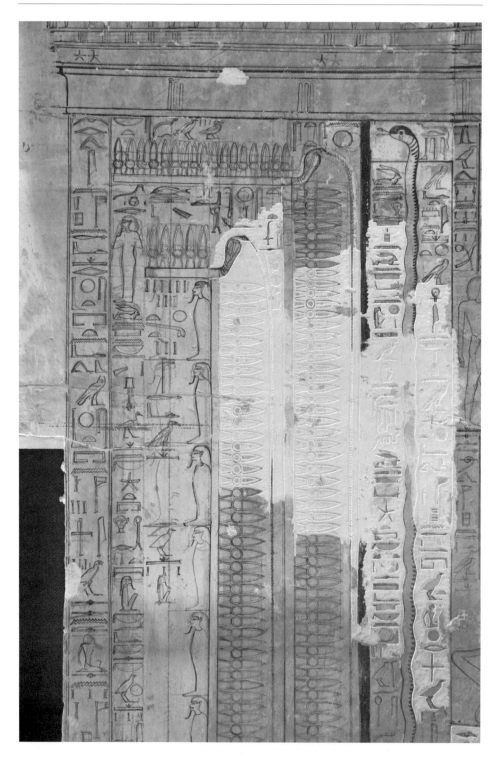

FIGURE 1.6.3. Detail of a wall under decoration in the burial chamber of the tomb of Horemheb in the Valley of the Kings, Biban el-Moluk (KV 57), showing material traces of the initial drafting, the finalized drawing or pattern, and the beginning of the stone cutting operation. Note the abbreviated sequence of motifs in the frieze of stars and the cavetto corniche. Author's picture.

history—private patrons endeavored—and competed—to hire the best and most polyvalent artists to work on their own monuments for pragmatic reasons (they are more autonomous and effective), but also, and maybe above all, for prestige. The negotiation that such a situation presupposes granted chosen artists more freedom to express their own style and artistic personality (e.g., Laboury 2013), even signing their own work; whereas the royal art production system almost always diluted individualities into a more rigid repertoire and a homogenized style, intentionally, for the sake of visual coherence, but also through the multiplication of actors involved in the creation of a single scene, panel, or monument—particularly when it was decorated with painted reliefs. Furthermore, the royal model allowed the integration into the *chaîne opératoire* of less talented craftsmen, regularly detectable in sloppy details (such as final paintings that unskillfully overlap the outlines of the reliefs they were meant to adorn) that one rarely comes across on private elite monuments. So in this sense, royal production was not necessarily synonymous with the utmost quality and artistic involvement due to the conditions of work and employment but also of creation itself.

Stylistic and quality discrepancies might also result from methods of training through apprenticeship and labor division. For instance, it has often been observed that symmetric structures, such as doorjambs and lintels, frequently display slight but consistent rendering differences between their left and right halves (Davies 2017), one of them being usually better detailed or decorated with a finer and surer hand (e.g., Krauss and Loeben 1996, especially 163, fig. 3); Laboury 2016–2017, 81–82), a divide that induces one to recognize a master artist working alongside his apprentice or a younger colleague, notably in the cases of mirroring inscriptions or decoration. In his analysis of unfinished reliefs in the temple of Seti I at Abydos, John Baines (1989, 18, 25–26) also noticed that some important or difficult features, such as faces of the king or complicated hieroglyphs, were left to be carved by "the principal artist," or master sculptor, while less prominent or repetitive—and boring—details "were rather crudely executed and may have been done by junior artists."

In this context, textual epigraphy imposed specific constraints, particularly because the alteration or omission of a single element in an inscription could compromise the latter's meaning and efficiency. Therefore, it was crucial to avoid any mistake. Though some indications could occasionally be noted in everyday tachygraphies (hieratic: Davies 1923, pl. 20; and later on, demotic and then Greek: e.g., Cannata 2012, 602) directly on the surface to be decorated, drafts for monumental inscriptions were usually—if not always—already prepared in linear or cursive hieroglyphs (see chapter by Vernus), much closer to proper monumental hieroglyphs in forms and disposition than to tachygraphies (Haring 2014). Long textual compositions could be dispatched—probably on site—on ordered and sometimes numbered ostraca (e.g., Tallet 2005; Lüscher 2013) in order to follow the right sequence, but also, and more importantly, to match perfectly with the surface meant to receive the inscription. Such a transcription system, of course, entailed a good knowledge of the corpus of hieroglyphic signs and, additionally, a well exercised ability to convert sketched cursive signs into full-fledged hieroglyphs. Nevertheless, mistakes—as might be expected—could sometimes occur.

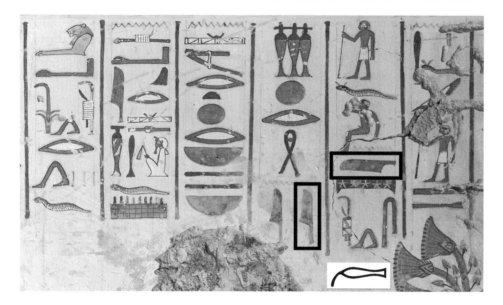

FIGURE I.6.4. Detail of the caption of a figure of the deceased in the tomb of Paser, TT 367 (Sheikh Abd el-Qurna), where the hieroglyph of the censer (Gardiner R5) was misinterpreted as a sloped reed leaf sign (compare with the column on the left), almost certainly from a draft in cursive hieroglyphs. Author's picture and montage.

An interesting example is to be found in an inscription of Theban Tomb 367 in the name of Paser, a military officer of the reign of Amenhotep II who was also "child of the (so-called) nursery" (ḥrd n kꜣp), a royal institution where the crown prince received education with a few selected classmates. The ideogram, depicting a censer (Gardiner R5), that is used to write the name of this institution is quite rare. In one of the inscriptions of the funerary chapel, the painter could not identify it correctly from the draft that was given to him, and he replaced the sign of the fumigation implement with a reed leaf sloped at a right angle (Figure I.6.4), a misinterpretation that could not derive from a confusion through hieratic, but only from a cursive hieroglyph difficult to understand. This case perfectly illustrates how enlightening the study of those epigraphic mistakes might be to understand the circumstances under which the monuments were decorated.

CONCLUSION

As Vanessa Davies (2017, 211) perfectly underlined, "Close study of wall decoration can sometimes give us an insight into a particular method of working a wall." There is indeed an intrinsic link between epigraphic and palaeographic study of monumental decoration and the way the latter was made, and hence, its makers. We ought to follow the example of ancient Egyptian artists themselves, when they studied the *oeuvre* of their predecessors, through their own practice of epigraphy and palaeography in order to train their eyes and hands and to consider and analyze the material marks of the life and making of those monuments, for those marks still allow us to investigate and better understand those who created them, their actions, and their thoughts. There is plainly a lot to gain both for art history and for Egyptian epigraphy and palaeography.

Bibliography

Allon, N., and H. Navratilova. 2017. *Ancient Egyptian Scribes: A Cultural Exploration.* London.

Andrassy, P. 2007. "Zur Organisation und Finanzierung von Tempelbauten im Alten Ägypten." In *Das Heilige und die Ware. Zum Spannungsfeld von Religion und Ökonomie*, edited by M. Fitzenreiter, 143–164. IBAES 7. London. http://www2.rz.hu-berlin.de/nilus/net-publications/ibaes7/beitraege.html.

Bács, T. A. 2011. "'…like heaven in its interior': Late Ramesside Painters in Theban Tomb 65." In *Proceedings of the Colloquium on Theban Archaeology at the Supreme Council of Antiquities, November 5, 2009*, edited by Z. Hawass, T. A. Bács, and G. Schreiber, 33–41. Cairo.

Baines, J. 1989. "Techniques of Decoration in the Hall of Barques in the Temple of Sethos I at Abydos." *JEA* 75:13–30.

Borchardt, L. 1910. *Das Grabdenkmal des Königs Saᵌḥu-Reʿ I: Der Bau.* WVDOG 14. Leipzig.

Cannata, M. 2012. "Funerary Artists: The Textual Evidence." In *The Oxford Handbook of Roman Egypt*, edited by C. Riggs, 597–612. Oxford.

Carter, H., and A. H. Gardiner. 1917. "The Tomb of Ramesses IV and the Turin Plan of a Royal Tomb." *JEA* 4:130–158.

Cherpion, N. 1999. *Deux tombes de la XVIIIᵉ dynastie à Deir el-Medina.* MIFAO 114. Cairo.

Clarysse, W., and U. Luft. 2012. "Demotic Contracts between Sculptors and the Bastet Temple at Tholthis." In *"Parcourir l'éternité": Hommages à Jean Yoyotte*, vol. 1, edited by C. Zivie-Coche and I. Guermeur, 323–335. BEHE SSE 156. Turnhout.

Connor, S. 2018. "Sculpture Workshops: Who, Where and for Whom?" In *The Arts of Making in Ancient Egypt: Voices, Images and Objects of Material Producers 2000–1550 BC*, edited by G. Miniaci, J. C. Moreno Garcia, S. Quirke, and A. Stauder, 11–30. Leiden.

Cooney, K. M. 2006. "An Informal Workshop: Textual Evidence for Private Funerary Art Production in the Ramesside Period." In *Living and Writing in Deir el-Medine: Socio-historical Embodiment of Deir el-Medine Texts*, edited by A. Dorn and T. Hofmann, 43–55. AH 19. Basel.

Cooney, K. M. 2012. "Apprenticeship and Figures Ostraca from the Ancient Egyptian Village of Deir el-Medina." In *Archaeology and Apprenticeship: Body Knowledge, Identity, and Communities of Practice*, edited by W. Wendrich, 145–170. Tucson.

Davis, T. M. 1912. *The Tombs of Harmhabi and Touatânkhamanou.* London.

Davis, W. M. 1989. *The Canonical Tradition in Ancient Egypt Art.* New York.

Davies, N. de G. 1923. *The Tombs of Two Officials of Tuthmosis the Fourth* (Nos. 75 and 90). TTS 3. London.

Davies, V. 2017. "Complications in the Stylistic Analysis of Egyptian Art: A Look at the Small Temple of Medinet Habu." In *(Re)productive Traditions in Ancient Egypt: Proceedings of the Conference Held at the University of Liège, 6th–8th February 2013*, edited by T. Gillen, 203–228. AegLeo 10. Liège.

Davies, W. V. 2009. "The Tomb of Ahmose Son-of-Ibana at Elkab: Documenting the Family and Other Observations." In *Elkab and Beyond: Studies in Honour of Luc Limme*, edited by W. Claes, H. de Meulenaere, and S. Hendrickx, 139–175. OLA 191. Leuven.

Derchain, P. 1970. "Review of Untersuchungen zu den ägyptischen Tempelreliefs der griechisch-römischen Zeit, by Erich Winter." *RdE* 22:242–243.

Derchain, P. 1990. "L'Atelier des Orfèvres à Dendara et les origines de l'Alchimie." *CdE* 65:219–242.

Dorman, P. F. 1991. *The Tombs of Senenmut: The Architecture and Decoration of Tombs 71 and 353*. PMMA 24. New York.

Dorn, A. 2011. *Arbeiterhütten im Tal der Könige: Ein Beitrag zur altägyptischen Sozialgeschichte aufgrund von neuem Quellenmaterial aus der Mitte der 20. Dynastie (ca. 1150 v. Chr.)*. AH 23. Basel.

Dorn, A. 2013. "Ostraka als Bildträger: Funktionen und Kontexte / Images sur ostraca: Fonctions et contextes." https://www.academia.edu/4736573/Ostraka_als_Bildträger._Funktionen_und_Kontexte_Images_sur_ostraca._Functions_et_contextes.

Eaton-Krauss, M. 2001. "Artists and Artisans." In *The Oxford Encyclopedia of Ancient Egypt*, vol. 1, edited by D. Redford, 136–140. Cairo.

Eichler, S. S. 2000. *Die Verwaltung des "Hauses des Amun" in der 18. Dynastie*. SAK Bh 7. Hamburg.

Eyre, C. J. 1987. "Work and the Organisation of Work in the New Kingdom." In *Labor in the Ancient Near East*, edited by M. A. Powell, 167–221. New Haven.

Fischer-Elfert, H.-W. 1998. *Die Vision von der Statue im Stein: Studien zum altägyptischen Mundöffnungsritual*. Schriften der Philosophisch-historischen Klasse der Heidelberger Akademie der Wissenschaften 5. Heidelberg.

Franke, D. 1994. *Das Heiligtum des Heqaib auf Elephantine: Geschichte eines Provinzheiligtums im Mittleren Reich*. SAGA 9. Heidelberg.

Freed, R. E. 1996. "Stela Workshops of Early Dynasty 12." In *Studies in Honor of William Kelly Simpson*, vol. 1, edited by P. Der Manuelian and R. E. Freed, 297–336. Boston.

Gabolde, M. 2008. "Des travailleurs en vadrouille." In *Hommages à Jean-Claude Goyon (offerts pour son 70e anniversaire)*, edited by L. Gabolde, 181–196. BdE 143. Cairo.

Galán, J. M. 2007. "An Apprentice's Board from Dra Abu el-Naga." *JEA* 93:95–116.

Georg, M. 2018. "Antiquity Bound to Modernity: The Significance of Egyptian Workers in Modern Archaeology in Egypt." In *The Arts of Making in Ancient Egypt: Voices, Images and Objects of Material Producers 2000–1550 BC*, edited by G. Miniaci, J. C. Moreno Garcia, S. Quirke, and A. Stauder, 49–66. Leiden.

Gervers, E. 2013. "Die Bildgraffiti des Neuen Reiches in Grab N13.1 in Assiut/Mittelägypten." MA thesis, Johannes Gutenberg Universität Mainz.

Habachi, L. 1957. "Two Graffiti at Sehel from the Reign of Queen Hatshepsut." *JNES* 16:88–104.

Hagen, F. 2013. "An Eighteenth Dynasty Writing Board (Ashmolean 1948.91) and The Hymn to the Nile." *JARCE* 49:73–91.

Haring, B. J. J. 2014. "Hieratic Drafts for Hieroglyphic Texts?" In *Ägyptologische "Binsen"-Weisheiten I–II. Neue Forschungen und Methoden der Hieratistik. Akten zweier Tagungen in Mainz im April 2011 und März 2013*, edited by U. Verhoeven, 67–84. AAWLM 14. Stuttgart.

Hayes, W. C. 1942. *Ostraka and Name Stones from the Tomb of Sen-Mut (No. 71) at Thebes*. PMMA 15. New York.

Hill, M. 2007. "Hepu's Hair: A Copper-Alloy Statuette in the National Archaeological Museum, Athens." *BES* 17:109–134.

Hornung, E. 1971. *Das Grab des Haremhab im Tal der Könige*. Bern.

Junker, H. 1959. *Die gesellschaftliche Stellung der ägyptischen Künstler im Alten Reich*. SÖAW 233(1). Vienna.

Kanawati, N. 2011. "Art and Gridlines: The Copying of Old Kingdom Scenes in Later Periods." In *Abusir and Saqqara in the Year 2010*, vol. 2, edited by M. Barta, F. Coppens, and J. Krejci, 483–496. Prague.

Kahl, J. 2016. *Ornamente in Bewegung: Die Deckendekoration der großen Querhalle im Grab von Djefai-Hapi I. in Assiut*. The Asyut Project 6. Wiesbaden.

Keller, C. A. 1991. "Royal Painters: Deir el-Medina in Dynasty XIX." In *Fragments of a Shattered Visage: Proceedings of the International Symposium on Ramesses the Great*, edited by E. Bleiberg and R. Freed, 50–86. Memphis.

Keller, C. A. 2001. "A Family Affair: The Decoration of Theban Tomb 359." In *Colour and Painting in Ancient Egypt*, edited by W. V. Davies, 73–93. London.

Keller, C. A. 2003. "Un artiste égyptien à l'œuvre: le dessinateur en chef Amenhotep." In *Deir el-Médineh et la Vallée des Rois: La vie en Égypte au temps des pharaons du Nouvel Empire. Actes du colloque organisé par le Musée du Louvre, les 3 et 4 mai 2002*, edited by G. Andreu, 83–114. Paris.

Klotz, D. 2015. "The Cuboid Statue of Ser-Djehuty, Master Sculptor in Karnak: Los Angeles County Museum of Art 48.24.8 + Cambridge University, Museum of Archaeology and Anthropology 51.533." *RdE* 66:51–91.

Krauss, R., and C. E. Loeben. 1996. "Die Berliner 'Zierinschrift' Amenemhets III als Beispiel für gebrochene Symmetrie." *JPKb* 33:159–172.

Kruchten, J.-M. 1992. "Un sculpteur des images divines ramesside." In *L'atelier de l'orfèvre: Mélanges offerts à Ph. Derchain*, edited by M. Broze and P. Talon, 107–118. Leuven.

Kruchten, J.-M. 1999. "Traduction et commentaire des inscriptions." In *Deux tombes de la XVIIIᵉ dynastie à Deir el-Medina*, edited by N. Cherpion, 41–55. MIFAO 114. Cairo.

Laboury, D. 2012. "Tracking Ancient Egyptian Artists, a Problem of Methodology: The Case of the Painters of Private Tombs in the Theban Necropolis during the Eighteenth Dynasty." In *Art and Society: Ancient and Modern Contexts of Egyptian Art. Proceedings of the International Conference held at the Museum of Fine Arts, Budapest, 13–15 May 2010*, edited by K. A. Kóthay, 199–208. Budapest.

Laboury, D. 2013. "De l'individualité de l'artiste dans l'art égyptien." In *L'art du contour: Le dessin dans l'Égypte ancienne*, edited by G. Andreu-Lanoë, 36–41. Paris.

Laboury, D. 2015. "On the Master Painter of the Tomb of Amenhopte Sise, Second High Priest of Amun under the Reign of Thutmose IV (TT 75)." In *Joyful in Thebes: Egyptological Studies in Honor of Betsy M. Bryan*, edited by R. Jasnow and K. M. Cooney, 327–337. Atlanta.

Laboury, D. 2016. "Le scribe et le peintre: À propos d'un scribe qui ne voulait pas être pris pour un peintre." In *Aere perennius. Mélanges égyptologiques en l'honneur de Pascal Vernus*, edited by P. Collombert, D. Lefèvre, S. Polis, and J. Winand, 371–396. OLA 242. Leuven.

Laboury, D. 2016–2017. "Senwosret III and the Issue of Portraiture in Ancient Egyptian Art." *CRIPEL* 31:71–84.

Laboury, D. 2017. "Tradition and Creativity: Toward a Study of Intericonicity in Ancient Egyptian Art." In *(Re)productive Traditions in Ancient Egypt: Proceedings of the Conference Held at the University of Liège, 6th–8th February 2013*, edited by T. Gillen, 229–258. AegLeo 10. Liège.

Laboury, D., S. Polis, A. Den Doncker, G. Pieke, and H. Tavier. Forthcoming. "Communication Marks in the Context of Artistic Production: The Case of the Nobles' Tombs of the 18th Dynasty in the Theban Necropolis."

Laboury, D., and H. Tavier. 2016. "In Search of Painters in the Theban Necropolis of the 18th Dynasty: Prolegomena to an Analysis of Pictorial Practices in the Tomb of Amenemope (TT 29)." In *Artists and Colour in Ancient Egypt: Proceedings of the Colloquium Held in Montepulciano, August 22nd–24th, 2008*, edited by V. Angenot and F. Tiradritti, 57–77. Montepulciano.

Lackenbacher, S. 2001. "Une lettre d'Égypte." In *Études ougaritiques I Travaux 1985–1995*, edited by M. Yon and D. Arnaud, 239–248. Ras Shamra-Ougarit 14. Paris.

Lazaridis, N. 2010. "Education and Apprenticeship." In *UCLA Encyclopedia of Egyptology*, edited by E. Frood and W. Wendrich. Los Angeles. http://digital2.library.ucla.edu/viewItem. do?ark=21198/zz0025jxjn.

Lüscher, B. 2013. *Die Vorlagen-Ostraka aus dem Grab des Nachtmin (TT 87)*. BAÄ 4. Basel.

Marée, M. 2009. "Edfu under the Twelfth to Seventeenth Dynasties: The Monuments in the National Museum of Warsaw." *BMSAES* 12:31–92.

Moeller, N. 2016. *The Archaeology of Urbanism in Ancient Egypt: From the Predynastic Period to the End of the Middle Kingdom*. New York.

Newberry, P. E. [1895.] *El Bersheh 1, The Tomb of Tehuti-hetep*. ASE 3. London.

Osing, J., and G. Rosati. 1998. *Papiri geroglifici e ieratici da Tebtynis*. Florence.

Owen, G., and B. J. Kemp. 1994. "Craftsmen's Work Patterns in Unfinished Tombs at Amarna." *CAJ* 4:121–146.

Petrie, W. M. F., and J. E. Quibell. 1896. *Naqada and Ballas: 1895*. BSAE/ERA [1]. London.

Phillips, J. 1991. "Sculpture Ateliers of Akhetaton: An Examination of Two Studio-Complexes in the City of the Sun-Disk." *Amarna Letters* 1:31–40.

Polz, D. 1987. "Excavation and Recording of a Theban Tomb: Some Remarks on Recording Methods." In *Problems and Priorities in Egyptian Archaeology*, edited by J. Assmann, G. Burkard, and V. Davies, 119–140. London.

Quack, J. F. 2014. "Die theoretische Normierung der Soubassement-Dekoration. Erste Ergebnisse der Arbeit an der karbonisierten Handschrift von Tanis." In *Altägyptische Enzyklopädien: Die Soubassements in den Tempeln der griechisch-römischen Zeit*, edited by A. Rickert and B. Ventker, 17–27. Wiesbaden.

Quirke, S. 1988. "'Art' and 'the Artists' in Late Middle Kingdom Administration." In *Discovering Egypt from the Neva: The Egyptological Legacy of Oleg D. Berlev*, edited by S. Quirke, 85–105. Berlin.

Quirke, S. 2009. "The Residence in Relations between Places of Knowledge, Production and Power: Middle Kingdom Evidence." In *Egyptian Royal Residences: 4th Symposium on Egyptian Royal Ideology, London, June 1st–5th 2004*, edited by R. Gundlach and J. H. Taylor, 111–130. KSG 4.1. Wiesbaden.

Ragazzoli, C. 2013. "The Social Creation of a Scribal Place: The Visitors' Inscriptions in the Tomb Attributed to Antefiqer (TT 60) (with newly recorded graffiti)." *SAK* 42:269–323.

Reeves, N. 2001. *Akhenaten: Egypt's False Prophet*. London.

Robins, G. 2001. "The Use of the Squared Grid as a Technical Aid for Artists in Eighteenth Dynasty Painted Theban Tombs." In *Colour and Painting in Ancient Egypt*, edited by W. V. Davies, 60–62. London.

Russmann, E. R. 2001. *Eternal Egypt: Masterworks of Ancient Art from the British Museum*. London.

Ryholt, K. 2005. "On the Contents and Nature of the Tebtunis Temple Library: A Status Report." In *Tebtynis und Soknopaiu Nesos: Leben im römerzeitlichen Fajum*, edited by S. Lippert and M. Schentuleit, 141–170. Wiesbaden.

Stauder, A. 2018. "Staging Restricted Knowledge: The Sculptor Irtysen's Self-presentation (ca. 2000 BC)." In *The Arts of Making in Ancient Egypt: Voices, Images and Objects of Material Producers 2000–1550 BC*, edited by G. Miniaci, J. C. Moreno Garcia, S. Quirke, and A. Stauder, 239–271. Leiden.

Stefanovic, D. 2012. "zš ḳdwt–The Attestations from the Middle Kingdom and the Second Intermediate Period." In *Art and Society: Ancient and Modern Contexts of Egyptian Art. Proceedings of the International Conference held at the Museum of Fine Arts, Budapest, 13–15 May 2010*, edited by K. A. Kóthay, 185–198. Budapest.

Tallet, P. 2005. "Un nouveau témoin des «Devoirs du Vizir» dans la tombe d'Aménémopé (Thèbes, TT 29)." *CdE* 80:66–75.

Tallet, P. 2017. *Les papyrus de la mer rouge I: Le "journal de Merer" (papyrus Jarf A et B)*. MIFAO 136. Cairo.

Traunecker, C. 1972. "Le 'Château de l'Or' de Thoutmosis III et les magasins nord du temple d'Amon." *CRIPEL* 11:89–111.

Vernus, P. 1990. "Les espaces de l'écrit dans l'Égypte pharaonique." *BSFE* 119:35–56.

Ward, W. A. 1977. "Neferhotep and His Friends: A Glimpse at the Lives of Ordinary Men." *JEA* 63:63–66.

Ware, E. 1927. "Egyptian Artists' Signatures." *AJSL* 43/3:185–201.

Wittmann, G. 1998. *Der Demotische Papyrus Rylands 9*. ÄAT 38. Wiesbaden.

CHAPTER I.7

···

AUDIENCES

···

HANA NAVRATILOVA

INTRODUCTION

AN outline of the history of audiences of art, architecture, and texts of ancient Egypt might embrace protean generations of people who were participants as well as observers of the ancient culture, inclusive of researchers in the role of interpreters of the culture. In this chapter, we are becoming spectators of the spectators.

Ancient Egyptian culture operated a range of visual and textual communication techniques including, but not limited to, those that are now accessible in the archaeological record, either material, visual, or written (Baines 2006; Seidlmayer 2006; Parkinson 2009; Baines 2013). The role of oral performance in Egyptian cultural communication has been evaluated more systematically only recently (Eyre 2013; Parkinson 2009), yet it was performances, not silent readings, of a ritual or poetry that were essential in transmission of texts and hence also cultural values (further observations in Parkinson 2009 and Simon 2013). We must also acknowledge a developing field of spatial analysis that locates social interaction in its built (or natural) environment. Although not pursued here in detail, this is an important line of inquiry and potentially very helpful to Egyptology (Fisher 2009; Lawrence and Low 1990; compare Baines 2013, 32–33, 49; Gutmann 2016).

A combination of visual and written record in tomb decoration programs often captured the tomb owner and his family as "audience" of grain collection, agricultural production, or a feast. New Kingdom dignitaries thematized the component of "seeing" or "inspecting" (for the spectator aspect, Tefnin 1983; specific New Kingdom phraseology, Popko 2006, 262–265; Baines 2013). They were in turn also seen—by the king and by their retainers—while performing their duties. Regarding audience (as well as nonroyal participants) of the public part of religious festivals, royal progresses, and royal receptions, only select depictions (compare Bickel 2013) and hints in texts survive (for access and exclusion of audiences, see Baines 2006), but the sense of audience, its gaze and listening-in, is reflected in the records.

The written record is but a fraction of the communications that enabled Egyptian society to function. Nonetheless, however limited to the ranks of the literate and however limited the access to some texts in specific spaces might have been, Egyptian texts were often composed, correspondingly to communication norms, with a "sense of dialogue" (Hagen 2012, 51). Cultural texts were meant to be received and transmitted as "a kind of normative and formative cultural program which conveys and reproduces cultural identity" (Assmann 1999, 7, but compare Hagen 2012, 56). An audience was implicit in Egyptian cultural norms, as well as manners and customs of a day-to-day social contact.

In terms of typologizing audiences, the main dividing line would seem to run between a participant in a culture, constituting an emic audience, and a later or outside observer, constituting an etic audience (Kottak 2006, 47). However, within the emic audience, we may want to further distinguish systemic and nonsystemic audience (compare Polz 1987). What constitutes the difference here? If emic and etic perspective groups could be characterized as Egyptians versus non-Egyptians, then systemic and nonsystemic have more ambiguous boundaries. A worshipper in a funerary temple could, for example, constitute an emic as well as systemic audience, even if s/he came several centuries after the temple had been in full active use. A person tasked with a thorough *damnatio memoriae* may be seen as a danger to the monument nowadays, but his or her impact on tomb or temple decoration was both emic and systemic, even if in the negative direction. Both the Amarna destructions (Eaton-Krauss 2003, 194–195; Gabolde 1998, 32–34) and the post-Amarna attacks on Amarna rulers would belong in this category (e.g., survey of *damnatio*, Wilkinson 2016; Atonist *damnatio*, Delia 1999; post-Amarna process, Brand 1999; see chapter by Brand).

The etic, observer role is not impartial either—it has expectations and limitations. In Egyptology, these are particularly well visible. An evolving, often limited, access to sources combined with influences of a concept of modern superiority has on occasion prompted judgments assessing the ancient culture as ultimately less sophisticated in areas of communication, interaction, and perception (Hagen 2012, 9).

However, "The possibilities of the past are, like those of the present, more varied than we often assume, and ancient experience more diverse than the surviving documentation might suggest" (Parkinson 2009, 40), and ancient communication experience and its conceptualizations, either implicit or explicit, are no exception (Baines 2013, 17, 263). It is almost tempting to say the observers were the ones lacking in subtlety, but that would constitute just another simplified and eventually unfair judgment, especially if projected onto previous generations of researchers (Fitzenreiter 2007, 330n25).

ADDRESSING ROYAL AND DIVINE SPECTATORS

Monumental edifice and text production of Egyptian royal and nonroyal origin proliferated, and kingship in particular relies on addressing different audiences as part of its legitimation strategies. "Legitimation has several basic strategies such as ritual and persuasive discourse…royal display, including works of art and major monuments, forms another crucial strand" (Baines 1995, 7). Both the performative aspects (ritual and court ceremony, including royal discourse embodied in practices and formalized behavior) and the monumental aspect relied on audiences. Royal ideological foundations included elements that needed to be communicated such as "royal action or efficacy…and myth" (Baines 1995, 7). The royal "audience" *stricto sensu* suggests the king hearing his subjects, but the ceremonial works both ways, the king—as well as his works and deeds represented in visual and written production (Baines 1995, 7)—is seen and heard too.

The king addresses gods and people—and possibly next generations of royalty. Especially in the Middle and New Kingdom, the terminology of royal "propaganda" is very rich and varied, as it belongs to the essential "fabrication" (Burke 1992, 12–13) of a monarch. New Kingdom kings had to combine several monarchical roles—to be Horus on earth, yet at the same time a divine surrogate on earth, fulfilling their functions as heirs to the long line of kings and responsible for correct discharge of their duties (Redford 1995, 161).

The king interacts mostly with deities. They are his/her communication partners, the primary royal audience as described by the visual and a large part of the textual record that was produced on royal command. The words of royal epithets, as well as larger stela and temple texts, address deities by enumeration of temple donations, victorious campaigns (*Ereignisgeschichte*, "history of events," Klug 2002, 496–497), and so on, contributing to a general sense that the king upheld *maat* in all its different aspects and setting the record for deities and people alike (e.g., Klug 2002, 96–106). This is also expressed in scenes of the king offering Maat to deities (Teeter 1997, 82–83). The essential communication a king had to maintain with deities required also a setting for a privileged approach. Temples, temple donations, and other environments set the conditions, and royal–divine contact was secured. In an Egyptian worldview, deities hear, listen to (as indeed they do in nonroyal context, compare *Ohrenstelen*), and speak to the king (as seen in New Kingdom texts), ultimately responding by providing the sovereign with their protection and power.

Deities are not the only royal audience, but since they provide the essential authority of kingship (Baines 1995, 33), the location of royal texts and stelae was often within temple precincts, with limited human access. It is a matter of future research to continue investigating the spatial arrangement of, for example, temple decoration as part of means of communication with the divine world (Arnold 1962; Hartwig 2015). Nonroyal mortals had limited rights to be depicted in a temple (Bickel 2013) and mostly (compare Kayser 1936), from the New Kingdom onward, obtained permission to locate statues there (Kjølby 2009). Susanne Bickel (2013, 24) also suggested that "identified non-royal men in primary temple decoration seem restricted to buildings with a strong emphasis on the cult of the pharaoh." It would almost suggest a decorous hierarchy of audience that permitted nonroyals in decoration schemes of a royal temple, whereas in the divine temple, the king had to dominate (and allowed for unnamed participants of feasts or other scenes).

Nonetheless, communication did not end with royal-divine dialogue. Although the king addressed his earthly audience only selectively, he always provided and commemorated, yet on earth, the mortal audience was there to express joy and recognition of a good reign. Different audiences are addressed implicitly by the very location and contents of a stela or text and scenes: temple stelae address gods (and priests), whereas, for example, Nubian rock stelae explicate the king's victory in the border region, possibly addressing other Egyptians in the area (via iconography, possibly also local inhabitants; Klug 2002, 496–497; also, the Tombos stela of Thutmose I, *Urk.* IV 82.3–86). The Sphinx stela of Amenhotep II (*Urk.* IV 1280.14, 14) relates the achievements of the sporting king, some of which were connected with the desert sports grounds nearby, and captures a staging of the king's bravado. Redford went as far as to consider it as "calculated insouciance for popular consumption…these were broadcast far and wide on stelae, the wording on which suggest the currency of a parallel oral tradition cultivated by the administration" (Redford 1995, 167). The sporting king's feats—or their representations—were possibly observed also by foreign audience who were to be in awe and respectful of the king's might (Manuelian 1987, 191–213; Decker 2011).

On occasion, the king's success was related in several different locations. Thutmoside and Ramesside stelae and temple texts tend to repeat important happenings, for instance, victories, booty, and Nubian and Syrian captured regions found in texts and scenes of Ramesses II in Theban, Abydene, as well as Nubian temples. Some of these scenes were located on the outside of temple walls and pylons to manifest king's power to any earthly audience that might have been close by, the visual message clear to all, literate and illiterate alike.

Areas of access to different groups of recipients are particularly delicate to assess, as the actual availability of texts to their respective audiences might have been limited. For instance, short-term and long-term physical and visual accessibility of royal stelae is a problematic issue (Klug 2002), even when we discount the difficulty of hieroglyphs not being the script of everyday use and hence of limited audience by definition (Parkinson 1999, 46–55). Some temple texts were clearly not read by the human audience on a regular basis, being physically inaccessible, either permanently (locations outside of usual visual range on temple walls) or temporarily (location in areas where only select personnel or celebrants were allowed). Temples, both divine and royal, became in any case accessible, however, to nonroyal statues of dignitaries (Kjølby 2009). One example among many is Amenmose, a scribe involved in the royal memorial cult of Ahmose Nefertari, who located his statue in Men-isut, the memorial temple of the queen, becoming her temple's eternal audience (Frood 2007, 183–188).

The king communicated by proxy of texts as well as in person with his earthly audience. Personal communication included court and select festivities of religious character and state ceremonies, and here, too, display and exclusivity were part of the message. The court was exclusive, not only by physical barriers but also by demands placed on the courtier in terms of character and ability (Baines 2013, 235–236). The king became a focal point of his earthly audience—the access of nonroyals to the king is thematized mainly in their texts and visual evidence. Courtiers were allowed access to the king's person and participation in court ceremony, and consequently, they manifested evidence of their court life in their tomb decoration program. In the Amarna period, the communication aspect was strengthened by the king imparting a new doctrine, and his attendants were judged with new accent on their ability to be an excellent and receptive audience of their king—not in the art of governance, but in religious doctrine. One of his foremost courtiers, Ay, sums up, "How prosperous is he that carefully listens to thy teaching of life," echoing traditional instructions with a new emphasis on the royal role (Redford 1995, 178, with references; Tobin 1986).

In turn, the dignitaries in nonroyal monumental discourse acknowledge the greatness of the king (plus, they desire to be in his presence or to demonstrate their ability in his presence). The king teaches the art of governance (including details of court proceedings, e.g., installation of vizier: van den Boorn 1988, 366), vizieral audience, as well as an ethical discourse (duties of the vizier: van den Boorn 1988), and his followers commemorate this act (Moreno García 2013). Rekhmire, vizier to Thutmose III, noted that his king "knew everything and was indeed (like) Thoth" (*Urk.* IV 1074.8–9).

The king promoted his ability in front of his court because royal legitimation had to be constantly renegotiated (Baines 1995; Redford 1995). In this perspective, Akhenaten's reform was a radical—and ultimately failed—renegotiation (compare Redford 1995, Janák forthcoming), which nonetheless had a powerful impact on communication patterns of the Egyptian elite of his time. Given the character of Egyptian administration, which was a "complex adaptive system" rather than a rigid departmentalized bureaucracy (see Shirley 2013), a constant emphasis on communication that operated on a day-to-day basis, as well as in monumental discourse, is appropriate for the structure.

Addressing Posterity: Memory on Earth

Egyptian nonroyal autobiographies also thematized one's abilities, achievements, and life well-lived and relied on an explicitly named audience to convey their message. Communicating with royal and divine spheres was significant, but for nonroyal Egyptians, the earthly audience was apparently essential and a key participant in their art of historical memory (Baines 2011). Egyptian autobiographies, but also more concise epithets (compare Frood 2007, 1–2), articulated the issues of audience and remembrance well and became a part of a larger historical communication.

Calls to the living enumerated different categories of expected audiences(s), as in this Eleventh Dynasty example: "O, priests (*ḥmw-nṯr*) and priestesses (*ḥmw.t-nṯr*), male and female singers, male and female musicians, the entire entourage of Abydos in the Thinite nome, it is my good name that you should remember" (Landgráfová 2012, 45; stela of Meru, Turin 1447).

The Thutmoside vizier Rekhmire specified, for instance, what these audiences should do: "Every skilled scribe excellent in his writings, who shall read in writings and interpret with his mind, keen of tongue, open of mind, who penetrates words, and whom an overseer has taught to do as should be done, deliberate and patient, daring in questioning, he is the knowledgeable one, who hears what the ancestors of former times have said" (translation after Gardiner 1925, 75).

Texts of this type, commenting on audience, appear in a variety of settings, such as tombs, stelae, and, mostly from the New Kingdom onward, statues. Audiences approached in these different locations were regulated by an interplay of seclusion and display in different contexts. The tomb and its chapel were accessible for funerary cult, and stelae, for example at Abydos, were accessible to participants in local Osirian feasts. Temple statues (Kjølby 2009) had a more tiered or nuanced audience, as select temple areas were probably accessible during important ceremonies or were periodically visited at least by temple personnel (compare Baines 2006). New Kingdom and later statues accordingly usually address a divine audience, plus—in calls to the living—often the temple staff.

Contents of biographies and further personal representations changed with the period. For instance, the Eighteenth Dynasty royal centrality in tomb decorations and biographical statements of the New Kingdom culminated in the Amarna Period (Murnane 1995, 107–204), while the preceding emphasis on the dignitary communicating his abilities and results of his work to his king and—in the tomb or on statue—to an earthly audience was replaced by a centrality of king as mediator between people and Aton. The Ramesside biography turned to other levels of communication, such as a dignitary's personal achievements, and added an emphasis on personal piety (Frood 2007).

PARTICIPATING AUDIENCE: SECOND AND THIRD HANDS ON THE MONUMENT

In the previous sections, we met textual and iconic narratives aimed at and assuming and desiring reaction of different audiences. This section is interested in responding audiences. Some of the audience interactions participated in a communicative process set up by the monuments' makers. Audience members may have reacted to the cultural and social message in a systemic way, while other responses were more differentiated.

Participating audiences left a mark of a second or third hand (Fischer 1974) on the monument. They included:

- Builders, artists, and their supervisors who decorated an edifice and became its first audience and engaged in correcting or modifying decoration if a mistake or inaccuracy was identified (Fischer 1974, 5–6). Possible inspecting marks that are open to various interpretations, were identified, for example, in the tomb of Senenmut (Dorman 1991, 146–147).

- People who were tasked with altering a monument's decoration when it was reused or usurped (see chapter by Brand).
- Inhabitants in dwellings and people in general in the urban space—one of the least studied groups, as settlements are attested selectively. However, cities were part of a larger landscape that was itself an arena to sacred and other cultural performances (Baines 2015a; Baines et al. 2015).
- Cult personnel in divine and funerary cult establishments. They entered in their own dialogue with existing decoration and on multiple levels. For instance, First Intermediate Period practitioners of the cult of Kagemni left graffiti in his tomb (Hamilton 2016). Cult practitioners might have left secondary texts containing prayers or hymns appropriate for the cultic setting that have the format of large graffiti (Kessler 1998, 1999; Gardiner 1928). Numerous graffiti affecting the temple walls were produced by local temple personnel and possibly by some distinguished visitors (Frood 2013; Salvador 2016).
- Artists and artisans as copyists visited monuments as a resource, as shown by copyists' grids attesting to direct copying, as well as by less direct, but still recognizable inspiration (Manuelian 1994; Laboury 2013).
- Visitors with as yet unknown or undefined purpose, but respecting the special character of the edifice. Makers of the visitors' graffiti in tombs and royal funerary precincts might be included in this category (Doncker 2012).
- Iconoclasts, operating still within Egyptian culture, such as those bent on individual *damnatio memoriae* or in a service of a systematic destructive campaign, such as that of Akhenaten against Amun and several other gods or later against Akhenaten.
- Restorers, such as in the post-Amarna Ramesside restoration campaign. Restorers might have had a more complex agenda than simply returning back what was damaged: Horemheb or Seti I combined restoration efforts with their own propaganda (Brand 1999, 2000). Of these groups, we further single out visitors and staff.

Graffiti

Attestations of an actual (if cast in a prescribed form) observation expressed by a member of the ancient Egyptian audience are found in different types of graffiti. The term "graffiti" sums up written and figural traces of a range of sociocultural practices, that, however, shared one element—a presence of audience in a significant space. Graffiti have been recently defined very aptly as secondary epigraphy (Ragazzoli 2017), that is, they are added mostly in an anthropogenic context to an already decorated or otherwise modified surface. As a category of historical evidence, secondary epigraphy is rather varied in terms of:

Script: Graffiti may be hieroglyphic, hieratic, figural, carved with much attention, written carefully, or scribbled in haste. They may have an almost formal character or be a brief, sketchy reaction.

Contents: From reaction to the visited edifice (comments in text or figural graffiti inspired by primary decoration) to devotional texts.

Writers: Named or, less often, anonymous and often titled staff of a temple, literati visiting funerary monuments, artists coming to copy scenes, etc.

TEMPLE VISITORS AND STAFF

In Egyptian temples, the audience carved, almost literally, its own epigraphic niche. From the New Kingdom to the Greco-Roman period, large divine temple precincts were marked by text and figural graffiti. These graffiti changed throughout the period, indeed, in some instances betraying a new understanding of temple spaces (Cruz-Uribe 2008, 199–225; Dijkstra 2012).

Hieratic New Kingdom graffiti in memorial temples and their neighborhood in Western Thebes betray different audiences with related, but not identical agendas. Many visitors to cave MMA 504 were from the Hatshepsut temple personnel in the Eighteenth Dynasty and applied both classical *Besucherinschrift* ("There came a scribe to see…") formulae and other formulae in the grotto that became a shop window of literate self-presentation and aspects of personal piety (Ragazzoli 2017). Such expressions were not found in the temple of Hatshepsut itself, which was probably out of bounds for such texts, unlike older funerary edifices and private funerary chapels, which were acceptable showgrounds.

In the Ramesside period, the Deir el-Bahri temples became a place for demonstrations of personal piety, often concentrating on Amun and Hathor, deities intensely connected with the West Theban sacred landscape. The temple of *Djeser-akhet* (Thutmose III) hosted a large audience in the Ramesside period—mostly literate visitors from Thebes, who came with votive interest and also on occasion of festivities. They often claimed divine help and protection by the phrase "Do good, do good, Amun (Hathor, Osiris)." The recognized value of the visited sacred area was implicit, and the edifice itself was seldom thematized.

Late New Kingdom and Third Intermediate Period temple graffiti were produced in large memorial and divine temple precincts, often on court walls or outer walls of the precinct or in service areas of large and fully operational temples. They have different nuances than West Theban graffiti and include a wide range of figural graffiti and hieroglyphic and hieratic texts, while each group had a different emphasis.

Some images appear in outer temple zones or directly on outer walls where access by a wider public is assumed—it would attract broader audiences to divine images, widening access to the sacred (Brand 2004). Some temple graffiti were carved and close to formal art. In Thebes (Frood 2013; Salvador 2016) and Abydos (Navratilova, forthcoming), temple graffiti represent deities worshipped in the temple precincts carved in relief with much care. Their writers, or rather, those who commissioned their making, were often connected to the temple as staff, on occasion—especially in Thebes—as dignitaries of considerable importance (Frood 2013). Their act was no doubt inspired by personal piety, but it also encroached on the temple sacred spaces—audience and participants of select rituals were appropriating temple space.

In both cases, the audience attending the temple, either from outside or inside, was participant in a change and manipulation of the edifice's message—and focused on its own benefit and commemoration of one's name. References to one's *ka* or name abound in the Third Intermediate Period graffiti and some of later Demotic graffiti. For instance, personnel of the temple of Khonsu composed brief texts "for the *ka* of the excellent one, AB, son of XY" (e.g., Jacquet-Gordon 2003, 14), on occasion provided with a protective formula. Later Demotic texts focused intensely on the survival of the writer's name (Thissen 1989).

Visitors' Graffiti and Copyists

Classical visitors' graffiti appeared mainly in the Eighteenth Dynasty and are located in private as well as royal funerary establishments. In older edifices, perhaps without a presence of consistent funerary cult, but still evidently recognized as sacred spaces, the graffiti affected any part of the edifice, although with a preference for accessible and highly visible locations. This is seen, for example, in the tomb of Senet (TT 60) (Ragazzoli 2013; Davies 1920; on Gardiner's unpublished records, Navratilova 2010/11) or in pyramid precincts in Dahshur and Saqqara (Navratilova 2013, 2015). Eighteenth Dynasty graffiti often contain references to the funerary edifice's appearance and ownership.

A model graffito would be "Coming of the scribe XY to see the temple of the Majesty of the Dual King NN and found it beautiful, more than any other temple." On occasion, identification of the edifice as pyramid appears in the Memphite area. In Thebes or Asyut, the owner is on occasion referred to as well. In Beni Hasan, the attribution was mistaken—confused with nearby temple institutions (Hassan 2016).

Although texts are relatively uniform and often apply an almost codified sequence of phrases, the motives behind them might have been more complex, depending on site and period. In the case of Memphite-area royal pyramid complexes, a motivation to analyze older royal edifices as art models is not to be excluded (see chapter by Bács). What is quite intriguing in this respect is the absence of larger numbers of Kushite- or Saite-era graffiti because the copying agenda was widespread at that time (Hussein 2011: texts perhaps copied from *Vorlage*-papyri, not copied from walls). Unequivocal copyists' traces on the original often consist of a grid drawn across a finished work of art.

Concluding Remarks

A complete history of those who interacted with Egyptian monuments (plus why and how they did so) would refer to use and reuse of culturally meaningful spaces, history of Egyptian religion, legitimation of power, cultural memory, and indeed aesthetic consumption (Baines 2015b) as well as to models of scholarship or to consuming reinterpreted history as entertainment. If personified by model figures, the audiences' crowd would look very much like an illustrated history: builders who had just finished a tomb chapel, priesthood performing a daily ritual, a king attending temple festival ceremonies, onlookers on a feast day, burial processions, curious visitors, callers seeking miraculous help in sacred places, iconoclasts motivated by order or by creed, restorers, stonemasons looking for recycled stone, locals believing in the magical power of an abandoned temple, travelers studious or fashionable, tourist guides, Egyptologists, epigraphers and so forth. The epigraphers also came with their own preconceptions and had to develop specific skills to be able to proceed with their task of recording und ultimately mediating the ancient records to new generations of audiences.

Bibliography

Arnold, D. 1962. *Wandrelief und Raumfunktion in ägyptischen Tempeln des Neuen Reiches.* MÄS 2. Berlin.

Assmann, J. 1999. "Cultural and Literary Texts." In *Definitely: Egyptian Literature: Proceedings of the Symposon "Ancient Egyptian Literature: History and Forms," Los Angeles, March 24–26, 1995,* edited by G. Moers, 1–15. LingAeg-StudMon 2. Göttingen.

Baines, J. 1995. "Kingship, Definition of Culture, and Legitimation." In *Ancient Egyptian Kingship,* edited by D. O'Connor and D. P. Silverman, 3–47. PdÄ 9. Leiden.

Baines, J. 2006. "Public Ceremonial Performance in Ancient Egypt: Exclusion and Integration." In *Archaeology of Performance: Theaters of Power, Community, and Politics,* edited by T. Inomata and L. S. Coben, 261–302. Lanham.

Baines, J. 2011. "Ancient Egypt." In *The Oxford History of Historical Writing, Volume 1: Beginnings to AD 600,* edited by A. Feldherr and G. Hardy, 53–75. Oxford.

Baines, J. 2013. *High Culture and Experience in Ancient Egypt.* Sheffield.

Baines, J. 2015a. "Ancient Egyptian Cities: Monumentality and Performance." In *The Cambridge World History III: Early Cities in Comparative Perspective, 4000 BCE–1200 CE,* edited by N. Yoffee, 27–47. Cambridge.

Baines, J. 2015b. "What Is Art?" In *A Companion to Ancient Egyptian Art,* edited by M. K. Hartwig, 1–21. Chichester.

Baines, J., M. T. Stark, T. G. Garrison, and S. Houston. 2015. "Cities as Performance Arenas." In *The Cambridge World History III: Early Cities in Comparative Perspective, 4000 BCE–1200 CE,* edited by N. Yoffee, 94–109. Cambridge.

Bickel, S. 2013. "Men in the Temple: World-order, Prestige, and Piety." In *Decorum and Experience: Essays in Ancient Culture for John Baines,* edited by E. Frood and A. McDonald, 205–213. Oxford.

Brand, P. J. 1999. "Secondary Restorations in the Post-Amarna Period." *JARCE* 36:113–134.

Brand, P. J. 2000. *The Monuments of Seti I: Epigraphic, Historical and Art Historical Analysis.* PdÄ 16. Leiden.

Brand, P. J. 2004. "A Grafitto of Amen-Re in Luxor Temple Restored by the High Priest Menkheperre." In *Egypt, Israel, and the Ancient Mediterranean World: Studies in Honor of Donald B. Redford,* edited by G. N. Knoppers and A. Hirsch, 257–266. Leiden.

Burke, P. 1992. *The Fabrication of Louis XIV.* New Haven.

Cruz-Uribe, E. 2008. *Hibis Temple Project, Volume 3: The Graffiti from the Temple Precinct.* San Antonio.

Boorn, G. P. F. van den 1988. *The Duties of the* Vizier: *Civil Administration in the Early New Kingdom.* London.

Davies, N. de G. 1920. *The Tomb of Antefoker, Vizier of Sesostris I, and of his Wife, Senet (no. 60).* TTS 2. London.

Decker, W. 2011. "Zuschauer beim altägyptischen Sport." In *Scribe of Justice: Egyptological Studies in Honour of Shafik Allam,* edited by Z. A. Hawass, K. A. Daoud, and R. B. Hussein, 119–126. CASAE 42. Cairo.

Delia, R. D. 1999. "Palimpsests, Copyists, Atenists and Others at the First Cataract." *JARCE* 36:103–112.

Dijkstra, J. H. F. 2012. *Syene I: The Figural and Textual Graffiti from the Temple of Isis at Aswan.* BBf 18. Darmstadt.

Doncker, A. Den. 2012. "Theban Tomb Graffiti during the New Kingdom. Research on the Reception of Ancient Egyptian Images by Ancient Egyptians." In *Art and Society: Ancient and Modern Contexts of Egyptian Art,* edited by K. A. Kóthay, 23–34. Budapest.

Dorman, P. F. 1991. *The Tombs of Senenmut: The Architecture and Decoration of Tombs 71 and 353.* PMMA 24. New York.

Eaton-Krauss, M. 2003. "Restorations and Erasures in the Post-Amarna Period." In *Egyptology at the Dawn of the Twenty-first Century: Proceedings of the Eighth International Congress of Egyptologists, Cairo, 2000/2,* edited by Z. Hawass and L. Pinch Brock, 194–202. Cairo.

Eyre, C. 2013. "The Practice of Literature: The Relationship between Content, Form, Audience, and Performance." In *Ancient Egyptian Literature: Theory and Practice,* edited by R. Enmarch and V. M. Lepper, 101–142. Oxford.

Fischer, H. G. 1974. "The Mark of a Second Hand on Ancient Egyptian Antiquities." *MMJ* 9:5–34.

Fisher, K. D. 2009. "Placing Social Interaction: An Integrative Approach to Analysing Past Built Environments." *JAA* 28:439–457.

Fitzenreiter, M. 2007. "Europäische Konstruktionen Altägyptens: der Fall Ägyptologie." In *Exotisch, weisheitlich und uralt: Europäische Konstruktionen Altägyptens,* edited by T. Glück and L. Morenz, 323–347. Münster.

Frood, E. 2007. *Biographical Texts from Ramessid Egypt.* WAW 26. Leiden.

Frood, E. 2013. "Egyptian Temple Graffiti and the Gods: Appropriation and Ritualization in Karnak and Luxor." In *Heaven on Earth: Temples, Ritual, and Cosmic Symbolism in the Ancient World,* edited by D. Ragavan, 285–318. Chicago.

Gabolde, M. 1998. *D'Akhenaton à Toutânkhamon.* CIAHA 3. Lyon.

Gardiner, A. H. 1925. "The Autobiography of Rekhmerē." *ZÄS* 60:62–76.

Gardiner, A. H. 1928. "The Graffito from the Tomb of Pere." *JEA* 14:10–11.

Gutmann, T. 2016. "Zur optischen (Außen-)Wirkung altägyptischer Monumentalbauten." In *Gebauter Raum: Architektur—Landschaft—Mensch: Beiträge des fünften Münchner Arbeitskreises Junge Aegyptologie (MAJA 5), 12.12. bis 14.12.2014,* edited by S. Beck, B. Backes, I-T. Liao, H. Simon, and A. Verbovsek, 111–125. Wiesbaden.

Hagen, F. 2012. *An Ancient Egyptian Literary Text in Context: The Instruction of Ptahhotep.* OLA 218. Leuven.

Hamilton, J. C. F. 2016. "'That His Perfect Name May Be Remembered': Added Inscriptions in the Tomb of Vizier Kagemni at Saqqara." In *Current Research in Egyptology 2015: Proceedings of the Sixteenth Annual Symposium; University of Oxford, United Kingdom, 15–18, April 2015,* edited by C. Alvarez, A. Belekdanian, A.-K. Gill, and S. Klein, 50–61. Oxford.

Hartwig, M. K., ed. 2015. *A Companion to Ancient Egyptian Art*. Chichester.

Hassan, K. 2016. "The Visitors' Graffiti in Two Tombs of *Beni Hassan* (Ameny and Khnumhotep II)." *JARCE* 52:33–53.

Hussein, R. B. 2011. "Notes on the Saite Copies of Pyramid Texts Spells in the Memphite and Heliopolitan Shaft-Tombs." In *Scribe of Justice: Egyptological Studies in Honour of Shafik Allam*, edited by Z. A. Hawass, K. A. Daoud, and R. B. Hussein, 217–234. CASAE 42. Cairo.

Jacquet-Gordon, H. 2003. *The Temple of Khonsu, Volume 3: The Graffiti on the Khonsu Temple Roof at Karnak. A Manifestation of Personal Piety*. OIP 123. Chicago.

Janák, J. Forthcoming. "Akhenaten: Monotheism or Monopoly?" In *Collapse and Regeneration in Complex Societies*, edited by M. Bárta and M. Kovář. Prague.

Kayser, H. 1936. *Die Tempelstatuen ägyptischer Privatleute im Mittleren und im Neuen Reich*. Heidelberg.

Kessler, D. 1998. "Dissidentenliteratur oder kultischer Hintergrund? Teil 1: Überlegungen zum Tura-Hymnus und zum Hymnus in TT 139." *SAK* 25:161–188.

Kessler, D. 1999. "Dissidentenliteratur oder kultischer Hintergrund? (Teil 2)." *SAK* 27:173–221.

Kjølby, A. 2009. "Material Agency, Attribution and Experience of Agency in Ancient Egypt: The Case of New Kingdom Private Temple Statues." In *"Being in Ancient Egypt": Thoughts on Agency, Materiality and Cognition. Proceedings of the Seminar Held in Copenhagen, September 29–30, 2006*, edited by R. Nyord and A. Kjølby, 31–46. Oxford.

Klug, A. 2002. *Königliche Stelen in der Zeit von Ahmose bis Amenophis III*. MonAeg 8. Brussels.

Kottak, C. 2006. *Mirror for Humanity*. New York.

Laboury, D. 2013. "Citations et usages de l'art du Moyen Empire à l'époque thoutmoside." In *Vergangenheit und Zukunft—Studien zum historischen Bewußtsein in der Thutmosidenzeit*, edited by S. Bickel, 11–28. AH 22. Basel.

Landgráfová, R. 2012. *It Is My Good Name That You Should Remember: Egyptian Biographical Texts on Middle Kingdom Stelae*. Prague.

Lawrence, D. L., and S. M. Low. 1990. "The Built Environment and Spatial Form." *ARA* 19:453–505.

Manuelian, P. Der. 1987. *Studies in the Reign of Amenophis II*. HÄB 26. Hildesheim.

Manuelian, P. Der. 1994. *Living in the Past. Studies in Archaism of the Egyptian Twenty-Sixth Dynasty*. London.

Moreno García, J. C., ed. 2013. *Ancient Egyptian Administration*. HdO 104. Leiden.

Murnane, W. J. 1995. *Texts from the Amarna Period in Egypt*. Edited by E. S. Meltzer. WA 5. Atlanta.

Navratilova, H. 2010–2011. "Gardiner and Graffiti." *EDAL* 2:171–186.

Navratilova, H. 2013. "New Kingdom Graffiti in Dahshur, Pyramid Complex of Senwosret III: Preliminary Report. Graffiti Uncovered in Seasons 1992–2010." *JARCE* 49:113–141.

Navratilova, H. 2015. *Visitors' Graffiti of Dynasties 18 and 19 in Abusir and Northern Saqqara: With a Survey of the Graffiti at Giza, Southern Saqqara, Dahshur and Maidum*. 2nd, rev. ed. Wallasey.

Navratilova, H. Forthcoming. "Graffiti in the Temple of Ramesses II at Abydos." In *The Temple of Ramesses II in Abydos*, vol. 2, edited by S. Iskander and O. Goelet. Atlanta.

Parkinson, R. B. 1999. *Cracking Codes: The Rosetta Stone and Decipherment*. London.

Parkinson, R. B. 2009. *Reading Ancient Egyptian Poetry: Among Other Histories*. Chichester.

Polz, D. 1987. "Excavation and Recording of a Theban Tomb. Some Remarks on Recording Methods." In *Problems and Priorities in Egyptian Archaeology*, edited by J. Assmann, G. Burkard, and V. Davies, 119–140. London.

Popko, L. 2006. *Untersuchungen zur Geschichtsschreibung der Ahmosiden- und Thutmosidenzeit: "…damit man von seinen Taten noch in Millionen von Jahren sprechen wird."* WSA 2. Würzburg.

Ragazzoli, C. 2013. "The Social Creation of a Scribal Place: The Visitors' Inscriptions in the Tomb Attributed to Antefiqer (TT 60) (with newly recorded graffiti)." *SAK* 42:269–323.

Ragazzoli, C. 2017. *La grotte des scribes à Deir el-Bahari. La tombe MMA 504 et ses graffiti.* Cairo.

Redford, D. B. 1995. "The Concept of Kingship during the Eighteenth Dynasty." In *Ancient Egyptian Kingship*, edited by D. O'Connor and D. P. Silverman, 157–184. PdÄ 9. Leiden.

Salvador, C. 2016. "Graffiti and Sacred Space: New Kingdom Expressions of Individuality in the Court of the Seventh Pylon at Karnak." In *10. Ägyptologische Tempeltagung: ägyptische Tempel zwischen Normierung und Individualität. München, 29.–31. August 2014*, edited by M. Ullmann, 111–128. Wiesbaden.

Seidlmayer, S. J. 2006. "Frohe – und andere – Botschaften: Kult und Kommunikation im alten Ägypten." In *Mediengesellschaft Antike? Information und Kommunikation vom Alten Ägypten bis Byzanz; altertumswissenschaftliche Vortragsreihe an der Berlin-Brandenburgischen Akademie der Wissenschaften*, edited by U. Peter and S. J. Seidlmayer, 93–111. Berlin.

Shirley, J. J. 2013. "Crisis and Restructuring of the State: From the Second Intermediate Period to the Advent of the Ramesses." In *Ancient Egyptian Administration*, edited by J. C. Moreno García, 521–606. HdO 104. Leiden.

Simon, H. 2013. *"Textaufgaben": Kulturwissenschaftliche Konzepte in Anwendung auf die Literatur der Ramessidenzeit.* SAK Bh 14. Hamburg.

Teeter, E. 1997. *The Presentation of Maat: Ritual and Legitimacy in Ancient Egypt.* SAOC 57. Chicago.

Tefnin, R. 1983. "Discours et iconicité dans l'art égyptien." *AHAA* 5:5–17.

Thissen, H.-J. 1989. *Die demotischen Graffiti von Medinet Habu: Zeugnisse zu Tempel und Kult im ptolemäischen Agypten.* DemStud 10. Sommerhausen.

Tobin V. A. 1986. "The Intellectual Organization of the Amarna Period." PhD diss., Hebrew University.

Wilkinson, R. H. 2016. "*Damnatio Memoriae* in the Valley of the Kings." In *The Oxford Handbook of the Valley of the Kings*, edited by R. H. Wilkinson and K. R. Weeks, 335–346. Oxford.

....

THE MATERIALS, TOOLS, AND WORK OF CARVING AND PAINTING

....

DENYS ALLEN STOCKS

INTRODUCTION

....

MONUMENTAL texts, often accompanied by figural depictions, were intended to serve as permanent records. As such, they were carved and painted on a variety of resistant, long-lasting materials, such as sedimentary, metamorphic, and igneous stones; plastered surfaces; wood; and metal. The two main sedimentary stones that were employed for the extensive carving of monumental texts and figural depictions in ancient Egypt were soft limestone (Mohs hardness 2.5) and sandstone (hardnesses variable from Mohs 2.5 for red sandstone up to Mohs 3.5). Fully and partially incised igneous structural components include the rose granite columns in the Nineteenth Dynasty Temple of Herishef at Heracleopolis. Additionally, reliefs were carved into the intractable igneous stone surfaces of stelae, shrines, obelisks, and specifically designed areas for inscribing texts on stone statuary. Texts and figural depictions were carved into wooden panels contained in tombs, and royal artifacts of gold and silver were inscribed with symbols.

STONE CARVING TOOLS

....

The manufacture of the tools needed to carve incised and raised figures into sedimentary stones began with the introduction of smelted and cast copper at the commencement of the Nagada II period (c. 3500–3200 BCE). As suggested by Flinders Petrie (1917, 1), working copper in this way enabled workers to imitate in metal the cutting edges of certain stone tools. Following this suggestion, the Predynastic flint end-scraper likely provided the original design shape for the copper chisel and for the conversion into copper of flint adze blades (Stocks 2003, 25). The widths of copper adze blades varied considerably, sometimes being markedly wider than chisels' tapers because an adze's edge was ground on one side of the blade only, usually on the outer side. The hafted, wide-bladed copper adze, when accurately swung so that the cutting edge makes a glancing blow against the stone, is useful for finishing soft limestone surfaces for the carving of hieroglyphs, a technique investigated by Ernest Mackay (1921, 163–164) in tomb chapels at Thebes. He also noticed that a driven chisel's line of travel would occasionally deviate from a straight line, a phenomenon known as chisel shake.

A driven chisel, however, has three distinct advantages. First, the worker is able to direct a chisel's cutting edge to an exact carving position before a blow is struck. Second, the worker can vary the force of a blow to be commensurate with the hardness of the stone and the required depth of penetration. Third, by governing a chisel's angle of attack from a nearly horizontal position through to the vertical, a worker enables the tool to remove in a controlled and delicate manner the stone still left in and around unfinished incised and raised reliefs.

Ancient Egyptian copper chisels developed into two basic shapes: the flat-tapered and the crosscut-tapered types. Both forms are still in use today. Workers created a flat-tapered chisel by hammering one end of a suitable copper casting into a wide or narrow double-tapered section, ending in an edge sharpened from both sides. Experimental (Stocks 2003, 56–62) copper, bronze, and iron chisels' tapers could easily be fashioned by beating the metal with hand-held, spherical stone hammers. Such tools were used in ancient times for beating metals into shape. When struck by a wooden mallet or by stone hammers, the wide, flat-tapered chisel quickly removes large areas of soft stone in preparation for further work by slimmer chisels and by adze blades swung with slanting blows against the chisel-prepared surfaces.

EXPERIMENTAL TOOLMAKING AND USE

In making a crosscut chisel, a copper casting already hammered into a double taper needs to be turned through a 90° angle and hammered into a second, narrower double taper. The crosscut chisel's shorter, sturdier taper concentrates a blow on a smaller cutting area. Wielded by an experienced ancient carver, the crosscut chisel's narrow blade allowed the controlled carving of intricate incised and raised reliefs into limestone, sandstone, plastered surfaces, and wood (Stocks 2003, 27–28).

Experimental casting and subsequent further manufacture (Stocks 2003, 56–57, Table 2.1) of ten replica, project-numbered small and large copper chisels and two numbered copper adzes contained varying small amounts of tin, lead, iron, and antimony. The shape of the experimental casts of chisels was formed by pouring molten copper into open sand molds. Some of the molds were created by impressing the required shapes and sizes into slightly damp sand with wooden patterns. Ancient sand molds, which could only be used once for a casting, are likely to have been shaped with small angular stone and wooden formers. Pottery molds later afforded the luxury of multiple uses for casting chisels and other simple tool shapes.

G. R. Gilmore's analyses (1986, 447–487) of edged copper artifacts in the Manchester Museum, including the ancient copper chisels that Petrie excavated at Kahun (1890, 29), have shown that the proportions of copper, tin, and iron, in addition to arsenic and antimony, differed significantly from tool to tool. The hammering experiments, completed by Stocks, including a 99.9% pure copper chisel, which was cast and beaten for comparison purposes, demonstrated that the additions of these elements, whether accidentally or deliberately added, significantly increased the hardness of copper chisels.

Eleven experimental bronze chisels were cast (Stocks 2003, 57, Table 2.1). In eight of them, the amount of tin alloy was raised in 2% increments, beginning with 1% tin content and continuing up to 15%, as the amounts of copper were correspondingly decreased. Three other bronze chisels contained 8%, 10%, and 12% tin respectively. This strategy allowed a group of seven bronze chisels to increase by a single percent tin content from 7% to 13% inclusive, facilitating a detailed comparison of increasing hammered hardness and the consequential ability to cut a variety of progressively harder stone types.

The hardness of ancient Egyptian copper and bronze tools depended on the cold hammering of these nonferrous castings. Experimental hammering (Stocks 2003, 43) of a bronze casting, raised to a bright red heat, demonstrated that within several seconds the metal fractured into several pieces. Red-hot copper and bronze become brittle at elevated temperatures because of changes to their crystal structures (Rickard 1932, 116). However, after a period of cold hammering, copper and bronze tools need to be annealed or softened by heating them to a dull red color and allowing the metal gradually to cool. Cold hammering can then be continued without cracking the metal. Quenching in water, a process normally employed rapidly to cool a red-hot ferrous chisel, is not desirable because of poor annealing of the crystal structure of copper and bronze.

The hardness of the hammered taper of an experimental copper chisel was then associated with the results of other stonecutting tests. Using an engineering Vickers Pyramid Hardness testing machine, a metal's hardness is expressed as a Vickers Pyramid Number (VPN). Hardness is measured by dividing a known load, which is applied to an inverted pyramid-shaped diamond indenter placed on a specimen's surface, by the area of the resulting indentation.

Evaluation of the hardness tests (Stocks 1988, I, 64–82, II, Appendix B) for copper chisels revealed that the hardest chisel could be cold hammered to a mean hardness of VPN 140, which is slightly harder than modern mild steel (VPN 131). A bronze chisel containing 8% tin could be cold hammered to hardness VPN 232, which exceeds that of cold-rolled mild steel (VPN 192). Bronze chisels containing 10% tin achieved hardness VPN 247, a value slightly harder than modern unworked chisel steel (VPN 235). By comparison, a hammered steel chisel's hardness is VPN 800.

The cutting tests on a variety of stones suggest that a bronze chisel made from 90% copper and 10% tin makes a superior cutting tool with regard to toughness and hardness. However, ancient bronze tools containing more than 10% tin content were in use. For example, two New Kingdom bronze chisels have been analyzed by J. Sebelien (1924, 8) and by M. A. Colson (1903, 190–192) and found to contain a tin content of 12% and 13.3% respectively. The experimental chisel of 12% tin content made a fine tool for accurately carving all sedimentary stones and all types of wood.

Experimental, eliminatory stonecutting tests (Stocks 1988, I, 83–99; 2003, 63–66) performed on soft limestone and sandstone, together with travertine (Mohs hardness 3–4), hard limestone (Mohs hardness 4-5), rose granite (Mohs hardness 7), quartzite (Mohs hardness 6–7), and diorite (Mohs hardness 7) by copper, bronze, and iron chisels determined their respective cutting abilities. All of the chisels cut soft limestone and red sandstone with ease, although the softer copper chisels suffered slight wear over extended periods of use. The cutting tests on the hard limestone and travertine demonstrated that the copper chisels suffered immediate blunting and jagged dents to their edges. Thus, copper chisels may be discounted as cutting tools for these stones. Only the bronze chisels containing 10% tin and over cut travertine well, but these required sharpening at intervals not consistent with the efficient use of the tools.

A study (Stocks 2003, 81) of carved hieroglyphs in ancient travertine artifacts indicates that they feature particular chipped and scraped tool marks. Travertine is sometimes referred to as calcite (calcium carbonate) or alabaster, resulting in some confusion in the literature (Aston, Harrell, and Shaw 2000, 59). Experiments with flint chisels, punches, and scrapers produced marks similar to those observed on these artifacts. The iron, flat-tapered chisel could cut travertine, hard limestone (Mohs hardness 4–5), but suffered expected severe damage on the rose granite, quartzite, and diorite (Stocks 2003, 64).

Experimental Carving and Incising of Sedimentary Rock, Wood, Plaster, and Metal

To test the carving of sedimentary stone, a raised, composite relief of the *was*-scepter and the *ankh* was marked out in red lines on a prepared flat surface of soft limestone (Figure I.8.1). Soft limestone is similar in hardness to gypsum plaster applied to rough limestone walls and allowed to dry. The hieroglyphs, which measure 8 cm in height, were carved with the experimental copper chisels. These sharp-edged chisels and sharp flint blades, both used as scrapers, gave finished, acute corners to the unfinished rounded elements of the carved signs. These experimental cutting tests suggest that the combined use of metal and flint tools would have been common in ancient times. Coarse and smoother sandstone grinders completed the two symbols. A total of two hours was needed for the carving of these raised reliefs.

Ancient sawyers discovered that serrated copper saws could efficiently cut sedimentary limestone (Arnold 1991, 266, fig. 6.23). Petrie (1917, 45) concluded that ancient workmen

FIGURE I.8.1. Two experimental raised reliefs carved in soft limestone and being adjusted with a copper chisel. Photograph: Jeffrey Stocks. Copyright: Denys Allen Stocks.

shaped hieroglyphs by drilling the corners of irregularly shaped hieroglyphs and sawing other signs, but he did not specify whether his remarks referred to incised or raised reliefs. However, some ancient raised hieroglyphs in soft limestone could have been sawn along straight edges of marked-out, elevated symbols, thereby ensuring that the background stone could safely be removed up to the saw cut and no further. This practice would protect the hieroglyph from damage, which was a far more critical concern when carving raised hieroglyphs as opposed to incised ones. It is unlikely that this technique was applied to interior straight edges within raised or incised hieroglyphs cut out of any stone type.

Some parts of the raised experimental *ankh* were completed employing a thinly hammered replica toothed copper saw. In later experiments, carried out at Aswan in 2005, a raised hieroglyph was cut on a red sandstone block with copper and bronze replica chisels and a small, thinly beaten replica toothed copper saw. The chisels and saw proved to be efficient for carving red sandstone.

Test drilling the sandstone with a small-diameter tubular drill and using sand as the abrasive cut a circular groove. This method, using different diameter drill-tubes, could have been used accurately to incise circular hieroglyphs in both sedimentary and igneous stones. The inner stone would then have been chipped out from the center downwards to the circular groove, and the resulting curved surface would have been smoothed and polished. Sand abrasive can also be used with copper, bronze and iron flat-edged saws to cut *accessible* edges of raised hieroglyphs to shape in all hard stones.

The experimental incised and raised hieroglyphs in sedimentary stone, wood, and gypsum plaster revealed that ancient incised hieroglyphs probably took considerably less time and effort to carve than raised hieroglyphs cut into the same types of materials. Nonetheless, the viewer, whether literate or not, of deeply incised, massive texts and figures on temple walls illuminated by the sun and combined with the consequentially dark shadows must have been overwhelmingly impressed by the magisterial authority of the texts and scenes.

Cutting tests indicate that all copper and bronze chisels, even those possessing a hardness equivalent to modern unworked chisel steel, are only truly effective for making incised and raised reliefs in sedimentary limestone and sandstone, gypsum plaster, and wood. Their lack of efficiency in carving harder stones suggests that stone tools must have been necessary for carving images into harder stones. As noted earlier, however, iron chisels could cut hard limestone of Mohs hardness 4–5. Subsequent hard stone carving tests revealed that the fashioning of raised reliefs in igneous stones would have necessitated huge numbers of stone tools and protracted effort just to complete one sign. Consequently, raised textual relief carving in igneous stones, such as diorite and granite, never became standard in ancient Egypt.

Metals like gold and silver (both Mohs hardness 2.5), however, have been incised with images and were employed for making ancient coffins, vessels, and other artifacts. Test incisions were made into copper sheet (Mohs hardness 3), a metal slightly harder than gold and silver. These tests demonstrated that copper sheets could be cut by a sharp flint tool. Each incision in the copper was V-shaped in cross-section, with each edge raised above the surface. These experimental cuts closely resemble V-shaped incisions on the surfaces of four copper razors, which are incised with the name Idy and currently located in the British Museum (EA 6079–82). Further tests indicated that no tools made of other materials could make the precisely incised hieroglyphs seen in gold, silver, and copper artifacts.

To produce raised reliefs in gold sheet, workers gently hammered the sheet over a wooden template or a wooden structure previously carved with raised reliefs, such as the shrines in Tutankhamun's tomb chamber (Cairo Museum JE 60686) and the embalming incision plaque of Psusennes I (JE 85821). By pressing the sheet with suitably shaped wooden tools, annealed and malleable gold would faithfully reproduce the fine details carved into the wood underneath.

Experimental Carving of Igneous Stones

An ancient written source, which was confirmed by experimental techniques (Stocks 1988, II, 246–273; 2003, 63, 83–95), strongly indicates that no metal tools, even iron chisels, could effectively cut into igneous stones, including granite, porphyry, and diorite. Even Egyptian quartzite, a silicified sandstone and slightly softer than igneous stones, cannot be carved with iron tools. The classical author Theophrastus writes in *History of Stones* (LXXII, LXXV), "As that some of the stones before named are of so firm a texture, that they are not subject to injuries, and are not to be cut by instruments of iron, but only by other stones... and others yet, which may be cut with iron, but the instruments must be dull and blunt: which is much as if they were not cut by iron."

A number of unfinished ancient hard stone artifacts display chisel and pitting marks. In some ancient objects, the pitting can be seen to become progressively smaller as the work moves toward completion. A black granite sarcophagus in the Musée du Louvre

(D10 N346) is incised with hundreds of small hieroglyphs on its inside surfaces. The crudely cut hieroglyphs have been left unfinished. The effort to fully scrape and grind the incised hieroglyphs in granite would have been enormous due to the length of time required to complete each sign, as indicated by the experimental carving of this stone with flint tools. However, the incised hieroglyphs carved into the interior surfaces of a greywacke (Mohs hardness 4–5) sarcophagus (D9 N345) are chiseled and scraped to a flat finish. Greywacke is considerably less hard than granite, making it practical to finish these incised hieroglyphs by scraping. The reliefs incised into a hard stone stela in the Manchester Museum (8134) also display an unfinished, pitted surface.

Stonecutting experiments (Stocks 2003, 83–94) positively indicate that only flint chisels, punches, and scrapers could carve incised hieroglyphs into igneous stone surfaces. Assessments of the reconstructed flint tools' performance for cutting other stones, like travertine, greywacke, and quartzite, show that the pitting marks created by chisels and punches are similar to those seen on ancient artifacts. However, experiments also confirm that iron chisels can carve hard limestone and stones of hardness Mohs 5 and below (Stocks 2003, 64).

The lidded stone sarcophagus of Ankhnesneferibre (BM EA 32), stated to be made of metamorphic schist (Mohs hardness 4–5) (James 1979, 76, 166, Figs. 25, 59), dates to the Twenty-sixth Dynasty, a period when tools of iron became commonly used in Egypt (Arnold 1991, 257). The sarcophagus lid displays small incised hieroglyphs on and underneath it, as well as a beautifully raised, carved figure of the deceased on its top surface. While the pitted appearance indicates that only flint chisels, punches, and scrapers carved the small hieroglyphs, iron chisels, used in conjunction with flint tools, may have been used to execute the figure of Ankhnesneferibre.

Carving both incised and raised reliefs in quartzite is exemplified on Tutankhamun's sarcophagus, still lying in his tomb in the Valley of the Kings. This stone is critically lower in hardness than truly igneous stones. In 2009, a skilled stonemason in York Minster's workshop, United Kingdom, made an experimental carving of details of the sarcophagus. A raised replica head of a goddess was cut out of the corner of a quartzite block using reconstructed flint chisels, punches, and scrapers. The head was similar in size to the heads of goddesses carved into each corner of Tutankhamun's sarcophagus. This experimental carving demonstrated that raised and incised figural depictions and texts could be achieved with these tools, but not with iron chisels and punches. Measurements of the volume of chipped-out stone indicated a carving rate of approximately 8 cm^3/hour.

Six rose granite columns formerly installed in the Nineteenth Dynasty Temple of Herishef at Heracleopolis are now located in various museums around the world: Adelaide, Australia, Boston and Philadelphia, United States of America, and Bolton, London, and Manchester, United Kingdom. The columns' curved surfaces have been incised with finished signs, which are attributable to Ramesses II. A sign's interior shape gradually curves from a minimum depth at its central part to a maximum depth of 2.5 cm at the edges. The incised hieroglyphs carved into the columns in Boston, Philadelphia, Bolton, London, and Manchester were examined and measured by the author. They are all cut to this depth. However, the column at Adelaide was not examined for this study. Other, unfinished signs on adjacent panels are ascribed to Merneptah. These later hieroglyphs are coarsely hacked out of the stone. The edges are extremely uneven, and quartz crystals protrude from them. Chisel marks of different sizes and at random angles to the signs' edges may be seen. Although the columns' curved, uncut surfaces are smoothed and polished, close examination reveals small pits left in them by the carvers. These pits are a consequence of the carvers using flint punches during the shaping of the columns. Completely removing the pitting by grinding and polishing would have greatly increased the time to accomplish such a long and tedious operation.

On the Manchester Museum column (1780), the wickerwork basket-shaped hiero-glyph representing the biliteral *nb*, has sharper edges. The sign measures 14 cm in length, 5 cm in width, and 2.5 cm in depth, with an approximate volume of 120 cm³. A test *nb* hieroglyph was carved onto a block of rose granite that had been prepared flat with stone hammers and coarse and smooth sandstone rubbers. This test hieroglyph measured 9 cm in length and 2.2 cm at its widest point. The experimental chiseling action on the rose granite proved to be more effective if, after each blow, a chisel's edge is twisted to a new angle of attack. In this way, account may be taken of the different quartz crystals' positions within the stone. After roughing out the test sign, pointed punches reduced the chiseled surface to a flatter finish, and the characteristic pitted appearance of the ancient carved signs soon appeared at the bottom of the test hieroglyph.

Four cubic centimeters of rose granite was removed in 45 minutes work, equaling a rate of 5.3 cm³/hour. This rate is slightly less than the rate of carving quartzite. The rose granite and the quartzite experimental signs were completed with flint scrapers. These tools are effective on hard stones as well as on all softer stones. Various sandstone grinding blocks of coarse and fine grades smoothed the sign's surfaces (Figure I.8.2).

The experimental granite-working results indicate that skilled ancient artisans prob-ably achieved a higher rate of chiseling and punching hieroglyphs into rose granite than did the author using these tools. The main reason is that ancient carvers struck a large mass of granite with their tools, allowing a chisel or punch to penetrate further into the stone. The experimental carving indicates a possible ancient cutting rate of approxi-mately 15 cm³/hour or about two to three times the experimental rate (Stocks 2003, 91). This rate of cutting is an extrapolation using my personal chiseling capabilities, both in mechanical engineering and during the experimental cutting of rose granite. Further, the relatively small test granite block caused a flint chisel to rebound when struck, coun-teracting some of the shock of a blow. The chisel did not effectively penetrate into the granite, as would happen with a very large mass of stone. Additionally, the necessarily smaller flint tools, and consequently lighter stone hammer blows, inflicted less stone removal, increasing the time to make an experimental hieroglyph (Stocks 2003, 91). This estimate of the ancient carving rate suggests a time of eight hours to cut out the *nb* sign carved into the column.

Anciently polished rose granite, because of the abundance of quartz crystals within its matrix, has a feel of glass (Figure I.8.3). The test hieroglyph carved in rose granite was polished by first gently abrading the surface with fine sandstone rubbers and then

FIGURE 1.8.2. Finished experimental *nb* hieroglyph incised into rose granite using flint tools, grinders, and a polishing lap. Photograph: Jeffrey Stocks. Copyright: Denys Allen Stocks.

buffing it with a leather lap and liquid mud. The tests show that these materials could have been used in ancient times. The polishing materials may also have included an intermediate, finely ground sand/stone/copper powder, a waste product from the tubular drilling and sawing of stone with sand abrasive. The finished test surface closely matched the ancient polished column surfaces.

Flat Surface and Relief Painting

In ancient Egypt, painting in various forms remained in use continuously from the Predynastic to the Roman Period. Ancient artists used pigments to replicate the color found in nature and to convey symbolic meaning (Aufrère 2001; Taylor 2001; Pinch 2001; on pigment, see Aston, Harrell, and Shaw 2000). Painting techniques that were employed on carved stone relief, flat stone surfaces, and wooden and cartonnage mummiform coffins developed from earlier experiences painting plastered mud brick structures, as well as wood, leather, linen, ostraca, papyri, and pottery (Lucas 1962). Painting also added detail to carved hieroglyphs and accompanying figural art and decorated different types of objects. Examples of decorated artifacts manufactured from disparate materials are the incised rose granite obelisk of Hatshepsut at Karnak, which still displays some painted reliefs, and a cartonnage coffin of Nespanetjerenpere of the Third Intermediate Period (Brooklyn Museum 35.1265), which exhibits precisely painted hieroglyphs.

FIGURE I.8.3. The rose granite obelisk of Ramesses II at Luxor Temple incised with deep hiero-glyphs. Its large mass ensures a maximum ability to cut out stone with flint tools. Photograph and copyright: Denys Allen Stocks.

Poor quality stone, as is found in the walls of Theban tombs, often could not be used as a carving surface. Instead, the tomb walls were roughly cut from sound limestone with large chisels and dressed flat with adzes and wide- and narrow-bladed chisels of copper, bronze, and iron, dependent on the period of tomb cutting. The wall surfaces were then faced with plaster or with a mixture of mud and a binding agent, such as straw or stone chips, that was then finished with plaster to be painted. (Lucas 1962, 76–79; Arnold 1991, 292–294; Laboury and Tavier 2010, 96.)

Before monumental texts could be inscribed or painted on any stone surface, a drafts-man often created a system of guidelines. Taking a string soaked in red paint, he would stretch the string across the surface to be worked and release it, creating a straight line (Robins 2001). This process was repeated until a suitable guide had been made on which figural representations were drawn (Davies 1901, pl. 17). Corrected figures indicate that the sketches were reviewed before being carved or painted (Ransom 1916, fig. 39). Practice pieces painted and carved on ostraca show workers' attempts at mastering their crafts (Brunner-Traut 1979, pl. 32:39; Minault-Gout 2002; Dorn 2013).

The production of paint pigments began with grinding minerals and compounds into fine powder and then mixing the powder with a binding agent, such as tree gum. The selected pigment color was brushed onto wood, stone, or plaster. At the Great Palace at Amarna, paint was applied to plastered floors while the plaster was still wet (Petrie 1894, 12; Weatherhead 2007). Plaster was also applied to raised and incised reliefs to complement stone carving and to repair defects natural to a stone's surface and errors made by the carvers (Nelson 1929, 22).

Shadowing was occasionally executed in paint (Davies 1922, 52). But experimental work in a tomb with lamps of the type used by ancient artists indicated that due to low light and the light's influence on the human eye's perception of color, artists were more likely to use bold colors and little shading (Tavier 2012, 211). Instead of shadowing, Egyptian artists frequently used color to depict fish-scales, animal fur, and birds' feathers (MMA 30.4.119, 30.4.48). Color was also used to create depth, as when figures that overlapped were rendered in alternating tones (MMA 30.4.37).

Large brushes would have been required to efficiently paint large areas of flat surfaces. The detailed work of painting incised and raised relief hieroglyphs needed smaller, defined brush heads (Polz 1997). Paintbrushes were manufactured from a commonplace Egyptian rush (*Juncus maritimus*). During the Ptolemaic Period, the common reed (*Phragmites communis*) was more frequently used as writing implement (Lucas 1962, 364–365). Rushes, palm fibers, wood, and reeds could be beaten to produce coarser or finer bristles that were bound together with string (Le Fur 1994; Laboury and Tavier 2010, 101n38; BM EA 36889, 36893; Cairo Museum SR 2120).

In 2005, the author conducted experiments in Egypt to recreate rush, palm rib, and common reed and wood brushes. These experiments demonstrated that while copper, bronze, iron, and flint knives all cut bound bristles to make brush heads, the most efficiently and cleanly cut brush bristles were cut by very sharp flint knives and small, pressure-flaked flint blades. These tools produced brush bristles of appropriate shapes and sizes for painting large areas and individual hieroglyphs, especially small incised signs. Examples of such detailed painting are found on the limestone walls of the Unas pyramid, where the bottoms and sides of incised hieroglyphs have been painted with a blue pigment so that the signs stand out clearly against the white background (Edwards 1986, 189).

Physical Conditions Affecting Stone Carvers and Painters

The experimental carving and painting of incised and raised relief hieroglyphs into limestone, sandstone, and granite involved tightly gripping copper, bronze, iron, and flint chisels and punches, as well as mallets, stone hammers, and brushes for extended periods of time (Stocks 2003, 63–65, 83–99, Figs. 2.54–2.55, 3.8–3.19). These circumstances, as well as the final shaping and smoothing of carved symbols with scrapers and sandstone grinders and their polishing with finely ground quartz sand powders and mud, indicate that ancient carvers and painters suffered from debilitating repetitive strain injuries to arms, wrists, and hands.

After many years of carving soft and hard stones, wood, and metals, it is likely that ancient workers' main thumb joints of both hands became worn and painful to use. This stress would have been caused by gripping tools and by a constant jarring of the hands and wrists at every blow of a mallet or stone hammer. Experiments reveal that the wrists and lower arms also experience permanent pain due to the necessity of twisting a chisel's cutting edge between each hammer blow in order rapidly to strike the stone at different angles to achieve the shape of a sign, whether carving incised or raised reliefs. Despite this strain to the body, the Instructions to Khety, a text that praises scribal work and disparages all others, warns its audience against becoming a sculptor or a goldworker not because of the physicality of the labor, but because the individual will not be known through his work (Laboury 2016, 377).

Even more serious for ancient carvers of igneous stone, the experimental incising of hieroglyphs with flint chisels and punches suggests that ancient stoneworkers risked serious eye injuries from very sharp fragments of flint that detached from the stone and from the tools' cutting edges. Besides producing splinters and particles that might injure carvers' eyes, the chiseling of limestone and sandstone also created fragments that caused slight pinprick injuries to carvers' arms and faces. Additionally, the work of building and decorating temples and tombs, with carvers chipping, cutting, drilling, sawing, scraping, and smoothing stone and plaster, would have generated a considerable amount of choking powders and dusts.

Finely ground powders and dusts produced in the experimental cutting of various stones have been examined under a scanning electron microscope. The SEM micrographs (Stocks 2003, 124–128, figs. 4.15, 4.18) showed that much of the powder and dust, particularly powders from working igneous stones, consist of extremely fine particles of silica. Many of these particles lie within the size range of 0.5–5 microns. Breathing fine particles of stone and quartz of this size range would cause lung damage. The microscopic quartz particles possess sharp, angular corners and, consequently, embed themselves into a worker's lung tissue. The lungs isolate these particles by surrounding each one with scar tissue, which does not permit carbon dioxide and oxygen gases to exchange like normal lung tissue. After prolonged exposure to these tiny fragments, lung efficiency progressively diminishes, causing severe incapacitation and eventually death (i.e., Park et al. 2002).

Stone carvers often worked high up on temple walls and within high tomb chambers. To reach these areas, carvers and painters likely employed short and longer wooden ladders, stools, reed scaffolding with planks (Davies 1943, 2:pl. 60), or convenient stone blocks and mounds of sand. Any of these situations risked injury to the worker who might fall. Inevitably, some injuries probably resulted from tiredness and carelessness when mallets, stone hammers, and chisels were dropped on oneself or others.

A misdirected hammer or mallet that missed the end of a chisel and struck the hand holding the tool must have been a fairly frequent occurrence. Experimental and professional use of hammers and chisels occasionally injured the author in this way and inflicted repetitive strain injuries. Ancient carving and painting in difficult locations placed stone carvers and painters in daily discomfort and danger.

Bibliography

Arnold, D. 1991. *Building in Egypt: Pharaonic Stone Masonry*. New York.

Aston, B. G., J. A. Harrell, and I. Shaw. 2000. "Stone." In *Ancient Egyptian Materials and Technology*, edited by P. T. Nicholson and I. Shaw, 5–77. Cambridge.

Aufrère, S. H. 2001. "The Egyptian Temple, Substitute for the Mineral Universe." In *Colour and Painting*, edited by W. V. Davies, 158–163. London.

Brunner-Traut, E. 1979. *Egyptian Artists' Sketches: Figured Ostraka from the Gayer-Anderson Collection in the Fitzwilliam Museum, Cambridge*. PIHANS 45. Leiden.

Colson, M. A. 1903. "Sur la fabrication de certains outils métalliques chez les Égyptiens." *ASAE* 4: 190–192.

Davies, N. de G. 1901. *The Mastaba of Ptahhetep and Akhethetep at Saqqareh. Part II. The Mastaba. The Sculptures of Akhethetep*. ASE 9. London.

Davies, N. de G. 1922. "The Egyptian Expedition 1921–1922: The Graphic Work of the Expedition." *BMMA* 17: 50–56.

Davies, N. de G. 1943. *The Tomb of Rekh-mi-Rēʿ at Thebes*. 2 vols. New York.

Dorn, A. 2013. "Ostraka als Bildträger: Funktionen und Kontexte," accessed May 6, 2016, https://www.academia.edu/4736573/Ostraka_als_Bildtr%C3%A4ger._Funktionen_und_Kontexte_Images_sur_ostraca._Functions_et_contextes. An abridged version appears as "Un cas particulier: Les ostraca figurés," *Dossier d'Archéologie, numéro spécial* 1: 24–29.

Edwards, I. E. S. 1986. *The Pyramids of Egypt*. Harmondsworth.

Le Fur, D. 1994. *La conservation des peintures murales des temples de Karnak*. Paris.

Gilmore, G. R. 1986. "The composition of the Kahun metals." *Science in Egyptology*, 447–487.

James, T. G. H. 1979. *An Introduction to Ancient Egypt*. London.

Laboury, D. 2016. "Le scribe et le peinture. À propos d'un scribe qui ne voulait pas être pris pour un peintre." In *Aere Perennius: Mélanges égyptologiques en l'honneur de Pascal Vernus*, edited by P. Collombert, D. Lefèvre, S. Polis, and J. Winand, 371–396. OLA 242. Leuven.

Laboury, D., and H. Tavier. 2010. "À la recherche des peintres de la nécropole thébaine sous la 18ᵉ dynastie. Prolégomènes à une analyse des pratiques picturales dans la tombe d'Amenemopé (TT 29)." In *Thèbes aux 101 portes: Mélanges à la mémoire de Roland Tefnin*, 91–106. Edited by E. Warmenbol and V. Angenot. MonAeg 12, Série IMAGO 3. Turnhout.

Lucas, A. 1962. *Ancient Egyptian Materials and Industries*. 4th ed. Edited by J. R. Harris. London.

Mackay, E. 1921. "The Cutting and Preparation of Tomb Chapels in the Theban Necropolis." *JEA* 7:154–168.

Minault-Gout, A. 2002. *Carnets de pierre: L'art des ostracas dans l'Égypte ancienne*. Paris.

Nelson, H. H. 1929. "The Epigraphic Survey of the Great Temple of Medinet Habu (Seasons 1924–25 to 1927–28)." In *Medinet Habu 1924–28*, 1–36. OIC 5. Chicago.

Park, R., F. Rice, L. Stayner, R. Smith, et al. 2002. "Exposure to Crystalline Silica, Silicosis, and Lung Disease Other Than Cancer in Diatomaceous Earth industry Workers: A Quantitative Risk Assessment." *Occupational and Environmental Medicine* 59(1): 36–43.

Petrie, W. M. F. 1890. *Kahun, Gurob and Hawara*. London.

Petrie, W. M. F. 1894. *Tell El Amarna*. London.

Petrie, W. M. F. 1917. *Tools and Weapons*. London.

Pinch, G. 2001. "Red Things: The Symbolism of Colour in Magic." In *Colour and Painting*, edited by W. V. Davies, 182–185. London.

Polz, D. 1997. "An Egyptian Painter's Utensils from Dra' Abu el-Naga." *EA* 10:34–35.

Ransom, C. L. 1916. "A Study of the Decorative and Inscriptional Features of the Tomb." In *The Tomb of Perneb*, 47–79. New York.

Rickard, T. A. 1932. *Man and Metals*. Vol. 1. New York.

Robins, G. 2001. "The Use of the Squared Grid as a Technical Aid for Artists in Eighteenth Dynasty Painted Theban Tombs." In *Colour and Painting*, edited by W. V. Davies, 60–62. London.

Sebelien, J. 1924. "Early Copper and Its Alloys." *Ancient Egypt* : 6–15.

Stocks, D. A. 1988. "Industrial Technology at Kahun and Gurob: Experimental Manufacture and Test of Replica and Reconstructed Tools with Indicated Uses and Effects upon Artefact Production." MPhil. thesis 13543. University of Manchester: Faculty of Arts.

Stocks, D. A. 2003. *Experiments in Egyptian Archaeology: Stoneworking Technology in Ancient Egypt*. London.

Tavier, H. 2012. "Pour une approche matérielle et expérimentale de la peinture thébaine." In *Art and Society: Ancient and Modern Contexts of Egyptian Art*, edited by K. A. Kóthay, 209–215. Budapest.

Taylor, J. H. 2001. "Patterns of Colouring on Ancient Egyptian Coffins from the New Kingdom to the Twenty-sixth Dynasty: An Overview." In *Colour and Painting*, edited by W. V. Davies, 164–181. London.

Weatherhead, F. J. 2007. *Amarna Palace Paintings*. EES EM 78. London.

....

RECORDING EPIGRAPHIC SOURCES AS PART OF ARTWORKS

....

GABRIELE PIEKE

Art and Text: Point of Departure

ANCIENT Egyptian culture has bequeathed a myriad of monuments and artworks, and there are many ways to approach them. A particularly strong interconnection of images and texts seems a basic condition for material inheritances and can be designated as a specific cultural phenomenon for ancient Egypt at least from 3000 BCE onward. Scholars like Henry George Fischer (1986, 24–50) even stated that art and writing were one in ancient Egypt. With countless pictorial representations, the study of multiple epigraphic, palaeographic, and philological questions has always been a main concern in Egyptology. Due to the field's genesis and tradition—with deciphering hieroglyphs at its nucleus—art historical studies are widely underrepresented, and the vast majority of artwork still lacks thorough documentation and research despite the fact that art in ancient Egypt is multifold and diverse, with many layers and polysemous iconic representations that fulfill various functions at the same time. In a widely illiterate Egyptian society, pictorial representations were key media for communicating a wide range of information to distinct audiences.

Images are perceptual containers and crucial instruments for knowledge production; iconic cognizance has been defined as exemplary thinking following its own logic (Boehm 2008; Bredekamp 2010). According to this premise, art history deals with historical and systematic problems of the visual arts. It tackles questions based on definition of forms, concept, and composition and asks about domains of iconography and typology of single artworks or monuments and stylistic criteria. The field explores a critical inventory of *oeuvre* and monuments, interpretations of single artworks and series of artworks, analysis of magical, religious, and social functions of art, the social framework and relevant conditions of art production, its direct implications on work process, and intended reception of images with respect to the beholder. Thus, historical-philological source criticism belongs to the traditional methodological frame. Against this background, recording and analyses of inscriptions as an integral part of many artworks, based on epigraphy, palaeography, and linguistic studies, seems a *conditio sine qua non* for any comprehensive understanding, not least because epigraphy provides essential information on ownership, prosopographical data, context, and purpose of artworks, chronological and topographical developments, and religious, historical, sociocultural, and many other types of evidence. Essential data can be gleaned about the role of and links between workshops and the relation and impact of clients. Art history, however, has its own demands for recording visual representations and their multiple layers. Naturally, research demands decision-making. In art history, documentation directly hinges on concrete questions about the artwork(s) and the addressed art genre. Therefore, and based on the interpenetration of visual and textual elements, it seems necessary to take epigraphy and palaeography as complementary sciences in order to arrive at a better understanding of written sources, the meanings they carry, and the artwork's coding.

With regard to recording and analyzing texts, the significance and importance of documenting the material quality of inscriptions has recently been emphasized (Polis and Razanajao 2016). Context and location of inscriptions are crucial for understanding, particularly when they are part of a larger concept and composition of an artwork (compare Fischer 1976; Eaton-Krauss 2009). Essential details include scrutinizing place and orientation of "picture writing" (Davies 1958) in relation to image and documenting the applied technique, for example, whether sunk or raised relief or painted or ink inscription. Yet in addition to classical epigraphic and palaeographic questions, for art history, some issues are relevant: What is the general concept of the writing with regard to the image it belongs to? What is the precise layout of the text? How does it interact with typology and concept? What is the semantic and syntactic relation between image and text? Which specific text formula is used, and is it linked to context and/or image? Is it interdependent with formal structures, such as back pillars, bases, negative spaces, main figures, smaller motifs, and larger wall compositions? Is there an interaction with the beholder's situation? Are there column lines, graphemes, or other items that enhance visibility and readability? Does the application technique for text correspond to the rest of the image or differ from it? Do details indicate individual "hands" of artists? Do the colors of the text correspond to or diverge from the rest of the composition? Is text contemporary to image, or is it part of a redesign and (re-)conceptualization? What is the work procedure, and are work zones visible? Is there a connection to workshop tradition(s), be it chronological or topographical? These and many questions can be raised in a holistic approach to studying epigraphic sources.

For art history, material quality is a natural starting point of this endeavor, and recording ancient texts is one part of the puzzle. Like in any other traditional comparative science, access to faithful illustrations is of utmost value. Difficulties of access and the wide lack of thorough documentation, however, mean that many art historical studies still deal with inscription as marginal. Also, the practice of separating texts and images in analyses of sculptures, stelae, tombs, and temples is still widely practiced despite this being scientifically unsatisfactory. Indisputably, this unconnected study constitutes a disadvantage for both fields due to a lack of context and proper understanding, which leads to misinterpretation or a distorted picture. A remedy for this profound deficiency seems overdue.

A vast number of objects, such as statuettes, furniture, coffins, or cosmetic articles, were designed to hold writings. Most of these artifacts belong to the field of decorative art, and they are not perceived as real works of "art" in a classical sense. Columns, obelisks, and shrines are here understood as architectural elements even though they regularly incorporate images in their conceptual layout. Yet in Egyptology, a proper distinction between art and decorative art, crafts, or architecture is often blurred. Stimulated by the *pictorial* and *iconic turn* (Mitchell 1994; Maar and Burda 2004) and in the context of image studies and visual culture (Belting 2001; Sachs-Hombach 2009; Davis 2014), these objects and monuments are rightly understood as essential carriers of multilayered information. However, due to more than four thousand years of pictorial tradition and several different art genres, each of which called for an adapted approach, the following remarks can only give a brief overview on dealing with artistic creations. Accordingly, the discussion focuses on documentation of "classical artworks," from relief and painting to sculpture in the round. Questions of graphemes, linguistic problems, or text semantics cannot be discussed in such an overview of diverse artworks due to their wide-ranging time period, material, and context, despite the reasonable numbers of unanswered questions about texts on sculptures, stelae, temples, and tombs.

A Line Is a Line: Different Techniques of Recording

Many art historians have stressed the importance of meticulous observation and study of artworks due to their complex nature. Certainly in-depth documentation is an essential basis for art historical analyses. A systematic, accurate recording is of intrinsic value and yields information of enormous significance. Thorough documentation, however, seems sufficient for tackling only some research questions, such as iconographic or typological studies, since interpretation, which transforms the object, distant in time and space to the present, is its very nature (Strudwick 2015). With regard to art history, most answers can only be given with the artwork in front of the observer. Given this awareness, Winckelmann implemented the "Autopsie" of artworks instead of studying illustrations (Graepler 2013, 119–121). For many art historical topics, for example, questions of stylistic features or in-depth understanding of the production of artworks can only be supported, but not substituted, by recorded information.

The main concerns have always been questions of authenticity (compare Fless et al. 2016) and objectivity. In his seminal work on the history of ancient art, Winckelmann

(1764, ix) criticized incorrect illustrations of sculptures and reflected on the quality of drawings and engravings. Regardless of faithful rendering or matters of objectivity and authenticity, illustrations of any kind do not reflect timeless statements, but rather time-bound ideas of a collective (Fless et al. 2016, 496). Visual rendering of artworks is deeply influenced by the creator's knowledge, understanding, and *zeitgeist*. For this reason, thorough studies are based on direct confrontation with artwork, while its documentation in whatever form can only be supportive and not replace the "autopsy" of the original.

With regard to authenticity, the widespread cultural practice in Egypt to usurp or adapt older monuments (Magen 2011; Eaton-Krauss 2015; Gilli 2016) constitutes an obstacle to correctly understanding them and causes specific challenges in recording. Due to the concept of "ideal image" (Laboury 2010; Bryan 2015), representation could easily be transferred to new ownership just by adding or altering name(s) and accompanying texts, sometimes combined with a stylistic or iconography remodeling (Fischer 1974, 7; Bács 2015; Pieke 2018; see chapters by Bács, Brand). Erasure and redecoration of monuments were common practices, whose evidence can only be gathered by close and prolonged examination, is easily missed if not actively sought (Spencer 1982, 26), and is often over-looked in recording, consequently leading to erroneous interpretation. Therefore, it is of the utmost importance to actively consider this issue and adjust research questions and documentation. In this regard, art historical research and connoisseurship can be of great benefit since stylistic analyses and material expertise belong to the field's core tasks.

LINE DRAWING

Line drawing plays an integral part of Egyptological documentation even though illustrations of three-dimensional artworks are much less common today. Conventions have been developed for graphic documentation and issues, such as relief techniques, paintings, supplements, and additions (Strudwick 2001; see chapters by McClain, Vértes). Digital epigraphy is now standard (see chapter by Manuelian). These so-called facsimile drawings (Strudwick 2001, 127–131) are not facsimiles in the proper sense. They are line drawings whose contours try to follow the original. In order to understand sculptors' hands, one must observe, among other considerations, whether contours are hard-edged or soft, angular or flat, without even extending the discussion to sequences of brush strokes (Figure I.9.1). Consequently, in terms of documentation and visualization of stylistic features, a line drawing is not enough. In addition, as mentioned earlier, many texts are not contemporary with images, a challenging issue for documentation by line drawing. The use of different artistic techniques might indicate the life-span of specific monuments, which were regularly used by family members and cult personnel to secure their own afterlife by appropriation of minor figures (Pieke 2018, 296–301).

Representations determine cognition and our level of awareness (Schürmann 2011). In epistemological terms, they have led to idiosyncratic analyses in Egyptology. In art

FIGURE I.9.1. The two lower registers of the Dynasty 11 stela of Meru (Museo Egizio, Turin, Drovetti collection [1824], C. 1447) demonstrate a potpourri of different artistic techniques. All figurative motifs and the main text are executed in raised relief, while the two lower registers demonstrate three different techniques. All text orientation follows the motif they accompany. The use of sunk relief for the list of offerings to the right might be explained by its placement on a higher relief plane, thus referring to Old Kingdom compositions of offering lists in a syntactically demarcated area. This text panel's particular form reveals a change of concept during the work process, further indicated by the slightly different color scheme in this area, while the captions in the bottom register are rendered in ink. This evidence suggests the later addition of minor texts, as well as a semantic hierarchy of motifs. Courtesy of Museo Egizio, Turin.

history, line drawings are useful only due to their diminution of the image. Accuracy of lines is vital in following an outer or inner contour line, distinguishing between losses and supplements, and being as neutral as possible. In addition, information of scale is essential. A critical stance toward drawings as a medium for accurate visualization of artworks is already reflected in seminal works of the early twentieth century (Capart 1907; Fechheimer 1913, 1921; Wreszinski 1923–1936; Mekhitarian 1954, who trusted the medium of photography more). Founded on archaeological and not art historical conventions, line drawings reduce the materiality and three-dimensionality of a complex representation to a number of lines. This reduction and readability seems advantageous for certain specific questions, but a drawing involves a complete loss of material quality, which is intrinsic for art history (compare Laboury and Tavier 2016). Therefore, line drawings are only of value as additional mediums for certain specific issues of the artwork's representations.

Photographic Documentation

Since its discovery in the first half of the nineteenth century, photography offers an effective technique of documentation and illustration of sites, architecture, artworks, and other finds (see chapters by Manniche, Emery). From William Henry Fox Talbot's pioneering book *The Pencil of Nature* (1844), the use of photography was established for documenting, reproducing, and copying as well as producing pictorial illustrations. The benefits of photography are a relative objectiveness and authenticity and a high level of accuracy. Photography, though, is also a spatial engagement (Shanks and Svabo 2013), which ought to be used consciously and based on specific concepts. In particular, camera perspective and lighting, as well as proximity, intensity, and direction of the light source, can have a strong impact on the motif's effect and can produce subjective images, rather than neutral ones required for research documentation.

Photography alone cannot capture all details. Taking and reproducing true color photography is now standard, at least as documentation, providing that the image is taken following professional principles regarding daylight-balanced light sources, use of color targets, and calibration of technical equipment (Langenbacher and Rivenc 2017). Since art history is a comparative science, accurate recording is of intrinsic value, and subjectivity must be reduced to a minimum. For qualitative comparison, a photographic procedure that involves color accuracy in the processing of digital data and printing is crucial. Unfortunately, high-quality reproduction is rarely achieved due to the limitations and financial constraints of academic publications. Yet compared to drawings, photography captures artwork at one moment and offers much more authenticity with multiplex information. Although photography is vital in epigraphic work (Bell 1995, 103) for its complementary control of line drawings, in art history, the reverse is true: a photo is much more valid than a drawing due to its higher convergence to materiality. The photographer, however, can only catch what s/he sees and understands, so photographic documentation needs direct Egyptological input.

Modern Techniques of Recording and Visualization

For scientific documentation and visualization, a well-rounded approach is fruitful for rendering data that is otherwise difficult to assess, and several modern, nondestructive techniques can aid in generating images of objects as a whole. Reflectance transformation imaging (RTI), in particular, can reveal otherwise hardly visible etching on degraded surfaces (see chapter by Wendrich), while x-ray radiography, UV-fluorescence, and infrared reflectography are well established in the field of restoration-conservation. Recently, multimodal imaging of subsurface texts produced promising results (Gibson et al. 2018), and these methods are also valuable for a better understanding of figurative images. For analyzing wall painting and polychrome layers, high intensity and pure UV light is suitable for documentation of specific artistic techniques, helping to enhance the visibility of images and texts depending on surface coating (for example, blue pigments and also varnishes: Parkinson 2008; Den Doncker and Tavier, 2018). Virtual modeling and reconstruction adds new dimensions particularly to the visualization of architecture and its decoration. As Lengyl and Toulouse (2014; Fless et al. 2016, 499–502) have rightly pointed out, however, the more realistic the visualization aims to be, the more it diverges from confirmed evidence and becomes fictional. For this reason, they have established a "visualization of uncertainty." Egyptology could profit immensely from this method to meet the highest requirements.

A main concern for computer simulation is colors, which presently cannot match the values and textures of original paint. In this regard, photography offers significant advances in capturing colors more accurately. High-end scanning is common in art collections in condition surveying, safeguarding artifacts, and state of the art research. For the future of our field, this high-resolution documentation offers undeniable benefits particularly for recording three-dimensional aspects, textures, or polychromy. In addition to classical photography, orthophotography or 3D scans are useful for a general understanding of the artwork's concept and of crucial importance for quick assessment and documentation of monuments (see chapter by Revez), especially in light of the immense quantity of artworks and their ongoing deterioration. The high-end scanning of Tutankhamun's painted burial chamber (www.highres.factum-arte.org/Tutankhamun/) testifies to this method's exceedingly authentic visualization, including many details of painting processes, technical issues of the "painter's hand" or surface structures, and soiling. Being extremely efficient, noninvasive, and offering high-resolution documentation and visualization, this process will play an essential role in the future.

Recording Colors

Colors are crucial media of artistic expression in all art genres though they are one of the most difficult fields to record, offering a potential for error both in documentation and in reproduction (Strudwick 2001, 132–137). Modern devices, such as spectrophotometers, allow the collection of objective data by on-site color measurements (Langenbacher and Rivenc 2017, 8–10; Strudwick 2016, 162–168). Certainly, it is important to document the actual state in long-term perspective. For everyday use in art history, charts with color codes are only partly feasible since comparative data exists only for very few monuments. A trained eye is a highly sensitive tool for perceiving and recording colors. The use of Munsell color order systems (Landa and Fairchild 2005), while perhaps only a subjective approximation (Beinlich-Seeber and Shedid 1987, 121–122), still seems helpful for quick recording particularly since software can translate all Munsell notation to color spectrophotometric data and vice versa. This color data can easily be integrated in future comparisons (e.g., Shedid 1988, 164–165; Strudwick 2016, 166).

The Devil Is in the Details: Dealing with Different Art Genres

Following these general comments, it is important to take a quick glance at specific issues in connection with the particular needs of certain art genres.

Living with Limitations: Recording Three-Dimensional Images

The most important medium to document sculpture is photography. Sculptural art appears in many forms, and each perspective can focus different aspects, hence defining the best angle or the right balance between light and shadow are only two of many challenges. Photographic illustrations strongly influence the scientific view and assessment of three-dimensional bodies, particularly the one of "portraits." Egyptology still lacks binding standards and a media-critical reflection on issues like focal length, shooting location, distance and camera angle, picture section, and lighting. Black and white photography offers much higher contrast value and is certainly preferable in many cases for the documentation of sculpture in the round, despite induced abstraction. In light of significant concerns about color authenticity in recording and reproduction, a visualization of corporeal vividness and perspectival figures in black and white photography offers advantages. However, color photography is essential for the visualization of material, like the color of the stone, its veins, and texture or staining. In addition, wider parts of statuary were originally bordered in color. Polychromy is a crucial instrument of Egyptian artists, and its recording is indispensable. In general, a formalized procedure is imperative in any comparative field, though, each artwork is different from the other and, depending on the precise position and viewing direction of the face, it is necessary to adapt the documentation (Kyrieleis 1988; Wiegand 1991, 33).

In sharp contrast to traditional art historical fields, line drawings were retained for the study of Egyptian statuary because of Egyptology's close association with nineteenth-century expeditions and with the archaeological approach of organizing material culture into typological series. Unrivaled are the eight volumes of slip boxes with drawings of distinct statue types published by the Danish sculptor and photographer Bodil Hornemann (1951–1969). The art historian Hans Gerhard Evers (1929), with his seminal work on Middle Kingdom sculptures, implemented the typology of iconographic and stylistic details by using line drawings as supportive medium in addition to photography.

FIGURE I.9.2. Dynasty 4 sitting figure of vizier Hem-iunu (Roemer-Pelizaeus-Museum Hildesheim, PM 1962) with inscription consisting of sunk relief with color-paste. This technique is extremely rare, the specific use is a direct dating criterion, and links the statue owner to the royal family in Meidum. Paste relief is otherwise attested in the tomb of prince Nefermaat, most likely the father of Hemiunu, who even claims to be the inventor of this technique. Thus, already on a purely visual level, the polychrome color paste points to prestige and social networks. With regard to the text itself, the particular use and omission of column lines for specific titles seems of interest, as well as their specific location on the statue base. The length of the lines indicate that they were carved before the hieroglyphs and not entirely in correspondence with them. Photo credit: Photo Archive Pelizaeus-Museum, Hildesheim.

Still today, researchers use this form of imaging for specific details, although drawings are no longer understood as the correct medium to visualize three-dimensional art in its complexity (Figure I.9.2). Drawings are commonly used to explicitly focus on specific features by omitting other aspects; to simplify representations of main form contours, stylistic details, or iconographic features; and in reconstruction drawings.

Because of publishing constraints and lack of access to high-quality photographs of sculptures, many publications use more easily reproducible visualization techniques in addition to photography. Drawings can be extremely useful to record statues' inscriptions, which might be tricky to display in photographs. For palaeographic comparison, a "facsimile" is essential, while the true haptic quality of hieroglyphs can only be understood by visual examination. In general, it is paramount to reflect the texts' concrete settings, which render information about concept, interconnections, and influences of distinct epigraphic choices, as well as the *Selbstthematisierung* of its owner (Assmann 1996).

Of particular importance are proper names given for monumental sculptures (e.g., Habachi 1969; Müller 1988, 72–73) that indicate certain functions of temple statues, in addition to ancient Egyptian terms for sculptures (Hoffmann, forthcoming).

From Low to Flat: Documenting Relief and Painting

As for relief and painting used in different art genres, the ultimate goal is a high level of detail and accuracy in rendering representations. Tomb and temple decoration are by definition closely related to architecture as its image carrier. Concept and composition have to react immediately on this concrete architectural setting. Thus, for understanding iconic references, semantic interaction, or interpretation of the overall concept of decoration, the connection with architecture, as well as specific placing of themes and motifs, is of the utmost importance. Since Lepsius's epigraphic campaign (see chapter by Loeben), tomb decoration has been documented by outline drawings with at least one sketch for each wall. Still today, this method is used to convey information about general conceptual layout and detailed organization of picture planes, and it offers an intelligible overview of the iconographic program, thus being a classical point of departure for art historical studies.

As mentioned earlier, line drawings almost completely disguise physical and artistic dimensions of artworks (Laboury and Tavier 2016, 60). A line drawing is the wrong medium to visualize haptic information or the wealth of variants and shades of colors of an original stroke drawn by a brush—all crucial for understanding of stylistic features or "hands" of particular artists (e.g., Beinlich-Seeber and Shedid 1987, 139–142; Shedid 1988, 88–92; Laboury and Tavier 2016). Indeed, close-up photography or high-end scanning are better solutions, maintaining higher levels of authenticity. The image carrier's material and the techniques used—sunk or raised relief and layers of architectural and pictorial coatings, primers, or colors—are essential information about individual strategies adapted to the monument (Figure I.9.3). Technical issues directly govern the production of images. Consequently, their understanding and recording is indispensable for art historical questions (for mural painting, see Beinlich-Seeber and Shedid 1987, 114–119; Tavier 2012; Laboury and Tavier 2016; Madden and Tavier, 2018; for painted relief, Williams 1932; Smith 1949, 244–272; Pieke 2011). In order to understand work process, information such as grids, guidelines, or corrections is as crucial as conceiving of work areas and processes (e.g., Bryan 2001; Wenzel 2007; Laboury and Tavier 2016).

The work of the Oxford Expedition to Egypt "Egypt in Miniature" series records relief-cut wall decorations and offers systematic, close-up (black and white) photography of scene details supplemented with descriptions, archaeological data, and line drawings (www.oxfordexpeditiontoegypt.com/index.html). This technique reveals surface structure, tool marks, erasures, additions, and details of relief cut. It is difficult, however, to

FIGURE I.9.3. Mutnofret offering to her parents in the Dynasty 18 tomb of Amenemope (TT 29). The wall paintings provide precise information about work procedures. An offering scene on the long hall's south side displays the daughter of Amenemope's cousin Sennefer offering to her parents. The image captions consist of eight columns each for Mutnofret and her parents, and the orientation of hieroglyphs follows the figures. The actual work process for the text panel was executed in two steps from left to right—the easier way for right-handers—as indicated by a decreasing quality of details in this direction. The area division is not text-/content-related, but based on ergonomic work conditions. The first column of the daughter's text belongs to the right work zone with the texts for Sennefer and his wife. Courtesy of Mission Archéologique belge dans la Nécropole Thébaine. Photo credit: Matjaz Kacicnik.

publish a huge monument using detail photography. Currently, therefore, photography combined with auxiliary "facsimile" drawings seems the most convincing way to deal with relief and paintings. Thereby, a clear vision is necessary in order to decide which information shall be include or omitted from drawings.

In general, the circumstances for recording tombs apply to relief and paintings in sanctuaries or on smaller monuments like chapels or stelae. The monumental character and large size of many temple walls, however, leads to much poorer accessibility and consequent problems for analysis. Perhaps for this reason, they generally lack proper art historical studies, and research still focuses on epigraphic and religious interpretation of monuments. Still awaiting research is the outstanding artistic contribution of the master conceptual mind who, acquainted with intellectual, sacral agendas, executed the highly sophisticated layout of a wall concept. Only an artist, the "layout designer," is capable of structuring large picture plans in different pictorial units. The textual is subordinate to the figurative program, as further documented by the working process. Another important point is physical accessibility (e.g., Fitzenreiter 2014) for makers, beholders, and researchers. Texts and motifs on upper parts of walls, in particular, must have been invisible due to height and bad lighting conditions. Art historical studies have emphasized that the position of the beholder was directly considered during the working process (Myśliwiec 1988, 9; Laboury 2008; Pieke 2011, 2015). Future studies should certainly reflect this relevant issue during documentation.

Let's Do It! An Appeal Instead of a Summary

The immense treasury of Egyptian images offers enormous potential and needs fundamental work to study and document preserved artworks. Indeed, regarding many art historical questions, we are just at the beginning. A media critical reflection for future documentation and analysis seems essential, while working with existing illustrations requires serious source criticism. Traditional and cutting edge methods of recording and analysis can make accessible a wide range of information coded in artworks, leading to a new understanding of work organization, relationship between makers and beneficiaries, and social hierarchy and art as powerful instruments to communicate certain meanings. A holistic approach seems indispensable due to the interwoven character of image and text. Epigraphic and art historical research can greatly benefit from mutual knowledge and understanding. The process of documentation in the past, present, and future calls for discussions, such as the development of standards for photography or digital visualizations. It is foreseeable that new technologies will soon become the dominant method of image capturing and will be integrated into professional protocols. For art history, however, documentation can act as a visual support, but cannot serve as a substitute for a direct confrontation with the original.

In its current state, epigraphy is widely explored by philologists, and documentation does not often facilitate art historical analyses other than for iconographic questions. Recording and analyzing texts is only one piece of a big puzzle. Allowing this research to stand alone without complementing it with the bigger picture, such as issues of form definition, iconographic program, and precise context, induces misinterpretation or a lack of understanding. In this regard, art history has much to offer Egyptology and can help in formulating new perceptions. Complex analyses can contribute better insights into all kinds of monuments, thus leading to thoughtful conclusions about culture. Because images were, and are, dominant communication tools, thorough studies in the future will bear much fruit and result in an appreciation of meaning, purpose, and structure of the material culture of ancient Egypt and its outstanding artworks. The dichotomy between an analysis predominantly of writing versus art historical studies with only a secondary integration of textual sources seems an unwelcome impediment in Egyptology, one that should be overcome. Artworks are a primary source of cultural knowledge and understanding of ancient Egyptian culture, thus requiring an "art history of complexity" (Kemp 1991). Egyptology would widely benefit from orienting toward nonlinear scholarship, developing new thinking and research habits, focusing on studies and recordings based on structural and dynamic complexity, and interacting better with different areas.

BIBLIOGRAPHY

Assmann, J. 1996. "Preservation and Presentation of Self in Ancient Egyptian Portraiture." In *Studies in Honor of William Kelly Simpson*, vol. 1, edited by P. Der Manuelian, 55–81. Boston.

Bács, T. A. 2015. "Some Aspects of Tomb Reuse during the Twentieth Dynasty." In *Joyful in Thebes: Egyptological Studies in Honor of Betsy M. Bryan*, edited by R. Jasnow and K. M. Cooney, 1–9. Atlanta.

Beinlich-Seeber, C., and A. G. Shedid. 1987. *Das Grab des Userhat (TT 56)*. AVDAIK 50. Mainz.

Bell, L. 1995. "New Kingdom Epigraphy." In *The American Discovery of Ancient Egypt: Essays*, edited by N. Thomas, 96–109. Los Angeles.

Belting, H. 2001. *Bild-Anthropologie: Entwürfe für eine Bildwissenschaft*. Munich.

Boehm, G. 2008. *Wie Bilder Sinn erzeugen: Die Macht des Zeigens*. Berlin.

Bredekamp, H. 2010. *Theorie des Bildakts: Frankfurter Adorno Vorlesungen 2007*. Berlin.

Bryan, B. M. 2001. "Painting Techniques and Artisan Organization in the Tomb of Suemniwet, Theban Tomb 92." In *Colour and Painting in Ancient Egypt*, edited by W. V. Davies, 63–72. London.

Bryan, B. M. 2015. "Portraiture." In *A Companion to Ancient Egyptian Art*, edited by M. K. Hartwig, 375–396. Chichester.

Capart, J. 1907. *Une rue de tombeaux à Saqqarah*. Brussels.

Davies, N. M. 1958. *Picture Writing in Ancient Egypt*. London.

Davis, W. 2014. *A General Theory of Visual Culture*. Princeton.

Den Doncker, A., and H. Tavier. 2018. "Scented Resins for Scented Figures." *EA* 53, 16–19.

Eaton-Krauss, M. 2009. "The Location of Inscriptions on Statues of the Old Kingdom." In *Sitting beside Lepsius: Studies in Honour of Jaromir Malek at the Griffith Institute*, edited by D. Magee, J. Bourriau, and S. Quirke, 129–153. Leuven.

Eaton-Krauss, M. 2015. "Usurpation." In *Joyful in Thebes: Egyptological Studies in Honor of Betsy M. Bryan*, edited by R. Jasnow and K. M. Cooney, 97–104. Atlanta.

Evers, H. G. 1929. *Staat aus dem Stein, Denkmäler, Geschichte und Bedeutung der Ägyptischen Plastik während des Mittleren Reiches*. 2 vols. Munich.

Fechheimer, H. 1913. *Die Plastik der Ägypter: Dreizehntes bis Siebzehntes Tausend*. Die Kunst des Ostens 1. Berlin.

Fechheimer, H. 1921. *Die Kleinplastik der Ägypter*. Die Kunst des Ostens 3. Berlin.

Fischer, H. G. 1974. "The Mark of a Second Hand on Ancient Egyptian Antiquities." *MMJ* 9:5–34.

Fischer, H. G. 1976. "Archaeological Aspects of Epigraphy and Palaeography." In *Ancient Egyptian Epigraphy and Palaeography*, 27–50. New York.

Fischer, H. G. 1986. *L'écriture et l'art de l'Égypte ancienne: Quatres leçons sur la palaeographie et l'épigraphie pharaoniques*. Collège de France. Essais et conférences. Paris.

Fitzenreiter, M. 2014. "(Un)zugänglichkeit: Über Performanz und Emgerenz von Schrift und Bild." In *Schriftträger–Textträger: Zur materialen Präsenz des Geschriebenen in frühen Gesellschaften*, edited by A. Kehnel and D. Panagiotopoulos, 179–208. Materiale Textkulturen 6. Berlin.

Fless, F., B. Graf, O. Dall, U. Franke, C. Gerbich, et al. 2016. "Authenticity and Communication." *eTopoi, Journal for Ancient Studies*, Special Volume 6, Space and Knowledge, 481–524.

Gibson, A., K. E. Piquette, U. Bergmann, W. Christens-Barry, G. Davis, et al. 2018. "An Assessment of Multimodal Imaging of Subsurface Text in Mummy Cartonnage Using Surrogate Papyrus Phantoms." *Heritage Science* 6 (1):1–13. https://doi.org/10.1186/s40494-018-0175-4.

Gilli, B. 2016. "How to Build a Capital: The Second Life of Pre-Ramesside Materials in Pi-Ramessse." In *Fenster in die Vergangenheit öffnen: Festschrift für Edgar B Pusch zum 70. Geburtstag*, edited by H. Franzmeier, T. Rehren, and R. Schulz, 137–175. FR 10. Hildesheim.

Graepler, D. 2013. "'Die Kupfer sind erbärmlich'—Die Reproduktion der Antike als quellenkritisches Problem im 18. Jahrhundert." In *Abgekupfert. Roms Antiken in der Reproduktionsmedien der frühen Neuzeit: Katalog zur Ausstellung Kunstsammlung und Sammlung der Gipsabgüsse, Universität Göttingen 27. Oktober 2013 bis 16. Februar 2014*, edited by M. Luchterhandt, L. Roemer, J. Bergemann, and D. Graepler, 115–132. Petersburg.

Habachi, L. 1969. *Features of the Deification of Ramesses II*. ADAIK 5. Glückstadt.

Hoffmann, F. Forthcoming. "Zu den Bild- und Statuenbegriffen im Ägyptischen." In *"Die Mittel der Kunst im Auge": Neue Studien zur Kunst des Alten Ägypten* I, edited by C.-B. Arnst. Norderstedt.

Hornemann, B. 1951–1969. *Types of Egyptian Statuary, Vols. I–VIII*. Copenhagen.

Kemp, W. 1991. "Kontexte: Für eine Kunstgeschichte der Komplexität." *Texte zur Kunst* 2:89–101.

Kyrieleis, H. 1988. "Ein klassischer Kopf, erneut betrachtet." In *Kanon: Festschrift Ernst Berger zum 60. Geburtstag*, edited by M. Schmidt, 108–111. Beiheft zur Halbjahresschrift Antiken Kunst 15. Basel.

Laboury, D. 2008. "Colosses et perspective: De la prise en consideration de la parallaxe dans la statuaire pharaonique de grandes dimensions au nouvel empire." *RdE* 59:181–230.

Laboury, D. 2010. "Portrait versus Ideal Image." *UCLA Encyclopedia of Egyptology*, edited by W. Wendrich, J. Dieleman, E. Frood, and J. Baines. Los Angeles. http://digital2.library.ucla.edu/viewItem.do?ark=21198/zz0025jjvo.

Laboury, D., and H. Tavier. 2016. "In Search of Painters in the Theban Necropolis of the 18th Dynasty. Prolegomena to Analysis of Pictorial Practices in the Tomb of Amenemope (TT 29)." In *Artists and Paintings in Ancient Egypt*, edited by V. Angenot and F. Tiradritti, 57–77. Studi Poliziani di Egittologia 1. Montepulciano.

Landa, E. R., and M. D. Fairchild. 2005. "Charing Color from the Eye of the Beholder." *American Scientist* 93 (5):436–443.

Langenbacher, J., and R. Rivenc. 2017. *Documenting Painted Surfaces for Outdoor Painted Sculptures: A Manual of Laboratory and Field Test Methods*. Los Angeles.

Lengyel, D., and C. Toulouse. 2014. "3D-Scans für die Rekontextualisierung antiker Skulptur." In *Elektronische Medien & Kunst, Kultur, Historie, Konferenzband*, edited by A. Bienert, J. Hemsley, and P. Santos, 135–142. Darmstadt.

Maar, C., and H. Burda, eds. 2004. *Iconic Turn: Die neue Macht der Bilder*. Cologne.

Madden, B., and H. Tavier. 2018. "Original Painting Techniques. Methods and Materials in 18th Dynasty Tombs, in the Valley of the Nobles, Egypt." In *Tracing Technoscapes: The Production of Bronze Age Wall Paintings in the Eastern Mediterranean*, edited by J. Becker, J. Jungfleisch, and C. von Rüden, 120–148. Leiden.

Magen, B. 2011. *Steinerne Palimpseste: Zur Wiederverwendung von Statuen durch Ramses II. und seine Nachfolger*. Wiesbaden.

Mekhitarian, A. 1954. *La peinture égyptienne*. Geneva.

Mitchell, W. J. T. 1994. *Picture Theory: Essays on Verbal and Visual Representation*. Chicago.

Müller, M. 1988. *Die Kunst Amenophis' III. und Echnatons*. Basel.

Myśliwiec, K. 1988. *Royal Portraiture of the Dynasties XXI–XXX*. Mainz.

Parkinson, R. B. 2008. *The Painted Tomb-Chapel of Nebamun: Masterpieces of Ancient Egyptian Art*. London.

Pieke, G. 2011. "The Evidence of Images: Art and Working Technique in the Mastaba of Mereruka." In *Old Kingdom, New Perspectives: Egyptian Art and Archaeology 2750–2150 BC*, edited by N. Strudwick and H. Strudwick, 216–228. Oxford.

Pieke, G. 2015. "Principles of Decoration: Concept and Style in the Mastaba of Mereruka in Saqqara." In *Proceedings of the Tenth International Congress of Egyptologists, University of the Aegean, Rhodes, 22–29 May 2008*, vol. 2, edited by P. Kousoulis and N. Lazaridis, 1791–1806. OLA 241. Leuven.

Pieke, G. 2018. "'Lass deinen Namen hervorkommen': Zur Appropriation von Einzelmotiven der Grabdekoration in Sakkara." In *"…Denn das eigentliche Studium der Menschen ist der Mensch," Beiträge aus der Ägyptologie, der Linguistik, der Medizin und ihrer Geschichte, der Musikwissenschaft, der Politikwissenschaft und der Provenienzforschung und der Rechtsgeschichte zu Ehren Alfred Grimms anlässlich seines 65. Geburtstags*, edited by B. Magen, 274–309. Wiesbaden.

Polis, S., and V. Razanajao. 2016. "Ancient Egyptian Texts in Context: Towards a Conceptual Data Model (The Thot Data Model–TDM)." *Institute of Classical Studies* 59/2:24–41.

Sachs-Hombach, K., ed. 2009. *Bildtheorien: Anthropologische und kulturelle Grundlagen des Visualistic Turn*. Frankfurt.

Schürmann, E. 2011. "Transitions from Seeing to Thinking. On the Relation of Perception, Worldview and World-Disclosure." In *Bilder–Sehen–Denken. Zum Verhältnis von begrifflich-philosophischen und empirisch-psychologischen Ansätzen in der bildwissenschaftlichen Forschung*, edited by K. Sachs-Hombach and R. Totzke, 93–105. Cologne.

Shanks, M., and C. Svabo. 2013. "Archaeology and Photography: A Pragmatology." In *Reclaiming Archaeology: Beyond the Tropes of Modernity*, edited by A. Gonzáles-Ruibal, 89–102. New York.

Shedid, A. G. 1988. *Stil der Grabmalereien in der Zeit Amenophis' II: Untersucht an den Thebanischen Gräbern Nr. 104 und Nr. 80*. AVDAIK 66. Mainz.

Smith, W. S. 1949. *A History of Egyptian Sculpture and Painting in the Old Kingdom*. 2nd ed. Oxford.

Spencer, A. J. 1982. "First and Second Owners of a Memphite Tomb Chapel." *JEA* 68:20–26.

Strudwick, N. 2001. "Problems of Recording and Publication of Paintings in the Private Tombs of Thebes." In *Colour and Painting in Ancient Egypt*, edited by W. V. Davies, 126–140. London.

Strudwick, N. 2015. "Interpretation." In *A Companion to Ancient Egyptian Art*, edited by M. Hartwig, 485–503. Chichester.

Strudwick, N., ed. 2016. *The Tomb of Pharaoh's Chancellor Senneferi at Thebes (TT 99), Volume I: New Kingdom*. Oxford.

Talbot, W. H. F. 1844. *The Pencil of Nature*. London.

Tavier, H. 2012. "Pour une approach matérielle et expérimentale de la peinture thébaine." In *Art and Society: Ancient and Modern Contexts of Egyptian Art: Proceedings of the International Conference held at the Museum of Fine Arts, Budapest, 13–15 May 2010*, edited by K. A. Kóthay, 209–215. Budapest.

Wenzel, G. 2007. "Die Funktion der Hilfslinien im Grab des Pepi-anch-Heni-kem (Meir A2)." *MDAIK* 63:337–358.

Wiegand, T. 1991. "Über das Fotografieren antiker Skulpturen." In *Apollon und Athena: Klassische Götterstatuen in Abgüssen und Rekonstruktionen*, edited by P. Gercke, 28–38. Kassel.

Williams, C. R. 1932. *The Decoration of the Tomb of Per-neb. The Technique and the Color Conventions*. New York.

Winkelmann, J. J. 1764. *Geschichte der Kunst des Alterthums*. Vol. 1. Dresden.

Wreszinski, W. 1923–1936. *Atlas zur altägyptischen Kulturgeschichte*. 7 vols. Leipzig.

PART II

HISTORICAL EFFORTS AT EPIGRAPHY

CHAPTER II.1

WHEN ANCIENT EGYPTIANS COPIED EGYPTIAN WORK

TAMÁS A. BÁCS

INTRODUCTION

COPYING, imitating, or referencing previous art, as in many visual cultures, if not all, was an integral part of that of ancient Egypt in all of its historic periods. Copying in the sense of visual repetition, however, has been addressed since the romantic and modernist movements in a discursive context of setting it opposite notions of variation and originality, creativity and innovation, or artistic genius. Moreover, its links to conceptions such as repetition and tradition were seen as a further unnecessary harness on inventiveness, the hallmark of artistic distinction. Although tempered today by postmodernism's appropriative stance toward copies and repetition, this negative perception understandably exerted its influence even in art education, where its use as understood by ancient rhetoricians, namely as an imitative practice, a conscious approach to improving skills had been mostly discarded.

In a culture like the ancient Egyptian, where a "perpetual dialogue with the past" (Baines 2007, 335–336) unavoidably involved the artistic, however, copying not only was a basic means of learning but also underlay the maintenance of tradition itself as well as being a highly valorized process of transmitting images and the ideas they expressed. Not surprisingly then, when engaging with the visual culture of ancient Egypt, Plato (*Laws* 2.656dl–657a2) famously expressed his admiration for what he perceived as the invariance and permanence of Egyptian artistic tradition (Davis 1979). To be understood in the context of his situating this tradition in opposition to the volatile artistic scene of contemporary Athens and in his conviction that "change, except in something evil, is extremely dangerous" (Pl. *Laws* 2.797d9—10), his idealizing perception of this permanence was predicated on how this was achieved.

Relevant foremost for what has been termed as "monumental discourse" (i.e., the Egyptian system of expression uniting or integrating hieroglyphic writing and pictorial representation, Assmann 1986, 533), Plato, though without expressing this explicitly, describes what is in effect an extreme example of a representational tradition based on copying, an ideal of reproduction.

Copying as Training

While Plato's description of Egyptian art was an ideal that never existed in this form, the distinct "canonical" rules (Davis 1989) or compositional principle, *hierotaxis* (Assmann 1987), defining the production of this art presupposes the practice of copying forming a central part of skill acquisition. While it is a commonplace to say then that copying from earlier art or artists is a recognized feature of the learning process, providing actual evidence for it is surprisingly difficult.

Pictorial evidence showing artists, artisans, or craftsmen, mostly in workshop settings, during different stages of their work is fairly well attested from most periods (e.g., Kanawati and Woods 2009, 5–27; Newberry 1893, pl. 4; Drenkhahn 1976). On the other hand, scenes related to copying are extremely rare. Only two examples have been identified, one being a fragmentary scene from the tomb of Niankhpepi that originally showed a master instructing an apprentice how to paint animals by imitating his figure style and no doubt palette (Lashien 2010, 82–84). Significantly enough, this very same scene may have actually served as a model for the other, better-known example at Beni Hasan (Lashien 2010, 83–85). The dependence of Baket III's scene on Niankhpepi's is hardly debatable, coincidentally drawing attention also to the extent to which artists were aware of earlier art and their access to and use of these as models.

The material record offers only a slightly better picture with actual objects attesting to the practice dating predominantly from the Nineteenth and Twentieth Dynasties. These so-called "teaching" ostraca (Keller 1991, 51) represent a special group within the larger corpus of figural ostraca produced by the Deir el-Medina community. In the professional context of this community, apprenticeship seems to have been the regular mode of learning crafts, particularly among draftsmen, painters, relief-carvers, and carpenters (Keller 1991, 51–54). Apprentices or assistants (both termed ḥr.y-ꜥ), within the framework of what may be seen as imitation pedagogy, would hone their skill by copying the model either drawn by or set out for them by their master. Unfortunately, however, the boundary between "sketch" and "teaching" ostraca are blurred, as indeed, many cannot be conclusively specified as belonging to one or the other category. (One straightforward example is MM 14116, Andreu-Lanoë 2013, no. 38.)

Evidence of a different type is provided by squared grids. Attested (introduced?) first in the reign of Senwosret I for human and animal figures, squared grids were used both as a proportioning method for larger compositions, especially with repetitive ones comprising multiple figures of the same type (e.g., rows of offering bearers), and as a teaching technique (Robins 1994). It is important to distinguish, however, between grids used during the creation of art and those laid over scenes well after the time of their making, mostly for the purpose of copying. Besides the well-known Saite gridlines on the Djoser panels (Friedman 1995) and those from the pyramid complex of Sahure (El Awady 2009, 49n313, 168, 219n1208), squared grids are also documented for a handful of Old Kingdom tomb chapels (Ptahshepses, Verner 1977, 29n2; Ptahhotep (I), Iymery, Pepyankh/Henykem, Kanawati 2011). That these grids only feature on parts of scenes and in certain cases, only on easily accessible wall spaces is strongly suggestive of these at least having served teaching, rather than copying, purposes (Kanawati 2011; El Awady 2009, 219n1208).

COPYING AS PRACTICE

Ancient Egyptian artworks, like other ancient ones, practically all had explicit religious, political, or social functions that motivated their manufacture. While aesthetic appreciation was sought after and practiced (e.g., so-called visitors' graffiti, Navrátilová 2007; Ragazzoli 2013), art was principally produced to serve an array of other purposes. Made to represent, articulate, or communicate, an assemblage of meanings adhered to them reflective of the society that created them. Accordingly, the practice of copying was present in all arenas of artistic media from architecture to the so-called minor arts, with variegated interaction and exchanges existing between artistic fields and crafts.

Before the advent of mass production technologies, mechanical reproduction methods were mostly confined to the minor arts where, for instance, the use of molds afforded objects to be manufactured in large quantities (e.g., bronze or faience industries). Where this was not possible, as was the case with stone statuary, reproductions of a model were created by members of the commissioned workshop (Oppenheim 2015, 27). In a strict sense, however, these cannot be considered copies, as they were all made within the context of (presumably) one workshop under one master's guidance. Such models or "master copies" were also used when the official royal image needed to be advertised and spread from a central workshop to others (e.g., bust of Nefertiti, Berlin 21.300). As in copying, in its making, casting and modeling played an important first step (e.g., workshop of Thutmose at Amarna, Laboury 2005). A significantly larger number of comparable "master copies" or apprentices' copies serving the same purpose survive from the Late and Ptolemaic periods (e.g., "sculptors' trial pieces" and votive types, Young 1964). Employing plaster casts in the process of copying other art forms was no doubt also more common than suggested by the only archaeologically attested examples, which were found in the pyramid temple of Sahure.

In its simplest form, copying could be done by direct observation without any intermediary medium of transference. Having mastered the technical procedure used to create the model, a competent copyist could then reproduce an original to almost near perfection, perfect copies being practically unattainable. Practice sketches done on the models themselves are a good testimonial of this (e.g., sketch of a jackal head in TT 60, Ragazzoli 2013, 284, fig. 10, 310).

The ability to reproduce an image from memory was an indispensable skill required of artists, a power or visual faculty that could be improved by training. Thus, there exist clear illustrations where artists would recall works, themes, or styles they had observed or were trained in, then repeat or "copy" them from memory (e.g., stela of Intef, Arnold 2015, 58–60). To satisfy the interests and expectations of his patron, the artist of the stela who worked in the distinct Theban artistic idiom of the day augmented this from memory (or memory aids) with Memphite iconographic and stylistic elements.

In order to facilitate producing some kind of copy, artists or artisans could also resort to squared grids, as the occurrence of "Late Standard" grids, or less correctly, grids of the "Saite Canon," on Old Kingdom monuments clearly show (Robins 1994, 169–170; Morkot 2003, 85–88).

No doubt, a valuable part of the working material of artists or workshops were sketches, drawings, and facsimiles on papyri and ostraca. However, identifying a sketch as a copy, basically a design or copy aid including only selective and incomplete information of the subject, and drawn with freer linework, is a particularly difficult exercise (e.g., Berlin 21442, depicting Ati, "Queen of Punt," may have been done after a pattern book rather than the relief at Deir el-Bahri (JE 14276), Breyer 2014, 88; Ćwiek 2014, 65).

The possibility that most ostraca of the type featuring rapid sketches with "stick figures" are replicas rather than aides-mémoires for future use can be also excluded in most cases (Dorn 2005, 7–11). As the western wall of the burial chamber of Kaiemankh (Junker 1940, 47–49, pls. 9–10) and the Amduat depictions of the Thutmoside royal tombs attest, the use of "stick figures" alongside cursive script was, more than anything else, specific to pattern books and ritualistic papyri (von Lieven 2007, 205–206).

Drawings and especially facsimiles, more than sketches, provided precise guidance and left little room for error. But while sketches survive in a relatively generous number, facsimiles are by far much rarer, although similarly difficult to identify. The laborious process involved in producing facsimiles meant that these were primarily made with the aim of transmitting their subjects, thus intended for archiving and not for direct transference (Haring 2015). A good example is furnished in TT 353, where Senenmut included texts and a scene originally copied from the Asyut tomb of Djefai-hapi I (Kahl 2014, 161–163). Despite the closeness of model and copy, as the inscription of Senenmut's statue from Mut Temple seems to confirm albeit indirectly, rather than direct copying, he used archival material, knowledge of which he proudly boasts (Kahl 1999, 312–313).

Characteristically, drawings on papyri or ostraca as a genre ancillary to painting and relief are viewed as mainly of preparatory function (e.g., ostraca from the tomb of Nespakashuty depicting liliform capitals with squared grids, which were intended to be included in the tomb decoration and were copied from the tomb of Montuemhat, Pischikova 2002). One exception to this are the "stelae ostraca," which mostly lack coloration, but which by all intents represent completed formal pieces (Dorn 2013, 3–8). One example is provided by an ostracon (Berlin 21447) that portrays the royal scribe, Huy, seated and writing (Andreu-Lanoë 2013, no. 39). The scribe's figure, as well as details, correspond enough to consider it a direct although creative copy from the tomb of Inherkhau, later deposited, like other "stelae ostraca," as a votive offering (Cherpion and Corteggiani 2010, 51, 59–61.).

DYNAMICS OF COPYING

Besides its role in training, copying also served a documentary function in that *record* copies were also expected to be produced. Official records made after the completion of a work are in evidence, for instance, in the celebrated cases of the New Kingdom royal tombs (e.g., plan of P. Turin 1885 recto of Ramesses IV's tomb or Ptolemaic and Roman papyri (handbooks) that detail the decoration of tomb and temple walls, Carter and Gardiner 1917; von Lieven 2007, 205–222). In many cases, however, the recurring mention of ancient models and their use may be mere rhetoric, a literary motif exploiting the authority of tradition and playing on the prestige bestowed on those who could access past knowledge (Eyre 2013, 286–315; e.g., stela of Neferhotep I, which explicitly details the act of copying, Grajetzki 2006).

While it is clear that, besides actual statues, inventories containing information about them on archival papyri or temple walls are known from eras as far apart as the Old Kingdom (pyramid temple of Khentkaus II, Vymazalová and Coppens 2011) or the Greco-Roman period (Dendera crypts, Cauville 1987), the purpose nevertheless was to conform to a *topos* with its preference for the textual over the visual that had dominated discourse on the subject throughout most periods. The same sentiment reflective of scribal *ethos* is expressed in the "Appeal to the living" type text of Ibi (Kuhlmann and Schenkel 1983, 71–73, pl. 23). By offering the chance to copy (*sph̲r*, Hagen 2011) his tomb decoration to those visitors who would have been able to read it, he aspires to immortalize himself, above and beyond the regular means provided by his mortuary cult, by becoming a model to be imitated (Eyre 2013, 288–289; Ragazzoli 2013, 285–286).

Textual descriptions of statues tend to concentrate on the (costly) materials used in their making (Hovestreyd 1997) and size (Hoffmann 2002) with only minimal reference to their form, this latter being supplied by illustrations. Drawings with squared grids of statues have survived on various media, such as drawing boards (EA 5601; Dra Abu el-Naga board, Galán 2007) or papyri (Andreu-Lanoë 2013, no. 56), but they are preparatory pieces, rather than copies.

Taking into account the full range of copying and every recorded use of reproduction that existed in ancient Egypt would exceed the limits of any article-length essay. All the more so, as scholarly research has tended to discuss copying not as a phenomenon in itself, but in the context of studies centered on such concepts as archaism, innovation, emulation, transmission of tradition, or more recently, intericonicity (Laboury 2017). Adopting a broad perspective and using examples from a wide chronological range may, within a certain framework however, illuminate the dynamics of it in the specific cultural and intellectual environment of Egyptian visual culture.

One of the principal issues when considering the nature of models is the matter of accessibility. The model has to be encountered in some manner for it to become the object of imitation or copying. The extent to which visibility could influence reception is well exemplified by the king Sekhemre-shedtawy Sobekemsaf of the Seventeenth Dynasty, an obscure ruler in the eyes of modern historiography otherwise, but who was described at the end of the Twentieth Dynasty as a "great ruler," precisely because his "(ten) monuments in Karnak" could be still cited as works to be admired (Peet 1930, 41). Awareness or ignorance, then, of what was and what was not accessible or visible in any given period seriously impacts the way in which artistic production can be evaluated (Bács 2017a). Is a lost older original being mediated through a copy or is it the first materialization of an innovation, for instance, is a question fundamentally influencing scholarly histories of Egyptian art.

That Egyptian landscapes and their monuments served as a source for the copying of texts is well attested in many periods, and even scribal "school excursions" are in evidence to different areas of the Memphite necropolis during the Thutmoside period, for example (Navrátilová 2007, 75–76). Like scribes, artists and artisans also left graffiti as direct testimony of their visiting particular monuments (The Epigraphic Survey 1980, 76–77; Bács 2017b). However, establishing that an artist or artists were familiar with specific models and the degree to which they used them as such at any given time relies on the recognition of dependence.

The way in which the meaning of monuments and their physical setting could be played on and exploited can be seen in the series of Amenhotep son of Hapu's scribe statues he set up at Karnak Temple. As an act of self-fashioning, he succeeded by copying and at the same time reviving a statue type used by Montuhotep, vizier under Senwosret I, to associate himself with both the first great builder of the temple as well as the sacred site itself (Sourouzian 1991).

Copying was also a way of relating to the distinguishing meanings and values bound up with a place that the art therein also projected. It was a manner in which the patron or commissioner of the work could identify with and embrace the tradition epitomized by it and appropriate the identity deriving from it (e.g., Freed 2000, 212). Sometimes the borrowing of a single motif was also sufficient for formal purposes (e.g., featuring an Old Kingdom wig-type in elite New Kingdom private tombs, Hofmann 2004, 146, fig. 171). Incidentally, as the tomb of Tia and Tia shows, this gesture of reverence toward the past was apparently made in conjunction with the dismantling of perhaps the very mastabas that provided the models for building material (Harpur 1994).

Physical access to models was not the only restrictive force circumscribing what was available for copying. The status of both commissioning patron and artist was equally determinant at any time period, as it could define the range of models the latter could work with. As the iconography of coffins of the famous Roman-period Soter family (c. 90–140 CE) attests, it seems safe to assume that decoration may have been shown or given to the artist by the patron or an informed representative of the patron. A number of rare iconographic elements, schemes, and the layout of several of the coffins have proven to derive from Ptolemaic decoration of the Deir el-Medina Hathor Temple, which offered only restricted access, however, as it was still a functioning institution when the coffins were made (Riggs 2006).

Access to models also came through a patron's ability to employ painters, sculptors, relief carvers, or other craftsmen who had privileged knowledge of and access to desired prototypes and templates, such as Amenhotep Sise's employment of the painter of Amun, Userhat, and Imiseba, who secured the services of the chief draftsman of Deir el-Medina, Amenhotep. Both individuals were chosen by their patrons because they could transfer through copying without considerable alteration iconography of royal temple scenes to the walls of their own private mortuary monuments (Laboury 2015; Bács 2001; also, Ser-Djehuty, who produced statues for himself that not only relied on past types and styles but also themselves became models that were widely copied, Klotz 2015).

The need for perfect copies or perceptual sameness was called for in situations when a duplicate was needed to replace an original, as an act of restoration, or when the copy was meant to be recognized as a purposeful repeat of the model. In the former, the model's meanings are transferred to the copy, while in the latter these are designed and expected to become demonstrably shared between the two. By faithfully reproducing Thutmose I's tableau on Hagr el-Merwa, a rock outcrop near Kurgus, but in his own name, Thutmose III was in essence making an assertive statement of equaling and identifying with his illustrious ancestor (Davies 2003, 23–31). As Thutmose III's intent in this case was not to emulate in the sense of outshine, but to repeat through copying his ancestor's political and military achievements, he chose the appropriate form of his visual communication accordingly.

Incidentally, Thutmose III also provides illustrative evidence for copying with the objective of restoration, conceived of as a ritual practice set within the framework of *wḥm mswt*, "Repeating birth." Associating himself with Senwosret I and his similarly named program of restoration/renovation, Thutmose III had matching scenes of himself and the king of the Twelfth Dynasty cut on the southern wall of the so-called Palace of Maat in Karnak Temple that were actually faithful copies of Senwosret's original albeit demolished scene (Habachi 1985; Gabolde 1998, §53–61; see Figure II.1.1). The rationale of such copying was to ensure that replacing elements of restored or even completely rebuilt temples or shrines did not unfavorably affect its meaning, a risk not to be underestimated regarding any cultic installation (see also Sekhemre Swadjtawy's reproduction at Medamud of a lintel of Senwosret III's, Cottevieille-Graudet 1933, pl. 5).

The practice of copying was more receptive of invention than it is credited for by modernist perceptions (e.g., interaction and dialogue between royal and nonroyal funerary art, Harpur 1987; van Walsem 2005). The elite and subelite tombs produced from the Fourth to the Eighth Dynasties display an extremely high variability and individuality in their decorative programs despite using a limited set of themes (van Walsem 2008). Of these, several have long histories of use (e.g., "the fording of cattle," Arnold 2008). Innovative tombs, where themes and/or subthemes first appeared (e.g., the vizier Ptahhotep (I), Kanawati 2011; Ti, Beaux 2011; Mereruka, Pieke 2011), naturally served as models, but once copied, these were then recopied from their secondary sources. A telling example is the tomb of Nimaatre at Giza (Roth 1995, 127–134) that

FIGURE II.1.1. Relief of Senwosret I reproduced by Thutmose III. © CNRS-CFEETK 175483/A. Chéné.

included at least one copied scene from the contemporary tomb of Senedjemib-Mehi only to have at least three other tomb-owners, Nefermesdjerkhufu, Rawer (II), and Kaiemankh, in turn copy from his (Bolshakov 2006, 53–59).

While attempting to identically reproduce the model is not unattested (e.g., Nisutnefer, who borrowed, albeit erroneously, from Seshathotep, Junker 1938, 68–77; Bolshakov 2006, 39–43), tombs in general reveal a high level of variation in their treat-ment of depictive content (see Figure II.1.2). The mode of copying this reflects then is best described as differential reproduction, the dynamics of which encouraged variation as an integral part of the copying process. Indeed, this mode also created a context in which displays of model emulation (*aemulatio*) were encouraged, an aspiration and technique not only merging the seemingly contradictory ambition of striving for corre-spondence and difference simultaneously but also implying competition with models defined as normative or ideal.

In ancient Egyptian visual culture, copying provided the means that kept the various artistic fields and their techniques advancing. It also created, however, the context in which "archaism" could exist, a "cultural behaviour" (Török 2011, 29) that exerted its influence most perceptively during the Twenty-fifth and Twenty-sixth Dynasties, but one that was neither restricted to those periods, nor exclusively to art (e.g., Bothmer 1960, xxxvii–xxxviii; Manuelian 1994; Assmann 1996, 375–382; Morkot 2003). Generally under-stood as a reversion to the past, for "archaizing" to apply to any work of art, the model has to belong to a verifiably discontinued or superseded tradition, regardless of the distance

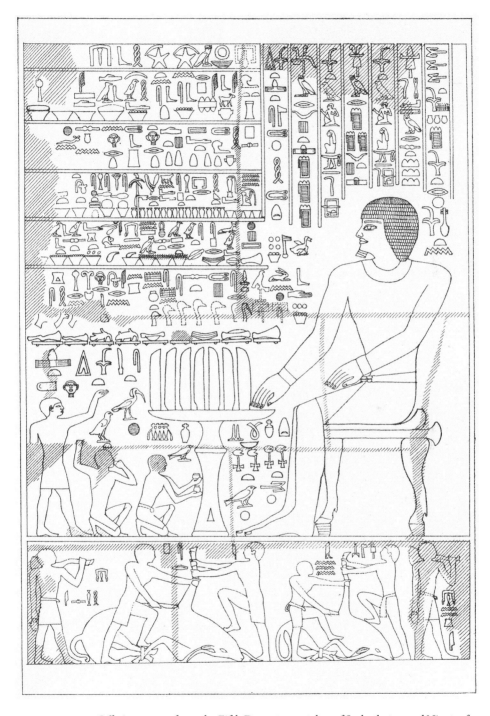

FIGURE II.1.2. Offering scenes from the Fifth Dynasty mastabas of Seshathotep and Nisutnefer. After Junker 1938, 74–75, fig. 9a–b.

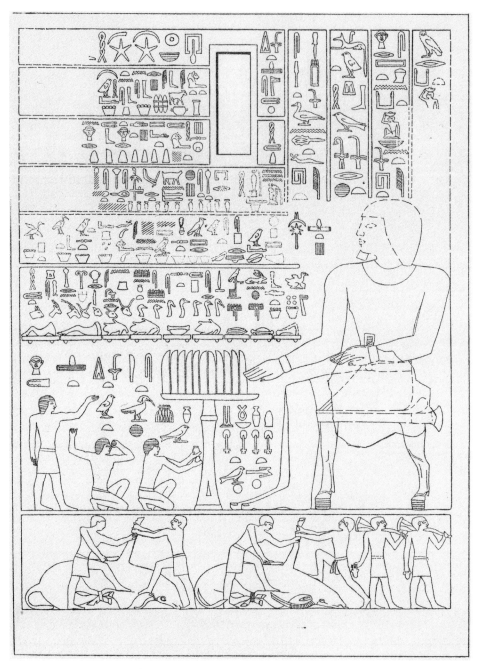

FIGURE II.1.2. Continued

in time separating it from the copy. In contrast, the designation "archaistic" has a more restricted referential meaning, pertaining specifically to artworks of the Twenty-ninth and Thirtieth Dynasties that imitated ones of the early Twenty-sixth Dynasty, which were themselves inspired by Old Kingdom models (Bothmer 1960, xxxvii).

In some cases, where past art was referenced or where artists can be seen consciously drawing directly from ancient works, this interest in ancient art originated in the aspiration to continue a tradition at the point it was abandoned. Thus in the context of self-positioning, the design of Senwosret I's pyramid complex at Lisht, rather than being a revival, was intended as a statement of carrying on the tradition interrupted at the end of the Sixth Dynasty (Baines 2007, 195). Similarly, the near-faithful transcriptions of local Theban Middle Kingdom tomb art in the early Eighteenth Dynasty was for the benefit of declaring those elites to be the immediate and legitimate successors of an idealized past age (Bács 2006, 6–7; Laboury 2013, 23–25).

The dominant artistic tendency of pre-Kushite art of the Third Intermediate Period was structured by the use of Thutmoside, "Tuthmosid-influenced earlier Ramesside," and late Ramesside prototypes (Fazzini 1997, 114–115). A different means of self-fashioning emerged, however, among the royalty and elite in the later part of the period in both Upper and Lower Egypt, one that turned with fresh interest toward the more ancient art of the Old and Middle Kingdoms (Becker 2012).

During the floruit of "archaism," the Twenty-fifth and Twenty-sixth Dynasties, the availability of models was again decisive in the selection of past works for those who recorded, collected, and imitated them. Although both Memphis and Thebes offered the possibility of identification with a revered past through association with ancient art, their abundant if damaged remains of ancient sculpture and architecture originated from different periods. In the north, the interest in and focus on predominantly Old Kingdom art was undoubtedly enhanced by the considerable remains of the Memphite necropolis (Morkot 2003). In Thebes, in contrast, Middle and New Kingdom models would have been available to its elite locally (Morkot 2003, 89–93).

For artists versed in this "archaizing" mode of presentation being in great demand and traveling between capitals, the most frequently cited example is Taharqa's trampling sphinx scene at Kawa with its origins in the scene in Sahure's pyramid temple (Morkot 2003, 81–84). Furthermore, perhaps one or more of the very same artists aided in the decorating of the Theban cenotaph of Harwa (Tiradritti 2013). Evidently, Harwa's so-called *tjeref*-dance scene is, to cite only one illustrative example, an emulative repetition of the one in the Giza tomb of Iymery, as underscored by the almost identical disposition of the accompanying hieroglyphic inscription (Tiradritti, forthcoming; see Figure II.1.3).

What lent "archaizing" Late Period copying its distinctiveness was basically its being eclectic imitation. It expressed a mode of repetition based on a well-thought-out selection of sources. It appealed to a conceptual and aesthetic mood that looked to encompass the entire repertoire of previous art and "living in citations" (Assmann 1993) and visualized the expectations of an audience conversant in knowledge, understanding, and appreciation of the references.

FIGURE II.1.3. Cenotaph of Harwa (TT 37); early seventh century BCE. Detail of the *tjeref*-dance scene. Rear wall of the courtyard, north portico. Photo by G. Lovera; © Associazione Culturale per lo Studio dell'Egitto e del Sudan ONLUS.

Whether considering the statuary or two-dimensional art of the period, "archaizing" reveals itself to have been rooted in a culture not only sensitive to how different period's styles worked, but also exploiting their different expressive values. Copying thus focused on schemes, themes, and specific details, as well as styles and stylistic traits. The monumental mortuary complexes of the Theban elite are quite explicit in how style was used to make compatible copies of a variety of scenes or vignettes from older tombs or from the Offering Chapel of Hatshepsut's Deir el-Bahri temple (Erman 1914). At the same time, a gradual shift from a preference for Old Kingdom style in Harwa's tomb to a more accentuated reliance on Eighteenth Dynasty styles can be seen in that of Montuemhat (Russmann 1994), further amplified subsequently in those of Basa (Assmann 1973), Ibi (Kuhlmann and Schenkel 1983), and Pabasa.

BIBLIOGRAPHY

Andreu-Lanoë, G. 2013. *L'art du contour: Le dessin dans l'Egypte ancienne*. Paris.
Arnold, D. 2008. "Egyptian Art—A Performing Art?" In *Servant of Mut: Studies in Honor of Richard A. Fazzini*, edited by S. H. D'Auria, 1–18. PdÄ 28. Leiden.

Arnold, D. 2015. "Stela of the Overseer of the Fortress Intef." In *Ancient Egypt Transformed: The Middle Kingdom*, edited by A. Oppenheim, D. Arnold, D. Arnold, and K. Yamamoto, 58–60. New York.

Assmann, J. 1973. *Grabung in Asasif 1963–1970, 2: Das Grab des Basa (Nr. 389) in der thebanishen Nekropole*. AVDAIK 6. Mainz.

Assmann, J. 1986. "'Viel Stil am Nil?' Ägypten und das Problem des Kulturstils." In *Stil: Geschichte und Funktionen eines kulturwissenschaftlichen Diskurselements*, edited by H. U. Gumbrecht and K. L. Pfeiffer, 519–537. Frankfurt.

Assmann, J. 1987. "Hierotaxis: Textkonstitution und Bildkomposition in der ägyptischen Kunst und Literatur." In *Form und Mass: Beiträge zu Sprache, Literatur und Kunst des alten Äypten. Festschrift für Gerhard Fecht*, edited by J. Osing, and G. Dreyer, 18–42. Wiesbaden.

Assmann, J. 1993 "Zitathaftes Leben: Thomas Mann und die Phänomenologie der kulturellen Erinnerung." *Thomas Mann Jahrbuch* 6:134–158.

Assmann, J. 1996. *Ägypten: Eine Sinngeschichte*. Munich.

El Awady, T. 2009. *Sahure—The Pyramid Causeway. History and Decoration Program in the Old Kingdom*. Abusir XVI. Prague.

Bács, T. A. 2001. "Art as Material for Later Art: The Case of Theban Tomb 65." In *Colour and Painting in Ancient Egypt*, edited by W. V. Davies, 94–100. London.

Bács, T. A. 2006. "The Tip of a Horn: The Possible Origin of an Iconographic Theme in the Elite Tombs of New Kingdom Thebes." *AAASH* 46:3–16.

Bács, T. A. 2017a. "Model Transfer and Style Repetition: On the Representations of the Processional Bark of Amun in TT 65." In *The Cultural Manifestations of Religious Experience: Studies in Honour of Boyo G. Ockinga*, edited by C. Di Biase-Dyson and Leonie Donovon, 173–184. ÄAT 85. Münster.

Bács, T. A. 2017b. "Traditions Old and New: Artistic Production of the Late Ramesside Period." In *(Re)productive Traditions in Ancient Egypt*, edited by T. Gillen, 305–332. AegLeo 10. Liège.

Baines, J. 2007. *Visual and Written Culture in Ancient Egypt*. Oxford.

Beaux, N. 2011. "The Decoration of the Portico from *Ti's Mastaba* at *Saqqara*: An Innovative Introduction to the Tomb." In *Abusir and Saqqara in the Year 2010/1*, edited by M. Bárta, F. Coppens, and J. Krejči, 223–232. Prague.

Becker, M. 2012. *Identität und Krise: Erinnerungskulturen im Ägypten der 22. Dynastie*. SAK Bh 13. Hamburg.

Bolshakov, A. O. 2006. "Arrangement of Murals as a Principle of Old Kingdom Tomb Decoration." In *Dekorierte Grabanlagen im Alten Reich: Methodik und Interpretation*, edited by M. Fitzenreiter and M. Herb, 37–60. IBAES 6. London.

Bothmer, B. V. 1960. *Egyptian Sculpture of the Late Period 700 BC to AD 100*. New York.

Breyer, F. 2014. "Vorlagen zur 'Punthalle' von Dair al-Baḥrī aus dem Alten Reich: philologisch-epigraphische, textkritische und ikonographische cruces im Zusammenspiel von Darstellungen und Inschriften." *SAK* 43:47–91.

Carter, H., and A. H. Gardiner. 1917. "The Tomb of Ramesses IV and the Turin Plan of a Royal Tomb." *JEA* 4:130–158.

Cauville, S. 1987. "Les statues culturelles de Dendera d'après les inscriptions pariétales." *BIFAO* 87:73–117.

Cherpion, N. and J. P. Corteggiani. 2010. *La tombe d'Inherkhaouy (TT 359) à Deir El-Medina*. MIFAO 128. Cairo.

Cottevieille-Giraudet, R. 1933. *Rapport sur les fouilles de Médamoud (1931): Les monuments du Moyen Empire*. FIFAO 9/1. Cairo.

Ćwiek, A. 2014. "Old and Middle Kingdom Tradition in the Temple of Hatshepsut at Deir el-Bahari." *ET* 27:62–93.

Davies, W. V. 2003. "La frontière méridionale de l'Empire: Les Égyptiens à Kurgus." *BSFE* 157:23–44.

Davis, W. M. 1979. "Plato on Egyptian Art." *JEA* 65:121–127.

Davis, W. M. 1989. *The Canonical Tradition in Ancient Egyptian Art*. New York.

Dorn, A. 2005. "*Men at Work*: Zwei Ostraka aus dem Tal der Könige mit nicht-kanonischen Darstellungen von Arbeitern." *MDAIK* 61:1–11.

Dorn, A. 2013. "Un cas particulier: Les ostraca figurés." *LDA* numéro spéciale 1:24–29.

Drenkhahn, R 1976. *Die Handwerker und ihre Tätigkeiten im alten Ägypten*. ÄA 31. Wiesbaden.

The Epigraphic Survey 1980. *The Tomb of Kheruef*. OIP 102. Chicago.

Erman, A. 1914. "Saitische Kopien aus Deir el bahri." *ZÄS* 62:90–95.

Eyre, C. 2013. *The Use of Documents in Pharaonic Egypt*. Oxford.

Fazzini, R. A. 1997. "Several Objects, and Some Aspects of the Art of the Third Intermediate Period." In *Chief of Seers: Egyptian Studies in Memory of Cyril Aldred*, edited by E. Goring, N. Reeves, and J. Ruffle, 113–137. London.

Friedman, F. D. 1995. "The Underground Relief Panels of King Djoser at the Step Pyramid Complex." *JARCE* 32:1–42.

Freed, R.E. 2000. "Observations on the Dating and Decoration of the Tombs of Ihy and Hetep at Saqqara." In *Abusir and Saqqara in the Year 2000*, edited by M. Bárta and J. Krejčí, 208–211. Prague.

Gabolde, L. 1998. Le "grand château d'Amon" de Sésostris Ier à Karnak. MAIBL 17. Paris.

Galán, J. 2007. "An Apprentice's Board from Dra Abu el-Naga." *JEA* 93:95–116.

Grajetzki, W. 2006. "Featured Pharaoh: Neferhotep I." *AncEg* 6:15–19.

Habachi, L. 1985. "Devotion of Tuthmosis III to His Predecessors: A Propos of a Meeting of Sesostris I with His Courtiers." In *Mélanges Gamal Eddin Mokhtar*, vol. 1, 349–359. BdE 97/1. Cairo.

Hagen, F. 2011. "The Hieratic Dockets on the Cuneiform Tablets from Amarna." *JEA* 97:214–216.

Haring, B. J. J. 2015. "Hieratic Drafts for Hieroglyphic Texts?" In *Ägyptologische "Binsen"-Weisheiten I–II. Neue Forschungen und Methoden der Hieratistik. Akten zweier Tagungen in Mainz im April 2011 und März 2013*, edited by U. Verhoeven, 67–84. AAWLM 14. Stuttgart.

Harpur, Y. 1987. *Decoration in Egyptian Tombs of the Old Kingdom: Studies in Orientation and Scene Content*. London.

Harpur, Y. 1994. "Stone Pillaging for the New Kingdom Tombs at South Saqqara." *Prudentia* 26 (1):1–15.

Hofmann, E. 2004. *Bilder im Wandel: Die Kunst der ramessidischen Privatgräber*. Theben 17. Mainz.

Hoffmann, F. 2002. "Measuring Egyptian Statues." In *Under One Sky: Astronomy and Mathematics in the Ancient Near East*, edited by J. Steele and A. Imhausen, 109–119. AOAT 297. Münster.

Hovestreyd, W. 1997. "A Letter to the King relating to the Foundation of a Statue (P. Turin 1879 vso.)." *LingAeg* 5:107–121.

Junker, H. 1938. *Gîza III. Die Mastabas der vorgeschrittenen V. Dynastie auf dem Westfriedhof*. Vienna.

Junker, H. 1940. *Gîza IV: Die Mastaba des K3jm'nh (Kai-em-anch)*. Vienna.

Kahl, J. 1999. *Siut-Theben: Zur Wertschätzung von Traditionen im alten Ägypten*. PdÄ 13. Leiden.

Kahl, J. 2014. "Assiut—Theben—Tebtynis: Wissensbewegungen von der Ersten Zwischenzeit und dem Mittleren Reich bis in Römische Zeit." *SAK* 43:159–172.

Kanawati, N. 2011. "Art and Gridlines: The Copying of Old Kingdom Scenes in Later Periods." In *Abusir and Saqqara in the Year 2010/2*, edited by M. Bárta, F. Coppens, and J. Krejčí, 483–496. Prague.

Kanawati, N., and A. Woods. 2009. *Artists in the Old Kingdom: Techniques and Achievements.* Cairo.

Keller, C. A. 1991. "Royal Painters: Deir el-Medina in Dynasty XIX." In *Fragments of a Shattered Visage: The Proceedings of the International Symposium on Ramesses the Great*, edited by E. Bleiberg and R. E. Freed, 50–86. Memphis.

Klotz, D. 2015. "The Cuboid Statue of Ser-Djehuty, Master Sculptor in Karnak." *RdE* 66:51–109.

Kuhlmann, K. P., and W. Schenkel. 1983. *Das Grab des Ibi, Obergutsverwalters der Gottesgemahlin des Amun (Thebanisches Grab Nr 36), Vol. 1: Beschreibung der unteriridischen Kult-und Bestattungsanlage.* AVDAIK 15. Mainz.

Laboury, D. 2005. "Dans l'atelier du sculpteur Thoutmose." In *La langue dans tous ses états: Michel Malaise in honorem*, edited by C. Cannuyer, 289–300. AOB 18. Brussels.

Laboury, D. 2013. "Citations et usages de l'art du Moyen Empire à l'époque thoutmoside." In *Vergangenheit und Zukunft: Studien zum historischen Bewusstsein in der Thutmosidenzeit*, edited by S. Bickel, 11–28. AH 22. Basel.

Laboury, D. 2015. "On the Master Painter of the Tomb of Amenhotep Sise, Second High Priest of Amun under the Reign of Thutmose IV (TT 75)." In *Joyful in Thebes: Egyptological Studies in Honor of Betsy M. Bryan*, edited by R. Jasnow and K. M. Cooney, 327–337. Atlanta.

Laboury, D. 2017. "Tradition and Creativity: Toward a Study of Intericonicity in Ancient Egyptian Art." In *(Re)productive Traditions in Ancient Egypt*, edited by T. Gillen, 229–258. AegLeo 10. Liège.

Lashien, M. 2010. "Artists' Training in the Old and Middle Kingdoms." *GM* 224:81–84.

Lieven, A. von. 2007. *Grundriß des Laufes der Sterne: Das sogenannte Nutbuch.* CP 8. CNIP 31. Copenhagen.

Manuelian, P. Der. 1994. *Living in the Past: Studies in Archaism of the Egyptian Twenty-sixth Dynasty.* London.

Morkot, R. 2003. "Archaism and Innovation in Art from the New Kingdom to the Twenty-sixth Dynasty." In *"Never Had the Like Occurred": Egypt's View of Its Past*, edited by J. Tait, 79–99. London.

Navrátilová, H. 2007. *The Visitors' Graffiti of Dynasties XVIII and XIX in Abusir and Northern Saqqara.* Prague.

Newberry, P. E. 1893. *Beni Hasan, Part II.* London.

Oppenheim, A. 2015. "Artists and Workshops: The Complexity of Creation." In *Ancient Egypt Transformed: The Middle Kingdom*, edited by A. Oppenheim, D. Arnold, D. Arnold, and K. Yamamoto, 23–27. New York.

Peet, T. E. 1930. *The Great Tomb Robberies of the Twentieth Egyptian Dynasty.* Vols. I–II. Oxford.

Pieke, G. 2011. "The Evidence of Images: Art and Working Techniques in the Mastaba of Mereruka." In *Old Kingdom, New Perspectives: Egyptian Art and Archaeology 2750–2150 BC*, edited by N. Strudwick and H. Strudwick, 216–228. Oxford.

Pischikova, E. 2002. "Two Ostraka from Deir el-Bahri and the Lily Flower Motif in Twenty-sixth Dynasty Theban Tombs." *JARCE* 39:197–206.

Ragazzoli, C. 2013. "The Social Creation of a Scribal Place: The Visitors' Inscriptions in the Tomb Attributed to Antefiqer (TT 60) (with newly recorded graffiti)." *SAK* 42:269–323.

Riggs, C. 2006. "Archaism and Artistic Sources in Roman Egypt: The Coffins of the Soter Family and the Temple of Deir el-Medina." *BIFAO* 106:315–332.

Robins, G. 1994. *Proportion and Style in Ancient Egyptian Art*. Austin.

Roth, A. M. 1995. *A Cemetery of Palace Attendants*. GMas 6. Boston.

Russmann, E. R. 1994. "Relief Decoration in the Tomb of Mentuemhat (TT 34)." *JARCE* 31:1–19.

Sourouzian, H. 1991. "La statue d'Amenhotep fils de Hapou, âgé, un chef d'oeuvre de la XVIIIe dynastie." *MDAIK* 47:341–355.

Tiradritti, F. 2013. "The Cenotaph of Harwa: Archaism and Innovation." *EA* 43:17–20.

Tiradritti, F. Forthcoming. "Memphis—Kawa—Thebes: On the Origin of the 25th Dynasty Theban Renaissance." In *Artists and Colour in Ancient Egypt, Proceedings of the Colloquium held in Montepulciano, August 22nd–24th, 2008*, edited by V. Angenot and F. Tiradritti. Montepulciano.

Török, L. 2011. *Adoption and Adaptation: The Sense of Culture Transfer between Ancient Nubia and Egypt*. Budapest.

Verner, M. 1977. *The Mastaba of Ptahshepses*. Prague.

Vymazalová, H., and F. Coppens. 2011. "Statues and Rituals for Khentkaus II: A Reconsideration of Some Papyrus Fragments from the Queen's Funerary Complex." In *Abusir and Saqqara in the Year 2010/2*, edited by M. Bárta, F. Coppens, and J. Krejči, 785–799. Prague.

Walsem, R. van. 2005. *Iconography of Old Kingdom Elite Tombs: Analysis and Interpretation, Theoretical and Methodological Aspects*. MVEOL 35. Leiden.

Walsem, R. van. 2008. *MastaBase: A Research Tool for the Study of the Secular or "Daily Life" Scenes and Their Accompanying Texts in the Elite Tombs of the Memphite Area in the Old Kingdom*. Leuven.

Young, E. 1964. "Sculptors' Models or Votives? In Defense of a Scholarly Tradition." *MMAB* 22:247–256.

WHEN CLASSICAL AUTHORS ENCOUNTERED EGYPTIAN EPIGRAPHY

JEAN WINAND

FOR centuries, Egypt attracted Greeks and Romans' attention more than any other countries of the *oikoumene*. In classical times and increasingly later, Egypt became an icon whence all wisdom was supposed to come. According to tradition, the greatest Greek philosophers visited Egypt to learn from the priests. Pythagoras was even credited with speaking Egyptian (Diog. Laert. 8.3). Among various topics, language and script(s) were regularly discussed, but most often in a marginal way (Marestaing 1913; Winter 1991; Iversen 1994; Winand 2005; for the relative lack of interest in other [?] foreign languages, see Thissen 1993, 240–241). It is symptomatic to observe that those who treated the matter in some detail were native Egyptians.

THE CORPUS

The list of authors who mentioned—however briefly—ancient Egyptian writings or language might at first sight seem impressive. Actually, the 120 different authors I have been able to identify can be reduced to 79 once very short notes and insignificant mentions have been dropped. The overwhelming majority (72 versus 7) unsurprisingly wrote in Greek. The time range covers nearly two millennia, from the fifth century BCE to the fourteenth century CE (Table II.2.1).

The time of composition, of course, greatly matters to assess the relevance of a text. As time passed, the number and quality of the informants—especially in Egypt—dramatically declined. After the second century CE, the number of those who still had a detailed knowledge of the written tradition had severely been reduced, to become virtually nonexistent after the fourth century.

Table II.2.1. Chronological Distribution of the Literary Sources, by Century

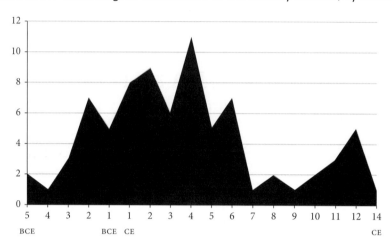

A significant number of authors were born and lived in Egypt, while many others visited Egypt and had the opportunity to discuss with Egyptian informants. A third category was never connected with the Nile Valley, but lived in places like Rome, where Egyptian monuments (genuine or not) could be seen and Egyptian intellectuals could be met. After the Arab conquest (640/1), knowledge of ancient Egyptian traditions increasingly rested on previous literature. The access to genuine monuments and artifacts became drastically limited and was to remain so until the Renaissance.

While the political situation can explain some occasional attitudes toward Egyptian culture, for example, in Rome in the aftermath of the battle of Actium, the sociocultural background of those who had to deal with Egypt and its traditions played a significant role. From the second century CE, the number of Christian authors rapidly increased. While they often—but not systematically—targeted old pagan traditions, they took a more polemical position toward neo-Platonic philosophers whom they had quickly identified as a direct and more dangerous threat to the new religion. The same kind of controversial attitude is also perceptible with the Jewish authors who occasionally dealt with Egypt.

The authors who constitute the corpus illustrate a remarkable diversity of genres:

1. Geographers and historians were foremost interested in reporting facts, more or less objectively, often mentioning their informants and their sources, but rarely trying to make sense of these facts within a general theory of human evolution.
2. Philosophers, especially Platonic and neo-Platonic ones (often engaged in polemics with early Christian theologians), tried to integrate hieroglyphic writing—and to a lesser extent Egyptian language—into a general epistemology. So also did people who had adopted more or less esoteric ways of wisdom, like alchemists or hermetic and gnostic authors.
3. Even if they showed partiality in their judgments, Christian theologians are another worthwhile category, for they are often our only source for pagan texts that are now lost.

4. Scientists, including people interested in natural sciences, physicians, and astronomers, constitute a minor category for the issues discussed here. They were mainly preoccupied with lexicon, giving Greek or Latin equivalents of Egyptian words, most often plants or animals.

5. Interest in vocabulary is obviously present with lexicographers, commentators, and epitomists, who constitute a large part of the Byzantine corpus.

6. Finally, and this is quite understandably one of our most precious sources, a small group of indigenous authors probably had a direct knowledge of Egyptian writing(s) and language(s) (for these treatises as the manifestation of antiquarian taste, see Fournet 2016). Except for Horapollo, whose work has at least partially come directly down to us, they are unfortunately known indirectly, by quotes, summaries, or translations.

Coptic sources are not discussed in this chapter. The Copts took no interest in the ancient Egyptian writings, which they saw as an evil abomination that must ultimately be destroyed (Hahn, Emmel, and Gotter 2008; Kristensen 2013). What comes closest to a description of how hieroglyphs superficially looked is a passage by the famous monk Shenoute (fourth–fifth century CE) à propos of an ancient shrine: "and if previously it is prescriptions for murdering man's soul that are therein, written with blood and not with ink alone—there is nothing else portrayed for them except the likeness of the snakes and scorpions, the dogs and cats, the crocodiles and frogs, the foxes, the other reptiles, the beasts and birds, the cattle, etc.; furthermore, the likeness of the sun and the moon and all the rest, all their things being nonsense and humbug" (transl. Young 1981).

The Sources

Quite understandably, the quality of the information given by the Greek and Latin authors is directly dependent on the kind of sources they had access to. I here first consider the monuments and artifacts, before turning to the informants.

For those who lived or stayed for a while in Egypt, monuments bearing hieroglyphic inscriptions were everywhere. Until the second century CE, the Ptolemaic and then the Roman rulers maintained an active building program, producing temples, obelisks, stelae, and statues. All these monuments and artifacts were covered with inscriptions that presupposed a mastery over the ancient writing systems and textual traditions. After the second century CE, a marked and irreversible decline in the knowledge of hieroglyphs can be observed (Sternberg-el Hotabi 1994).

Outside Egypt, genuine monuments were found only sparsely, with the exception of Italy, especially Rome, where there was a concentration of imported monuments and objects. Rome and other places in Italy also witnessed the production of monuments directly inspired from Egypt (Winter 1991, 85–87). While some inevitably displayed only a superficial layer of Egyptian culture, in the vein of Egyptomania, others bore witness of the skills of Egyptian specialists who lived in Italy (Iversen 1994).

As can be easily guessed, the Greek and Latin authors were foremost attracted by hieroglyphic inscriptions or iconographic compositions that were closely linked in their mind to the writing system. It seems dubious that they had any informed access to the papyrological material, but some descriptions seem to indicate that at least some had the opportunity of seeing papyri.

The quality of the Greek and Latin authors' informants was, of course, of utmost importance. Occasional visitors probably passed through various hands of more or less specialized or scrupulous guides (dragomen) as they strolled across the Nile Valley. In Greek and Roman times, the knowledge of the ancient Egyptian writings, especially the hieroglyphic script, was deposited in the hands of a handful of the so-called *hierogrammateis* (Derchain 1991). While some authors certainly had the chance of being directly in touch with these famous Egyptian scholars in Egypt or elsewhere, others probably must have relied on second- or third-rate information.

The majority of the authors could not of course read the Egyptian texts, but were wholly dependent on previous sources, as shown by Eusebius (*Praep. evang.* 10.13.1), for instance, who wrote that as he could not use himself the original texts, he had to follow Manetho, who had a direct access to the Egyptian sources.

The Terminology

The terminology we still use in modern Egyptology to name the different types of writings (hieroglyphic, hieratic, and Demotic) come from the Greek tradition. In this section, I first give an overview of the terms found in the Greek and Latin literature, before turning to the practice found in the documentary texts coming from Egypt.

The Literary Sources

The Egyptian writing was sometimes referred to under the generic label "Egyptian letters" (αἰγύπτια γράμματα; Herodotus 2.106 and 125). A more specific, much rarer, term, which alludes to the specific use of the hieroglyphs in epigraphy, was "engraving" (χαράγματα αἰγύπτια, see Julian, *Epistle* 59.17). The Egyptian writing was also commonly called by the Greeks the "sacred letters" (ἱερὰ γράμματα, see Diodorus 1.81) in reference to what they perceived was its main raison d'être. In most cases, this denomination clearly refers to hieroglyphic and/or hieratic texts, as opposed to non-religious ones, but it was sometimes used as a cover term without distinction.

The adjective ἱερογλυφικός is regularly used in Imperial and Byzantine times. Its Latin correspondent *hieroglyphicus* is attested in Ammianus Marcellinus (17.4.8), who also opted, without apparent reason, for the variant *hierographicus* (22.15.30), and

Macrobius (*Sat.* 1.19.13). There is also a related adverb, ἱερογλυφικῶς, which seems to be a technical term in the magical texts. These texts, whose lexical creativity is well-known, sometimes used the adverb ἱερογλυφιστί, which seems to refer to the language, more than the script: "I invoke you, Lord, in bird-like language (ὀρνεογλυφιστί) 'arai,' in hieroglyph-like language (ἱερογλυφιστί) 'lailam'" (*PGM* XIII.81). Finally, there is a verb ἱερογλυφεῖν "draw hieroglyphs" found in "Horapollo" (2.34) and late Byzantine sources like Eustathius and Michael Italicus.

George Syncellus (seventh–eighth century; 41.3–5) seems the only one to make a real distinction between ἱερογλυφικός and ἱερογραφικός. He reports that Manetho used stelae written in a sacred dialect in sacred letters (ἱερογραφικοῖς γράμμασι) by Thoth, which were later translated in hieroglyphs (γράμμασι ἱερογλυφικοῖς). In this text, the first term seems more neutral, being disconnected from the technical process of engraving.

The adjective ἱερατικός can be used in a general and a technical way. The former is the most common. As noted by Damascius, *hieratike*, as opposed to philosophy, means the priestly art (*In Phaed.* 1.172), the service of the gods (θεῶν θεραπεία, *Isid.* 3.9). In some rare cases, *hieratike* seems to have a technical meaning pointing to the cursive writing. In Olympiodoros the alchemist (*Comm. in Arist. Graeca* 2.80.9–11), a distinction is made between what is engraved on the obelisks and what is on/in the hieratic writings. As the subject matter concerns in both cases religious matters, it is tempting to take the latter expression as referring to what Egyptologists in a narrow sense call hieratic writing or cursive hieroglyphs. The same kind of ambiguity occurs in a magical papyrus (*PGM* I.233–237), where the expression λαβὼν χάρτην ἱερατικὸν "(lit.) taking a hieratic sheet of papyrus" can refer to a papyrus covered with hieratic signs or used for the cult. As the purpose of hieratic texts had at the time become exclusively religious, it is probably useless to give an univocal answer to this question.

A special use of the adjective *hieraticus* is made by Pliny (*HN* 13.74) to describe the best quality of a sheet of papyrus. The *hieraticus* was first reserved for the sacred books, but in Augustan times, this top quality papyrus was renamed after Augustus, and *hieraticus* was subsequently applied to a third-rate quality papyrus.

While most authors made no distinction in the written production of ancient Egypt, some were well aware of the complexities of the system as it was in Late Antiquity. I first deal with those who organized the Egyptian scripts according to a binary division, before discussing the tripartite organization that was proposed by a second group of authors.

The binary division is an ancient one, already advanced by Herodotus (2.36), who stated that the Egyptians use two kinds of letters, the ones that are called sacred (ἱρά) and the ones that are called popular (δημοτικά), in the sense of profane. The adjective δημοτικός has been retained in Egyptology for qualifying the script and the language of nonreligious texts. The very general term ἱ(ε)ρός may equally apply to hieroglyphic and hieratic writing systems as both were used at that time almost exclusively for sacred matters. It is unknown whether Herodotus ever had the chance of seeing texts written in hieratic or cursive hieroglyphs. Diodorus reported twice on Egyptian writings in much the same spirit. In 1.18, he differentiates between sacred letters and those whose learning is simpler. In 3.3, when discussing the education of scribes, he says that one has to learn first what is called public letters (τὰ μὲν δημώδη προσαγορευόμενα) before moving to sacred letters (τὰ δ'ἱερὰ καλούμενα). According to Diodorus, this last category was accessible only to priests who learned it from their fathers. Much later, Heliodorus of Emesa (*Aeth.* 4.8.1), when describing a small text, says that it was not written with Demotic letters (δημοτικοῖς), but with a royal script (βασιλικοῖς), analogous to what the Egyptians call hieratic (ἱερατικοῖς). He might here refer to what Egyptologists technically call hieratic or perhaps cursive hieroglyphs (see Lucarelli chapter, Ali chapter). As the purpose focused on a strip of cloth (ταινία), one cannot exclude that Heliodorus deliberately opted for a term that was connected with the cursive script. One can also mention here the distinction made by Manetho (frag. 42), when discussing the etymology of the noun Hyksos, between the sacred language (καθ' ἱερὰν γλῶσσαν) and the common language (κατὰ τὴν κοινὴν διαλεκτόν).

The tripartite division adopted in Egyptology is found in Clement of Alexandria's *Stromata* (5.4.20). When dealing with the Egyptians' educational system (as already made by Diodorus), he says that they begin with the system used for epistolary purposes, they then learn the system called the sacred one that is used by the *hierogrammateis*, and the ultimate state is that of the *hieroglyphike*. The word "epistolographic" explicitly refers to the practice of using Demotic (language and script) for business matters, be it sending letters or the redaction of commercial or private contracts. This term did not succeed in Egyptology, which instead adopted the Herodotean name, although it was sometimes used in this sense by scholars in the nineteenth century. Finally, a tripartite division is also found in Porphyry (*Vit. Pyth.* 11–12) regarding three kinds of writings in Egypt: one for correspondence by letters (ἐπιστολογραφικός), then what he calls the hieroglyphic (ἱερογλυφικός) letters, and the symbolic (συμβολικός) letters. As is clear, Porphyry, whose source is probably Clement, whom he could not fully understand, based his classification on uses of the writing systems that he perceived as important, hence his division between hieroglyphic and symbolic.

The Egyptian Documentary Sources

The documentary texts from Egypt give a welcome supplement of information. One can here consider the epigraphic material and the countless resources of the documentary papyrological texts.

In business matters, it was not uncommon to have, at least, partial bilingual (Greek and Egyptian) documents. References could also be made to a version written in the other language. There were several expressions to refer to Demotic (without distinguishing between script and language). One common appellation was ἐγχώρια γράμματα, "script of the country." This terminology is found on the Rosetta Stone (l. 14), where it is stipulated that the decree will be inscribed in sacred letters (ἱεροῖς γρ.) (i.e., in hieroglyphs), in indigenous letters (ἐγχωρίοις γρ.), (i.e., in Demotic), and in Greek (ἑλληνικοῖς γρ.). The corresponding hieroglyphic and Demotic versions call the hieroglyphs "(lit.) script of the divine words" and the Demotic *sš n sẖj* "(lit.) script of the letter," which is the prototype of the word ἐπιστολογραφική used by Clement. In other Ptolemaic temple decrees, however, Demotic is more simply called αἰγύπτια γράμματα (Canopus l. 74). This corresponds with what the Demotic language was sometimes called: one regularly finds expressions like "the language of the Egyptians" (ἡ τῶν αἰγυπτίων φωνή) or more simply the adverb αἰγυπτιστί (P.Cair.Goodsp. 3), which is reminiscent of the formulations found in the magical papyri.

As in the literary texts, the word ἱερατικός means "cultic, priestly." One must here note the existence of an extraordinary document attesting that a candidate to the priesthood has the required social background and technical skills (P.Tebt. 291.41–44, dating to 162 CE; Sauneron 1962). After stating that the candidate comes from a family of priests, the text adds that he was able to show in front of the *hierogrammateis* his knowledge of hieratic and Demotic writings by reading from sacred books brought by priests. The word ἱερατικός comes twice. If the translation "cultic, sacred" gives a satisfactory meaning when applied to books, in the second occurrence, one is closer to the modern sense where [ἱε]ρατικὰ qualifies a type of script (γράμ[ματ]α).

The adjective δημοσία, "popular" or "profane" as opposed to sacred (*IFayoum* 2.182), could also be used; it is reminiscent of the terms already found in the classical literature.

The adjective ἱερογλυφικός derives from ἱερογλύφος, which is attested in Ptolemaic times. This noun refers to a category of craftsmen, meaning sculptor. From Byzantine times comes a rare variant, ἱερογλύπτης, glossed "those who know how to engrave the sacred (script)" (Georgios Lekapenos, *Letters*, 7n, 98). The first attestation of ἱερογλύφος might well be from *Nectanebo's Dream*. The job of Petesis, the ἱερογλύφος, is precisely described as "the epigraphy of the sacred texts in stone buildings." In the Demotic versions, it is rendered *ḥm-(n-)sˁnḫ* (Ryholt 2002, 230). The modern noun "hieroglyph" (Fr. *hiéroglyphe*) to name the hieroglyphic sign is consequently unfortunate. It was actually "reinvented" in the Renaissance by Amyot, the famous translator of Plutarch, from the adjective "hiéroglyphique," which is attested in 1529 (Geoffroy Tory, *Champs Fleury* fol. 43ʳ and 73ʳ; Winand 2005, 91–92).

DESCRIBING A HIEROGLYPHIC TEXT?

When they attempted to describe Egyptian writing, the authors largely remained impressionistic. They unsurprisingly mentioned the presence of natural entities like men, animals, and trees, occasionally alluding to the presence of tools and geometric lines.

Even if it was common enough to designate the hieroglyphic signs with the generic noun γράμματα, some authors contrasted the letters as used in the Greek and Latin alphabet with what they call the σημεῖα and the χαρακτῆρες of the Egyptian writing (Lucian, *Hermot.* 44.1–7), or their ἀγάλματα (Plotinus, *Enn.* 5.8.6). The distinction is clearly made by Plutarch (*Cat. Min.* 23.3.3–4), who states that the hieroglyphic signs (σημεῖα) in small and concise forms (τύποι) have the value or power (δύναμις) of several letters.

As already noted, hieratic is not often discussed. One exception could be the well-known passage in Apuleius (*Met.* 11.22.8), where the author notes that one could see the books brought by priests "have their meaning protected from the curiosity of the uninitiated by letters that are intricate, twisted into themselves like a wheel, and thickly knotted like vine-tendrils" (transl. Keulen et al. 2015, 377).

Understanding the Mechanisms, Principles, and Uses of Ancient Egyptian Writing

When trying to understand the mechanisms and purpose of hieroglyphic writing, the theories put forward by classical authors repeatedly cluster around four major points: sacred, secret, symbolic, and wisdom. They also quite understandably opposed this enigmatic writing to their own alphabetic system.

Mechanisms and Purpose of the Hieroglyphic Writing

The *sacrality* of the hieroglyphs is inscribed in the first component ἱερα-/ἱερο- that appears in many Greek words connected with the Egyptian writing. The knowledge of hieroglyphs was entirely deposited into the hands of specialized priests (the so-called *hierogrammateis*) and only transmitted within this caste. According to Clement of Alexandria, the knowledge of hieroglyphs was the last stage that could be reached by a priest, an observation also supported by P. Tebt. 291.

The exclusive link of the hieroglyphs with the temple and the small number of experts who could handle them naturally suggested that the script and the texts must be kept *secret* and hidden (Porphyry, *Anebo's Letter* 2.12.2). Apuleius (*Met.* 11.22.29) notes that the books presented to Lucius come from a hidden place of the sanctuary and that the texts must be kept away from the curiosity of the noninitiated. Clement, in a passage already discussed (5.4.20), notes that knowledge of hieroglyphs was only communicated to priests and to those who were destined to become kings. The hieroglyphic writing—or something that had the appearance of it—was also an important ingredient in many magical formulae.

Hieroglyphic texts must be kept secret because they concealed a *wisdom*, an ancient one that was transmitted unaltered from the origin (compare Flavius Josephus 1.28; Ammianus Marcellinus 16.4.8). This antique wisdom was about mysteries (John Tzetzes, twelfth century), more precisely the true nature of the gods and the immortality of the soul (Chaeremon frags. 12 and 2, resp.). Hieroglyphic texts also dealt with natural phenomena (Pliny, *HN* 36.71), like the geography of the Nile (Heliodorus, *Aeth.* 2.28.2), the movements of stars (Claudius Aelianus, *HN* 11.10.24–25), and the cosmos (Olympiodoros). Generally speaking, hieroglyphic symbols conveyed a philosophy

(Philo of Alexandria, *Vit. Mos.* 1.23; Clement, *Strom.* 1.23.152; *Suda* 1.159.7). The *hiero-grammateis*, who were the depositors of hieroglyphic writing, were not infrequently credited with the capacity of predicting the future (Flavius Josephus 2.205; Synesios, *Aegyptii sive de providentia* 1.18.53; *Suda* 1.176.1). According to some authors, hieroglyphs could record more mundane affairs, like a victory inscription (Herodotus 2.106.12) or even workers' daily rations (Herodotus 2.125.17). In this respect, the interpretation of a Roman obelisk reported by Ammianus Marcellus remains unique. It was not properly speaking a translation, but a relatively fair attempt at giving a sense of the inscriptions (Winter 1991, 88–89; Nobbs 2013). Unfortunately, it did not find many echoes among the scholarly world of the Renaissance and early modern times. Some isolated signs had also survived in memory, such as the so-called crux, actually the *ankh* sign (*ʿnḫ*), which was correctly interpreted as meaning "life."

The *symbolic* function of hieroglyphs was very often discussed and debated. A semantic link was supposed to exist between what a sign represents and the word expressed by this sign. When Ammianus Marcellinus (16.4.8) reports that the picture of a bee means "king," he explains it by a connection between the activities of the bee and the expected behavior of a beneficent king. This kind of explanation was widespread. Diodorus (3.4) notes that Egyptians depict a vulture or a crocodile to signify entities or properties that can metaphorically be transferred from the behavior or aspect of these animals. The same kind of explanation is given by Damascius (*Isid.* 98) when discussing the choice of the hippopotamus to express injustice.

In Byzantine times, the symbolic nature of hieroglyphs has become a topos that was endlessly repeated without much comment. For instance, Michael Psellos (eleventh century), while conceding that the Egyptians' viewpoint was not very clear, flatly stated that everything was symbolic (ἀλλὰ πάντα συμβολικά). In Imperial times, the idea that hieroglyphs were symbolic in nature was already firmly rooted. When discussing Pythagoras's stay in Egypt, Plutarch (*De Is.* 354E8) says that he imitated the Egyptians' symbolic way and their mysteries and that he mixed up his dogmas with enigmas. Thus, Plutarch concludes, Pythagorean precepts are not very different from what we call hieroglyphic writing. Secrecy and symbolism were complementary, as is clear from a fragment of Chaeremon (frag. 12; Van Der Horst 1984), who explains that the hieroglyphic script was invented "to conceal the theory about the nature of the gods . . . by way of such allegorical symbols and characters." The symbolic approach culminates in Horapollo's *Aegyptiaca*, which appears as the last testimony of a specialist issued from a well-known family of scholars living in Egypt in Late Antiquity. According to a paper presented by Jean-Luc Fournet in June 2018 (Collège de France), Horapollo's Aegyptiaca should now be considered a pseudepigraphical work written by a Byzantine scholar around the sixth or seventh century. The schema of exposition adopted by Horapollo is roughly like this: "when the Egyptians want to express X, they draw Y, because there is the following relation between X and Y." While the connection between a hieroglyph and a given meaning can be proven as correct in many cases, the explanation given (or transmitted) by Horapollo often takes its origin in later philosophical speculations or in more or less well documented knowledge in the natural sciences. For instance, when he states (sec. 26) that Egyptians draw the image of a rabbit (Gardiner E34) to mean "open," which is correct, he fails to see that the connection is made through the phonetic value of the sign/wn/, which is the same as the word *wn*, which means "open." According to the presupposition that the link between the *significans* and the *significatum* is symbolic in essence, he explains that the image of a rabbit is appropriate here because it always keeps its eyes open, an opinion that was common in Late Antiquity scientific treatises, like the Physiologus or Aelianus' De Natura Animalium.

By exclusively focusing on this aspect of hieroglyphic writing, classical authors probably did not contribute to a quick (re)discovery of the original system in modern times, but it must be stressed that a strong semantic link was actually present in the mechanisms of writing. If, for instance, words connected with greed were often written with the crocodile as classifier, or words dealing with anger with the porcupinefish, whose body covered with sharp spines can inflate when attacked, it was probably because the Egyptians had perceived some similitudes between the behavior of these animals and these social behaviors (Vernus 2003). Thus, the *interpretatio graeca* should not be dissociated from a genuine Egyptian tradition. Several Egyptian texts coming from Ptolemaic and Roman times persuasively show that this kind of reasoning was common enough in the practice of the temple culture. The most elaborate texts that survive so far are P.Carlsb. VII (third/second century BCE), dubbed a hieroglyphic dictionary by its editor (Iversen 1958; see also Assmann 2003; von Lieven 2010, with previous literature; Bolshakov and Soushchevsky 2003), and P.Tanis (= P.Brit.Mus. ESA 10672, first century CE). The same mode of reasoning was also at work in religious treatises (P.Jumilhac) and literary texts (P.Mythus).

One probably also has to take into account iconographic representations that could in a sense be "read" in the same way that emblems, allegories, or heraldic compositions of the Renaissance would also be interpreted and glossed (Winand 2013). Indeed, some classical authors, when dealing with hieroglyphs, seem to rather describe monumental scenes than actual writing. For instance, Clement (*Strom.* 5.20.3) describes a scene from Diospolis where one can see a child and an old man surrounded by a hawk, a fish, and a crocodile. He then suggests the following "translation" of this symbolic representation: "Io you who are born and die, do not forget that God hates shameless-ness." The two "hieroglyphs" of the child sitting on a lotus bud and of the god in the sun bark discussed by Iamblichus (7.2) also belong to what Assmann (2003, 50) felici-tously calls an iconogram. In the same spirit, the example of the hippopotamus that was mentioned earlier, even if parallels in later texts can be found, can also be related to well-known representations of the king killing this wild beast with a harpoon as a metaphor for triumphing over chaos. In doing so, ancient classical authors are very close to what some scholars now call "visual poetry" (Morenz 2008). It is important to note here that this component of hieroglyphic writing was not first intended to be cryptic, but rather aimed at arousing the spectator's curiosity by showing the inventiveness of high-skilled scribes.

The neo-Platonists' ideas on the place of writing in a general theory of wisdom could not but welcome a direct link between the *significans* and the *significatum* as they could perceive it in the Egyptian writing system. What was an important—but not exclusive—

epistemological tendency in the temple scholarship of Hellenistic and Roman Egypt captured the attention of Late Antique philosophers who systematized and paradigmatized these explanatory etymographies (in the sense of Assmann) into a coherent and unified system. This conception reached its most refined expression with Plotinus (5.8.6), who says: "for me, that is what the Egyptian wise men have realized, whether by exact knowledge or spontaneously: to name what they wish in wisdom, they do not use the forms of letters (τύποις γραμμάτων), which give way to discourses and sentences and which imitate sounds and propositions of reasoning; they rather draw pictures, each one being for one distinct entity; and they engrave them in the temples for presenting all the details of this entity. Each image (ἄγαλμα) is a science, a wisdom, a real thing, an immediate unity, and not (something coming out of) reasoning or deliberation."

The hieroglyphic writing and—to some extent—the Egyptian language itself had an intrinsic efficiency (*energeia*) that could not be preserved when transposed or translated, a concept that was most forcefully expressed in the *Hermetic Corpus* (XVI).

Hieroglyphs versus Alphabet

Although some authors curiously saw no difference between Egyptian writing and their own, except for the forms of letters (τύπος τῶν γραμμάτων: Stephanus of Alexandria, *Int. Arist.* 1.18–22), the majority more or less intuitively knew how differently both systems worked. While many authors stick to the general idea that Egyptians used letters, γράμματα, some, like Lucian, explicitly preferred to speak of signs and characters. According to Chaeremon (frag. 12), Egyptians do not have letters for their characters; for this, he uses the expression στοιχεῖα γραμμάτων, which usually refers to the alphabet.

The idea that there was no connection between hieroglyphic signs and any kind of phonetic expression was common enough (Plotinus, *Enn.* 5.8.6: "they don't use the shape of letters nor do they try to imitate the sounds of words"). This is what Diodorus (3.4) has in mind when he writes that the meaning does not come out of a composition of syllables (ἐκ τῆς τῶν συλλαβῶν συνθέσεως).

Among these various, sometimes contradictory, conceptions, the concise but detailed report made by Clement of Alexandria stands out as an exception. After naming the three main types of writing, Clement proceeds to detailing the hieroglyphic script. Roughly speaking, Clement's presentation can be summarized as follows: "the Egyptians use a kind of alphabet (like the Greeks), but their writing can also have some other uses." He first makes a binary distinction between what he calls the kyriologic and the symbolic manner (Table II.2.2). Kyriologic, which means "simple, clear," is here defined as "with the first radical letters" (διὰ τῶν πρώτων στοιχείων). Clement has in mind the simplified form of hieroglyphs (uniliteral signs) that functioned at the time as an alphabet. Under the category symbolic, kyriologic once more occurs. Three types of symbols are here considered: kyriologic (i.e., by direct representation of ideas), tropic (i.e., by transposing a sign in another domain), and allegoric (i.e., enigmatic) (Vergote 1941; Derchain 1991; Assmann 2003; Winand 2005).

Table II.2.2. The System of Egyptian Writings in Clement of Alexandria

After this brief presentation, Clement gives some examples as illustrations. It should be noted that Clement (or his source) does not mention the existence of classifiers (semantic determinators).

CONCLUSION

The impact of classical authors—above all, philosophers—on subsequent scholarship must be appreciated with some nuance. The symbolic approach, of course, paved the way for the studies that were en vogue during the Renaissance and the first half of the modern times. This branch of premodern Egyptology would finally reach its climax with Kircher, who unwillingly made the final proof that it led to a dead end (Winand 2018). But what preoccupied the antique Greek and Latin authors does now experience a second life that meets some concerns of contemporary scholars, who take a renewed interest in the semantic potentialities of hieroglyphic writing.

BIBLIOGRAPHY

Assmann, J. 2003. "Etymographie: Zeichen im Jenseits der Sprache." In *Hieroglyphen: Stationen einer anderen abendländischen Grammatologie*, edited by A. Assmann and J. Assmann, 37–64. ALK 8. Munich.

Bolshakov, A. O., and A. G. Soushchevsky. 2003. "Образ и письменность в восприятии древнего египтянина" (Image and script in the perception of the ancient Egyptians). Вестник древней истории 1:45–59.

Derchain, P. 1991. "Les hiéroglyphes à l'époque ptolémaïque." In *Phoinikeia Grammata: Lire et écrire en Méditerranée. Actes du colloque de Liège, 15–18 novembre 1989*, edited by C. Baurain, C. Bonnet, and V. Krings, 243–256. Leuven.

Fournet, J.-L. 2016. "Alexandrie et la fin des hiéroglyphes." In *Alexandrie la Divine: Les sagesses barbares: Échanges et réappropriation dans l'espace culturel gréco-romain*, edited by S. Aufrère, 599–607. Geneva.

Hahn, J., S. Emmel, and U. Gotter, eds. 2008. *From Temple to Church: Destruction and Renewal of Local Cultic Topography in Late Antiquity*. RGRW 163. Leiden.

Horst, P. W. van der. 1984. *Chaeremon: Egyptian Priest and Stoic Philosopher*. EPRO 101. Leiden.

Iversen, E. 1958. *Papyrus Carlsberg nr. VII. Fragments of a Hieroglyphic Dictionary*. Copenhagen.

Iversen, E. 1994. "Egypt in Classical Antiquity: A résumé." In *Hommages à Jean Leclant* III, edited by C. Berger, G. Clerc, and N. Grimal, 295–305. BdE 106. Cairo.

Keulen, W. H., S. Tilg, L. Nicolini, L. Graverini, S. Harrison, S. Panayotakis, and D. van Mal-Maeder. 2015. *Apuleius Madaurensis Metamorphoses, Book XI: The Isis Book*. Leiden.

Kristensen, T. M. 2013. *Making and Breaking the Gods: Christian Responses to Pagan Sculpture in Late Antiquity*. ASMA 12. Aarhus.

Marestaing, P. 1913. *Les écritures égyptiennes et l'antiquité classique*. Paris.

Morenz, L. 2008. *Sinn und Spiel der Zeichen: Visuelle Poesie im Alten Ägypten*. Pictura et Poiesis 21. Cologne.

Nobbs, A. 2013. "Egypt in Late Antiquity: The Evidence from Ammianus Marcellinus." *BACE* 24:81–88.

Ryholt, K. 2002. "Nectanebo's Dream of the Prophecy of Peteisis." In *Apokalyptik und Ägypten: Eine kritische Analyse der relevanten Texten aus dem griechisch-römischen Ägypten*, edited by A. Blasius and B. U. Schipper, 221–241. OLA 107. Leuven.

Sauneron, S. 1962. "Les conditions d'accès à la fonction sacerdotale à l'époque gréco-romaine." *BIFAO* 61:55–57.

Sternberg-el Hotabi, H. 1994. "*Der Untergang der Hieroglyphenschrift: Schriftverfall und Schrifttod im Ägypten der griechisch-römischen Zeit*." *CdE* 69:218–248.

Thissen, H.-J. 1993. "…αἰγυπτιάζων τῇ φωνῇ…: zur Umgang mit der ägyptischen Sprache in der griechisch-römischen Antike." *ZPE* 97:239–252.

Vergote, J. 1941. "Clément d'Alexandrie et l'écriture égyptienne." *CdE* 16:21–38.

Vernus, P. 2003. "Idéogramme et phonogramme à l'épreuve de la figurativité: Les intermittences de l'homophonie." In *Philosophers and Hieroglyphs*, edited by L. Morra and C. Bazzanella, 196–218. Turin.

von Lieven, A. 2010. "Wie töricht war Horapollo? Zur Ausdeutung von Schriftzeichen im Alten Ägypten." In *Honi soit qui mal y pense: Studien zum pharaonischen, griechisch-römischen und spätantiken Ägypten zu Ehren von Heinz-Josef Thissen*, edited by H. Knuf, C. Leitz, and D. von Recklinghausen, 567–574. OLA 194. Leuven.

Winand, J. 2005. "Les auteurs classiques et les écritures égyptiennes: Quelques questions de terminologie." In *La langue dans tous ses états*, edited by C. Cannuyer, A. Schoors, R. Lebrun, J.-M. Verpoorten, and J. Winand, 79–104. AOB 18. Brussels.

Winand, J. 2013. *La réception des hiéroglyphes de l'Antiquité aux Temps modernes*. L'Académie en poche 29. Brussels.

Winand, J. 2018. "Un Frankenstein sémiotique: Les hiéroglyphes d'Athanase Kircher." In *Signatures: (Essais en) Sémiotique de l'écriture/(Studies in the) Semiotics of Writing*, edited by J.-M. Klinkenberg and S. Polis, 213-251. Liège.

Winter, E. 1991. "Hieroglyphen." In *Reallexikon für Antike und Christentum* XV, col. 83–103.

Young, D. W. 1981. "A Monastic Invective against Egyptian Hieroglyphs." In *Studies Presented to Hans Jakob Polotsky*, edited by D. W. Young, 348–360. East Gloucester.

....

INTERPRETATIONS AND REUSE OF ANCIENT EGYPTIAN HIEROGLYPHS IN THE ARABIC PERIOD (TENTH–SIXTEENTH CENTURIES CE)

....

ANNETTE SUNDERMEYER

OVERVIEW

....

THE Ancient Egyptian writing systems ceased to be used in the fifth century CE. The end of their use is marked by the last dated hieroglyphic inscription in the temple of Philae from the year 394 CE and the last Demotic inscription dating about 100 years later. Also of fifth-century origin is Horapollo's compilation of explanations of hieroglyphs, which hint at still existing knowledge about the possible functions of individual signs, seemingly without a deeper understanding of the sign function classes of the hieroglyphic script. Horapollo's *Hieroglyphica* is generally considered the endpoint of the antique and late antique interpretations and ideas about the hieroglyphic script. Historians of the reception of hieroglyphs (e.g., Iversen 1961; Assmann and Assmann 2003) usually start only with the works of European Medieval or Renaissance authors and leave a gap corresponding to the Arabic period, beginning with the conquest of Egypt in 640 CE. Notable exceptions are Edgar Blochet (1914–1915, 50–51), who mentioned a group of Arabic manuscripts containing hieroglyphic characters in the Bibliothèque Nationale in Paris, and more recently Okasha El Daly (2005), who included a chapter on what he calls the "decipherment" of hieroglyphs in his book on medieval Arabic efforts to explain ancient Egyptian culture.

A vast corpus of literature dedicated to the wonders of Egypt reflects the fascination the ancient remains evoked in Arabic authors. (For an overview, see Reitemeyer 1903.) Hieroglyphs took a central place in the literature on the mysteries of Egypt since they constituted a long-forgotten script and a key to treasures—material as well as immaterial—concealing the secret antediluvian knowledge of mankind (see Graefe 1968, 4 on Maqrīzī [d. 1442]; for an overview: Pasquali 2016). Hieroglyphs as a script are mainly incorporated in so-called alphabet books, works that deal with foreign and "secret" alphabets, but are also found in the wider context of occult literature. Unlike the preserved Greek and Latin works on hieroglyphs, there are rarely verbal descriptions of signs but rather drawn images. All extant manuscripts are late copies and date from the sixteenth to the eighteenth centuries. This implies a long history of transmission and almost inevitably considerable modifications of the original signs.

Okasha El Daly (2005, 59–73) not only describes the interest of Arabic authors in the hieroglyphic script and relates some still-existing knowledge about its function but also aims to demonstrate that medieval Arabic scholars had the means to and did decipher parts of the ancient writing system. He refers almost exclusively to some phonetic signs that, according to his judgment, they correctly explained—an assessment that is rejected by other scholars (i.e., Colla 2008, 136) and the present author. In this article, a few examples will illustrate various ways the Arabic scholars interpreted hieroglyphs.[1] Some cases clearly document a still-existing knowledge about the original function of a particular sign, while others highlight more imaginative explanations and the creative reuse of hieroglyphs. The main focus is on so-called alphabet books and the alchemical work *The Book of the Seven Climes*.

With regard to alphabet books, two different traditions of interpreting hieroglyphs are visible with little correspondence: one is represented by the tenth-century work *The Book of the Long Desired Fulfilled Knowledge of Occult Alphabets*, the other by a group of works dating from the thirteenth to fifteenth centuries.

TENTH CENTURY CE: *THE BOOK OF THE LONG DESIRED FULFILLED KNOWLEDGE OF OCCULT ALPHABETS*

The first (and most extensive) alphabet book containing Egyptian characters is *The Book of the Long Desired Fulfilled Knowledge of Occult Alphabets* (*Kitāb shawq al-mustahām fī maʿrifat rumūz al-aqlām*), which is attributed to early tenth-century Iraqi alchemist Ibn Waḥshiyya (d. 930–931 CE). Five manuscripts of the text are preserved and is the only alphabet book that has been edited.

---

[1] This article is an overview of my dissertation, which I am currently preparing at Humboldt-University in Berlin with the kind financial support of the Excellence Cluster Topoi.

Editions and Manuscripts

In the nineteenth century, the work was edited on the basis of a single manuscript and published with an English translation by the Hungarian orientalist Joseph Hammer (-Purgstall) (1806). Based on Hammer's English translation, Alleau (1977) prepared a French translation. Jumʿa and Ibn-Waḥšīya (2010) introduced a new edition, which is supposedly based on a manuscript in a private collection, but reprints Hammers signs. To my knowledge, at least five manuscripts of the work exist in the following libraries: Bibliothèque Nationale, Paris (MS arab. 6805), Österreichische Nationalbibliothek, Vienna (MS 68) (which is actually the manuscript Hammer used, although it has been described as lost; El Daly 2005, 68), Bayrische Staatsbibliothek, Munich (BSB arabe 798), National Library, Cairo (346), and an incomplete copy (without the appendix) in the Staatsbibliothek zu Berlin (12 Mf. 708). Another manuscript, which is said to be located in the National Library of Tehran, was published as facsimile by Ṭabbāʿ (2003; without manuscript number), but it rather seems to be a copy of Hammer's edition. All extant manuscripts were written between 1750 and 1800 CE, and all claim to refer to a single archetype produced in the year 1022 CE, with only minor deviations. (For more information on the manuscripts and their interrelation, see Toral-Niehoff and Sundermeyer, 2018.)

Ibn Waḥshiyya al-Nabaṭī is primarily known as the author of *Nabataean Agriculture* (*Kitāb al-filāha al-nabaṭiyya*) (Hämeen-Anttila 2006), which was intensely debated by European scholars in the nineteenth century (for a summary, see Hämeen-Anttila 2006, 4–6). In the end, Ibn Waḥshiyya was determined to be a forger of ancient wisdom, and this assessment has dominated considerations of the author ever since. Ibn Waḥshiyya is mentioned as the author of the present work only in the colophon of the extant manuscripts (except in the Berlin manuscript, which lacks the appendix), and for this reason, the work is widely considered a pseudoepigraphon (see, e.g., Hämeen-Anttila 2006, 21n45). Based on a detailed analysis of the content, it is suggested that only the appendix should be attributed to Ibn Waḥshiyya, while the main parts are likely of Egyptian origin and more or less contemporary with Ibn Waḥshiyya (Toral-Niehoff and Sundermeyer, forthcoming). For the sake of convenience, the name Ibn Waḥshiyya will be used for the author of the whole work throughout this article.

Hieroglyphs in *The Book of the Long Desired Fulfilled Knowledge of Occult Alphabets*

Besides the descriptions of pagan rituals, of a temple, and of descendants of Hermes Trismegistos, this work contains ninety-three "secret" alphabets attributed to, for example, the planets, antique sages, and signs of the zodiac (Toral-Niehoff and Sundermeyer, forthcoming). Individual signs resembling hieroglyphic, hieratic, and Demotic characters occur throughout the book, but hieroglyphs are mainly covered in the eighth chapter and in the appendix. The latter comprises one "alphabet" of thirty-eight hieroglyphic characters, all interpreted as phonograms (the *shīshīm alphabet*, Hammer 1806, ١٢٨–١١٩/ 43–48), as well as descriptions of pictographic signs and copied inscriptions. Due to the brevity of this article, the appendix is not included in the following analysis. The eighth chapter (Hammer 1806, ١١٣–٨٧/14–40) offers a description of some properties of the indigenous Egyptian script and a list of about 450 signs. Among these are clearly recognizable hieroglyphs as well as additional signs from other sources, all with a logographic Arabic interpretation. The system is called the "script of the Hermesians" and explained in a way that resembles classical Greek or Latin descriptions of hieroglyphs: the script is said to comprise an innumerable set of signs, not corresponding to modern alphabets of the *abjd* or *abc* types, but rather based on the secrets of nature, with an appropriate sign for every expression, going back to an order established by Hermes. Every expression is said to have a sign of its own, which might be modified or augmented for further specification (Hammer 1806, ٨٠–٧٩/15–16).

The list of signs is clearly structured, dividing the signs into four groups: celestial, living, botanical, and mineral objects. Within these divisions, the logograms are again grouped according to semantic categories (for example, planets or diseases) and yet again, for example, on the level of synonyms and antonyms. The assessment of this work and the interpretation of individual signs is controversial. In general, the signs and their suggested meanings are considered to be ad hoc inventions (Ullmann 1972, 284n3). El Daly (2005), however, considers the list the outcome of a successful decipherment of the hieroglyphic script by Arabic scholars. Both points of view are unsustainable. In fact, the Arabic "translations" of hieroglyphs result from a blend of then still-existing historical knowledge, conjectures about the function of hieroglyphs, and the specific conditions of the receptive literary genre.

Assessing the Sign Interpretations

Horapollo's explanations of individual hieroglyphs unknowingly refer to different original functions of the signs. Sometimes his explanations refer to the original standard use as a logogram or a classifier, occasionally to more specialized applications in wordplays or so-called cryptographic texts, and he also provides other interpretations (especially in the second part of the second book) that are not directly related to the genuine Egyptian writing system at all (van de Walle and Vergote 1943; Thissen 1998). There is evidence in his work for different paths of knowledge transmission, as is also the case in the book of Ibn Waḥshiyya.

Selected List of Interpreting Strategies

A. Correct knowledge about individual signs also found in other contexts

Clear-cut connections between the interpretations of hieroglyphs in this work and other antique or late antique works are scarce. The [FALCON] (Gardiner sign list G5) as a sign for "god" was widely known in ancient times and is also mentioned by Horapollo

(Thissen 2000, 5). Aside from this glyph, there is only one other sign that may be traced back to the Horapollonian tradition with a fair degree of probability: Horapollo translates the [DOVE] as "ungrateful/unjust to his benefactor" (Thissen 2000, 35), and in the present work, there is also a bird, possibly a dove, with the translation "injustice" (al-ẓulm). The lack of more connections between the known Greek or Latin and the Arabic analyses of hieroglyphs may be simply due to different selection strategies: while in the classical works, anthropomorphic and animal-shaped signs are commonly described, such signs are rarely treated in the Arabic works. The only exception is bird signs, which were seen as characteristic of the hieroglyphic script, also called "bird script" in Arabic (qalam aṭ-ṭair; on the special role of bird-shaped hieroglyphs, see Kammerzell 2001, 129–31 and 154n44).

B. Correct sign interpretations (iconicity)

It is very unlikely that the city sign (O49) or the nbw-sign (S12) could have been correctly recognized as a [CITY MAP WITH CROSSROAD] and a [PECTORAL], respectively, solely by means of their iconic value, which forms the basis of the given interpretations as "world" and "wealth." These can only be explained as transmitted knowledge.

C. Incorrect sign interpretations that may originate from authentic information about hieroglyphs of a similar shape

The [REED LEAF] (M17) is translated as "poverty," which seemingly has no connection to the ancient Egyptian usage. Nevertheless, because of an imprecise knowledge and/or copying of the signs, it is possible that it was confused with the [FEATHER] (H6), which is—because of its phonetic value—used in the writing of the word šw, "emptiness."

D. Sign interpretations that can be explained due to the respective shape in hieratic

Thissen (1998, 14) has argued that the source of Horapollo's Hieroglyphica was a sign list with hieroglyphic, hieratic, and Demotic signs, that probably even included Coptic pronunciations. (For actual pharaonic sign lists, see Kammerzell 2001, 125–129.) While in the other alphabets listed in this work, there are some signs resembling Demotic and hieratic forms, only one sign's interpretation might actually be related to a hieratic form. The [HEAD] (D2) is translated as "life," and while the [HEAD IN PROFILE] (D1) in temple inscriptions of the Greco-Roman Period is sometimes used for ꜥnḫ "live; life," the interpretation of [HEAD] (D2) can more likely be traced back to its shape in hieratic, which closely resembles the standard ꜥnḫ-sign (S34) (compare Möller 1909, 80).

Signs with explanations that reflect a still extant knowledge of their usage in pharaonic times are not numerous (about 2 percent), and the Arabic text does not offer any explication for the other interpretations. Nevertheless, the approach to the interpretation of hieroglyphs (or signs listed as hieroglyphs) in this particular work is all in all rather systematic. It commonly surpasses a simple image-iconic interpretation, according to which the shape of the sign is similar to the object it refers to. Some examples of iconic signs are the following:

E. The [MOON] (N12a) for "moon" and the [GRAPE] for "grape"

Table II.3.1. Ibn Waḥshiyya's Sign Interpretation with the Respective Ancient Egyptian Usage

	Mode of interpretation	Sign, in Hammer (1806)	Arabic "translation"	Hieroglyph	Sign use in Old Egyptian
Transmitted knowledge					
a.	Connection to other sources	p. 82	god	G5	logogram: *Horus* pt. period: logogram: *god*
b.	Non iconic interpretations	p. 83	world	O49	classifier.: *city, settlement* logogram: *village*
		p. 85	wealth	S12	logogram,: *gold* classifier: *precious metal*
c.	Related meaning	p. 85	poverty	M17	logogram: *reed* phonogram: *j*
				H6	*šw – lack, shortage*
d.	Hieratic form	p. 85	life	D2	logogram: *face, sight* phonogram: *ḥr*
				I:80 (Möller)	logogram: *life* phonogram: *ꜥnḫ*
Mechanisms of interpretation					
e.	Image-iconic	p. 83	moon	N11	logogram: *moon*
		p. 102	grape	---	---
f.	Container//liquid	p. 103	aloe	W14	classifier/logogram: *jar* phonogram: *ḥz*
g.	Part//object	p. 84	lion/leo	F22	logogram: *rump* phonogram: *pḥ*
h.	Individual//collective	p. 84	earth	N33	classifier: *salt, sand*
i.	Metonymic-functional	p. 85	the waking	D6	classifier: *sleep*
		p. 85	the sleep	---	---
		p. 86	the action	D40	classifier: *strength - activities*
Groups					
j.	Semantic group	p. 82	the subduer (name of god)		
		p. 88	the rule	A42	classifier: *king, l, master*
		p. 103	king's clover		
Other contexts					
k.	Alchemical sign	p. 108	mineral water	---	---
l.	Christian sign	p. 82	the merciful (name of god)	---	---
m	Connection to Christian beliefs (?)	p. 85	sin	I12	classifier: *uraeus snake*
		p. 86	deceitfulness	I10	logogram: *cobra, snake* phonogram: *d*
		p. 86	deceiver	I9	phonogram: *f*
		p. 88	enmity		

The relation between the iconic referents of the signs and their Arabic interpretation might rather be explained as metonymic. Most frequently, signs of containers—some resembling actual hieroglyphs, some not—are used for various liquid substances. In other cases, there is a meronymic relation between the sign and its Arabic rendering. Both methods are used in hieroglyphic sign formation as well (Goldwasser 2002; Lincke 2011; Lincke and Kammerzell 2012; Lincke and Kutscher 2012).

F. Container//liquid

[VESSEL] for "aloe"

G. Part//object

[RUMP OF A LION] (F22) for "lion/Leo" *(astronomy)*

H. Individual//collective

[GRAIN OF SAND] (N33) for "earth" *(element)*

Human figures are rarely included in the sign list; instead, there are signs resembling body parts. Daniel Werning (2014, 119) has shown for the ancient Egyptian script that a body part might stand for an associated action, which also seems to rule the interpretation of these signs in Ibn Waḥshiyya's work.

I. Metonymic-functional relation: body parts interpreted as activities

[CLOSED EYE] for "the sleep," [OPEN EYE] for "the waking," [ARM/HITTING ARM] (D36/D40) for "the doing"

These examples show the fuzzy edges between transmitted knowledge and a possible iconic, secondary interpretation of the respective signs. While the first sign, [CLOSED EYE] does not occur in hieroglyphic texts at all and the second has a different function than the one described, the third should probably be seen as a case of transmitted knowledge. Especially in the Vienna manuscript, the sign clearly resembles the [HITTING ARM] (D36). Thus, its interpretation is probably related to its function as a classifier for various energetic actions (Kammerzell 2015, 1405–1406, 1409–1410).

A further difficulty in attempting to explain the intention of the Arabic interpretations of individual signs is the fact that certain signs may reoccur with varied interpretations in different sections of the booklet. Most of the translations are, however, semantically connected.

J. Semantic group
[SITTING MAN HOLDING A FLAGELLUM] (A42) appears in the celestial objects category as "the Subduer" (Islamic name of God), in the human objects as "the rule," and

interestingly, in the plant section as "king's clover." All translation terms are clearly related to the sphere of king and kingship.

The mechanisms mentioned above do not explain all interpretations found in the work: (1) Many signs are not recognizable as icons, either simply due to the fact that they were not based on hieroglyphic signs or due to incorrect copying. (2) In some cases of recognizable signs, we should consider the production conditions of the receptive Arabic genre: the science of alchemy is frequently described by Arabic authors as originating in Egypt (Ullmann 2012). Thus, it is not surprising that a number of signs in this list of hieroglyphs are actually of alchemical origin (for example, Table II.3.1:K). Alchemical considerations also play a role in the order of the signs in the four groups. Looking at the Arabic terms in the explanations, the alchemical focus is apparent as well. Only one other manuscript presents logographic interpretations of signs (Bib. Nat., Paris: MS arabe 2703: fol. 43r–46r). Even though that text contains no recognizable hieroglyphs or other symbols corresponding to Ibn Waḥshiyya's signs, 65 percent of the Arabic terms used as explanations are identical.

Summing up, the lists in the eighth chapter of *The Book of the Long Desired, Fulfilled Knowledge of Occult Alphabets* contain (1) authentic hieroglyphs with explications that imply still existing transmitted knowledge about individual signs' functions, (2) a systematic approach to the interpretation of signs, and (3) symbols and explications whose existence is related to the overall alchemical context and the perception of Egypt as the land of alchemy. The path of transmission is not clearly definable. There is no apparent direct connection to the late Egyptian sign lists (P. Tanis and P. Carlsberg). The selection of signs does not correspond to the preserved classical sources, and the images could not have been drawn based on the typical Greek descriptions of signs without access to pictorial prototypes. Mentioning the excerpt of an invective attributed to Shenoute (fifth century CE), Young (1981) argues for a still-existing interest in hieroglyphs in Coptic monasteries (Thissen 1994, 256; El Daly 2005, 61). This view is reflected in Arabic historical anecdotes, which often grant Coptic monks a constitutive role in the interpretation of ancient scripts (Graefe 1968, 22). Unfortunately, in the interpretation of the signs, there is only sparse evidence for this otherwise quite plausible explanation of knowledge transmission (in the form of recognizable Christian transformations). A sign introduced into the list of Christian and not pharaonic origin is a Byzantine angel who is listed as "the Merciful" (Islamic name of God) in the section on celestial objects (Table II.3.1:L). Also the ʿnḫ-sign (S34), which was used as a cross symbol by the Coptic Church (Cramer 1943, 31), is once interpreted as "cross" (Hammer 1806, 86, but compare 88). Another indicator of a decidedly Christian interpretation of signs may be the explications of signs resembling snakes (Table II.3.1:M). Four snake-shaped signs more or less resembling I9, I10, and I12 are explained in negative terms from a seemingly biblical context: "sin," "deceitfulness," "deceiver," and "enmity." Even though negative associations with snakes exist in Islam as well, the connection to the fall of mankind—which is not only defining for the Christian view, but seemingly also for the interpretation of the signs in this context—is absent from the Qur'an (i.e., Qur'an 2:36.)

LATER ALPHABET BOOKS (THIRTEENTH TO FIFTEENTH CENTURIES)

The texts addressed here as "alphabet books" are works transmitted under different titles with widely consistent content. They include mainly identical alphabets and between these alphabets, recurring textual passages in differing order. The works are sometimes transmitted as one individual work (Bib. Nat., Paris MS arabe 2675, 2676, 2726, Princeton Garrett no. 52b) and sometimes as parts of larger works, either completely (Bib. Nat. MS arabe 2727) or only in parts (Bib. Nat., Paris MS arabe 2688). All of these manuscripts are described as anonymous in the catalogs, but nevertheless two names can be found in connection to them: the thirteenth-century alchemist Abū l-Qāsim al-ʿIrāqī and ʿAbd al-Raḥmān al-Bisṭāmī (fifteenth century), who is mostly known for his works on the "science of letters." El Daly (2005, 67) points out that in MS arabe 2703—which differs slightly from the other works—Abū l-Qāsim al-ʿIrāqī is mentioned as the author (fol. 23v). He is additionally named in MS arabe 2676 (fol. 45v). MS arabe 2727 is actually a corrupted and partial copy of ʿAbd al-Raḥmān al-Bisṭāmī's *Excitement of the Explanation of the Function of Occult Alphabets* (*Kitāb mabāhij al-aʿlām fī manāhij al-aqlām*, University Library Leiden Or.14.121), while MS arabe 2688 is also attributed to this author.

For all the alphabets in these books, the signs are exclusively explicated with Arabic letters (except the previously mentioned alphabet of MS arabe 2703, 43r–46r). The topics covered in these books differ widely from the aforementioned work. They predominantly cover (1) the revelation of twenty-four scripts to as many prophets as a present from God, (2) historical and religious statements about the Arabic script, and (3) philosophical statements about the intellect.

The twenty-four prophetic scripts constitute the core of the scripts dealt with in these books, considerably enlarged by additional alphabets. The first script was revealed to Adam and then successively to his descendants and the following prophets. The Egyptian context is not mentioned explicitly, but hieroglyphs are mainly found in the alphabets of Seth (son of Adam), Kenan, and Akhnūkh/Idris (Hebraic: Enoch), who was identified with Hermes Trismegistos (Siggel 1937; on the Arabic Hermes-tradition, see van Bladel 2009). In Arabic historical accounts, those three prophets are often described as rulers of Egypt (see Ibn Iyās 2008, 64 [fifteenth century]). The hieroglyphic characters in the different manuscripts were copied carefully; only slight differences in the order and in single signs are apparent. Nevertheless, discrepancies in the sequence of the signs (Arabic, as well as "secret") give little reason to justify a connection with the original Egyptian phonetic values, as El Daly (2005, 72) assumed. There is apparently no relationship to Ibn Waḥshiyya's work and his interpretations of hieroglyphs.

Remarkably, most of the textual passages in these works seem to consist of citations and anecdotes from the Qur'an and Hadith (the traditions of Muhammad) that are also found in other works. The Qurʾanic verses all deal with the importance of writing (96:3–5, 80:12–15, 82:10–12) as being a gift from God. All of the remaining myths about the Arabic script (its origin, transmission, distribution, and superiority) are common in works dealing with script from the ninth century onward (for a brief overview, Endress 1982, 169). Also included is Aristotle's definition of language from the first chapter of *De interpretatione*, which had already been translated into Arabic in the early ninth century and is frequently cited in statements about language and writing, for example, in the tenth-century work for secretaries by al-Ṣūlī (1922, 33). The Hadiths cited in these books do not deal with writing and are not included in the canonical collections. They place great emphasis on the intellect, calling it God's first creation in concordance with the Greek doctrine of emanation (already criticized in the fourteenth century; see, e.g., Ibn Taymiyya [1964?], 218–219). Not surprisingly, these hadiths were prominent mostly within intellectual groups dealing with Platonic and Neoplatonic wisdom (Goldziher 1909, 318–320). All the textual passages found in the alphabet books are typically also found in works on the so-called science of letters. Originally, this science was an onomastic method of divination—using solely the Arabic script—which developed into a complex technique in mysticism. A further link between the manuscripts cited here and this domain is ʿAbd al-Raḥmān al-Bisṭāmī, who is mentioned in three of the manuscripts and who is one of the primary representatives of the "science of letters" (Gril 2005). This connection requires further research. The "science of letters" nevertheless constitutes a different receptive genre of the scripts—it is not the picture-like value that seems important in that context, but their transformation into the Arabic script.

It is remarkable that the hieroglyphic signs included in the late alphabet books are also found in the larger context of occult literature, for example, in a manual of treasure hunting in the Bibliothèque Nationale (MS arabe 2764:70r) and in *The Book of the Seven Climes*.

THE BOOK OF THE SEVEN CLIMES ON THE SCIENCE CALLED THE ART

The *Kitāb al-aqālīm as-sabʿa fī-l-ʿilm al-mausūm bi-ṣ-ṣanʿa*, a thirteenth-century work by the Iraqi alchemist Abū l-Qāsim al-ʿIrāqī, shows varying uses of hieroglyphs. Of this beautiful work with many illustrations, only one complete manuscript exists, in the National Library, Cairo (V:376) (Holmyard 1926, 403). In addition, four manuscripts in European libraries contain portions of the second half of this text as part of collective manuscripts, which are commonly referred to under the same title: British Library (Add. 25724), Forschungsbibliothek Gotha (MS orient 1261), Chester Beatty Library, Dublin (ar.5433, 5579, 5642 [5579 according to Ullmann 1972, 236]).

For the Arabic phonetic interpretations, El Daly (2005, 72) again postulates a successful decipherment of individual phonetic signs. However, the reason for assigning Arabic phonetic values to the hieroglyph-like signs is a different one. The Arabic letters are substitutes for the elements occurring in what appear at first glance to be only decorative, pseudo-hieroglyphic inscriptions and offer the code to read and understand most of these—as Arabic (!) texts. On three folios (8a, 23b, 24a), hieroglyphs and pseudo-hieroglyphs are accompanied by single Arabic letters above or below them. In three of the accounts, the individual Arabic letters next to the secret signs reproduce the line written in the Arabic text above them (8a, 23b on top, 24a), which is not immediately apparent because of the different shape of Arabic letters written individually or in cursive. The only real deviation is the letter *dhal* (ذ), which is consistently written as *dal* (د). On Folio 23b (Figure II.3.1), the title reads, "This is the description of the circle of stars," followed by a line of (pseudo-)hieroglyphic signs accompanied by Arabic letters written in their isolated shapes:

(haḏihi ṣifatun dāʾirati falakin)	و هذه صفة دايرة قلك
(h-ḏ-h-ṣ-f-t-d-ā-ī-r-t-f-l-k)	و ه د ه ص ف ة د ا ي ر ة ف ل ك

The conversions of the secret signs into Arabic letters function as a code. By applying this code to the (pseudo-)hieroglyphs around the picture of folio 6b (Figure 2), they become easily readable: The three lines of signs are again a duplication of the Arabic text in the line above them, the inscription running through the top line, and the lines on the left and right sides of the picture ("This is the description of the cold and moist soul, which is the quicksilver of the West and its examples you see here"). The substitution of the Arabic letters with the "secret signs" is executed with little deviation. The gray letters in Table II.3.2 indicate that the sign is not included in the list of deciphered signs, but is commonly used as this particular letter throughout the book. The third line of every section contains the Folio number on which the "deciphered" sign is found.

Not every Arabic letter has a corresponding counterpart in these lists, but many of the secret signs used here are also included in the hieroglyphic alphabets in the alphabet books (c. 80 percent), while fewer signs have identical Arabic explications (c. 50 percent).

As indicated earlier, in the European manuscripts, *The Book of the Seven Climes* is the first of several tractates ending with the colophon on Folio 39a (Gotha). In the following texts, there are two different approaches to hieroglyphs: El Daly (2005, 72) describes a copy of the hieroglyphs from a stela of Amenemhat II (fol. 50r). The original is apparently lost now, but on the basis of that illustration in the manuscript, Hallum and Marcel Marée (2016) have recently prepared a reconstruction.

The other approach links back to the alphabet books and ʿAbd al-Raḥmān al-Bisṭāmī: Folio 52r shows a table with various "secret" signs for every Arabic letter, which is attributed to ʿAbd al-Raḥmān al-Bisṭāmī, who lived about two hundred years after Abū l-Qāsim al-ʾIrāqī, and which corresponds closely to the sign lists in the alphabet books, without any connection to the use of hieroglyphs in the first part of the manuscript.

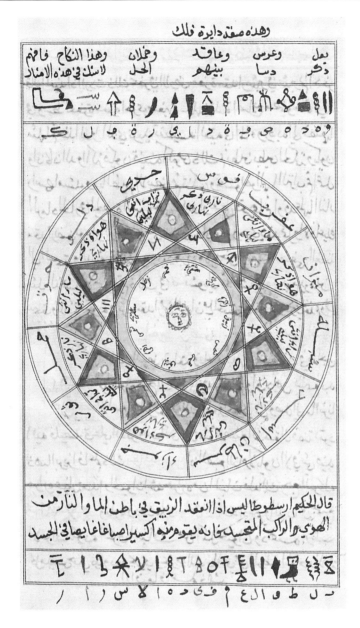

FIGURE II.3.1. *Kitāb al-aqālīm as-sabʿa* (Forschungsbibliothek Gotha of the University Erfurt, MS orient. 1261, 23b).

FIGURE II.3.2. *Kitāb al-aqālīm as-sabʿa* (Forschungsbibliothek Gotha of the University Erfurt, MS orient. 1261, 5v).

As has been shown previously, the hieroglyphs in the alphabet books must have been known in Abū l-Qāsim al-ʿIrāqī's time, even though his authorship remains unclear. For the time being, it seems that the thirteenth-century author and the fifteenth-century author used the (pseudo-)hieroglyphs quite differently: as a code in the context of alchemy in the case of Abū l-Qāsim al-ʿIrāqī and as a substitution

Table II.3.2. Analyses of the "Hieroglyphic Script" around the Picture on Folio 6b, Gotha Ms orient 1261

Arabic text above	البارد	الروح	صفة	هي	وهذه
First line (right to left)					
"deciphered sign" fol.-nr. (left-right)	8r-23v-8r-8r-24r	8r-8r-8r-()-()	8r-8r-23v	8r-23v	24r-23v-23v-8r
Arabic text above	الغريب	الرقيق	وهو		الرطب
Second-third line (left)		الزيبق			
"deciphered sign" fol.-nr. (left-right)	()-23v-8r-()-()	8r-23v-()-8r-()-()-8r	8r-24r-8r		8r-8r-8r-()-()
Arabic text above		ترى	كما		وكذلك
Fourth line (right)			ان امع		
"deciphered sign" fol.-nr. (left-right)		8r-8r-8r	()-()-8r		8r-24r-86-8r-23v-23v

code for Arabic letters in the context of the "science of letters" in the case of ʿAbd al-Raḥmān al-Bisṭāmī.

CONCLUSION

Not surprisingly, Arabic-speaking scholars were fascinated by the script that covered great parts of the surfaces of the ancient monuments in Egypt. In the tenth century, the reception of hieroglyphs was governed by a persistent tradition of the knowledge of individual signs, as well as by a mystical imagination of Egypt's past. The perception of hieroglyphs as an overall pictorial system was consistent with the classical sources, while the correct knowledge of the function of individual signs must have come from different sources. Ibn Waḥshiyya, the assumed author of the early work on hieroglyphs, is also mentioned in one of the later alphabet books as an authority on secret scripts (Bib. nat. Paris MS arabe 2675, 46r). Scripts appear in that work, as well as in the later works, but they do not include hieroglyphic signs. The later alphabet books assemble texts and alphabets of a fairly fixed tradition, even though they differ with respect to the ordering of the various parts. The (pseudo-)hieroglyphs, which are also found in other occult literature (e.g., the alchemical work on the Seven Climes), obviously form parts of this tradition too. The fact that the hieroglyphs are explicitly interpreted phonetically in the late alphabet books can be neither traced back to historical knowledge about their authentic function nor taken as an indicator of a successful decipherment of the Egyptian writing system. It is rather most likely due to the specific requirements of the receptive genre (alchemical code, equalization with the Arabic script in the "science of letters"). The interpretation and secondary usages of hieroglyphs as documented in Arabic manuscripts have close parallels with the European tradition and deserve a prominent role in the history of the reception of hieroglyphs.

BIBLIOGRAPHY

Alleau, R., ed. 1977. *La magie arabe traditionelle*. Paris.

Assmann, A., and J. Assmann, eds. 2003. *Hieroglyphen: Stationen einer anderen abendländischen Grammatologie*. ALK 8. Munich.

Bladel, K. van. 2009. *The Arabic Hermes: From Pagan Sage to Prophet of Science*. Oxford.

Blochet, E. 1914–1915. "Études sur le gnosticisme musulman." *RSO* 6: 5–67.

Colla, E. 2008. "Review of *Egyptology: The Missing Millenium Ancient Egypt in Medieval Arabic Writings*, by Okasha El Daly." *IJMES* 40(1): 135–137.

Cramer, M. 1943. *Das altägyptische Lebenszeichen im christlichen (koptischen) Ägypten: Eine kultur- und religionsgeschichtliche Studie*. 2nd ed. Wiesbaden.

Daly, O. El. 2005. *Egyptology: The Missing Millenium; Ancient Egypt in Medieval Arabic Writings*. London.

Endress, G. 1982. "Die arabische Schrift." In *Grundriss der arabischen Philologie, Band I: Sprachwissenschaft*, edited by W. Fischer, 165–197. Wiesbaden.

Goldwasser, O. 2002. *Prophets, Lovers and Giraffes. Wor(l)d Classification in Ancient Egypt*. GOF 38. Wiesbaden.

Goldziher, I. 1909. "Neuplatonische und gnostische Elemente im Hadīṯ." *ZDMG* 22: 317–344.

Graefe, E., ed. and trans. 1968. *Das Pyramidenkapitel in al-Makrīzī's "Ḥiṭaṭ" nach zwei Berliner und zwei Münchner Handschriften unter Berücksichtigung der Būlāker Bruckausgabe*. LSS V, 5. Leipzig. First published 1909.

Gril, D. 2005. "Ésotérism contre hérésie: ʿAbd al-Rahmān al-Bisṭāmī, un représentant de la science des Lettres à Bursa dans la pemière moitié du XVe siècle." In *Syncrétismes et Hérésies dans l'Orient Seldjoukide et Ottoman (XIVe–XVIIIe siècle): Actes du colloque du Collège de France, Octobre 2001*, edited by G. Veinstein, 183–198. Paris.

Hallum, B., and M. Marée. 2016. "A Medieval Alchemical Book Reveals New Secrets." Retrieved from https://blog.britishmuseum.org/a-medieval-alchemical-book-reveals-new-secrets/

Hämeen-Anttila, J. 2006. *The Last Pagans of Iraq: Ibn Waḥshiyya and His Nabatean Agriculture*. IHC 63. Leiden.

Hammer, J., trans. 1806. *Ancient Alphabets and Hieroglyphic Characters Explained, with an Account of the Egyptian priests, Their Classes, Initiation, and Sacrifices*. London.

Holmyard, E. J. 1926. "Abu' l-Qasim al-Iraqi." *Isis* 8(3): 403–426.

Ibn Iyās al-Ḥanafī, A. M. 2008. *Badāi az-zuhūr fī waqāi ad-duhūr*. Edited by M. Muṣṭafā. 3rd ed. Cairo.

Ibn Taimiyya, A. [1964?]. *al-Ǧawāb aṣ-ṣaḥīḥ li-man baddala dīn al-masīḥ*. Edited by A. Madānī. Cairo.

Iversen, E. 1961. *The Myth of Egypt and Its Hieroglyphs in European Tradition*. Copenhagen.

Jumʿa, J., and A. Ibn-Waḥšīya. 2010. *Šauq al-mustahām fī maʿrifat rumūz al-aqlām*. Beirut.

Kammerzell, F. 2001. "Die Entstehung der Alphabetreihe: Zum ägyptischen Ursprung der semitischen und westlichen Schriften." In *Hieroglyphen, Alphabete, Schriftreformen: Studien zu Multiliteralismus, Schriftwechsel und Orthographieneuregelungen*, edited by D. Borchers, F. Kammerzell, and S. Weninger, 117–158. LingAeg-StudMon 3. Göttingen.

Kammerzell, F. 2015. "Egyptian Verb Classifiers." In *Proceedings of the Tenth International Congress of Egyptologists, University of the Aegean, Rhodes, 22–29 May 2008*, edited by P. Kousoulis and N. Lazaridis, 1395–1416. 2 vols. OLA 241. Leuven.

Lincke, E.-S. 2011. *Die Prinzipien der Klassifizierung im Altägyptischen*. GOF 38. Wiesbaden.

Lincke, E.-S., and F. Kammerzell. 2012. "Egyptian Classifiers at the Interface of Lexical Semantics and Pragmatics." In *Lexical Semantics in Ancient Egyptian*, edited by E. Grossmann, S. Polis, and J. Winand, 55–112. LingAeg-StudMon 9. Hamburg.

Lincke, E.-S., and S. Kutscher. 2012. "Motivated Sign Formation in Hieroglyphic Egyptian and German Sign Language (DGS): Towards a Typology of Iconic Signs in Visual Linguistic Systems." In *Lexical Semantics in Ancient Egyptian*, edited by E. Grossmann, S. Polis, and J. Winand, 113–140. LingAeg-StudMon 9. Hamburg.

Möller, G. 1909. *Hieratische Paläographie: Die ägyptische Buchschrift in ihrer Entwicklung von der fünften Dynastie bis zur römischen Kaiserzeit, Vol. I,: Bis zum Beginn der achtzehnten Dynastie*. Leipzig.

Pasquali, S. 2016. "Les hiéroglyphes égyptiens vus par les auteurs arabes du Moyen Âge *ou* L'aura du passé pharaonique." In *À l'école des scribes: Les écritures de l'Égypte ancienne*, edited by L. Bazin Rizzo, A. Gasse, and F. Servajean, 213–225. CENIM 15. Montpellier.

Reitemeyer, E. 1903. *Beschreibung Ägyptens im Mittelalter aus den geographischen Werken der Araber*. Leipzig.

Siggel, A. 1937. "Das Sendschreiben: Das Licht über das Verfahren des Hermes der Hermesse dem, der es begehrt." *Der Islam* 24: 287–306.

Ṣūlī, M.al-. 1922. *Adab al-kuttāb*. Edited by A. H. Basaj. Cairo.

Ṭabbāʿ, I. 2003. *Minhağ taḥqīq al-maḫṭūṭāt*. Damascus.

Thissen, H.-J. 1994. "Horapollinis Hieroglyphika Prolegomena." In *Aspekte spätägyptischer Kultur: Festschrift für Erich Winter zum 65. Geburtstag*, edited by M. Minas-Nerpel and J. Zeidler, 255–264. Mainz.

Thissen, H.-J. 1998. *Vom Bild zum Buchstaben, vom Buchstaben zum Bild: Von der Arbeit an Horapollons Hieroglyphika*. AAWLM 3. Mainz.

Thissen, H.-J., ed. and trans. 2000. *Des Niloten Horapollon Hieroglyphenbuch*. AfP 6. Munich.

Toral-Niehoff, I., and A. Sundermeyer. 2018. "Doing Egyptian in Medieval Arabic Culture: The Long-Desired Fulfilled Knowledge of Occult Alphabets by Pseudo-Ibn Waḥshiyya." In *The Occult Sciences in Pre-Modern Islamic Culture* Cultures, edited by N. El-Bizri and E. Orthmann, 249–264. Beirut and Würzburg.

Ullmann, M. 1972. *Die Natur- und Geheimwissenschaften im Islam*. Leiden.

Ullmann, M. 2012. "al-Kīmiyāʾ." In *Encyclopaedia of Islam*, edited by P. Bearman, T. Bianquis, C. E. Bosworth, E. van Donzel, and W. P. Heinrichs. 2nd ed. Retrieved from http://dx.doi.org.54943987otwo.erf.sbb.spk-berlin.de/10.1163/1573-3912_islam_SIM_4374.

Walle, B. van de, and J. Vergote. 1943. "Traduction des *Hieroglyphica* d'Horapollon." *CdE* 18(35): 39–90; 18(36): 199–239.

Young, D. W. 1981. "A Monastic Invective against Egyptian Hieroglyphs." In *Studies Presented to Hans Jakob Polotsky*, edited by D. W. Young, 348–360. East Gloucester.

Werning, D., 2014. "Der 'Kopf des Beines,' der 'Mund der Arme' und die 'Zähne' des Schöpfers: Zu metonymischen und metaphorischen Verwendungen von Körperteil-Lexemen im Hieroglyphisch-Ägyptischen." In *Synthetische Körperauffassung im Hebräischen und den Sprachen der Nachbarkulturen*, edited by K. Müller and A. Wagner, 107–162. AOAT 416. Münster.

....

THE RECEPTION OF ANCIENT EGYPT AND ITS SCRIPT IN RENAISSANCE EUROPE

....

LUCIE JIRÁSKOVÁ

ANCIENT Egyptian pyramids, particularly those at Giza, attracted the attention and provoked the fantasy of many European scholars in the past. The hieroglyphic script was more fascinating in the eyes of Medieval and Renaissance Europe, however. Due to its simple visual demonstration on the one hand and the impossibility to understand it on the other hand, it became a source of inspiration for many generations of scholars in various branches of early science, philosophy, and art. A slow rise of interest in ancient Egypt and its culture in the final part of the Middle Ages became an enchantment in the Renaissance era. The ancient Roman culture resurrected in the sixteenth century enabled the return to more ancient roots of European civilization by means of ancient Egyptian or Egyptianizing objects found in Rome (e.g., Roullet 1972; Curl 1994; Wittkower 1977; Iversen 1968). The growing trend was supported by the first translations of "hermetic texts" that were brought to Italy from Greece at approximately the same time. These two points were the milestones of the Egyptian revival, starting in early Renaissance Italy and later spreading to the north and affecting the development across Europe.

EARLY TRAVELERS TO EGYPT AND EGYPTIAN MONUMENTS IN EUROPE

....

Although it is difficult to divide Renaissance science into specific fields as they are classified today, the influence of the interpretation of ancient Egyptian culture might be perceived in philosophy, art, chemistry, astronomy, medicine, and other natural sciences. The word "interpretation" is of the utmost importance, since the available information on ancient Egypt and its culture was limited. Nobody could read hieroglyphs anymore, ancient Egyptian monuments were already buried under thick layers of sand, and the "genuine ancient texts" available in Europe later proved to be much younger. There were only a few sources of inspiration accessible in Europe, such as real historical monuments brought to Italy from Egypt during the Roman rule or the "Hermetica" mentioned earlier.

Encounters with Egypt through travels to this (at that time) rather distant country were important as well, reflecting a growing interest in the ancient Egyptian culture. Between 1250 and 1517, the country was under the rule of the Mamluks, who were defeated by Sultan Selim I in the battle of Cairo in 1517. After that time, Egypt became part of the Ottoman Empire. Medieval travelers to Egypt were attracted primarily by places connected with biblical stories (Donadoni, Curto, and Donadoni Roveri 1990, 42). They sometimes also visited the Giza pyramids, for these were situated close to Cairo and easy to see from a distance due to their height. However, even the pyramids were perceived as a feature mentioned in the Bible rather than as ancient Egyptian monuments.

Renaissance travelers to Egypt were likewise above all faithful Christians, and they followed in the footsteps of earlier visitors. (A list of travelers to Egypt from Antiquity to the early twentieth century can be found in Kalfatovic 1992.) In this respect, their first steps led to Alexandria (those who traveled from Italy landed there), then Cairo (Heliopolis-Matareia) and Sinai (Saint Catherine Monastery and Mount Sinai, the mountain of Moses). However, as "real" Renaissance men (and they were mostly men), they were also tempted to visit ancient Egyptian monuments connected with the kings who had ruled over Egypt long before. The Giza pyramids, which had been described as "Joseph's granaries" in the Middle Ages (best known from the mosaic in the church of Saint Mark in Venice), became generally accepted as giant tombs of ancient kings. Educated European noblemen included the Greco-Roman monuments in Alexandria, the Great Sphinx, various obelisks, and the Saqqara tombs with mummies in their itineraries. Unfortunately, many challenges faced those who tried to reach distant areas in the south. Yet even this part of Egypt did not remain unknown, as it had been described by ancient Greek and Roman writers, and Renaissance travelers often quoted from these works in their travelogues. However, it took some time until the southern part was "rediscovered" by Christian missionaries during the Baroque period.

Renaissance travelers did not just have a brief look at the monuments, but paid enough attention to sometimes extensive descriptions in their travelogues. Moreover, some Renaissance travelers were not merely curious to see these giant wonders of the world, but made the first steps to a scientific study of them. Among these were Jacques de Villamont with his attempts to measure the pyramids (Villamont 1971, 198–203) and Cardinal Marco Grimani, who described and measured the Great Pyramid and its interior (Curran 2007, 156). Many visitors also enriched their printed travelogues with illustrations. Travelogues, usually printed after the author's return from travels, became a popular literary genre, and the pattern of their distribution, which often reached beyond the author's home country, testifies to their general accessibility (e.g., the Czech Lands in Jirásková 2007).

Apart from plentiful memories recorded and later published in the form of books, most European Renaissance travelers probably brought real objects back to Europe as well. European artists knew mostly the large stone pieces that had survived in Rome from antiquity, above all sphinxes and obelisks. The first wave of restoration of Egyptian and Egyptianizing monuments came with the plan for the restoration of ancient Rome endorsed by Pope Leo X, who was followed by Sixtus V (Figure II.4.1). The erection of the first obelisk at Piazza di San Pietro by Domenico Fontana in 1586 aroused interest not only in Italy, but across Europe. Since that time, many other obelisks were discovered in Rome and its vicinity, and some of them were re-erected (Iversen 1968; Iversen 1993; Curran 2007).

Obelisks, which soon found their place in Renaissance architecture, were not the only ancient Egyptian monuments that attracted attention at that time. Sphinxes and pyramids were also dominant features, and soon they found their way to various collections. Already Pope Sixtus IV had some Egyptian and Egyptianizing objects exhibited in the

FIGURE II.4.1. The red granite obelisk originally erected at Heliopolis during the Nineteenth Dynasty was brought to Rome by Augustus to become part of the Circus Maximus. In 1589, it became a central feature of Piazza del Popolo. Credit: Egyptian obelisk at Piazza del Popolo. © Lucie Jirásková.

Capitol Museum, which was founded in 1470 (Curl 1994, 52). Italy was a rich source of inspiration for the rest of Renaissance Europe, and its influence soon reached other countries mainly through royal courts. The earliest documents of Egyptian motifs outside Italy could be seen at the court of King Francis I and later in other places in France (Curl 1994, 67). It took some time, however, before the central and northern parts of Europe started to follow the trend.

The interest in ancient Egyptian monuments, hieroglyphs, and their study was supported and spread across Europe also by publications that described them, such as *De re aedificatoria* (known as *Ten Books on Architecture*) by Leon Battista Alberti (1404–1472) published in 1485 (Curran 2007, 69–76). Although this work received much attention and found its way to France and Germany soon after its publication, a much more popular publication appeared a few years later, in 1499. It was *Hypnerotomachia Poliphili* by Fra Francesco Colonna (1433/4–1527) (Figure II.4.2). The work, accompanied by beautiful

FIGURE II.4.2. One of the most popular illustrations in Colonna's *Hypnerotomachia Poliphili* was an obelisk situated on the back of an elephant. The idea was later, in 1667, realized by Lorenzo Bernini at Piazza della Minerva. Credit: Egyptian obelisk at Piazza della Minerva. © Lucie Jirásková.

woodcuts, described a fictional journey through the Egyptian land covered by monuments inscribed in hieroglyphs, either real or imaginative (Volkmann 1923, 11–23). The last key publication with respect to the mediation of ancient Egyptian monuments and hieroglyphs to European scholars was *Hieroglyphica sive de sacris Aegyptiorum aliarumque gentium literis* by Pierio Valeriano (1477–1558) from 1556. It consisted of fifty-eight books, each dealing with various "hieroglyphs": animals, body parts, objects, plants, and so forth (Volkmann 1923, 11–40; Curran 2007, 146–156).

Besides inscribed obelisks, sphinxes, and pyramids, there were also other ancient Egyptian objects present in Europe at that time, usually of smaller sizes, not attracting so much attention, but serving either a practical function or as a means of studying ancient history. A "practical" ancient Egyptian artifact was a mummy. The European tradition knew it primarily as a medicament rather than as an embalmed ancient body (Germer 1991, 17–18). According to a Renaissance traveler to Egypt, Kryštof (Christopher) Harant of Polžice and Bezdružice (1564–1621), a piece of such "medicine" was to be found in every better equipped pharmacy in Europe (Harant 1972, 193). Pharmacies sold pieces of mummies ground into dust, and most people probably had no idea of their origin, but there was also another way of experiencing this object. At least from the time of the Renaissance, whole mummies were brought to Europe to be sold as curiosities (Curran 2007, 284). Again, Kryštof Harant mentioned a mummy shop in Cairo that had just sold several mummies to Venice (Harant 1972, 193). Another marketplace for ancient Egyptian objects was Constantinople. The first ancient Egyptian artifact still in the collection of the Kunsthistorisches Museum in Vienna was bought by Ogier Ghislain de Busbecq, the emissary of Holy Roman Emperor Francis I, in Constantinople in 1560 (Satzinger 1994, 7–9).

The period also saw the foundation of many collections of works of art, natural curiosities, and ethnographic objects (Lhotsky 1941–1945; Schlosser 1978; Scheicher 1979). One of the best known, probably the largest in Europe, was established and stored in Prague by the Holy Roman Emperor Rudolf II (reigned 1576–1612). (The longest inventory was published by Bauer and Haupt in 1976.) It contained an amazing mixture of artifacts that were intended to represent the whole world known at that time. The emperor gathered all these wonderful items in various chests in several rooms so that he and some other chosen specialists could study them in detail (Schultze and Fillitz 1988; Konečný, Bukovinská, and Muchka 1998). Ancient Egypt was included in the ethnographic part, represented by mummies (human and possibly also animal), pottery, and statuettes (Jirásková 2005). The purpose of the remarkable collection was highlighted by the presence of a study room as the center of the "Kunstkammer." Apart from the three rooms filled with various objects, it was mostly equipped with scientific machines, a library, and a large study desk in its center. From the point of view of studying ancient Egypt, it is necessary to mention geographic works and emblematic studies, such as *Thesaurus Hieroglyphicorum* by Johann Georg Herwarth von Hohenburg. (For details on the work, see Curran 2007, 283.) These specific books served the emperor in his scientific study of the collected objects and indicate the Renaissance approach to these objects and way of thinking.

EARLY APPROACHES
TO HIEROGLYPHIC SCRIPT

The work on hieroglyphs mentioned earlier led to another perspective of ancient Egypt in the Renaissance period. The rediscovery of ancient monuments in Rome represented mainly by obelisks increased the interest in the script that was engraved in them. There was no knowledge of its reading in Europe any more, and also in Egypt very few people could have possibly been able to read hieroglyphs at that time, since several Arabic sources mention Coptic monks who could read the ancient script in the Middle Ages (Pasquali 2016). The Coptic language, the only surviving piece of ancient Egyptian linguistic culture, was slowly turning into a merely liturgical language and ceased to be actively used in everyday communication in the sixteenth century. Moreover, it was written in Greek letters.

Some particular Arabic works presented not only the stories mentioning Coptic monks, who were the only living Egyptians able to understand the ancient script written on various monuments, but also offered explanations and interpretations of the hieroglyphs (see chapter by Sundermeyer). Unfortunately, these works were not generally accessible in Renaissance Europe and had no influence on the European view of the script. In this respect, other ways of interpreting hieroglyphs must have been developed by Europeans.

Although the Arabic writings were not available to the early Renaissance scholars and humanists, various explanations of the ancient Egyptian script were generally accessible in the works of ancient Greek authors. A new impetus came with an interesting work that appeared in Florence in 1419. *Hieroglyphica*, by Horapollo of Nilopolis, allegedly originally written in the ancient Egyptian language and later translated into Greek (first published in 1505), was translated and printed in Latin in 1517 (Volkmann 1923, 8; Horapollo 1950). The text was a manual for the reading of hieroglyphs, the mysterious script of ancient Egyptians, and through its simple but mysterious interpretation, it soon gained much attention. Despite the existence of an earlier reading of hieroglyphs in Clement of Alexandria's *Stromata*, Horapollo's way of reading was preferred. It probably better corresponded with the period's trends than the more complicated explanation of Clement, who divided the signs into several classes representing either sounds or objects (Donadoni, Curto, and Donadoni Roveri 1990, 45). Even Clement wrote of a "secret code" related to a group of signs, but Renaissance scholars chose solely the way of reading presented and elaborated by Horapollo and applied it to all the signs. Therefore, they saw the structure of hieroglyphs as a basic concept of each word written with a single sign. (Interestingly, not all of them were wrong; Champollion found thirteen correctly translated signs in the work of Horapollo [1950, 29].) Moreover, the reading was hindered by the symbolic representation of the objects meant and drawn. It is necessary to add that Horapollo's approach was supported by the narratives of Pliny, Plutarch, and Plotinus, who also spoke of ancient wisdom hidden in the ancient Egyptian temples, recorded in enigmatic hieroglyphs that could keep it secret (see chapter by Winand).

Many scholars were influenced by the numerous Greek texts translated into Latin in the fifteenth and sixteenth centuries as well as by Horapollo's work or by *Asclepius* and *Corpus Hermeticum*. Scholars such as Alberti and Valeriano, whose theses were mentioned earlier, paid much attention to "Egyptian" hieroglyphs in their publications (Figure II.4.3). They also followed the outline of neo-Platonic way of perception, that is, of secret knowledge hidden in the lines of the pictorial script (Curran 2007, 72–73; Laboury 2006).

Encouraged by Horapollo's approach, Renaissance scholars did not (in fact) so much try to read the genuine ancient texts, but rather attempted to develop and write their own records. Such a study of the hieroglyphs benefited by heraldry, antique symbolic, imprese, and other sources of inspiration led to a new branch of art, which is called emblematics (Giehlow 1915; Volkmann 1923; Henkel and Schöne 1976; Wittkower 1977; Morenz 2003). One of the key works on emblems, *Emblematum liber* by the Italian Andrea Alciato (1492–1550), was published in Augsburg in 1531. He defined the meaning of the Renaissance "emblem." The book contained 104 emblems, each consisting of three parts—a short title (motto), an illustration, and an explanation in verse giving the key to the meaning of the emblem (Volkmann 1923, 41–45).

The view of Egypt as a country of wisdom and secret knowledge that was accessible only to a particular group of people satisfied the needs of Renaissance scholars and humanists, who therefore preferred the symbolic reading of hieroglyphic signs. Unfortunately, it was a dead end that prevented any progress toward real understanding of ancient texts. Interestingly, although the hieroglyphic signs were an important source of inspiration, there was no effort at all to use similar signs in emblematic works. In this respect, the method was more important than the language and the script itself (Wittkower 1977, 118).

The Renaissance publications of the discovered monuments, including the epigraphic work, were of two kinds. Many artists who drew the ancient Egyptian or Egyptianizing monuments and artifacts put no emphasis on the real visual aspects of hieroglyphs. Others tried to make true copies. Most artists, who tended to approach the script through emblematics and the Hermetica, neglected the true shape of signs, whereas architects, such as Cronaca (Simone del Pollaiolo), an Italian architect who documented the Vatican obelisk (Donadoni, Curto, and Donadoni Roveri 1990, 55) and who drew "technical" illustrations, attempted to be accurate.

Athanasius Kircher was the first scholar who got slightly closer to the reading of hieroglyphs, due to a completely new approach. He did not belong to the group of Renaissance humanists anymore, but rather represented the upcoming Baroque age. However, the influence of Hermetism and the strong Christian thinking of Kircher can still be followed in his work. Kircher's approach to hieroglyphs and their study was not straightforward. He first came across several Coptic works that attracted his attention and directed his future steps. These books, including Coptic grammars and Coptic-Arabic vocabularies, were brought to Europe by Pietro della Valle, who not only traveled

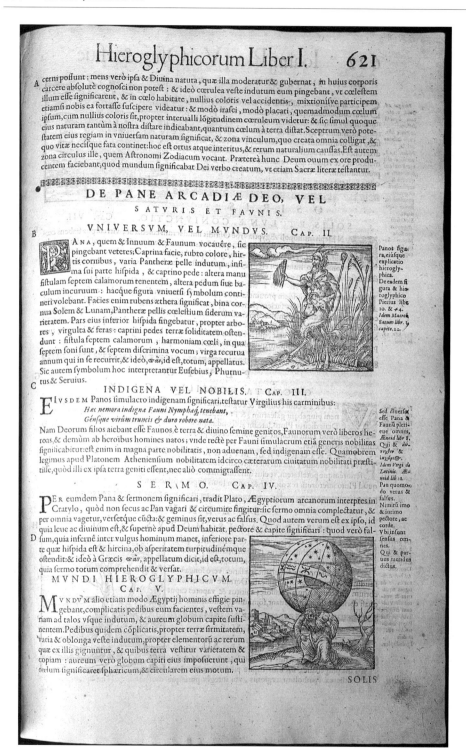

FIGURE II.4.3. Renaissance hieroglyphs from Pierio Valeriano's publication followed the period trends and did not correspond to original Egyptian signs. Credit: Pierio Valeriano. *Hieroglyphica sive de sacris Aegyptiorum aliarumque gentium literis.* Library of the Czech Institute of Egyptology. Sign. F 872. © Czech Institute of Egyptology. Faculty of Arts. Charles University.

to Egypt but also spent many years in other Oriental countries and brought back many valuable objects. (Curran 2007, 284).

The Coptic language was almost unknown and neglected by scholars at that time, except for a few people, such as Nicholas-Claude Fabri de Peiresc, who recommended Kircher as a translator of the aforementioned manuscripts. Kircher emphasized the similarity between "modern" Coptic and ancient Egyptian. The awareness of the historical succession of the two languages led to the scientific study of Coptic and the production of the first Coptic grammar available to other scholars in Europe. The intense study of Coptic language subsequently aided in the first steps toward the reading of hieroglyphs (even Jean-François Champollion learned Coptic before deciphering hieroglyphs).

Although Kircher was successful in reading Coptic, he followed a blind alley when trying to apply his knowledge on the reading of the hieroglyphic script. He thought that the letters used to record Coptic language were developed straight from hieroglyphs (and much later adopted by Greeks), as was the spoken language. In this respect, he attempted to "reconstruct" the hieroglyphic alphabet, which would have served as a paradigm for the Coptic alphabet. Moreover, influenced by Hermetism, he was still not able to abandon completely the symbolic interpretation of hieroglyphs (Beinlich 2002, 89–92; Curran 2007, 286).

Apart from introducing Coptic and its grammatical system to European readers, Kircher's contribution to hieroglyphic studies was also significant in the area of the publication of existing texts. Contrary to his Renaissance predecessors, who often "published" ancient Egyptian monuments of Rome regardless of the original signs, inventing their own hieroglyphs, Kircher copied the texts in detail, presenting real ancient Egyptian signs (Donadoni, Curto, and Donadoni Roveri 1990, 61–65). Due to his authority, he was also able to access numerous private collections that included ancient Egyptian objects. Kircher later published their drawings and descriptions in his work *Oedipus Aegyptiacus* (Beinlich 2002, 97).

RISE OF HERMETISM

The symbolic reading of hieroglyphs was supported by the wave of Hermetism that influenced many areas of Renaissance science. Once again, it originated in Italy, particularly at the Academy of the Medici in Florence as the center of translations of ancient Greek texts into Latin. It was there that one of the key works, a manuscript called *Corpus Hermeticum*, appeared in 1460. In 1471, it was translated into Latin by order of Cosimo de Medici and became generally accessible through print as *Pimander*. In the original manuscript, *Pimander* was the name of the first part (dialogue) dealing with the creation of the world. The corpus consisted of fourteen parts of incoherent forms and contents that must have originally been written by different authors. Its neo-Platonic thoughts were acceptable to the society of that time, since the primary objective of the numerous translations of Greek texts was an effort to find Christian features in ancient works.

Indeed, many were found in *Corpus Hermeticum*, which rapidly gained in popularity and was printed in sixteen editions in the Latin translation by the end of the sixteenth century. Of great importance was always the commentary of the editor, who set the work in context (Donadoni, Curto, and Donadoni Roveri 1990, 43–44; Curran 2007, 90–92).

Another important publication was titled *Asclepius*. This piece of text has never been found in its original Greek version, but became known only through the Latin translations appearing in the works of earlier philosophers and patriarchs, such as Lactantius or Augustine. It seems that the corpus consisted of three parts, again written by three different authors (Yates 1964, 8). Lactantius discussed Hermes Trismegistos and his supposed thesis *Asclepius* partly in *De ira Dei* and more thoroughly in *Divinae institutiones* (Lactantius 1871). Like his Renaissance successors, Lactantius attempted to find Christian motives in *Asclepius* and due to a positive approach to *Asclepius*, he admired and defended Hermes as the one who was able to see the (Christian) truth in pagan times. Augustine (1957–1972) dealt with Hermes in his work *De civitate Dei*, which was also primarily meant as a defense of Christianity. His approach to *Asclepius* was different, however. Although Augustine also admitted that Hermes was able to get closer to the "right" view of the world, he rather concentrated on the problematic points of Trismegistos's teaching. In this respect, Augustine perceived Trismegistos as a traditional representative of a pagan religion.

The sources of inspiration for the composition of *Corpus Hermeticum* and *Asclepius* had roots in Late Antiquity. Due to the similarity of thoughts and arguments in the Hermetica and in philosophical studies from the early years after Christ, Renaissance humanists thought that the Greek philosophers had taken over the best ideas of Hermes Trismegistos available at their time and worked with them in their own theses. Hermes (the Greek version of Egyptian Thoth) was mostly associated with astral science and magic in Late Antiquity, but philosophical and religious texts connected with him also existed (Hermes Trismegistus 1924, 1). *Asclepius* and *Corpus Hermeticum* were probably created between 100 and 300 CE. Mostly neo-Platonic thoughts, influenced by stoicism, Jewish thought, and probably also Persian religion (Yates 1964, 3), were presented through a dialogue of Hermes as the master and one of his disciples, such as Tat, Asclepius (who resembles ancient Imhotep), or Ammon.

Renaissance scholars perceived Hermes Trismegistos (the epithet was a Greek version of Egyptian "ꜥꜣ ꜥꜣ ꜥꜣ" used for Thoth) as a real person who had lived a long time ago. They knew that his existence had been accepted and his thoughts discussed by the patriarchs Lactantius and Augustine, who were still strong authorities at the time of the Renaissance. Inspired by Medieval works on Trismegistos, Marcilio Ficino, the Florentine translator of *Pimander*, added to his translation a genealogy of Hermetic wisdom (Hanegraaff 2005, 476–477). However, the main influence on Renaissance science and philosophy dwelled in two areas. One of them was represented by Christian motifs; the other, more important from the point of view of reading ancient Egyptian script, was the idea of sacred wisdom that was supposed to be kept secret in ancient Egyptian temples. This wisdom was accessible only to a limited number of chosen people who were taught to read and write hieroglyphs as the means of codification of this sacred wisdom. In this respect, the obelisks inscribed with hieroglyphs were sacred symbols of knowledge, and the sphinxes were the guardians of the ancient wisdom.

Such an approach inspired many scholars of that time, Giordano Bruno being the best known (Yates 1964). The end of the Renaissance Hermetic wave stimulated by *Asclepius* and *Corpus Hermeticum* came with the philological analysis by Isaac Casaubon published in 1614 in *De rebus sacris et ecclesiasticis exertationes XVI*. He was the first to deny that Hermes Trismegistos could have been the author of these two works. Casaubon did not disclaim his existence, but merely assigned the works to an unknown Christian author. Moreover, he claimed that the texts could not have been written before the second or third centuries CE (Yates 1964, 398–403; Iversen 1984, 27–28).

Although the critical study denied the supposed origin of the Hermetica, the magical-esoteric thought still attracted many people and has survived into modern times in various forms (Thorndike 1929–1958). In contrast to that, the Renaissance perception of hieroglyphs and its "innovative" approach to them was abandoned in favor of a real scientific study of the script represented by Athanasius Kircher and his followers.

Kircher's main contribution to hieroglyphic studies was a new perspective from which he studied hieroglyphs. Most of the Renaissance humanists perceived the signs as individual words, whereas Kircher tried to search for particular letters, that is, the sounds of the ancient speech. Also, the visual aspects of the hieroglyphic signs, which were of minor importance for the Renaissance humanists, played a significant role in his publications. These two features of his "Egyptological" work were the first steps to a scientific work and divided the Renaissance "fascination" from modern science, although many years were to pass until the script of the ancient Egyptians was finally deciphered by Champollion.

Bibliography

Augustine. 1957–1972. *City of God*. Edited and translated by G. E. McCracken, W. M. Green, D. S. Wiesen, P. Levine, E. M. Sanford, and W. C. Greene. Cambridge.

Bauer, R., and H. Haupt. 1976. "Das Kunstkammerinventar Kaiser Rudolf II: 1607–1611." *JKSW* 72:1–140.

Beinlich, H. 2002. "Athanasius Kircher und die Kenntnis vom Alten Ägypten." In *Magie des Wissens: Athanasius Kircher 1602–1680. Universalgelehrter, Sammler, Visionär*, edited by H. Beinlich, C. Daxelmüller, H.-J. Vollrath, and K. Wittstadt, 85–98. Dettelbach.

Curl, J. S. 1994. *Egyptomania: The Egyptian Revival; A Recurring Theme in the History of Taste*. Manchester.

Curran, B. A. 2007. *The Egyptian Renaissance: The Afterlife of Ancient Egypt in Early Modern Italy*. Chicago.

Donadoni, S., S. Curto, and A. M. Donadoni Roveri. 1990. *Egypt from Myth to Egyptology*. Milan.

Germer, R. 1991. *Mumien: Zeugen des Pharaonenreiches*. Zürich.

Giehlow, K. 1915. "Die Hieroglyphenkunde des Humanismus in der Alegorie der Renaissance, besonders der Ehrenpforte Kaisers Maximilian I." *JKSAK* 32:1–232.

Hanegraaff, W. J., ed. 2005. *Dictionary of Gnosis and Western Esotericism*. Leiden.

Harant, K. 1972. *Voyage en Egypte de Christophe Harant de Polžic et Bezdružic 1598.* Translated by C. Brejnik and A. Brejnik. Cairo.

Henkel, A., and A. Schöne. 1976. *Emblemata: Handbuch zur Sinnbildkunst des XVI. und XVII. Jahrhunderts.* Stuttgart.

Hermes Trismegistus [pseud.]. 1924. *Hermetica: The Ancient Greek and Latin Writings Which Contain Religious or Philosophic Teachings Ascribed to Hermes Trismegistus.* Vol. 1. Edited and translated by W. Scott. Oxford.

Horapollo. 1950. *The Hieroglyphics of Horapollo.* Edited by G. Boas. New York.

Iversen, E. 1968. *Obelisks in Exile, Vol. 1: The Obelisks of Rome.* Copenhagen.

Iversen, E. 1984. *Egyptian and Hermetic Doctrine.* Copenhagen.

Iversen, E. 1993. *The Myth of Egypt and Its Hieroglyphs in European Tradition.* New Jersey.

Jirásková, L. 2005. "The Reception of Ancient Egypt in the Collection of Emperor Rudolf II." In *Egypt and Austria I. Proceedings of the Symposium,* edited by J. Holaubek and H. Navrátilová, 71–79. Prague.

Jirásková, L. 2007. "Ancient Egypt in Private Czech and Moravian Renaissance Libraries." In *Egypt and Austria III. The Danube Monarchy and the Orient. Proceedings of the Prague Symposium, September 11th to 14th, 2006,* edited by J. Holaubek, H. Navrátilová, and W. B. Oerter, 133–144. Prague.

Kalfatovic, M. R. 1992. *Nile Notes of a Howadji: A Bibliography of Travelers' Tales from Egypt, from the Earliest Time to 1918.* London.

Konečný, L., B. Bukovinská, and I. Muchka, eds. 1998. *Rudolf II, Prague and the World.* Prague.

Laboury, D. 2006. "Renaissance de l'Égypte aux temps modernes: De l'antérêt pour la civilisation pharaonique et ses hiéroglyphes a Liège au XVIᵉ siècle." In *La Caravane du Caire: L'Égypte sur d'autres rives,* edited by Eugène Warmenbol, 43–68. Louvain-la-Neuve.

Lactantius. 1871. *The Works of Lactantius.* 2 vols. Translated by W. Fletcher. Edinburgh.

Lhotsky, A. 1941–1945. *Die Geschichte der Sammlungen. Erste Hälfte: Von den Anfängen bis zum Tode Kaiser Karls VI 1740.* Vienna.

Morenz, L. D. 2003. "Neohieroglyphs of the Italian Renaissance Tradition and Its Invention." In *Philosophers and Hieroglyphs,* edited by L. Morra and C. Bazzanella, 50–69. Turin.

Pasquali, S. 2016. "Les hiéroglyphes égyptiens vus par les auteurs arabes du Moyen Âge ou l'aura du passé pharaonique." In *À l'école des scribes: Les écritures de l'Égypte ancienne. Site archéologique Lattara—Musée Henri Prades, Lattes 9 juillet 2016–7 janvier 2017,* edited by L. Bazin-Rizzo, A. Gasse, and F. Servajean, 213–225. Milan.

Roullet, A. 1972. *The Egyptian and Egyptianizing Monuments of Imperial Rome.* Leiden.

Satzinger, H. 1994. *Das Kunsthistorische Museum in Wien: Die Ägyptisch-Orientalische Sammlung.* Mainz.

Scheicher, E. 1979. *Die Kunst- und Wunderkammern der Habsburger.* Vienna.

Schlosser, J. von. 1978. *Die Kunst- und Wunderkammern der Spätrenaissance: Ein Beitrag zur Geschichte des Sammelwesens.* Braunschweig.

Schultze, J., and H. Fillitz, eds. 1988. *Prag um 1600: Kunst und Kultur am Hofe Rudolfs II.* Freren.

Thorndike, L. 1929–1958. *A History of Magic and Experimental Science.* Vols. I–VIII. New York.

Villamont, J. de. 1971. *Voyages en Egypte des années 1589, 1590 et 1591.* Edited by C. Burri, N. Sauneron, and P. Bleser. Cairo.

Volkmann, L. 1923. *Bilderschriften der Renaissance: Hieroglyphik und Emblematik in ihren Beziehungen und fort Wirkungen.* Leipzig.

Wittkower, R. 1977. *Allegory and the Migration of Symbols.* Boulder, Colorado.

Yates, F. A. 1964. *Giordano Bruno and the Hermetic Tradition.* London.

THE EPIGRAPHY OF EGYPTIAN MONUMENTS IN THE *DESCRIPTION DE L'ÉGYPTE*

ÉRIC GADY

PUBLISHED between 1809 and 1828, the *Description de l'Égypte* may be roughly summarized as a scientific victory born of a military failure. As part of their extensive work, Bonaparte's scholars copied and made available a huge amount of genuine Egyptian art and texts, an approach to the ancient material that was completely revolutionary at the time, especially since Europe had been disconnected from Egypt for more than a millennium and exclusively based its perception of Pharaonic culture on Greek and Roman comments, (selected) imports, and imitations. Although the French expedition to Egypt might not be called an "epigraphic survey" in the current and modern sense of that term, the work that was accomplished was an important step in providing Europe with Egyptian inscriptions and iconographic material.

WHO WERE THE SCIENTISTS WHO COPIED EGYPTIAN MONUMENTS?

Bonaparte brought with him to Egypt 40,000 soldiers, but also about 150 to 160 scientists who constituted the *Commission des sciences et des arts* (Commission for Sciences and Arts). The fact that it was a collective expedition (the first scientific collective expedition that was not maritime; Bourguet 1999, 23) was completely new at that time. Bonaparte's scientists were able to produce a work of greater significance than all their predecessors.

They were numerous, but above all, they quickly "formed tighter bonds" (Burleigh 2007, 91), which allowed them to work in a collective spirit.

Few of them were destined to study ancient Egypt specifically; only three were *antiquaires* (specialists in antiquity), but none were famous for that, and there were no historians or epigraphers, except a few who specialized in other areas of the ancient Near East. There were also architects, doctors, botanists, mineralogists, chemists, and other experts, but most of the scientists who were the "architects and builders" (Gillispie 1999, 45) of the ancient part of the *Description de l'Égypte* were in fact engineers (nearly one-third of the scientists; Laissus 1998, 523–525), in particular, students from the École des ponts et chaussées, the brand new École polytechnique. Although their famous teachers, such as Monge, Berthollet, and Denon, had almost not participated in the *Description*, these young men would become famous: Jomard, Jollois, Viard, Villiers du Terrage, Chabrol, Lancret, and Dubois-Aymé, among others. Others were professional draftsmen, such as Dutertre or Redouté. As students, the engineers were very young. The average age of all the scientists was about twenty-five. The youngest was barely fifteen years old. None of them even knew the exact destination of the expedition. In fact, although these young scientists may have had a solid classical background, they discovered a country they knew little of before (Malaise 2003; Winckelmann 1764). They were not prepared with a knowledge of ancient Egypt, but as engineering students, they were thoroughly trained in drawing (half of their teaching program at the École polytechnique, for example), in particular scientific drawing and also mathematics, physics, and other sciences. They were prepared to make drawings with scientific rigor and precision. For these engineers, measurement of everything was the priority. But most of all, they were young, enthusiastic about all they were going to discover, worked hard and worked together, and were eager to make note of and draw everything they could. The spirit of this scientific expedition in the Age of the Enlightenment prompted these young scientists to produce a work that had no equivalent.

What Was the Scientists' Mission?

Most of the scientists, especially the younger ones and the engineers, had agreed to leave on the expedition without knowing its exact destination. The French government (the *Directoire*) had given only three objectives to Bonaparte: to take control of the Red Sea; to cut off the Suez isthmus from the British; and to improve the lot of the Egyptians. For this last objective, Bonaparte wanted to add scientists to the expedition. But the expedition was hastily prepared (in about three months), and for this reason, the French Institute did not have time to write precise instructions for the scientists, as the Académie royale des sciences did, for example, for the La Pérouse expedition thirteen years earlier (Laissus 2009, 7). When they left France, the scientists simply did not know what they would be doing. Moreover, the team assembled for the expedition and the fact that there were no historians among them shows clearly that the recording for Egyptian texts was by no means the first objective (Forgeau 1998, 33).

When they arrived, the scientists turned their attention to the natural history of Egypt and to modern and ancient Egypt. They set their own agenda, took measurements of what they saw, drew up maps, and so forth. But the young engineers were also fascinated by the ancient monuments, especially by pharaonic architecture, which was, to them, a revelation. The first scientist who went to Upper Egypt was not a young engineer, but an artist who was already very famous: Vivant Denon. He followed Desaix's army in Upper Egypt in 1798 and 1799. He was immediately enthusiastic about Egyptian architecture, especially when he discovered the temple of Dendera. But working alone and always on the move, he was unable to copy any Egyptian texts. His drawings, published beginning in 1802 to much acclaim, are the fruit of an artist, not of an engineer, and absolutely not those of an epigrapher. The hieroglyphic characters are very roughly and inexactly drawn (Golvin 1989, 333–338).

At about the same time, a small expedition directed by the engineer Girard went to Upper Egypt to collect information about agriculture, art, and other topics. The expedition was made up of engineers, such as Jollois, Villiers du Terrage, Dubois-Aymé, Dupuy, and an artist, Casteix. These young men became captivated by ancient sites. Each day, after their official work, they drew all they saw, but not as Denon did. They worked as engineers, taking measurements of the monuments. They wanted to produce not artistic drawings but scientific drawings, following a methodical plan of work. At Dendera, Villiers du Terrage and Jollois wanted to make an exact reproduction of the zodiac. They worked as archaeologists still do, to understand rather than to simply appreciate the monuments. They carefully recorded the scenes sculpted as bas-reliefs. They did this work in their spare time, on their own initiative, and had no official orders to do so. The expedition's director, Girard, did not approve of their pastime, and he chastised them, saying that it was not their mission "to make hieroglyphs" (Villiers du Terrage 2001, 142).

In Cairo, Denon showed his drawings to Bonaparte, who, before leaving again for France, named two scientific missions, one directed by Costaz and the other by Fourier, to explore Upper Egypt. When the two missions met Girard's expedition, back in Cairo, they understood the importance of the work Jollois and Villiers du Terrage had already done. They decided not to duplicate their work, but to use it as the basis for the final product. The majority of the plates in the *Description* about the monuments of ancient Egypt stems from the work of all of these engineers (Golvin 1989, 347).

In the *Description*'s Preface, Fourier sums up the engineers' work: "on levait les plans topographiques; on dessinait les divers aspects du paysage et plusieurs vues pittoresques du même édifice (…); on imitait fidèlement les tableaux peints ou sculptés, et les caractères hiéroglyphiques dont ils sont couverts" (Fourier 1809, LXII). (We were making topographical plans; drawing the various aspects of the landscape and many picturesque views of the same building [...]; faithfully imitating the painted and carved scenes, along with the hieroglyphic characters with which they are covered.) This is surely accurate, but again, this work was not planned from the start. In fact, the engineers arrived in Egypt with "no definite program. They worked as they wished, choosing their topics themselves, coming back to the places they were particularly interested in" (Pinault Sørensen 1999, 164–165).

How Did They Work?

The scientists and draftsmen of Bonaparte's expedition were not specifically trained nor were they prepared to carry out an epigraphic survey of Egypt, and they did not have much time to teach themselves. (None of them, of course, knew how to read hieroglyphs.) They used the simplest tools: paper and pencils. Along with sticks of glue, these were the only things that Villiers du Terrage was ordered to prepare before the departure to Upper Egypt (Gillispie 1989, 339). The *Description* often shows Bonaparte's soldiers or scientists in the monuments. In approximately two dozen plates, the figure of one of Bonaparte's draftsman, with his hat, his typical gabardine coat, and his portfolio, can easily be identified (for example, *Description de l'Égypte* III, pls. 20, 48 [hereafter cited as *Desc.* and *Expl. Planches*]). Only once does the explanation clearly mention a "French engineer engaged in copying the Greek inscription" (*Desc.* IV, pl. 59). In most of the plates, the engineers stand up just in front of the object or inscription to draw (*Desc.* III, pl. 48, 6); and occasionally, they are represented seated, using their portfolio as a table (*Desc.* I, pl. 67, 1). This confirms Denon's words, writing later that he had drawn "most of the time on his knee, or standing, or even on horseback" (Laissus 1998, 234–235). Engineers are never seen using ladders to copy inscriptions at the top of columns, for example, only because they had none with them. They pointed out that at Qus, they were able to approach and copy the upper part of the door because it had deteriorated and fallen to the ground (*Desc.* II, 68). They copied only what they were able to see, which was not always easy. A plate of the *Description* presents only six inscriptions on the terrace roof of the south great temple at Karnak, "the most important and visible" inscriptions (*Desc.* III, pl. 57). They also sometimes made casts in order to have exact copies of inscriptions or parts of monuments. Casts were made with sulfur (most of the time), but also plaster, wax (*Desc.* II, 444), and even metal in the case of a sarcophagus. The casts provided models for the draftsmen and the engravers of the *Description* (*Desc.* II, 448). The Rosetta Stone was reproduced by three ways: hand drawing (imagined by Jean-Joseph Marcel), lithography (by Nicolas-Jacques Conté), and a sulfur cast made by engineer Adrien Raffeneau-Delile (Laissus 1998, 256–258).

The engineers' objective was to precisely copy all of the hieroglyphs they could, as Fourier wrote in the Preface to the *Description*: "on s'est attaché, dans un grand nombre de ces dessins [= bas-reliefs], à transcrire exactement les caractères hiéroglyphiques; et l'on a conservé non seulement les formes individuelles, mais encore l'ordre et la disposition respectives de ces signes" (Fourier 1809, LXXX). ("We set out, in most of these drawings [of reliefs] to faithfully transcribe the hieroglyphic signs; and we copied not only the individual forms, but also the order and disposition of those signs.") On many occasions, the *Description* stresses the importance the engineers attached to the very faithful reproduction of scenes and hieroglyphs. The plates of the Rosetta Stone and of the zodiac of Dendera were prepared with the most "religious care" (*Desc.* V, 152).

The scientists encountered several difficulties. They realized that the hour of the day and the way that the sun shone on the inscriptions affected copying and could explain different versions of the same text produced by various travelers (*Desc.* II, 69; see Qus citation earlier). It was often difficult to work at midday, so they preferred to work in the morning or evening. The zodiac of Dendera was very "long and arduous" to copy, but Jollois and Villiers du Terrage, who endured suffocating heat in the black room lit only by their torches for several weeks, succeeded in copying the zodiac: "using string, they divided the intricate ceiling frieze into eight sectors and worked on a scale of one to five, reproducing every inch of it" (Burleigh 2007, 178–179). Another difficulty was the lack of paper or pencils. In Upper Egypt, Villiers du Terrage ran out of pencils, but employing their boundless ingenuity, the engineers melted down bullets and, with reeds, improvised writing implements (Villiers du Terrage 2001, 153–154). It must also be noted that the scientists were moving through a land at war and had to work under the protection of the French soldiers. They also were faced with the loss of the notes they had taken. The Greco-Roman inscriptions of the colossi of Memnon had been taken by a certain M. Coquebert, who died prematurely and whose papers were lost (*Desc.* I, 309).

The most important difficulty was the lack of time. The men most regretted not copying all they had seen. For example, at Edfu, Jomard merely indicated that there were seventy-five columns of hieroglyphs; it was not possible to copy the full set of inscriptions (*Desc.* I, 171). He also lamented not being able to copy a unique scene in a temple at Armant "with all of its hieroglyphic inscriptions" (*Desc.* I, 218). About the Theban rock-cut tombs, he wrote, "as for the possibility of drawing so many details, it would have been necessary to have a prodigious amount of time: twenty people occupied for six months in a row to copy the rock tombs' paintings would not draw the tenth part" (*Desc.* I, 557). Although they were aware that they could not make a complete survey, they thought that it was a job for future travelers, who could use prints and other "mechanical means" to make copies (*Desc.* I, 609; II, 114). The engineers noted that once, in the Suez desert, they had no time to stop and copy a "Persepolitan" (i.e., a Persian) bas-relief. Thus, they decided to remove some fragments, which they took with them in order to publish them at a later date (*Desc.* II, 533). In their understanding, Egypt was a land for future scientists: "combien de tableaux et de sujets il reste encore à dessiner dans les monuments! Nous attachant, comme nous devions le faire, à recueillir des scènes complètes, nous donnions à chacune un temps considérable, et nous n'avons pu réussir, malgré nos efforts, qu'à en copier une faible partie: tant est grande la richesse, l'étendue ou la quantité de tableaux hiéroglyphiques" (*Desc.* I, 586). ("How many scenes and subjects are still to be drawn in the monuments! Setting out, as we had to, to collect complete scenes, we devoted to each one of them a considerable amount of time, and despite our efforts, we could only copy a small part of them: the richness, the extent, and the quantity of hieroglyphic tableaus are so great.")

What Was the Result of Their Work?

The *Description de l'Égypte* presents the result of the scientists' collective work: five volumes of plates, entitled "Antiquités," and four volumes of texts ("Descriptions" and "Mémoires"). For each archaeological site, the presentation of the plates is always the same: the view begins with large landscapes, zooms in to views of monuments, and then details of parts of these monuments. Hieroglyphs play their part on the plates. Even on the plates showing full views of monuments, hieroglyphs are represented. This is not systematically done, however, on the plates showing details of the monuments. Some plates feature scenes and small columns of texts, but in many other scenes, texts are missing or columns of texts are represented, but without any hieroglyphs (for example, *Desc.* I, pl. 82).

If the expedition members did not copy all the hieroglyphs, it was clearly because of a lack of time. They mention as much, for example, in reference to their work at Philae (*Desc.* I, pl. 12 and *Expl. Planches* I, 12). A few plates later, the *Description* presents six scenes. Three of them are complete, with figures and hieroglyphs, but the others are not: "les tableaux 2, 4 et 6 sont complets; ils peuvent donner une idée parfaitement exacte de ceux dont on n'a pas recueilli les hiéroglyphes et, en général, de tous ceux qui décorent les monuments égyptiens" (*Expl. Planches* I, 22). ("Scenes 2, 4, and 6 are complete; they may provide a perfectly accurate idea of those whose hieroglyphs we could not record and, in general, of all those that decorated Egyptian monuments.") Similar comments are also made with regard to Edfu, "On n'a pu dessiner qu'une partie des hiéroglyphes de ce tableau curieux" (*Expl. Planches* I, 59). ("We could only draw a portion of the hieroglyphs of this intriguing scene.")

The scientists clearly intuited that the hieroglyphs and large-scale figures are different parts of the same scene. Indeed, they noticed the presence of the same items in both the figures and the hieroglyphs around those figures, and they concluded that the hieroglyphs were linked to the figures. For example, the *Description* notes in regard to a scene at Philae: "l'offrande du prêtre est une coiffure composée de deux pièces; on la voit aussi en tête de la colonne hiéroglyphique placée devant le prêtre. [...] Ce même signe prouve le rapport de sens qu'il y a entre l'action du personnage et la phrase hiéroglyphique dont il est accompagné. [...] Divers tableaux que le lecteur peut consulter conduisent au même résultat" (*Expl. Planches* I, pl. 22). ("The offering presented by the priest is a headgear made of two pieces; the latter can also be seen at the top of the hieroglyphic column in front of him. [...] This same sign proves the semantic relation between the action of the figure and the accompanying hieroglyphic sentence. [...] Many scenes that the reader might consult lead to the same conclusion.") For this reason, they wanted to copy the hieroglyphs in the most accurate way: "On s'est attaché à copier les hiéroglyphes avec la plus parfaite exactitude. Les scènes très intelligibles que ces hiéroglyphes accompagent pourront servir à leur interprétation si, comme tout le démontre, les inscriptions hiéroglyphiques ont du rapport avec les tableaux" (*Expl. Planches* I, pl. 68). ("We set out to copy the hieroglyphs as faithfully as possible. The very intelligible scenes that those hieroglyphs accompany can be used for their interpretation if, as everything indicates, the hieroglyphic inscriptions are connected with the scenes.") They understood that the text and image work together. "On a le droit de conclure que ces colonnes de hiéroglyphes placées devant chaque personnage ont un rapport avec la scène du tableau et l'action du personnage" (*Expl. Planches* I, pl. 10). ("We may conclude that the columns of hieroglyphs set in front of each figure are related to the scene and the action of the figure.") They also noticed that texts and images were in the same direction: "Ainsi qu'il est d'ordinaire, les signes d'écriture sont tournés dans le sens des personnages qu'ils environnent" (*Desc.* II, 446). ("As is usual, the writing signs are oriented according to the direction of the figures they surround.")

Although the copyists took care to record images along with hieroglyphs, it was not possible for them to do this systematically. Champollion's private judgment of the authors of the *Description* seems to be very negative. When he traveled in Egypt, he carried with him a copy of the *Description*. He wrote in a private letter to his brother about his extreme disappointment: "il faudrait fouetter en place publique la *Commission d'Égypte* [. . .] [qui a] osé publier des croquis si informes de ces grandes et belles compositions" (Champollion 1824, 455). ("One should flog in the public arena the *Commission of Egypt* [. . .] [who] dared to publish such rough sketches of those great and beautiful compositions.") His judgment was rather stern, primarily because he and his brother disliked Jomard, who was responsible for the publication of the *Description*. Champollion had other good reasons to express that opinion to his brother when he compared the plates of the *Description* with what he saw on the monuments:

- Lacunas are numerous in the *Description*. Many columns of hieroglyphs on the plates are empty (for example, Medinet Habu, *Desc.* II, pl. 11, completely anepigraph). This is due to a lack of time and to the fact that the scientists preferred empty columns to the invention of fanciful signs, as Vivant Denon had done a few years earlier (Van Essche-Merchez and Broze 1993, 73). Some lacunas are clearly mentioned, but others, are not (for example *Desc.* pl. I, 67, where the copyist forgot to note that there were also hieroglyphs).
- The scientists sometimes preferred to copy only one column of the temple and then reproduce that column for all of the other columns, rather than copying each individual column's set of signs (for example, Dendera, *Desc.* IV, pls. 7, 9–10, 29–30).
- Mistakes are numerous (for example, a plate drawn by Redouté at Esna: *Desc.* I, pl. 81). Redouté had difficulty reading the names inscribed in the cartouches at the top right of the wall. He should have left them empty, but he preferred to fill the cartouches with signs he had seen in others cartouches, rather than try to accurately read the signs there. Below that, Redouté tried to restore a lacuna in the text, but he failed. Under the king's arms, he drew five animals (which should have been rams, but clearly are not) instead of four, and he forgot the cross and the three small plural strokes. Before the cartouches above the figure of the king, he omitted the signs for "King of Upper and Lower Egypt," "Son of Re," etc. (Van Essche-Merchez and Broze, 1993, 80). This example is not unique, and similar mistakes are rather frequent.

- And no less significantly, especially in the perspective of this book, despite their strong and explicit will to produce faithful copies of what they saw, Bonaparte's scholars created images in which the impact of their own visual culture is plain to see. Because of their classical background and, for many of them, of their reading of J. J. Winckelmann's seminal *Geschichte der Kunst des Altertums* (*History of the Art of Antiquity*, 1764), which set Greek art as the ultimate standard for the appraisal and perception of any other art form from antiquity, the style of their drawings is noticeably Hellenized or contaminated by classical imagery. In many respects, their work looked like ancient Roman copies of Egyptian monuments (such as those one can still see on the so-called Sallustiano obelisk in front of the Trinità dei Monti church in Rome, an early third-century CE copy of the Heliopolitan obelisk of Seti I and Ramesses II now in the center of the Piazza del Popolo). Very interestingly, this Hellenization or classical influence varies according to what may be called the iconographic genre: for instance, the depiction of the Memnon colossi in the archaeological *vedute* genre (*Desc.* II, pl. 20) is much more accurate, and hence genuinely Egyptian, than the reconstitutions in full front, side, and back views of the very same statues (*Desc.* II, pls. 21–22), whose appearance strongly resembles the Egyptianizing sculptures of Antinous made in the time of Emperor Hadrian. This was certainly shocking for Champollion, who was a great admirer of ancient Egyptian art per se, not in comparison with ancient Greek art (Champollion 1824). Moreover, the Hellenized style of ancient Egyptian monuments as they appear in the *Description* perfectly illustrates the almost inevitable impact of cultural background on every epigraphic recording attempt since epigraphy is always an interpretation (as Bonaparte's scholars seem to have already been aware of). To put it another way, it is an unavoidable cognitive fact that we do not see with our eyes but with our brain, which involves our visual culture and reference thesaurus, in addition to the issue of our understanding of what is looked at.

But these "mistakes" should not diminish the value of the publication. Indeed, the work done in the *Description* is without comparison among the books published by the engineers' predecessors. The five volumes about antiquity offered to the world so many scenes, texts, and signs inscribed and painted on the walls of monuments, on objects, or in manuscripts (for example, the plates from the papyri from the Theban Hypogées, *Desc.* II, pls. 60–75). The quantity of texts and scenes published and the precision with which they were recorded make this work much more important than collections of Egyptian scenes that were published up to that point. The scientists' adherence to their "methodology" was not as rigorous as they might have wanted, but none of them was an Egyptologist, a concept that in any case did not exist at that time. "They copied thousands of hieroglyphs without understanding the slightest bit of it" (Gillispie and Dewachter 1988, 28). They were, of course, much more familiar with Greco-Roman inscriptions than hieroglyphs. But the collective work they produced, which is sizable, prefigured the first great Egyptological expeditions of the mid-nineteenth century. The same work of the same quality could not have been produced by other men who knew nearly nothing about hieroglyphs before going to Egypt. Egyptologists of the world took decades in the nineteenth and twentieth centuries to publish all the texts and scenes carved on the monuments of ancient Egypt. How can one blame the young engineers who were not Egyptologists for not succeeding in publishing an exhaustive work without a single error? This is perhaps why Champollion's public judgment of their work was rather different from the opinions he expressed in a private letter to his brother. In the famous *Lettre à Monsieur Dacier* published in 1822, Champollion paid homage to the authors of the *Description*. He did the same in his *Précis du système hiéroglyphique* (374–375) two years later: "c'est de l'apparition du bel ouvrage exécuté par les ordres du gouvernement français, la *Description de l'Egypte*, que datent seulement en Europe les véritables études hiéroglyphiques. Ce sont les nombreux manuscrits égyptiens gravés avec une étonnante fidélité dans ce magnifique recueil […] qui seuls ont pu servir de fondement solide aux recherches des archéologues de tous les pays." ("Real hieroglyphic studies in Europe date back only to the appearance of the excellent work, the *Description of Egypt*, made on the orders of the French government. Only the numerous Egyptian manuscripts recorded with a surprising faithfulness in this magnificent compendium could provide a solid basis for the research of archaeologists of any country.")

BIBLIOGRAPHY

Bourguet, M.-N. 1999. "Des savants à la conquête de l'Égypte? Science, voyage et politique au temps de l'expédition française." In *L'expédition d'Égypte, une entreprise des Lumières*, edited by P. Bret, 22–36. Paris.

Burleigh, N. 2007. *Napoleon's Scientists and the Unveiling of Egypt*. New York.

Champollion, J.-F. 1824. *Lettres à M. le Duc de Blacas d'Aulps*. Paris.

Description de l'Égypte, publiée par les ordres de sa Majesté l'Empereur Napoléon le Grand, édition impériale 1809–1828. 2006. Les grandes expéditions scientifiques du 19ᵉ siècle. Directed by Jean-Yves Empereur. DVD. Paris.

Essche-Merchez, E Van., and M. Broze. 1993. "La contribution de Henri-Joseph Redouté à la *Description de l'Égypte*: Reliefs, peintures et inscriptions." In *Henri-Joseph Redouté et l'Expédition de Bonaparte en Égypte*, edited by A. Dierkens and J.-M. Duvosquel, 60–83. Saint Hubert.

Forgeau, A. 1998. "Le repérage des sites de l'Égypte pharaonique par les membres de la commission des Sciences et des Arts." In *L'invention scientifique de la Méditerranée. Égypte, Morée, Algérie*, edited by M.-N. Bourguet, B. Lepetit, D. Nordman, and M. Sinarellis, 33–52. Paris.

Fourier, J. 1809. *Description de l'Égypte: Préface historique*. Paris.

Gillispie, C. C. 1989. "Aspects scientifiques de l'expédition d'Égypte (1798–1801)." In *L'expédition d'Égypte, 1798–1801*, edited by H. Laurens, 371–396. Paris.

Gillispie, C. C. 1999. "Les polytechniciens face à l'Égypte." In *L'expédition d'Égypte, une entreprise des Lumières*, edited by P. Bret, 45–51. Paris.

Gillispie, C. C., and M. Dewachter. 1988. *Monuments de l'Égypte: L'édition impériale de 1809*. Paris.

Golvin, J.-C. 1989. "L'expédition en Haute-Égypte à la découverte des sites ou la révélation de l'architecture pharaonique." In *L'expédition d'Égypte, 1798–1801*, edited by H. Laurens, 333–350. Paris.

Laissus, Y. 1998. *L'Égypte, une aventure savante, 1798–1801*. Paris.

Laissus, Y. 2009. *Description de l'Égypte: Une aventure humaine et éditoriale*. Paris.

Malaise, M. 2003. "La Révolution française et l'Égypte ancienne." *Bulletin de la Classe des lettres et des sciences morales et politiques de l'Academie Royale de Belgique* 1–6: 193–231.

Pinault Sørensen, M. 1999. "Du dessin d'artiste ou d'ingénieur au dessin archéologique." In *L'expédition d'Égypte, une entreprise des Lumières*, edited by P. Bret, 157–171. Paris.

Villiers du Terrage, E. 2001. *L'expédition d'Égypte: Journal et souvenirs d'un jeune savant*. Paris.

Winckelmann, J. J. 1764. *Geschichte der Kunst des Altertums*. Dresden.

···

THE ROSETTA STONE, COPYING AN ANCIENT COPY

···

ILONA REGULSKI

"I embarked with the Rosetta Stone, determining to share its fate…"[1]

INTRODUCTION

THE decipherment of Egyptian hieroglyphs in 1822 is often acclaimed as the most important event in the history of Egyptology. There had been no proper understanding of the ancient Egyptian language and script until the discovery of the Rosetta Stone and its eventual decryption. This extraordinary achievement encouraged exploration of one of the longest chapters of human history. However unique to the history of Egyptology, the Rosetta Stone was but one of a mass-produced series of stelae designed to perpetuate an agreement issued by a council of priests. The decree, inscribed in three ancient scripts (Greek, Egyptian Demotic, and hieroglyphic), affirmed the royal cult of the thirteen-year-old Ptolemy V Epiphanes on the first anniversary of his coronation (196 BCE). Its purpose was to testify to the king's benevolence toward his people and his piety toward the gods.

Long the single most popular object in the British Museum, the Rosetta Stone has become an icon of all decipherments and attempts to access the ancient past. "Rosetta Stone" has become synonymous with any type of key used to unlock a mystery; a company that creates computer-based language-learning programs made "Rosetta Stone" their registered trademark, and a European project to investigate comets in deep space

---

[1] Extract from a letter by Major General Turner (1810, 214).

has been termed the Rosetta Mission. Visitors to the museum feel compelled to possess a personal record of the inscription; images of the stone or details of its inscriptions are constantly reproduced in the form of postcards, facsimiles, booklets, and printed objects.

The power of this bilingual icon cannot be underestimated, but it should be remembered that the decipherment eventually succeeded by examining copies rather than the Stone itself. At the time of the most groundbreaking stage of his decipherment, Champollion had never visited England nor seen the Rosetta Stone, but was able to work with copies that were available in Paris and accurate enough for his purpose. The same was true at that time of other inscriptions found in Egypt, which could only be studied in the form of drawings or the occasional squeezes (impressions of reliefs in paper made pliable by soaking in water). Only in the spring of 1824 did Champollion travel to London with his brother to visit the British Museum.[2] It was the first and only time that the decipherer saw the original Rosetta Stone, as opposed to copies of its inscription.

The Rosetta Stone did not only provide the means to decipher ancient Egyptian, it elicited an unprecedented appreciation for accurately copied inscriptions. The editors of the current *Handbook of Egyptian Epigraphy and Palaeography* therefore requested a reassessment of the Rosetta Stone as an epigraphic instrument. Hence, this contribution focuses both on the Stone as an ancient copy itself and on the early copying of the Stone (for additional bibliography and more detail on the discovery and decipherment of the Stone, see Ray 2007).[3]

THE ROSETTA STONE, A CONTEMPORARY COPY

According to the inscription on the Rosetta Stone, an identical copy of the decree was to be placed in every sizable temple across the country. Whether this happened is unknown, but copies of the same bilingual, three-script decree (the so-called Memphis Decree-Rosettana) have been found and can be seen in other museums (Cairo and smaller collections in Egypt, and Paris; Clarysse 1999).

Recent research on the Rosetta Stone text has been devoted to its significance as the end product of a complex composition and transmission process. As one of a mass-produced series of stelae designed to disseminate an agreement issued by a council of priests, the Rosetta Stone is itself an ancient copy of another document.

The decrees are essentially honorary Greek texts in composition, terminology, and ideology (Clarysse 1999). The active priestly involvement in state affairs and the near exclusion of the Ptolemaic rulers from important religious decisions and practices

---

[2] The visit is not well documented, and some Egyptologists have doubted that it ever took place (Hartleben 1983, 267; Parkinson 1999, 38).

[3] I thank my colleague Patricia Usick for her help with researching our archive.

conveyed in the Rosetta Stone are not typical of Egyptian documents; in the earlier pharaonic period, decrees (of a different type) would have been issued by the king (Valbelle 1999). Because of this deviation from earlier pharaonic practices and the numerous concessions toward the priests on the part of the royal household, the Rosetta Stone has been understood as historical evidence of the political disarray and decline during the second century of Ptolemaic rule (200–100 BCE). In 204 BCE, Ptolemy IV was assassinated in a palace coup, and several months later, his six-year-old son, Ptolemy V, was named pharaoh. With parts of the country in revolt, the palace was losing control of its territories abroad, and Rome soon intervened in Egyptian politics. Central authority was weak, and the priests who commissioned this stela would have been extremely powerful. However, the fact that the Rosetta Stone was a copy of a template created in the heyday of Ptolemaic rule shows that the decree should not be interpreted as a historic reflection of its time.

The *do-ut-des* principle, which here refers to the mutually beneficial rapport between a powerful priestly class and the Ptolemaic rulers, was already present in the Alexandria Decree of 243 BCE; the earliest of the Ptolemaic decrees (el-Masry, Altenmüller, and Thissen 2012). The Alexandria decree dates to the fifth regnal year of Ptolemy III (the third of December 243 BCE) and provided the template for the later bilingual Canopus Decrees. With its text appearing in three scripts and its availability to the priestly and literate public (thanks to copies present in temples), this decree set the standard for subsequent ones.

Scholars have debated whether the Rosetta Stone's Memphis Decree-Rosetanna had a single or several authors. Rather than the result of an intensive collaborative revision process involving Egyptian priests and Greek officials (Sethe 1916, 299; Spiegelberg 1922, 20), it seems likely that the three versions—Greek, Demotic, and hieroglyphic—were composed by the same Egyptian priest(s) (Clarysse 1999). By the time of the Rosetta Stone inscription, Egyptian priests were Hellenized enough to prepare Greek texts of an official nature because they belonged to the ruling class of the Ptolemaic administration. The hieroglyphic version of the decrees was guided by the priests' desire to make them "look old" in comparison with Demotic. At the time the Rosetta Stone text was inscribed in stone (196 BCE), the usage of hieroglyphs was even more than before restricted to a priestly elite. As the Stone itself tells us, the ancients' words were "the writing of the words of the gods." Distinguishing this script from the day-to-day scripts and languages of Egypt was a means for the priests to display their authoritative knowledge and, thereby, their status. Rather than using an earlier language phase to achieve this goal, they searched for synonyms or euphemisms. For example, instead of translating the Greek ψήφισμα "decree" or "resolution" with the commonly used *wḏ*, they favored *sḫꜣw*, "memorandum," because *wḏ* is too close to *wt* in Demotic.

Texts on the Rosetta Stone therefore do not represent conscious editions and adaptations reflecting priestly resistance to the rule of Ptolemy V (Sethe 1916, 284–297; el-Masry, Altenmüller, and Thissen 2012, 182). The relations between the priests and king probably did not change much in the second century. Both parties benefited from collaboration, whereas the distance between the powerful priests and the Egyptian population probably grew increasingly wider.

THE ROSETTA STONE AS A PRINTING BLOCK: THE FIRST COPIES MADE IN EGYPT

Almost two thousand years later, the Rosetta Stone was once again the vehicle for transmitting knowledge. When Napoleon Bonaparte launched his invasion of Egypt in 1798, he was accompanied by the Commission des Sciences et des Arts, a French learned body of 167 technical experts assembled on March 16, 1798, with the aim of documenting the geography and culture of Egypt. Despite its members' inability to read hieroglyphs, the French expedition was a landmark in Egyptology's modern history for providing, for the first time, one-to-one, hand-drawn facsimiles based on original monuments (see Gady chapter). The expedition lasted fifteen months (1798–1801) and reached the Nile's Second Cataract, which formed Egypt's southern frontier. On its way back to Lower Egypt, the Commission had an extended stay in the Valley of the Kings, where inscription after inscription was recorded. It was in this climate shaped by the Enlightenment intention to systematize the acquisition of knowledge that the Rosetta Stone was discovered.

Soldiers in Napoleon's army found the Rosetta Stone in 1799 while digging the foundations of an addition to Fort Saint Julien near the town of El-Rashid (Rosetta). The engineering officer in charge of the demolition, Lieutenant François-Xavier Bouchard, at once recognized the potential of its texts for providing information critical to revealing the nature of the ancient Egyptian script and notified General Menou, then in command at Rosetta (Gillispie and Dewachter 1987, 21). A public announcement of the discovery appeared in the official *Courier de l'Egypte* in September (No. 37). The subsequent rush to produce accurate copies reflects the *Zeitgeist* in which the French savants operated. The Stone was moved to the Institut d'Égypte in Cairo, where the first copies were made.

The Stone's lightly incised inscriptions proved difficult to reproduce by hand. The first copies were therefore made through (plaster) casts[4] or print technique. Bonaparte's Commission included twenty-two lithographers specialized in Latin, Greek, and Arabic scripts; hence, the first attempts at copying used the Stone as a printing block. The earliest prints were produced by the French expedition's senior orientalist Jean-Joseph Marcel (1776–1854), a printer, engineer, and gifted linguist working at the Institut d'Égypte in Cairo. Marcel was the first to recognize that the middle text of the Rosetta Stone, originally thought to be Syriac, was in fact the Egyptian Demotic script (Parkinson 1999, 20). Demotic was not typically used for stone inscriptions and therefore seldom seen by scholars at that time. Following a "relief" printing technique, whereby the ink is applied to the original surface, rather than the (proto-)lithographic technique, as suggested by previous scholars, Marcel produced a reverse image with the hieroglyphs in white on a black background on January 24, 1800 (Gillispie and

---

[4] In this article, the word "cast" refers to a thin cast of the top layer of the stone (usually between five and ten centimeters thick) made in a mold, rather than full-sized replicas.

Dewachter 1987, 21–22; Iversen 1993, 127; Parkinson 1999, 20).[5] For this purpose, he had the surface washed and meticulously cleaned, leaving the carved signs moist so that they would not take ink. Following the reverse "intaglio" approach, whereby the ink is applied to the engraved part (Stijnman 2012, 40–41, fig. 37), copies were also produced by the artist and inventor Nicolas-Jacques Conté, who is probably best known for inventing the modern graphite pencil (Adkins and Adkins 2000, 10). His workshop in Cairo manufactured the necessary drawing tools for the French expedition.[6] Conté used the Stone as "an engraved plate, producing prints with the hieroglyphs in black on a white background" (Parkinson 1999, 20; Gillispie and Dewachter 1987, 21–22). In the latter case, ink would have been harder to remove.

With remarkable speed, these copies were circulated to scholars in several European countries including England, with which France was still at war. Even before the French surrendered antiquities to the Anglo-Turkish forces in 1801, copies of the facsimiles of the Stone were circulating amongst the European intelligentsia (Figure II.6.1). Already in 1804, annotated versions of the copies made by Marcel and Conté were published to facilitate attempts at explaining the hieroglyphs and translations of the Greek text (Palin 1804). Champollion later complained that these copies were insufficiently detailed (as the exact shape of signs may not have been understood; see in what follows), but especially the facsimile published by Palin in 1804 (reproduced in 1830) shows the meticulous detail with which these copies were executed (Figure II.6.2). In a letter from 1830, the scholar Hubert Pascal Ameilhon (1803, 1–4) remembers the excitement these copies caused among the French intelligentsia when brought back by General Dugua and handed over to the "Institut National" in Paris. In contrast, the disappointment that the Stone itself was captured by the British was equally passionate.

According to the articles of the Capitulation of Alexandria, all antiquities held by the French, including collections and papers, should be ceded to the British. In 1801, the diplomat and antiquary William R. Hamilton (1777–1859), secretary to Lord Elgin, who was later a Trustee of the British Museum, landed in Egypt to help oversee the French evacuation. The French claimed that many items were personal possessions, including the Stone, which General Menou had taken back to Alexandria. Menou claimed these items as "his private property; and therefore as exempt from requisition as the linen of his wardrobe, or his embroided saddles" (Clarke 1817, 327; Usick 2016). The savants who were packing their drawings, plans, and maps, explained that literary acquisitions had nothing whatsoever to do with the private collections or journals of individuals. They threatened to burn their papers rather than hand them over.

Through Hamilton's intervention, the Commander of the British army in Alexandria, General Lord Hely-Hutchinson, finally relented somewhat, and the French delegation managed to retain their records for the planned *Description de l'Égypte*. Dominique

---

[5] Marcel only used the principle of immiscibility of grease and water. Modern examples of the relief technique are woodcut or woodblock, wood engraving, linocut, and metal cut.

[6] When supplies did not reach the savants in the south, they improvised pencils by melting lead bullets (Adkins and Adkins 2000, 29).

FIGURE II.6.1. Nineteenth-century charcoal rubbing of the hieroglyphic section of the Rosetta Stone (AES Ar.574, no. 46). © Trustees of the British Museum.

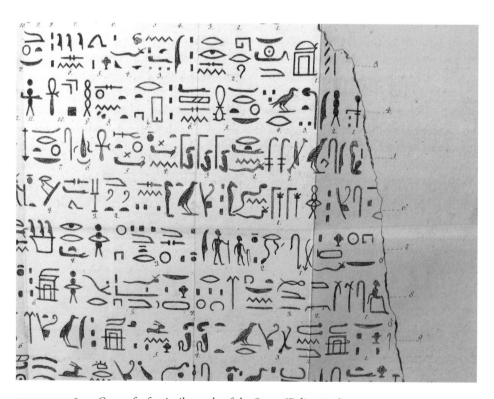

FIGURE II.6.2. Copy of a facsimile made of the Stone (Palin 1804).

Vivant Denon (1747–1825), an artist, collector, curator, diplomat, and author who served as Napoleon's minister of arts and was the first director of the Musée Napoléon (the Louvre), returned to France and swiftly published an illustrated account, *Voyage dans la basse et la haute Égypte*, which was a sensation when it appeared in 1802 (see chapter by Manniche) (Figure II.6.3).

The French scholars were allowed to take casts of the Stone before they left Egypt at the end of September 1801.[7] A letter, written by Colonel Tomkyns Hilgrove Turner (1766–1843), who accompanied the Stone from Cairo to England (on a captured French frigate!), explains that such permission was granted "provided the Stone should receive no injury" (his letter was published in Royal Society of Antiquaries, London 1810, 213). Turner was most likely referring to the effects of physical contact with the Stone, which, at this point, must have been covered with printing ink used to produce the earlier copies. His letter suggests that, during the production of the cast, the Stone was "well cleared" of the ink.

Alire Raffeneau Delile made a cast of the inscription using a sulfur-based material. This cast, which was brought to France and handed over to the "Institut National" (Iversen 1993, 127),[8] would provide the basis for the published copies of the Demotic and Greek inscriptions in Volume V of the Antiquities section (1822) of the *Description* (Vol. V, 53–54, reproduced in Gillispie and Dewachter 1987). The plate (Vol. V, 52) showing the hieroglyphs was reproduced from a plaster cast that Jomard made in 1815 during a visit to the British Museum (Gillispie and Dewachter 1987, 22).

Colonel Turner and Hamilton were assisted by the traveler and scientist Edward Daniel Clarke (1769–1822), who was to ensure the security of the Rosetta Stone. The British Museum possesses correspondence between Clarke and General Hely-Hutchinson. In a letter dated September 13, 1801 (BM EA76744; O'Connell 2016), Hutchinson urges Clarke not only to safeguard the stone but also to recopy the inscription:

My Dear Sir,

I shall be very much obliged to you to copy the inscription from the stone. I send you the former copy which you say is inaccurate. Tell Colonel Turner that not only the stone but every thing which we get from the French should be deposited in some place of security. I do not regard much the threats of the French savants, it is better however not to trust them. Have you heard of any more Coptic or Arabic manuscripts

I have the honor to be

Dear Sir

your most obedt humble servt

J Hely Hutchinson

---

[7] I was not able to retrieve more information about this first cast. We can assume it has disappeared, but was made of plaster of Paris, which was used for the later casts.

[8] The whereabouts of this cast are uncertain. Communication with several institutions in Paris was not successful in reconstructing its present depository.

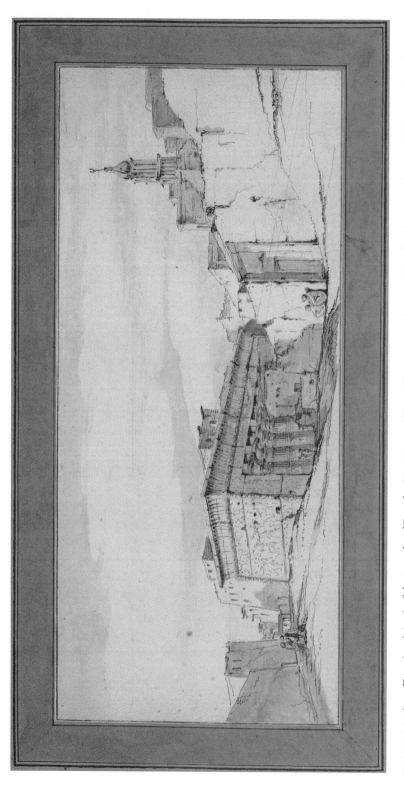

FIGURE II.6.3. Drawing (1802) of the temple of Esna by Dominique Vivant Denon; one of two studies for Plate 53 of the artist's "Voyage dans la Basse et la Haute Egypte, pendant les campagnes du Général Bonaparte" (1836,0109.75). © Trustees of the British Museum.

In Clarke's published account (Clarke 1817, 328), he refers to the "former copy" mentioned earlier: "... His Lordship had already obtained an impression from the stone, made with red chalk, upon paper, by some member of the French Institute; but the characters so impressed were too imperfectly marked to afford a faithful representation of the original: this he consigned to our care as likely to assist us in the undertaking." This red chalk impression of the Stone, probably a rubbing as shown in Figure II.6.1, was Clarke's main means of documentation. The Coptic and Arabic manuscripts referred to in Hutchinson's letter were also conceded and are now in the British Library.

Hutchinson's urgent note encapsulates the dramatic circumstances of the surrender of the Rosetta Stone and shows that the copies and notes of the inscription were considered almost equally valuable. The Rosetta Stone would soon bear two extra inscriptions on the sides: "Captured in Egypt by the British Army 1801" and "Presented by King George III." By applying these inscriptions, the British follow an ancient (Egyptian) tradition of legitimizing ownership by appropriating through writing an object that radiates ancient authority.

Sic Vos Non Vobis ("For You But Not Yours")

As soon as the Rosetta Stone arrived in Portsmouth, England, in February 1802, numerous casts were taken.[9] At this point, the Stone remained at the apartments of the Society of Antiquaries until it was removed to the British Museum. On April 29, the Society's Council resolved that a sulfur cast of the inscriptions on the Stone be taken and invitations were sent to several scholars in England to inspect and copy the Stone if they wished (Whitehouse 1997). Already in the same month, translations of the Greek inscription were presented by Rev. Stephen Weston (a member of the Society; published in Society of Antiquaries' 1810 report, 215–228) and Professor Heyne from Göttingen (Iversen 1993, 128). A final translation proved difficult as the idiom used by the Ptolemaic administration was unfamiliar to scholars at the time, but the general content of the text was clear.

In July, the Society of Antiquaries ordered four more casts to be taken, by Mr. Papera, in "plaster of Paris."[10] These were dispatched, together with a letter from the Secretary of the Society, to the Universities of Oxford, Cambridge, Edinburgh, and Dublin. All of them survive until this day but, apart from the Oxford cast (Whitehouse 1997), they

---

[9] *Sic Vos Non Vobis*, the words Vergil wrote on the wall when Bathyllus, another poet, had plagiarized his work, seem particularly appropriate in this situation where the British take the Stone from the French, but then distribute copies of the text and expect first insights into the translations.

[10] This gypsum plaster, named after a large gypsum deposit at Montmartre in Paris, is easily shaped when wet, yet dries into a robust and lightweight structure.

remain unpublished.[11] The Dublin cast, presently at Trinity College, was part of an exhibition entitled "Napoleon, Emperor of the French" in 2009.[12]

At the same time, a full-sized facsimile engraving was issued and copies were widely distributed throughout Europe and beyond to various institutions including the Vatican, the National Library in Paris, the universities of Leiden and Uppsala, and the Philosophical Society of Philadelphia (Palin 1804, 1830; Simpson 1996, 8–9).[13] Matthew Raper specifies that copies were sent to General Garth, "for his Majesty;" members of the Society, and "to those foreign Universities, to which the Society usually send present of their work." The list of institutions published by Raper (1810, 208–209), shows that within one year of the Stone's arrival in England, every western European country was in possession of a copy of the Rosetta Stone.

In 1810, the Society expresses its disappointment that no further translations or communications on the content of the stone were sent to them in return for their generous distribution of the copies (Raper 1810, 209). This expressed concern perhaps suggests that the initial incentive of the Society was to maintain an exclusive control over the intellectual output of the translation work. When this failed, the Society decided in 1810 to publish Weston's translation and the letter they had received from Professor Heyne with a Latin version of the text (Royal Society of Antiquaries 1810, 215–228 and 229–246, respectively). Hamilton's *Aegyptiaca* with a transcript and translation of the Greek text of the Rosetta Stone had already appeared separately in 1809. These early publications show a major shift in publishing ancient Egyptian text culture from incorporating the script into figural art toward proper text editions.

EPIGRAPHY AS A SOURCE OF NATIONALISTIC COMPETITION

In June 1802, the Stone itself was transferred to the British Museum in Bloomsbury (Parkinson 2005, 30–32). Early in its museum history, the Rosetta Stone's incised signs were filled in with white chalk to make the text more legible to the public

---

[11] The Edinburgh cast was donated to the university by the Society of Antiquaries of Scotland (Jervise 1864–1866, 400–401). When the Society's museum was amalgamated with the Royal Scottish Museum to become National Museums Scotland (NMS), the cast became part of the latter. I thank Margaret Maitland, senior curator of the Ancient Mediterranean collections at the NMS, for providing this information. Several casts still exist at Cambridge. One is "on display" on the second floor landing of the Faculty of Asian and Middle Eastern Studies, formerly Oriental Studies Faculty. I thank Catherine Ansonge for this information.

[12] http://www.tcd.ie/news_events/articles/glucksman-symposium-and-library-exhibition-on-napoleon/3605 (last checked February 24, 2017). General Hutchinson had an intimate link with Trinity College Dublin, as his father, John Hely-Hutchinson, was provost from 1774 until 1794. I thank Zuleika Rodgers from Trinity College for confirming the whereabouts of the Dublin cast.

[13] The arrival of copies at the Philosophical Society of Philadelphia resulted in a highly decorated report of the Committee appointed by the Philomathean Society of the University of Pennsylvania (1859) with translations and commentaries. This report also alludes to the arrival of a plaster cast.

(Parkinson 1999, 23). Carnauba wax was applied to the surface to help protect it (Parkinson 2005).

For international distribution, reproductions of the Stone continued to be "printed" using ink and paper rather than handcopying, which would later become the more common practice. Further casts must have been made in the following years as one was registered in the Hunterian Museum in Glasgow in 1812 (Whitehouse 1997, 110n12).

Simultaneously, European scholars started the work of translating the text on the Rosetta Stone, which culminated just over twenty years later, in 1822, when Jean-François Champollion outlined his thoughts about the workings of the hieroglyphic writing system in a letter to the secretary of the Académie des Inscriptions et Belles-Lettres. In that first quarter of the nineteenth century, the accuracy of copies of inscriptions was a persistent problem. In 1814, Champollion requested a new cast from the Royal Society. Their foreign secretary was Thomas Young, who was making his own contributions to the decipherment of the Rosetta Stone. In his letter, Champollion complained that the engraving of the Stone made earlier by the English Royal Society and the French copy in the *Description* differ in some respects. Since the French scholars who prepared the *Description* were not able to read hieroglyphs, their recording of individual signs was often approximate. It is uncertain whether the request was approved immediately, but in 1815, the French cartographer, engineer, and archaeologist Edme-François Jomard traveled to London and made a new cast of the Stone in the British Museum (Gillispie and Dewachter 1987, 22). This cast was certainly taken back to Paris, as it provided the basis for plates 52–54 in Vol. V of the *Description*. Its current whereabouts are unclear.

In October 1839, Hawkins (then Keeper of Antiquities at the British Museum) reported that Richard Lepsius had applied for a cast of the Stone "and as other persons had occasionally expressed a similar wish," he proposed that a mold should be made. The following month, the Trustees agreed to a mold and a cast of the Stone.[14] This is the first specific reference to a mold of the Stone, but it should be remembered that the earlier casts also required the fabrication of a mold. The British Museum still possesses such a mold, made out of a rubber-like material, but it is unclear from the object itself when it was made. From the museum's departmental "Officers" Reports, we know that a further cast of the Stone was agreed at their meeting of June 27, 1840, to be presented to Mr. Harris and another was agreed to be sent to the Vatican on July 6, 1844.[15] A considerable number of casts remain in the British Museum, but it is unclear when each of them was made.[16]

---

[14] Officers Reports, vol. 23, p. 6567. Trustees agreement: November 2, 1839.

[15] Presumably A. C. Harris (1790–1869), collector and dealer. Departmental Reports Minutes vol. p. 5217, 5415.

[16] One cast has been seen by the author at the Bloomsbury site. But at least three more are probably preserved in off-site storage. These are currently inaccessible, and the author was therefore not able to verify this information. The uncertainty of this number is related to the fact that the substantial cast collection stored at Blythe House has never been cataloged. Our colleague, Patricia Usick, is preparing a more detailed study of the entire cast collection of the British Museum. The Bloomsbury site also contains full-sized replicas.

Despite intensive exchange between research institutions, epigraphy was becoming a source of nationalistic competition in the following years. In order to complement the texts on the Rosetta Stone, both the French and English eagerly gathered copies of other inscriptions during travels in Egypt or facsimiles of monuments that were shipped to Europe. Young and Champollion (Solé and Valbelle 2006; Ray 2007, 38–55) both compared the Greek names appearing on the Stone with the Ptolemy and Cleopatra that later turned up on the Bankes obelisk (see chapter by Manniche). This obelisk is one of two found at Philae in Upper Egypt in 1815 and soon afterward transported to England by the collector and connoisseur William John Bankes to beautify his estate at Kingston Lacy in Dorset, England (Habachi 1977; Sebba 2004). This bilingual inscription in Egyptian hieroglyphs and ancient Greek records a petition by Egyptian priests at Philae and the response by Ptolemy VIII Euergetes and queens Cleopatra II and Cleopatra III (118 or 117 BCE). Already in February 1818, Young wrote a letter to Bankes in which he gives the hieroglyphic equivalents for thirty-six names or other words (Ray 2007, 49). Like the Rosetta Stone, the obelisk played an invaluable role in identifying hieroglyphs as (partly) phonetic script.

In the 1820s, enthusiastic young copyists accompanied consul-collectors in the field with the sole purpose of capturing Egypt's antiquities, landscape, and modern society with brush and pen. Unfortunately, apart from Champollion and Rosellini, their published works are meager and often unillustrated. In the opinion of another epigrapher, Ricardo Caminos (1976, 11), one of the earliest remarkable exceptions, where meticulous facsimile recording resulted in first-rate publication, is "the voluminous production of Norman de Garis Davies. His facsimile copies, as seen in his books, are for the most part direct tracings of the walls mechanically reduced by the printer to the required scale."

Once initial papers on the Rosetta Stone were published in the beginning of the nineteenth century, scholars were able to build up a larger hieroglyphic character set by turning to copies of other inscriptions from Egypt that were beginning to reach Europe in ever greater numbers (Magee and Malek 1991; Delange 2011). In particular, drawings and casts or squeeze impressions from the great temple of Karnak produced the names of more Ptolemies and several Roman emperors. Champollion was able to do much the same for the more common signs that appeared in the Demotic register. These too tended to occur in sequences, spelling out the various Greek names that corresponded to those in the Greek register. It was this hieroglyphic and Demotic alphabet that Champollion announced with confidence in the "Lettre à Monsieur Dacier" (Parkinson 1999, 36–37).

I hope this article was successful in illustrating that, apart from the groundbreaking work with regard to the ancient Egyptian writing system, the subsequent recognition that direct access to objects was the basis for solid research, is equally impressive. Progress has been made since, but it has lacked persistence. The industrious French Institute later designed one of the world's best and richest fonts for Egyptian hieroglyphs. Perhaps as a result, their gifted epigraphers did, in the last century, show a distinct preference to reproduce the inscriptions typographically (rather than facsimile recording). Such editorial publications are still used in many universities to teach the Egyptian language to students when there is not an opportunity to a glance at the originals. Attention is now given to both epigraphy and palaeography, as seen in, for example, the palaeography series published by the IFAO.

BIBLIOGRAPHY

Adkins, L., and R. Adkins. 2000. *The Keys of Egypt: The Race to Read the Hieroglyphs*. London.

Ameilhon, H. P. 1803. *Éclaircissemens sur l'inscription grecque du monument trouvé a Rosette*. Paris.

Caminos, R. 1976. "The Recording of Inscriptions and Scenes in Tombs and Temples." In *Ancient Egyptian Epigraphy and Palaeography*, 3–25. New York.

Clarke, E. D. 1817. *Travels in Various Countries of Europe, Asia and Africa: Part 2, Greece, Egypt and the Holy Land*. Sec. 2, Vol. 5. London.

Clarysse, W. 1999. "Ptolémées et temples." In *Le Décret de Memphis: Colloque de la Fondation Singer-Polignac à l'occasion de la célébration du bicentenaire de la découverte de la Pierre de Rosette: Paris, 1er juin 1999*, edited by D. Valbelle and J. Leclant, 41–65. StudHell. Paris.

Delange, É. 2011. "Prisse et l'égyptologie." In *Visions d'Égypte: Émile Prisse d'Avennes, 1807–1879*, 17–52. Paris.

Gillispie, C., and M. Dewachter, eds. 1987. *Monuments of Egypt: The Napoleonic Edition; The Complete Archaeological Plates from la Description de l'Égypte*. Old Saybrook.

Habachi, L. 1977. *The Obelisks of Egypt: Skyscrapers of the Past*. Edited by C. C. Van Siclen III. New York.

Hamilton, W. R. 1809. *Remarks on Several Parts of Turkey, Part I: Aegyptiaca, or, Some Account of the Ancient and Modern State of Egypt, as Obtained in the Years 1801, 1802*. London.

Hartleben, H. 1983. *Jean-François Champollion: Sa vie et son œuvre, 1790–1832*. Translated by D. Meunier and R. Schumann Antelme, with an introduction by C. Desroches-Noblecourt. Paris. First published 1906.

Iversen, E. 1993. *The Myth of Egypt and Its Hieroglyphs in European Tradition*. 2nd ed. Princeton.

Jervise, A. 1864–1866. "Note Regarding Cist and Urn Found at Invergowrie." *Proceedings of the Society of Antiquaries of Scotland* 6:394–395.

Magee, D. N. E., and J. Malek. 1991. "Squeezes in Grantham Museum Made by Alice Lieder in 1851–2." *JEA* 77:195–197.

el-Masry, Y., H. Altenmüller, and H.-J. Thissen. 2012. *Das Synodaldekret von Alexandria aus dem Jahre 243 v. Chr.* SAK Bh 11. Hamburg.

O'Connell, S. 2016. "Napoleon and Egypt." *The British Museum Newsletter Egypt and Sudan* 3:9.

Palin, N. G. 1804. *Analyse de l'inscription en hiéroglyphiques du Monument trouvé à Rosette contenant un décret des Prêtres de l'Égypte en l'honneur de Ptolémée Épiphane*. Dresden.

Palin, N. G. 1830. *Nouvelles recherches sur l'inscription en lettres sacrées du Monument de Rosette*. 2nd ed. Florence.

Parkinson, R. 1999. *Cracking Codes: The Rosetta Stone and Decipherment*. London.

Parkinson, R. 2005. *The Rosetta Stone*. London.

Philomathean Society of the University of Pennsylvania 1859. "Report of the Committee Appointed by the Philomathean Society of the University of Pennsylvania to Translate the Inscription on the Rosetta Stone." Philadelphia.

Raper, M. 1810. "An Account of the Rosetta Stone, in Three Languages, Which Was Brought to England in the Year 1802." *Archaeologica* 16:208–211.

Ray, J. D. 2007. *The Rosetta Stone and the Rebirth of Ancient Egypt*. London.

Sebba, A. 2004. *The Exiled Collector: William Bankes and the Making of an English Country House*. London.

Sethe, K. 1916. "Zur Geschichte und Erklärung der Rosettana." *NGWG* 275–314.

Simpson, R. S. 1996. *Demotic Grammar in the Ptolemaic Sacerdotal Decrees*. Oxford.

Solé, R., and D. Valbelle. 2006. *The Rosetta Stone: The Decipherment of the Hieroglyphs*. Edited by W. V. Davies. Translated by S. Rendall. London.

Spiegelberg, W. 1922. *Das Verhältnis der griechischen und ägyptischen Texte in den zweisprachigen Dekreten von Rosette und Kanopus*. Papyrusinstitut Heidelberg, Schrift 5. Berlin.

Stijnman, A. 2012. *Engraving and Etching: A History of the Development of Manual Intaglio Printmaking Processes*. London.

Turner, H. 1810. "Letter from Major General Tomkyns Hilgrove Turner." *Archaeologica* 16:212–214.

Usick, P. 2016. "New Acquisition: General Menou's Proclamation." *The British Museum Newsletter: Egypt and Sudan* 3:19.

Valbelle, D. 1999. "Les décrets égyptiens et leur affichage dans les temples." In *Le Décret de Memphis: Colloque de la Fondation Singer-Polignac à l'occasion de la célébration du bicentenaire de la découverte de la Pierre de Rosette: Paris, 1er juin 1999*, edited by D. Valbelle and J. Leclant, 67–90. StudHell. Paris.

Whitehouse, H. 1997. "Cast of the Rosetta Stone (no. 12)." In *Canova: Ideal Heads*, edited by K. Eustace, 106–110. Oxford.

THE EPIGRAPHIC WORK OF EARLY EGYPTOLOGISTS AND TRAVELERS TO EGYPT

LISE MANNICHE

THIS chapter is about some outstanding early epigraphers who with different backgrounds and skills recorded Egyptian artifacts in Europe or went out to Egypt with a desire to explore the ancient land. They traveled individually or in teams, for private or public means. In the days before photography, being able to draw accurately was an essential qualification. Many made valuable contributions not only to the history of Egyptology but also to the corpus of primary records of monuments, many of which are now damaged or lost. The immediate impact of their laborious fieldwork depended on the equally complicated process of printing and distribution.

GEORGE ZOËGA (1755–1809)

Zoëga was born in southern Jutland, Denmark, as son of the local vicar. He studied classics at Göttingen and Leipzig. He had the opportunity to travel in Europe, and, once in Italy, he continued his ancient studies. With the intention of appointing him curator of the royal collection of coins and medals, the then prime minister took him under his wings and gave him a grant to study abroad. However, for personal and subsequently, financial reasons, he never returned to Denmark but stayed in Rome for twenty-seven years. Most of his working life became devoted to the study of ancient Egypt, and it is fair to consider him one of the pioneering Egyptologists.

Zoëga's lasting legacy was his book on the obelisks of Rome, *De origine et usu obeliscorum*, published in Rome in 1797. Until recently, it was less well known that he had made a groundbreaking study of the hieroglyphic language at a time when a print of the Rosetta Stone was still locked up in Paris (Frandsen 2015, 161–172, esp. n. 24). To this end, he made copies of a great many objects with hieroglyphic inscriptions (Figure II.7.1). His work, which reveals that he was also a skilled and meticulous draftsman, remains unpublished. In the early days of Egyptology, his papers, now mostly kept in the Royal Library in Copenhagen, would have been of invaluable use, as would also his attempts at classifying the corpus of hieroglyphic signs, handcopied from the available monuments, such as the Lateran obelisk and objects in the Borgia collection, and worked into intricate numbering systems.

The Napoleonic Expedition

Before the days of the great French expedition to Egypt, few travelers drew and published subjects at a standard that would qualify as being epigraphy. As part of Bonaparte's campaign to conquer Egypt, a Commission of Arts and Science embarked on a visionary task: an exploration of the legendary land of Egypt, past and present, spearheaded by the newly founded Institut d'Égypte in Cairo with Bonaparte himself as its vice-president (see chapter by Gady).

The French team, notably the gifted draftsman Vivant Denon (1747–1825), later director of Musée Napoléon, made substantial contributions to the first volume of the *Description de l'Égypte*, the majority of the plates being architectural drawings of Egypt from Alexandria to Philae. Obliged to stay with the army, Denon literally made some of his drawings on the hoof. His own account, *Voyage dans la basse et la haute Égypte, I–II*, was published in Paris in 1802 in advance of the great work and made a substantial impression on the Egyptian Revival in French art and architecture. He was of a noble family, and, having abandoned his law studies for art and literature, he had become a favorite of Louis XV and embarked on a diplomatic career. He had a natural talent for drawing and also mastered the arts of etching and engraving. He survived the revolution and chose to side with Bonaparte. In his capacity as director of the Musée Napoléon, he was responsible for the looting from Rome in 1812 of Egyptian artifacts that were bound for the museum in Paris.

Another valuable member of the expedition was André Dutertre (1753–1842), a painter who drew portraits of his colleagues, in addition to painting landscapes and reconstructing temples on paper, such as those at Kom Ombo, Esna, and Dendera. All of this would not have been possible without the ongoing efforts of Nicolas-Jacques Conté (1755–1805), who not only drew numerous scenes of craftsmen at work but also had invented and, during the campaign, manufactured all the graphite and clay pencils needed for the field recording.

The *Description* was published in ten volumes of text and thirteen folio volumes of plates from circa 1809 to 1822. The work was supervised by Edmé-François Jomard (1777–1862), who also produced some plates and wrote up the majority of the final

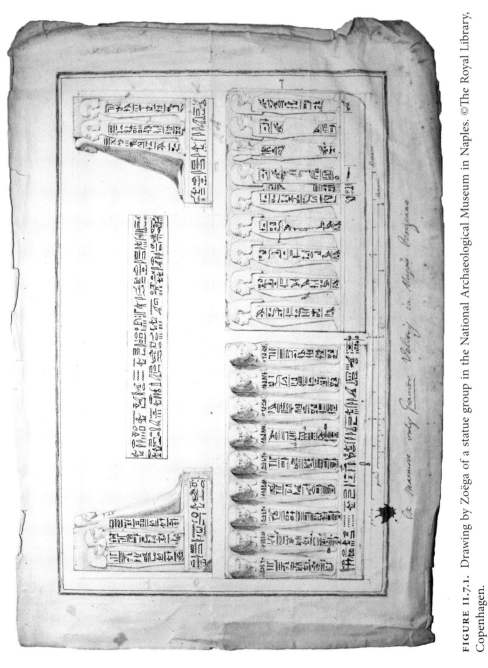

FIGURE 11.7.1. Drawing by Zoëga of a statue group in the National Archaeological Museum in Naples. ©The Royal Library, Copenhagen.

accompanying text. Some 400 engravers were involved, special paper was manufactured, and the whole enterprise was a monumental effort. Its fame was great, but the print run was modest, and few people had the chance to consult it. A second edition was decreed by Louis XVIII with the 900 plates reproduced once more and published in 1821–1826. The original drawings are now kept in the Bibliothèque Nationale and Archives Nationales in Paris.

To complete the epigraphic work of the expedition of Bonaparte, the German-born architect François Christian Gau (1790–1853), later city architect of Paris, went to Nubia in 1817. He produced sixty-eight drawings and plans, which were published in Stuttgart and Paris (Gau 1822), involving many of the engravers responsible for the *Description*.

Frédéric Cailliaud (1787–1869)

After the advent of the rule of Muhammad Ali in 1805, Egypt was opened up to foreigners. Among the indefatigable pioneers who were also able draftsmen must be reckoned the French naturalist Frédéric Cailliaud and Linant de Bellefonds. Both traveled intensively in Egypt and, joining Ismail Pasha and the Egyptian army, penetrated deep into Upper Nubia, where they were the first to record the Meroitic monuments.

Cailliaud was primarily a mineralogist, but he first trained as a jeweler and an artist. On a search for minerals for his collections, he traveled to Greece and was for a while in the employment of the Ottoman sultan. Egypt became a natural next step. After his arrival there in 1815, he made the acquaintance of the French vice-consul Bernardino Drovetti, whom he joined on a journey to Wadi Halfa. He was appointed court mineralogist of Muhammad Ali, who sent him to the Eastern Desert in pursuit of emerald mines. A stay in Thebes aroused his interest in the private tombs and their wall decoration, which in many cases reflected his own profession as a craftsman. After a pioneering excursion to the Kharga Oasis, he returned to Paris in 1818 with the bulk of his records and became involved in the publication of the *Description de l'Égypte*. He sold his drawings and his collection of antiquities to the French government, which sent him to Egypt the following year to complete the recording of the oases and Nubia. On his way back from Siwa and the oases of the Western Desert, he received news of Ismail Pasha's campaign to conquer the Sudan and exploit its minerals. Cailliaud and his cartographic assistant, naval officer Pierre-Constant Letorzec, joined the troops with the aim of discovering gold mines south of Khartoum. Due to problems with their papers, they ended up traveling on their own and hence had ample time on their way south to visit all the ancient monuments. Countless drawings and plans were made at sites such as Semna, Kumma, Sai, Argo, Soleb, Sedeinga, Sesebi, and Kerma. At Gebel Barkal, which they believed was the Meroe of the classical texts, they caught up with the army. While officially on the search for gold and diamonds, they made it all the way to Meroe, Naga, and Musawwarat el-Sufra. A five-months stay at Omdurman enabled Cailliaud to organize his notes and records, most of which he later published in the 1820s.

In Luxor in 1823, he continued his work in the private tombs, being particularly interested in subjects that concerned daily life. He organized his material as a collection of plates depicting aspects of arts and crafts. *Recherches sur les arts et métiers* was published between 1831 and 1837 with a print run of 100, although half of the 100 copies were accidentally destroyed while in storage. Only the volume of hand-colored plates appeared during his lifetime. He never completed his intended text. After his death, his notes vanished, only to reappear in 2002 at a sale where they were purchased by a London bookdealer along with eighty original plates and a collection of other notes and sketches. The collection was finally published in English and French by the American University in Cairo Press (Bednarski 2014).

Cailliaud may have achieved less fame that some of his immediate successors, but not only was he the one who traveled furthest afield. He was, in many cases, the first scholar on the site. His architectural drawings are of the highest quality and, having passed through the hands of engravers who inevitably left their own touch, the reproduction of his renderings of reliefs and paintings are as faithful to the originals as can be expected. His impressive plates of wall decoration were reproduced from annotated tracings that were then inked, reduced, engraved, and finally hand-colored for the final publication. One incident mars his otherwise fine reputation: the removal of a large fragment of wall-painting from TT A5 that can now be seen in the Louvre (Manniche 1988, 44–45).

Louis Maurice Adolphe Linant de Bellefonds (1789–1883)

After early years in the navy, when he was involved in charting and surveying the coast of the northern United States and Canada, Linant, born in Lorient, traveled in the Middle East as a draftsman. He arrived in 1818 in Cairo, where he obtained employment in the services of Muhammad Ali. He joined William Bankes and his party and traveled with them in Nubia. After a journey to the Siwa Oasis, and still in the employment of Bankes, he was sent to explore even further up the Nile in 1821–1822 with the aim of identifying the city of Meroe, known from classical writers. Like Cailliaud, Linant followed the campaign of Ismail Pasha, initially accompanied by the physician-*cum*-draftsman Alessandro Ricci, as far south as Gebel Barkal, which Linant correctly identified as ancient Napata. There, the two parted company, and Linant continued on his own, recording the ruins of Musawwarat el-Sufra, which he believed to be Meroe, and Naga (coinciding with Cailliaud and Letorzec). On March 25, 1822, Linant reached Meroe, but failed to identify it as the famous city. Although the temples were more or less deserted at that time, the battlefield was never far away. However, his corpus of drawings does include numerous scenes of daily life and folklore.

In 1826, the African Association, a British club that encouraged the mapping of Africa charged Linant with following the course of the White Nile to its sources. William Bankes was involved in commissioning Linant for this project without himself taking part in the expedition. On the way, Linant recorded and drew the monuments in Nubia and the Sudan, including watercolors of selected motifs, but he was forced to abandon the real aim of his journey. After his return to Egypt, he focused on engineering enterprises and became involved in the planning of the Suez Canal. Linant was appointed Egyptian Minister of Public Works and later was made Pasha. He made an invaluable contribution to recording the sites and monuments, many of which are now damaged or even lost. Over the years he also copied monuments for Robert Hay and Champollion. His notebooks, drawings, plans, and maps of Egypt were donated to The Louvre by his descendants. Some documents relating to the expedition in the Sudan for Bankes are kept with the Bankes papers.

WILLIAM BANKES (1786–1855)

Bankes was the eldest surviving son of a wealthy and distinguished family in England. Although not himself a skilled artist, he was involved in many of the important enterprises in the early nineteenth century that are relevant to the subject. He organized and sponsored expeditions, in particular employing Linant de Bellefonds, collected antiquities, notably the Philae obelisk, which provided the original hieroglyphic text as well as an inscription in Greek, and identified the name of Cleopatra, which proved to be of vital importance for scholars struggling with the decipherment of the hieroglyphs. For his further travels in 1818 he had received instructions from Thomas Young to collect inscriptions, especially names of kings and gods that accompanied the relevant figures. The Abydos king-list of Ramesses II, which he copied but did not remove, was a major discovery. His copy, with annotations, was published as a frontispiece to Salt (1825). Bankes's papers are kept with his collection of antiquities at his family estate at Kingston Lacy in Dorset.

GIOVANNI BATTISTA BELZONI (1778–1823)

With a past as strong man in a circus and in hydraulic engineering, "The Great Belzoni," as he was known, is perhaps most famous for his enterprises following employment in the service of Muhammad Ali with the aim of bringing Egypt into the modern technological era. However, his special field became clearing monuments and transporting large antiquities. He discovered and partly excavated the temple of Abu Simbel and later the tomb of Seti I in the Valley of the Kings. With the assistance of Ricci, he recorded the decoration of this tomb in wax impressions and drawings. Back in London, this was worked into a splendid show held at the already existing Egyptian

Hall in Piccadilly in 1822 and, without other Egyptian paraphernalia sold at auction, in Paris that same year. It featured a 1:1 model in plaster of Paris, cast in sections from his wax molds and colored from his and Ricci's annotated drawings, of two of the chambers of the tomb, as well as a complete model of the tomb, mounted on canvas frames, made from Ricci's 1:6 drawings. Also displayed were a 1:120 open wax model of the pyramid of Chephren and a 1:30 model of the temple at Abu Simbel with another of the portico of the temple of Isis at Philae.

Belzoni (1835) wrote a popular account of his adventures in Egypt. His watercolors of the tomb of Seti I are now in the Bristol Museum. Although not strictly facsimile copies, the results of his artwork are impressive for their time, and, due to their media appeal in the early days, they greatly contributed to the interest in aegyptiaca.

John Gardner Wilkinson (1797–1875)

Wilkinson was a "gentleman scholar" whose main claim to fame was to make ancient Egypt known to the West by publishing his research in an affordable format rather than the exclusive and expensive publications of his predecessors. By doing so, he influenced the general public in Britain for several decades of the mid-nineteenth century. His parents had died while he was still a child but had left him enough means to be financially independent. His grandfather had encouraged his interest in history, and his mother had taught him the early steps of drawing. At school (Harrow), Wilkinson had the chance to meet Thomas Young. He studied and practiced cartography at Oxford with the aim of later joining the army. After leaving Oxford, Wilkinson embarked on a Grand Tour. In Italy, he met the classical archaeologist William Gell, who encouraged him to go to Egypt as a traveler with a scholarly purpose. With James Burton, Wilkinson began to study Arabic. He read the relevant literature available in Gell's library, and he was introduced to the then-known rudimentary basics of ancient Egyptian, copying inscriptions he saw in collections in the area. He was thus well prepared for his future career. In November that year, he found himself in Alexandria. His ultimate destination was Thebes, but he also visited the oases in the Western Desert and the Eastern Desert, and eventually went as far upriver as the Second Cataract. Not until 1833 did he return to England. He made a further three visits to Egypt later in life.

The greater part of Wilkinson's years in Egypt was spent on the west bank of Thebes, where from time to time many of his friends and colleagues joined him. In 1828, he published *Materia Hieroglyphica*, an illustrated account of the deities, kings, and language of ancient Egypt. Of outstanding importance is the very detailed map he drew of the Theban necropolis, published in 1835 as *A Topographical Survey of Thebes*. He drew countless scenes from the walls of tombs and temples, and he filled small notebooks with sketches and detailed notes. Along with rubbings and squeezes of reliefs, this material later formed the basis of his major publication *Manners and Customs of the Ancient*

Egyptians, which was published in three volumes in 1837. The genre as such already existed for contemporary manners and customs of foreign lands, but Wilkinson also made the journey back in time. Instead of being organized topographically, Wilkinson's book dealt with various topics of interest. It came out in a number of editions with supplements, and an abridged edition in two volumes was reprinted several times. In 1878, three years after the author's death, a revised version that included notes taken from Wilkinson's manuscripts was edited by Samuel Birch of the British Museum. The book was affordable, it was in English, and it contained numerous illustrations made from Wilkinson's field sketches and reproduced as lithographs (carried out with the assistance of Joseph Bonomi and the architect and painter Francis Arundale) or for the later editions, woodcuts.

In 1838 Wilkinson went to Rome, where he copied inscription on obelisks with Bonomi and then back home to England. In 1841 he went to Egypt again to work on a travelers' guide, and then, in 1848–1849 he traveled in Nubia as far as Gebel Barkal. Wilkinson realized that his efforts were one step on the long road to understanding the ancient Egyptians, but with his first-hand knowledge of the originals, he felt that he was in a position to give an unbiased description of what he saw. By using just pen, pencil, and his notebooks, he was able to communicate the motifs that mattered to the Egyptians. Although the drawings were not facsimile copies, they had the advantage of actually being made available to a large circle of readers. Overall, Wilkinson's artwork, though executed by freehand and thus not true facsimiles and without the benefit of collation from a second party, is fairly accurate, reflects the artistic style, and is sympathetic to the originals. For a long time, the corpus of his manuscripts and drawings were in the possession of Wilkinson's heirs. Eventually, they were loaned to the Griffith Institute to be microfilmed, and they are now kept in the Bodleian Library in Oxford.

ROBERT HAY (1799–1863)

Epigraphy in the modern sense of the word entered Egyptology with an expedition mounted by the Scottish nobleman, Robert Hay. As a young naval cadet, he had visited Port Said. After the death of his two older brothers, he came in possession of the family estate, and he decided to explore the land of the pharaohs, not as a tourist but as a scholar. With the proper permissions and personnel, which included Joseph Bonomi (1796–1878), a sculptor and draftsman who also worked for other early travelers, Hay set off in 1824 on the first of several expeditions. Their equipment included "large sheets of paper" and tins of yellow, blue, white, green, and black paint as well as oil and varnish. The "tins of paint" left few traces in the documents, if any at all. Hay also brought a camera lucida, a drawing gadget patented in 1807 that enabled the draftsman to inspect his motif with one eye through a sequence of prism, lens, and mirror, while the other followed the lines of his pen on a sheet of paper, producing a rather accurate line drawing, at a scale smaller than the original, which could later be filled in with watercolor (see chapter by Emery). The camera lucida could also be used for reducing large tracings to a more manageable format. This drawing aid became commercially available in the 1820s.

On March 18, 1825, at Abu Simbel, Hay managed to have enough sand removed from the head of one of the colossi to draw it with his camera lucida. Working inside the temple with a substantial amount of sand still remaining was a demanding task in a constant temperature of 86°F: "I am obliged to strip to my drawers & then I am perspiring as much as in a Turkish bath wh. is no agreeable thing for drawing. The paper becomes quite damp with the atmosphere and a very curious thing I have remarked is that an HH pencil wh. is in this climate as soft as an HB in a cold climate becomes so hard that it even scratches the paper...on quitting the temple (it) is soft again" (Tillett 1984, 22).

In spite of summer approaching, the group continued south. In the temples of Kalabsha and Derr, Hay and his team made use of the gypsum they had brought along to make casts of the wall decoration. At the small temple at Beit el-Wali, they had made notes of the color scheme, perhaps anticipating that the painted surface would be damaged during the operation, which is exactly what happened. These latter casts with their added coloration can now be admired in the Nubian room in the British Museum.

At Thebes, Hay made his greatest contribution to Egyptology. Having spent time there on the way up the Nile, the team returned in October and after a break in Cairo, came back once more in May 1826 and stayed until January 1827. Bonomi was still with Hay, as well as a draftsman by the name of A. Dupuy, who penciled notes on colors in French on many of the tracings (Figure II.7.2). Along with the camera lucida, the artists now made use of large sheets of paper that were made semitransparent by applying drying oils and resins. This enabled the artists to do proper 1:1 tracings. Considering the fact that they would have worked in conditions where light (natural or artificial) was scarce, the quality of these tracings is truly remarkable and compares with many modern tracings executed with proper pens and the benefit of electric light on clear tracing paper, acetate, or the like. However, the sheets being applied directly to the walls, this method is bound to have placed the original paintings at risk.

The results of Hay's efforts, forty-nine volumes of drawings and diaries now kept in the British Library, remain a true treasure trove to this day because all that he managed to publish was a folio volume of drawings of Cairo. The tracings were usually done on the equivalent of a modern A3 paper size. Because they were drawn in a 1:1 scale, a number of sheets were joined together to cover a full wall. Transforming the penciled tracings to a printed plate at a reduced scale would have involved a third party, an engraver, and this transferring process would have influenced the original accuracy of the artwork. In two major publications on lost Theban tombs, the present writer chose to trace and ink the lines of the early travelers' drawings, filling in double contour lines where clearly the original on the wall would have had just a single one (Manniche 1988, 2011). The Hay archive is invaluable for several reasons, the two main ones being that a number of the subjects he and his team drew are now damaged or no longer in existence, and because of the innovative drawing aids that he introduced.

FIGURE II.7.2. Tracing of a scene in TT C4 from the Hay MSS with color annotations in French. ©The British Library Board, Add. 29852, f. 256–7.

JOSEPH BONOMI (1796–1878)

Soon after Bonomi's birth in Rome, his architect father took the family to England. Bonomi trained as a sculptor and draftsman and, after further studies in Rome, he went to Egypt in 1824 to assist Robert Hay and other scholars. He stayed there for eight years and even went as far upstream as to Dongola in the Sudan with Linant de Bellefonds. Hay demanded greater accuracy from the artists even in awkward drawing situations. Bonomi devised a drawing frame, a viewfinder-type device equipped with a sight and a string or wire grid, to help them draw the temples' interior decorations. At the temple of Kalabsha, Bonomi labored to produce several plaster casts of the reliefs. After their return to Thebes, the two fell out, and in 1826, Hay replaced him with William Lane, the Arabic scholar and draftsman. Bonomi then worked for Wilkinson, and back in England, he was instrumental in preparing many of Wilkinson's drawings for publication. Subsequently, Bonomi joined Lepsius's 1842 expedition (see chapter by Loeben). Bonomi made the first hieroglyphic font in England. From 1861 until his death, he was curator of Sir John Soane's Museum, during which time he lithographed the sarcophagus of Seti I in that collection, as well as objects in countless other collections. Being immensely productive he left a substantial mark on early Egyptological publications.

James Burton (1788–1862)

Burton, the son of a property developer, studied mathematics at Cambridge, but found it difficult to focus on a career, for years to come being financially supported by his father. At some point, he traveled to Italy, where he made the acquaintance of Wilkinson and other persons with similar interests. Though having no formal training in such matters, he was invited by Muhammad Ali to take part in the 1822 Geological Survey of Egypt, mainly with the aim of finding coal. Two years later, he joined Hay and Wilkinson in their individual pursuits at Thebes. In 1825, he traveled up the Nile and also into the Eastern Desert. He returned to Egypt again in 1830–1835. During his peregrinations, he made a vast number of plans, drawings, and sketches, mostly unpublished, now bound in sixty-three volumes kept in The British Library. His chief claim to fame in epigraphy, however, was the publication in 1825–1828 with Joseph Bonomi of *Excerpta Hieroglyphica*, a corpus of sixty-four plates with no accompanying text that provided the early decipherers of hieroglyphs with original texts for their study. The plates were printed in Cairo on Burton's newly acquired printing press and sent in four installments to scholars in Europe.

Jean François Champollion (1790–1832), Ippolito Rosellini (1800–1843), and the Franco-Tuscan Expedition 1828–1829

The year 1822 and the famous "Letter to M. Dacier" mark the formal occasion of the decipherment of hieroglyphs by Champollion (see chapter by Regulski). Having received his education in Grenoble and Paris, he had authored works on ancient Egypt and was awarded a teaching position at Grenoble. Through royal patronage, he was able to work in museums in Italy, being subsequently appointed curator at the Louvre in 1826, a year before its official opening as a museum. In 1829, he organized a joint expedition to Egypt with Rosellini with the specific purpose of testing his philological hypotheses and seeing the context of the inscriptions. In 1831, he held the first chair in Egyptology at the Collège de France, but the following year, while preparing the publication of the expedition, he died from a stroke. Four folio volumes, including 446 plates, appeared in Paris (Champollion 1835–1847), his 1,641 pages of field notes being published in two volumes (Champollion 1844–1899).

Rosellini was born in Pisa, where, after studies in Bologna, he was appointed professor of Oriental languages. He met Champollion and studied with him in Paris for a year. He became head of the Tuscan section of their joint expedition, sponsored by Leopold II, grand duke of Tuscany, and Charles X, king of France. He lived to see most of his great folio volumes published by the press in Pisa (Rosellini 1832–1844; in total 395 plates and 3,300 pages of text), and his diaries were published in 1925. His papers are kept in the library of Pisa University.

In addition to the philologist heads of the expedition, the team comprised a classicist, six artists (including Nestor l'Hôte and Alessandro Ricci), two architects, and two naturalists. They arrived in Alexandria in August 1828, and from October and until September of the following year, they traveled to the Second Cataract and back, working intensively all the while. Only at Thebes did they linger, from March to September. Champollion was a keen observer of anything he met on his way. By studying the monuments, he was confirmed in his belief that his understanding of the hieroglyphic system was correct. He was also the first to alert the authorities (i.e., the Pasha) of the risks to the monuments from illicit digging, inexpert handling, vandalism, and the general encroaching of modern settlements on the ancient sites (a ban on the export of antiquities was eventually implemented with other measures in 1835, and the first plans for a museum to house and protect artifacts were made).

Nestor l'Hôte (1804–1841)

L'Hôte was as one of eleven French members of the Franco-Tuscan expedition. For years, he earned a living in the customs service. He was an established painter and an accurate copyist of hieroglyphs, making an impressive contribution to the published folio volumes of the expedition. Despite ill health, he went out to Egypt on two subsequent occasions. He wrote a book on obelisks, notably the one that ended up in Paris, and also published some of his letters home before he died at the age of thirty-eight. His papers are mostly kept in the Bibliothèque Nationale, and his drawings and watercolors are in the Louvre.

CONCLUSION

The inspiration and motives for these early epigraphers were as diverse as were the circumstances of their travels and their financial backing. Pioneering epigraphic work was carried out in Rome by dedicated scholars who never set foot in Egypt. A major opportunity to explore the ancient country was offered by the expedition of Bonaparte at the turn of the nineteenth century. During its second decade, when traveling was almost obligatory for craftsmen, some went for general professional reasons and, having made their way to Italy or Istanbul, found themselves attracted by the prospects offered by new schemes developing in Egypt. Opportunities to travel further upstream and into the Sudan offered themselves at the fringe of military operations that paved the way. Some travelers had a wealthy, or at least a comfortable, background and were motivated by a genuine interest in Egypt and its ancient history, art, architecture, and language. Many were skilled at drawing and had studied the available literature. They wanted to visit and draw the sites and, if possible, to bring back antiquities for resale to the newly established museums in Europe.

The success of their efforts at the time should be assessed on the impact they made: the samples of hieroglyphs privately distributed to early linguists in the early days; exhibitions, temporary or permanent; and publications of their artwork and descriptions, including the influence it had on contemporary Egyptianizing design. During the second half of the nineteenth century, these works were overtaken by rapidly moving new research and techniques. In retrospect, when we realize that entire monuments have disappeared and others have suffered substantially from modern civilization, unlawful appropriation, neglect, or vandalism, the original records of the early travelers, many of which remain unpublished, have become the focus of renewed attention.

BIBLIOGRAPHY

Bednarski, A., ed. 2014. *The Lost Manuscript of Frédéric Cailliaud*. Cairo.

Belzoni G. 1835. *Narrative of the Operations and Recent Discoveries within the Pyramids, Temples, Tombs and Excavations in Egypt and Nubia*. Brussels.

Champollion, J. F. 1835–1847. *Monuments de l'Égypte et de la Nubie d'après les dessins exécutés sur les lieux, sous la direction de Champollion le jeune*. Paris.

Champollion, J. F. 1844–1899. *Notices descriptives conformes aux notes rédigées sur les lieux par Champ. le jeune*. Paris.

Frandsen, P. J. 2015. "A Concealed Attempt at Deciphering Hieroglyphs." In *The Forgotten Scholar: Georg Zoëga (1755–1809): At the Dawn of Egyptology and Coptic Studies*, edited by K. Ascani, P. Buzi, and D. Picchi, 160–173. CHANE 74. Leiden.

Gau, F. C. 1822. *Antiquités de la Nubie, ou monuments inédits des bords du Nil, situés entre la première et la seconde cataracte, dessinés et mesurés, en 1819*. Stuttgart.

Manniche, L. 1988. *Lost Tombs: A Study of Certain Eighteenth Dynasty Monuments in the Theban Necropolis*. London.

Manniche, L. 2011. *Lost Ramessid and Post-Ramessid Private Tombs in the Theban Necropolis.* CNIANES 33. Copenhagen.

Rosellini, I. 1832–1844. *I Monumenti dell'Egitto et della Nubia, disegnati dalla spedizione scientifica letteraria Toscana in Egitto.* 12 vols. Pisa.

Salt, H. 1825. *Essay on Dr. Young's and M. Champollion's Phonetic System of Hieroglyphics.* London.

Tillett, S. 1984. *Egypt Itself: The Career of Robert Hay, Esquire of Linplum and Nunraw, 1799–1863.* London.

KARL RICHARD LEPSIUS AND THE ROYAL PRUSSIAN EXPEDITION TO EGYPT (1842–1845/6)

CHRISTIAN E. LOEBEN

BEFORE the nineteenth century, it was extremely difficult in Europe to get authentic pictures of Egypt. For example, the Freemasons, who were formed in 1717 in London and were fascinated by ancient Egypt early on, saw images of Egypt in the among them widely distributed and richly illustrated work of Noël Antoine Pluche *Histoire du Ciel…*(1739/40), which essentially showed figures in classical robes. This is not surprising, since the most important source for these pictures was Bernard de Montfaucon's fifteen-volume work *L'antiquité expliquée et représentée en figures* (Paris 1719–1724) in which it was obviously not possible to create a clear distinction of *Aegyptiaca* ("things Egyptian"), which could come from either the pharaonic or Greco-Roman periods of Egypt. It is no surprise, then, that Mozart's opera, originally named *The Egyptian Secrets* and renamed *The Magic Flute* in Vienna shortly before its premiere in 1791—not only the most-performed opera in the world but also the most important artwork of Freemasonry—in the stage sets of the premiere, apart from a pyramid, looked like a production of a Greek comedy.

IMAGES FROM EGYPT BEFORE LEPSIUS

The dissemination of the first authentic images from the land of the pharaohs happened in the Western world as a result of the first scientific exploration of the Nile Valley by the military expedition to Egypt by Napoléon Bonaparte (1798–1801), the *Description de l'Égypte* (eleven volumes of tables and nine volumes of text), published between 1809 and 1828, at that time the largest publication project of human kind (see chapter by Gady). With the addition of Nubia, which was unresearched by the French, the *Description* was completed by the expedition of Franz Christian Gau (1818–1820) and his publication in French and German in Paris from 1821 to 1827. But only the 1822 decipherment of hieroglyphs by Jean-François Champollion (1790–1832) made it clear that the images of the *Description* and all other formerly published works were unfit for intensive scientific study of the monuments that are littered with hieroglyphic inscriptions. Because the artists among the 156 savants traveling with Napoléon did not yet understand hieroglyphs, the copies are inaccurate and unusable for scientific purposes. This problem was addressed by the hieroglyphic decipherer himself, who created a first remedy by conducting together with the Pisa-born Orientalist Ippolito Rosellini the Tuscan-French expedition to Egypt from 1828 to 1830, the first real "Egyptological" state-sponsored survey. The resulting works, *Monuments de l'Égypte et de la Nubie*…(four volumes, 1835–1847) and *I monumenti dell'Egitto e della Nubia*…(nine volumes, 1832–1844), show consistently readable copies of hieroglyphs, but feature only small sections of the diversity of monuments in the country and thus do not remotely measure up to the quasi-encyclopedic scope of the *Description*.

Lepsius's Formative Years

The explicit aim of the Royal Prussian Expedition to Egypt and Ethiopia (1842–1845/6) was to replace the *Description* with exact pictures of the monuments of Egypt, particularly in the same size folio format. The initiator of this huge undertaking, which scientifically eclipsed all previous expeditions, was Karl Richard Lepsius, who was born on December 23, 1810, in the town of Naumburg on the Saale and died in Berlin on July 10, 1884. From 1829 to 1833, he studied classical antiquity and philology as well as comparative linguistics at the Universities of Leipzig, Göttingen, and Berlin, where he received his doctorate with a work about the Iguvine bronze tablets, inscribed in Latin and Umbrian and discovered in 1444 in Gubbio (central Italy). The publication of this work ("De tabulis Eugubinis") in 1833 attracted much attention because with it, Lepsius had rediscovered the language now called Oscan-Umbrian. Thus, the work immediately attracted the interest of the archaeologist Eduard Gerhard (1795–1867), who was just at that right moment visiting Berlin from Rome. In Rome, the future first professor of archaeology at the University of Berlin, was, along with Bunsen and Kestner, one of the founders of the archaeological group "the Roman Hyperboreans" (1823), which became "Instituto di Corrispondenza archeologica" on Winckelmann Day (December 9,) 1828 in the presence of the Prussian crown prince, later King Friedrich Wilhelm IV. Gerhard took up Lepsius's idea that he would continue and expand his language studies in Paris, the "home" of the decipherment of ancient Egyptian. In Paris, Lepsius could also work, which came in handy for Gerhard, for the French section of the "Instituto…" established there.

On July 17, 1833, exactly sixteen months and ten days after the death of Champollion, Lepsius arrived in Paris, where he was to stay for three years. There, in the lectures of Jean Antoine Letronne for the first time he came in contact more intensively with ancient Egypt and its archaeological and linguistic legacies, the latter of which interested him more as a linguist. For this reason, he learned Coptic in Paris with the famous Arabist Baron Silvestre de Sacy (1758–1838) and Demotic from Champollion's pupil Francesco Salvolini (1809–1838). Through these studies, especially of the originals in the Louvre—up until his departure, he copied the hieroglyphic texts of all (!) of the Egyptian objects in the museum—Lepsius immediately realized that one of the prerequisites for further work with the ancient Egyptian script and language would be to accurately document Egyptian original inscriptions. Only from this, he was convinced one could, among other things, develop an exact palaeography of hieroglyphic writing, the same way Lepsius provided a palaeography of Sanskrit on which he had worked for some time and which he finished in Paris (published in 1834 as: "Paleography as a Means of Linguistic Research First Demonstrated in Sanskrit").

Lepsius's work with ancient Egypt was not without reason and was initially not particularly welcomed by himself. In November 1833, he had already received in Paris the challenge of his Berlin mentor, the Prussian diplomat Christian Karl Josias Freiherr von Bunsen (1791–1860), to apply himself to Egyptian, after all one would not want to leave the young science of Egyptology only to the French, but would really like to leave it also "to a German scholar with diligence and love."

In this respect, von Bunsen, who was working on a monumental work "Egypt's Place in World History" (published in five volumes 1844–1857), extended his offer to Lepsius that he would try to get a stipend for Lepsius in Berlin so that he could go from Paris directly to Rome to deepen his Latin, Umbrian, and Etruscan studies at the "Instituto…" as editorial secretary, as well as to employ himself more intensively with the Egyptian monuments there in Rome and the monuments available in greater number in the new Egyptian Museum in Turin. This "Instituto," the predecessor institution of today's "German Archaeological Institute," was the first in the world to be founded specifically for archaeological and antiquarian research. It is noteworthy that it had been established in the first draft of its statute to deal also with ancient Egyptian monuments—albeit not in the framework of field projects in Egypt, at least as a subject for publication in the Institute's forthcoming journal series. Including ancient Egypt from the outset as a research subject, for an archaeological institute based in Rome and thus mainly concerned with research conducted in Italy, certainly goes back to the influence of August Kestner (1777–1853) with the founding of the "Instituto…." Kestner lived in Rome almost continuously from 1817 until his death in 1853, for most of that time as a kind of ambassador of the Kingdom of Hanover and thus also of England. There, he developed over time into an enthusiastic collector of antiquities, who spared no effort in acquiring objects from Egypt even in Italy. For this reason, he can be regarded worldwide not only as the first important private collector of Egyptian art but also as one of the first researchers of Egypt. He was, in fact, personally informed about the progress of deciphering hieroglyphs by no less a figure than Jean-François Champollion (see chapter by Regulski).

He met with Champollion twice in Rome, in 1825 and 1826, and during one of those stays made a portrait of him. Certainly, Kestner personally knew Champollion and appreciated him as a true hieroglyph decipherer—as opposed to his compatriot Gustav Seyffarth (1796–1885), who was on the wrong track in this regard—something Lepsius, as Champollion's later "successor," was denied, which made Lepsius and Kestner close friends for life. At the end of his two years as editorial secretary in Rome, Lepsius was also drawn by August Kestner on January 28, 1838. Lepsius himself later described his time in Rome as his happiest and most formative, although while there he had to bury his brother Reinhold, who died during a visit.

He himself already having been in Paris and then also in Turin before Lepsius agreed to the terms to work intensively with Egyptian monuments with Ippolito Rosellini in Pisa and two years in Rome, he got assurances from his mentor von Bunsen that this would really lead to a job in the civil service, because the rather young science of Egyptology obviously had no visibly attractive career opportunities for the then twenty-four-year-old. Only the assurance that he could take over the management of the Egyptian collection in Berlin—at that time more than six thousand pieces, definitely one of the world's largest collections of this kind—convinced him to agree to do Egyptian in Paris and to deepen these studies in Rome from 1836 to 1838.

As an aside, although Lepsius had been promised the position of director of the Egyptian Museum in Berlin in 1833, he did not receive the position until 1865 after he had shared it for almost ten years with the acting director Giuseppe Passalacqua (1797–1865). He had worked his way up from an Italian horse dealer in Egypt to become a civil servant of the Prussian state because in Paris, he had sold the antiquities he collected in Egypt to the royal collections in Berlin and could therefore call himself a director for life. However, for Lepsius, this position was in the meantime only an "honorary position," because on January 15, 1842, just in time for his Egyptian expedition, he became an associate professor (*ausserordentlicher*) and in August 1846 became a full professor and thus the first chair of Egyptology at the University of Berlin, after Paris, the second Egyptology chair in the world. Incidentally, for Lepsius, the highlight of his career was to be appointed Royal High Librarian in 1873.

The Establishment of the Prussian Expedition

Being awarded the prestigious university post was a direct consequence not only of Lepsius's much-noticed "Lettre à M. le professeur Hyppolite Rosellini sur l'alphabet hiéroglyphique" of 1837, in which he considerably clarified the Champollionic hieroglyphic system, but above all because of his great success as head of the Royal Prussian Expedition to Egypt and Ethiopia, as the area of today's Sudan was normally called. The stated goal of this expedition, which lasted exactly from September 1, 1842, to May 23,

1846, and which ultimately cost the Prussian state 34,600 Thaler, was on the one hand, a precise inventory of primarily the monuments of the Old and Middle Kingdoms—the latter was at that time not identified as such—and on the other hand, the legacies of Nubian cultures should be traced in detail, even the basics of which were not known at that time, namely, whether they were older or younger than the Egyptian cultures. The expedition was sent far into today's Sudan in order to clarify that. Also on the expedition's agenda was the acquisition of originals for the Egyptian Museum in Berlin, in the planned "Neues Museum" on the Museum Island. At its conclusion, 613 originals, over fifteen hundred individual pieces, were sent to Berlin with special permission from the Egyptian khedive Muhammad Ali, among them three complete mastaba tombs. This represented a considerable increase of the collection, particularly of pieces with secure provenance, something that other Egyptian collections in Europe so far, up to that time, had not been able to produce; they had simply just been collected by agents of the consuls of various European nations without any information about exact find spots in Egypt.

In the end, it was the personal commitment of the Prussian king Friedrich Wilhelm IV, who had been enthusiastic about archaeological things since his youth, that made a Prussian expedition to Egypt at all possible. He came into contact with Egypt early because the educator of his brother Carl was none other than Heinrich Menu Freiherr von Minutoli (1772–1846), who from 1820 to 1821 undertook a first Egyptian expedition financed by the Prussian state from which he also brought objects to Berlin, although, unfortunately, the most important pieces were lost on the night of March 12, 1822, during a storm in the Elbe estuary off Cuxhaven. After his return from Rome, incidentally, again via Paris, Lepsius had several opportunities to personally meet the crown prince in Berlin and at the latest one, after he had written the title and name of his wife Elisabeth in hieroglyphs, developed a kind of friendship with the two of them. Having come to the throne in 1840, the new king devoted himself in particular to the advancement of research and the Berlin Museum as a "sanctuary for art and science." The monarch pledged great profit for both of these areas in the realization of an "Egyptian venture," as he called the planned expedition. Within just two weeks, Lepsius had to work out a plan for such a venture, assisted by two famous expedition-experienced researchers, both members of the Academy of Sciences. On the one hand, there was no one less than Alexander von Humboldt (1769–1859), whose brother, Wilhelm (1767–1835), a linguist and founder of the Berlin University, was extremely enthusiastic about Lepsius's early linguistic work, but unfortunately died early. Lepsius knew Alexander von Humboldt well because of time spent together in Paris, and no one could bring more experience in the planning and execution of expeditions (the Americas 1799–1804 and Russia 1829). On the other hand, the experience of the naturalist Christian Gottfried Ehrenberg (1795–1876), who was a member of the Minutoli Egyptian expedition, could, of course, be drawn from extensively for the planning of the new Egyptian expedition. In an audience with the king on December 26, 1840, the expedition was approved by cabinet orders to the satisfaction of all involved. Finally, in June 1841, the positive vote of the commission, composed mainly of members of the Academy of Sciences, was concluded on the basis of the "Memorandum on the journey to Egypt to be taken on the orders of his Majesty, King Friedrich Wilhelm IV" written by Lepsius. Furthermore, the commission extended the expedition to three years and to five accompanying persons, and granted lavishly the funds of 31,100 Thaler. Lepsius could then buy materials in Paris and London, including books and maps, for the expedition. In London, where his mentor von Bunsen was now ambassador, Lepsius received from Berlin not only vases from the Royal Porcelain Factory, which were intended as gifts to the viceroy of Egypt, but also the final travel order of the Prussian government on the basis of which Lepsius finally set the launch of the expedition on September 1, 1842, with his departure from Southampton.

In order to achieve the hoped-for goals, the expedition needed a well-selected staff. The success of the expedition depended—not surprisingly, according to what is stated earlier—very much on the draftsmen. These were the brothers Ernst (1818–1882) and Max Weidenbach (after 1818–1892), who like Lepsius came from Naumburg, as well as the Basel landscape painter Johann Jacob Frey (1813–1865), who had already worked for Lepsius in Rome. The latter, however, became so ill at the beginning of the expedition that he had to return to Europe in 1843, which, understandably, seriously threatened the success of the expedition. The fact that the expedition still did not fail is again due to the friendship of Richard Lepsius and August Kestner. Lepsius regularly wrote letters to Rome to inform Kestner about Egypt and the progress of the expedition. Thus, in a letter dated August 30, 1843, he asked him to send a German or Italian draftsman to Egypt and to disburse the necessary travel expenses: "I would not know who would be better to turn to in this matter than to you." Kestner's arrangement was to get to the expedition the artist Friedrich Otto Georgi (1819–1874), who, as a result of his stay in Egypt, was to become the most important representative of the German "Orientalist" school of painters. The theologian and linguist, later advisor to Bismarck, Heinrich Hermann Abeken (1809–1872) was a member of the expedition and, along with Lepsius, another close friend of August Kestner. Abeken lived from 1831 to 1838 in Rome, where he was drawn by Kestner after his return from Lepsius's expedition in 1846. For a short time, members of the Egyptian expedition were also the sculptor and draftsman and well Arabic-speaking expert on Egypt, Joseph Bonomi the Younger (1796–1878), Roman-born, though usually living in England, and the English architect James William Wild (1814–1892)—later both, incidentally, were successively curators of the Sir John Soanes Museum in London. From Naumburg also came the gypsum sculptor Carl W. Franke (1814–?), whom Lepsius, however, had to send back home from Nubia without replacement after two arguments with him in 1844.

Besides the draftsmen, however, the most important member of the expedition—actually, the assistant director—was the architect and geodesist Georg Gustav Erbkam (1811–1876). He was responsible for making most of the topographical plans and the architectural drawings of individual monuments. Even today, the accuracy with which he made his drawings during the limited duration of the expedition at the various locations is admirable. Many of his plans are still unrivaled in their exact documentation of excavation sites. In addition to Lepsius, he also kept along the entire route of the expedition a

"Diary of My Egyptian Journey," whose three volumes are published on the Internet (Erbkam 2007) and together with his journey notes, which are published in book form (Freier 2013), are definitely worth reading because they convey a very personal impression of the everyday life of the expedition and the hardships of the lives of its members in Egypt.

The Prussian Expedition in Egypt

On September 13, 1842, the expedition members Erbkam, Franke, and Ernst Weidenbach, who had traveled through Trieste and Greece, arrived in Alexandria. Lepsius, Bonomi, Wild, and Max Weidenbach traveled from Southampton completely by sea, where they picked up in Malta the painter Frey, who was coming from Rome. They arrived in Alexandria five days later, on September 18. On September 23, the entire official delegation traveling by the order of His Majesty King Friedrich Wilhelm IV of Prussia was presented by the consul general of Sweden and Norway in Egypt, Giovanni Anastasi (1780–1860), who was also responsible for German interests in Alexandria, to the Egyptian khedive Muhammad Ali and was received by him with all honors in his summer residence in Alexandria for half an hour. Shortly before leaving Alexandria on September 30, Lepsius received the "firman" of the khedive, the letter that was to grant him aid throughout the country and contained various special provisions, including the previously strictly prohibited collection and export of Egyptian antiquities. In exchange for the vases of the Royal Porcelain Factory in Berlin, admired as exceptional for their quality by the khedives, all antiquities collected by the expedition were meant to become a personal gift of the khedive to the Prussian king at the end of the voyage. On October 5, the expedition members finally arrived in Cairo. Ten days later, the "emblematic" event occurred with which the expedition will probably always be connected: On the top of the pyramid of Cheops, the birthday of the Prussian king Friedrich Wilhelm IV was celebrated. This event was recorded not only in a watercolor by Johann Jacob Frey that found distribution at home as a frequently reproduced lithograph but also in a text translated by Lepsius into Egyptian that he had carved in eleven hieroglyphic columns directly above the ancient entrance to the pyramid and that until today has elicited irritation from many visitors to Giza.

The itinerary then developed as follows: region of Memphis (October 1842–May 1843), Fayum (three months), Middle and Upper Egypt, as well as Nubia and shortly beyond Khartoum (summer 1843–summer 1844), and finally in detail the Theban region (November 1844–May 1845). During the evening before the departure from "hundred-gated Thebes," Lepsius gave to all of the expedition members a memento of the expedition, reported by Erbkam in his travel diary entry of May 16, 1845, as follows: "Yesterday, Leps[ius] gave each of us a scarab with our name, made of glazed stone...." Lepsius had these scarabs—which looked astonishingly authentic and not at all like fake antiquities—made by local artisans in Luxor not only for the members of his expedition but also for his dear friend August Kestner, for whom he obviously also brought real antiquities from Egypt. Kestner's copy from among this group of freshly made scarabs seems to be the only one that has survived. It is preserved in the Museum August Kestner in Hannover (Figure II.8.1), and its inscription, written in six hieroglyphic lines, can be easily read. It is translated as follows: "Thebes. NN (Name of the respective expedition member, in this case: Kestner). Regnal year 6 under the Majesty of the King (literally: "Son of Re") "Friedrich Wilhelm," the lord of the lands of Prussia, may he be given life forever." Remarkably, the word FRIEDRICH is not simply written in letters, but is written phonetically so that the hieroglyphs themselves are also readable and translatable as "The Sun of the Subjects." At the end of the expedition, there was on the program a visit to the Sinai peninsula and the return to Cairo (Summer 1845).

When they arrived in Cairo, all of the finds were packed, including three completely dismantled mastaba tombs. On July 7, 1845, Lepsius officially released from service his expedition team members, who then returned to Germany, traveling across the Eastern Delta and through Palestine and Lebanon as well as Italy on their way. In Rome, Erbkam informs us, they visited August Kestner on October 28 and November 2, 1845, and reported extensively to him about the expedition. Lepsius himself stayed on longer in Cairo, where during the closing audience with the khedive on September 16, almost

FIGURE II.8.1. Scarab inscribed for August Kestner. Museum August Kestner, Hanover, Inv. No. 2151. The six-line hieroglyphic inscription includes Kestner's name (QJSTNJR), the name of King Friedrich Wilhelm (P3 R' TJRHYT WYLHJLM) in the cartouche, and in the following line, Prussia (PRJWSSJN).

exactly three years after their first meeting in Alexandria, Lepsius received the official export license for all ancient objects as gifts for King Friedrich Wilhelm IV. Then, on October 2, Lepsius left Egypt for Palestine and visited Jerusalem, Beirut, Damascus, and Constantinople and returned to Berlin scarcely four months later. On May 23, 1846, the materials from the expedition reached Berlin, marking the official end of the Egyptian expedition, even though Lepsius had already submitted his final report on March 12.

RESULTS OF THE EXPEDITION

The essential work of the expedition consisted of the best possible documentation of the existing monuments. Only where necessary, for example, when these were partially covered with sand, were excavations carried out with the help of local workers. Maps and architectural drawings, as well as copies of reliefs and paintings, were meticulously made. In addition to impressions in plaster of the three-dimensional reliefs, so-called squeezes were produced. These are imprints made when moistened, thick paper was placed on areas of relief images and firmly tapped with a wet brush. When dry, they were faithful three-dimensional impressions that had to be carefully transported without being crushed. Unfortunately, such squeezes also have the extremely dramatic side effect that the always water-soluble Egyptian colors were dissolved from the walls by this method and thus Egyptian paint is still preserved on the back of these paper imprints today. Nondestructive copies of paintings and reliefs were made by manually drawing them, although Lepsius was also interested in the young method of photography, which had only appeared in 1839. Shortly before the expedition, in July 1842, in England, Lepsius met with William Henry Fox Talbot (1800–1877), an inventor of a photographic process and also an Orientalist colleague of his (see chapter by Emery). Lepsius also grappled demonstrably with the daguerreotype, which was patented in 1841 and elicited enthusiasm among many scientists. In the end, he decided not to use any of these techniques, which required a great deal of technical work, during his expedition to Egypt. Shortly thereafter, Egypt became the destination of the world's first photographic expedition, which was conducted by the Frenchman Maxime du Camp from 1849 to 1852 and attended by the young author Gustave Flaubert. Immediately after this trip, du Camp published the first photobook about Egypt in 1852.

Draftsmen on the expedition trained in hieroglyphs made exact copies of the paintings and reliefs using the so-called camera lucida. This instrument was developed at the beginning of the nineteenth century and is a simple device, screwed to a drafting table or sketchbook, that has a prism that allows a draughtsman to see simultaneously the object being copied and the draftsman's own drawing, which means that only what was to be seen on the paper had to be traced, an easy, confident, and quick method of copying.

THE *DESCRIPTION* BECOMES LEPSIUS, *DENKMÄLER*

The main output of the expedition was this mass of two thousand drawings and plans, as well as countless paper squeezes and fifteen thousand plaster casts made in Egypt. All these documents form the basis of the 894 plates that are published in twelve folio volumes, *Denkmäler aus Aegypten und Aethiopien*, whose last volume appeared in 1859, after more than ten years' labor of editing the complete set (1849–1859). This work, however, which quite clearly adopted the 78 × 61 format of the *Description de l'Égypte* of the Bonapartian expedition as its model, overshadows it in an Egyptological sense. Lepsius, *Denkmäler*, as the publication is known for short, is still considered the largest publication in the field of Egyptology, and even today, there is hardly any Egyptological publication that does not refer to its plates. The "Blätter" (leaves), as the plates of the twelve "Bände" (volumes) are called, are divided into the following chapters called "Abtheilungen" (sections, abbreviated Abt.).

- Abt. I: Maps and plans, as well as views of the ancient sites (145 Blätter/Tafeln in Bände 1–2)
- Abt. II: Old and Middle Kingdom (153 Blätter, Bände 3–4)
- Abt. III: New Kingdom (304 Blätter, Bände 5–8)
- Abt. IV: Ptolemaic and Roman times (90 Blätter, Band 9)
- Abt. V: Nubia (75 Blätter, Band 10)
- Abt. VI: Ancient texts (127 Blätter, Bände 11–12)

Lepsius's expedition diaries, titled from the scientific, "Egyptian journey," could only be published after his death from 1897 to 1913. Appearing as five volumes of text, they were an even more enormous work that is owed to a student of Lepsius's, the Swiss man Édouard Naville (1844–1926), and the final editorship of Kurt Sethe (1869–1934).

LEPSIUS'S ACHIEVEMENTS FOR CURRENT RESEARCH

Finally, as an example of the success of the expedition, notice should be made of an important accomplishment of Lepsius's work for current Egyptological research, namely, the rediscovery of the so-called Amarna period (Loeben 2008–2009). This period, connected with the names of rulers of Egypt quite famous to everyone, Akhenaten, Nefertiti, and Tutankhamun, and called Amarna after el-Amarna, the modern site of Akhenaten's newly founded capital city, was virtually unknown before the expedition. Lepsius himself, it must be said, called the pharaonic protagonist of the era Chuenaten.

Both on the route up the Nile and on the return journey down the Nile, the expedition stayed in Middle Egypt. According to the aforementioned goals of the expedition, to focus on the monuments of the Old and Middle Kingdoms, it is not surprising that the expedition spent seventeen days (August 30–September 14, 1843, and June 15, 1845) in Beni Hasan, an important center for Middle Kingdom monuments. Accordingly, Beni Hasan is represented in Lepsius, *Denkmäler* by four plates among the plans (Abt. I), thirteen plates in the chronological part of the plates, and nearly forty pages in the text volumes. While Lepsius was working at Beni Hasan, he became aware of the not far away, but previously virtually unknown Amarna, and the expedition then stayed at that place for a total of eleven days (September 19–21, 1843 and June 7–14, 1845). Amarna monuments accordingly only take up three plans, twenty-one plates, and just under twenty-three pages of text. Nevertheless—and the relatively large number of plates illustrates this clearly—just the use of Amarna and its monuments in Lepsius, *Denkmäler* represents an absolute "rediscovery," because before Lepsius, travelers to Egypt paid no significant attention to the ruins of Amarna. It can almost be said that Lepsius was successful in having rediscovered, along with the place of Akhenaten's city, Akhetaten, also his era. In Egyptology, therefore, Lepsius also plays the role of the first researcher to work purely scientifically on the time of Akhenaten and his archaeological legacies. Based on his documents and finds from Amarna, Lepsius was the first Egyptologist in a position to formulate, in the framework of a report to the Prussian Academy of Sciences in Berlin in 1851, a synthesis of all knowledge about the period now known as the Amarna era. The year 1851 can thus be regarded as the birth of "Amarna research."

In the context of Lepsius's Egyptian expedition in 1844, there was also an Egyptological achievement, which was to last almost 150 years, namely, the first exact plan of the city of Amarna. This record of the topography of the main city of Akhetaten is the work of the aforementioned, brilliant architect and geodesist Georg Gustav Erbkam. The plan of Amarna, which Erbkam prepared in only eleven days—three days in September 1843 and another eight days in June 1845—was only superseded in 1993 by the publication of the new survey of the region of Amarna, which was set up by Barry J. Kemp and later Salvatore Garfi on behalf of the Amarna research of the London-based Egypt Exploration Society in nine excavation seasons between 1977 and 1989. Plans made in the meantime, such as, for example, the English expeditions of Petrie 1891/92 and Pendlebury 1921–1936, as well as the German expedition of Borchardt 1911–1914, concerned only the concrete area assigned to these expeditions through the concessions of the Egyptian Antiquities Organization, never the entirety of the city of Amarna.

The eleven days spent by Lepsius's expedition at Amarna, however, not only yielded this important topographical plan of the Amarna city complex (Lepsius, *Denkmäler*, Bd. 1, Abt. I, Bl. 64) but also the first publication of scenes from the private tombs of both the northern and the southern group of Amarna (Lepsius, *Denkmäler*, Bd. 2, Abt. III, Bl. 91–111). While the plan was replaced by a publication only in 1993, in the meantime, the tombs of Amarna were known to have been the subject of an expedition by the Englishman Norman de Garis Davies. His drawings of the reliefs of all the rock tombs were published in six volumes from 1903 to 1908, *The Rock Tombs of El Amarna*, a

FIGURE II.8.2. Detail of the publication by Lepsius (Bd. IV, Abt. III, Bl. 103) (in gray) of the "gold of honor" scene in the tomb of Ay in the southern group at Amarna in comparison with a modern epigraphic drawing of a plaster cast that was moulded before the destruction of the scene in 1890 (Drawing: Christian E. Loeben, digital montage: Frank Joachim).

publication that essentially replaced the drawings in Lepsius, *Denkmäler*. Nevertheless, the author of this chapter together with the Egyptologist Rolf Krauss (Krauss and Loeben 2003) recently demonstrated in a publication that the drawings Davies published do not possess the overall precision that Egyptologists generally assume. In the example of the famous "Gold of Honor" scene in the tomb of Ay, the later pharaoh—as Lepsius

FIGURE II.8.3. Detail of the publication by Davies (*The Rock Tombs of El Amarna* VI, pl. 29) (in gray) of the "gold of honor" scene in the tomb of Ay in the southern group at Amarna in comparison with a modern epigraphic drawing of a plaster cast that was moulded before the destruction of the scene in 1890 (Drawing: Christian E. Loeben, digital montage: Frank Joachim).

already correctly supposed him to be—and famous successor of Tutankhamun, we were able to show that Lepsius's lithograph (*Denkmäler*, Bd. IV, Abt. III, Bl. 103; Figure II.8.2) is more accurate on a number of points than is Davies's drawing (Figure II.8.3). It is always, therefore, worthwhile to refer back to Lepsius's *Denkmäler*, not just for certain details. The achievements of Karl Richard Lepsius's 1842–1845/6 Egyptian expedition for all areas of Egyptology, as well as for Nubian and Meroitic studies, are not be underestimated even after over 160 years.

BIBLIOGRAPHY

Davies, N. de G. 1903–1908. *The Rock Tombs of El Amarna*. 6 vols. ASE 13–18. London.

Erbkam, G. G. 2007. "Tagebuch meiner egyptischen Reise." Transcribed by E. Freier and S. Grunert. Edited by the Arbeitsgruppe Altägyptisches Wörterbuch der Berlin-Brandenburgischen Akademie der Wissenschaften. Berlin. http://pom.bbaw.de/erbkam/

Freier, E. 2013. *"Wer hier hundert Augen hätte…" G. G. Erbkams Reisebriefe aus Ägypten und Nubien*. Berlin.

Kemp, B. J., and S. Garfi. 1993. *A Survey of the Ancient City of El-Amarna*. Occasional Publications 9. London.

Krauss, R., and C. E. Loeben (in collaboration with F. Joachim). 2003. "Epigraphiker-Kopien eines Amarna-Reliefs im Vergleich zu seinem Gipsabgus." In *Es werde niedergelegt als Schriftstück: Festschrift für Hartwig Altenmüller zum 65. Geburtstag*, edited by N. Kloth, K. Martin, E. Pardey, 231–246. SAK Bh 9. Hamburg.

Lepsius, K. R. 1849–1859. *Denkmäler aus Aegypten und Aethiopien: nach den Zeichnungen der von Seiner Majestät dem Koenige von Preussen Friedrich Wilhelm IV nach diesen Ländern gesendeten und in den Jahren 1842–1845 ausgeführten wissenschaftlichen Expedition*. 12 vols. Berlin. (http://edoc3.bibliothek.uni-halle.de/lepsius/); Supplement, Leipzig 1913; Text, published by É. Naville, edited by K. Sethe. 5 vols. Leipzig 1897–1913.

Loeben, C. 2008–2009. "L'expédition en Égypte de Karl Richard Lepsius (1842–1845) et la naissance des études égyptologiques sur la période dite 'amarnienne.'" *EAO* 52:21–30.

....

NINETEENTH-CENTURY FOUNDATIONS OF MODERN EPIGRAPHY

....

VIRGINIA L. EMERY

WHEN John Gardner Wilkinson landed in Alexandria on November 22, 1821, Champollion was ten months from publishing his famous *Lettre à M. Dacier*, but already the need for reliable copies of Egyptian hieroglyphic texts was recognized and growing (Thompson 1992; see chapter by Regulski). Wilkinson knew that a critical component of Egyptologists' work would be accurately to record Egyptian monuments—their images and their texts—developing and practicing early modern epigraphy (Thompson 1992, 2015–2017). The major epigraphic players of this era, Wilkinson, Auguste Mariette, and Georges Legrain, as well as the photographers William Henry Fox Talbot, Félix Teynard, and Francis Frith, worked through the dramatic political and cultural shifts of the nineteenth century that made it possible to be physically present in Egypt and benefited from landmark discoveries and inventions that improved the means of recording and disseminating epigraphic materials, alongside other historical information, to the world beyond Egypt.

HAND-DRAWN IMAGES OF SIR J. G. WILKINSON

....

Although Wilkinson reached Egypt before Champollion's landmark announcement, he arrived with the benefit of having had some instruction in the script that he copied. In the three months before his departure to Egypt, Wilkinson had been tutored by Sir William Gell, a scholar of the classical world, in what was known about hieroglyphs at that time

(Thompson 1992, 2015–2017, 1). Wilkinson's arrival in Egypt at the cusp of decipherment shaped what he recorded and his later presentation of it in publications, resulting in an emphasis on tying Egyptian culture to that of the classical world and a focus on working out Egyptian chronology from internal sources. (See Figure II.9.1.)

For example, his first publication, *Materia Hieroglyphica* (1828), was fundamentally a primer for Egyptology as it stood at that point, including in a single work the basics of language, religion, and history from the Egyptian perspective, though paradoxically influenced by the value placed on those subjects in the study of the Classics. It included fifty-one plates picturing major deities of Egypt, along with accompanying inscriptions, as encountered on a variety of temple walls. Published in black and white, deities' figures are pictured with internal details, whereas the hieroglyphs are printed in black block form, filled with ink and preserving no internal detail. Architectural details are not provided, and the site of a scene's source is only variably included in the accompanying discussion (Wilkinson 1828, pls. 1–51). Wilkinson provided commentary for each scene, explaining the Egyptian gods with extensive cross-referencing to classical ones (Wilkinson 1828, 1–65). A five-page, handwritten introduction to Egyptian grammar preceded the commentary, and lists of hieroglyphic phonetic values and English-Coptic-hieroglyphic word equivalences followed it (Wilkinson 1828, unnumbered, Appendix 2). By including information on hieroglyphs—phonetics, translations, and grammar—Wilkinson made such information accessible beyond networks of scholars like Gell, permitting an interested reader to work through the inscriptions for themselves, which served to create a broader audience for future publications. Wilkinson thus ushered in the era of *modern* palaeography, publicly displaying how hieroglyphs could be reduced clearly to their simplest elements to be recorded by hand and demonstrating the informative nature of hand-copies as simplified means of textual publication that allowed for greater flexibility when editing and excerpting texts (Wilkinson 1828; James 1997, 113). Until the first hieroglyphic printing font was developed later in the nineteenth century and expanded in the early twentieth (Chassinat 1907; Gardiner 1962, 42), publications with handwritten copies were the norm and a readable hieroglyphic "hand" was a requirement of the profession.

Materia Hieroglyphica also included five plates presenting Wilkinson's collection of royal names to date and extended commentary about his work on establishing an internal chronology for ancient Egypt. The cartouches, which come from a selection of sources, are presented in an Egyptianizing grid distinguishing the constituent components of the royal titulary; all are relatively standardized in size and proportions, and the hieroglyphs within are printed in black block form (Wilkinson 1828, Part 2:pls. 1–5). For this subject, Wilkinson draws an even sharper distinction between a narrative, interpretive discussion that compares the Egyptian sources to the classical sources of Manetho, Herodotus, and Diodorus (1828, 69–106) and the detailed commentary on individual plates and names (1828, 108–134). He reproduced the King List from Abydos explicitly to correct mistakes in previous copies, his own and others' (1828, Part 2:132–133, pl. 9); in his next work, Wilkinson (1830, 23, pl. 4) included the list of ancestors from the Chamber of Kings at Karnak. Wilkinson was to add to his original list of kings, presenting successive versions in hieroglyphs and in English in most of his publications (1835, pls. 1–3; 1847, 17–26), sometimes including a list of the Caliphs and Sultans of Egypt (1847, 27–42).

With his study of the Turin king list, Wilkinson (1851) hoped to lay to rest controversy over the positioning of smaller fragments of papyrus (Wilkinson 1851, v). Although he received permission from the museum to trace both sides, he elected to work from a facsimile copy of the recto made by Lepsius (see chapter by Loeben), in order better to preserve the papyrus; presumably, however, he traced a copy of the verso (Wilkinson 1851, 3–6). In addition to copying the hieratic, Wilkinson transcribed royal names from hieratic to hieroglyphs, to aid in their comparison with cartouches as preserved on other monuments; in this process, he indicated conjectural reconstructions with hash marks, leaving blank locations where signs were too insecure to reconstruct (Wilkinson 1851, 5). By including his work on Egyptian chronology as it evolved, Wilkinson not only presented additional texts for his readers but also provided improved historical context for his audience, making the ancient Egyptian world and culture more accessible to them and allowing them to place cartouches and the monuments where they appeared in a more fully realized historical context.

In addition to historical context, Wilkinson sought to provide physical context in his publications, drawing, throughout his career, on the extensive portfolio of hand-drawn images, maps, and notes he had made during his first sojourn there. His multivolumed, multieditioned *Manners and Customs of the Ancient Egyptians* (1837, with supplement 1841 and revision 1878) is perhaps the best example of this; even more notably than in the earlier *Materia Hieroglyphica*, the images in *Manners and Customs* illustrate Wilkinson's textual narrative, providing visual support for his analysis and interpretation of aspects of the daily lives of ancient Egyptians. The images in the work are of several types, including lithograph vignettes of contemporary landscape scenes (1837, 1:40, vig. B) and, occasionally, an ancient interior (1837, 3:263, vig. I), and woodcut prints of excerpts of tomb scenes illustrating myriad aspects of Egyptian life and recording at least the site whence the scene came. Lithographs and woodcuts were usefully paired to show similarities and differences between modern and ancient worlds, as in the use of the *shadoof* (1837, 2:1, vig. D, and 4, nos. 74–75) and windcatchers or *mulquf* (1837, 2:93, vig. E, and 121, no. 110). Larger plates were also included, some in pull-out form, providing a better sense of the scene as it was encountered on the wall, either with multiple registers (1837, 1:406 [opposite], pl. 4; 3:222 [opposite], pl. 12) or simply providing more detail because at a larger scale (1837, 1:106 [opposite], pl. 1). Some plates, particularly the frontispieces, employ color, though the red, yellow, and green used generally fail to accord with an Egyptian aesthetic (1837, 1:333 (opposite), pl. 3); the bulk of the images are presented in black and white.

With this simple color scheme, the woodcuts stand out as capturing well the essence of the originals. Overview scenes showing action are coupled with images of a specific item or animal in a range of variants, illustrating a surprising scope of Egyptian art relatively compactly. The overview scenes frequently include their accompanying hieroglyphs, rendered in miniature in black block print; prints of illustrations of variations of an object less frequently include the hieroglyphs (e.g., 1837, 1:298–309, nos. 17–36, 2:345–355, nos. 246–257), though Egyptian names for animals usually were included in small-scale, black block style (1837, 3:39, no. 328, 41, no. 339, 50, no. 340). While Wilkinson's eye for detail was usually exquisite, occasionally scenes suffer from a slide toward classical style: his reproduction of the famous fowling scenes from the Theban Tomb of Nebamun is immediately recognizable as such (1837, 3:42, no. 337) and includes an accurate copy of the hieroglyphs accompanying the scene (with the omission of a B [Gardiner D58] at the top of line 3), but the profiles of the figures, especially that of Nebamun's wife, are decidedly Hellenic! This may have been an aberration: his images of Ramesses III from Medinet Habu compare well stylistically to later copies (Wilkinson 1837, 1:106 (opposite), pl. 3; The Epigraphic Survey 1930, pl. 24). In the case of Medinet Habu, Wilkinson seems to have mixed and matched the scenes to best effect, as when he brought together two scenes from different parts of the East High Gate (Wilkinson 1837, 1:420, no. 295, figs. 1–2, no. 296, figs. 1–2; The Epigraphic Survey 1970, pls. 638, 640, 654).

In contrast to *Manners and Customs*, Wilkinson's travel guide (1847) did not include many images (though one startling exception illustrates the use of a sleeping bag-mosquito net contraption that rendered the occupant mummiform; 1847, 3), relying instead on the physical panorama that would have surrounded the traveler. However, the depth of Wilkinson's portfolio is indicated by the maps and plans in the work, demonstrating the range of his contextual information gathering while on the ground (e.g., Wilkinson 1847, 80, 165, 332; the number increased by the 1873 edition). Besides producing site plans and architectural drawings, and recording landscapes, wall decoration, and vignettes of modern life, Wilkinson also incorporated sources from other ancient cultures, primarily the classical authors with whom he was best acquainted, but also occasionally other Near Eastern material, such as figures from Persepolis (Wilkinson 1837, 1:369, no. 64). For Wilkinson, the accurate copying of texts and scenes from the walls of a single monument with the aim of facsimile publication was not the goal; immersing himself, and by extension the reader, in a contextualized perspective of the ancient Egyptians was the primary aim, coupled with the acknowledgment that he would make mistakes and would seek to correct himself as was possible (Wilkinson 1828, iv).

Many elements of Wilkinson's *oeuvre* became standard practice in epigraphic publications, though some were eventually superseded as Egyptology developed. When Georges Legrain published his first work (1890), he included textual exegesis interspersed in his translation, together with a word-by-word index of each chapter and a glossary to encourage readers to follow the development of words through time, much as Wilkinson had done in *Materia Hieroglyphica*. Legrain presents the entire text of the four-meter-long Louvre Demotic Papyrus 3452—a funerary text of Ptolemaic date—in facsimile copy in black ink, including the original illustrations and reproducing their sketch-like character (Legrain 1890). In the years between Wilkinson's first publication and Legrain's, Egyptology had become focused enough and established enough that constant comparison to the classical sources no longer was required in epigraphic publication; the concomitant contextualization that situated the culture of ancient Egypt within physical and temporal landscapes also waned with time.

TECHNOLOGY IN EARLY MODERN EPIGRAPHY

For all his work, Legrain had access to a technology not available to Wilkinson: photography. Photography allowed for direct reproduction of ancient Egyptian inscriptions without the interpretation inherent in handcopies and improved the ability to publish hieroglyphic texts, thereby providing better access to them beyond Egypt's borders (Buckland 1980, 89; Caminos 1966; Roberts 2000, 60–63).

A self-taught artist and surveyor, Wilkinson recorded temple and tomb decoration, along with the landscape views he used to contextualize them, by eye (see Figure II.9.1), preferring that method to the use of the camera lucida, a mounted prism and the best technology to facilitate fast facsimile copy in his day (Thompson 1992, 88; 2015–2017, 1:240–241; Flynn 1997, 14, item 32). In contrast, Wilkinson's contemporary, Robert Hay and his team of artists, including Joseph Bonomi, who had worked with the camera lucida's inventor, did use that technology, though not without mixed feelings (Thompson 1992, 88; James 1997, 138–139; also, Hoskins 1835; see chapter by Manniche). In either case, publication relied on a copy of a copy, whether a wood cut or lithography, which required handcopying the image with a crayon onto a limestone slab then used as the printing negative. Lithography was employed by the multivolume publications of the Napoleonic, Franco-Tuscan, and Prussian Expeditions, but it could lead to mistakes in perspective and other matters left to artistic interpretation (Jammes 1972, 10–11).

Frustration with the camera lucida inspired William Henry Fox Talbot to experiment with and ultimately perfect the positive-negative photographic process (Jammes 1972; Roberts 2000, 7–10). Returning to England from his 1833 honeymoon in Italy, where he failed to capture satisfying representations of the countryside with his camera lucida, Talbot began experimenting with the camera lucida's older cousin, the camera obscura, and paper made photo-sensitive by a series of chemical washes. By 1835, Talbot was able to produce the first negative image or "Talbotype" (Buckland 1980, 26–31; Jammes 1972, 7; Roberts 2000, 8). The positive-negative photographic process held an advantage over other contemporary photographic processes, like the Daguerreotype, because the negative of Talbot's process could be used to produce multiple prints of the image without the additional step of lithography (Buckland 1980, 13–15; Jammes 1972, 7–9). Talbot himself was the man behind the camera of the first published photos of Egyptian hieroglyphs, a three-page brochure entitled "The Talbotype Applied to Hieroglyphs," which appeared in 1846 (Caminos 1966). Ironically, the pamphlet published a near-facsimile copy of the rock-cut stela of Seti I and his Nubian Viceroy Amenemope near Qasr Ibrim drawn by Joseph Bonomi—a handcopy likely produced using the camera lucida—together with a translation by Samuel Birch of the British Museum and a description of the stela's physical

FIGURE 11.9.1. Wilkinson's unpublished handcopy of Eighteenth Dynasty decoration at Amada Temple, Nubia, made in 1821–1822, MS. Wilkinson dep. a 14, Fol. 29, copyright Bodleian Library, Oxford, by permission of the National Trust.

setting by A. C. Harris (Caminos 1966, pls. 13–15; Roberts 2000, 60–61). With the publication, Talbot demonstrated the potential for photography to replace the cumbersome lithographic reproduction process, facilitating the publication of facsimile copies of hieroglyphic texts for all future epigraphic endeavors, expanding exponentially the access to Egyptian texts in accurate copy.

In addition to ease of publication, positive-negative photography permitted the direct recording of monuments, their texts, their landscape situations, and their state of preservation. Following initial experimentation with Daguerreotypes by Venet, Goupil-Fesquet, Bouton, and Joy de Lothbière in 1839, the Frenchman Félix Teynard traveled to Egypt in 1851 with a camera that produced salted paper negatives. An independent traveler, Teynard set out explicitly to produce a photographic companion, published as *Égypte et Nubie* in 1858, to the lithographs of the *Description de l'Égypte*, drawing influence as well from the lithographic images in Frantz-Christian Gau's *Antiquités de la Nubie* (Howe 1992, 139–144). Similarly, the Englishman Francis Frith journeyed through Egypt and the Holy Land with a wet collodion camera between 1856 and 1861, drawing inspiration from David Roberts' hugely popular lithographic scenes of Egypt to produce a series of publications, most famously 1857's *Egypt and the Holy Land* (Frith 1857; Manchip White and van Haafted 1980, vii–xix; Vercoutter 1992). Frith's and Teynard's works served to make the visible reality of Egypt accessible to those who could not visit the country and also helped fuel a burgeoning tourist trade, a trade subsequently encouraged by the distribution of photographic stereoscopic series (Nicholson 2009) and the new literary genre of travel guides (Mariette 1872a, 1878b, 1890, 1892; Reid 2002, 69–73; Wilkinson 1847, 1857).

Auguste Mariette

The influence of the Napoleonic Expedition and its *Description de l'Égypte* extended beyond the photographic world to the world of museums across France, in turn influencing the careers of Egyptologists and the course of Egyptology as practiced both in Europe and in Egypt (see chapter by Gady). At the museum in Boulogne, which had acquired the personal collection of Denon, who had participated in the Napoleonic Expedition, the Frenchman Auguste Mariette began his Egyptological career (Le Guilloux 2000, 48; Tourneur d'Ison 1999, 15–18; Reid 2002, 99–107). Mariette's interest in Egypt was sparked when his family inherited the papers of Nestor l'Hôte, a cousin who had accompanied Napoleon to Egypt (Le Guilloux 2000, 48). Tasked by his father with cataloging the papers, Mariette became intrigued with ancient Egyptian culture and soon started haunting the Egyptological section of the local museum, teaching himself hieroglyphs and practicing them by reading and recording inscriptions on objects in the museum. Unbeknownst to him, his efforts were somewhat foiled by inaccurate "restorations" made by the Napoleonic savants before the objects reached the museum (Le Guilloux 2000, 48; Tourneur d'Ison 1999, 15–18).

From Boulogne, Mariette worked his way to the Louvre, where he made handcopies of all the inscriptions then in the collection (Bierbrier, Dawson, and Uphill 1995, 275). Only upon Mariette's entrance into this professional Egyptological position did Egypt itself become accessible to him. He was sent to Egypt in 1850 to purchase Coptic and Syriac manuscripts for the Louvre, but when the Coptic Patriarch refused to sell, Mariette instead, and without permission, used the money to fund an excavation that eventually uncovered the Serapeum. Mariette sent the bulk of his finds back to the Louvre, much to the museum's delight and much to the consternation of the Egyptians; he had conducted all his excavations without holding a *firman* granting him permission to dig or export objects (Le Guilloux 2000, 50–51; Tourneur d'Ison 1999, 59–105).

Mariette's early career demonstrated the impact of growing European interest in ancient Egypt, fueled by increased access to information about and materials from Egypt accessible beyond the borders of the country. When Mariette was invited by Saïd Pasha to organize and head the newly founded Egyptian Antiquities Organization in 1858, the Frenchman settled in Egypt permanently (Reid 2002, 99–107). As its first director, Mariette limited the exporting of artifacts, channeling his energy and antiquities into a new museum in Boulaq, a suburb of Cairo, importing the European practice of museum development to Egypt itself and adding another point of potential access to the culture of the ancient Egyptians (Le Guilloux 2000, 51–55; Tourneur d'Ison 1999, 131–189).

Although Mariette produced graceful reproductions of ancient Egyptian monuments (Marshall 2010, 66, 110–111) and also employed his artistic talents on caricatures (e.g., Marshall 2010, 25, 38, 46–47), he more often than not employed artists and draftsmen, most notably Ernst Weidenbach, for publications (Caminos 1976, 3–4; Bierbrier, Dawson, and Uphill 1995, 434–435). He would give them the resources he assembled in Egypt—paper squeezes, notes, and handcopies (e.g., Marshall 2010, 110–111)—which they used to work up copies of the monuments while in Europe (Caminos 1976, 5). With these resources, the artists produced drawings that, not surprisingly, tended to reproduce the figures more carefully than the hieroglyphs, as squeezes and handcopies would have preserved the larger figures in greater detail than they would the smaller scale hieroglyphic signs (Mariette 1872b, 1875).

This method produced line drawings published in black and white with hieroglyphs rendered in a nicely legible hand, but reduced to the essentials required for recognition, neglecting most internal details and a sense of the original style (Mariette 1872b, 1875). On rare occasions, a hieratic inscription was included, traced in outline (Mariette 1875, pl. 46). Damage within lines of texts tends to be indicated with hash marks (Mariette 1872b, 1875), with obscured and partial hieroglyphs being filled in where possible (e.g., Mariette 1875, pls. 36, 45). Where parts of a monument were missing, lines of text could be left blank; in these instances, a simple reconstruction generally is offered, indicating the surviving edge of the monument, and, where relevant, boundary lines between rows of hieroglyphs frequently were dotted in across the reconstruction (e.g., Mariette 1872b, pls. 1 [recto], 4 [verso]). Damage was also indicated with hashing, which, in some cases, seems to attempt to replicate the appearance of the original (e.g., Mariette 1872b, pl. 7). Being larger, the figures tend to be more detailed and give the impression of having been traced from the original or from rubbings of the original (e.g., horse on the lunette of the Victory Stela of Piye; Mariette 1872b, pl. 1). This impression is reflected in the fact that the figures do accord better with the development of Egyptian artistic style than do the hieroglyphs (compare earlier monuments, such as the Stela of Wahankh Intef II or the Tomb of Horemheb, to later monuments, such as the Ptolemaic temple at Aswan or the stela of Alexander II; Mariette 1872b, pls. 49, 74–75 and 23–25, 14).

Although Mariette's contextual scope, as reflected in his publications, was not necessarily as expansive as Wilkinson's, the images and illustrations included in Mariette's publications do address context, with maps, plans, and isometric drawings appearing in many of his works. Mariette's practice of focusing his publications on single sites led him to provide a different level of context than Wilkinson was wont to. Scenes from the temple of Ptah at Karnak (Mariette 1872b, pls. 80, 84) are situated clearly in their architectural context, with doors and color-block borders included and with scenes presented in the same order and relationships as they appear on the temple walls. The coffin of Akh-Hor was pictured together with its related assemblage, illustrating the material culture context of the body (Mariette 1872b, pl. 51). Atmospheric views of the *dromos* and the interior of the catacomb of the Serapeum constituted three of ten total plates in one volume, adding landscape context (Mariette 1856, pls. 2–4). Mariette also published graffiti from the landscape surrounding sites where he worked (Mariette 1872b, pls. 26u, 70–73) or from otherwise uninscribed walls (Mariette 1875, pl. 46). In his own notebooks, drawings of objects stand next to excerpts of texts from those objects (Marshall 2010, 110–111), and this pairing is occasionally maintained in his publications (e.g., Mariette 1872b, pl. 101). Mariette had the flexibility to include photographs in his publications, alongside the line drawings of texts and lithographs of landscape views (e.g., Mariette 1872b, pl. 20).

In addition to his image-heavy publications, and like Wilkinson, Mariette produced a string of unillustrated or minimally illustrated publications intended to serve as commentary for what lay before the reader, though unlike Wilkinson, these publications included not only travel guides/travelogues (Mariette 1872a, 1878b), but also guides to Egyptian and Egyptianizing installations at Exhibitions Universelle in France (Mariette 1867a, 1878a) and a guide to the galleries at the Boulaq Museum (Mariette 1869). In addition, Mariette produced histories in the same mold, which were translated into English (e.g., Mariette 1867b, 1892). These works served to expand the audience for all Egyptological publications, even the more technical ones, creating an audience of educated amateurs with a desire to know more about Egypt.

GEORGES LEGRAIN

Upon Mariette's death in 1881, the position of Director of the Egyptian Antiquities Organization passed in the hands of another Frenchman, Gaston Maspero, and subsequently to Jacques de Morgan in 1892, a position that he took up after working in the

Caucasus Mountains and Persia. Trained as an engineer, he assembled an able team to continue the archaeological projects of the Antiquities Service (Bierbrier, Dawson, and Uphill 1995, 278, 297). The core of the team consisted of Georges Legrain, a young Egyptologist whom de Morgan quickly placed as the director of work at Karnak (Bierbrier, Dawson, and Uphill 1995, 246); Gustave Jéquier, a Swiss Egyptologist who worked with de Morgan in Persia (Bierbrier, Dawson, and Uphill 1995, 217); and Urbain Bouriant, director of the French Archaeological Mission (Bierbrier, Dawson, and Uphill 1995, 59). De Morgan assembled this team to excavate and record work at Dahshur in 1894; the collective went on to work together throughout Upper Egypt (Bierbrier, Dawson, and Uphill 1995, 297). The publications of these projects were jointly authored, with de Morgan most commonly taking the lead (Morgan et al. 1894–1909; Morgan et al. 1895; Bouriant, Legrain, and Jéquier 1903). Their work reflects the efforts of a government-funded team, like the Napoleonic, Franco-Tuscan, and Prussian Expeditions, but a team of archaeologists and epigraphers funded by the Egyptian government, rather than a foreign government (Thompson 2015–2017, 2:65–66).

Of this team, the career and work of Georges Legrain stands out; though probably best known for his archaeological work at Karnak, and specifically for the discovery of the Karnak Cachette in 1903, Legrain began his Egyptological career with a thesis on a Ptolemaic funerary papyrus (Legrain 1890). Legrain's career spanned the period in which photography was increasingly employed to record objects and texts, a trend that his epigraphic work and publications epitomize. Where his earliest publications make use of hand-drawn copies of texts, through time, his works increasingly rely on photography for facsimile reproduction, frequently, for inscribed objects, coupled with a version of the text in hieroglyphic font copy (compare Legrain 1890, 1906–1925). In Legrain's work, this trend may in part be explained as a matter of convenience, especially for those volumes published after the discovery of the Cachette, but they do follow a broader pattern in publication initiated by Talbot himself.

As part of de Morgan's team, Legrain contributed catalogs of objects, illustrations of architectural detail, and object drawings to publications, though others, particularly de Morgan and Jéquier, also drew architecture and objects (e.g., Morgan et al. 1895, V–VI). At Dahshur, Legrain's contribution followed the style of his earlier efforts, with textual descriptions of objects illustrated by detailed black and white line drawings sensitive to the artistic style of the original (e.g., Morgan et al. 1895, 39, 78, 79). In addition, Legrain produced the colored plates illustrating princesses' jewelry found in the course of excavations (Morgan et al. 1895, pls. 15, 19). A publication of inscriptions from Ptolemaïs to which Legrain contributed facsimile copies of and textual commentary on Demotic graffiti similarly drew on his expertise based on previous experience copying demotic papyri at the Louvre, though included less translation than was his norm, the texts being highly formulaic (Morgan, Bouriant, and Legrain 1894, 372–379).

Expanding his repertoire for the team's work at Amarna, Legrain wrote the bulk of the text, copied scenes from the South Tombs, and contributed some of the photographs included in the publication (Bouriant, Legrain, and Jéquier 1903, III, 13). In his text, Legrain not only provided descriptions of the scenes and their states of conservation but also quoted extensively from previously published materials providing both philological and archaeological context for the tomb scenes presented and compiling a summary of work done at Amarna to that point (Bouriant, Legrain, and Jéquier 1903, IV). In this publication, the tomb scenes are presented in black and white line drawings with black and white photographs of details (e.g., Bouriant, Legrain, and Jéquier 1903, pls. 2–3, 7–8). Despite the line drawings' inclusion of detail on figures and the reproduction of the distinctive Amarna-style art, the hieroglyphs are presented in a handcopy, reductionist manner, not fully preserving the original style (e.g., pls. 16–17). This may suggest that the final copies for publication were produced from resources compiled in the field, but not completed with immediate reference to the wall. The drawings were prepared in 1894, but, due to various other and more pressing engagements, the material was not published until 1903, which did allow for subsequent cross-checking of drawn copies with the originals on the wall (Bouriant, Legrain, and Jéquier 1903, I). In a single instance, hieroglyphs are reproduced completely filled in with black ink (pl. 30). Intralinear damage is indicated with hash marks, sometimes mimicking the reconstructed placement of individual signs or sign groups (pl. 15) and sometimes simply indicating the absence of legible hieroglyphs in the entire line or column (pls. 22, 63).

De Morgan and his team also worked at sites further south, most notably recording the Ptolemaic double temple of Kom Ombo (Morgan et al. 1894–1909). The team began recording the materials for the Kom Ombo volumes in the winter of 1893–1894, but more pressing obligations quickly diverted the attentions of de Morgan, Jéquier, and Bourriant; ultimately, Legrain saw the material through to publication, being in closest proximity to Kom Ombo from his home base at Karnak and thus best able to visit the site and proof copies of the scenes and texts (Morgan et al. 1894–1909, 3:1–2).

Unlike Legrain's and the team's earlier publications, no translations were included in the volumes, and a minimum of commentary accompanies the images; this was done explicitly to allow those scholars whose work it was to draw such deductions from the scenes and texts to do so unimpeded (Morgan et al. 1894–1909, 2:5), a perhaps questionable aspect of the presentation, given the simplification of both figures and hieroglyphs in the subsequent plates. All volumes in the Kom Ombo series present figures and text in black and white line drawings and in simplified form, a feature likely born of the speed with which the temple was recorded. The Kom Ombo volumes do not include photographs, relying instead solely on line drawings. Though simplified, the figures are presented in more detail than are the hieroglyphic signs (e.g., the usual Ptolemaic beading on broad collars, striped detailing on head cloth lappets, etc.). Architectural plans, elevations, and photographs of the temple and the surrounding landscape before (Morgan et al. 1894–1909, 2:3) and after (Morgan et al. 1894–1909, 2:4) clearance provide some context for the line drawings (Morgan et al. 1894–1909, 2:1–5, 3:1–2). The Kom Ombo volumes follow in the tradition of Mariette's publications focusing on single sites and participate in the shift away from the synthetic epigraphic and historical perspective of the early nineteenth century epitomized by Wilkinson's work, appealing instead to an increasingly professionalized audience of Egyptologists as specialist scholars.

Like the Kom Ombo volumes, Legrain's subsequent publications seem to reflect increasing pressure to publish accurately but quickly. He increasingly made use of photographs rather than line drawings and a hieroglyphic font instead of handcopies

(Legrain 1912, 14–18, 1906–1925). Legrain equally relied on photography and hieroglyphic print font in lieu of line drawings for his publications relating to the Karnak Cachette (Legrain 1906–1925), a trend curious to compare to more recent publications of the same material (Goyon et al. 2004).

CONCLUSION

The development of early modern epigraphy and the techniques and technology it employed throughout the course of the nineteenth century was shaped by waves of increasing access to the physical land of Egypt, to ancient Egyptian monuments, and to the voices of the ancient Egyptians themselves. The published work of John Gardner Wilkinson expanded exponentially the audience for Egyptological literature, both hieroglyphic texts and commentary on them, establishing the standards for subsequent publications while simultaneously presenting a synthetic perspective on ancient Egyptian culture and history unmatched later in the century and deemed increasingly unnecessary as Egyptology was professionalized into a discipline distinct from classics. The pioneering work of Wilkinson, Mariette, Legrain, and their contemporaries continued to open the world of ancient Egypt to those not yet able to make the voyage to Egypt itself, by presenting Egyptian texts and their contexts in publication, by embracing and improving museology to accommodate Egyptian artifacts, and by contributing to the ever-developing understanding of hieroglyphs, hieratic, and Demotic.

BIBLIOGRAPHY

Bierbrier, M. L., W. R. Dawson, and W. P. Uphill. 1995. *Who Was Who in Egyptology*. 3rd rev. ed. London.

Bouriant, U., G. Legrain, and G. Jéquier. 1903. *Monuments pour servir à l'étude du culte d'Atonou en Égypte*. MIFAO 8. Cairo.

Buckland, G. 1980. *Fox Talbot and the Invention of Photography*. Boston.

Caminos, R. 1966. "The Talbotype Applied to Hieroglyphs." *JEA* 52:65–70.

Caminos, R. 1976. "The Recording of Inscriptions and Scenes in Tombs and Temples." In *Ancient Egyptian Epigraphy and Palaeography*, 3–25. New York.

Champollion, J.-F. 1822. *Lettre à M. Dacier*. Paris.

Chassinat, E. 1907. *Catalogue des signes hiéroglyphiques de l'Imprimerie de l'Institut Français du Caire*. Cairo.

The Epigraphic Survey. 1930. *Medinet Habu I: Earlier Historical Records of Rameses III*. OIP 8. Chicago.

The Epigraphic Survey. 1970. *Medinet Habu VIII: The Eastern High Gate*. OIP 94. Chicago.

Flynn, S. J. A. 1997. *Sir John Gardner Wilkinson: Traveller and Egyptologist, 1797–1875*. Oxford.

Frith, F. 1857. *Egypt and Palestine: Photographed and Described*. Vol. 1. London.

Gardiner, A. H. 1962. *My Working Years*. London.

Goyon, J.-C., C. Cardin, M. Azim, and G. Zaki, eds. 2004. *Trésors d'Égypte: La "cachette" de Karnak, 1904–2004*. Grenoble.

Hoskins, G. A. 1835. *Travels in Ethiopia, Above the Second Cataract of the Nile*. London.

Howe, K. S. 1992. *Félix Teynard: Calotypes of Egypt*. New York.

James, T. G. H. 1997. *Egypt Revealed: Artist-Travellers in an Antique Land*. London.

Jammes, A. 1972. *William H. Fox Talbot: Inventor of the Negative-Positive Process*. Luzern.

Legrain, G. 1890. *Le Livre des Transformations (Papyrus Démotique 3452 du Louvre)*. Paris.

Legrain, G. 1906–1925. *Statues et Statuettes de Rois et des Particuliers*. 4 vols. Cairo.

Legrain, G. 1912. "The Paintings and Inscriptions of the Painted Vaulted Chamber of Teta-Ky." In *Five Years' Exploration at Thebes*, edited by Carnarvon and Carter, 14–18. London.

Le Guilloux, P. 2000. "Auguste Mariette: Une vie pour l'archéologie Égyptienne." *EAO* 16:47–55.

Manchip White, J. E., and J. van Haafted. 1980. *Egypt and the Holy Land in Historic Photographs: 77 Views by Francis Frith*. New York.

Mariette, A. 1856. *Choix de monuments et de dessins découverts ou exécutés pendant le déblaiment du sérapeum de Memphis*. Paris.

Mariette, A. 1867a. *Description du parc Égyptien*. Paris.

Mariette, A. 1867b. *Aperçu de l'histoire ancienne d'Égypte pour l'intelligence des monuments exposés dans le tempe du parc égyptien*. Paris.

Mariette, A. 1869. *Notice des principaux monuments exposés dans les galeries provisoires du Musée d'Antiquités Égyptiennes de S. A. le Vice-Roi à Boulaq*. 3rd ed. Paris.

Mariette, A. 1872a. *Itinéraire de la Haute-Égypte*. Alexandrie.

Mariette, A. 1872b. *Monuments divers recueilles en Égypte et en Nubie*. 2 vols. Paris.

Mariette, A. 1875. *Karnak: Étude topographique et archéologique avec un appendice comprenant les principaux textes hiéroglyphiques découvertes ou recueillis pendant les fouilles exécutées a Karnak*. 2 vols. Leipzig.

Mariette, A. 1878a. *La galerie de l'Égypte ancienne à l'exposition rétrospective du Trocadéro*. Paris.

Mariette, A. 1878b. *Voyage dans la Haute-Égypte*. Paris.

Mariette, A. 1890. *The Monuments of Upper Egypt*. Boston.

Mariette, A. 1892. *Outlines of Ancient Egyptian History*. Translated by Mary Brodrick. New York.

Marshall, A. 2010. *Auguste Mariette*. Paris.

Morgan, J. de, M. M. Berthelot, G. Legrain, G. Jéquier, V. Loret, and D. Fouquet. 1895. *Fouilles à Dachour, Mars–Juin, 1894*. Vienna.

Morgan, J. de, U. Bouriant, and G. Legrain. 1894. *Les carrières de Ptolemaïs*. Paris.

Morgan, J. de, U. Bouriant, G. Legrain, G. Jéquier, and A. Barsanti. 1894–1909. *Catalogue des monuments et inscriptions de l'Égypte antique*. 3 vols. Vienna.

Nicholson, P. T. 2009. "Egyptology for the Masses: James Henry Breasted and the Underwood Brothers." In *Sitting beside Lepsius: Studies in Honour of Jaromir Malek at the Griffith Institute*, edited by D. Magee, J. Bourriau, and S. Quirke, 381–422. OLA 185. Leuven.

Reid, D. M. 2002. *Whose Pharaohs? Archaeology, Museums, and Egyptian National Identity from Napoleon to World War I*. Berkeley.

Roberts, R. 2000. *Specimens and Marvels: William Henry Fox Talbot and the Invention of Photography*. New York.

Thompson, J. 1992. *Sir Gardner Wilkinson and His Circle*. Austin.

Thompson, J. 2015–2017. *Wonderful Things: A History of Egyptology*. 3 vols. Cairo.

Tourneur d'Ison, C. le. 1999. *Mariette Pacha ou le rêve égyptien*. Paris.

Vercoutter, J. 1992. *L'Égypte à la chambre noire: Francis Frith, photographe de l'Égypte retrouvée.* Paris.

Wilkinson, J. G. 1828. *Materia Hieroglyphica.* 2 parts in 1 vol. Malta.

Wilkinson, J. G. 1830. *Topographical Survey of Thebes, Tapé, Thaba, or Diospolis Magna.* London.

Wilkinson, J. G. 1835. *Topography of Thebes and General View of Egypt.* London.

Wilkinson, J. G. 1837. *The Manners and Customs of the Ancient Egyptians.* 3 vols. London.

Wilkinson, J. G. 1847. *A Handbook for Travellers in Egypt.* London.

Wilkinson, J. G. 1851. *The Fragments of the Hieratic Papyrus at Turin.* 2 vols. London.

Wilkinson, J. G. 1857. *The Egyptians in the Time of the Pharaohs.* London.

....

LATE NINETEENTH- AND EARLY TWENTIETH- CENTURY SCIENTIFIC DEVELOPMENTS IN EPIGRAPHY

....

VANESSA DAVIES

THE discipline of Egyptology gradually became formalized and systematized in the nineteenth and early twentieth centuries. With growing scholarly and popular interest in Egyptology came new concerns with regard to copying texts and images, spurred on by everything from new photographic techniques developed in the nineteenth century, to standardized hieroglyphic typefaces used in publications, to a burgeoning concern with protecting monuments. During this era, epigraphic work moved from the realms of independent scholars and motivated travelers, such as Robert Hay and J. G. Wilkinson, and efforts funded by states, such as the Napoleonic (see chapter by Gady), Prussian (see chapter by Loeben), and Franco-Tuscan expeditions (see chapter by Manniche), to scholars affiliated with universities and research societies. Likewise, a change came about in the way that the work was described. Scholars of this era frequently referred to the "science" of epigraphy (Naville 1870, iii; David 1999, 100; Newberry 1893, ix; Breasted 1933), modeling their language on that of the earlier state-sponsored expeditions and signaling their perception that the recording of decoration was a systematic field of study.

WORK HISTORY

With Champollion's decipherment of hieroglyphs and the subsequent study of Egyptian texts, Egyptology emerged as a scientific discipline, as described by de Rougé (1867, 3), who referred to Champollion's grammar as "the basis of all science" (see chapter by Regulski). The young field's scholars, who were mostly of European origin, developed the methods of study and practice that would be carried out in Egypt. Standards of work began to emerge or be discussed; objectives were set; rules were put into effect concerning who was authorized to work at particular sites and what objects could be removed from Egypt. Scientific work, that is, work carried out according to the field's generally approved methodologies, contrasted with what those scholars viewed as the indiscriminate recording and removal of objects by Egyptians, interested tourists, and would-be scholars.

Following the pattern set by the Napoleonic, Prussian, and Franco-Tuscan expeditions, many early epigraphic missions visited a wide range of sites, copying carved and painted decoration and seeking out texts that had not been previously published (Brugsch 1862; Mariette and Maspero 1872–1889; de Morgan et al. 1894). By the end of the nineteenth century, the approach to epigraphic work had changed. Many epigraphic missions narrowed the focus of their efforts, concentrating on one site at a time (Mariette 1870–1875; Daressy 1900), and sometimes widened the range of material covered by reporting on archaeology and epigraphy in the same volume (Quibell 1908; Borchardt 1910–1913; Peet 1914; Junker 1929). With scholars spending more time at a particular site and making a more complete study of the site's decoration, tombs and temples were published partially or in full as stand-alone monuments, not as one of many monuments in a large collection.

The site-centric approach coincided with an increased emphasis on work history. Consulting earlier records of work on a monument became a standard of research. The publication of the first volume of the *Topographical Bibliography* (Porter and Moss 1927) greatly facilitated the research of decoration and previous epigraphic work at sites. During the following decades, new volumes in this series and revisions of earlier volumes ensured this invaluable compendium's place in epigraphic research.

In his publication of Pediamenopet's tomb at Thebes, Johannes Dümichen (1884, x) acknowledged the previous work there of J. G. Wilkinson and Richard Pococke. When Percy Newberry's mission arrived at Bersha in November 1891, they found many sections of wall decoration in the tomb of Djehutyhotep that had been destroyed. Newberry's knowledge of the tomb's previous state was informed by a variety of sources, including drawings and notes from Lepsius's expedition; those of Joseph Bonomi and Francis Arundale, who were sent to work there by Robert Hay, Nestor l'Hôte, and J. G. Wilkinson; rough sketches of the interior by a Mr. Bankes and a Mr. Beechey, who traveled with the explorer Giovanni Belzoni; and a photograph of a section of wall taken in 1889 by a Major Brown of the Egyptian Irrigation Department. Newberry ([1894?], 3–5) incorporated the older records into his own. The portions of decoration known to him only from those sources were rendered in outline rather than his usual block figures.

In the late 1920s, the Mission française du Caire resumed publication of their *Tombes thébaines* after World War I had interrupted and changed their work. In a long introduction, George Foucart (1935, x–xi) expressed admiration for the color plates in Norman de Garis Davies's Robb de Peyster Tytus Memorial series published by the Metropolitan Museum of Art, but he nevertheless defended the line drawings of his publication series as both accurate and less expensive to reproduce. Looking to the old scientific method as a benchmark for epigraphic work, he compared the line drawings of Marcelle Baud to those of Robert Hay (see chapter by Manniche), which were in the British Museum. As a signal of the quality of the Mission française's work, he proudly reported that Baud's drawings were found to be almost identical to Hay's.

When James H. Breasted and Alan H. Gardiner began their ambitious, decades-long compilation of the Coffin Texts, earlier copies of texts provided them with valuable information. Originally, the team included Pierre Lacau, who had already studied many coffins. Lacau's duties as director-general of the Egyptian Service des Antiquités, however, proved too great for him to continue work on their project. Instead, he generously gave Breasted and Gardiner access to his notes and copies of Coffin Texts that he had made. Once again, older documentation came to the rescue of an epigraphic mission. Lacau's records proved crucial when the team encountered texts that had since fallen into disrepair (de Buck 1935, x).

Techniques and Standards of Recording

Standard epigraphic recording involved making squeezes and freehand drawings and tracing decoration. Following techniques employed by epigraphers working on Greek and Latin inscriptions, epigraphers in Egypt made squeezes by applying wet paper to stone surfaces to obtain imprints of inscriptions. Yet, a unique problem existed for Egyptian inscriptions that did not factor into the recording of most Greek and Latin inscriptions: paint. In 1874, Amelia Edwards (1888, 323) lamented the effects on vibrantly colored paint done by Egyptologists' wet squeezing, which, along with tourists' graffiti and collectors' appropriations of artifacts, she identified as the main causes of the destruction of Egyptian monuments. Her despair at the situation was channeled into the formation of the Egypt Exploration Fund (EEF), whose purpose was to document ancient monuments and to raise awareness about their protection.

The head of the EEF's first excavation, Édouard Naville, began his career working with carved and painted decoration, and that would continue to be a focus of his scholarly energy. After studying under Lepsius (see chapter by Loeben), Naville toured Egypt for five months in 1868, reading and copying monumental texts for publication. He spent sixteen days at Edfu Temple, recording texts related to the Horus myths. Over the summer in Geneva, he completed his drawings and made a second visit to the temple to check them against the originals. Two years after his initial trip, Naville's first epigraphic publication (1870) appeared in print.

Naville's wife, Marguerite, played a substantial role in his work. She took notes and photographs in the field, painted watercolors, and redrew and edited her husband's drawings. Determining that her husband's strengths lay elsewhere, she took responsibility for the presentation of texts and vignettes in many of his publications, eliciting praise from Reginald Stuart Poole of the British Museum, who likened her work to that of an "Egyptian basilicogrammate" (i.e., royal scribe) (Maurice-Naville, Naville, and Eggly-Naville 2014, 93). With his wife's collaboration, Naville pursued his passion for recording and translating texts. In a letter bemoaning the copying errors of his colleague, W. M. Flinders Petrie, Naville (1886a, COR.005.d.12) wished Petrie would make squeezes so that others "could work them out."

Petrie, who is better known for establishing archaeological methods, was also quite an active epigrapher. His (1885) assessment of the importance of epigraphy can be seen in the quote by the poet George Herbert that introduces his volume on Tanis: "Copy fair what Time hath blurred; Redeem truth from his jaws." In his publication of the Meidum tombs, Petrie echoed Amelia Edwards's concern with damage to tombs. Collectors and vandals cut out and damaged portions of scenes, and wet squeezing removed paint from walls. To avoid further damage, Petrie made dry squeezes. With one hand, he held three-foot long, one-foot wide sheets of paper on the wall. Using the other hand, he either folded paper over the lip of sunk-relief carving or used his finger to trace and emboss the shape of raised-relief carving on paper. He then drew the images on the paper, comparing the squeeze to the original so as to produce a copy that was accurate both in detail and in artistic sensibility (Petrie 1892, 2, 23).

Petrie's comparison of squeeze and original was important for communicating what the eye perceived when looking at a raised-relief image. He realized that the edges of raised-relief images had a small amount of curvature, a sort of border, and that if he traced along the outermost edge of the border, the resulting image appeared bloated in comparison to the original. To both account for the border and avoid swollen-looking images, he traced along the curved ledge of the border. Then he used the impression as a guide to draw in the scene's major elements, and he filled in smaller details by sight (Petrie 1892, 2, 23).

Back in England, the sheets were taped together to recreate the wall decoration. Over the course of about a month, the drawings were inked in preparation for photo-lithography. Petrie preferred his methodology to wet squeezing because it did far less damage to wall surfaces. He also felt that his results were sufficiently precise to allow detailed studies of decoration.

Although Petrie and Naville approached epigraphic work differently, they sought similar goals in their work. They valued text as a means of exploring questions of chronology, geography, and biblical interpretation. Petrie, however, perceived yet another purpose to copying texts. He saw the potential for new avenues of study centered on the analysis of artistic detail, and he engaged (1892, 29–34) with questions concerning the forms of hieroglyphs. His former student, Francis Llewellyn Griffith (1896, 1898), expanded this line of study, where he discussed the pictorial quality of hieroglyphs, their individual uses in writing, and various general writing conventions. Palaeographic study of Egyptian papyri was practiced already in the nineteenth century (Maspero 1875; Borchardt 1891). But without facsimile copies of wall decoration, epigraphy could not be paired with palaeography.

Petrie observed palaeographic details and noticed the artists' hands in the way that they formed hieroglyphs and larger images. While working at Meidum, Petrie (1890) wrote to Percy Newberry, urging Newberry to track variations, such as shapes of birds' claws, number of wedges in water signs, and curvature of barbs on feathers. He also informed Newberry that he was recording even offering bearers' fine facial details, which he referred to as portraiture. In the letter, Petrie illustrated for Newberry how the slightest differences in outlines of human lips convey to the viewer markedly different expressions (Figure II.10.1). Petrie's influence can be seen in the growing level of detail included in Newberry's publications over time.

Newberry's epigraphic method was similar to Petrie's, but the results were quite different. Like Petrie, Newberry did not take squeezes. Rather, he (1893 ix–x; [1894?] viii; James [1992] 2001, 25) attached to tomb walls large sheets of paper and traced images onto them. The pencil drawings were inked in England after the season was over. In the first Beni Hasan volume (1893), however, very little internal detail of human figures or hieroglyphs was recorded. Male bodies, for example, are typically completely black with some small details, such as hairline or sclerae of the eyes, indicated in thin white lines. White kilts stand in stark contrast to black bodies, and thin black lines indicate a belt, a fold, or legs under the kilt. Most items held in the figure's hands are also outlined only. Exceptions to this standard occur, such as when pairs of wrestlers are depicted as one black, one white. This helps to avoid confusion when limbs overlap and intertwine in unexpected ways.

When a young Howard Carter joined Newberry's team at the end of 1891, Newberry was presented with a way to do the detailed recording that Petrie had urged of him. Carter was skilled at and eager to draw the wall scenes freehand. Slowly, a new style of epigraphic recording creeps into Newberry's publications. In the plates of the Beni Hasan and Bersha volumes, Carter's preference for drawing freehand copies with considerable internal detail can be seen alongside Newberry's technique of rendering figures as mostly solid black images. The new technique was better suited for palaeographical study. Later, Newberry

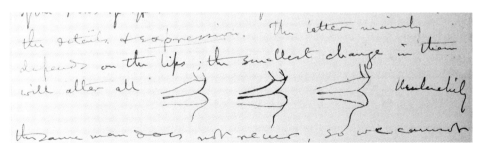

FIGURE II.10.1. Excerpt from letter written by W. M. F. Petrie to P. E. Newberry, December 23, 1890. Copyright Garstang Museum, University of Liverpool.

largely abandoned the block forms of human figures and thin, reed-like hieroglyphs found in the Beni Hasan and Bersha volumes. In his Rekhmire volume (Newberry 1900), most scenes and inscriptions are published in outline form.

Because of the wide range of sites that he worked, Petrie developed different epigraphic techniques that were suited to the situation at hand. Despite his published distaste for wet squeezing, he did make wet squeezes on occasion, but typically only on surfaces already devoid of paint. To record images located high atop Theban monuments, he (Petrie 1888, 4) descended on a rope ladder, which was held in place by another person, hung on to the ladder with one arm, unrolled sheets of wet paper that had been wound around a brush, beat the paper into carved lines, and left it there to dry. Petrie's perilous method of squeezing resulted in casts that were exhibited in England, thus bringing 3D images out of Egypt without actually removing artifacts from the country.

At Tanis in 1884, Petrie exercised a novel technique that proved useful on more than one occasion. When inspecting large blocks, Petrie upended them to check the undersides for decoration. With very large blocks that could not be overturned, he simply cleared earth from under the center, and with the ends supported by the ground, he lay underneath the stone to copy its inscription (1931, 45). Petrie (1897, 26; 1931, 160) had Wilhelm Spiegelberg use this technique to copy the Israel stela at the temple of Merneptah.

At Abydos, another creative method was needed to record the limestone markers on retainers' graves because wind and sand erosion had worn down surfaces to such an extent that carved detail did not appear in photographs. Petrie (1901, 32–33) devised the ingenious solution of filling in the hollows of carved surfaces with enough sand so that the relief just emerged over the edge of the sand (Figure II.10.2). Each stela was subjected to two separate preparations, once for drawing and once for photographing, thus keeping the two processes of recording entirely separate from one another. To draw stelae, Petrie (1901, 33) made a frame of threads and placed it on the stone to serve as a scale that corresponded to lined paper that he placed under thin drawing paper.

As Naville did with Marguerite, Petrie relied on his wife, Hilda, in his work life. She drew reliefs, plans, and artifacts, cataloged objects, edited his writing, and managed salary payments to the crews of Egyptians who worked for him. In the 1904–1905 season, Hilda led a small team of epigraphers to Saqqara to record Old Kingdom mastaba reliefs, and then she and another epigrapher joined Petrie's epigraphic mission at Wadi Maghara in the Sinai.

Petrie's team in the Sinai found that in the intervening decades since the last major expedition there, inscriptions had suffered damage on account of mining work and other causes. One evening, while the team ate dinner, the very inscriptions that they had been recording were deliberately vandalized. Petrie (1906, 47–48) decided to carve away the remainder to save them from further harm. An additional setback occurred when Petrie's quarter-mile-long roll of printing paper was stolen. With the team unable to carry out their copying work, Faris Nimr, editor of the newspaper *Al Mokattam*, provided them with a fresh supply of paper (1906, xi).

FIGURE 11.10.2. Stela found near the tomb of Djer, photographed as seen by the naked eye (left). The same, photographed with sand sprinkled over it (right). Copyright of the Egypt Exploration Society.

The married couple Norman and Nina de Garis Davies became renowned for their style of epigraphic recording, although only Nina had had any artistic training. Norman de Garis Davies first worked in Egypt with Petrie in 1896 as an excavator and copyist at Dendera. After they married in 1907, the couple worked for many missions, including for the Egypt Exploration Society, the Metropolitan Museum of Art, and The Oriental Institute. They initially copied decoration in ink and watercolors and later in egg tempera because it more accurately represented opaque Egyptian paint. Plates as vibrantly colored and produced with such meticulous accuracy as theirs were often unobtainable for missions because of the prohibitive costs associated with publishing (Foucart 1935, ix–xi). Even photographs, which had become more and more a standard of publication in the twentieth century, were dismissed by Gardiner (1935, viii) as "a needlessly expensive luxury" in his publication of hieratic papyri.

Painting techniques like the de Garis Davieses' easily communicated vibrant colors to viewers. Line drawings, however, presented a challenge to the epigrapher, who had to contend with how, or whether, to represent paint colors and paint lines that did not correspond with carved lines. Some authors noted when the presence of color was particularly vibrant, well preserved, or otherwise striking (de Morgan et al. 1894; Newberry [1894?]; Quibell 1908). Blackman (1911) went further, writing the colors of the images' various segments on his line drawings. Davies (1917) and Lefebvre (1923–1924) included rich discussions of how ancient artists used color.

Another challenge for epigraphers was how to represent large areas of damage and decoration that was partially or completely obscured due to damage. Areas of damage to large figures were sometimes outlined with the interior left blank (Bouriant, Legrain, and Jéquier 1903; de Morgan et al. 1894), while smaller spots of damage, such as a distinct part of a figure or a few individual hieroglyphs, were marked out with shaggy, light lines (de Morgan et al. 1894) or crosshatching (Dümichen 1867).

At the heart of the tension between whether to represent scenes in their original forms or in their contemporary states was what type of information the author wished to communicate to viewers. In the Beni Hasan series, Griffith (1896, 2) noted that Marcus Blackden depicted scenes as he felt they had looked prior to being damaged, and Howard Carter and Percy Brown drew scenes as they appeared at the time. Clearly marking out uncertain or damaged areas proved to be a compromise between these positions. When faced with considerable damage to scenes at Deshasha, Petrie (1898) opted to include the fairly certain restorations in dots to distinguish conjectured areas from undamaged areas, which were rendered, as usual, by solid lines. Carter's challenge was even greater when he worked with Naville (1895–1908) at Deir el-Bahri, because of the large number of damaged wall scenes. He drew most scenes freehand relying only occasionally on measurements and guidelines as reference points (James [1992] 2001, 60). To mark out damage, he adopted an earlier technique (Brugsch 1862; Mariette and Maspero 1872–1889) of using crosshatching and including hieroglyphs in the crosshatching when visible.

A publication's approach to epigraphic decoration sometimes favored the function of hieroglyphs over their particular, exact shapes. For the author focused primarily on how to read passages, the publication might focus solely on a clear reproduction of hieroglyphs as recognizable constituents of language. The author interested in forms of images, both hieroglyphs and accompanying depictions, might seek to represent all of those elements of the text. Limited staff and resources, however, sometimes interfered with the ability to make and publish copies with such careful attention to detail.

Brugsch's (1862) epigraphic recording from a variety of sites reproduced the layout of hieroglyphs in columns or rows, but only sometimes included images that accompany hieroglyphic texts (i.e., pl. 28). Dümichen (1867), likewise, gave precedence to the linguistic function of hieroglyphs in his publication of texts at Edfu Temple. He devoted some, but only partial, attention to figures that accompanied hieroglyphs. For example, when he reproduced offering scenes, he included with the lines of hieroglyphs the items held in offering bearers' hands along with a short German caption that explained the person's action. Gaston Maspero's (1873) publication of the stela Louvre C1 does not reproduce the stela's decoration, but he describes the image in the lower corner.

When Petrie and Griffith copied graffiti, they took a similar approach to reproducing inscriptions. Petrie's publication (1888) included handcopies of inscriptions, but images that accompanied texts were only sometimes reproduced. Instead, English captions often explain who was depicted and what action took place. Griffith (1888–1889, 1889–1890) described accompanying images and reproduced some deities' crowns in a standard font, but he did not include drawings. When he published tomb inscriptions (Griffith 1889), however, he laid out his handcopies of hieroglyphs in rows or columns, as appropriate to the original. With the difficult task of copying palimpsest walls, he reproduced some, though not all, of the nonhieroglyphic decoration.

In contrast, the plates in Naville's Edfu volume (1870) reproduce entire scenes, as if the viewer of the book is looking at the wall, with background noise removed. His volumes on Deir el-Bahri (1895–1908) provide lively commentary, as well as translation and recordings of wall decoration made under the direction of Howard Carter. In his publication of the Book of the Dead (1886b), Naville took a slightly different approach, treating text and image separately. One volume lays out versions of the same spells side by side, and another volume reproduces vignettes, often with their associated text.

Some publications reproduced hieroglyphic texts in a typeface. Readers could not view text as it appeared on the wall, but the font's standardized shapes facilitated visual scanning of a text and allowed for hieroglyphic texts to be easily interspersed with the printed translation and commentary (i.e., Maspero 1894). Printed fonts were quite successful in reproducing Greek and Latin inscriptions because of the fixed number of letters used and because drawings and photographs showed the placement of text on the object (Breccia 1911).

Complications arose when the ancient text used uncommon or unique hieroglyphs and no corresponding sign in the font existed. Such limitations forced Ahmed Kamal (1904–1905) to inaccurately reproduce texts because the available typeface could not always accommodate hieroglyphs found on Ptolemaic and Roman stelae. He counseled the reader (1:vi) to consult the volume's plates to view the hieroglyphs' actual forms. Maspero (1873) faced a similar issue with Louvre stela C1. Because some of the typically horizontal signs were oriented vertically, he opted to handwrite hieroglyphs in that publication. The difficulties of rendering hieroglyphs in typeface would be solved by Émile Chassinat (1907), who designed a hieroglyphic font for the IFAO printing house (see chapters by Emery, Traunecker).

Kurt Sethe (1908–1922) handwrote his copies of the Pyramid Texts, as Emanuel de Rougé had done in his *Chrestomathie* (1867) and in contrast with Maspero's (1894) font-based Pyramid Texts. Sethe touted (1908–1922, 1:vi–vii) the advantages of his approach, where he could more accurately reproduce the very particular hieroglyphic spellings of words and the placement of hieroglyphs in relation to one another. Yet, he also acknowledged (1:xi) the limitations of the copies, which could not be studied for palaeographic purposes, but assured readers that the shapes generally corresponded to the hieroglyphs' actual forms.

In Sethe's (1903) first and subsequent volumes of his *Urkunden* series, he also transcribed hieroglyphs in his simplified and consistent handwriting. Hieroglyphs from the Old Kingdom tomb of Ibi at Deir el-Gebrawi appear in the same recognizable penmanship as do those from a New Kingdom inscription of Djehuty originally found at Thebes. Ignoring both hieroglyphic and nonhieroglyphic forms, Sethe did not reproduce larger images that accompany hieroglyphs, but instead provided brief narrative headings in German. By focusing exclusively on the linguistic functions of hieroglyphs, he gave precedence to the compilation of texts rather than individual constituent parts.

Sethe was involved in another project that took the opposite approach and did not prefer function to form. The 1903–1904 epigraphic season at Saqqara saw Margaret Murray directing tomb excavations and leading the artists Freda Hansard and Jessie Mothersole in recording scenes. Murray's volumes of decoration (1905–1937), which supplemented the handcopies and sketches previously made by Auguste Mariette, devoted tremendous attention to all of the raw data of her epigraphic mission, describing each scene in detail and noting all sorts of important features, such as presence or absence of plaster and paint and whether images had been carved or painted. Sethe translated the texts that Murray's team copied. A hieroglyphic font was used for words that were interspersed with his narrative explanations.

Adriaan de Buck (1935) followed the example set in Sethe's *Urkunden* volumes when he opted to publish handwritten copies for the Coffin Texts project that was begun by Breasted and Gardiner. The painstaking process of recording Coffin Texts involved not just reading and copying signs, but also correctly translating those signs from the original cursive script to the hieroglyphs of the copy sheets and the publication. A further complicating factor on this project was the need to disassemble coffins in order to study the texts. The scholarly and physical effort and the risk of damage to coffins should they be handled too often prompted a particularly rigorous method of collation, where every transcription was reviewed and agreed on by two other people, and the text's translation was also settled.

Like Sethe's *Urkunden*, the Coffin Texts project gave priority to words over image despite the intention of "reproducing the original as faithfully as possible" (de Buck 1935, xiii). The epigraphic team did not reproduce the original signs, and they did not record nonhieroglyphic images, such as offering tables, false doors, or eyes. Texts were effectively removed from their contexts because epigraphers did not note where signs appeared on coffins. (For the reversal of this process, see chapter by Wendrich.)

Other epigraphers took great care in how they presented nonhieroglyphic images. Eschewing traditional black, Newberry (1900) printed his Rekhmire line drawings in red because he felt that the more subtle contrast with the paper made for easier viewing. When Lefebvre (1923–1924, 1:vi) was working at the tomb of Petosiris, Pierre Lacau, then director-general of the Service des Antiquités, visited twice. Seeing the importance of epigraphic recording, Lacau secured the cooperation of the artist Hamzeh Carr, who reproduced the tomb's decoration in line drawings and watercolors, which the author admitted would have been woefully underwhelming in photographic form alone. Breasted's other major epigraphic endeavor, The Epigraphic Survey (see chapter by McClain), did not observe the Coffin Texts project's inattention to hieroglyphic detail, accompanying images, or location of inscription or paint on the surface. So great was the regard for detail that the Survey's first two years' work was discarded when it was realized that the scale of reduction obscured valuable detail in the hieroglyphs and the sketches of accompanying images failed to convey either adequate detail or artistic aspects (Nelson 1929, 13). Walter Wreszinksi (1923–1936) connected image and artifact through epigraphy, publishing photographs and drawings of scenes alongside photographs of three-dimensional objects that were depicted in images. Contrary to epigraphic missions that treated each site separately, his three-volume work included scenes from various royal and private monuments.

CONSERVATION

As now, epigraphy was then closely tied to the protection, excavation, and preservation of monuments. Mariette's appointment in 1858 as Conservator of Egyptian monuments reflected a growing awareness in the latter half of the nineteenth century that sites were being damaged or destroyed by locals and visitors. Organizations established in the 1880s to undertake scientific research and preservation include the École du Caire, the predecessor of the Institut français d'archéologie orientale (IFAO), the Egypt Exploration Fund (later: Society), and the Committee (later: Society) for the Preservation of the Monuments of Ancient Egypt. Wet squeezing on painted surfaces gradually ceased, thanks in part to Petrie's outspoken criticism, but not before many walls had been damaged. In 1886, August Eisenlohr petitioned Gaston Maspero, then Director of Museums and Excavations, to retask the IFAO as an epigraphic coalition funded by various European governments (David 1999, 145–146). The cooperation engendered by the international body would surely have further standardized epigraphic practice. Although Eisenlohr's idea never reached fruition, these organizations, joined in 1929 by the Deutsches Archäologisches Institut in Kairo, attracted international bodies of scholars.

The interest in Egyptian culture generated by scholars and research societies produced varied consequences. Egyptian law forbade the removal of antiquities from the country without permission. An August 1897 decree greatly expanded Muhammad Ali's 1835 ban on the export of antiquities by defining punishments for those who illegally excavated government lands, removed a government antiquity, or damaged an ancient artifact or site. Decrees in 1912 and 1921 further regulated excavations and the trade and export of antiquities. Nevertheless, antiquities continued to exit Egypt, bound for private collections and museums.

The public's enthusiasm for new discoveries sometimes endangered the very antiquities that researchers sought to protect. To safeguard painted floors that he discovered at Amarna, Petrie (1894, 1) had a building constructed over them. He singlehandedly built a long raised, wooden platform so that viewers could walk over the floors without damaging the delicate surfaces. But because no path to the site had been laid out, visitors traipsed through agricultural fields to arrive at their destination. After Petrie concluded his work, someone, he reported (1931, 138), had been motivated to discourage streams of curious tourists and destroyed the painted surfaces.

Whether reproduced in photographs, line drawings, paintings, or any other method, epigraphic recording remains subject to what is captured by the viewing eye, human and technical. Each method of copying images is limited by a variety of factors, including constraints of technologies, such as photography and printing, the physical location of texts, and external factors, such as light and amount of time available to devote to work. The human factor, however, constitutes the most significant component affecting the recording of decoration. The reproduction, then, results from a complex combination of the epigrapher's aims, such as an emphasis on words versus images, training, both artistic and Egyptological, personality, and cultural and historical background, where, for example, familiarity with classical art (see chapter by Manuelian) might influence the epigrapher's conceptualization and recording of a scene. Whether Petrie's zeal in dangling from a rope ladder by one arm and unfurling paper with the other or Gardiner's rejection of photography as an extravagance, each scholar's approach to decoration ultimately shapes the way that the viewing audience perceives it.

BIBLIOGRAPHY

Blackman, A. M. 1911. *The Temple of Dendûr*. Cairo.

Bouriant, U., G. Legrain, and G. Jéquier. 1903. *Monuments pour servir à l'étude du culte d'Atonou en Égypte. Tome premier: Les tombes de Khouitatonou*. MMAF 8. Cairo.

Borchardt, L. 1891. "Die Wandlungen häufiger Zeichen der Cursivschrift des mittleren Reiches." *ZÄS* 29: 45–47.

Borchardt, L. 1910–1913. *Das Grabdenkmal des Königs Śaḥu-Re'*. 3 vols. WVDOG 14, 26. Leipzig.

Breasted, J. H. 1933. *The Oriental Institute*. Chicago.

Breccia, E. 1911. *Iscrizioni Greche e Latine*. CGC 57. Cairo.

Brugsch, H. 1862. *Recueil de monuments égyptiens, Prèmiere partie*. Leipzig.

de Buck, A. 1935. *The Egyptian Coffin Texts I: Texts of spells 1–75*. OIP 34. Chicago.

Chassinat, É. 1907. *Catalogue des signes hiéroglyphiques de l'Imprimerie de l'Institut Français du Caire*. Cairo.

Daressy, G. 1900. "Le mastaba de Mera." *MIE* 3: 521–574.

David, É. 1999. *Gaston Maspero 1846–1916: Le gentleman égyptologue*. Paris.

Davies, N. de G. 1917. *The Tomb of Nakht at Thebes*. Robb de Peyster Tytus Memorial Series 1. New York.

Dümichen, J. 1867. *Altägyptische Tempelinscriften in den Jahren 1863–1865, I. Weihinschriften aus dem Horustempel von Edfu (Apollinopolis Magna)*. Leipzig.

Dümichen, J. 1884. *Der Grabpalast des Patuamenap in der thebanischen Nekropolis, Erste Abtheilung*. Leipzig.

Edwards, A. B. 1888. *A Thousand Miles Up the Nile*. 2nd ed. New York.

Foucart, G. 1935. *Le tombeau d'Amonmos, première partie*. MIFAO 57. Cairo.

Gardiner, A. H. 1935. *Hieratic papyri in the British Museum. Third series: Chester Beatty gift*. London.

Griffith, F. Ll. 1888–1889. "Notes on a tour in Upper Egypt." *PSBA* 11: 228–234.

Griffith, F. Ll. 1889. *The Inscriptions of Siût and Dêr Rîfeh*. London.

Griffith, F. Ll. 1889–1890. "Notes on a tour in Upper Egypt." *PSBA* 12: 89–113.

Griffith, F. Ll. 1896. *Beni Hasan, Part III*. ASE 5. London.

Griffith, F. Ll. 1898. *A Collection of Hieroglyphs: A Contribution to the History of Egyptian writing*. ASE 6. London.

James, T. G. H. (1992) 2001. *Howard Carter: The Path to Tutankhamun*. London.

Junker, H. 1929. *Gîza I. Die Mastabas der IV. Dynastie auf dem Westfriedhof*. Vienna.

Kamal, A. 1904–1905. *Stèles ptolémaïques et romaines*. 2 vols. CGC [20–21]. Cairo.

Lefebvre, G. 1923–1924. *Le tombeau de Petosiris*. 3 vols. Cairo.

Mariette, A. 1870–1875. *Dendérah: Description générale du grand temple de cette ville*. 6 vols. Paris.

Mariette, A., and G. Maspero. 1872–1889. *Monuments divers recueillis en Égypte et en Nubie*. Paris.

Maspero, G. 1873. *Un gouverneur de Thèbes au début de la XIIe Dynastie (Stèle C, 1, du Louvre)*. Paris.

Maspero, G. 1875. *Mémoire sur quelques papyrus du Louvre*. Paris.

Maspero, G. 1894. *Les inscriptions des pyramides de Saqqarah*. Paris.

Maurice-Naville, D., L. Naville, and C. Eggly-Naville. 2014. *La plume, le pinceau, la prière, l'égyptologue Marguerite Naville (1852–1930)*. Geneva.

Morgan, J., de, U. Bouriant, G. Legrain, G. Jéquier, and A. Barsanti. 1894. *Catalogue des monuments et inscriptions de l'Égypte antique. Première série. Haute Égypte. Tome premier. De la frontière de Nubie à Kom Ombos*. Vienna.

Murray, M. A. 1905–1937. *Saqqara Mastabas*. 2 vols. London.

Naville, É. 1870. *Textes relatifs au mythe d'Horus recueillis dans le temple d'Edfou et précédés d'une introduction*. Geneva.

Naville, É. 1886a, June 10. To Reginald S. Poole. Egypt Exploration Society, Lucy Gura Archive.

Naville, É. 1886b. *Das Aegyptische Todtenbuch der XVIII. bis XX. Dynastie aus verschiedenen Urkunden*. 3 vols. Berlin.

Naville, É. 1895–1908. *The Temple of Deir el Bahari*. 6 vols. MEEF [13, 14, 16, 19, 27], 29. London.

Nelson, H. H. 1929. "The Epigraphic Survey of the Great Temple of Medinet Habu (Seasons 1924–25 to 1927–28)." In *Medinet Habu 1924–28*, 1–36. OIC 5. Chicago.

Newberry, P. E. 1893. *Beni Hasan, Part I*. ASE 1. London.

Newberry, P. E. [1894?] *El Bersheh, Part I*. ASE 3. London.

Newberry, P. E. 1900. *The Life of Rekhmara*. Westminster.

Peet, T. E. 1914. *The Cemeteries of Abydos, Part II, 1911–12*. MEEF 34. London.

Petrie, W. M. F. 1885. *Tanis, Part I, 1883–4*. MEEF 2. London.

Petrie, W. M. F. 1888. *A Season in Egypt, 1887*. London.

Petrie, W. M. F. 1890, December 23. To Percy E. Newberry. Garstang Museum of Archaeology, University of Liverpool.

Petrie, W. M. F. 1892. *Medum*. London.

Petrie, W. M. F. 1894. *Tell el Amarna*. London.

Petrie, W. M. F. 1897. *Six Temples at Thebes, 1896*. London.

Petrie, W. M. F. 1898. *Deshasheh 1897*. MEEF 15. London.

Petrie, W. M. F. 1901. *The Royal Tombs of the Earliest Dynasties, 1901, Part II*. MEEF 21. London.

Petrie, W. M. F. 1906. *Researches in Sinai*. London.

Petrie, W. M. F. 1931. *Seventy Years in Archaeology*. London.

Porter, B., and R. L. B. Moss. 1927. *Topographical Bibliography of Ancient Egyptian Hieroglyphic Texts, Reliefs, and Paintings I: The Theban Necropolis*. Oxford.

Quibell, J. E. 1908. *Excavations at Saqqara 1906–07*. Cairo.

de Rougé, E. 1867. *Chrestomathie égyptienne, Première partie*. Paris.

Sethe, K. 1903. *Urkunden des alten Reichs*. Urk. 1. Leipzig.

Sethe, K. 1908–1922. *Die altaegyptischen pyramidentexte nach den papierabdrücken und photographien des Berliner museums*. 4 vols. Leipzig.

Wreszinksi, W. 1923–1936. *Atlas zur altägyptischen Kulturgeschichte*. 7 vols. Leipzig.

PART III

TRADITIONAL AND NEW TECHNIQUES OF EPIGRAPHY

....

HOW TO PUBLISH AN EGYPTIAN TEMPLE?

....

CLAUDE TRAUNECKER

How should we go about publishing an Egyptian monument? You would imagine that this problem has been solved in the two centuries that have passed since the beginnings of Egyptology and that epigraphy is a technique based on codified rules, processes, and a method known to all. That is far from the case.

The great variability in quality and especially of requirements in this field are due, I believe, to factors at times technical and economic, but also human. In this contribution, I do not dwell on the techniques of survey strictly speaking. That subject has been treated extensively, and I myself have previously published a kind of field epigraphy manual in which I took stock of survey and copying (Traunecker 1987). In that text, I presented my method of rapid epigraphic survey, or what I call *copie proportionnelle*, in as instructional a way as possible. It was the result of Serge Sauneron's teaching and my experience in the field. It has its good qualities and its faults and, though old, remains usable. What has changed since then is the considerable progress due to the introduction of digital drawing and digital photography and, more recently, processing techniques in the digital imaging space.

I witnessed the introduction of personal computers in the field in the early 1980s. But on those early machines, image processing was not more than rudimentary, if not impossible. Although computing quickly became a big help to topographers, it was not until digital cameras in the late 1990s and suitable laptops that we could see the progress and applications for our discipline. Digital drawing methods were introduced at that time (Manuelian 1998). As for photographic survey techniques combined with topography and three-dimensional reproductions, the results are dazzling (Onézime and Pollin 2014; see chapter by Revez). Reflectance transformation imaging (RTI) allows shooting in optimum lighting (Frood and Howley 2014; see chapter by Wendrich). Faced with these results, one might think that the time has come for me to put my lined paper, graphite pencils, yardstick, and mirror (see the list of materials in Traunecker 1987, 285) in a display case in an epigraphy museum. In absolute terms, this is true provided you have the means at your disposal in terms of personnel, material, and time to carry out current cutting-edge techniques and that the monument is suited to these techniques. What should be done when not all of these conditions are met?

There is one aspect of epigraphic projects that depends very little on the material conditions of making documentation: the publication options. I mentioned this aspect in the introduction to my old publication (Traunecker 1987, 262–265). In this short contribution, I would like to draw colleagues' attention to certain points that seem important to me on the principles of publishing temples.

Precursors and Major Options for Publishing Temples

The first major epigraphic project that published an entire temple's hieroglyphs was that of Auguste Mariette (1870–1875) for the temple of Dendera, consisting of five volumes of drawings totaling 350 plates (see chapter by Emery). The position of scenes is indicated in a purely descriptive manner. The rooms are numbered by letters, from facade to sanctuary, then following the side chapels in a rather incoherent succession. The sketches of figures were by Mariette's hand. The whole thing was redesigned by Weidenbach, a former colleague of Lepsius's on the *Denkmäler* (see chapter by Loeben) with checks by Vassali and Devéria. These epigraphic units were selected and did not aim at a complete treatment of the monument.

The first major project that aimed at exhaustive coverage and ease of consultation by the reader was Jacques de Morgan's publication of Kom Ombo (Morgan et al. 1895; see chapter by Emery). This project was very innovative and modern. All accessible scenes were drawn, text and image on a single plate. They are numbered sequentially (881 in all), and their position within the architecture is rendered by very realistic architectural drawings. Unfortunately, it seems that the drawings were done by sight and, therefore, are impossible to check in the absence of photographs. The copying, however, was frequently inaccurate, so the Institut français d'archéologie orientale (IFAO) commissioned a new publication of Kom Ombo in 1995 (Gutbub 1995; Labrique and Bedier, forthcoming).

Around 1860, two technologies appeared that would heavily influence publication methods:

1. Photography. In 1868, at the instigation of Wilhelm I of Prussia, the future German Kaiser, Johannes Dümichen (1869) organized the first epigraphic expedition to use photography and published the results. But contemporary photographic processes and the capabilities of print publishing were not adapted to the constraints and objectives of the publication of temples (dark places, difficulty of lighting, reproduction costs).
2. Appearance of hieroglyphic fonts. The first ones date to 1840 (Janssen 1972). This tool allowed for typesetting hieroglyphic text following the format of Western languages

and writing, that is, in a line reading from left to right. From then on, the temptation would be great to rip the temple texts from the medium and context of the wall and to treat them as philological objects, similar to the Latin and Greek texts of classical authors. Émile Chassinat, director of the IFAO beginning in 1898, was trained as a typographic craftsman and, with support from Gaston Maspero, created the famous IFAO font and published the catalog of it in 1907 (Anonymous 1983; see chapter by Emery).

So began the IFAO's impressive publications of the great Ptolemaic temples: Edfu, beginning in 1897 (from the squeezes of Rochemonteix), then Dendera beginning in 1934. The work is navigated via a system of codes and descriptive conventions that, while certainly rigorous, are unwieldy and hardly user-friendly for a person infrequently consulting it.

But above all, the researcher who uses these works does not have reference to the temple and its walls, but to a printed volume with a reference to a page and a line. Thus, the text's identity becomes that of a paper publication (see chapter by Pieke).

As a result of this development, two key schools of thought regarding temple publication emerged.

1. Publications where the hieroglyphic text is reproduced in its original layout. This option often involves a publication that aims to provide the reader with an image as faithful as possible to the temple wall, with plates showing texts and images in the locations where they appear on the wall.

2. Publications where the hieroglyphic text is reconstructed according to the criteria of Western languages and writing. This tradition uses a hieroglyphic font, and the texts are arranged in horizontal lines reading left to right without taking into account breaks in the version on the temple wall.

Within these two options, there are numerous variants according to the survey's methods and the process of reproduction used. Recently, advances in photographic technologies have allowed for a third option:

3. Photographic publications. Let us briefly consider this option and its recent developments.

Hieroglyphic Text Reproduced in Its Original Layout

Publication in Single Plates

This is obviously the most appropriate solution for the ease of the library researcher. This method, one of oldest, has met with more or less success. As early as 1895, Jacques de Morgan (Morgan et al. 1895) used it for the temples of Kom Ombo. His entire publication has 881 drawings of scenes and texts accompanied by a localization scheme. It was a very rational and innovative idea for epigraphic publication. Unfortunately, the drawings and copies are not very faithful, so a "modern" edition, initiated by Adolphe Gutbub (1995), is ongoing (Labrique and Bedier, forthcoming).

The most prestigious achievements are the Epigraphic Survey's publications, particularly the temple of Medinet Habu, the reliefs of the Luxor colonnade, and many others (e.g., Epigraphic Survey 1930, 1994; see chapter by McClain). The drawings are made directly on orthophotos. These are chemically treated so that only the drawing remains visible. These documents are collated several times by draftsmen and Egyptologists, the walls being meticulously drawn. Our colleagues at Chicago House have adapted to the possibilities of the digital world, and currently, drawings and collations are done on tablets (see chapter by Vértes). More modestly, around 1949, H. Nelson, director of Chicago House in Luxor, drew the wall decoration of the great hypostyle hall of Karnak by himself, but died in 1954. In 1979, W. Murnane undertook alone, in his free time, the collation of that volume (Nelson 1981). The layout is very convenient thanks to large folding plates at the end of the volume that reproduce in smaller size the entire decoration of the room.

German publications of Philae (Junker 1958; Junker and Winter 1965), with line drawings including texts, appeared at the same time. Key plans are printed on separate sheets with scene numbers referring to book pages. Texts, accompanied by translations, are reproduced opposite the drawing either in a clear font (Junker 1958) or in transliteration (Junker and Winter 1965) with subdivisions by verse and translations. In 1961, the IFAO published the seventy-four magnificent plates of P. Clère (1961) reproducing to a 1/100 scale all the decoration of the door of Euergetes at Karnak.

Around 1974, under the direction of Serge Sauneron, we began publication of the Achoris Chapel at Karnak (published in 1981), inspired by the methods of our Chicago House colleagues. A. Bellod made metric photos of the walls that were printed on transparent film and used as the basis for Françoise Le Saout's drawings. She worked on a light table and drew in ink on tracing paper. She also meticulously drew the condition of walls on a second sheet intended for printing in sepia (Figure III.1.1). This conception of the condition of walls is crucial. It makes it possible to distinguish an intended gap in decoration from an accidental gap due to deterioration of the surface. Epigraphic units have been numbered continuously from 1 to 21, starting from the facade and giving priority to the visitor's left. The set includes seventeen plates (Traunecker, Le Saout, and Masson 1981). The visual layout is two drawings in perspective (vol. II, pl. 17). In the text volumes, the epigraphic material is analyzed, and the analyses are illustrated with handwritten copies.

Mention should be made of the publication of the Mut gateway at Karnak, initiated by Serge Sauneron (1983), with the magnificent drawings of Leïla Ménassa, the architectural study of F. Laroche-Traunecker, and a glossary of texts by S. Cauville.

Sylvie Cauville (1993) published in the *Bulletin de l'Institut français d'archéologie orientale (BIFAO)* the Barque Chapel door, a model publication: sequential numbering (twenty-four total) and alternating around the opening to the right, line drawings with condition of walls, transliteration, translation, index, and vocabulary. This edition is exemplary.

In 1992, we initiated with Jan Quagebeur the Temple of Chenhour (Shenhur) project. I used as much as possible my experience of Karnak and Coptos. Unfortunately,

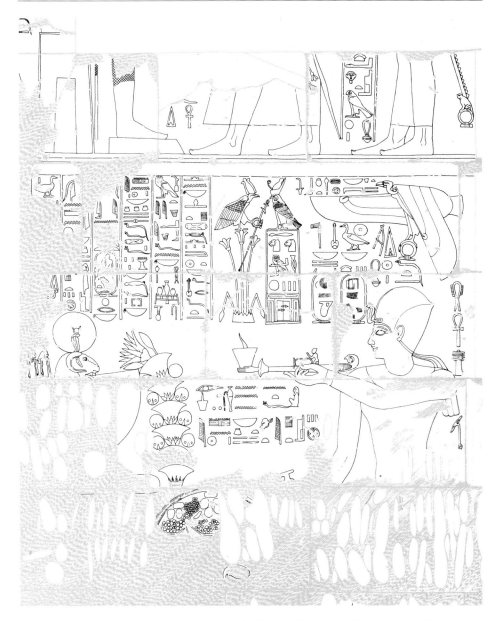

FIGURE III.1.1. Chapel of Achoris at Karnak. The condition of walls is in sepia; Traunecker, Le Saout, and Masson 1981, pl. XI, scene 19.

Jan Quaegebeur died in 1995. I took leadership in 1996, then codirected it with Harco Willems until 1999. The first volume of the temple publication appeared in 2003 (Willems, Coppens, and De Meyer 2003; Minas-Nerpel 2018). Based in part on our work, this publication applies my processes generally: sequential numbering (1–98), key plans with exploded-view of rooms, drawings on single plates with condition of the wall in sepia (on the model of Achoris.) The only twist to the system is that the authors used a linear numbering of scenes from below to above, thus, nonanalytical and nonsymmetrical, which makes interpretation according to the principles of "temple grammar" more difficult (Quaegebeur and Traunecker 1994, 206; see chapter by Pantalacci). Fundamentally, it does not matter, since the reader who is knowledgeable and perceptive about this type of reading will find a way to reestablish the natural order of scenes thanks to the layouts copied in our publication of the temple of el-Qal'a. Unfortunately, I did not participate directly in the production of this volume, but I must recognize its quality. Incidentally, I thank René Preys, who kindly sent me a copy.

In the same category, the very beautiful and complete edition of the Ptolemaic portal of Karnak-Nord by S. Aufrère (2000) appeared with alternating sequential numbering, key plans, complete line drawings, translations, and commentaries. Also important to mention is the publication of the Armant crypt in single plates in "facsimile," unfortunately, without wall condition (Thiers and Volokhine 2005).

Publication in Original Layout of Texts, but Separated from the Image

When it comes to publishing more modestly, with fewer institutional resources and where texts are often traced, we have the Opet temple in Karnak with copies by C. de Wit (1958–1968) and key plans.

In my edition of the monuments of Coptos-Sud, I published handwritten copies of texts in original position referring to my drawings of scenes. The overview of sequential numbering (69 numbers) is provided through key plans in perspective printed on a separate sheet (Traunecker 1992).

In 1982, we began with Laure Pantalacci publishing the temple of el-Qal'a in Coptos. Faced with the terrible epigraphic conditions of this monument, with its decoration very poorly engraved in a very hard stone and barely leveled, we gave up on any attempt at "facsimile." Scenes are drawn schematically, but with wall conditions. Texts are drawn by me and made into clean readings, respecting as much as possible the signs' distinctive features, which are often difficult to discern. During this work, we developed the principles of key plans in exploded-view on separate sheets (Pantalacci and Traunecker 1990–1998).

Finally, to conclude with this type of publication, I cite some examples, modest in scope, but illustrating the possibilities of simple manual processes. I published several small monuments of Karnak. The drawings were made on site, to scale, on graph paper: figures and texts. My inking was limited to specific elements of decoration: position, crowns, objects held. They are not "facsimiles," but iconographic notes supplemented by proportional copies (Figure III.1.2). These principles and survey techniques are described in my paper from the Heidelberg symposium (Traunecker 1987). This is how I "published" the decoration of the Hout-noub (ḥw.t-nb) of Thutmose III at Karnak (Traunecker 1989). I used the same techniques in 2010 to "make public" the entire set of decoration of the Osiris chapel "Lord of Eternity-neheh" at Karnak (Traunecker 2010). It is important to draw the architectural framework to scale, always on graph paper, so one can assess gaps or even graphically replace fallen blocks.

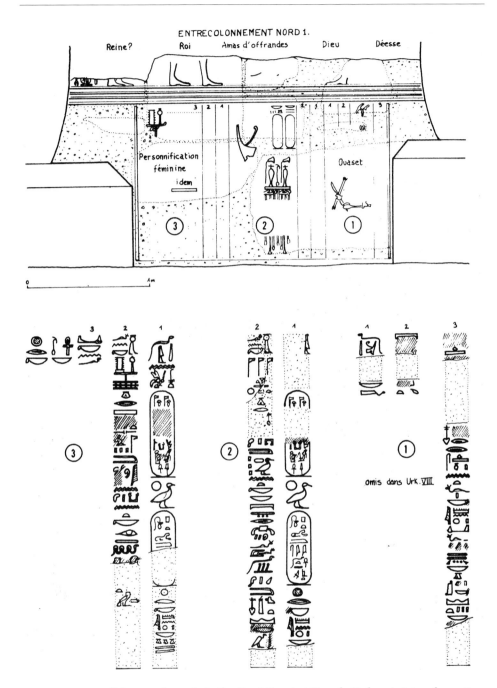

FIGURE III.1.2. Taharqa colonnade in the Great Court at Karnak. Ptolemaic intercolumnation. Proportional copy and architectural setting. Plan and drawing C. Traunecker; Traunecker 1989, 293.

As a final example, I published Ptolemaic decoration in a room (XVA) in the sector known as the *magasins nord* (north storehouses) at Karnak. I used the same technique (manual proportional copy excluding image) except that, having excellent photographs, I reproduced opposite the copies the photographs themselves with a line indicating the original heights of columns and their numbering. Thus, we have a graphic view of the lacunae (Traunecker 2013).

Hieroglyphic Text Reconstructed in Rows

This type of publication was established at the end of the nineteenth century. Georges Bénédite (1893–1895) published in a white font the texts of Philae with some plans and drawings of the temple. The overview is descriptive, but the entire thing is not easy to use, and furthermore, Bénédite's copies include many errors. In 1892, the first volume of the monumental publication of the temple of Edfu by Émile Chassinat appeared, based on, among other things, the squeezes of Maxence de Chalvet, Marquis de Rochemonteix, who unfortunately died in 1891. Initially, Chassinat used a white font, but appointed director of the IFAO in 1895, this former typographer created the prestigious printing house of the IFAO and, in particular, a magnificent black hieroglyphic font. This font, which has more than seven thousand signs, is capable of transcribing Ptolemaic texts (Anonymous 1983). The publication of Edfu Temple contains fourteen volumes, published from 1892 to 1934. If the readability and beauty of Chassinat's black font is undeniable, we must recognize that this publication is not practical. The weight of volumes, descriptive overview, absence of sequential numbering and of master plans, and separation of photographic graphic data in the final volumes (IX–XIV) does not help the consultant navigate the monument. In 1934, E. Chassinat put into practice the same principles, publishing the temple of Dendera as F. Daumas, his successor, would (vols. V–VIII). Sylvie Cauville (1999, 2007a, vols. IX–XV) would modernize these legendary publications.

The contradiction between the prestigious single-plate publications of Chicago, for example, and publications in a font disconnected from the reality of the wall, like Edfu, would be partly reduced.

The impetus for this revival was provided by Serge Sauneron and his publication of the temple of Esna. The first volume of text published in 1963 marks a true turning point in the history of the publication of hieroglyphic texts (Sauneron 1959, 1963). It reintroduced the principle of sequential numbering. For each epigraphic unit, such as an offering scene, the reader has a line drawing with columns of hieroglyphs numbered, a site plan, and an elevation diagram of the facade with the position of the scene concerned. Then follows a short bibliography with possible reference to an older publication and finally, the text rendered in the beautiful black font of Chassinat. So unlike Edfu and Dendera, it is very easy to maneuver in Esna Temple, though truly, it is architecturally simpler than Edfu and Dendera. These principles would profoundly influence the publications of Ptolemaic temples for fifty years.

From 1980 on, a series of publications model Esna (sequential numbering, sheets with key plans, drawing of scenes associated with texts), except they do not use a font, but publish a handcopy reordered in lines as if it were in a font: thus are published the temples of Deir Chelouit (Zivie 1982–1986) and Tod I (Grenier et al. 1980). This rather strange option that manually imitates a font is due, among other things, to material circumstances. Kom Ombo I (Gutbub 1995), the last volume of the IFAO composed in black font, attempts to align that publication with the principles of S. Sauneron. Its distinctive feature is, among other things, to use in its numbering and descriptions not actual orientations, but the symbolic (Gutbub 1995, XII–XV). The publication of the temple of Deir el-Medina (Bourguet 2002), published in black font, was on hold for a long time at the IFAO printer. Luc Gabolde adapted it to the principles of Esna: sequential numbering and sheets with key plans. It is a shame that the numbering does not observe the rule of symmetry. Leïla Ménassa's line drawings with wall conditions are exemplary. In addition, there is complete photographic coverage.

In 1997, the black font, too expensive in typesetting, was abandoned, and the first volumes of Dendera appeared in the digital font of Hallof and Van der Berg (Cauville 2007b, VIII). The traditional system of Chassinat was preserved, but supplemented by a volume of photographic plates (full coverage) with overviews, numbering of columns, and references to pages in the text volume (Cauville 2007a). A DVD that allows you to enlarge photographs at will to observe details is added to this volume of images. Volumes II and III of the temple of Tod publication (Thiers 2003) are very complete and, in a way, double, since texts are given in line drawing as well as Western font. Layouts are very clear thanks to plans and elevations attached to each scene. Volume III gives complete photographic coverage. The same characteristics are in publications of the temple of Ptah at Karnak (Thiers and Biston-Moulin 2016) and the temple of Athribis (Leitz and Mendel 2017a, 2017b; Leitz, Mendel, and El-Masry 2010). The Kom Ombo II volume (Labrique and Bedier, forthcoming) is composed in a digital font, but partially includes the options of Kom Ombo I. Thus, the editions in font partially meet the requirements of the single-plate editions.

Photographic Publication

The most recent achievements of the IFAO are accompanied by complete photographic coverage. Given the state of preservation of certain walls, line drawing, copying, or typographic transcription remains necessary. Certain monuments, however, given the necessary equipment and technicians, can lend themselves to purely photographic publication. In addition, DVD publication allows for enlargements useful to examine the detail of texts.

O. Onézime and G. Pollin (2014) emphasize the benefits of photogrammetry and orthophotography (see chapter by Revez), which they present as new techniques. I would simply have us keep in mind that this technique appeared in Egyptology during the UNESCO campaign to save the monuments in Nubia (1955–1968). As for orthophotography,

A. Bellod (1982), photographer of the CFEETK, developed a metrical process of photography in 1975–1976, using a tracking rail, a carriage with shooting column designed for this use, and a modified 13 × 18 Linhof chamber. The whole setup was placed on a theodolite under the supervision of a topographer. He thus produced orthophotos of excellent quality. In particular, I wish to mention the interior walls of the sanctuary of Alexander and the facade of the pylon of Khonsu Temple. Of course, this technique, despite its good qualities, is of another time, a time before the digital. Compared to current techniques of photogrammetry, it is very unwieldy and time con-suming, but I would still like to remind readers of the existence of this important phase in the history of field techniques.

With digital photogrammetry, we are operating on a completely different level. The results are truly dazzling for scholars of my generation (Onézime and Pollin 2014). The work of data collection is fast and performed with light equipment. By contrast, post-processing has some genuine constraints. When processing large areas, powerful computers are needed, and the images rendered are sometimes very cumbersome. RTI is accessible to all and provides remarkable results when photographing difficult-to-reach spaces (Frood and Howley 2014, Capelle 2017; see chapter by Wendrich). As indicated at the beginning of this chapter, everything is a question of means and circumstances.

Notes, Tips, and Some Rules

Sequential Numbering

The importance of this option does not need to be demonstrated, and it is now quite widespread. It is regrettable that the publishers of Edfu and Dendera did not adopt this principle initiated by J. de Morgan. At my instigation, one of my students developed a sequential numbering mock-up for the temple of Edfu: he counted 2,356 units (Becker 2008, unpublished). The epigraphic unit that it involves can be an offering scene, but also any element of decoration. The order of numbering is not trivial. It will determine a sense of reading and publishing and will depend on the condition of the monument. In the case of a well-preserved monument, it seems logical to proceed from rooms at the back of the temple toward the exterior, following a sort of chronological progression. I would add that ancient scribes would not have repudiated this option: in the famous *manuel du temple*, unfortunately very fragmentary, the description of the ideal temple and its arrangement goes from interior to exterior (Quack 2003, 13; 2004, 9; 2014, 24). The sequential numbering of epigraphic units is not contradictory to a system of designations of rooms, preferably by function. Above all, designate left and right in the objective sense of the visitor.

How to Number Decorative Elements in a Room

1. Number in the direction of the visitor, beginning from the left. This side is to the right of the deity and preeminent, as demonstrated by the distribution of titles and hierarchy of persons depicted (e.g., the two Cleopatras, second and third wives of Ptolemy VIII Euergetes II) (Pantalacci and Traunecker 1990, 14–15; Traunecker 1992, 139, 141; Traunecker 2009, 46–47; Figure III.1.3).
2. Symmetric numbering. The designers of these decorative elements followed a logic of symmetry. This logic, therefore, should be respected as much as possible. For example, scenes framing a door should be numbered in pairs, register by register, from bottom to top of the two doorposts. Priority is given to the scene on the left of the entering viewer.
3. Numbering of scenes in a room.
   a. First register, left series, up to the axis of symmetry on the back wall, then right series, from the other side of the door, up to the axis of symmetry on the back wall.
   b. Second register, left series, up to the axis of symmetry on the back wall, then right series, from the other side of the door, up to the axis of symmetry on the back wall.
   c. Left *soubassement*, read from the axis of symmetry, then right *soubassement*, read from the axis of symmetry.
   d. Finally, the same procedure for the *couronnement*.

"Facsimiles" and Epigraphic Drawing

It has been customary to call line drawings "facsimiles." It is an abuse of language (Traunecker 1987, 269–270). In the strict sense of the term, a facsimile is a copy in three dimensions. A line drawing is only an interpretation of a complex reality (Le Saout 1984, 206). The draftsman is forced to use conventions and image processing. The drawing is therefore an object close to the original, as much as is possible, but it is different. Whatever the medium and technique used, a drawing made mechanically from a photograph is an interpretation of the original. We must agree on graphic conventions (with or without line strength) and the conditions of walls (hacked out, damaged, etc.). We must above all try to reproduce not the injury to the stone, but the line of the ancient artist's hand. Sometimes extreme fidelity to the accidental aspect of the document hinders its readability (compare Grimal 1981, pls. IV, XII).

Many projects are using—or used, because the Egyptian authorities have forbidden it—the method of tracing the wall on a plastic sheet. This method is to be avoided and has many disadvantages including the difficulty of drawing life-size (Traunecker 1987, 279–281). Moreover, it is not faithful and distorts the document (Onézime and Pollin 2014, 392, pl. 5).

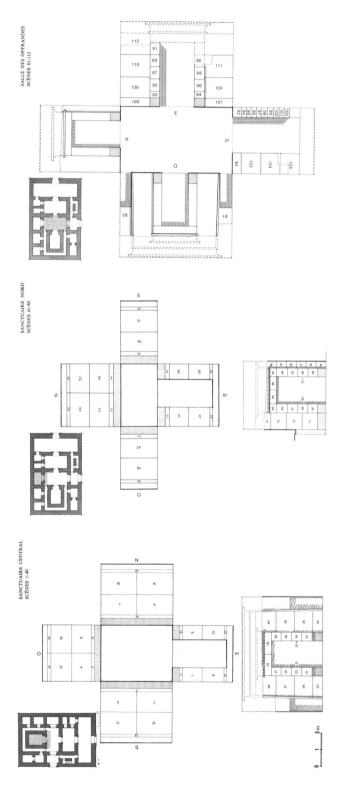

FIGURE III.1.3. Key plans of the scenes in the axial and the northern sanctuaries and the offering hall of the temple of el-Qalʿa. Exploded views on separate sheets. Drawing by C. Traunecker; Pantalacci and Traunecker 1990.

Field Procedures

Personally, I separate "mechanical" harvesting of data, that is to say, essentially photographic coverage, from field observations, properly speaking. Of course, if there are significant means and the monument is suitable, "mechanical" survey by digital photogrammetry would be very useful.

As an exaggeration, one can imagine two extremes: on the one hand, highly ambitious projects, removed from all economic constraints in terms of financial means, staffing, and time, with constant access to the monument, and on the other hand, epigraphy under difficult circumstances, a small team, short of time, with low levels of technical support. I would even dare say, guerrilla epigraphy! In this second picture, the crew must be truly multitalented in epigraphic drawing, of course, but also in architectural drawing, metric photography, and other areas.

Whatever the circumstances, I remain very attached to the method of copying by hand. For me, this phase of work, especially if we follow the procedure that I advocate, is crucial. It provides an invaluable base document and allows all field observations to be recorded live. Additionally, if we respect the three rules of the field epigrapher's work, it is the product of a real group workshop.

1. All primary documents are prepared using fine lead pencil on graph paper. They must include reference to location, be signed by authors, and be dated. Do not forget indications of orientation and scale.

2. Work in pairs as much as possible, whether together or in turns. This method ("copying with four eyes") generates a constant discussion of readings. All philological comments and observations, of structure, grammar, parts of translations, and other points, will be recorded on the copy sheet. One must not hesitate to attempt translation and philological commentary on the spot. At el-Qal'a, we always had a copy of the Wörterbuch with us to make headway in this difficult epigraphic situation. Today, information technology facilitates these consultations.

3. All copies and documents are collated systematically, if possible, by or with a colleague who did not participate in the initial copying. These collations are recorded on the copy sheet with a different colored pencil and also signed and dated. One of the methods of collation that Serge Sauneron taught me consists of systematically checking the text sign by sign, but backward, for example, from bottom to top for columns or, for lines, from end to beginning. This avoids the shortcuts and lack of attention of a reader drawn along by the content of the text and its particular orthographic conventions.

Constant conflicting views, especially in the case of difficult texts, is salutary for the work's quality. Epigraphy should not be solitary work. It teaches epigraphic humility, even when we have a reading that seems satisfactory to us, to listen objectively to the suggestion of a colleague, whoever that may be. When one has identified a plausible solution, one does not tend to notice other possible paths.

For the process, I propose, at least in the case of epigraphy with modest means, the following three stages:

1. Set up a drawing at 1/20 scale of the wall on graph paper. Note stone joints, restored areas, and other features. Measurements are taken directly with a wooden yardstick of two meters and possibly a *téléscomètre* (rigid telescopic meter). This reference document, which does not replace the architectural survey possibly done by an architect or topographer, is easy to make and is immediately available. It will be very useful for establishing the overview drawings.
2. Establish a plan on graph paper of each epigraphic unit at 1/10 scale. Precisely record the dimensions of columns of text, frames, thrones, and other features. Note crowns and objects held.
3. Finally, proceed to manual copying of texts on the same lined sheet (cadrat of 1 cm). It will be used for collation and to note various remarks.

I know this process is very traditional, from another time, even for some, old-fashioned. I get it. But it makes it possible to store all epigraphic information and context in real time. It is enough at the end of the mission to scan this documentation to preserve it and possibly disseminate it.

One might be surprised about the importance I attach to drawing. Drawing, even if one does not have a very sure hand, is above all observing and concentrating on the object. But is that not the essence of the epigrapher's profession? An excellent draftsman can render with great talent the document in its aesthetic qualities, but neglect the minute detail that will ascertain a reading. But this detail is not the domain of artistic feeling, but rather the knowledge of the observer and the ability to imagine, in the case of texts, possibilities about the reading. The ideal, of course, is that artist and scientist are one and the same person. But we can also work in pairs.

Another advantage of on-site work, especially copying, is psychological. The act of copying requires time, concentration, and calm. I have often found that this phase is intellectually fertile especially when working in comfortable conditions.

On the contrary, I remember some slightly difficult copying and collation sessions, especially in Coptos, with the screams of children leaving school, even stone throwing. This is a good way to test the epigrapher's concentration and resilience in trying circumstances (Traunecker 1992, 13–14, §11, 14). The passage of time in the copyist's work allows the mind to explore paths that flow from place and document. Dare I say that a field epigrapher can have "contemplative" practices and taste, with the tip of a pencil, in front of the wall, pleasures that a digital font, however user-friendly, will not provide.

Publishing Options

From this primary documentation and its supplements, the head of a project must, with the team, make decisions about publishing options. We examined those in the first part of this chapter. They are numerous, and the choice once again depends on economic and material opportunities. We saw that the "single plate" and "font" distinction is no longer appropriate. But above all, whatever the team adopts, it should not forget the purpose of any epigraphic publication: to provide the reader or library consultant a substitute for the monument, easy to understand, immediate reading delivering to the knowledgeable and the visitor all information and impressions that the ancient Egyptians left for posterity. It is also, as it were, a way of assuring the permanence of the monument.

As a Conclusion

It is clear from this journey into the history of publishing techniques that Egyptology is a science in constant evolution and open to modern techniques. In the early days of epigraphy, there reigned a technique today forgotten, but to which I would like to pay tribute: squeezing on paper, a true "facsimile." I even experienced its last spasms, especially of its less durable avatar, the latex imprint (Lauffray et al. 1970, 96). The legacies of nineteenth-century Egyptologists are preserved in the tens of thousands of squeezes made by Champollion, Mariette, Rochemonteix, Dümichen, Legrain, and many others. These processes are currently prohibited by Egyptian authorities. While fully respecting the reasons for this ban, I regret it. Working on an imprint was very convenient: the document was unrolled on the worktable, and details could be explored under the best lighting angle (Rives and Bellod 1979, 62). Let us hope that innovative photographic techniques (digital photogrammetry, RTI shooting) will be new substitutes for the squeezing papers with which our illustrious predecessors were lining the monuments!

BIBLIOGRAPHY

Anonymous. 1983. *Catalogue de la fonte hiéroglyphique de l'imprimerie de l'I.F.A.O. (nouvelle édition)*. Cairo.

Aufrère, S. H. 2000. *Le propylône d'Amon-Rê-Montou à Karnak-Nord*. MIFAO 117. Cairo.

Becker, G. 2008. *Proposition: Une numérotation continue au temple d'Edfou*. Mémoire de Master d'archéologie (unpublished). Université de Strasbourg.

Bellod, A. 1982. "La photographie métrique." In *Karnak, L'Égypte grandiose*, 104–106. Dijon.

Bénédite, G. 1893–1895. *Le temple de Philae*. MMAF 13. Paris.

Bourguet, P. du. 2002. *Le temple de Deir al-Médîna*. MIFAO 121. Cairo.

Capelle, J. 2017. "Reflectance Transformation Imaging (RTI) et épigraphie." *RAAN* (blog), *Institut de Recherche sur l'Architecture Antique*. February 20, 2017. https://raan.hypotheses.org/1326.

Cauville, S. 1993. "La chapelle de la barque à Dendara." *BIFAO* 93:79–172.

Cauville, S. 1999. *Le temple de Dendara: La porte d'Isis*. Cairo.

Cauville, S. 2007a. *Dendara: Le temple d'Isis*. 2 vols. Cairo.

Cauville, S. 2007b. *Le temple de Dendara 12*. 2 vols. Cairo.

Clère, P. 1961. *La porte d'Évergète à Karnak*. Deuxième partie. Cairo.

Dümichen, J. 1869. *Resultate der auf Befehl sr. Majestät des Königs Wilhelm II im Sommer 1868 nach Aegypten entsendeten archäologisch-photographische Expedition*. Berlin.

Epigraphic Survey. 1930. *Medinet Habu I: Earlier Historical Records of Rameses III*. OIP 8. Chicago.

Epigraphic Survey. 1994. *The Festival Processions of Opet in the Colonnade Hall*. OIP 112. Chicago.

Frood, E., and K. Howley. 2014. "Applications of Reflectance Transformation Imaging (RTI) in the Study of Temple Graffiti." In *Thebes in the First Millennium BC*, edited by E. Pischikova, J. Budka, and K. Griffin, 625–638. Newcastle.

Grenier, J.-C., É. Drioton, G. Posener, and J. Vandier. 1980. *Tôd: Les inscriptions du temple ptolémaïque et romain I: La salle hypostyle, textes nos 1–172*. FIFAO 18. Cairo.

Grimal, N.-C. 1981. *La stèle triomphale de Pi('ankh)y au Musée du Caire: JE 48862 et 47086–47089*. MIFAO 105. Paris.

Gutbub, A. 1995. *Kôm Ombo I: Les inscriptions du naos (sanctuaires, salle de l'ennéade, salle des offrandes, couloir mystérieux)*. Edited by D. Inconnu-Bocquillon. Cairo.

Janssen, J. M. A. 1973. "Les listes de signes hiéroglyphiques." In *Textes et langages de l'Égypte pharaonique: Cent cinquante années de recherche 1822–1972* 1, 57–66. BdE 64. Cairo.

Junker, H. J. B. 1958. *Der grosse Pylon des Tempels Isis in Philä*. DÖAW Sonderband. Vienna.

Junker, H. J. B., and E. Winter. 1965. *Das Geburtshaus des Tempels der Isis in Philä*. DÖAW Sonderband. Vienna.

Labrique, F., and S. Bedier. Forthcoming. *Kom Ombo II: Les inscriptions de la salle médiane et des chapelles annexes*. Cairo.

Lauffray, J., S. Sauneron, R. Sa'ad, and P. Anus. 1970. "Rapport sur les travaux de Karnak: Activités du Centre franco-égyptien en 1968–1969." *Kêmi* 20:57–99.

Le Saout, F. 1984. "L'épigraphie, un métier de l'égyptologie." In *Egypte*, 205–215. Paris.

Leitz, C., and D. Mendel. 2017a. *Athribis III: Die östlichen Zugangsräume und Seitenkapellen sowie die Treppe zum Dach und die rückwärtigen Räume des Tempels Ptolemaios XII*. 2 vols. Cairo.

Leitz, C., and D. Mendel. 2017b. *Athribis IV: Der Umgang L 1 bis L 3*. 2 vols. Cairo.

Leitz, C., D. Mendel, and Y. El-Masry. 2010. *Athribis II, Der Tempel Ptolemaios XII.: Die Inschriften und Reliefs der Opfersäle, des Umgangs und der Sanktuarräume*. 3 vols. Cairo.

Manuelian, P. Der. 1998. "Digital Epigraphy: An Approach to Streamlining Egyptological Epigraphic Method." *JARCE* 35:97–113.

Mariette, A. 1870–1875. *Dendérah: Description générale du grand temple de cette ville*. 6 vols. Paris.

Minas-Nerpel, M. 2018. "The Contra-Temple at Shanhûr." In *Hieratic, Demotic and Greek Studies and Text Editions: Of making many books there is no end. Festschrift in honour of Sven P. Vleeming*, edited by K. Donker van Heel, F. A. J. Hoogendijk, and C. J. Martin, 32–45. PLB 34. Leiden.

Morgan, J. de, U. Bouriant, G. Legrain, G. Jéquier, and A. Barsanti. 1895. *Catalogue des Monuments et Inscriptions de l'Égypte Antique*. Première série, tome 2. Vienna.

Nelson, H. H. 1981. *The Great Hypostyle Hall at Karnak, Volume 1, Part 1: The Wall Reliefs*. Edited by W. J. Murnane. OIP 106. Chicago.

Onézime, O., and Pollin G. 2014. "La place de la photogrammétrie en égyptologie et en archéologie égyptienne: Réflexions méthodologiques et premiers résultats." *BIFAO* 114:375–396.

Pantalacci, L., and C. Traunecker. 1990–1998. *Le temple d'el-Qal'a*. 2 vols. Cairo.

Quack, J. F. 2003. "Le manuel du temple: Une nouvelle source sur la vie des prêtres égyptiens." *EAO* 29:11–18.

Quack, J. F. 2004. "Organiser le culte ideal: Le manuel du temple." *BSFE* 160:9–25.

Quack, J. F. 2014. "Die theoretische Normierung der Soubassement-Dekoration: Erste Ergebnisse der Arbeit an der karbonisierten Handschrift von Tanis." In *Altägyptische Enzyklopädien. Die Soubassement in den Tempeln der griechisch-römischen Zeit: Soubassementstudien I*, vol. 1, edited by A. Rickert and B. Ventker, 17–27. Wiesbaden.

Quaegebeur, J., and C. Traunecker. 1994. "Chenhour 1839–1993: État de la question et rapport des travaux de 1992 et de 1993." *CRIPEL* 16:167–209.

Rives, J., and A. Bellod. 1979. "Un service photo à la dimension des temples de Karnak." *Le Photographe* n°1358, 56–71.

Sauneron, S. 1959. *Quatre campagnes à Esna*. Esna 1. Cairo.

Sauneron, S. 1963. *Le temple d'Esna*. Esna 2. Cairo.

Sauneron, S. 1983. *La porte ptolémaïque de l'enceinte de Mout à Karnak*. MIFAO 107. Cairo.

Thiers, C. 2003. *Tôd. Les inscriptions du temple ptolémaïque et romain, II–III*. FIFAO 18. Cairo.

Thiers, C., and S. Biston-Moulin. 2016. *Le temple de Ptah à Karnak*. 2 vols. BiGen 49. Cairo.

Thiers, C., and Y. Volokhine. 2005. *Ermant I: Les cryptes du temple ptolémaïque*. MIFAO 124. Cairo.

Traunecker, C. 1987. "Les techniques d'épigraphie de terrain: Principes et pratiques." In *Problems and Priorities in Egyptian Archaeology*, edited by J. Assmann, G. Burkard, and V. Davies, 261–298. London.

Traunecker, C. 1989. "Le château de l'Or de Thoutmosis III et les magasins nord du temple d'Amon." *CRIPEL* 11:89–111.

Traunecker, C. 1992. *Coptos: Hommes et dieux sur le parvis de Geb*. OLA 43. Leuven.

Traunecker, C. 2009. "Le temple de Qasr el-Agoûz dans la nécropole thébaine." *BSFE* 174:29–69.

Traunecker, C. 2010. "La chapelle d'Osiris seigneur de l'éternité neheh à Karnak." In *Le culte d'Osiris au Ier millénaire av. J.-C.*, edited by L. Coulon, 155–194. BdE 153. Cairo.

Traunecker, C. 2013. "Thèbes, été 115 avant J.-C. les travaux de Ptolémée IX Sôter II et son prétendu 'Château de l'Or' à Karnak." In *Documents de Théologies Thébaines Tardives (D3T 2)*, edited by C. Thiers, 177–226. ENiM 8. Montpellier.

Traunecker, C., F. Le Saout, and O. Masson. 1981. *La chapelle d'Achôris à Karnak*. 2 vols. Paris.

Willems, H., F. Coppens, and M. De Meyer. 2003. *The Temple of Shanhûr I: The Sanctuary, the Wabet and the Gates of the Central Hall and the Great Vestibule (1–98)*. OLA 124. Dudley, MA.

Wit, C. de 1958–1968. *Les inscriptions du temple d'Opet, à Karnak*. 3 vols. BÄ 11–13. Brussels.

Zivie, C. M. 1982–1986. *Le temple de Deir Chelouit*. 3 vols. PIFAO. Cairo.

CHAPTER III.2

EPIGRAPHIC
TECHNIQUES USED BY
THE EDFU PROJECT

DIETER KURTH

THE early Egyptologists' attempts to record the written sources of ancient Egypt focused on giving as much information as possible about the astonishing achievements of this early and highly developed culture. Reliable recording and scientific objectivity were not neglected, but this was not the main interest. For instance, Heinrich Brugsch sometimes went so far as to emend an obvious mistake made by the ancient Egyptians without any commentary on what is actually written in the original. In a passage of the Edfu inscriptions, Emile Chassinat (1897–1934, 5:400,2 with n3) rendered a hieroglyph as the *rnpỉ* sign (Gardiner M7), just as he saw it in the original, adding a "sic."[1] This sign obviously does not fit the context and is correctly indicated by Chassinat's "sic." Brugsch, however, emended this unequivocal mistake of the ancient scribe or stone mason rendering the sign in question as the mortar and pestle (U32), and this is the hieroglyph we have to expect as determinative of the word *dns*, the heavy one (the hippopotamus) (*Wb.* 5:469,12).

The reliability of the early copies of hieroglyphic temple inscriptions varies between fairly reliable and rather faulty. To get an impression thereof, it suffices to take a glance at the footnotes in Chassinat's publications of the inscriptions of the temples of Edfu and Dendera, where each mistake of his predecessors is relentlessly identified and corrected.

Chassinat was not the first to put a lot of effort into rendering the inscriptions correctly, but his publication of the Edfu inscriptions marks a considerable change. The conviction had become stronger that a faithful and appropriate treatment of these historical sources demanded the strict separation of a sober reproduction of an inscription on the

---

[1] Strictly speaking, Chassinat's rendering is not quite correct, since the little sprout that forms part of the sign (usually depicted in the middle of the stem) is absent in the original (Kurth, forthcoming, *sub voce*).

one hand and its translation and interpretation on the other, somewhat comparable to the corresponding imperative in modern journalism to separate information and commentary. This somewhat idealistic method, however, is unlikely to overcome all the difficulties of hieroglyphic epigraphy as I will try to show in what follows.

Various methods to meet the new epigraphic credos were elaborated. Translations were often dispensed with and postponed for future work, and instead epigraphers tried to render the exact condition of an inscription as regards the position of the hieroglyphs, lacunae, and damages. For example, Harold H. Nelson (1981) separated the remaining parts of reliefs and inscriptions from the destroyed parts by means of outlines. Others, for instance, Claude Traunecker (Traunecker, Le Saout, and Masson 1981) and Harco Willems (Willems, Coppens, and de Meyer 2003), marked the destroyed areas off with colored hatching.

The creation of hieroglyphic fonts and a typographic text edition are comfortable for the user on the one hand, but they are "dangerous" on the other since they always represent an interpretation of the original (see Caminos 1976, 11). This, however, is not a problem in most cases, but there are also examples of an incorrect understanding of a text due to the wrong choice in rendering an indistinct sign. The same is true of an ambiguous arrangement of hieroglyphs in the original that is transposed in a wrong order. To avoid this source of error, some Egyptologists, for example, K. A. Kitchen (1975) and Christiane M. Zivie (1982–1986), render all the texts in an autographic edition, thus returning to the methods used by the early Egyptologists in the nineteenth century. Others, like Serge Sauneron (1968, e.g., 3:14, 94, 120, 286–287), reproduce only indistinct or questionable signs or passages in facsimile.

Epigraphic work based solely on the sober reproduction of the inscription reaches its limits where an extremely indistinct form of a sign renders a choice between the possible readings of it nearly impossible. In such a case, it is not the epigrapher's eye, but only the philologist's understanding of the text that can help to find a plausible solution. There are a few late temples the hieroglyphic inscriptions of which can only be copied if the epigrapher is able to understand most of the text; this is exemplified in the almost illegible inscriptions of the temples of el-Qal'a (Pantalacci and Traunecker 1990–1998; see chapter by Traunecker) and Deir el-Shelwit (Zivie 1982–1986).

An excellent way of approaching the problems of epigraphy was chosen by Hermann Junker and Erich Winter in their edition of the temple of Philae. In the first volume (Junker 1958), a page containing a facsimile of the hieroglyphic text is juxtaposed with a page rendering the same text typographically combined with a translation. The font-based text and the translation are separated into phrases rather than reflecting the divisions on the wall. A feature most comfortable for the user was the insertion of the inscription into the drawing of the ritual scenes and other parts of the decoration. This arrangement saved the user from searching for the exact position of an inscription. In the second volume (Junker and Winter 1965), the typographical rendering of the hieroglyphs was dispensed with in exchange for a phonetic transcription. The transcription is helpful for those not familiar with the writing system of the Greco-Roman temple inscriptions.

The use of the temple editions is much facilitated if the position of the inscription within the temple is indicated by means of a sketch showing ground plan and elevation such as provided, for example, in the editions of the temples of Esna (Sauneron 1968) and Tôd (Thiers 2003; Kurth 2014).

Sylvie Cauville continued Émile Chassinat's and François Daumas's work and finished the publication of the inscriptions of the temple of Dendera (Cauville 1997–2008). She communicated the texts in a typographic text edition and photographs. Most parts of the temple were also translated with transcription and commentary. Cauville's work is excellent and reliable in general, but there are passages where the user would appreciate a more detailed discussion of the inherent epigraphic problems.

The following presentation of the epigraphic methods applied by the Edfu Project is a case study. Owing to the particular aims of the project and also to the peculiarities of Chassinat's publication, the methods of this project, of course, cannot be applied to epigraphic undertakings that have other underlying requirements and conditions.

The Edfu Project was founded by myself in 1986, and it still exists. Its aim is a reliable translation, transcription, and commentary of all the inscriptions that were carved into the walls and columns of the temple of Edfu. For the benefit of the user, the secondary literature is also being collected up to date and referenced. The project is confined to the inscriptions, and the representations of the kings and deities, their artistic style, and so forth are excluded.[2] Nevertheless, the numerous figural depictions are considered and evaluated if they help to understand the texts, since the representations and the inscriptions are closely interconnected and often complement one another.

From the beginning, it was obvious that this task would take some decades since the huge main temple of the archaeological site Edfu is one of the best preserved temples of Egypt. Its inscriptions, which were copied by the eminent French scholar Émile Chassinat (1897–1934), make up eight volumes of text, two volumes of line drawing, and four volumes of photographs.[3]

In the beginning, I had thought that Émile Chassinat's rendering of the hieroglyphic texts in his vast publication was fully reliable. But in the course of the work, the existing photographs showed that—despite the admirable work done by Chassinat—many mistakes had crept in. A lot of these were more than trifles, as they hindered the understanding of the text or even resulted in wrong translations, some of which persisted in Egyptology for a rather long time.

---

[2] Regarding the line drawings, see, for instance, Chassinat (1897–1934, vols. 9–10). Bartels (2009) contains the line drawings of the pylon and the outer face of the enclosure wall and thus fills a gap in Chassinat's publication. Mysliwiec (1969, 64–79) analyzes the human figures represented in the temple of Edfu and their different stylistic periods.

[3] Strictly speaking, it was Le Marquis de Rochemonteix who started copying the inscriptions, but his work was only just started when he died, and it was Chassinat who prepared all the volumes for publication. (See Chassinat's complaint and rectification in 1897–1934, 5:XII–XVI, 14:III–VII). Later, a few smaller inscriptions overlooked by Chassinat were published (Cauville and Devauchelle 1985; Kurth 1998, 224–227, 267–272, figs. 1–4; Kurth 2004, 318–321, 469). A revised edition of volumes I and II was published by S. Cauville and D. Devauchelle (Rochemonteix and Chassinat 1984–1990).

So it was necessary to figure out an epigraphic technique adequate to meet the requirements of the work and at the same time to keep in mind that Chassinat's copy of the hieroglyphic texts is reliable in general on the one hand, but contains mistakes on the other. Just to give an impression of the number of mistakes: Within the 170 pages of the volume Edfou VIII that renders the inscriptions of the pylon, no less than about 750 copy mistakes were found (Kurth 1998).

This surprised me because the copy of the inscriptions in the volume Edfou VIII was generally considered to be reliable, and this had been the reason to start the project by translating this volume first. In contrast to this, every Egyptologist knew that the volumes Edfou I and II contained way too many mistakes, which had led the French Institute in Cairo to initiate a revised and corrected re-edition (Rochemonteix and Chassinat 1984–1990).

In order to avoid unnecessary work, my first attempt to solve the problem was to mark, during the process of translating the texts in our institute in Hamburg, only those hieroglyphs that did not make sense and therefore seemed to be incorrect. They should be scrutinized later during several epigraphic campaigns in Edfu.

In Edfu, however, it appeared that this method was not likely to secure an overall epigraphic reliability, which, of course, is the basis of a reliable translation. This became clear to us when we were standing in front of the walls comparing the copy with the original. Whenever we looked beyond the hieroglyphs we had marked, we realized that there were a lot of other mistakes in Chassinat's copy that had not been noticed by us during our work in the University of Hamburg because we had concentrated solely on those parts of the inscription which gave us reason to suspect that they were copied wrongly. What also surprised us was the fact that sometimes the false copy made sense as well, although it did not correspond to the original—and this had been the reason why we had not discovered these mistakes and marked them.

So it was decided to examine not only the questionable passages, but all of the inscriptions. When searching for an appropriate method, taking squeezes was excluded from the outset. It would have caused unnecessary effort because a complete copy already existed. Therefore, a twofold method of recording the inscriptions was chosen: On the one hand we now compare all the inscriptions of the temple with Chassinat's copy, and on the other we take as many photographs as possible, from different angles and at different times of the day. The reason for the latter is that the interaction of light and shadow has an enormous influence on what we see on the wall. For instance, a hieroglyph could appear as a vulture (ꜣ) in the morning and as an owl (*m*) at noon. Taking photographs is important for other reasons too. In some areas, Chassinat had arranged the hieroglyphs for typographic reasons in a way that misleads the modern reader, whereas in the original, the text is perfectly clear and makes good sense immediately. Moreover, the photographs form the basic material for the continuation of our epigraphic work at home in the institute (see *infra*).

As for the inscriptions on the dadoes, the first register of the girdle wall, and the outer walls of the main fabric of the temple, the complete review could be executed without any problems. If necessary, we used ladders, the tops of which had been wrapped up in rugs to protect the inscriptions. The upper registers, however, were not within reach when we tried to scrutinize the inscriptions. Since we did not have the equipment of the French Institute at our disposal, for instance, the wheeled scaffolds used in Dendera, we had to look for another solution.

Sometimes it chanced that the local authorities of antiquities had placed scaffolds at the walls in order to seal the deeper cracks and holes in the walls where, in the course of time, myriads of sparrows had covered the inscriptions with a layer of their excrements. If done carefully, the sealing of the holes was a useful piece of work. If not, patches of concrete covered parts of the hieroglyphs and rendered our work more difficult. Nevertheless, apart from this, the scaffolds offered an opportunity to collate the texts of the upper registers. Permission was given by the authorities, and we were able to work where the scaffolds happened to be placed. But it goes without saying that the range of this activity is rather limited because it depends on the time and the place of the scaffolding—and to make an arrangement turned out to be rather difficult.

So we opted to make use of optical instruments. In the beginning, we continued our work in the upper registers by using magnifying glasses and a telescope with a magnifying factor of 60. The latter enabled us to decipher hieroglyphs up to the highest spots of the pylon, even at a height of 30 meters.

Regarding the comparison of the original inscriptions with Chassinat's copy, the following method is applied: One colleague turns to the original inscription and reads out each single sign to another colleague who compares them with those rendered in Chassinat's publication and takes down each divergence. This work demands that collaborators have a rather good ability to read Ptolemaic inscriptions and understand them at first glance, because many signs are damaged or have left only tiny traces. Furthermore, colleagues have to be aware that there is a difference between our "physical eye" and our "intellectual eye" and that we have to use both of them in a well-balanced manner, since the former tends to lack imagination and the latter tends to lack objectivity. In ambiguous cases, we can use the Berlin *Wörterbuch* and our computer, especially the "Edfu explorer," which contains a huge collection of formulae occurring in the texts. Sometimes, and more often in texts written in sunken relief, it is helpful to pay attention to the thin white lines in the deepest layer of a damaged or blurred sign (Figure III.2.1). They can show us the outlines of the sign because they are the remains of the gypsum coating that was used to cover the decorated surface before the colors were put on. There are also spots where a powerful electric flashlight renders good service.

We were aware, of course, that some of the higher parts of the temple would cause considerable difficulties concerning collation as well as photography. And indeed, the space between the girdle wall and the temple is too small to use a telescope or a camera, especially in the corridors that connect the ambulatory and the court on both sides of the pronaos, where the walls have a ground distance of not more than about one meter apart from one another. So we had to figure out how to continue the epigraphic work from the second register onward, up to the frieze.

FIGURE III.2.1. The temple of Edfu, part of an inscription on a door of the court showing hieroglyphs whose outlines are abraded but still show up in white, which is the remains of the gypsum coating. Edfou V, 392,14–393,2, montant du côté gauche, H'-J'2'; image 2754 of the Edfu Project.

Some inventive ideas to solve the problem, for instance, to employ an alpinist, were quickly abandoned. Finally, we bought an apparatus that resolved our difficulties. It consists of a telescope mast that can lift a camera fixed on top up to a height of 15 meters. Standing on the ground, we can see the image on a display and move the camera to the right spot. The photographs are excellent. Up to this day, the number of pictures taken by means of our "Goliath" tripod and the other cameras totals 21,000.

There are also other obstacles to epigraphic work in Edfu. The temple is always open to the public from the morning until the late afternoon. So it sometimes happens that a tourist lifts his son up to our unattended telescope to let him look through it, with the result that the lens is smeared and we have to align the telescope anew. And we have to suffer a lot of noise and sometimes silly questions. The worst incident was when someone took malicious pleasure in shaking the scaffolds like an apple tree in order to make us fall off.

At home, while preparing the translations and the commentary for publication, the epigraphic work is continued by evaluating both the photographs and the corrections we have taken down into the copies of Chassinat's publication. In order to prevent us from leaving out a hieroglyph and to detect hieroglyphs left out by Chassinat, this final work is executed in the following way: One colleague reads the phonetic transcription of the text aloud from the photograph, and the other compares it with the text in Chassinat's publication.

In spite of the good photographs and the rectifying entries in our copies of Chassinat's publication, some passages, however, remain unclear. They are collected and entered into the schedule of a following epigraphic campaign.

We also make use of photographs taken in former times. The best of them are those in Chassinat's publication. They are also one of the main bases for the future work to be done in the inner parts of the temple. Another starting point is the corrected second edition of the volumes Edfou I and II published by Sylvie Cauville and Didier Devauchelle (Rochemonteix and Chassinat 1984–1990). Both resources will reduce the future epigraphic work in the temple to a minimum.

Older photographs, for example, those taken by de Rougé ([1865]) (see Emery chapter) or by the Prussian Expedition (photographs dating to the years 1908–1910, e.g., Beinlich 2010; see Loeben chapter), are very useful especially if they depict inscriptions or representations that are now damaged or even lost. A comparison of our photographs and the older ones shows that some of the inscriptions have suffered a lot in the course of more than one hundred years.

Older copies of the inscriptions are evaluated, too. Nearly all of them are quoted by Chassinat, for instance, the copies of Brugsch, Dümichen, Naville, Piehl, and de Rougé. In almost every case, Chassinat's copy is better, but there are also a few spots where the photographs reveal that the older copy is more accurate, even despite a *sic* in Chassinat's publication. It is true for all photographs that the manipulation of the image with the help of a computer can be very useful.

There are also some results of our epigraphic work in the Edfu temple that do not directly concern the translations, but are more or less incidental discoveries. One of them is that we observed several self-corrections of the ancient workmen whose task was to incise the inscriptions (e.g., Kurth 1998, 104n1; 2004, 262n5). The normal procedure

FIGURE III.2.2. An ancient self-correction. The Edfu Project, Photo 3905–3908.

to correct a mistake in a sunken relief was to fill the wrong sign with gypsum up to the level of the surrounding surface and to engrave the correct sign over the wrong one. In cases where the gypsum had fallen off over the course of time, both signs are visible again and look like a picture puzzle (Figure III.2.2).[4]

Instances like this one led us to pay more attention to the ancient methods of decorating a wall with images and inscriptions. Among the entries in the index of the publications of the Edfu Project, the reader will find the item *Werkverfahren* where instances of this kind are listed (see, e.g., Kurth 2004, 756). Based on our observations of unfinished inscriptions, I can say that the normal method in the temple of Edfu comprised the following main steps:

- The craftsmen marked the outlines of the areas destined for the inscription with red ink.
- The inscription was written with red ink on the bare wall in characters wavering between ordinary hieroglyphs and cursive hieroglyphs.
- The outlines of the signs were engraved.
- The details inside the hieroglyphs were fashioned, for example, the cheeks of the face, the muscles of the body or the feathers of a wing. This part of the work demanded a well-trained and skilled artist.
- Then the inscription was covered with a thin coating of liquid gypsum.
- Finally, the colors were applied.

There is an inscription in the temple itself that describes a part of the procedure and at the same time confirms our observations (Kurth 2004, 8–9): "Work was resumed…in year 30 of this king: the tracing out of the inscriptions (with ink) and the carving with bronze tools…the laying on of the colours…in superb workmanship executed by the best craftsmen." This inscription is rich in details and it also reports "the embellishing of the walls with gold." And indeed, there is clear evidence that certain parts of the decoration that had an outstanding religious importance were gilded (Aufrère 1991, 2:377–379).

The decoration has preserved its original colors in several areas of the walls and the ceilings. Some of them have been cleaned recently and show their former splendor and beauty. The symbolism of the colors of the hieroglyphs and its possible contribution to the decipherment of damaged parts of the inscriptions is a special task planned to be executed later in combination with a general study of the colors in the temple of Edfu.

Some single hieroglyphs, not only in Edfu but also in Esna and in other temples of the Greco-Roman period, have a style that strongly resembles cursive characters, to wit, hieratic, demotic, and cursive-hieroglyphs (for the latter, see, e.g., the plates in Vandier 1961). In almost every case, they do not show the exact cursive form, but a

---

[4] The explanation of this picture puzzle is given by Kurth (2004, 477n6): The phrase *ḥnꜥ mwt.f* [*ꜣst*] had been engraved erroneously. Then the wrong signs were covered with gypsum and thus prepared for the engraving of the correct phrase *nṯr ꜥꜣ nb pt*. For another example, see Kurth (1983, 84–85n26).

mixture of the hieroglyph and its cursive form. They were designed in this way in order to make the true cursive sign fit the style of the hieroglyphic script. Some of them had been used since pre-Ptolemaic times, while others did not appear before the Ptolemaic era. For example, the sign ⎯⎯, which was derived from the hieratic ⎯ and adapted to the hieroglyphic script, corresponds to the long bread roll hieroglyph (X5) (for the hieratic, see Kurth 1999, 75,a).

A lot of mistakes in the hieroglyphic inscriptions are due to the fact that two different hieroglyphs sometimes have a very similar form in the cursive. If the scribe whose task it was to transcribe the cursive characters of a hieratic original or copy into hieroglyphics chose the wrong alternative and traced it out on the wall, then the stonemason incised a hieroglyph that does not make sense in the text. For example, the vulture head (H4) is written in mistake for ⎯ (for the hieratic, see Kurth 1999, 79,y).

It could also happen that a scribe transferred the typically cursive orthography of a word into hieroglyphs, character by character, with the result that this word appeared in the hieroglyphic text as an alien element, which in certain cases can confuse the modern reader. See, for instance, the unorthodox writing ⎯ (Kurth 1999, 72–73 ḫꜣswt).

There is a tendency among the scribes to confuse signs that have similar sizes. What lies at the root of many mistakes of this kind, however, is their similarity not in hieratic, but in cursive hieroglyphs (Kurth 1999, 86–94). The animal belly and tail (F32) is written in error for the column (O29) (Kurth 1999, 87 bu) or the crossroads (O49) in error for the placenta (Aa1) (Kurth 1999, 92 ds).

The aforementioned phenomena had not attracted much attention among the Ptolemaists, and so only a relatively small number of these signs had been collected and communicated up to 1986, when the Edfu Project started. However, in the course of the epigraphic work, it became evident that the knowledge of these phenomena had some bearing on the understanding of the inscriptions. Therefore, a corresponding study was carried out (Kurth 1999, 69–96).

Having reached the field of the mistakes made by the ancient scribes and craftsmen, it is worthwhile to give some more examples of signs that were confused with one another. Due to the different reasons given above and some others we find, for example, the cowskin sign (F28) is written in error for the mace (T3) (Kurth 1999, 78 p); the plucked bird (G54) is written in error for the flower and stem (M11) (Kurth 1999 79 x); the stairway (O40) is written in error for the crocodile skin (I6) (Edfou I, 317,5); a circle (D12) is written in error for a *nw*-pot (W24) (Kurth 1999, 89 cl).

There is a special kind of mistake that gives insight into the ancient Egyptians' way of planning and organizing the decoration of a temple. In Chassinat's publication of the temple of Edfu, we find that the western *Bandeau Supérieur* of the column 2´ in the pronaos occupies the position where we would expect the eastern one. Since the decoration pattern of the columns in the pronaos is perfectly valid without exception, we must conclude firstly that each inscription had been written on a separate piece of papyrus to be handed over to the scribe who had to trace out the hieroglyphs on the bare wall, and secondly that the western and the eastern copies had been mixed up by mistake (Kurth 1983, 281,

284–287, 362–363; for similar mistakes, Kurth 2004, 688–689 under "Formaler Aufbau, Abweichungen und Besonderheiten").

A survey of the Egyptian temples of all periods shows that quality of epigraphy differs between the temples and also changes over the course of time. The number and kind of mistakes made by the ancient scribes and workmen reflect the standards of education, instruction, and training acquired by the authors, scribes, artists, and workmen. Sometimes we find inscriptions that have a poor artistic quality or that teem with orthographic mistakes beside others that are quite correct (see, e.g., Chassinat 1897–1934, 8:29n1). In some of these cases, the scribes' or workmen's superiors and their lack of review must be blamed for it. In others, the occurrence of qualitative distinctions is due to the fact that the work was normally executed by different gangs.

Here and there, we meet a single hieroglyph or a part of one traced out with red ink and left unfinished. There are also longer passages of an inscription totally traced out with red ink, but not carved (Chassinat 1897–1934, 5:158, 3–4 and n1, fig. 3 (image 2969 of the Edfu Project), 5:178, 5–6 and n1; Figure III.2.3).

As I have already pointed out, lists of mistakes and related phenomena are appreciated by Egyptologists who want to corroborate the translation of a word based on the correction of the ancient text. The existence of the same mistake in other inscriptions does not

FIGURE III.2.3. A column of hieroglyphs traced out with red ink. The Edfu Project, Photo 2969.

prove the correctness of a conjecture, of course, but nevertheless it can corroborate the correction of an ancient text which—without the lists and the parallels in them—would be carried out solely on the grounds of semantics and context. The usefulness of such lists of mistakes was recognized not only by myself (Kurth 2009, 1:147–447; examples can be found among the first footnotes of every entry) but also by other colleagues (e.g., Junker 1910, 27–32; Cauville 2001, 253–258; Thiers 2003, 297–299).

As concerns the future work of the Edfu project, it is planned to create a computer simulation that enables the user to have an artificial walk through the temple, pointing to a spot on a column or a wall, thus opening a window that shows the respective image, inscription, translation, and commentary. But this, like the completion of the entire project, depends on institutions ready to finance it. I have to thank the Deutsche Forschungsgemeinschaft and the Akademie der Wissenschaften zu Göttingen for their generous financial support over the course of three decades.

Bibliography

Aufrère, S. 1991. *L'univers minéral dans la pensée égyptienne.* 2 vols. BdE 105. Cairo.

Bartels, U. 2009. *Edfu: Die Darstellungen auf den Außenseiten der Umfassungsmauer und auf dem Pylonen. Strichzeichnungen und Photographien.* Die Inschriften des Tempels von Edfu, Abteilung II Dokumentationen 1. Edited by D. Kurth. Wiesbaden.

Beinlich, H. 2010. *Die Photos der Preußischen Expedition 1908–1910 nach Nubien. Teil 1: Photos 1–199.* SRaT 14. Dettelbach.

Caminos, R. 1976. "The Recording of Inscriptions and Scenes in Tombs and Temples." In *Ancient Egyptian Epigraphy and Palaeography,* 1–25. New York.

Cauville, S. 1997. *Le temple de Dendara X: Les chapelles osiriennes.* 2 vols. Cairo.

Cauville, S. 2001. *Dendara: Le fonds hiéroglyphique au temps de Cléopâtre.* Paris.

Cauville, S., and D. Devauchelle. 1985. *Le temple d'Edfou.* Edfou 15. MMAF 32. Cairo.

Chassinat, É. 1897–1934. *Le temple d'Edfou.* 14 vols. MMAF 10–31. Paris.

Junker, H. 1910. *Die Stundenwachen in den Osirismysterien: Nach den Inschriften von Dendera, Edfu und Philae.* DAWW 54. Vienna.

Junker, H. 1958. *Der große Pylon des Tempels der Isis in Philä.* DÖAW Sonderband. Vienna.

Junker, H., and Winter, E. 1965. *Das Geburtshaus des Tempels der Isis in Philä.* DÖAW Sonderband. Vienna.

Kitchen, K. A. 1975. *Ramesside Inscriptions, Historical and Biographical, I.* Oxford.

Kurth, D. 1983. *Die Dekoration der Säulen im Pronaos des Tempels von Edfu.* GOF 11. Wiesbaden.

Kurth, D. 1998. *Die Inschriften des Tempels von Edfu, I/1. (Edfou VIII).* Wiesbaden.

Kurth, D. 1999. "Der Einfluß der Kursive auf die Inschriften des Tempels von Edfu." In *Edfu: Bericht über drei Surveys; Materialien und Studien,* edited by D. Kurth, 69–96. Die Inschriften des Tempels von Edfu, Begleitheft 5. Wiesbaden.

Kurth, D. 2004. *Die Inschriften des Tempels von Edfu, I/2. (Edfou VII).* Wiesbaden.

Kurth, D. 2009. *Einführung ins Ptolemäische: Eine Grammatik mit Zeichenliste und Übungsstücken.* Teil 1. Hützel.

Kurth, D. 2014. *Die Inschriften des Tempels von Edfu, I/3. (Edfou VI).* Gladbeck.

Kurth, D. Forthcoming. *Die Inschriften des Tempels von Edfu I/4. (Edfou V).*

Mysliwiec, K. 1969. "Une esquisse du décorateur du temple d'Horus à Edfou." *ET* 3:63–79.

Nelson, H. H. 1981. *The Great Hypostyle Hall at Karnak, Volume 1, Part 1: The Wall Reliefs*. Edited by William J. Murnane. OIP 106. Chicago.

Pantalacci, L., and C. Traunecker. 1990–1998. *Le temple d'el-Qal'a*. 2 vols. Cairo.

Rochemonteix, M. de, and É. Chassinat. 1984–1990. *Le temple d'Edfou, I, 1–2*. 2 vols. Rev. and corr. by S. Cauville and D. Devauchelle. MMAF 10–11. Cairo.

Rougé, E. de. [1865]. *Album photographique de la mission remplie en Égypte par le Vte Emmanuel de Rougé, accompagné de M. le Vte de Banville et de M. Jacques de Rougé, attachés à la mission, 1863–1864*. Paris.

Sauneron, S. 1968. *Le Temple d'Esna*. Esna III. Cairo.

Thiers, C. 2003. *Tôd: Les inscriptions du temple ptolémaïque et romain, II: Textes et scènes nos 173–329*. FIFAO 18/2. Cairo.

Traunecker, C., F. Le Saout, and O. Masson. 1981. *La chapelle d'Achôris à Karnak II*. 2 vols. Recherche sur les grandes civilisations. Synthèse 5; Mémoires du Centre Franco-Égyptien d'Étude des Temples de Karnak 2. Paris.

Vandier, J. [1961.] *Le papyrus Jumilhac*. [Paris.]

Willems, H., F. Coppens, M. de Meyer. 2003. *The Temple of Shanhûr, Volume I: The Sanctuary, the Wabet and Gates of the Central Hall and the Great Vestibule (1–98)*. With the Collaboration of Peter Dils. OLA 124. Leuven.

Zivie, C. M. 1982–1986. *Le temple de Deir Chelouit*. 3 vols. Dessins de Yousreya Hamed Hanafi. Cairo.

CHAPTER III.3

....

THE SO-CALLED
KARNAK METHOD

....

CHRISTOPHE THIERS

WHEN faced with a hieroglyphic relief or inscription, the Egyptologist has a variety of options available to document it: photography, manual copies, proportional copies, smears, latex/silicone squeezes (in an underwater environment, for example), stamps, and facsimiles (Caminos 1976; Traunecker 1987; Dorman 2008). There are numerous variations in the use of these different techniques, which are obviously not mutually exclusive. They all have their own advantages and disadvantages, depending on the situation, the intended use of the copy, and above all, the time and resources available. Notes and copies on the site, accompanied by a photograph, are often sufficient evidence for Egyptologists' personal archives, while he/she awaits the opportunity (possible, but not always forthcoming) to publish the findings.[1]

In the framework of wide-ranging documentation and/or publication programs, whether individual or collective, the end goal is different. It is therefore necessary to use a more proven method to capture the essential features of the object being studied. The hand copy is thus the only option capable of accurately rendering reliefs and inscriptions and particularly the arrangement and relative proportions of hieroglyphic figures and signs (Dorman 2008, 83–85). Once published and accessible to the scientific community, it can then be used for other purposes (proposals to restore lacunae, palaeography, etc.). A careful examination, as close as possible to the wall, ensures the optimum rendering of epigraphic features, especially if the relief has been damaged or subject to hammering/erasure/second engraving. This work must usually be preceded by a preparatory copy (manual copy into a notebook), which acts as a first approach to the text and helps to familiarize the epigrapher with the object in question. Nevertheless, a direct copy of the wall "makes the epigrapher more keenly aware of the idiosyncrasies of the artists who decorated the wall," and "the practice of making facsimiles helps in understanding

[1] Project supported by LabEx ARCHIMEDE from "Investissement d'Avenir" program ANR-11-LABX-0032–01.

the texts much more than a mere transcription ever can" (Willems, Coppens, and De Meyer 2003, 2–3).

Since the relief is three-dimensional, a true facsimile can only be carried out using a cast (plaster, latex/silicone squeezes, or even stamped paper). We therefore often use the term "facsimile" in its more limited sense, that is, reproducing a three-dimensional object in two dimensions, but taking great care to render the epigraphic features of the object as accurately as possible (for this distinction, see Traunecker 1987). Facsimiles have been and are often still created based on photographic media, and the final drawing is therefore highly dependent on the quality and accuracy of the shot (see chapter by McClain and *infra*). The Karnak method allows us to avoid using a photographic intermediary when making copies.

The So-Called Karnak Method

Tradition has it that this technique was introduced at Karnak in 1983:

> Tous les égyptologues précités, chargés du relevé de séries de blocs épars, ont appliqué une méthode commode inaugurée par Luc Gabolde en 1983. Elle consiste sur le terrain à décalquer le bloc sur un film transparent souple, en suivant le contour de tous les textes et reliefs au stylo feutre, ce qui permet d'en obtenir aisément le dessin grandeur nature, puis à repasser au bureau le dessin obtenu avec un stylo feutre plus épais afin qu'il soit possible d'obtenir des photos-réductions de bonne qualité. Celles-ci permettent ensuite de réaliser graphiquement l'assemblage des blocs et les dessins de restitution des parois. Le procédé est particulièrement performant lorsque les blocs sont très fragiles ou difficiles d'accès et ne peuvent donc être transportés ou être photographiés [i.e., "All of the Egyptologists mentioned above, responsible for making copies of a series of scattered blocks, used a convenient method introduced by Luc Gabolde in 1983. In the field, it consists of tracing the block on a flexible transparent film, following the outline of all texts and reliefs using a felt-tip pen. This allows us to easily create a life-size drawing, and then to go over it again later in the office with a thicker felt-tip so that it is possible to obtain good-quality photographic miniatures. In turn, this allows us to graphically assemble the blocks and/or reproductions of the walls. This process is particularly reliable when the blocks are very fragile or difficult to access and therefore cannot be transported or photographed"]. (Abd el-Hamid, Golvin, and Goyon 1985, 31n79)

But the so-called Karnak method does not belong to Karnak, and its origins actually lie elsewhere: it was used by P. Clère while working on the publication about the temple of Esna, to remedy the problem of drawing the column scenes, which could not be photographed (Sauneron 1963). The same process was used by Chicago House epigraphers to copy the columns of the temples of Luxor and Khonsu at Karnak (Caminos 1976, 11).

Although this method systematized the use of completely transparent plastic film, in reality, it is merely the evolution of an older practice (the "Howard Carter method"). This was originally carried out using natural tracing paper and then later on thicker and more rigid polyester tracing paper (such as Kodatrace and Rhodoïdes, depending on the manufacturer, which are plastic films made of cellulose acetate, in individual sheets or rolls). This was often used with precision to partially reproduce a relief, inscription (statues, tablets), graffiti, or cave carving (e.g., Devauchelle 1984; Jacquet-Gordon 1988, 11; Leclant 1989, 171; Jenni 1998, 11; Schiff Giorgini 1998, IX–XI; Leclant 2001, 3–4; Jacquet-Gordon 2003; Willems, Coppens, and De Meyer 2003). This method of creating a 1:1 copy facilitated the use of plastic film on a larger scale, often being used after or simultaneously alongside polyester tracing paper during the same mission (Gasse and Rondot 2007). Although polyester tracing paper is less transparent than plastic film, it is still frequently used to reproduce inscriptions of smaller dimensions for which the tip of a graphite pencil (lead pencil) is thinner than that of a felt-tip pen (super fine tip: 0.4 mm).

As indicated in the *Karnak* 8 report mentioned earlier, this method using plastic film was first developed at Karnak to inventory collections of scattered blocks that could not easily be moved and represented a method of documenting and supporting the study which was easy to put into practice. Indeed, the study of sets of scattered stones has long been favored by the Centre Franco-Égyptien d'Étude des Temples de Karnak (CFEETK), overshadowing the publication of temples and monuments themselves. The method subsequently spread across the entire field of epigraphic documentation. When done carefully, it does not degrade the wall or block at all (prior restoration work can be carried out if the condition of the block calls for it; consolidation with ethyl silicate, for example). Depending on the state of the wall or block, the plastic can also be held in place by a wooden frame. In every instance, the common sense of the epigrapher should prevail, and the condition of the stone should always come first when applying the plastic film. However, the dramatic reality of the combined effects of human (touristic) and climactic factors in wearing down the Nile Valley monuments makes the impact of this method completely insignificant with regard to the conservation of the monuments. On the contrary, this method allows us to document and preserve blocks and walls that unfortunately are likely to undergo significant degradation.

GENERAL PRINCIPLES

The method implemented in the 1980s is simple (Pécoil 2000, 31; Biston-Moulin and Thiers 2016, XI–XIII). Carefully apply a plastic film to the block or wall and, using a permanent felt-tip pen (fine tip 0.6 mm, or super fine tip 0.4 mm), trace (life-size) the outlines and forms of the figures, hieroglyphs (unlike publications that harmfully categorize iconography and inscriptions separately), joints, re-engraved areas, hammered areas, fractures, any epigraphic information likely to be used to understand the inscription and its condition. Once the copy has been made and the plastic dusted down, the drawing is retraced on the back with a thicker felt-tip (medium point 1.0 mm) using solid or dotted lines, depending on the conventions settled on. The original drawing on the front is erased with an alcohol or acetone solution, a scale (30 or 50 cm long) is traced and all the necessary information is added (inventory number, material, type of relief, location, date and author of the drawing, etc.). The plastic film (max. size 1.40 × 1 m) on a 1:1 scale is then photographed against a bright wall. For the frequent cases where the dimensions of the scene exceed the maximum size of the plastic, it is sufficient to note points of reference (crosses) between the plastic sheets with enough of an area overlapping to ensure precision when assembling them later. In the days of film photography, paper prints of the negatives (reduced to 1:10 scale) were needed for study and for publication. Manually assembling these paper prints allowed the Egyptologist to prepare a study of a set of stones or to reproduce an entire wall. Naturally, in between these steps the drawing is verified several times (via trips to the monument and the use of photographs) before the final photographs of the copy are taken.

It is clear that this method is more appropriate for reproducing sunken reliefs, since the film is placed as close as possible to the inscribed wall and the relief lines can be easily followed; however, its usage with raised relief is also possible.

There are two fundamental disadvantages of this method. First, although reducing the scale to 1:10 allowed the drawing's imperfections to be largely eliminated, the use of felt-tip pen did not always allow for a uniform outline, both in terms of thickness and density. Second, although it was always possible to erase a line and replace it using a technical pen (Rotring 0.1 mm), the correction process remained impractical to implement once the paper copy had been made without reproducing the entire drawing on tracing paper.

This technique therefore underwent various changes that attempted to address these difficulties. The first (in the late 1990s) was to change the plastic for a polyester crystal film that was totally transparent, thin (50 microns), more rigid, and did not distort at high temperatures (unlike the "nappes de nylon achetées au souq de Louqsor" (i.e., "nylon tablecloths bought in the souq of Luxor": Sauneron 1963). The quality of the drawing was therefore greatly improved. This type of film is still used today on a number of missions. It can be purchased in rolls of various sizes and lengths or in individual sheets and can be reused if needed (by erasing the existing drawing with an alcohol or acetone solution).

To remedy the potential irregularities resulting from the use of a felt-tip pen, a change was made when finalizing: based on the photograph/scan of the copy, reduced to 70 percent, the final outline was done using India ink (Rotring technical pen) on conventional polyester tracing paper. The line was therefore more uniform, and it was easier to make corrections during the verification process (Figure III.3.1). This method was used in particular for the blocks of the Chapelle Rouge (Burgos and Larché 2006) and the Speos Artemidos (Bickel and Chappaz 1988). After the original had been reduced, the final drawing could always be made on tracing paper using a lead pencil (Jordan, Bickel, and Chappaz 2015).

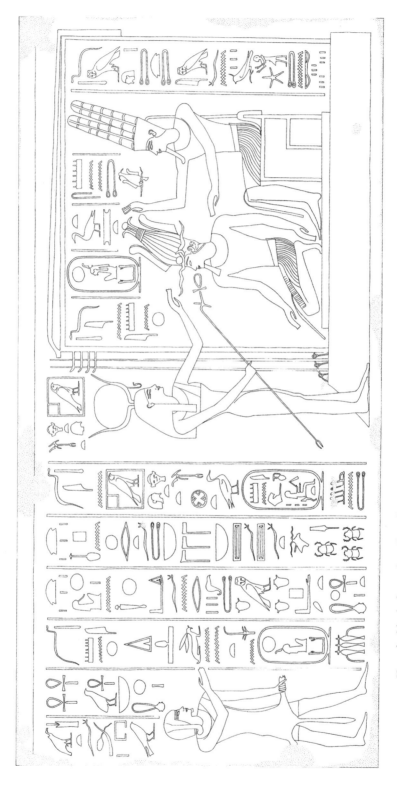

FIGURE III.3.1. Karnak, block from the Chapelle Rouge. Credit: CNRS-Centre franco-égyptien d'étude des temples de Karnak © Cnrs-Cfeetk/ H. Zacharias.

This method with its various modifications was mainly used at Karnak, as mentioned, to document and publish sets of stones, some of them significant (e.g., the festival court of Thutmose II, Gabolde 1993; the calcite bark-shrine of Thutmose III, Arnaudiès-Montélimard 2003; Netjery-menu, Gabolde 2005; the great pillared court of Thutmose IV, Letellier and Larché 2013; the obelisks at Karnak, Gabolde 2007; and in numerous articles, especially those published in *Cahiers de Karnak*). It has also proved to be effective in documenting monuments ("Botanical garden," Beaux 1990; Akhmenu, Pécoil 2000; gate of the tenth pylon, Jordan, Bickel, and Chappaz 2015), and notably thousands of scattered blocks whose records and handcopies are kept in the archives of the CFEETK, which are often the only evidence of stones that have unfortunately largely deteriorated over time. In other places, different teams have appropriated this method, improving it as needed (e.g., Beaux and Karkowski 1993; Karkowski 2003; Beaux, Grimal, et al. 2012; Beaux, Karkowski, et al. 2016; see *infra*).

Vectorization of Epigraphic Copies

The evolution of computer programs (photography and vector graphics) has profoundly changed the method, even if the philosophy behind it remains the same. Nowadays, the on-site copy done on plastic film, dusted down, and annotated (with information concerning the drawing, grid, etc.), is photographed or scanned directly. With the aid of the grid transferred onto the plastic, it is easy to obtain the desired scale by simply manipulating the image on a computer. The digital file is then used to create the final vectorized image using Adobe Illustrator software. This type of design software lets us apply a range of features, such as colors (*infra*), and to modify the scale of the work ad infinitum. As well as improving the rendering, it also makes it easier to transfer it to the final document intended for publication (Biston-Moulin and Thiers 2016). In addition, paper versions of old copies can now be digitized and vectorized to improve the quality and make it easier to assemble images or reproduce them (e.g., Thiers 2009); documentation work done in the past therefore remains perfectly usable for editing or publishing purposes now.

Color notation has largely been excluded from copies for a long time. As with other methods, thinner or dotted lines giving the impression of a gray line could indicate color on the plastic copy with a more or less exhaustive list of any traces of colors preserved in the reliefs being provided in the body of the publication (e.g., Jacquet-Gordon 1988, 9 nos. 1, 264; Pécoil 2000, 9–20; Thiers 2003, 295–296). Traces of color could also be indicated directly on the final drawing with letters/abbreviations (e.g., Jenni 1998, 11). Nowadays, software offers tools to represent the entire range of colors encountered. Beforehand, the epigrapher annotates the copy to indicate traces of color; the use of indelible color pens also simplifies the process. The drawing is finalized with the aid of a high-definition color photograph (orthophotography) and verification against the original (Figure III.3.2). At each stage, a paper copy can be annotated with the corrections

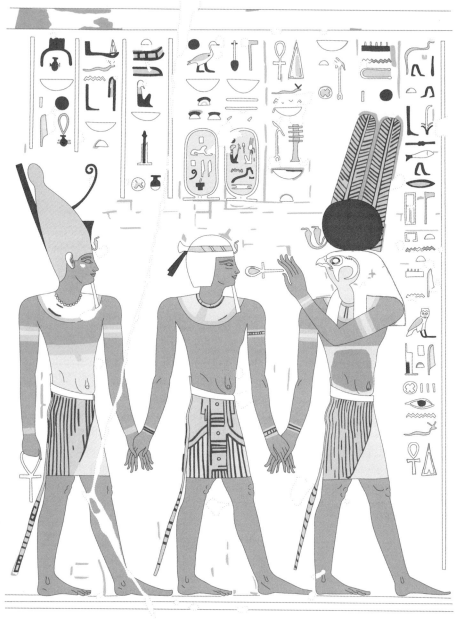

0   50 cm

P.C.

Philippe-Arrhidée, Mur Sud, Scène 24

FIGURE III.3.2. Karnak, outer southern wall of Philipp Arrhidaeus' bark shrine. Credit: CNRS-Centre franco-égyptien d'étude des temples de Karnak © Cnrs-Cfeetk/P. Calassou.

made to the digital copy. The decrease in publishing costs thanks to the use of digital presses means that nowadays copies of scenes can be printed in color, accompanied by a full-color photographic cover if necessary. Color can also be used to effectively and aesthetically differentiate between the outlines of scenes and inscriptions as opposed to broken areas/joints (Willems, Coppens, and De Meyer 2003; Willems 2007) or hammered/re-engraved areas (Karkowski 2003; Beaux, Grimal, et al. 2012; Beaux, Karkowski, et al. 2016; Biston-Moulin and Thiers 2016).

Whether for temple walls or any other inscribed object, digitizing copies also means that we can consult the results of archived research (drawings and old photographs), allowing us to better understand the condition of inscriptions and reliefs; vectoring allows us to easily show (using a different color) information provided by the archives in relation to the current state/deterioration of the wall (e.g., Shenhûr, Willems, Coppens, and De Meyer 2003, 3; Ayn el-Muftella, Labrique 2014, 163–164).

For publications concerning temples, having the handcopy accompanied (alongside it, if possible) by a normalized digital version of the hieroglyphs (online, with critical apparatus), a layout plan (of the temple and the wall), and finally a photographic copy gives the reader access to all the information essential for Egyptology (Karkowski 2003; Thiers 2003; Jordan, Bickel, and Chappaz 2015; Biston-Moulin and Thiers 2016; Figure III.3.3). This is a major improvement over typographical editions offering only the typography (old lead cast or digitized) running from right to left (Edfu, Dendera, Kom Ombo, Esna, Athribis) or traced editions (Opet, Deir Shelwit, Tod I) accompanied by an indicative summary of the iconography or the scenes depicted—but without taking into account the hieroglyphs—and sometimes by layout plans. An intermediary method of presenting a proportional copy showing the hieroglyphs as arranged in the original scene (Traunecker 1987) but usually separating them from the iconography (Coptos, el-Qal'a, Qasr elAguz) has also been proposed. All these methods proved their worth during the time they were used, in terms of not only the scope of the task in hand but also the readability of the reliefs studied and the economic constraints of publications.

Some Remarks

The choice of method when making an epigraphic copy therefore depends largely on the resources available (financial and human) and consequently on the time that we are willing to dedicate to documenting a relief or inscription that could deteriorate quickly in order to provide access to Egyptological information. A copy that is extremely accomplished but that takes years to be accessible to the scientific community is perhaps not the most suitable, if it deprives many researchers of the information they need to further their studies. The ambiguous concept of productivity in the humanities remains significant when it comes to documenting monuments that were last documented a long time ago or that have never been published before, as far too many examples attest to irreversible destruction or disintegration over time.

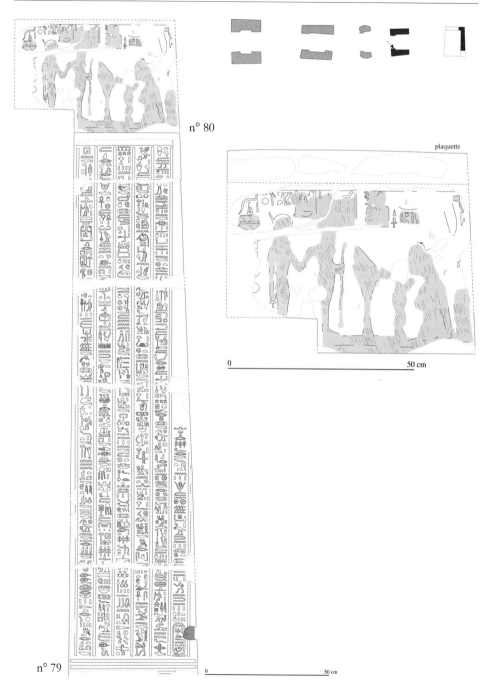

FIGURE III.3.3. Karnak, temple of Ptah, hymn dedicated to Imhotep. Credit: CNRS-Centre franco-égyptien d'étude des temples de Karnak © Cnrs-Cfeetk/Chr. Thiers.

This practical, easy, and inexpensive method, which does not require lengthy training, allows us to produce a rendering of an inscription or relief in order to document it or to support and illustrate a publication on Egyptology. This level of rendering does not aim to be a definitive reproduction of the relief or inscription: it must be comprehensive, legible, and show the reader all the key epigraphic features. The final drawing is therefore not to be considered an artistic work by any means—this is not its function. Obviously, we tend toward an aesthetically pleasing drawing where possible, one that is faithful to the original and nice to look at for the reader who flicks through the work in which it is published, but the inclusion of epigraphic/Egyptological features takes priority over the artistic value. "L'idéal est atteint lorsque l'égyptologue est également un artiste" (i.e., "The ideal is achieved when the Egyptologist is also an artist") (Traunecker 1987, 265n8).

Every drawing is an interpretation of how the object being drawn appears in reality, and the choices made when rendering the outlines are the result of collective rules or individual practices. A copy made by even the most brilliant artist is merely an interpretation of the reality of the relief or inscription in question even if he/she has access to photographs without optical distortion (tilt-shift or orthoimages). It is possible to obtain the maximum possible objectivity of the supporting material—and we can consider that this is the case when using geo-referenced orthoimages alongside a theodolite—but the objectivity of the copy will always depend on the ability of the epigrapher to interpret the relief or inscription, especially when the supporting material has been highly modified. This interpretation, however, must remain objective and faithful to the original.

We can only welcome recent technological improvements (orthoimages, Reflectance Transformation Imaging, depth maps) that can now act as supporting material and can often be decisive in epigraphic analysis. However, they cannot always be a substitute for the trained eye and Egyptological knowledge of the epigrapher.

Since this method of making a copy is not binding, there is no definitive style guide. It is enough for the copy to be internally consistent and for its role to be clearly defined beforehand (rendering the limits of blocks, joints, outlines of figures, breaks, cupules, post-restoration mortar remnants, etc.) (e.g., Beaux 1990, 351; Schiff Giorgini 1998, IX–XII; Pécoil 2000, 32; Karkowski 2003, pl. A; Biston-Moulin and Thiers 2016, XI–XIII).

Sometimes used in certain publications, a thicker shadow line tends to indicate the existence of a theoretical light source situated above and to the left of the object (at an angle of 45°) and therefore indicates the nature of the relief (sunken or raised). This shadow line is typically absent from *Karnak* copies. Using photography, which must nowadays be systematically published (on paper, CD-ROM, or online) along with the handcopy (see Caminos 1976, 19), allows us to visualize the nature of the relief, which can also be indicated in the publication (Schiff Giorgini 1998, XI; Thiers 2003, 295). This avoids having the shadow line interfere with the drawing and distort the work of the ancient sculptor, who was not thinking about a conventional light source above the pattern on the left when he carved it. The use of the shadow line is sometimes ambiguous in certain publications, where it is applied to reliefs but not to smaller hieroglyphic signs. But as mentioned, the method is not prescriptive, and this convention may therefore be adopted if desired, being even easier nowadays thanks to the digitization of copies. It is a technical and/or aesthetic decision, whichever method is used to make the epigraphic copy.

A wide variety of renderings is therefore possible, from the most succinct to the most aesthetically accomplished. However, since the handcopy is intended as a supporting material when reading, understanding, and studying a relief, it is not usually necessary to note the slightest scratches or the internal details of breakages on the plastic film. By contrast, areas that have been lost, as well as cupules, need to be clearly defined (by a dotted line or dashed/shaded areas); failing to note broken areas is extremely damaging, resulting in a loss of information since there is no longer any way of distinguishing between a nonengraved area and an area that has been damaged (accidentally or intentionally). The Egyptologist's job of editing and reproducing texts is therefore not possible using such copies.

The strengths of this technique are its flexibility, based on a copy scale of 1:1, and the speed with which it can be carried out. It is very easy to perform and has therefore been adopted by many missions and by inspectors from the Egyptian Ministry of Antiquities, allowing them to better document the various monuments unearthed during excavations or during inventories of sets of stones by the Ministry. The few studies noted here are, of course, just an indication. It is impossible to list the hundreds of publications (monographs and articles), monuments (temples, blocks, statues, etc.), and documentation/inventory projects that have benefited from this quick and simple technique throughout Egypt, bringing together a considerable collection of documents for Egyptologists to study.

Technological Developments

The growing contribution of digital photography, the increase in computing power, and the appearance of specialized software all allow us to further develop the old techniques of photogrammetry and thus to obtain high-definition orthoimages with no optical distortion. Thanks to these media, digital epigraphy at Karnak is applied to large-scale programs where the traditional method would not be suitable. For example, the entire Eighth Pylon was recently drawn in this manner based on high-definition orthoimages. The same process was used for the chapel of Alexander at Akhmenu where the extremely well preserved colors, after an extensive period of restoration, made the use of plastic film inadequate. Again, each method has its advantages and disadvantages, and we must choose the most suitable according to the variables involved, subject to the characteristics of the supporting material, the time dedicated to making the copy, and the final use that the epigrapher intends for it.

The so-called Karnak method is just one tool among many others.

BIBLIOGRAPHY

Arnaudiès-Montélimard, E. 2003. "Un reposoir de barque en calcite édifié par Thoutmosis III dans le temple d'Amon-Rê à Karnak." *Karnak* 11:159–234.

Beaux, N. 1990. *Le cabinet de curiosités de Thoutmosis III: Plantes et animaux du "Jardin botanique" de Karnak.* OLA 36. Leuven.

Beaux, N., N. Grimal, G. Pollin, J. Karkowski, and E. Majerus. 2012. *La chapelle d'Hathor: Temple d'Hatchepsout à Deir el-Bahari, I: Vestibule et sanctuaires.* 3 vols. MIFAO 129. Cairo.

Beaux, N., and J. Karkowski. 1993. "La chapelle d'Hathor du temple d'Hatchepsout à Deir el-Bahari. Rapport préliminaire." *BIFAO* 93:7–24.

Beaux, N., J. Karkowski, E. Majerus, and G. Pollin. 2016. *La chapelle d'Hathor: Temple d'Hatchepsout à Deir el-Bahari, II: Façade et salles hypostyles, 1: Figures et planches.* MIFAO 133. Cairo.

Bickel, S., and J.-L. Chappaz. 1988. "Missions épigraphiques du fonds de l'égyptologie de Genève au Spéos Artémidos." *BSEG* 12:9–24.

Biston-Moulin, S., and C. Thiers. 2016. *Le temple de Ptah à Karnak I: Relevé épigraphique (Ptah, n°s 1–191).* TravauxCFEETK, BG 49. Cairo.

Burgos, F., and F. Larché. 2006. *La chapelle Rouge: Le sanctuaire de barque d'Hatshepsout 1.* Paris.

Caminos, R. 1976. "The Recording of Inscriptions and Scenes in Tombs and Temples." In *Ancient Egyptian Epigraphy and Paleography*, 3–25. New York.

Devauchelle, D. 1984. *Les graffites du Gebel Teir: Textes et démotiques grecs.* RAPH 22. Cairo.

Dorman, P. F. 2008. "Epigraphy and Recording." In *Egyptology Today*, edited by R. H. Wilkinson, 77–97. Cambridge.

Gabolde, L. 1993. "La 'cour de fêtes' de Thoutmosis II à Karnak." *Karnak* 9:1–100.

Gabolde, L. 2005. *Monuments décorés en bas-relief aux noms de Thoutmosis II et Hatchepsout à Karnak.* MIFAO 123. Cairo.

Gabolde, L. 2007. "An Atlas of the Obelisks of Karnak in Preparation." *EA* 37:33–35.

Gasse, A., and V. Rondot. 2007. *Les inscriptions de Séhel.* MIFAO 126. Cairo.

Hamid, S. Abd el-, J.-C. Golvin, and J.-C. Goyon. 1985. "Les travaux du Centre Franco-Égyptien de 1981 à 1985. Rapport général." *Karnak* 8:9–39.

Jacquet-Gordon, H. 1988. *Karnak-Nord VI: Le trésor de Thoutmosis Ier. La décoration.* FIFAO 32. Cairo.

Jacquet-Gordon, H. 2003. *The Temple of Khonsu III: The Graffiti on the Khonsu Temple Roof at Karnak. A Manifestation of Personal Piety.* OIP 123. Chicago.

Jenni, H. 1998. *Elephantine XVII: Die Dekoration des Chnumtempels auf Elephantine durch Nektanebos II.* AVDAIK 90. Mayence.

Jordan, M., S. Bickel, and J.-L. Chappaz. 2015. *La Porte d'Horemheb au Xe pylône de Karnak.* CSEG 13. Geneva.

Karkowski, J. 2003. *The Temple of Hatshepsut: The Solar Complex.* Deir el-Bahari 6. Varsovie.

Labrique, F. 2014. "Chronique des travaux en Égypte. Chronique 2014. 1. Ayn el-Mouftella." *Dialogues d'histoire ancienne* 40/1: 163–179.

Leclant, J. 1989. "Mise au point sur le progrès de l'étude des nouveaux textes des pyramides de Saqarah." In *Akten des vierten internationalen Ägyptologen Kongresses München 1985*, edited by S. Schoske, 171–181. SAK Bh 3. Hamburg.

Leclant, J. 2001. *Les textes de la pyramide de Pépy Ier.* 2 vols. MIFAO 118. Cairo.

Letellier, B., and F. Larché. 2013. *La cour à portique de Thoutmosis IV.* EE 12. Paris.

Pécoil, J.-F. 2000. *L'Akh-menou de Thoutmosis III à Karnak. La* Heret-ib *et les chapelles attenantes. Relevés épigraphiques.* Paris.

Sauneron, S. 1963. *Le temple d'Esna II.* Cairo.

Schiff Giorgini, M. 1998. *Soleb V: Le temple. Bas-reliefs et inscriptions.* Cairo.

Thiers, C. 2003. *Tôd: Les inscriptions du temple ptolémaïque et romain II. Textes et scènes nᵒˢ 173–329.* FIFAO 18/2. Cairo.

Thiers, C. 2009. "Les 'quatre ka' du démiurge (à Tôd)." In *Verba manent: Recueil d'études dédiées à Dimitri Meeks par ses amis et collègues,* edited by I. Régen and F. Servajean, 425–437. CENiM 2. Montpellier.

Traunecker, C. 1987. "Les techniques d'épigraphie de terrain: principes et pratique." In *Problems and Priorities in Egyptian Archaeology,* edited by J. Assmann, G. Burkhard, and V. Davies, 261–298. New York.

Willems, H., F. Coppens, and M. De Meyer. 2003. *The Temple of Shanhûr I: The Sanctuary, the Wabet and the Gates of the Central Hall and the Great Vestibule (1–98).* OLA 124. Leuven.

Willems, H. 2007. *Dayr al-Barsha I: The Rock Tombs of Djehutinakht (17K74/1), Khnum-nakht (17K74/2), and Iha (17K74/3). With an Essay on the History and Nature of Nomarchal Rule in the Early Middle Kingdom.* OLA 155. Leuven.

THE CHICAGO HOUSE METHOD

J. BRETT McCLAIN

INTRODUCTION

THE Epigraphic Survey is a core expedition of the University of Chicago's Oriental Institute and an essential component of the Institute's mission to explore, record, analyze, and evaluate the textual and archaeological remains of the ancient Near East. Since 1924, the Survey has engaged in systematic facsimile documentation of the reliefs and inscriptions in Egyptian temples and tombs, primarily within, though not limited to, the region of ancient Thebes. The expedition's objective is to document the scenes and texts contained in these monuments, along with their architectural context, at an optimum level of accuracy, such that the resulting publications will form the definitive and permanent record of the structures and their inscribed content, serving as a primary resource for academic research and standing in place of the original monuments themselves, as their physical deterioration takes its inevitable course. The distinctive recording methodology devised by Professor James Henry Breasted at the inception of the Epigraphic Survey, and employed by the expedition throughout its history, has come to be known as the "Chicago House Method," after the name of the Institute's field headquarters in Luxor. In the following paragraphs, our methodology will be presented in detail. It should be noted from the outset that several excellent presentations thereof have been given over the years, by Breasted himself (1930, 1933) and by former field directors Nelson (1930), Hughes (1952), Nims (1972), Bell (1987), Dorman (2008), and Johnson (2012), all of which the reader is urged to consult, and that our approach remains fundamentally the same as in these earlier descriptions. As part of a handbook on Egyptian epigraphy, however, it is appropriate that the principles and procedures of the Method be laid out concisely, making its theory and practice available to the users of this volume, and also that its application be discussed in the context of the Survey's current field research projects.

Breasted devised the Chicago House Method in response to a twofold problem. His early fieldwork in Egypt had demonstrated that existing copies of hieroglyphic inscriptions, made during the pioneering years of Egyptology in the nineteenth century, were often to a greater or lesser degree inaccurate, and that many of these same inscriptions were, even in the early decades of the twentieth century, rapidly deteriorating, with the result that irreplaceable evidence of Pharaonic civilization was being lost forever. At first, Breasted considered the possibility that photography, a relatively new technology at the time, could provide the solution—an objectively accurate, yet rapid and efficient way to capture the image of an inscribed surface. Experimentation showed, however, that even the most careful photographs were often insufficient to illustrate all of the details of a relief or inscription. To make a readable photograph, the decorated surface must be illuminated from a single direction, but the choice of this direction inevitably reveals some details by light and shadow, while concealing others, depending upon the angle of lighting. Moreover, the camera lens impartially records both the inscribed details and the other elements on the surface, such as discoloration, damaged areas, and areas of historical modification of the relief, with equal emphasis. Epigraphic minutiae, such as partially damaged hieroglyphs, eroded internal details of signs or figures, traces of earlier decorative stages, or faded paint lines, which are detectable by careful study of the wall, often remain invisible in the photo. Breasted realized that the impartial accuracy of the photograph needed to be combined with observation and interpretation by the Egyptologist in such a way that the historically significant features of the inscription would be highlighted, de-emphasizing the obscuring elements, such as damage or discoloration. The photograph should therefore be used to provide the proportionally accurate basis for a line drawing in which the inscribed and/or painted elements would be given priority. To make a high-quality drawing, however, it would also be necessary to employ the skills of an artist trained in scientific illustration techniques, capable of observing and setting down the details with sufficient care and accuracy as to give a true representation of the ancient carved lines. The combination of these three elements— the expertise of the professional photographer, the skills of the scientific draftsman, and the philological and historical knowledge of the Egyptologist—was Breasted's ingenious solution to the problem of accurate epigraphic documentation, and this remains an underlying principle of the Chicago House Method.

Our methodology is based on the high-quality, large-format film photograph. In fact, as Bell (1987) has already pointed out, a preliminary "Epigraphic Survey" of many of the monuments of Thebes is already in existence, in the form of over twenty thousand large format negatives (4" × 5", 5" × 7", and 8" × 10") that form the core of the Chicago House photographic archive. Assembled over the past nine decades, this collection of images not only is fundamental to the Survey's documentation projects but also serves as a resource for the academic community, and it has recently been made available online in digital form.[1] The importance of this archive is enhanced by the fact that many of the

---

[1] The Chicago House large format archive may be consulted via the Oriental Institute Integrated Database at: http://oi-idb.uchicago.edu/.

older photographs depict scenes and inscriptions that have since decayed or suffered damage, and are thus the only attestation of features that are now lost. Although now supplemented by extensive digital photography, the continued development of the large format film archive remains a fundamental part of the Epigraphic Survey's research program.

It should be pointed out that, in some cases, where the level of preservation of a decorated surface is exceptionally high, the photograph alone can in fact provide sufficient detail for publication. If a scene is relatively free of damage or discoloration, or in cases where there has been no deliberate modification (such as usurpation or stylistic recarving), it is often unnecessary to devote the extensive time and effort needed to produce a facsimile line drawing. Some sections of the monuments published by the Epigraphic Survey are given in photographic plates only or as hand-enhanced photographs accompanied by epigraphic commentary. The facsimile line drawing is a highly intensive and specialized type of record, necessary only in cases where the information visible on the wall requires clarification and in-depth interpretation to make it fully understandable to the reader. It is also the case, however, that the Survey typically selects and prioritizes monuments or parts of monuments that are damaged or threatened with decay or that exhibit complex epigraphic problems to which our specialized methodology is particularly applicable. For this reason, the facsimile line drawing is and has always been the Survey's main product, precisely and accurately depicting inscribed details that would be largely incomprehensible if presented in photographs only.

DESCRIPTION

The photographic negative, then, is the initial step in the recording process. Prior to starting a project, the field director and the expedition staff will have reviewed the available photographic negatives and selected the best one available for each inscription or scene, commissioning new photographs as needed. The photographer takes careful measurements prior to each shot in order to minimize distortion and to provide consistent lighting across the inscribed surface, usually making several negatives of each wall section. The scale of reduction at which each scene or section of the wall will be drawn is decided in advance, as well. From the negative, an enlargement is made to this scale on heavyweight matte photographic paper, the coating of which is selected to provide a durable surface for pencil and ink lines. The photographer takes care to print the enlargement in such a way that as many details as possible are clearly visible, minimizing in particular the intensity of cast shadows. An alternate print is made from the same negative and kept for reference. Other photographic prints, taken, for example, from old negatives whereon elements now damaged or lost may be detectable, as well as detail shots of problematic sections, may also be requested as aids for the artist. Sometimes, depending on the architectural configuration of the wall surface, it is necessary for the photographer to shoot a scene in two or more sections, taking care to provide sufficient overlap at the edge of each image so that the parts drawn separately can be joined for publication. Also prior to starting the drawing, the project's Egyptologists may provide additional background information, such as earlier published or unpublished copies of the scene or text, that may be useful during the drawing process, so that the artist will have at hand all useful information about the visual content of the area to be recorded. Careful planning and coordination during the initial stages of the process can save much time and frustration later on.

When the enlargement has been prepared, the artist takes it to the site and measures it carefully, comparing it to the scene in question to verify that the scale and proportions are correct. Once this is done, penciling begins. Observing the wall closely, using sunlight reflected with mirrors or artificial lighting to rake the relief from every angle, the artist pencils the lines of the inscription directly onto the surface of the photograph. Great care is taken not only to reproduce the lines and details of the figures and hieroglyphs, but also to capture the style in which the relief is carved. Years of experience have given the Survey's artists a familiarity with the stylistic nuances of relief carving from a variety of historical periods, and these will be reflected in the rendering of the facsimile. In cases where the relief has been modified in antiquity (such as with divine names and figures erased in the reign of Akhenaten and subsequently restored), any visible traces of the earlier versions of the carving are also painstakingly indicated, along with any remaining vestiges of the painted decoration of the scene. Significant non-inscriptional features, such as deliberate iconoclastic hacking of signs or figures, areas of ancient plaster repair, and architectural elements are also included, but the indication of damage to the stone surface is limited to places where it affects or interrupts a carved line, thus maximizing the emphasis on the carved or painted elements. The artist also makes extensive notations while at the wall in order to facilitate the subsequent stages of the drawing and publication process.

After the on-site penciling of the enlargement is complete, the drawing proceeds to the inking stage, which is carried out in the artist's studio at Chicago House or during the summer, after the expedition returns from the field. Using technical drafting pens, the artist carefully inks over the penciled lines of the inscription and other features, once again directly on to the surface of the photograph. The Epigraphic Survey has adopted a set of scientific drawing conventions to indicate the character of the relief, whether raised/*bas*-relief, or incised/sunk relief. In all of our drawings, a theoretical light source is posited at the upper left, raking the surface at a forty-five-degree angle. Raised relief features will therefore show thinner (sun) lines at the upper left, and thicker (shadow) lines at the lower right, while these conventions will be reversed for elements carved in sunk relief. Traces of earlier versions of the relief are shown using an even thinner line, while the outlines of any preserved painted details are shown using a dotted line convention. Additionally, there are conventions specifically employed for damaged areas, remains of ancient plaster, and architectural features (such as wall corners, architraves, torus molding, etc.), the goal being to show these elements, which form the context of the decoration, clearly and realistically. Again, when inking the lines, care is taken to remain true to the historical and stylistic features of the relief. The inking conventions may be modified to suit various unusual situations encountered at the wall, but in general they are adhered to quite closely in order to guarantee consistency of rendering from one facsimile to another, even if drawn by different artists. Since the inking stage must necessarily take place off-site, the artist's annotations are helpful in ensuring that the features are inked as they were observed at the wall.

When the inking of the enlargement is complete (Figure III.4.1), it is returned to the photographer for bleaching. A chemical bath consisting of a solution of iodine is prepared, and the enlargement is immersed therein for a fixed length of time. The solution causes the photographic emulsion to fade and then disappear, leaving only the inked lines on the surface. Following this delicate procedure, the paper is dried and re-flattened, and then it is returned to the artist. The artist then cleans the enlargement carefully to remove any vestiges of dirt or dust, along with stray pencil marks, although the penciled annotations, especially those concerning the eventual joining of separate drawings for publication, and questions regarding other features of interest, may be retained for reference.

FIGURE III.4.1. Photographic enlargement with inscription inked by the artist using sun-shadow convention. TT 107 (Nefersekheru). Photograph by Y. Kobylecky; drawing by S. Osgood. Courtesy of the Oriental Institute of the University of Chicago.

Once cleaned, the drawing (Figure III.4.2) is ready for collation, or checking, at the wall. The collation of the drawing is the task of the epigrapher, an Egyptologist who has received specialized training in the study of inscriptions and relief scenes. In order to avoid damage to the inked enlargement itself, the collation must be carried out using copies of the drawing. It is returned once again to the photographer, who makes first a negative and then a positive duplicate using blueprint paper, exposed either to the sun or to artificial ultraviolet light. The original drawing is carefully stored for the time being, though photocopies may also be taken for further reference. Blueprinted copies of the drawings are particularly suitable for the collation process, as they allow penciled annotations to be made in clear juxtaposition to the existing inked lines. Two blueprints are made for each drawing; one of these is kept whole for reference, while the other is cut up into sections, each containing a manageably sized portion of the scene. These sections are pasted onto sheets of white paper, each of which is labeled with the number of the scene (using the Nelson numbering system) and given its own unique sub-number. These are the collation sheets (Figure III.4.3), the basic unit of the epigraphic collation process.

A given scene or group of related scenes is assigned to a first epigrapher, who is responsible for making the initial collation. Prior to beginning work at the site, it is the responsibility of the first epigrapher to assemble a dossier of all available information concerning the wall section that is to be examined, including all earlier published and unpublished copies of the scene(s), any earlier photographs, and published or unpublished translations, commentaries, or notes on the area in question. With proper planning, this archival research may be carried out in the summer, when the expedition is not in the field, but the extensive field library at Chicago House also serves as a ready resource when needed during the winter season. The epigrapher should thus have a thorough familiarity with the material before approaching the wall itself.

When it is time to carry out the collation, the epigrapher examines the wall carefully, using raking light from various angles in the same manner as used by the artist, and checks every line of the drawing against the inscribed original. Knowledge of the texts and iconography will often allow the epigrapher to observe details that the artist may have missed, or to clarify difficult sections of a text or other decorative elements. Experience has shown that careful and repeated observation of problematic features or damaged areas of the surface, often extending over a period of several days, under varying lighting conditions, and keeping in mind the inscriptional and historical context of the monument, can reveal a great many previously unnoticed details, sometimes minute but nevertheless crucial for the interpretation of the scene. When the epigrapher observes a detail that needs to be added to the drawing or an existing line that should be modified, the addition or change is sketched in pencil on the blueprint, and an explanatory note is added in the margin of the sheet. Additional notes on philological, iconographic, or historical questions, etc., may also be added, enclosed within a box to avoid confusion. Each sheet will thus be annotated in turn as the epigrapher works over the whole scene. Corrections to the paint lines are usually indicated on a photocopy of the drawing, since the dotted lines are more easily seen in black and white, and notes on the color scheme and its preservation are included as well.

FIGURE III.4.2. Enlargement bleached to produce facsimile line drawing. Medinet Habu, Small Amun Temple (MH.B 27). Drawing by M. De Jong and W. Johnson. Courtesy of the Oriental Institute of the University of Chicago.

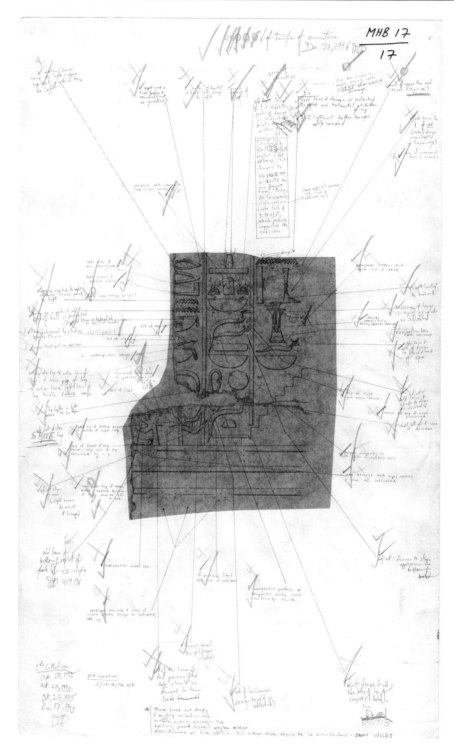

FIGURE III.4.3. Collation sheet with corrections and epigraphic commentary. Medinet Habu, Small Amun Temple (MH.B 17). Drawing by S. Osgood; collation by J. Darnell, A. Baumann, and the author. Courtesy of the Oriental Institute of the University of Chicago.

The objective of the collation is to create a set of recommendations for modifying the drawing that are clear, concise, and accurate. In addition, the collation process gives the epigrapher the opportunity to study the inscribed wall more closely than anyone else is likely to have the chance to do and thereby to master its contents. Based on this careful examination of the scene or inscription, the epigrapher writes up a preliminary translation, with notes and epigraphic commentary, containing all features noted during the process, along with any questions raised at the wall. This will form the basis for the formal translation and commentary that will be included in the published volume.

When all of the first epigrapher's work is complete, the collation packet, containing all the information assembled for the scene, is passed on to a second epigrapher. The second epigrapher takes the sheets to the site and repeats the collation process, carefully checking every line of the drawing against the original wall relief, and must indicate agreement or disagreement with every correction suggested by the first epigrapher, noting down the reason for the disagreement in brackets. Moreover, the second epigrapher also notes down any additional changes based on this second collation. The value of having at least two Egyptologists check each facsimile drawing in the presence of the original inscription cannot be overstated. Each scholar brings a unique individual background of specialized knowledge to bear on the problems that may be encountered when interpreting an inscription, and a consensus of interpretation produces far greater depth and accuracy than would the work of a single collator. The task of the second epigrapher must be therefore be executed as carefully as that of the first. When finished, the sheets are returned to the first epigrapher, who then rechecks each of the second epigrapher's comments at the wall. Then the two epigraphers review each of the sheets together on-site and discuss any points of disagreement or other questions that have arisen during the process, until consensus is reached. By the time the collation is complete, the two epigraphers must be in agreement about every change that is to be suggested to the artist.

The completed collation packet is then returned to the artist, who takes the annotated sheets to the wall and, in the presence of the original scene, checks each correction that the epigraphers have recommended. If the artist disagrees with or has a question about any of the annotations, this is indicated on the sheet; when the artist's wall check is finished, these points are discussed with the first epigrapher until agreement is reached. The artist and the epigraphers must be in full agreement on every point regarding modification of the facsimile before the corrections to the original inked drawing are made. The artist uses the collation sheets as a guide to making these changes, deleting, modifying, or adding to the ink lines using pens and a surgical scalpel, a process that is facilitated by the high-quality surface of the photographic paper. Since this process takes time, it is also usually performed as summer work during the "off-season."

Once the artist has entered all of the corrections to the drawing, it is returned to the first epigrapher, along with the collation sheets, and each correction indicated on the sheets is verified. Only when the transfer of each and every correction to the inked drawing has been checked will it be submitted to the field director for approval. The final director's check is also carried out at the wall, with all relevant materials—original drawing, alternate photographs, collation sheets, translation, commentary, and notes—at hand so that the results of the work can be evaluated, and additional work on the scene can be assigned if warranted.

When the field director gives final approval, the drawing is ready to be published and, along with the photographs and other supporting documentation, is placed in storage until all of the drawings for a given publication have been completed. The entire dossier of drawings, collation sheets, notes, and other materials is then transported back to the Oriental Institute in Chicago to be edited for publication in the Survey's characteristic large-format folio volumes, each of which will simultaneously be released online in electronic form. Insofar as warranted by the nature of the relief, each scene is published both as a black-and-white photograph and as a facsimile line drawing, accompanied by a detailed translation and epigraphic/iconographic commentary, placing the inscribed wall in its historical and art-historical context. In cases where painted colors and details are well preserved, scenes may be presented in color photographs or color facsimile drawings as well. The goal is to provide the reader of our publications with the entire results of the Survey's research, making all of the visual and textual information available, so that, as noted earlier, the published volume can stand in the place of the original monument or section thereof, both making the ancient records widely available for scholarly research and preserving them for the future in those cases, sadly all too frequent, where the monument is in a progressive state of decay.

VARIATIONS

The most important principle of the Chicago House Method has been made clear in the foregoing description: the highest level of accuracy in the photograph-based facsimile drawing is achieved by means of a series of multiple observations and cross-checks, carried out in the presence of the original wall surface by a team of professionals, each of whom (photographer, artist, epigraphers, field director) contributes specialized knowledge and skills to the process. The result is the product of a collaborative effort, incorporating the fruits of intensive, repeated study of the inscribed surface. Although the steps of producing the facsimile are technically complex, it is in fact this series of checks and discussions in situ that is the most time-consuming part of the Method. In order to extract and record the maximum amount of information from an ancient decorated wall surface, *there is no substitute for taking the time to make multiple examinations of the wall, with multiple collations of the copy against the original.* The technical aspects of the Chicago House Method may be, and on many occasions have been, modified to suit particular or unusual field conditions or varied types of inscribed evidence, depending on the situation and the nature of the material. The basic principles just outlined, however, must be respected at all times. As long as the team adheres to these principles, modifications of the procedures used to create the photographs and drawings can provide a wide and flexible range of approaches to a variety of field documentation tasks. It will be useful to give a couple of examples of these variations of the tools and techniques used to execute the Method on the Survey's current field projects.

Documentation of the reused fragments taken from dismantled older monuments and built into the floors, walls, and roof of the Ramesside Khonsu Temple at Karnak is a good example of how the Chicago House Method has been adapted to suit unusual conditions. Starting in 2008, the Epigraphic Survey carried out a program of recording the reused blocks in conjunction with a restoration project sponsored by the American Research Center in Egypt (Kimpton et al. 2010). The restoration work has allowed access to cracks in the floor, walls, and roof of the temple structure, through which many blocks with inscribed surfaces, commonly turned inward by the Twentieth Dynasty builders, could be detected. These narrow interstices between the blocks, sometimes as small as one centimeter, preclude the use of photographs in most cases. Instead, sheets of aluminum foil are inserted into the cracks and used to create rubbings of the surfaces, whether in raised or sunk relief. (See Schenck chapter.) Often, the decorated surfaces are located so deep within the gaps that they cannot be seen at all, but nevertheless may be "felt" by using wooden skewers wrapped in cotton, permitting the foil impression to be taken from otherwise completely inaccessible surfaces. The process is painstaking, often requiring dozens of foil impressions to capture the whole of the accessible surface. The outlines of the decoration captured on the foil are then traced by the artist onto clear acetate at 1:1 scale. Once the artist has built up the complete image of the decorated block, the resulting drawing is collated on site by the epigraphers, using the same foil-impression method. The aluminum foil thus functions as a substitute for the camera of the photographer and for the eyes of the artists and epigraphers, but the series of cross-checks remains the same, within the physical limitations of the material and its context. Occasionally, hand-mirrors can be inserted into the cracks to examine hard-to-reach surfaces, but this is the exception rather than the rule. Even during the final checks by the field director, additional foil rubbings may be taken to verify specific points of interpretation. The completed 1:1 tracings are then scanned, reduced, and inked (either on vellum or by digital means) using the standard Epigraphic Survey line weight conventions. The result is a series of cross-checked facsimile drawings, made to the Survey's standards of accuracy, of a corpus of inscribed material that would otherwise have remained entirely unrecorded.

The ongoing documentation of the monuments at Medinet Habu remains a core concession of the Epigraphic Survey. Although the process of making inked facsimiles from photographic enlargements continues to furnish the primary means of documenting the wall reliefs at the site, particular areas have required innovative adaptation of our tools and procedures. A current example of such adaptation is part of the Survey's work in the Eighteenth Dynasty temple, where newly available digital drawing technologies have been applied to decorated wall sections presenting unusually convoluted epigraphic problems. The west exterior wall of the Thutmoside bark shrine, for instance, preserves evidence of five stages of decoration: the original carved and painted relief from the time of Thutmose III, desecration of divine names and images during the reign of Akhenaten, restoration of these in the aftermath of the Amarna period, an episode of repainting early in the Ptolemaic Period, and wholesale architectural reworking and restoration of the doorway and adjacent panels in the reign of Ptolemy VIII Euergetes II. Due in particular to the extensively preserved but bewilderingly complicated paint layers successively juxtaposed over the relief, there was no way to capture all the information on a single line drawing in a way that would be clearly understandable. Digital drawing has offered the answer. The process whereby all of the stages of decoration on this portal and the flanking wall sections have been recorded, organized, and set down in facsimile in an orderly fashion are described in detail by Epigraphic Survey artist Krisztián Vértes in a separate article. (See Vértes chapter.) Here it is sufficient to note that separating the various stages of the decoration into discrete layers using Adobe Photoshop software has allowed each phase to be documented in full and that the use of a portable tablet computer for drawing on site has been essential to the success of the procedure. It is critical to observe, however, that the procedures used to create and verify the multilayered digital drawing conform to the Chicago House Method. All sections of the facsimile were based on photographs, in this case a combination of digital photos and older large-format film negatives. These photographs, worked into digital composites, formed the basis of digitally penciled drawings, made on the tablet computer, based on an intensive in situ study of the decorated surface. It was even possible to import scanned copies of older inked drawings for inclusion in the ensemble. Damage, painted details, and architectural features are indicated in accordance with the Epigraphic Survey's drawing conventions. Collation of the component drawings in their various stages is in progress and will be completed by the epigraphic team according to the prescribed methodology, followed by on-site discussions, the transfer of corrections, transfer check, and final approval by the field director. Therefore, although the *tools* and *techniques* used to create this sophisticated digital facsimile are significantly different from those of the usual pen-and-ink drawings, having been especially selected and utilized to suit this particular situation, the *methodology* remains the same as in all of our documentation projects. The highly sophisticated digital technology employed for recording at Medinet Habu has greatly expanded the ways in which inscribed information can be recorded and processed, but can in no way replace the time and care taken on site to observe, understand, and interpret what is preserved on the wall.

EVALUATION

The Chicago House Method was devised by Professor Breasted for a specific purpose: to make an accurate facsimile record of ancient Egyptian wall reliefs and inscriptions. Its application is therefore particular to this type of material. It is not well-suited to recording some other types of decoration, such as polychrome painted tomb scenes, or for the illustration of sculpture in the round, although some principles of the Method, such as multiple collations of the copy in the presence of the original, are useful in any field documentation program. Moreover, the Epigraphic Survey is organized in such a way as to provide favorable conditions for application of our methodology, with a lengthy six-month field season each winter providing the time on site necessary to undertake the time-consuming drawing and collation processes. It is understood that, for many expeditions, the types of material to be recorded will dictate substantially different approaches to documentation and the exigencies of fieldwork and the limitations of time and resources will require a more abbreviated approach. In fact, it is inconceivable that all of Egypt's monumental heritage, with its great quantity and variety of textual and iconographic records, could be documented at such a high level of accuracy and detail as is characterized by the Survey's publications, and this was clearly understood by our founder. Breasted's vision was that a representative selection of the most significant Pharaonic records should be documented and published in an optimum fashion. Even this circumscribed objective could not always be achieved. The Oriental Institute expedition to Saqqara, which was originally intended to copy and publish the scenes in an extensive list of mastaba tombs in the Old Kingdom necropolis, had to be concluded after less than a decade in the field (1931–1940) due to lack of funds, with only one tomb (that of Mereruka) partially completed (The Sakkarah Expedition 1938). Today, funding and logistical considerations continue to delimit what the Epigraphic Survey can expect to accomplish in any given six-month field season, especially given the additional commitments to conservation and site management that our expedition has taken on during the past twenty years. Nevertheless, to preserve a representative sample of Egyptian inscribed scenes and written records through accurate documentation and high-quality publication remains the primary goal of our work. Our current dossier of epigraphic projects includes both standing and fragmentary monuments in the Medinet Habu temple precinct, thousands of relief fragments in the Luxor Temple blockyard, late Roman fresco decoration in the temple's Imperial Chamber, reused blocks in the Khonsu Temple at Karnak, and the exquisite but heavily damaged inscriptions in the Eighteenth Dynasty tomb of Nefersekheru (TT 107) in the Theban necropolis. For each of these sites, and for any future projects, the Chicago House Method will continue to provide the guiding methodology whereby the purpose of our expedition is to be fulfilled.

BIBLIOGRAPHY

Bell, L. 1987. "The Epigraphic Survey: Philosophy of Egyptian Epigraphy after Sixty Years' Practical Experience." In *Problems and Priorities in Egyptian Archaeology*, edited by J. Assmann, G. Burkard, and V. Davies, 43–55. London.

Breasted, J. H. 1930. Foreword. In *Medinet Habu I: Earlier Historical Records of Ramses III*, by the Epigraphic Survey, ix–xi. OIP 8. Chicago.

Breasted, J. H. 1933. "The Epigraphic Expedition." In *The Oriental Institute*, 187–223. The University of Chicago Survey XII. Chicago.

Dorman, P. F. 2008. "Epigraphy and Recording." In *Egyptology Today*, edited by R. H. Wilkinson, 77–97. Cambridge.

Hughes, G. R. 1952. "Recording Egypt's Ancient Documents." *Archaeology* 5:201–204.

Johnson, W. R. 2012. "The Epigraphic Survey and the 'Chicago Method.'" In *Picturing the Past: Imaging and Imagining the Ancient Middle East*, edited by J. Green, E. Teeter, and J. A. Larson, 31–38. OIMP 34. Chicago.

Kimpton, J. L., J. B. McClain, K. Vértes, and W. R. Johnson. 2010. "Preliminary Report on the Work of the Epigraphic Survey in the Temple of Khonsu at Karnak, 2008–2009." *JARCE* 46:113–124.

Nelson, H. 1930. Introduction. In *Medinet Habu I: Earlier Historical Records of Ramses III*, by the Epigraphic Survey, 8–10. OIP 8. Chicago.

Nims, C. 1972. "The Publication of Ramesside Temples in Thebes by the Oriental Institute." In *Textes et langages de l'Égypte pharaonique: cent cinquante années de recherches 1822–1972. Hommage à Jean-François Champollion*, 89–94. 2 vols. BdE 64. Cairo.

The Sakkarah Expedition. 1938. *The Mastaba of Mereruka*. 2 vols. OIP 31, 39. Chicago.

....

TYPICAL, ATYPICAL, AND DOWNRIGHT STRANGE EPIGRAPHIC TECHNIQUES

....

WILLIAM SCHENCK

MY interest in epigraphy goes back to my first excavation in Egypt. It was the late 1970s, and I had just graduated with a degree in Egyptology from Cambridge University. I arrived at Saqqara to work on the EES (Egypt Exploration Society) excavation at the tomb of Horemheb directed by Geoffrey Martin and Hans Schneider. Essentially, I was there to help with the drawing of the small finds, but I soon became fascinated by the drawings that Geoffrey was making of the tomb's carved wall relief. He would take rolls of plastic to the tomb and copy the decoration with markers, then return to the dig house in the evening and trace what he had drawn onto tracing paper. He would then erase the original inkings so he could reuse the plastic the next day. It was in this way that he slowly built up a record of the tomb's decoration that would culminate in its publication (Martin 1989). The copying of the decoration was very much the provenance of Geoffrey Martin. I looked on enviously, but only had a chance to try my hand at some epigraphy at the very end of the season, when I was asked to plan and draw the freestanding shrines in the rear courtyard of the tomb.

I guess they could be considered very large "small objects." Though essentially undecorated, they did display some graffiti: the outline of feet in several locations. So I got my chance to borrow some of Geoffrey's plastic and markers and copy the footprints in order to add them to the elevations I had already done of the shrines. I will always remember the pleasure of drawing directly from the object and trying to capture something of the nature of the roughly scratched and incised graffiti. It was very satisfying to try and duplicate the exact appearance of the original. In a way, this helped establish a direct link to the individual who had first stuck a foot up against the limestone slab and roughly scratched its outline. At that moment, I understood Geoffrey's proprietorial efforts in copying the tomb's decoration. It was something very personal. Just as I felt linked to the graffiti, I could only imagine how rewarding it must be for Geoffrey to translate the artistry of the ancient Egyptian sculptors into a new, modern medium. I could only dream of emulating him someday, though I never forgot the pleasure of drawing those footprints! I kept the memory at the back of my mind, but it would prove to be over a decade before I could return to epigraphy.

A Journeyman Illustrator

For the next several years, I was a journeyman archaeological illustrator working at sites in Egypt, Syria, Cyprus, and Greece, drawing primarily pottery and small objects. In 1980, I joined the Department of Egyptian Art in the Metropolitan Museum as the resident draftsman, drawing material in the collection for publication. Yet again, this was essentially drawing pottery and small objects, although, I was working my way up to coffins and furniture. I was also involved in the department's excavations in the field, directed by Dieter Arnold (1988) primarily at the Middle Kingdom pyramid site at Lisht. Although this work entailed surveying and planning architecture, I was still no closer to epigraphy. Ironically, after I left the department the site yielded masses of beautiful relief fragments that my successors had the pleasure to draw. I, on the other hand, would have to wait several more years before finding my way back to epigraphy.

Recording Reused Blocks

I left New York in 1990 and returned to England, working once again for the EES over several seasons drawing pottery at Memphis under the direction of Janine Bourriau. It was while in Egypt that I was approached by Horst Jaritz, director of the Swiss Institute in Cairo to lend a hand to Susanne Bickel, who had been given the task of recording a small group of reused Amenhotep III blocks. These limestone blocks had been found at the institute's excavations at the mortuary temple of Merneptah on the West Bank, Luxor. I confess I jumped at the chance, but despite Horst's faith in me, I had no clear idea how to proceed. The method I remembered Geoffrey Martin using at the tomb of Horemheb seemed inadequate for the size and scale of these enormous blocks. The Swiss Institute did not appear to have any preferred method or procedure, something I was to find was not unusual in the various organizations and projects for which I would work in the future, Chicago House being the notable exception. Susanne likewise had had no experience of epigraphy. So like two babes in the wood over the next several years we were to learn together.

Many of the blocks had been exposed for centuries on the site. They were badly worn and showed clear evidence of having been reused by Merneptah, with the later carving cutting across that of Amenhotep III usually at a completely different orientation. This was a characteristic feature that would have to be incorporated into the documentation. Since I was far more comfortable using pencil as opposed to marker, I opted to use matte acetate that would take pencil. A drawback to this decision was that the matte acetate was only semitransparent, but I hoped this would not be a problem since both the raised and sunk relief was deeply carved with clear edges. It would often prove helpful to clarify the carving with the fingertips and the sense of touch. Since the blocks were in full sun, it was necessary to construct awnings over them to diffuse the sunlight and prevent glare from the acetate. Finally, because of the size of many of the blocks, it was practical to cut the rolls of acetate into manageable sheets that could be overlapped so as to cover the entire carved surface.

This system worked well and fortunately proved flexible enough to accommodate a major group of even larger Amenhotep III limestone blocks that were discovered buried face down in a clean bed of sand serving as the foundations for the long vanished Merneptah second pylon. The blocks were magnificently carved with well-preserved paint. The sunk relief scenes, painted yellow, depicted Amenhotep III worshipping before different gods. The multicolored, raised relief blocks depicted the king's sed festival. Susanne realized that the blocks made up the outer walls and passage of a large gate that probably once stood in the southern enclosure wall of Amenhotep III's mortuary temple, which was originally located to the north of the site.

The first of these blocks to be discovered had to be raised up approximately fifty centimeters on car jacks in order for both Susanne and me to slide in on our backs and transfix the matte acetate sheets to the underside of the multi-ton block. We then proceeded to very gently draw the carved decoration. Fortunately, it proved to be sunk relief, and we were able to trace the well-preserved edges as much by feel as by sight. Light was virtually nonexistent, as one might imagine. Needless to say, health and safety did not really come into it, although there was a log tucked in under the block in case the jacks gave way. Ironically, as more blocks were found, they were all raised to a standing position by a rented crane, even the one we had been forced to crawl underneath, making them simplicity itself to draw (Figure III.5.1).

The decision to record the carving in pencil now proved fortuitous. The painted raised relief blocks had such detail and subtlety of carving that I felt it would have been difficult to convey with a marker. At this point in my career, I had next to no experience using markers and felt they were a clumsy medium for copying anything finely carved. I would eventually come to realize that the use of the marker could come to match that of the pencil, but that mastery would only come with future practice. My next project would provide me with that experience, and my method of recording would change again to meet the circumstances. I find that this is a defining feature of my epigraphy; the ability to adapt and modify my techniques according to the situation. For the Amenhotep III relief the pencil and matte acetate method had successfully communicated the delicate subtlety of the carving. The individual sheets were ultimately reduced by photocopy, joined together where necessary to make a complete block, and then

FIGURE III.5.1. The Amenhotep III block supported by a car jack and log at the Temple of Merneptah. Credit: William Schenck.

inked on a separate sheet at a scale of 1/3. The results of this, my first foray into epigraphy, can be seen in the Swiss Institute publication by Susanne Bickel (1997).

TOMB OF SUEMNIWET

In the early 1990s, I was working from site to site in Egypt mostly still drawing pottery and small objects but observing and absorbing ideas about epigraphy. I often visited Chicago House while in Luxor, and although their lauded documentation method was impressive, it was not particularly pertinent to my hands on, low-tech approach to epigraphy. Of more interest to me was the work being done by John Darnell and Debbie Darnell on their Desert Roads Project (Darnell et al. 2002). They used their weekends while working at Chicago House to go into the desert to record inscriptions and graffiti they found along the ancient tracks. For this purpose, they used cheap rolls of clear plastic bought in the local souq. The plastic was intended to cover car seats and upholstery. Despite being unstable and particularly vulnerable to heat, the plastic's very softness allowed it to be easily molded over irregular surfaces, and therefore, it was ideal for recording rock carvings. The facsimile copies could be made with permanent marker, but would need to be transferred to tracing paper, very much as Geoffrey Martin had done all those years ago at the tomb of Horemheb.

At this time, I joined the work that Betsy Bryan (2001) was doing in TT 92, the painted Eighteenth Dynasty tomb of Suemniwet on the West Bank in Luxor. Although I was employed to draw the objects, I saw that the Johns Hopkins students on the excavation were using large sheets of acetate and a variety of colored markers to indicate the different layers of paint on the many unfinished walls. For me, this was a revelation. I thought how useful color might be in recording different kinds of epigraphic information. Although not necessarily using it in the same way as did Betsy and her students, I imagined how color might indicate the treatment of the wall, almost like a conservator's condition report. A range of colors could indicate a variety of features such as carving, recarving, painting, underpainting and gridlines, damage, and even deliberate mutilation and usurpation. I was pulling together different strands from my recent work: precut, consistently sized, overlapping sheets from the Amenhotep III drawings at the temple of Merneptah, clear acetate or plastic and permanent markers borrowed from the Darnells' Desert Road Project, and the use of color markers lifted from the Johns Hopkins work in the tomb of Suemniwet. All I needed now was somewhere to apply my ideas! But before that was to happen, I journeyed down a kind of epigraphic cul-de-sac, a short detour, interesting but something I would not develop further. Ironically, it would be taken up in, of all places, Chicago House many years later!

More Reused Blocks

In the mid-1990s, while working regularly drawing pottery at Memphis, Ray Johnson, former artist and newly installed director of Chicago House, and I came up with a project to record some of the reused blocks in the Small Temple of Ptah at Memphis. Ray would take a short break from his duties in Luxor and spend some time at the EES dig house, "Beit Emery," a kind of working holiday. Ray, an expert on the decorative style of the reign of Amenhotep III, wrote his doctoral dissertation on the colonnade hall in Luxor Temple. Through observation, he had discovered on stylistic grounds that some of the blocks in the temple walls came from a structure dating to the time of Amenhotep III (Giddy et al. 1996). The only difficulty was that the decoration on the blocks was only visible either within the narrow gaps between the individual blocks where the mortar had fallen away, or under water, or both! The sad truth was the Small Temple of Ptah was partially submerged in a noxious lake of filthy ground water and possible sewage. Ever intrepid, Ray and I devised a system of using small squares of kitchen foil, approximately twenty by twenty centimeters, that I would place delicately over the areas of relief. I would then, often blindly, press gently but firmly over the surface with my fingertips to fix an impression of the carving. With sunk relief, I had to be very careful not to push too hard or I would tear the foil. Once the impression was complete I would raise the sheet out from between the blocks or from under the water and deposit it lightly in a large plastic carrier bag. It felt a bit like catching fish! One had to be very careful not to crush the foil sheets by packing too many sheets into the bag. If crushed or flattened the impressions would become distorted. In this way, as with the far larger Amenhotep III blocks, I gradually collected a series of overlapping foil sheets that would hopefully cover the entire decorated surface. In the evenings back at the dig house, I would outline the relief with black marker so as to make it more visible. Then would begin the painstaking procedure of transferring the decoration from the overlapping sheets to larger sheets of acetate, assembling a composite image of the decoration. Gradually, from sheet to sheet, block to block, Ray realized we had the makings of a barque shrine from the reign of Amenhotep III. The most impressive raised relief block revealed that it was in fact a barque shrine including the carved image of the barque of the god Ptah-Sokar-Osiris and in all likelihood must have been a part of the Amenhotep III expansion of the Path Temple complex. At some point it was pulled down and used as building material for the much later Small Temple of Ptah. From what I understand, this use of foil sheets was resurrected much later by Chicago House to take impressions of carved inscriptions between the flooring slabs of the Temple of Khonsu at Karnak (see chapter by McClain). I can only imagine that Ray Johnson never forgot those malodorous days on our hands and knees pushing kitchen foil into the cracks between stones rising up from a bog at Memphis!

Tomb of Hormose

In 1996, the opportunity to put my epigraphic ideas to use presented itself with Renee Friedman's invitation to work at Hierakonpolis. Although the site is renowned for its early Egyptian monuments, I was asked to copy one of the last New Kingdom tombs, that of Hormose from the reign of Ramesses XI for which she had received an ARCE (American Research Center in Egypt) grant to conserve and record. It was a painted, rock cut tomb badly blackened and would need to be cleaned before it could be drawn. Betsy Bryan (1999, 2000), through a fortunate stroke of serendipity, was to study the tomb from an art historical perspective, and we would often be able to work in the tomb together (Schenck 1999). For me, this would be an excellent opportunity to pass my thoughts by her and incorporate her comments and criticism into my evolving drawing methods. The tomb of Hormose was to prove for me a kind of epigraphic laboratory, a chance to put my ideas about epigraphy into practice.

Perhaps the best way to explain the method I devised for recording the tomb of Hormose and used in much of my subsequent work is to describe a usual day and the drawing decisions made accordingly. I began each day by unfurling a sheet of clear acetate, carefully cut the night before to the standard dimensions of sixty by ninety centimeters. This was not an arbitrary decision. The roll of acetate was sixty centimeters wide, and the ninety-centimeter width provided for a generous portion of any scene to be copied. And as I had already learned, these dimensions still meant that the sheet could be run through a standard photocopying machine. The sheets would eventually need to be reduced and joined together to create complete scenes as I had done at the temple of Merneptah. It should be said that I had already drawn a diagram plotting where each of the sheets would go and how much overlap would be required. A numbering system allowed me to identify each sheet and to be certain of covering the entire painted wall in a systematic fashion. The sheets needed to be placed gently against the wall and secured by small balls of Blu-Tack and masking tape carefully affixed only in damaged areas so as not to harm the fragile painted plaster.

On this particular day, I was intending to copy a badly faded group of mourning women. I was putting into effect my proposed method of using different colored permanent markers to denote the condition of the decoration. I made no attempt to reproduce the colors of the pigment used to paint the figures, as the range of color was far too large and the subtle blending of color too painterly. I began by outlining all of the damaged areas with the red pen. This usually took some time since so much of the plaster had fallen away. Before starting with the drawing itself, I had already inked simple blue crosses onto small squares of masking tape that were fixed to the wall. These crosses could then be copied onto the sheet to indicate the points of overlap with surrounding sheets as well as noting the vertical distance from a standard horizontal line measured throughout the tomb. This information would be critical when it came to joining up the individual sheets for publication. Next, I checked for areas of plaster that had popped off the wall, leaving behind a ghost outline of the original painted design. It seemed to be a feature of this tomb that particular paints, usually blue or green, reacted this way chemically with the plaster. These I would outline in red as well but mark with the letter *c* to distinguish them from the other less informative damage. All these years later, I have no idea what the *c* signified. Perhaps I used it because it was quick and simple to draw. Next, I would check for areas of color that were not originally outlined in red or black by the ancient Egyptian artists. Sometimes the final outlining did not match the placement of the underlying color. This color could extend over the outline or sometimes not even reach it. When this was the case, I would copy it in green. Often because of the damage to the painted surface or the removal of the upper layers of paint, red guidelines or even gridlines might show through. Wherever I found these lines, I added them in purple to clearly differentiate them from the final painted outlines. Finally, I was ready to begin the real job of copying the outlined scene with a black, superfine marker.

The group of women mourners was drawn by the ancient Egyptian artist in an almost sketch-like manner. Many lines indicating legs and arms seemed to vanish in a tangle, and it was hard to make out which limbs belonged to which women. After outlining several heads, I tried to follow their bodies through to the arch of their feet often ending up with too many legs! This was weird. Fortunately, the scene was fairly standardized in New Kingdom painting. And I would think of well-known examples like the painted funeral scene in the tomb of Ramose on the West Bank at Luxor and stare at the wall some more. This is a characteristic of my ongoing approach to epigraphy. Working at the wall is the time to understand what it is you are copying, not to just slavishly copy without actually understanding the sense of the scene. One would never have a better opportunity to understand the decoration than at that moment. And one should never remove the plastic without resolving the meaning of all the lines.

On this occasion, I remember when the penny dropped. At last, I made a crucial discovery. In and among the jumble of lines in the center of the grouping, I found what certainly must be a nose and lips. Directing a beam of sunlight with foil-covered cardboard, in the raking light, I saw three or four heads, shoulders, and sidelocks of little girls mixed in the scrum with the women. I finally understood all those extra legs! As a matter of principle, I tried to remove each sheet of acetate before the end of the day and not leave it up overnight. Therefore, I now needed to finish the ladies before the end of the working day. It would be a race against time. Once I knew what I was looking for, the work went much faster, and I would see more small details that I had missed earlier: curled fingers, locks of hair, etc. This is but one small example of the detective work needed in copying the tomb of Hormose.

Once the sheet was finished, it needed to be peeled gently from the wall, rolled, and placed in a plastic tube for safekeeping. I had learned through hard experience that the acetate contained static electricity and could on no account touch any of the dust in the tomb, of which there was inevitably a great deal! If this happened, the plastic seemed to suck the dust up like a Hoover. Any attempt to wipe off the dust would scratch the surface of the acetate, rendering it opaque. This was another good reason for removing each sheet every day, so there was no risk of the sheet falling down during the night. Adequate time was always needed for this operation, so that the hours and hours of hard work were not jeopardized in a rushed few minutes. Only at this point was I done for the day.

The painted tomb of Hormose was a baptism by fire. The complexity of the decoration demanded an extensive use of various colored markers. For future, simpler epigraphy, I would reduce my color range to four: black for outlines, red for damage, blue for crosses and measurements, and green for painted edges. But in Hormose's tomb, I had learned that my copying method worked and that it had the advantage of being flexible enough to expand or contract according to what a painted or carved scene demanded. The basic tenets of overlapping measured sheets, clear acetate, and colored permanent markers I would rely on for all future work.

SAQQARA, MUT TEMPLE, AND A RETURN TO SUEMNIWET

My next three major projects provided me with the opportunity of applying what I had learned in Hormose. The first, beginning in 1999, launched my ongoing association with Alain Zivie and the documentation of the New Kingdom tombs at Saqqara excavated by the MAFB (French Archaeological Mission at the Bubasteion). Over the next decade, I copied the rock cut tombs of Thutmose ("the Tomb of the Artist," I.19), dating to the reign of Amenhotep III, Raia/Hatiay, dating from the transition between Akhenaten to Tutankhamun (I.27), and Maïa (I.20), dating to the reign of Tutankhamun. Interestingly, the first tomb I worked in was that of Thutmose, who was a "scribe of the necropolis" and seems to have decorated his own tomb with examples of his work. Some walls were either fully carved or fully painted, while others were left unfinished with only the red guidelines and roughly sketched figures visible. There was even one painted standing image of Thutmose himself, proudly holding his scribal kit bearing the cartouche of the king, Amenhotep III. The tomb of Maïa, on the other hand, was entirely carved primarily in raised relief, depicting magnificent images of herself in her role as wet nurse to the young king Tutankhamun. The tomb of Raia/Hatiay, entirely painted in the Amarna style, consists of small registers, which are densely packed with groups of figures and are very reminiscent in style of the tomb of Hormose. I drew all three of these tombs and later others as well, using the techniques developed at Hierakonpolis. The results can be seen in Alain's publications (2009, 2013).

From 2004 to 2008, I rejoined Betsy Bryan for her work at the Temple of Mut in Karnak. The Johns Hopkins excavation had been finding masses of decorated blocks from the Hatshepsut/Tuthmosis III temple structure used as foundation material for the later temple. This consisted of both raised and sunk relief but as was to be expected, very little remaining paint. The blocks often needed both consolidation and conservation because of damage from water and salts. Since the blocks had been parts of standing walls for many centuries, they often exhibited evidence of massive recarving. The real challenge of this work was to try and find the telltale signs of any alteration to the surface or reconfiguration of the carved figures and inscriptions. I had had earlier experience with these issues when working on the Amenhotep III material reused by Merneptah, but there, the older blocks were primarily reused as building material. At the Temple of Mut, the situation was far subtler since the decoration had been modified while the blocks were still a part of a standing monument. Again, selecting a particular color to indicate recarving came to my rescue and helped tremendously in disentangling often contradictory evidence. Recarving and repainting is so common in Egyptian temples and tombs that I was pleased that the Mut material gave me the opportunity to come to grips with it. As in the tomb of Hormose, I again greatly benefited from Betsy's wealth of experience and insight in adapting my epigraphy method to this new challenge. In a sense, this working relationship was to come full circle when she asked me to return to the tomb of Suemniwet to instigate an epigraphy program to copy the painted decoration that could complement the earlier work of the students, which had initially focused on the painting process.

Over two seasons, beginning in 2009, I returned to TT 92, Suemniwet's tomb that dates to the reign of Amenhotep II. I was able to put together a small team including Keli Alberts with whom I had worked at the Temple of Mut and using the talents of both the MoA (Ministry of Antiquities) inspectors, Omar Abou Zaid and Hassan Ramadan Aglan, over subsequent seasons. The large decorated first room with its broad walls and high ceilings was ideal for letting each individual take over one entire scene. We often needed to stand on ladders and tables in lieu of scaffolding. Since neither Keli nor either of the inspectors had ever done this kind of large-scale epigraphy, I found I was instructing them in the method that I had been using now for a number of years. It seems

FIGURE III.5.2. Keli Alberts and Hassan Ramadan Aglan copying scenes in the Tomb of Suemniwet, TT 92. Credit: William Schenck.

unsurprising in retrospect that I had moved somehow from a kind of epigraphy apprenticeship, picking up skills as I went along, to a mature period when I had a flexible system that I could adapt to a variety of circumstances, and finally reach the point where I was teaching others my own personal method of epigraphy. The drawing in the tomb of Suemniwet was the first time I experienced the satisfaction of training and then working with a team of epigraphers (Figure III.5.2). This experience led to the most recent phase of my epigraphic career, training and encouraging a new, younger generation of archaeological illustrators.

Teaching Epigraphic Recording

Since 2005, I had been teaching archaeological illustration at Giza on behalf of AERA (Ancient Egypt Research Association), to inspectors of the MoA. Although initially limited to pottery and object drawing, I was able to incorporate an element of epigraphy thanks to the access we had to the Giza monument field. The first generation of advanced illustration students was able to copy a large carved stone lintel, suspended over the courtyard of the Fifth Dynasty mastaba of Nensedjerkai, G 2100-II. They worked simultaneously with markers on large, overlapping clear plastic sheets, four meters above the pavement below. Eventually, the sheets were reduced and joined together, producing a facsimile of the complete lintel. I took this memory with me of how epigraphy could be taught to students if there was the possibility of access to an actual standing monument, either tomb or temple, carved or painted, which could become a kind of classroom.

The opportunity came in 2014, when I was approached by JJ Shirley and ARCE to teach epigraphy in TT 110, the New Kingdom tomb of Djehuty, which dates to the reigns of Hatshepsut/Tuthmosis III. The clearance of the tomb and its subsequent excavation and conservation had already facilitated field schools for local MoA inspectors focusing on archaeology and conservation. Now it would be possible to use the cleared and cleaned tomb for teaching epigraphy. For me, this was a dream come true. JJ and I created a syllabus that included not only drawing but also the research skills that would allow the students to fully publish any monument they recorded. We were both in complete agreement that the drawings the students produced would be an integral part of any publication of the tomb. My experience at Giza with AERA had impressed on me that the students would work more diligently if they appreciated that what they were doing was for real. The epigraphy method I have elucidated in this chapter has become my teaching template for ERFS (Epigraphy and Research Field School). Because of the restrictive size of the tomb, only five students could be taken at a time. But an advantage to the small number of students meant that JJ and I could give them one-on-one attention (Figure III.5.3). This intensity was increased with the assistance of Sayed Mamdouh

FIGURE III.5.3. William Schenck teaching epigraphy in the Tomb of Djehuty, TT 110, during the Epigraphy and Research Field School. Credit: JJ Shirley.

and Yaser Mahmoud Hussein, both of whom were already familiar with the tomb because they had taught illustration in the earlier ARCE field school.

As I had done at Suemniwet and at Giza, I wanted the students to feel that they were part of a team, not in competition with one another, but rather sharing and helping one another. Despite the tight conditions inside the tomb, each student had an assigned area of a wall to copy. Only the two carved stelae, false door, doorjambs, and lintel were appropriate for teaching purposes, so it was primarily inscriptions that were being copied. They worked on sized acetate sheets that would eventually be joined together. They worked with color markers indicating carving, damage, measurements, paint traces, and so forth. They learned to look for the bevel of the sunk relief and to appreciate the use of the chisel in creating the inscription. They developed sympathy for the characteristic early Eighteenth Dynasty style of the carving. They paid particular attention to traces of recarving especially in reference to the images, names, and titles of Hatshepsut. They learned to clean and collate their drawings at the end of the school. They maintained a portfolio of copies of their work that they were able to take away with them, as well as the epigraphic drawing kit provided by the field school.

They now had a comprehensive understanding of one particular method of epigraphy, which, of course, is not to say it is the only method. The individual sheets drawn from the walls or the blocks or any other surface could now be photocopied and reduced, joined together, and then inked manually. They could also be scanned into the computer, stitched together using various softwares, and then digitally inked. This process opens up all kinds of exciting possibilities for the future, but is at the same time firmly grounded in the past. It is something that was missing at the beginning of my career: a formulated method of epigraphy. I feel that, at the very least, this is something my work and my teaching has addressed.

Bibliography

Arnold, D. 1988. *The Pyramid of Senwosret I: The South Cemeteries of Lisht 1*. PMMA 22. New York.

Bickel, S. 1997. *Untersuchungen im Totentempel des Merenptah in Theben 3: Tore und andere wiederverwendete Bauteile Amenophis' III*. BBf 16. Stuttgart.

Bryan, B. M. 1999. "The Artists in the Tomb of Hormose." *Nekhen News* 11:20.

Bryan, B. M. 2000. "The Artists in the Tomb of Hormose, Part II." *Nekhen News* 12:23.

Bryan, B. M. 2001. "Painting Techniques and Artisan Organization in the Tomb of Suemniwet, Theban Tomb 92." In *Colour and Painting in Ancient Egypt*, edited by W. V. Davies, 63–72. London.

Darnell, J. C., D. Darnell, R. Friedman, and S. Hendrickx. 2002. *Theban Desert Road Survey in the Egyptian Western Desert, I: Gebel Tjauti Rock Inscriptions 1–45 and Wadi el-Hôl rock Inscriptions 1–45*. OIP 119. Chicago.

Giddy, L., D. Jeffreys, J. Bourriau, G. T. Martin, P. T. Nicholson, et al. 1996. "Fieldwork, 1995–6: Memphis, Saqqara, North Saqqara, Tell el-Amarna, Buto, Gebel Dokhan, Qasr Ibrim." *JEA* 82:1–22.

Martin, G. T. 1989. *The Memphite Tomb of Ḥoremḥeb, Commander-in-chief of Tutʾankhamūn, I: The Reliefs, Inscriptions, and Commentary*. EES EM 55. London.

Schenck, W. 1999. "An Artist in Hormose: A Day in the Life." *Nekhen News* 11:22–23.

Zivie, A. 2009. *La tombe de Maïa: Mère nourricière du roi Toutânkhamon et Grande du Harem; (Bub. I.20)*. Les tombes du Bubasteion à Saqqara 1. Toulouse.

Zivie, A. 2013. *La tombe de Thoutmes, directeur des peintres dans la Place de Maât (BUB. I.19)*. Les tombes du Bubasteion à Saqqara 2. Toulouse.

CHAPTER III.6

··

ONLINE PUBLICATION
OF MONUMENTS

··

WILLEKE WENDRICH

EPIGRAPHY is closely linked to the publication of monuments, because almost all texts and images that are its subject occur on the walls of temples or tombs. In an overview of the history of epigraphy published in 1976, Caminos discussed a century of different approaches. Rather than starting his account in 1875, he felt compelled to commence with the 1849–1859 twelve-volume publication by Lepsius, whom he praised for what he clearly saw as the most important aspects of epigraphic work: high standards of accuracy, draftsmanship, presentation, and completeness. He stressed the importance of conveying "*the actual appearance of the wall*" (Caminos 1976, 5) by which he meant that the publication should provide not only the direction and grouping of the hieroglyphs, but also indications of damage, gaps, block edges, and frames. He criticized editions with printed hieroglyphs, such as those by the specialized press of the Institut français d'archéologie orientale, and reproductions of the texts from left to right in horizontal lines with standardized hieroglyphic forms, such as Sethe's Pyramid Text edition (1908–1922). His emphasis on the importance of the context was, however, very limited: he defined epigraphic context as the figures, frames, and other graphic elements that surround and in his view merely complement the texts.

Earlier epigraphic publications actually had a broader understanding of the context of inscriptions or wall paintings, encompassing the relative location of themes, texts, and images, but also the orientation of the inscribed wall and the location in the tomb or temple. To do this on paper required an organization of the publication that enabled placement of drawings or photographs through visual protocols. There are different ways to express the location and orientation of texts and decorative schemes. Perhaps the best known approach is that of the sketch plan with wall numbers and the in-text specification of location and register (e.g., Porter and Moss 1927). The combination of plans with wall elevations on which wall sections were numbered and correlated to published plates was a more precise way of indicating location and was common in many early publications (e.g., Blackman 1911).

With the increased use of technology, the approach to epigraphy has changed markedly. Photography is a standard part of the workflow. Digital photography as the basis for digital vector drawings is another innovation that influences the epigraphic methods (Manuelian 1998). Apart from the possibility to make corrections, working with layers of visual information that can be shown or hidden greatly facilitates the work. Vector drawings are, furthermore, small and can yet be printed at high quality, as well as stored and easily shared.

There are many other advantages to working digitally. The application and potential of digital techniques in epigraphy, as well as archaeology, have increased exponentially in the past decade. Three-dimensional scanning has become an affordable and exact way of documenting surfaces. Enhanced photography, such as cross-polarized light and infrared photography, reflectance transformation imaging (RTI), and polynomial texture mapping (PTM), surpass the human eye in capability of discerning worn hieroglyphs, toolmarks, use traces, and intentional or accidental damage (Piquette 2016). At present, these techniques are used in concert with traditional epigraphy, for instance in the Corpus of Ptolemaic Inscriptions (CPI 2014).

Photography, scanning, tracing, or drawing can only convey what is present. Deeply carved damage and wall surface destruction, dismantling of temples, and reuse of building material all have taken their toll on the vulnerable stone surfaces. Reconstruction of ancient structures has proven to be possible, especially for the Karnak Temple complex, which has known a long history of construction, deconstruction, remembering, and forgetting (Wendrich 2014). Epigraphy of blocks that have been reused has proven to provide vital information on the possible existence of earlier temple phases, such as a New Kingdom Khonsu Temple. This temple, which originally was dated to the Twentieth Dynasty, when under Ramesses III older monuments were quarried, includes many reused blocks, some of which are from monuments on the West Bank of the Nile, but many are from structures that seem to have been part of at least two New Kingdom phases of the Khonsu Temple. Blocks from the early New Kingdom (Thutmose IV) attest to an Eighteenth Dynasty temple, while remains dated to several Nineteenth Dynasty kings (Seti I, Ramesses II, Merneptah, usurped by Seti II) were found, as well as a blosck of Herihor. The shape of the sandstone blocks, together with the texts and scenes in relief, might enable a reconstruction of the hall or court of Seti I that was dismantled, while the blocks were reused in the subfloor of the court. The order in which these blocks were built into the new structure provides additional evidence (Kimpton et al. 2010; McClain et al. 2011).

Using computers to aid in the reconstruction of relief scenes is not new. Organizing the *talatat* blocks recovered from the ninth pylon of Karnak Temple was in fact one of the earliest applications of computerized analysis in relation to epigraphy and architecture, an effort that is still ongoing (Smith and Kristof 1970; Prévôt 2013). Advanced computerized techniques are also used in palaeographic research, making use of image recognition, measurements of ink stroke thickness and direction, and character forms and variations to recognize individual hands. These are combined qualitative and quantitative methods, used mostly on handwritten cursive texts in different scripts and languages (e.g., Aussems and Brink 2009; Rajan 2017).

In Egyptology, however, the earliest hand-drawn epigraphic records provide vital information on those monuments that today are less complete or long gone. Combining such records with a restudy of the same monuments with modern technology adds information, also because research interests have shifted. Emphasis on sculpting methods, use marks, or graffiti provide insight in the formation, use, and *nachlass* of monuments. It enables the consideration of the visual record of tombs and temples in relation to the architecture and use of sacred space, an approach that, although to some extent speculative, enriches the understanding of the relationships between texts, imagery, and placement.

Caminos's admonitions that Sethe's text editions have lost their context is, however, equally true for the epigraphic works he so admired. Even if the publication indicates where a certain relief was situated, it has become isolated from the three-dimensional space, and consequently it has become very difficult to understand the visual message in the context of the entire tomb or temple because location, elevation, orientation, and narrative development through space are key factors in the religious decorative program. This can only be understood if epigraphic publications take the space into account. With the technology available today, it is possible to present the results of detailed epigraphic work in a way that retains the sense of space and the relationships between the different elements of the visual program.

To fully explore the spatial and visual relationships within the epigraphic record, monuments should be studied as three-dimensional objects. This is possible using a variety of digital techniques that allow the creation of three-dimensional models of the monuments and all wall surfaces. High quality three-dimensional virtual reality (3DVR) models can be created in different ways, but have in common that they can be used both as a record in themselves, or as scaffolding for epigraphic records obtained by other (including nondigital) means. Linked to 3D modeling as a research method, ideally the models should also be published, to be accessible together with a printed publication or integrated in a digital publication.

In this contribution, I survey the different methods of 3DVR modeling, outline their advantages and challenges, and provide a discussion of existing initiatives and current options for publication. Central in the assessment of whether a method and the result-ing model are suitable is the question *whether the 3DVR publication explicates its goals and attains these*. 3DVR models come in many forms from simple wire frames to hyper-realistic alternate realities, and from crude impressionistic outlines to highly researched interpretations. The criteria that follow are not a means to determine what the "best" type of modeling is, but rather tools to define different approaches and their suitability in addressing particular goals.

a. The model is explicitly linked to a research goal.
b. The model gives an adequate representation of the space and the visual program.
c. The model allows the discovery of new information, by combining existing information in new ways.
d. The model indicates levels of (un)certainty and interpretation.

e. The model is interactive, it allows users to move through the virtual spaces at will.

f. The interface allows searches.

g. The model is accessible and sustainable.

My proposition is that for Egyptology there are three main forms of 3D online publication of monuments that are highly relevant and a fundamental improvement on traditional ways of publishing epigraphy in printed books or as online fixed texts with illustrations such as PDFs. The first is an interactive reconstruction of a monument, textured with high-resolution photographs or drawings in the correct positions on the walls.

The second is a model of the monument to which localized documents are linked. Each wall section can have multiple documents attached to it, such as photos under different kinds of light, drawings, 3D wall scans (see chapter by Revez), commentary, and interpretations. The third is an architectural model with a focus on layout, routing, or immersive elements, such as acoustics and lighting. The first type of 3DVR model would address criteria b and e: the model should be an adequate presentation of the space through which users can move freely. The second type is characterized by criteria b and c: by using the space as interface, through which the researcher interacts with aggregated documents and media, new information and insights can be gained.

The third type would be guided by criteria a, b, and c: designed to explore particular questions, such as how sound travels, how much space a sacred bark would need to make a turn, or what part of the texts gets highlighted by the sun through a roof opening at a certain time of the day or year. These types of questions can be explored in a 3DVR model, provided the reconstruction is based on solid, documented information and users can move through freely.

For model types 1 and 3, the textured and architectural models, it is, furthermore, crucial to indicate levels of (un)certainty and interpretation (d), while for model type 2, linked to the aggregate of sources, it is probably important to build in a search functionality (f). Other desiderata might be the ability to create references to the model, or particular parts of it, to enable interaction with printed or online textual arguments. Such references are also important to allow others to cite the model and refer to particular parts of it that illustrate an argument.

For all types of interactive models, the last point (g) may be of vital importance: how important is it that these models be preserved? In other words: should they be accessible in five years' time? Ten years' time? And should they be accessible in the same form, or is it sufficient to preserve the underlying data for the long term? In digital preservation, it is recommended to decide what the "significant properties" of an asset are in order to determine how to proceed with preservation.[1] Publication of monuments using 3DVR models requires models that can be shared and accessed. The software in which models are constructed potentially hampers the scholars' ability to distribute 3DVR publications.

---

[1] The Archaeological Data Service has published guidelines on this: http://guides. archaeologydataservice.ac.uk/g2gp/3d_3-1.

The main rule in a constantly changing technological environment, with new commercial as well as open source products becoming available each year, is to only work with software that can both read standard formats and can save every aspect of the produced or reworked 3DVR models into standard formats. Typically, a 3DVR project employs several software packages to reach the desired result, and with each import and export, the software might break or distort some of the information. Access is at present dependent on having the appropriate soft- and hardware, but this is a rapidly changing technological landscape. Nonproprietary file formats, such as OBJ, COLLADA (COLLAborative Design Activity) and X3D, facilitate access to models despite changes to commercial software packages. Real-time VR requires continuous recalculation of the geometry from which the model is built and takes considerable computing power. The video card is another element that needs to be up to displaying these changes without hitches. High-end gaming computers are the hardware of choice at this time, because computer games are dealing with the same issues.

So what software and workflow steps are we discussing, if we want to create 3DVR models? In general, such models are at present created in three different ways: through 3D scanning, through Structure from Motion and thirdly, through building a geometry from architectural drawings and measurements (CAD and 3D modeling).

Computer-aided design (CAD) drawings can be made from maps, plans, and elevations, which have been published in historical reports. These can be based on measurements taken by early explorers of buildings that are no longer extant. The accuracy of measurements varies and can be checked through ground truthing if the buildings still exist. This is the method used by the Ancient Egyptian Architecture Online (Aegaron) project,[2] which publishes standardized plans and elevations, but not 3D reconstructions (Figure III.6.1). Depending on how well a building has been preserved, 3D modeling usually requires a high to very high level of speculation. Wall heights and roof constructions usually are unattested and have to be reconstructed. Door openings, the location of windows, and wall paintings or reliefs may have been located above the level that was preserved, and therefore their location and appearance have to be surmised. CAD software exists in commercial and open formats, such as BRL-CAD, FreeCAD, and LibreCAD. It is possible to link additional information to each part of the model, or the model as a whole by using BIM (Building Information Modeling), or adaptations focused on cultural heritage (HBIM) or a more general scholarly application (SBIM).

While CAD software was developed for architectural and engineering purposes, there are a variety of other 3D modeling software tools that can be used to create reproductions. This type of software is a tool to construct and modify 3D graphic models of almost anything, including human forms, and allows users to store and export the models once they are completed. Most of these software packages are commercial, but there are some free packages that support exporting to commonly used file types with extensions such as .obj and .dfx. Examples of modeling freeware are SketchUp and Blender 3D.

---

[2] http://dai.aegaron.ucla.edu, a collaboration between UCLA and the DAIK, funded by the National Endowment for the Humanities (NEH) and the Deutsche Forschungsgemeinschaft (DFG) under grant numbers HG-50012–09 and HG-50046–13.

PLATE I Image of Atet, Meidum. © Boyo Ockinga. See Chapter I.3.

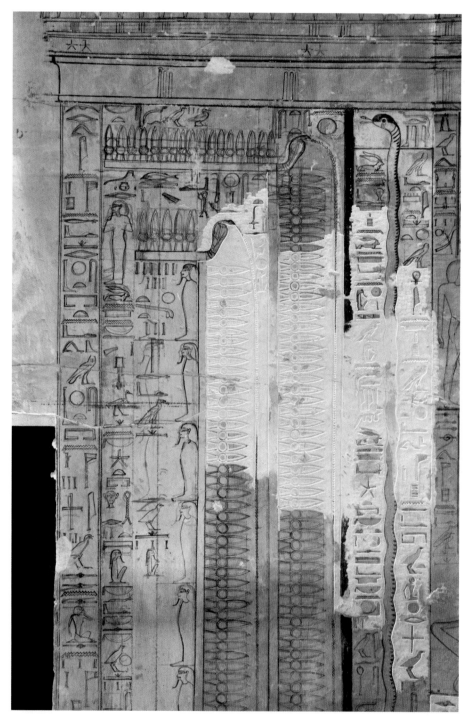

PLATE II Detail of a wall under decoration in the burial chamber of the tomb of Horemheb in the Valley of the Kings, Biban el-Moluk (KV 57), showing material traces of the initial drafting, the finalized drawing or pattern, and the beginning of the stone cutting operation. Note the abbreviated sequence of motifs in the frieze of stars and the cavetto corniche. Author's picture. See Chapter I.6.

PLATE 11 Mutnofret offering to her parents in the Dynasty 18 tomb of Amenemope (TT 29). The wall paintings provide precise information about work procedures. An offering scene on the long hall's south side displays the daughter of Amenemope's cousin Sennefer offering to her parents. The image captions consist of eight columns each for Mutnofret and her parents, and the orientation of hieroglyphs follows the figures. The actual work process for the text panel was executed in two steps from left to right—the easier way for right-handers—as indicated by a decreasing quality of details in this direction. The area division is not text-/content-related, but based on ergonomic work conditions. The first column of the daughter's text belongs to the right work zone with the texts for Sennefer and his wife. Courtesy of Mission Archéologique belge dans la Nécropole Thébaine. Photo credit: Matjaz Kacicnik. See Chapter I.9.

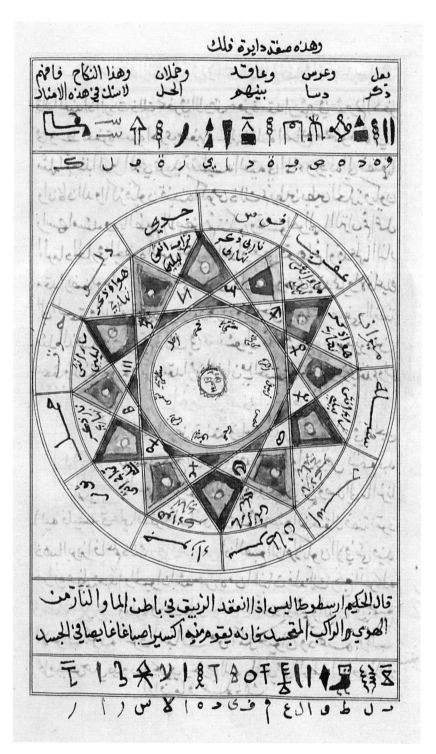

PLATE IV *Kitāb al-aqālīm as-sabʿa* (Forschungsbibliothek Gotha of the University Erfurt, MS orient. 1261, 23b). See Chapter II.3.

PLATE V Chapel of Achoris at Karnak. The condition of walls is in sepia; Traunecker, Le Saout, and Masson 1981, pl. XI, scene 19. See Chapter III.1.

P.C.

Philippe-Arrhidée, Mur Sud, Scène 24

PLATE VI Karnak, outer southern wall of Philipp Arrhidaeus' bark shrine. Credit: CNRS-Centre franco-égyptien d'étude des temples de Karnak © Cnrs-Cfeetk/P. Calassou. See Chapter III.3.

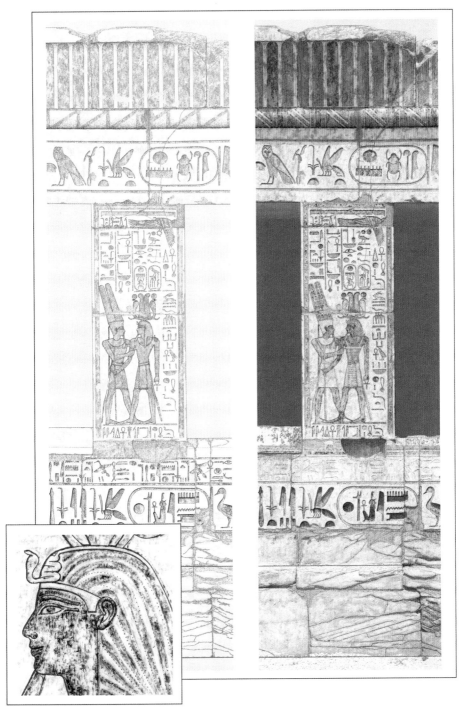

PLATE VII Color-enhanced representation of the Eighteenth Dynasty façade in the Small Amun Temple at Medinet Habu comparing the late Ramesside and Ptolemaic (with photo background) appearance of the same section (detail). Courtesy of the Oriental Institute of the University of Chicago. See Chapter III.7.

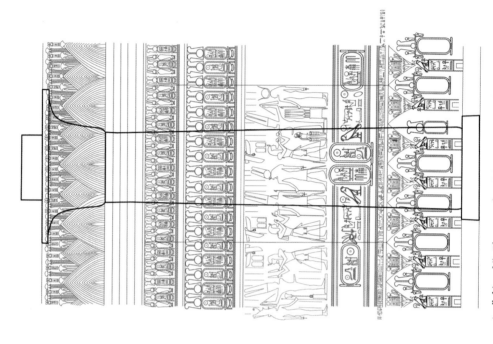

PLATE VIII Orthophoto of an unwrapped column ("first generation" déroulé). Photo credit: ATM-3D. Facsimile of an unwrapped column based on déroulé. Photo credit: E. Feleg. See Chapter III.8.

PLATE IX 3D visualization of the west wall of the subterranean chapel of Queen Meresankh III, Giza mastaba G 7530-sub, based on HU-MFA Expedition epigraphy from the 1920s. 3D model by David Hopkins and the Giza Project, Harvard University. See Chapter III.9.

PLATE X A view of the Sennefer Hotel, in the hamlets of Sheikh Abd al-Qurna, prior to demolition. Credit: Gemma Tully 2008. See Chapter III.16.

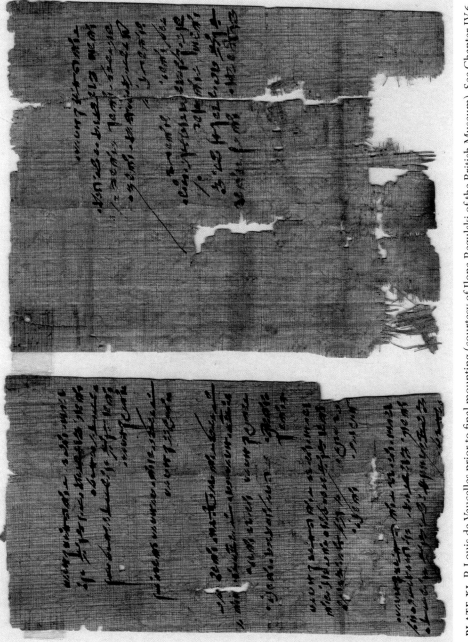

PLATE XI P. Louis de Vaucelles prior to final mounting (courtesy of Ilona Regulski of the British Museum). See Chapter IV.6.

PLATE XII Part of a hymn from year 2 Ramesses V with Amennakht's signature in the antepenultimate line (O. Turin CG 57002 verso; © Museo Egizio di Torino). See Chapter IV.10.

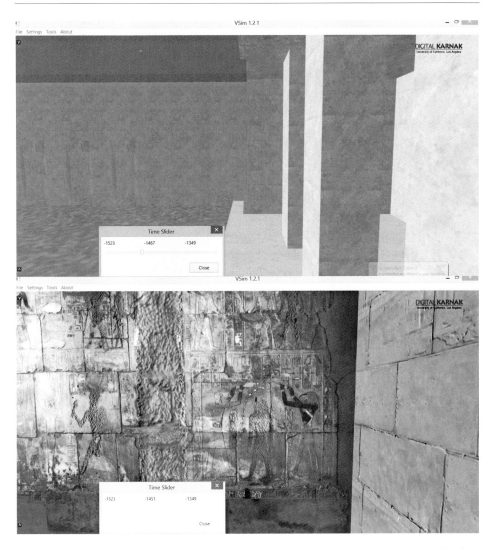

FIGURE III.6.1. The Middle Kingdom court of Karnak Temple (top) and the north wall of the Palace of Maat built in this same spot. The relief shows the present condition, with erasure of the figure of Hatshepsut as part of the *damnatio memoriae* by Thutmose III.

A 3DVR model of the Temple of Amun at Karnak was created with (commercial) 3D modeling software (3ds Max and Maya). The model could not be made available online because it was too large to download and run. Instead the model was used to create stills and fly-through videos for the Digital Karnak website.[3] The strength of the Karnak model is twofold, because it shows spatial relations as well as development through time (Figure III.6.2). It was created by modeling the geometry of the architecture in different

[3] http://dlib.etc.ucla.edu/projects/Karnak/archive, a UCLA project, funded by the National Endowment for the Humanities (NEH) under grant number EE-50432–07.

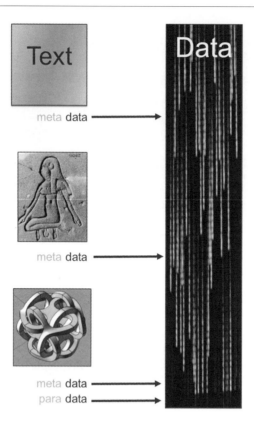

FIGURE III.6.2. Relationship between texts, images, models, and the datasphere.

phases of its existence, based on the publications of the Centre franco-égyptien d'étude des temples de Karnak (CFTEEK) and others who worked in this large religious complex. The resulting architectural wire frame was textured with repeated generic photographs of the Karnak mudbrick and limestone walls. Where available, the texturing was done with photographs of the actual wall reliefs in situ, which enables the user of the model (but not the website) to explore a variety of questions focused, for instance, on the location of particular ritual reliefs in relation to the place where the rituals were performed. The development of the temple complex through time can be explored by making use of a 3DVR viewer, VSim, developed at UCLA.[4] This viewer includes a time slider with which the user can see the construction and demolition of buildings in Karnak. Similarly, the Digital Giza Project at Harvard University has made several fly-through videos of the 3D model of the Giza Plateau available as part of the extensive archives of photographs, notebooks, and drawings on Giza from eleven different institutions that are made available through the website.[5]

---

[4] https://idre.ucla.edu/research/active-research/vsim, a UCLA project directed by Lisa Snyder, funded by the National Endowment for the Humanities (NEH) under grant numbers HD-50958–10 (DH start-up) and HK-50164–14 (DH Implementation).

[5] http://giza.fas.harvard.edu/, a Harvard University project directed by Peter Der Manuelian.

3D scanning requires specialized hard- and software and produces a point cloud in which the position of each point is defined in space by an X, Y, and Z coordinate. The resulting files are usually very large, depending on the resolution and size of the scan. To record an entire temple would require a set-up of the scanner in each room or courtyard as well as at positions all around the outside of the temple. The advantage of scanning over 3D modeling is that this method also records the reliefs in three dimensions and can be performed at a very high resolution so that the scan is a millimeter-precise record of the wall reliefs at the moment of scanning. This technique is, therefore, also suited to monitor the condition of reliefs. Because the scanners can be combined with high resolution cameras, the point cloud can be textured with the photograph, providing a very detailed reproduction of the original.

Structure from Motion (SfM) is a method in which an algorithm recreates the motion of a photo camera in relation to a building or object and based on this, calculates the position and shape of the object in three dimensions. Any digital camera, even a camera phone, can be used to create a large number of overlapping photographs ranging from many-sided overviews to detail shots. The geometry of the building or object is reconstructed and the resulting model can be automatically textured with the photographs, including the reliefs and wall paintings that are present at the time of the photographic recording. Depending on the resolution and camera positions, the reliefs can be shown in considerable detail. No specific equipment is needed, but georeferencing of control points provides greater accuracy. There are several commercial software solutions for this type of model building.

A substantial difference between the major methods of model creations is that 3D scanning and Structure from Motion produce a record of extant remains only, while CAD and modeling software allow the user to create elements that no longer exist. This becomes important when we use older records from a period when more of the monument was intact. The latter two also enable the creation of more far-reaching reconstructions and even allow the use of the model to test or present theories. In the Egyptological literature, this has been done so far through drawings, for instance, the three different theories on how the upper level of the temple of Montuhotep II in Deir el-Bahri should be reconstructed: with a pyramid, a square top, or a tumulus (Naville 1910; Arnold 1974; Stadelman 1991). If we want to create a three-dimensional representation of early epigraphic records, we will need to engage in substantial reconstruction especially if both the reliefs or paintings, and the walls on which these rested, no longer exist.

The look and feel of 3DVR models should depend very much on their purpose and can range from schematic to photorealistic. For a three-dimensional display of drawings or photographs made by eighteenth-, nineteenth-, or early twentieth-century travelers or researchers, a schematic reconstruction of the walls is more effective than an attempt to create an "authentic" atmosphere by imitating the structure and color of the local stone. It also enables the modeler to indicate which part of the model is no longer extant and had to be reconstructed. Transparency or dotted lines can be used to show that a wall or roof height reconstruction is uncertain. Photorealistic models can be useful for specific research questions related to experiential archaeology, which attempts to define the factors that would have influenced the experience of the users of a space. Introducing variations of natural light, oil lamps, or torches can be relevant in relation to understanding what parts of the texts and other visual clues would actually have been visible and legible. Photorealism or hyperrealism in a VR model also changes the interaction and sets expectations. Because of the similarity to gaming, research models that aim to be photorealistic are usually disappointing, because they do not reach the hyperrealistic environment that the multimillion dollar gaming industry offers. A realistic environment also might create subconscious expectations that the model offers an interactive environment with moving avatars. More problematic, however, is the suggestion of reality, truth, and veracity that a hyperrealistic environment presents:, it colors the understanding and dampens a critical approach.

For the scholarly use of 3DVR, it is of utmost important that every modeling decision be made explicit and be available with the model, either as a separate document or embedded. Descriptions, images, and other sources should be listed, together with a list of decisions that are based on these. In the Aegaron project, this is done by providing a drawing log for each downloadable drawing. In Digital Karnak, it is a separate document. The website for Digital Karnak mentions for each architectural element what the reconstruction of appearance and placement is based on.[6] The term used for the information that underlies reconstructions is *paradata*. These differ from metadata, because they give information on the sources and creation process for a 3DVR model, rather than on the model itself. The creators of the model are mentioned in the metadata, and the publications and drawings on which the model is based are the paradata. These two terms, "metadata" and "paradata," are sometimes useful, but the more we consider the digital realm as a knowledge continuum, the less important the distinction becomes. Ultimately the model, the digitized sources, and the names of persons are all data that come into play depending on the research questions we formulate.

Already in the development phase, when the basic research is done, and during the modeling phase, decisions have to be made on how to present the model and the related information. As mentioned previously, output in widely used formats, such as OBJ, X3D, RXF, or DAE will enable more users to interact with the model. Of course, the researcher can use the 3D representation of the visual program of a temple or tomb as basis for a traditional printed publication, but it would be much more useful to make the model itself available to colleagues as a 3DVR publication. Although still early days, this is becoming feasible. I will highlight three platforms than can be used as publication: VSim, 3D GIS, and Unity 3D.

Elaine Sullivan and Lisa Snyder have created a publication that includes a scholarly argument within the digital model of Karnak and are presenting this model using the VSim platform (Sullivan and Snyder, 2017).[7] VSim enables users to import a model and create a predefined movement path through the model. This path can contain pauses

---

[6] See for instance http://dlib.etc.ucla.edu/projects/Karnak/feature/AmenhotepICalciteChapel.
[7] https://idre.ucla.edu/research/active-research/vsim.

where the user's attention is focused on a particular view. VSim also allows resources to be embedded, such as explanatory texts or comparative images, which can either be activated by the user or can be programmed to appear automatically when the user reaches a certain viewpoint (Figure III.6.3). At any point, the user is free to step out of the predefined narrative path and explore the model independently. The embedded resources can be used to support the narrative, but also as an independent interactive information aggregator, where all texts, images, and video that pertain to the model as a whole, or to a specific part of the model, are connected to a point in virtual space. For an epigraphic publication, the model could show a monument in its present state and in reconstruction, with each wall showing the original decoration, but also linking to commentaries, parallels, literature, alternative interpretations, or other information that the author of the model considers relevant.

The 3D Saqqara project is a 3D GIS (Geographic Information Systems) model of the built landscape at the necropolis of Saqqara (Sullivan 2017) and will be published as part of a larger born-digital monograph examining the creation of sacred landscapes in the Egyptian Nile Valley. Like the Karnak project, it emphasizes free interaction by the user and allows a reader to explore the 3D model independently, as well as through curated views or paths. Created in a GIS urban simulation program (ESRI CityEngine), the model will be accessed directly online, eliminating the need for software downloads, an increasingly possible option for 3D scholarly content. The GIS format additionally allows for each model to be directly linked to robust (meta- or para-) data, all accessible within the 3D space. As part of the overall publication, the individual geometry of each custom-modeled monument (approximately one hundred structures based on over a century of field publications on the site) will be available for free download by researchers and the public. While the landscape-scale focus of the project means that many of the models do not contain a great deal of interior detail, quite a few are still suitable for exploring the context of artwork or inscriptions, and the downloaded versions can be manipulated freely by the user. As entire sites or landscapes are modeled in 3D, there is new potential for thinking about texts in their individual context (a single monument), but also in the larger site or on a regional scale.

A third 3DVR resource that can be employed as a publication tool is the game engine Unity 3D.[8] Although developed as a game development platform, Unity 3D is used increasingly in cultural heritage research and presentation. The platform has several drag and drop functions, but requires programming in C Sharp (C#) for many tasks and utilities, such as movement and action triggers by touch. The advantage of using Unity 3D is that importing a 3DVR model is very easy and allows the user to instantly move around and explore the 3D representation of a monument. Providing atmospheric context is quite straightforward as well, because programmers usually want to include "natural" surroundings to a game. Any interaction within the model requires programming, but the code of many open source assets can be found online and can be adapted for scholarly purposes. This enables us to develop a 3DVR model through which we can

[8] https://unity3d.com/.

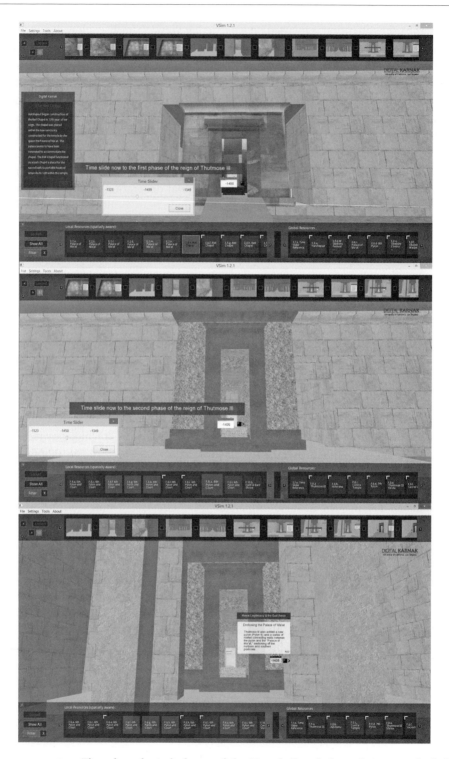

FIGURE III.6.3. Three hypothetical phases of the Karnak Temple boat shrine, one built by Hatshepsut and two Thutmose III phases. VSim screen layout with at the top the narrative, or scholarly argument, and at the bottom the embedded resources (texts, photographs, videos, and web links). The time slider maintains the same view, but shows different period reconstructions.

layer information that comes up when we touch a part of a monument to which that information (e.g., original photographs, drawings, PDFs of publications) is linked. Apart from accessing the model through a keyboard and 2D screen, the digital environment can be exported to formats supported by virtual reality headsets, such as the Oculus Rift or the HTC Vive. This is a market that is in very rapid development, driven by the multimillion dollar gaming industry, which has surpassed the film industry in revenue.[9] Interaction of a 3DVR model through a virtual reality headset allows the user to physically walk through a virtual monument, walk up to walls, reach out, and touch virtual inscriptions or lift virtual objects. At present, a research project at UCLA is developing an interactive interface as part of a project titled the Immersive Humanities. The virtual Karnak Temple can now be entered on foot, while the user can move around and look up to inscriptions and decorative programs on the walls for which that information is available. Another cultural heritage environment that is in development for this platform is the Digital Nubia Project, a collaboration between UCLA, the Museo Egizio, and the Politecnico di Torino in Turin, Italy, on reconstructing the landscape of Nubia that was inundated after the construction of the Aswan High Dam in the early 1960s (Tamborrino and Wendrich 2017).

If we consider three-dimensional models as a means of publication of epigraphic records, then it is important to consider not only how they should be published but also how we can assess their quality. Peer review of 3DVR models has been difficult, because there is no tradition of scholarly publication that is partly visual and interactive. Moreover, in spite of the prohibitively large size and the advanced computer requirements of running real-time VR projects, it is gradually becoming possible to deliver the models in a way that they can be accessed and shared via the Internet. Using VSim or Unity 3D as publication platforms opens the possibility to share models and embedded arguments and to incorporate peer review into the production of scholarly 3DVR publications. This is a review that has a broader focus than the epigraphic components. The methods, design, and workflow of the project should be transparent: it should be clear why and how the work was done, who contributed, and who financed it. These new avenues of publication do not mean that every epigrapher should learn how to create 3DVR models. Digital Humanities projects typically are multidisciplinary and collaborative, combining contributions of an epigrapher, an architect, an archaeologist, and a modeler. Often large 3DVR projects such as Digital Karnak, Digital Giza, Digital Nubia, and 3D Saqqara have a scholarly board that oversees and discusses the work in all its stages.

Digital publication should rightly be concerned with the long-term preservation of the results. With a constantly changing landscape of digital media, system requirements, web browsers, and formats, it is easy to predict that whatever is developed will be outdated in about five years' time and stop functioning in about a decade. For disciplines such as ours that rely on scholarly communications, that is an unacceptably short life span. Project design should, therefore, take into account that elements that together

[9] http://www.nasdaq.com/article/investing-in-video-games-this-industry-pulls-in-more-revenue-than-movies-music-cm634585.

create the 3DVR model and all related elements, such as the texts, images, and videos associated with it, should be preserved individually. This can be accomplished by depositing these files in a repository specialized in long-term preservation of accepted formats (e.g., .tif, .pdf, .txt, .csv). Ultimately, 3D models consist of lines or point clouds, and these can be stored in a sustainable manner. The task of data repositories is not just to serve as a backup, but also to migrate data to new versions of software and hardware systems. The way we access the assets we develop, and the relation between them, can be updated or reconstituted in the new digital environment. This clarifies that the value of epigraphic work, and the significance of interpreting epigraphic evidence in a three-dimensional environment, are independent of any particular program, system, or technology.

Finally, we do need to return to the question of perception. Does an epigraphic study reach the goal as formulated by Caminos to convey "the actual appearance of the wall?" Certainly, a 3DVR model provides better insight in the location and orientation of texts and decorative schemes, but how much do we gain by analyzing or presenting our epigraphic results in a reconstructed space in which we can interact with the walls of a monument as if we were there? Or does the 3DVR representation give misleading impressions that we are not even aware of, because the reconstructed environment influences our interpretation at a subconscious level? These questions clarify why any representation of our understanding of the past should be done critically and should be presented with a very explicit account of the information we base our decisions on and all the steps we have taken along the way (see chapter by Manuelian). In this way, we can aim for an ultimate purpose that is not to provide the actual appearance, but to approach the actual perception and meaning.

Bibliography

Arnold, D. 1974. *Der Tempel des Königs Mentuhotep von Deir el-Bahari: 1. Architektur und Deutung*. AVDAIK 8. Mainz.

Aussems, M., and A. Brink. 2009. "Digital Palaeography." In *Codicology and Palaeography in the Digital Age*, edited by M. Rehbein, P. Sahle, and T. Schaßan, 293–308. Schriften des Instituts für Dokumentologie und Editorik 2. Norderstedt.

Blackman, A. M. 1911. *The Temple of Dendûr*. Les temples immergés de la Nubie. Cairo.

Caminos, R. A. 1976. "The Recording of Inscriptions and Scenes in Tombs and Temples." In *Ancient Egyptian Epigraphy and Paleography*, 3–25. New York.

CPI. 2014. "Corpus of Ptolemaic Inscriptions at the University of Oxford." http://cpi.csad. ox.ac.uk/about/.

Manuelian, P. Der. 1998. "Digital Epigraphy: An Approach to Streamlining Egyptological Epigraphic Method." *JARCE* 35:97–113.

Kimpton, J. L., J. B. McClain, K. Vértes, and W. R. Johnson. 2010. "Preliminary Report on the Work of the Epigraphic Survey in the Temple of Khonsu at Karnak, 2008–2009." *JARCE* 46:113–124.

Lepsius, C. R. 1849–1859. *Denkmäler aus Ägypten und Äthiopien*. 12 vols. Berlin.

McClain, J. B., J. L. Kimpton, K. Alberts, K. Vértes, and W. R. Johnson. 2011. "Preliminary Report on the Work of the Epigraphic Survey in the Temple of Khonsu at Karnak, 2009–2010." *JARCE* 47:159–179.

Naville, É. 1910. *The XIth Dynasty Temple at Deir el-Bahari, Part II*. MEEF 30. London.

Piquette, K. E. 2016. "Documenting Early Egyptian Imagery: Analysing Past Technologies and Materialities with the Aid of Reflectance Transformation Imaging (RTI)." In *Préhistoires de l'écriture: Iconographie, pratiques graphiques et émergence dans l'Égypte prédynastique*, edited by G. Graff and A. Jiménez Serrano, 87–112. Aix-en-Provence.

Porter, B., and R. L. B. Moss. 1927. *Topographical Bibliography of Ancient Egyptian Hieroglyphic Texts, Reliefs, and Paintings I: The Theban Necropolis*. Oxford.

Prévôt, N. 2013. "The Digital Puzzle of the *Talatat* from Karnak: A Tool for the Three-Dimensional Reconstruction of Theban Buildings from the Reign of Amenhotep IV." In *Texts, Languages and Information Technology in Egyptology: Selected Papers from the Meeting of the Computer Working Group of the International Association of Egyptologists (Informatique & Égyptologie), Liège, 6–8 July 2010*, edited by S. Polis and J. Winand, 129–138. AegLeo 9. Liège.

Rajan, V. 2017. "Quantifying Scripts: Defining Metrics of Characters for Quantitative and Descriptive Analysis." *Digital Scholarship in the Humanities* 32, 3: 602–631. doi: https://doi.org/10.1093/llc/fqw030.

Sethe, K. 1908–1922. *Die altaegyptischen pyramidentexte nach den papierabdrücken und photographien des Berliner museums*. 4 vols. Leipzig.

Smith, R. W., and E. Kristof. 1970. "Computer Helps Scholars Re-Create an Egyptian Temple." *National Geographic* 138 (5):593–655.

Stadelman, R. 1991. *Die ägyptischen Pyramiden: Vom Ziegelbau zum Weltwunder*. 2nd ed. KAW 30. Mainz.

Sullivan, E. 2017. "Seeking a Better View: Using 3D to Investigate Visibility in Historic Landscapes." *JAMT* 1–29. doi: 10.1007/s10816-016-9311-1.

Sullivan, E., and L. M. Snyder. 2017. "Digital Karnak: An Experiment in Publication and Peer Review of Interactive, Three-Dimensional Content." *Journal of the Society of Architectural Historians* 76 (4):464–482. https://jsah.ucpress.edu/content/76/4/464.

Tamborrino, R., and W. Wendrich. 2017. "Cultural Heritage in Context: The Temples of Nubia, Digital Technologies and the Future of Conservation." *Journal of the Institute of Conservation* 40 (2):168–182. doi: 10.1080/19455224.2017.1321562.

Wendrich, W. 2014. "Visualizing the Dynamics of Monumentality." In *Approaching Monumentality in Archaeology: Proceedings of the IEMA Postdoctoral Visiting Scholar Conference on Theories and Methods in Archaeology*, edited by J. Osborne, 409–430. Buffalo.

CHAPTER III.7

....

TRADITION AND INNOVATION IN DIGITAL EPIGRAPHY

....

KRISZTIÁN VÉRTES

FOR the specialist intending to incorporate computer technology into the epigraphic documentation process, it is essential to become familiar with a host of perhaps unfamiliar technical terms, software management, and advanced computer skills. Digital drawing tools evolve and change so rapidly that one might find the necessity of keeping up with them exhausting and occasionally counterproductive. For this reason, in order to present digital documentation principles in a way that will both conform to the limited space available in this volume and stay relevant for the foreseeable future, reference to specific technical details or software features must be minimized, and the same is true for discussion of computer hardware (Vértes 2014). Instead, the emphasis must be on the digital implementation of the basic principles of documenting and interpreting ancient Egyptian art, in order to present visual data digitally in a meaningful way. Nevertheless, the usefulness of incorporating these newly emergent techniques for field documentation can only be fully appreciated by presenting some specific digital projects wherein the advantages of the digital approach have been utilized.

First of all, the purpose of epigraphic documentation should be clarified. When studying a work of art, fine details must be appreciated just as much as the whole composition. Understanding and interpreting the "message" of an artwork requires a unique set of skills and knowledge. This special knowledge is even more important when representing art. It must be acknowledged that any method of copying a work of art deducts from the original, regardless of what technique is used. For some purposes, the copy ought to simplify the original, thus focusing on the important details, while in other cases it is considered undesirable to make this kind of selection, leading to a preference for using photography in order to achieve objectivity (Epigraphic Survey 2009, fig. 3 and pl. 139). The possible objectives of making a copy of an artwork, either by traditional or by digital means, may be categorized as follows:

- Preservation: Present an ancient artwork in its original context as realistically and precisely as possible, with the highest level of stylistic accuracy.
- Interpretation: Synthesize and indicate all information that the expert can learn about an ancient artwork in an understandable form.
- Representation: Create an artistic rendition of a scene that is comparable to the original in quality and which itself can be appreciated as a stand-alone work of art.
- Integration: Show the relationship between fine details and the whole by treating the ancient artwork as part of a larger context.

When an argument has to be made for selecting one documentation technique over another, providing a list of the drawbacks of an older method and extolling the advantages of a newer one is naturally to be expected. One might easily draw up such an argument even without possessing any particular knowledge of digital drawing techniques, simply based on some of the myths with which computer technology is associated. It is generally believed that by choosing digital methods over traditional (i.e., manual or paper-based) documentation techniques, one saves time and money, while relying less on advanced artistic skills or knowledge of the subject matter. Likewise, digital epigraphy is often confused with a computer-generated and automated rendition of visual data, favoring appearance over substance.

It is undeniable that there is much room for improvement in many traditional epigraphic recording methods. First of all, an overwhelming amount of these methods rely on direct physical contact with the monuments. 1:1 direct tracing, which is accurate with regard to details and proportions and is relatively easy to apply, may cause damage to the surface itself. Its result is often a static rendering of whatever the artist/epigrapher finds important, necessitating another drawing whenever the focus shifts to different data. As a consequence, scholars often prefer textual communication over visual documentation, based on the assumption that the more data that is visually represented, the more confusing the end result will become. Furthermore, static, nondigital drawings are difficult to correct or to modify stylistically. Additionally, when a drawing is digitized for publication, the recording procedure often degrades its quality and generates background noise.

On the other hand, dragging digital equipment out to the field poses a number of basic logistical problems. Drawing on site often requires sitting, standing, or occasionally lying in awkward positions while copying hard to reach areas, sometimes in conditions of physical discomfort. Further problematic factors include the need to seal off devices against airborne dust, avoiding heat and direct sunlight on computer screens, and providing electricity to keep devices supplied with power. Preparation and determination of task sequences is essential for making good progress in the field. For these reasons, in order to keep digital field drawing as close as possible to the traditional drawing experience, it is desirable to use lightweight equipment with minimal software interaction. This makes it possible to mimic the basic drawing experience, leaving the more sophisticated retouching processes that involve complex hardware for the studio. In accord with these principles, large custom-made drawing boards were created for the work of the Epigraphic Survey to accommodate graphics tablets and enhance the drawing experience by adding a better grip and more elbow room to the setup. This seemingly banal detail demonstrates rather well how digital fieldwork can occasionally feel somewhat alien. From a more scientific point of view, the artist has many digital tools in his/her arsenal, from precalibrated pressure sensitive brushes through special erasers to vector tools for replicating the original decoration as accurately as possible (i.e., Ligon 2010; Beccia 2012, 2014; Covey 2012).

Furthermore, to help with the digital artist's work in the field, the Epigraphic Survey introduced templates for Adobe Photoshop: preset, custom-designed transparent digital canvases in certain scales, containing all the standardized layers, including a proper scale and a tool for double-checking the drawing's measurements against the wall. The epigrapher imports the scanned negative into the appropriate template before taking the file to the field and adjusting its size as needed, using the digital scale in tandem with the physical meter stick, which was included in the original photograph. These accessories and preparatory steps simplify the digital field recording process as much as possible. This certainly does not mean that the final results of digitally interpreted wall scenes should not be complex and extensive; on the contrary, many recent projects reached an unprecedented level of sophistication, thanks to the use of computer technology. The basic considerations in integrating digital techniques with traditional documentation methods can be demonstrated by presenting four recent projects that were designed with the principles listed earlier in mind, although each achieved its goal in a different way. All four methods are based on proven traditional documentation principles, and each is the product of the digital evolution and enhancement of conventional procedures.[1]

RECONSTRUCTING THE OUTER WEST DOORWAY OF THE THUTMOSIDE BARK SANCTUARY IN THE SMALL AMUN TEMPLE AT MEDINET HABU

For this project, Photoshop software on the Cintiq Companion was used to produce the drawings in the field. The complexity of the task—documentation of an entire wall section—required careful planning and many preparatory steps. First, an accurate

---

[1] I thank the Oriental Institute of the University of Chicago and Gábor Schreiber for granting me permission to present parts of the extensive unpublished documentation associated with digital projects I am currently involved with.

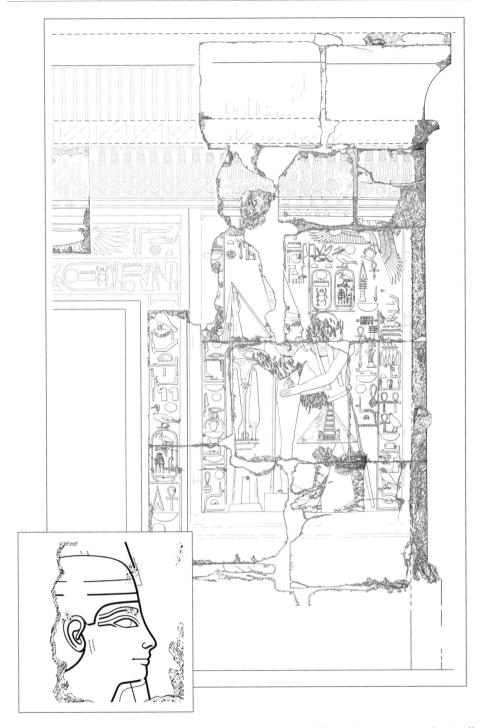

FIGURE III.7.1. Representation of the outer west doorway of the Bark Sanctuary in the Small Amun temple at Medinet Habu indicating the hypothetical reconstruction of the Thutmoside lintel (detail). Courtesy of the Oriental Institute of the University of Chicago.

architectural elevation of the entire wall surface was created, integrating all of the three-dimensional features, such as torus molding, cavetto cornice, and the doorway itself. This digital line drawing provided the framework for the actual field drawing. In the next step, all of the existing photographic documentation of the monument was scanned and digitally assembled onto a separate layer, laid over this architectural plan, while additional detail photographs were taken and integrated wherever necessary for clarification. Often, archival photographs showing features that were better preserved in the past were used to incorporate the maximum amount of detail. Once fully prepared, this complex digital background provided the template for digital penciling executed on the site. In this case, using the Companion, a full-function computer for the initial field drawing proved to be a good choice, due to the complexity of the pencil drawing itself. This particular decorated surface included more than one historical paint layer in very fragmentary states of preservation, so the artist used a variety of digital aids (such as templates for *kheker* and torus elements, specific to a given historical period) for identifying and distinguishing these paint traces.

To keep the drawing experience as close as possible to working with a real pencil, special pressure- and size-sensitive brushes were created in Photoshop for the initial capturing of the scenes. Although the entire drawing method was designed to let the artist work with the software with minimal technical complexity, there were some digital tools that proved to be useful even at this early stage. Digital French curves were used for testing the precise alignment of long curved elements, and guidelines, clone stamps. Transformation tools (such as scale, rotate, distort, and warp) were applied whenever a previously penciled element needed to be adjusted. Likewise, the added flexibility provided by the layer system was taken advantage of throughout the process (Faulkner and Conrad 2015). Once the on-site work was completed, another series of preparatory tasks had to be carried out in the studio before *digital inking* could be started. The resolution of the field drawing had to be upscaled to match the Survey's standards, and previously downscaled inked drawings were replaced with their high-resolution counterparts accordingly. The rather complex final background system consisted of more than twenty layers of architectural elements, pencil drawings, previously inked scenes, templates, and photographs, all digitally assembled as a single file.

The digital inking method itself was designed to resemble closely the Chicago House method, so as to remain virtually indistinguishable from traditional drawings created on paper using Rapidograph pens. Some of the more crucial attributes of this technique were:

- The pencil line underneath the digital ink could be made visible by using a semitransparent brush stroke so the relationship between the two could be controlled.
- Proper line weight transitions for the sun-shadow convention could be built up by keeping the brush stroke relatively thin.
- The right curvature for a more elegant brush stroke could be predetermined by using Photoshop's vector tools, especially when creating long curved lines.

- Repetitive elements could be drawn much faster by creating special brushes for dotted and dashed lines while keeping even distances and providing a consistent size.
- Damage or plaster patterns at a large scale could be applied by creating randomized patterns while maintaining the hand-drawn feel (Vértes 2014, 97–148).

Stylistic continuity with traditional drawings is indispensable when creating a digital method, since each new drawing has to be part of a much larger preexisting system. For this reason, the Survey's sun and shadow conventions, along with the trademark damage, paint, and trace representations were carefully imitated when inking digitally, but at the same time they were made easier to apply and modify, if necessary. Different types of information were represented on separate layers, allowing the epigrapher to use a much broader variety of indications and line work than would have been possible on paper.

By inking digitally, multiple versions of the same wall could be represented within the digital environment, which was particularly rewarding in the case of the doorway. Its outer doorjambs contain two interesting blocks, originally part of the Thutmoside lintel and cavetto cornice, that were reused as a segment of this later version created in the time of Ptolemy VIII (Hölscher 1939, 56–59). Their proportions and the traces on their surfaces revealed their original positions above the doorway and allowed the precise reconstruction of the Eighteenth Dynasty layout. Using the same digital templates as when penciling in situ and comparing the other Thutmoside doorways preserved within the temple complex provided enough information for the artist to recreate the original doorway as a layer underneath the drawing of the features as currently preserved. Further paint studies confirmed the existence of two paint episodes on top of one another, both on the wall scenes on either side of the doorway and on the reused blocks as well, suggesting a very complex decorative history to this particular area of the wall. Capturing and indicating these decorated surfaces separately while representing their relationship and historical development was made possible by the complex layer system, a feature that only the computer can provide (Figure III.7.1.).

ENHANCED COLOR COMPARISON DRAWINGS OF THE EIGHTEENTH DYNASTY FAÇADE IN THE SMALL AMUN TEMPLE AT MEDINET HABU

There is a vast, largely unexplored territory in epigraphy that is underrepresented in publications, namely the visual representation of color (Strudwick 2001, 132–135). In the early days of documentation, painted details were either omitted for the sake of clarity or indicated only to mark painted outlines. When fully represented, painted details were

FIGURE III.7.2. Color-enhanced representation of the Eighteenth Dynasty façade in the Small Amun Temple at Medinet Habu comparing the late Ramesside and Ptolemaic (with photo background) appearance of the same section (detail). Courtesy of the Oriental Institute of the University of Chicago.

usually shown with some sort of black and white pattern fill. Several outstanding field projects, however, created color copies of certain scenes to indicate the original's vivid colors and elaborate decorative elements. Today, since digital photography provides accurate and cost-effective color representation, there has been less impetus for the inclusion of color information in epigraphic recording. Nevertheless, representing color as a visual part of the drawing can be very rewarding in certain cases, and digital color enhancement can open up a new level of data distribution. A good candidate for presenting a scene in color is when the degree of paint preservation visible on the wall does not sufficiently reflect the original quality of detail.

Color texturing was added to some of the traditional line drawings of the square pillars at the Small Amun Temple because the colors on these scenes were so faded that neither photography nor the regular Chicago House Method could capture them properly. To recreate a semblance of the original decoration based on faded paint scars and to enhance the colors preserved on the wall surface, fieldwork began in a nondigital way by using color pencils on matte acetate. It was decided that a crosshatched texture applied on a separate layer would provide the actual color information over the regular line drawing. These drawings did not add any new color values beyond the pigment traces existing on the walls, but rather enhanced them by strengthening their intensity and clarifying the details. The authenticity of the colors was ensured by the choice of tools: Derwent color pencils provided the color palette for the scenes and gave the necessary control for capturing the fine lines. Combining three basic hues for each color allowed the artist to apply a large variety of transitions when faithfully replicating every bit of pigment on the wall. In the next stage, these color pencil textures were digitized, and artificial brush strokes were created based on their texture and style, preserving the hand-made feel of the original. Various types of these color pencil "brushes" were designed in Procreate and tested out in the field. As soon as the result became satisfactory, the artist could apply these digital color enhancements over a much larger area, achieving the quality of the color pencil work while exercising greater control over the process. In this way, traditional and digital brush strokes were used to complement each other and to blend together seamlessly on the digital canvas.

Two different devices were used to capture the color information for the color-enhanced representation of the façade in the Small Amun Temple. The iPad Pro was used to add digital color pencil strokes over smaller, sensitive areas, where hair-thin outlines represented the rich painted details. A Wacom tablet, connected to a powerful computer equipped with Photoshop, allowed the artist to apply the same color texture over large homogeneous painted surfaces such as torus moldings, cavetto cornices, or deep-cut Ramesside hieroglyphs, where the same texture with individual hatching would have taken impossibly long. Once again, the decorated surface contained more than one paint episode, so the main goal was to indicate the evolution of the decoration scheme over the monument's history.

The central gateway to the temple was heavily modified in later times, so it would have been impossible to include the entire façade in representations of the earlier stages without adding a certain hypothetical element. Aside from this, most of the pillar faces did not show enough traces of either one of these painted layers to provide enough information for a confident representation. For these reasons, one vertical section, including the pillar with the best preserved paint traces, was selected to represent the entire six-pillared façade. Instead of recreating the original appearance with an immaculately restored look for each phase, the artist enhanced only the areas of pigment that were still present on the surface by adding much more prominent color values for the traces. The final drawings present each separate paint stage with a worn appearance, and the same areas of damage were included for each stage. The façade background was modified according to each representation, thus erasing later additions, such as Ramesses III's and Pinudjem's marginal inscriptions, from the earlier phases.

Naturally, the existing line drawings served as the background for the digitally enhanced color drawing. Some sections above and below the pillars had to be drawn in Photoshop, because they were not originally planned for inclusion with the epigraphic publication. With this specific data, the façade's different decorative stages could be shown without much artificial reconstruction. For the same reasons, all of the damaged areas were left as originally drawn, adding another naturalistic element to these representations. Additional modifications enriched the overall appearance: a gray panel behind the scene provided a homogeneous background for the composition and helped to indicate the tone of the original whitewash on the surface wherever it was still visible. White paint was such a crucial element of the original decoration that being able to represent it digitally was a welcome addition to the overall appearance of the reconstruction. Finally, an additional version of each phase was created with the enhanced form of the original color photograph set up as background, providing further dimensionality to the more deeply cut elements, architectural features, and Ramesside hieroglyphs.

As a result, these digital color representations showed the temple façade as if it had been left unmodified after a certain period and gradually decayed to the point of showing the currently visible damage and faded colors. In this manner, the artist could distinguish four significantly different stages of the façade's decoration, from the early Thutmoside Period through the Ramesside and late Ramesside additions, to the final Ptolemaic redesign of the entire color scheme. The entire sequence could be presented as part of the same file by adding each layer on top of the other, making it possible to study the relationships between them simultaneously (Figure III.7.2.).

Representing Painted Walls in Grayscale in Theban Tomb 179, the Eighteenth Dynasty Tomb of Nebamun

Yet another completely different method had to be invented to document the large colored scenes in this private tomb, where the painted colors are much better preserved than in the Small Temple at Medinet Habu, therefore digital photography could be used to provide the necessary color information. The wall scenes are, however, marred by numerous damaged areas, intentionally vandalized sections, and natural cracks resulting from geological activity, making visual representation of the overall compositions difficult. It has always been desirable to capture tomb scenes in their entirety, but up until now it was impossible to present such an enormous quantity of data on a single sheet of paper without sacrificing quality and understandability. When this author developed the so-called Imiseba method about twenty years ago for the documentation of TT 65, every step of the procedure had to be carried out manually on paper. Transparent paper sheets were used to produce the initial drawings of the walls, and a complex system was created for labeling different types of data to avoid confusion during inking. Later on, these transparent paper sheets, containing the drawings at 1:1 scale (with some walls as large as 4 by 10 meters), were manually reassembled and taped onto the floor and were painstakingly retraced with Rapidograph pens, maintaining the scale at 1:1 to preserve the line quality. When completed, the line drawings were scanned and printed at 1:4 scale for further processing. These reassembled, reduced versions of the painted outlines provided the background for color coding, the application of a simple dotted texture specific to each basic color in the scenes. The overall tone of these carefully created black and white patterns resembled the actual colors as they would appear on a grayscale photograph taken of the wall. Although the practice of presenting colorful tomb scenes as black and white drawings originated from the high cost and low quality of color printing, such a method also added a certain amount of clarity to the graphic representations, and so it has remained relevant until today. Of course, applying the color-coded pattern manually, dot by dot, over such large surfaces, while keeping the density consistent, was a time-consuming and tedious process. When finished, the drawings were scanned at the highest possible resolution and prepared for publication. Adding any modifications during the drawing process and cleaning up background noise was almost impossible and involved applying white tempera over the ink (Vértes 2015, 1577–1588).

For the documentation of TT 179, yet another hybrid method was designed for capturing multiple layers of information over the same wall surface. Representing painted relief with the grayscale color-code system required two sets of copies of the same scene, one capturing the relief on clear acetate using permanent markers and another one indicating the painted details on opaque matte acetate using regular pencils. Preserving the exact relationship between these two layers was critical since carved and painted outlines of the same pictorial elements rarely align and often additional details are added exclusively in paint. Although the idea of including layers on top of each other was already present at this early stage, field computer technology was not advanced enough to have a useful impact on the first drawings that were made in 2011. As soon as computers became powerful enough to handle such large amounts of data, the need to create in situ copies could be eliminated. Photogrammetric software was used to provide a complete montage of each wall that indicated the correct perspective and proportions without any distortion. Smaller sections of these montages based on a basic grid system offered the same color background for both relief and paint, eliminating the possibility of misaligning

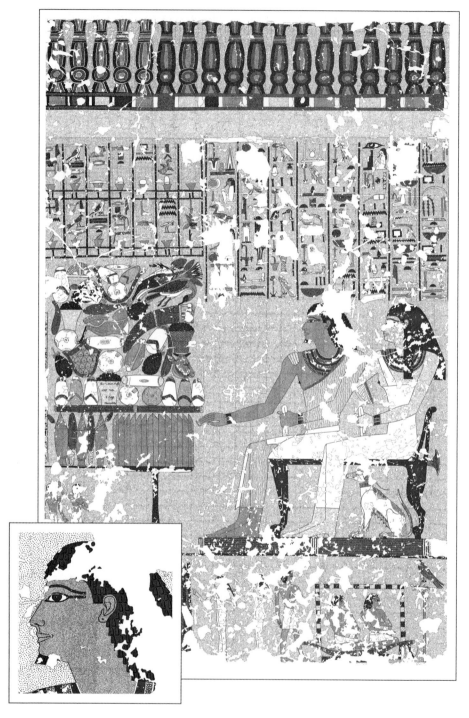

FIGURE III.7.3 Representation of the painted decoration of the west wall in Theban Tomb 179, the Eighteenth Dynasty tomb of Nebamun (detail). Courtesy of Gábor Schreiber.

the two layers. Notes, including color labels, were included within the digital drawing on a separate layer, providing extra information and making studio work significantly easier. But the most notable addition to the digital field drawing versus the earlier method was to eliminate the need to produce an "inked" duplicate of the entire copy in the studio. Although inking the relief layer required the kind of precision that was established by the digital Chicago House Method, thereby needing to be done in the studio, nevertheless, the initial copy of the painted layer was precise enough to represent the painted outlines, thus immensely speeding up the inking process.

Digitization and automation of the grayscale color-coded pattern were based on its hand-drawn counterpart for consistency. A large panel with each color-code layout was created manually on paper, then scanned and multiplied to provide an infinite pattern that could be applied over any surface as a simple brushstroke. A combination of computer-generated pattern and individual hand-drawn dots were used over small details and sensitive areas. The key element of this method was that the pattern, being based on a hand-drawn texture, became virtually indistinguishable from its manually color-coded predecessors. At a later stage, the artist was able to complete the damaged areas, reconstructing the entire composition on a variation of the color-coded layer. Technically, it meant that the epigrapher had to mask the damaged sections by painting their interior white, while recreating every missing bit of decorated surface underneath them. Introducing yet another unobtrusive and nondestructive drawing technique meant the reconstructed parts could gradually be revealed just by turning the opacity of the damage fill layer up and down, while all of the existing layer information remained intact (Figure III.7.3.).

Documenting and Reconstructing the Late Roman Murals in the Emperor's Chamber at Luxor Temple

The documentation of these frescos is the most unconventional of the four digital projects introduced here. The murals are in a very fragmentary condition, due to continuous abuse and to the lack of interest in non-Pharaonic remains typical of the last century. Today, most of the Late Roman paintings in the chamber are lost, and their remains are exposed to pollution and to the effects of thousands of birds visiting the monument each day. Most of the top layer containing the bulk of the details is gone; only paint scars are preserved, with very little pigment remaining on the surface. In some instances, these traces do not even form any recognizable features, so the main goal of epigraphic recording in this case is to isolate the visible pigment and to synthesize the data detectable on the surface.

Most of the in situ documentation was carried out in the Survey's traditional fashion (see McClain chapter). Inventing yet another hybrid method allowed us to focus on the

FIGURE III.7.4. Representation of the late Roman murals of the southeast wall in the Emperor's Chamber at Luxor Temple (detail). Courtesy of the Oriental Institute of the University of Chicago.

task by keeping the process simple. Once again, crosshatched texturing was chosen to represent the graphical impression of the scenes. The artist reinforced every little pigment spot over the photo by adding a pencil texture with variable strength. After the photographic background was bleached away, the scanned pencil drawing was ready for digital enhancement. As part of the fieldwork stage, some contextual information was provided by indicating a narrow strip of the original Eighteenth Dynasty background, which is mostly preserved around the edges of the fresco remains. As an attempt to simplify this process, these line drawings were made on the iPad Pro by using Procreate, a lightweight combination of tool and software. Procreate has a relatively simple interface, but allows the separation of certain categories of information into layers. Of course, the use of a less powerful digital drawing board, such as the iPad Pro (with Apple Pencil), entailed careful planning in advance: as with the outer doorway of the Bark Sanctuary at Medinet Habu, a detailed, proportional, and perspective-corrected photo mosaic of each wall section had to be created on a much more powerful computer in the studio, and this became the master background for the entire project. This immense file was divided into smaller sections with some overlap, and it was downgraded to a manageable resolution before being transferred for work on the iPad.

In the studio, the in situ record of each wall was carefully reassembled over the master background and upscaled to the Survey's standard high resolution in preparation for inking. A new digital inking method had to be invented that would reflect the appearance and style of the fresco. Between 2005 and 2008, the fresco remains were thoroughly photographed in concert with the restoration efforts carried out by an Italian conservation team. Most of their results have recently been published, along with a detailed historical, art historical, material, and methodological analysis containing many recent color photos and other archival material (Jones and McFadden 2015). Our work supplemented this with drawings in grayscale that emphasize the recognizable details and features rather than the preserved color information. The pigment texture layer that was captured in situ on photo paper became the medium tone layer in the final presentation and was redrawn stroke by stroke by using a tilt-sensitive Photoshop brush that was specifically created for this application.

To be able to show the stylistic differences between the Roman paintings and pharaonic art, two more paint-specific layers were introduced in order to emphasize perspective and depth in the fresco. One strengthened the details, such as facial and costume features, well definable objects, and so forth, and represented dark areas, especially black panels. The other, much lighter layer showed the painted background wherever it was preserved. Both additional layers operated with the same texture style as the medium tone layer, but the opacity of the layers varied according to their importance. In this way, the artist was able to paint with the same black brush over the entire canvas and still produce a drawing with gray brush strokes of variable shades. The end result became a graphic impression of the original mural with a close resemblance to the Late Roman painter's style, indicating even the least prominent individual brush strokes on the eroded surface, while eliminating much of the background noise that is an inseparable feature of the photographs. Meanwhile, the few small areas where some of the finest details, such as the dotted designs on the figures' shoulders, are still preserved were copied at the wall and were added over the inked surface on a separate masking layer to achieve maximum accuracy.

The Pharaonic relief carvings were indicated on multiple layers according to the regular digital Chicago House Method, with one unique difference: all of these layers were represented in a light gray tone in order to keep them in the background and to emphasize the fresco. By tweaking the opacity of each layer, the same black brush stroke could be used on all elements yet again, while each layer's prominence could be changed at any time. With such flexibility, any type of data from this complex data pool could be emphasized or omitted, making the file an unprecedented compilation of visual information. However, when assembled to integrate with the entire wall section, the sporadically preserved sections of the fresco appeared disconnected, like separate islands on the wall. As a solution, a single weight line drawing of the essential components of the Pharaonic background relief was created to provide a unified background and hold the composition together. This discreet line drawing was confined to the representation of the carved lines, distinct from the strip around the fresco edges, and no damage or plaster was included, while the level of detail was kept to a minimum, creating a lightweight wall map of the Pharaonic decorative program for each wall.

Luckily, a dossier of archival photographs and watercolor paintings was recovered during the extensive research carried out for the recent publication, showing some exquisite details on the walls that were removed and/or damaged during the subsequent decades (Jones and McFadden 2015, 156–167 and figs. 4.6, 4.10–4.13, 4.18–4.19, 4.21, 6.11).[2] The information gained from these sources (most importantly the numerous watercolor paintings made by Gardner Wilkinson shortly after the excavation of the room) could be used to enhance the documentation in a meaningful way, however, no overall reconstruction of the scenes was planned, simply because there was not enough data to be certain about the entire composition. For the most battered of all the walls, a digital "overhaul" became possible. The eastern short wall once held a magnificent mural depicting soldiers and horses above the imitation opus sectile dado that is today reduced to a few faint painted contours. The master background, based on the Survey's recent high-resolution photographs, provided the base for a reconstruction. First, all of the recent epigraphic documentation, traditional and digital alike, was imported and set up properly, enhancing and emphasizing the remaining features on the wall. Next, the only surviving French archival photograph, which framed the entire wall and was contemporary with the excavation, had to be upscaled, perspective-corrected, and adjusted to align with the master background. Before it was made part of the same set, Wilkinson's watercolor of the entire corner of the room was cropped and similarly corrected. The drawings and the master background provided the landmarks for the proper alignment of both photo and watercolor, which were adjusted to match exactly. The sum of these layers formed a unique foundation for the reconstruction, which was based on the

---

[2] I thank Michael Jones for his immense help finding and providing high-resolution scans of most of the archival photographs and watercolor paintings used for the epigraphic reconstruction.

actual features that once were seen and photographed on the wall. As with the other supporting layers, the reconstruction layer's opacity was lowered to a distinctly lighter tone than the preserved remains to avoid confusing the two with each other. Although this hypothetical extension was created with the usual texture-based technique in mind, only one light gray tone represented the fresco expansion, along with a greatly simplified relief representation. The result was a graphical collection of all the available information, both historical and contemporary, that our team was able to assemble about this unique fragmentary artwork (Figure III.7.4.).

CONCLUSION

It must be reiterated that creating the proper digital workspace, toolbox, layers, and file system is just as important as the drawing process itself. Flexibility and sensitivity in documentation is critical. Drawing digitally does not necessarily mean easy and fast documentation. Creating stylistically correct, highly accurate representations of ancient Egyptian art is a very time-consuming process, which must also incorporate the necessary background research. The four digital projects detailed in this chapter, while differing in their appearance, use the same design language and philosophy when dealing with the disparate types of material. Each approach is oriented toward the larger context and treats the represented data within a unified system, which offers an answer for every single issue regarding the actual project.

Digital epigraphy and epigraphy in general can only stay relevant within this larger context when the epigrapher creates a close connection between the ancient artwork and its interpretation. In the four instances introduced here, this connection is provided by using hybrid techniques that were based on proven methods of creating handmade drawings conventionally on paper. The personal contact that modern epigraphers have with the ancient artists when studying the walls, sitting in front of them holding pen and paper, is not eliminated, but rather enhanced by effectively employing complementary digital tools. These digital representations, from the simplest brush stroke to the most complex color texture, are always based on their conventional counterparts, providing comparability and continuity when made part of the broader documentation scheme. Whenever one encounters a method's shortcomings, a new method should be invented, especially in such a rapidly changing field as digital epigraphy. Nevertheless, the documentation process, especially digital field drawing, should be kept as clean and simple as possible. Last, but not least, one has to preserve the human touch, which becomes even more indispensable when drawing on the computer.

BIBLIOGRAPHY

Beccia, C. 2012. *Digital Painting for the Complete Beginner*. New York.
Beccia, C. 2014. *The Digital Renaissance: Classic Painting Techniques in Painter and Photoshop*. New York.

Covey, S. 2012. *Photoshop for Artists: A Complete Guide for Fine Artists, Photographers, and Printmakers*. New York.

Epigraphic Survey, The. 2009. *Medinet Habu IX: The Eighteenth Dynasty Temple, Part I: The Inner Sanctuaries, with Translations of Texts, Commentary, and Glossary*. OIP 136. Chicago.

Faulkner, A., and C. Chavez. 2015. *Adobe Photoshop CC Classroom in a Book: 2015 Release*. San Francisco.

Hölscher, U. 1939. *The Excavation of Medinet Habu, Volume 2: The Temples of the Eighteenth Dynasty*. OIP 41. Chicago.

Jones, M., and S. McFadden, eds. 2015. *Art of Empire: The Roman Frescoes and Imperial Cult Chamber in Luxor Temple*. New Haven.

Ligon, S. 2010. *Digital Art Revolution: Creating Fine Art with Photoshop*. New York.

Strudwick, N. 2001. "Problems of Recording and Publication of Paintings in the Private Tombs of Thebes." In *Colour and Painting in Ancient Egypt*, edited by W. V. Davies, 126–140. London.

Vértes, K. 2014. *Digital Epigraphy*. Chicago. Retrieved from https://oi.uchicago.edu/research/publications/misc/digital-epigraphy.

Vértes, K. 2015. "Ten Year's Epigraphy in Theban Tomb 65: Documentation of the Late Twentieth Dynasty Wall Paintings in the Tomb of Imiseba." In *Proceedings of the Tenth International Congress of Egyptologists, University of the Aegean, Rhodes, 22–29 May 2008*, edited by P. Kousoulis and N. Lazaridis, 1577–1585. 2 vols. OLA 241. Leuven.

3D SCANNING, PHOTOGRAMMETRY, AND PHOTO RECTIFICATION OF COLUMNS IN THE KARNAK HYPOSTYLE HALL

JEAN REVEZ

INTRODUCTION

FREE-STANDING stone columns have been an essential feature of Egyptian architecture as far back as the Old Kingdom (c. 2686–2160 BCE) (Phillips 2002, 51–60). Used rather sparingly at first in royal funerary temples, their number increases dramatically with the advent of the New Kingdom (1550–1069 BCE), when they were erected in clusters inside hypostyle halls of divine temples. Built mostly from that time on out of sandstone, a more durable type of rock than limestone that was commonly used earlier, temple columns are by then massive structures offering complex and varied styles. Relatively devoid of inscriptions initially, columns are increasingly filled with a large number of texts and scenes, to the point that recording them becomes a daunting challenge for Egyptologists who, among other things, must deal with the cylindrical shape of the surface on which the texts are carved and the sheer height of some inscriptions above the ground. Using the Hypostyle Hall inside the temple of Amun-Re in Karnak as a case study, this chapter examines the advantages and challenges of using 3D scanning, photogrammetry, and photo rectification, three complementary processes based on measurements from photographs, to record and reconstruct columns three-dimensionally in digital form (Luhmann et al. 2014, 2–9).

The Relevance of the Hypostyle Hall at Karnak as a Case Study for Testing Newly Emergent Techniques

Located in Upper Egypt in what was then known as the fourth Upper Egyptian nome, the Temple of Amun-Re in Karnak represents an ideal laboratory to assess the use of new emergent techniques in epigraphy and paleography. As the temple was the focus of religious attention for more than two millennia (2000 BCE–100 CE), during which time all important kings built, added to, or restored the site dedicated to one of the most important dynastic gods of Egypt (Golvin and Goyon 1987; Blyth 2006), the complex serves as a unique model to study the evolution of Pharaonic epigraphy, art history, and architecture. Erected in the heart of this religious complex is the Hypostyle Hall, which in its current state, was decorated under the reign of at least five rulers: Seti I, Ramesses II, Ramesses IV, Ramesses VI, and Herihor (Brand 2000, 192–219; Revez and Brand 2012). Not only does the Hall offer a broad range of inscriptional and iconographical styles that can be investigated but also the widespread practice of recarving (a process by which artisans erase or scrape off older inscriptions in order to engrave newer ones in their stead) makes it also an excellent testing ground to analyze ways computer-aided tools can facilitate reading palimpsests. Finally, as the Hall measures 100 m in length and 50 m in width, it is the largest surviving example and certainly the best preserved hypostyle hall in Egypt, with most of its 134 columns still standing. Of these, the twelve open-bud columns of the central colonnade reach 20 m in height, while the 122 close-bud lateral columns are 13 m high.

In addition to these larger attributes, there are specific features that make the Hall a very fertile ground for experimenting with emerging techniques for epigraphic purposes:

- *Constraint of height*: Recording the epigraphy in the traditional analogic way usually involves drawing with a felt-tip pen on a plastic transparent sheet applied directly over the surface of the stone relief to be copied or penciling onto an enlarged photograph print set of the scene to be collated (see chapters by McClain, Thiers). Applying this method to record textual and iconographic evidence located high up in the uppermost parts of shafts, capitals, and abaci of the smaller columns is a particularly great challenge because of the logistics involved in moving around heavy and cumbersome equipment inside a confined space, such as ladders, scaffolding, and even a scissor lift (see chapters by Gaber, Kurth). Proceeding in this way for the towering central colonnade inside the Hall becomes an unsurmountable feat.

- *Constraint of surface*: Taking a full series of pictures at 90 degrees of scenes carved into the flat surface of a temple wall is one thing; doing so for reliefs engraved on columns is another matter, since the nonplanar, cylindrical shape of the structure creates high distortion, especially along the rim. Exploiting digital photographs as background material for drawing scenes by hand or by computer-aided tools without the help of photogrammetry turns out to be an all but impossible task.

- *Constraint of apparent redundancy:* Carrying out a thorough epigraphic survey of 134 columns covered in large part with a deceitfully repetitive and conventional textual and iconographic repertoire may at first glance look like a rather poor investment in time, energy, and money, especially when one takes into account the overwhelming number of decaying Pharaonic monuments that have yet to be recorded; we shall see in the next section that such stereotyped decoration is actually very rich in information. Admittedly, collating this type of material without the help of 3D scanning and photogrammetry can prove to be extremely time-consuming and laborious (Brand, Laroze, and Revez 2011–2012, 22).

Using Photogrammetry and Photo Rectification to Record Planar Surfaces: The Case of the Abaci Inside the Hypostyle Hall

Column shafts at Karnak are cylindrical in form, but the abaci that lie on top of the capitals are square. Seen from this perspective, the Hypostyle Hall offers opportunities for experimenting with photogrammetry and photo rectification both on planar and nonplanar surfaces.

Each face of the abaci is engraved with the large cartouche of a king. Since 134 columns originally stood inside of the Hall (of which six are either truncated or totally gone), there were altogether 536 cartouches inscribed on all the faces of the abaci. On the face of it (to use a bad pun), it would seem repetitive and pointless to record each and every side of abaci. Yet, the information contained on the abaci sums up, to quite a large extent, the chronology of the decoration of the entire Hall. The various spelling of the kings' names written inside the cartouches (Seti I to the north and Ramesses II to the south), together with the type of carving involved (raised or sunk relief) are in this case clearly indicative of six differing ranges of dates of engraving (Revez and Brand 2012, 17–22). The complete recording of every single abaci face allowed us to find out that the rows lining the two main processional ways were decorated before the ones located further away from the main axes. One could also get a much better understanding of the logistics used by the various artisans to decorate the Hall by doing a paleographical study of the hieroglyphic signs and their distribution inside the Hall. Finally, the quality of workmanship differs quite significantly inside the hall, depending on the location of the abaci faces in relation to the main processional ways (Revez and Brand 2015, 10–13).

In a nutshell, a consistent and systematic recording of all the abaci inscriptions has proven to be a very rewarding exercise. R. Caminos did transcribe the cartouches carved on all the abaci in the 1950s, but this unpublished data was mostly collated from ground level up, with the simple use of binoculars, a method that led him to overlook some palimpsest inscriptions. Had photogrammetry been an option in his time, recording these cartouches would have been an easier task, an observation that leads us to examine the various steps involved in photogrammetry to record and process the data of the abaci.

One needs first to set up a Total Station Laser Theodolite at different locations inside the Hall to shoot points from ground level up. Six predefined reference points, chosen randomly but spread out evenly on the entire surface of each abacus face, have to be acquired in order for the photogrammetry post-production process to be feasible. Some precautions must be taken in order to optimize the entire operation. The hieroglyphic signs must be sufficiently visible so as to find remarkable points on the picture (one uses reflection from the sun on handheld mirrors that throw light on the abaci), the angle at which points are measured must be relatively wide (though not necessarily at a 90 degree angle), and the surface of the stone must not be excessively irregular. Ideally, it is best to relate the internal coordinate system of the photo image with the ground system of geographic coordinates of the temple, a process called georeferencing. Once the points are recorded, the process of image rectification can begin, by projecting the tilted or oblique photographs on to a horizontal plane. The rectified photos can thus serve as basis to draw facsimiles of the abaci (Gobeil 2022).

We have previously stated that reaching the upper sections of the columns in the Hall has always been a great challenge for shooting pictures that would later be rectified. In the case of the twelve open-bud gigantic papyriform columns erected in the central axis, not only is sheer height an insurmountable obstacle, as we have mentioned before, but the open-bud shape of the capitals hides the view (partially if not entirely) of the abaci from ground level. One could naturally set up a tripod with a camera on top of the architraves of the lower lateral columns that lie more or less at the same height as the open-bud abaci, a solution that has been used, at least for the abaci located on the northern side of the axis, but this alternative still only offers a partial view of the other faces.

The ideal solution to overcome this problem would be to operate a flying camera or unmanned aerial vehicle (or UAV, commonly known as a drone) around the abaci to take pictures of them from different angles. We obtained the authorization from the Egyptian government to use a DJI Phantom 4 Pro UAV in our 2017 field mission. There was enough space between columns to allow the flying camera to navigate freely without colliding with the architectural elements. We took advantage of this unique opportunity (it was to our knowledge the first time ever that a flying camera was used at Karnak for scientific purposes) to produce scaled photogrammetric models of the architraves, abaci, clerestories, and top sections of the adjoining walls of the Hall. Open-air areas outside of the Hall where loose drum fragments, originally belonging to the columns, are now stored, were also flown over in order to generate an overview map showing the location of all such free blocks.

Nonemerging and Emerging Techniques Used in Past Projects to Record the Nonplanar Surfaces of Columns Inside the Hypostyle Hall at Karnak: A Brief Survey

Nonemerging Techniques

Most of the research that has been carried out on the columns inside the Hypostyle Hall at Karnak is quite varied in scope. Topics range from the account of ancient and modern restoration of the columns to the analysis of individual scenes or cartouches carved on them and the use of the columns as case studies for virtual 3D reconstruction of the Hall. Surprisingly, though, for a monument of this magnitude and resplendence (the grandiose nature of the Hypostyle Hall at Karnak has not escaped the attention of tourists who regularly flock in large numbers to visit the monument, and by so doing, make work more complicated), no thorough and systematic recording of the scenes and inscriptions carved on the columns of the Hall has ever been carried out (see however now Biston-Moulin 2016, § 5.2, for the inscriptions inside the main scenes). The closest that we have to a monograph dealing extensively with the columns is L.-A. Christophe's *Les divinités des colonnes de la grande salle hypostyle et leurs épithètes* (1955); the book contains a wealth of raw data dealing with textual occurrences of deities' names in text captions, but it includes only a limited number of pictures of the columns as such. The first published scientific illustrations of the columns at Karnak go at least as far back as J.-F. Champollion and R. Lepsius at the end of the eighteenth and during the mid-nineteenth century respectively; unpublished archives in the 1950s comprise carefully handcopied drawings made by H. H. Nelson of the texts of each and every single column inside the hall; the iconographic features of the scenes are by contrast only sketched out. All of this invaluable material is still of great use today, as the state of preservation of the columns was certainly better centuries or even just decades ago than at the present time. Unfortunately though, no palaeographical studies can be made out of the hieroglyphic signs traced in these copies, since the drawings were produced by hand and not made to scale. The information is thus recorded in an analogic way (i.e., without involving the electronic process of the data), since digital and computerized means did not exist at the time (Revez and Brand 2012, 13–14).

Emerging Techniques

The advent of emerging technologies in the 1990s opened up new ways to record epigraphy on columns. Successful attempts at using orthophotography, a process by which scanned and georeferenced pictures of one and the same column are assembled, stitched together, and then unrolled (an operation akin to flattening a three-dimensional globe in order to transform it into a bidimensional world map), were made on smaller-size columns at Karnak through the use of a camera set on a wheeled platform that circled around columns on narrow Decauville railroad tracks (Chéné, Foliot, and Réveillac 1999, 119–122; see chapter by Traunecker). This system worked fine for individual columns that are relatively isolated from one another, but proved inadequate for the clustered forest of columns inside the cramped space of the Hypostyle Hall.

In the 2000s, the Groupe de Recherche en Conception Assistée par Ordinateur (GRCAO) at Université de Montréal used a column inside the Hypostyle Hall and several others elsewhere at Karnak to apply the technique of orthophotographic *déroulés* on larger-size columns. Exploiting the well-known Autocad software that is both widely used by architects and capable of being programmed for specific needs, newly inserted functions made it possible to, among other things, record the shape and size of each hieroglyphic sign geometrically and allow damaged signs to be restored by means of completion (Meyer et al. 2006; Revez et al. 2007).

Emerging Techniques Used in Current Projects to Record the Nonplanar Surfaces of Columns inside the Hypostyle Hall at Karnak

More recently, a true 3D computer simulation of the Hall was created by ATM-3D, a French private firm, through the recording of close to a trillion points using a Riegl LMS Z 390 scanner that was set up in three hundred different spots across the Hall. The École nationale des sciences géographiques (ENSG) carried out a field mission not long afterward, during which time some four thousand photographic images were taken of all the columns. Each column was divided up into eight sections, and four overlapping cameras perched on an eight-meter-long pole were used to make full photographic coverage of each of those sections. Using photogrammetry, it was then possible to paste these pictures on the 3D computer model of the columns and then to unroll each of them. An original feature of these orthophotos (which we will designate conveniently as "first generation" déroulés) is that the flattened images could be texturized, allowing the viewer to see the depth of the carving on each column (Chandelier et al. 2009; Laroze and Chazaly 2009).

While these "first-generation" orthophotos represented huge progress and were of great use, as we shall explain later on, two constraints prevented us from exploiting them fully.

- *Constraints of lighting:* Optimal lighting for the photography of carved scenes is a key issue in order for a campaign to be successful. Obtaining a light source that hits the surface of the column at an oblique angle in order for the highly contrasted stone relief to be best readable is a challenge. There are many factors regarding lighting that have to be taken into account: the position of the sun changes during the year so that the parts of columns best lit vary according to the time of the day and the season; to be able to obtain best raking light, it would theoretically be important to take pictures at different points during the year in order to cover the full circumference of a column. While almost all of the roofing of the Hypostyle Hall in Karnak is gone, the architraves that supported it are still very much in place. The shade cast by these features on the columns makes it very difficult to obtain homogeneous lighting all through the déroulés. In the process of producing the first generation of déroulés, the decision had been made to take pictures of the columns in the shade in order to obtain uniform lighting throughout and avoid sharp contrasts. The downside of this choice was that poor lighting made it impossible for epigraphers to use the déroulés to draw digitally with a sufficient level of accuracy small hieroglyphic signs, highly damaged sections of the texts, and scenes or palimpsest inscriptions.

- *Constraints of resolution*: By using nonreflective Canon G9 material that is both of reasonable weight and easily manipulated, the quality of the photos obtained was sufficient for the objectives that the mission of the ENSG had set in 2008. Our project required, however, images at much higher resolution so that we could read the tiniest details of the scenes to be collated and then reproduced in facsimiles. When we zoomed in on a detail of the image in order to enlarge it, we were quickly confronted with a problem of pixelation, which made it impossible to read the scenes sufficiently well.

Since 2013, the Karnak Hypostyle Hall Project, through a joint University of Memphis-Université du Québec à Montréal epigraphic mission, has laid out a program to produce a new set of higher-resolution and optimized "second-generation" déroulés, focusing this time only on the main central scenes carved out in the middle sections of the columns (Figure III.8.1A–B). Several series of photographic tests, set solely on optimizing the resolution and the quality of the luminosity of the main columns, were carried out.

The use of a lightbox has proven to be a very effective method, both for improving the reading of palimpsest inscriptions and for attenuating the shadows created by natural light. This system, designed specifically for our project by our photographer, Owen Murray, relies on the use of a white tarpaulin of frosted and translucent plastic stretched over the scene to be photographed, that allowed artificial light coming from a studio strobe set up just above the scene to irradiate homogeneously over the entire surface of the stone. This technique guaranteed consistency and ensured that external/environmental ambient light conditions were not a factor in lighting the scenes; all in all, one hundred fifty shots were necessary to produce high-resolution images of each scene (Murray, Forthcoming).

Once work in the field is completed, the next step is to program the commercialized Agisoft 3Dscan software to filter the data contained in the "first-generation" déroulés in

FIGURE III:8.1A. Orthophoto of an unwrapped column made up of a mosaic of pictures. Photo credit: O. Murray/Y. Egels.

FIGURE III.8.1B. Orthophoto of an unwrapped column ("second generation" déroulé). Photo credit: O. Murray/Y. Egels.

order to produce a new, improved "second-generation" set of orthophotos. A software developed by our photogrammetrist Yves Egels, *Cumulus*, is used for georeferencing and point cloud processing, before stitching all the individual photos together into high-quality déroulés.

THE FUNCTIONALITY OF ORTHORECTIFIED DÉROULÉS OF COLUMNS

Contrary to a flat wall or an abacus face whose entire surface can be seen completely in a single glance, a column by definition is always cylindrical in shape, which means that a large portion of its circumferential decoration is always hidden from view. Thanks to the unrolled orthophotos, which show each individual column in its entirety, it is possible to establish a very precise typology of all the columns of the Hall based on size, number of decorative segments, and type of carving (raised or sunken relief). One can also have a full and instant appraisal of the complexity of the various registers that make up the decoration of a whole column and get a much better understanding of the spatial layout of the scenes and bandeau texts and of the interrelationship between stereotyped (or conventional) and nonstereotyped (or unconventional) decoration. Considered traditionally as "conventional" decoration are the deceptively repetitive (but nevertheless highly significant) elements of the decoration, namely: the plant motifs engraved on the base and at the top of columns; the friezes of royal cartouches that adorn substantial sections of the columns; the hieroglyphic inscriptions carved in horizontal bandeaux; and the so-called *rekhyet* birds engraved at the bottom of columns that symbolically represent the Egyptian people. The main central scenes, located halfway up the columns, are not part of the "conventional" decoration, as their more original content show a much greater abundance and variety of themes and treatments.

By using the orthorectified déroulés as substrata, it is possible to produce digital facsimiles that outline the main features and the chronology of the decoration of each column (Figure III.8.2A–B).

As shown in Figure III.8.2b, we can distinguish between no fewer than four stages of carving and recarving, carried out by four different pharaohs on one of the twelve open-bud papyriform columns of the central colonnade. For the 122 closed-bud lateral columns, up to seven successive stages were counted. The almighty Ramesses II, due to the extraordinary length of his reign, distinguishes himself from other pharaohs by the scale and magnitude of his interventions that number at least four.

The data that had previously been used to create a digital 3D model of the Hall also led to the production of longitudinal sections of column rows that are greatly useful for the architectural study of the Hall. Thus, the apparatus of the column drums seems to be uniform inside the whole monument, which would lead one to think that the columns were all erected at approximately the same date, a conclusion that would run counter to the conclusion of recent studies according to which the columns of the Hypostyle Hall were raised during the course of several construction campaigns (Carlotti and Martinez 2013). Such longitudinal sections can also be used to study the typology of columns erected in and around Karnak during Ramesside times (Egels and Laroze, Forthcoming).

The Functionality of 3D Scanning

Producing a 3D digital model of the Hall offers numerous advantages.

A More Accurate Way of Representing Space

W. Helck (1976) was able to demonstrate that there was a consistent and coherent spatial arrangement of the alternating figures of Amun-Re and Amun-Re-Kamutef on the

FIGURE III.8.2A. Orthophoto of an unwrapped column ("first generation" déroulé). Photo credit: ATM-3D.

FIGURE III.8.2B. Facsimile of an unwrapped column based on déroulé. Photo credit: E. Feleg.

columns and that the location of female and male deities inside the Hall also followed a logical pattern. A lot of such valuable information is lost in the process of converting the essential and distinguishing tridimensional attributes of the Hypostyle Hall into a bidimensional reality; large plates of orthophotos and facsimiles of columns published in traditional paper folio format are of immense assistance, as shown previously, but these media are inappropriate to express the complex relationship that exists among columns in terms of repertoire of scenes and texts. On the contrary, a 3D scanned computer model of the monument proves to be far more suitable in conveying the intricate spatial relation between divine and royal figures carved on the columns, for instance, as well as understanding the implicit logic of the layout of the different offering scenes depicted inside the Hall (see chapter by Wendrich).

A Process That Highlights Features of the Columns Conveniently

With a digital 3D model, it is also possible to create a search engine that can bring out on request certain features that a user would like to visualize, such as the areas inside the Hall decorated under the reign of a particular pharaoh, the sections of columns where there is evidence for palimpsest, or the locations inside the hall where any specific form of a given god is to be found.

The Capacity to Store Data for Archival Purposes

Despite the efforts to counter with conservatory measures the effect of pollution, natural and human-made erosion, and the action of saltpeter, the columns inside the Hall are subject to an ongoing and almost irreversible process of deterioration. In parts of the southern section of the Hall, clear signs of the slow decaying of the sandstone are visible. Scanning the Hall enables the Egyptologist to store what amounts to a virtual three-dimensional computerized archive of the monument.

The Ability to Enhance Reality

The Hall was a lively place where important religious and political ceremonies occurred that involved people moving around and others gathering in designated areas of the Hall. One of the most popular features of 3D models is their capacity to show the interior of buildings from different moving perspectives. The viewer is thus in the very convenient position of circulating inside the Hall virtually, reproducing in so doing the experience of the priest carrying the sacred barque along processional ways or the happy few who could attend the annual festivals inside the monument (e.g., Eccetta 2013; Sullivan 2012). Being able to look at the Hall through the eyes of the people who designed it in ancient times allows us to gain incredible insight into what impression the decoration of the monument made on its visitors. This is very important, since we know, based on supporting evidence from our field missions in Karnak, that the order of priority of the space to be engraved on the columns and abaci depended to a very large extent on the principle of visibility, namely, that the sections of the columns to be decorated in precedence and the portions that show the highest standards of workmanship are the ones facing the two major processional ways of the Hall (Revez and Brand 2015). One could virtually experiment with different cases of scenarios and settings inside the Hall.

A Testing Ground to Validate Hypotheses of Restitution

Virtual 3D models are also very useful in the process of restoring ancient buildings back to their original state. In the case of the Hypostyle Hall, significant parts of the northern half of the monument collapsed at the end of the nineteenth century (Azim and Réveillac 2004, 123–166; for other damage on the columns: Brand 2001; Rondot and Golvin 1989). Georges Legrain, the French *maître d'œuvres*, who was then in charge of rebuilding the massive columns after they had fallen, is generally and rightly credited for having accomplished this amazing feat successfully. However, during our last epigraphic mission of the Karnak Hypostyle Hall Project in winter 2016–2017, we were able to expose hitherto undetected errors made by Legrain in his reconstruction of certain columns. Faults could be uncovered on the basis of the wrong orientation of some scenes, the misplacement of standard texts, the misalignment of divine and human figures, and/or the inconsistent presence of palimpsest royal cartouches on some sections of columns. Judging from the experiment successfully carried out by R. Vergnieux in his ATON-3D research project in Bordeaux (Prévôt 2013), a digital 3D model of the Hall could likewise serve as a testing ground to validate new hypotheses about the reconstruction of the columns. Such a model would also allow us to put back in their virtual original position some of the hundreds of fragmentary and complete loose abaci or drum blocks that are currently stashed away just outside the Hall. Those are blocks that Legrain was not able to place physically back inside the Hall, but that could eventually be integrated again in a digital model.

The Process of Wrapping Columns

Agisoft Photoscan, a user-friendly software that can be of great help in the treatment of unfurling columns photogrammetrically, as we have mentioned in an earlier section, is actually used normally for the exact opposite operation, that is, wrapping columns back around their three-dimensional projection. It does this by processing an impressive

FIGURE III.8.3. 3D model of a column created through the Agisoft 3DScan software. Photo credit: P. Brand.

number of photos in order to produce a 3D model of any architectural feature at a record-setting time, with a high degree of accuracy in terms of resolution. In the case of our columns, we simply have to provide the software with all the photos taken from a given column in order to produce a point cloud of the model showing the position of the camera of each photo in three-dimensional space (Figure III.8.3). It is also possible to generate a polygonal mesh model of the column or one with high texture that can be exported out of the software into another file where it can be saved more conventionally in .jpg or .pdf format. More interestingly, the model can also be uploaded in the Sketchfab resource so as to be viewed three-dimensionally online. This mode of presentation is particularly useful because it allows the user to rotate the column at will and to observe it under different angles, creating in the process the same impression as someone who would be circling around the column inside the temple. The software can project artificial raking light on the column as it rotates, optimizing the view in the process. The user also has the option to zoom in on any section of the column deemed worthy of a closer look. Last but not least, it is possible to label certain features of the columns inside the model or to create hyperlinks inside virtual windows that can contain all sorts of information relating to them.

Enhancing Colors Virtually

Until now, we have not used DStretch (for decorellation software), a very valuable digital tool that enhances painted pictographs that are otherwise not perceptible by the eye. This device is particularly effective for faded color scenes painted on plaster inside tombs, but also on some temple walls (e.g., the Epigraphic Survey project in the small Eighteenth Dynasty temple at Medinet Habu, where DStretch is successfully used to detect Demotic and Christian graffiti). However, we have used the open source, Java-based image processing program called ImageJ, that enables poorly preserved color pigmentation to be intensified. Although the coloration on columns has disappeared to a very large extent (to the point that it is nowadays difficult to imagine that the surface of columns was initially totally covered with paint), traces of color do remain. The software was able to demonstrate that Egytian artists went to great lengths in choosing a variety of colors associated with specific hieroglyphic signs (Poiron, Forthcoming). By scanning certain well-preserved colored sections of columns, it would be possible to restore other more damaged portions of the colonnade virtually, a process used for instance by the private Spanish firm Factum Arte in its restored full-size three-dimensional model of the tomb of Tutankhamun.

Conclusion

Using computer-aided devices such as photogrammetry and 3D scanning in order to help epigraphers optimize their work is a trend that is becoming ever more widespread (see chapter by Wendrich). The gains obtained in productivity, exactitude, and breadth of data recording and processing, as well as the opportunities of exploring new research avenues have been nothing short of spectacular. Obstacles do remain, however, in terms of financial investment and technological update (see chapter by Manuelian). Indeed, what at first usually begins as a very costly and complicated technique used only by top-notch developers becomes within a relative short span of time a mainstream and relatively affordable tool, before becoming obsolete with the advent of a new generation of more sophisticated devices. Another challenge is finding a common ground between the objectives of the computer scientist and those of the epigrapher. These objectives may differ in content and scope; what can be considered challenging from the computer developer's point of view may be deemed useless by the epigrapher and vice versa. Keeping up with the state of the research in this field is also a great challenge, since by the time an article is published describing and analyzing a specific method of recording, newer techniques are already being tested and implemented. Problematic also is the fact that some computer scientists and photogrammetrists are content with developing their prototypal software at an experimental stage, allowing potential users to be fully aware of the greats gains that could be made by embracing their innovative ways of working, but not converting their technology into a more user-friendly format. Finally, one must not underestimate a certain reluctance from part of the community of Egyptologists, which is naturally prone to use time-tested traditional techniques, to work with more sophisticated computer tools. One must reckon that such resistance is luckily becoming evanescent with time, as younger generations who grew up with computers feel at ease working with them.

Looking into the future, a revolutionary technological breakthrough in the field of artificial intelligence that is currently under way, but is still at a relatively early stage, may have a phenomenal impact on the way upcoming Egyptologists will work in the field. High-tech companies such as Google and Ubisoft have been heavily investing in a process known as "Deep Learning," where machines are taught to learn on their own, rather than being taught, as was the approach up to now. Whereas computers had to be fed information that had been previously processed in order for them to "think," the next generation of computers will be able to think for themselves, simply by filtering and processing out the data they are being provided. Huge advances in image recognition and natural language processes will allow for much greater accuracy in identifying damaged iconographic units or individual hieroglyphic signs, as well as proposing more correct restitutions of missing texts.

Acknowledgment

The project discussed in this chapter is a joint University of Québec in Montreal—University of Memphis epigraphic mission that has been ongoing since 2011. For current and past financial support, we thank the Social Sciences and Humanities Research Council of Canada, the National Endowment for the Humanities, The American Research Center in Egypt, The University of Memphis, The University of Quebec in Montreal, and the Tandy Institute at Southwestern, and the Centre National de la Recherche Scientifique (CNRS). For their invaluable collaboration and assistance during our field seasons in Karnak, we are very grateful to the Centre franco-égyptien d'étude des temples de Karnak (CFEETK. MAE-CNRS USR 3172), the Egyptian Ministry of Antiquities, and the Chicago House in Luxor for having allowed us to use their flying camera (UAV) in December 2017.

Bibliography

Azim, M., and G. Réveillac, G. 2004. *Karnak dans l'objectif de Georges Legrain: Catalogue raisonné des archives photographiques du premier directeur des travaux de Karnak de 1895 à 1917*. 2 vols. Paris.

Biston-Moulin, S. 2016. *Inventaire des monuments, objets, scènes et inscriptions des temples de Karnak*. Montpellier.

Blyth, E. 2006. *Karnak: Evolution of a Temple*. London.

Brand, P. J. 2000. *The Monuments of Seti I: Epigraphic, Historical and Art Historical Analysis*. PdÄ 16. Leiden.

Brand, P. J. 2001. "Repairs Ancient and Modern in the Great Hypostyle Hall at Karnak." *Bulletin of the American Research Center in Egypt* 180:1–6.

Brand, P. J., E. Laroze, and J. Revez. 2011–2012. "Le projet américano-canadien des colonnes de la salle hypostyle de Karnak. Objectifs globaux et méthodologie." *JSSEA* 38:17–34.

Carlotti, J.-F., and P. Martinez. 2013. "Nouvelles observations architecturales et épigraphiques sur la Grande Salle Hypostyle du temple d'Amon-Rê à Karnak. *KARNAK* 14:231–277.

Chandelier, L., B. Chazaly, Y. Egels, E. Laroze, and D. Schelstraete. 2009. "Numérisation 3D et déroulé photographique des 134 colonnes de la Grande Salle Hypostyle de Karnak." *Revue XYZ, Revue de l'association française de topographie* 120:33–39.

Chéné, A., P. Foliot, and G. Réveillac. 1999. *La pratique de la photographie en archéologie*. Paris.

Christophe, L.-A. 1955. *Temple d'Amon à Karnak: Les divinités des colonnes de la grande salle hypostyle et leurs épithètes*. BdE 21. Cairo.

Eccetta, K. 2013. "Access to the Divine in New Kingdom Egypt: Royal and Public Participation in the Opet Festival." In *Current Research in Egyptology 2012: Proceedings of the Thirteenth Annual Symposium, University of Birmingham 2012*, edited by C. Graves, G. Heffernan, L. McGarrity, E. Millward, and M. Sfakianou Bealby, 1–21. Oxford.

Egels, Y., and E. Laroze. Forthcoming. "The Use of Photogrammetry in Unfurling the Columns of the Hypostyle Hall: Interim Report on the Joint University of Memphis & the Université du Québec à Montréal Epigraphic Mission at Karnak" (provisional title; manuscript in preparation).

Gobeil, C. 2022. "Surveying the Hall: Interim report on the joint University of Memphis & the Université du Québec à Montréal Epigraphic Mission at Karnak" (provisional title; manuscript in preparation).

Golvin, J.-C., and J.-C. Goyon. 1987. *Les bâtisseurs de Karnak*. Paris.

Helck, W. 1976. "Die Systematik der Ausschmückung der hypostylen Halle von Karnak." *MDAIK* 32:57–65.

Laroze, E., and B. Chazaly. 2009. "Relevés des colonnes de la grande salle hypostyle de Karnak." *CRAIBL* 153:669–685.

Luhmann, T., S. Robson, S. Kyle, and J. Boehm. 2014. *Close-Range Photogrammetry and 3D Imaging*. Berlin.

Meyer, E., C. Parisel, P. Grussenmeyer, J. Revez, and T. Tidafi. 2006. "A Computerized Solution for Epigraphic Surveys of Egyptian Temples." *Journal of Archaeological Science* 33:1605–1616.

Murray, O. 2022. "Photography Field Season: Interim report on the joint University of Memphis & the Université du Québec à Montréal Epigraphic Mission at Karnak" (provisional title; manuscript in preparation).

Phillips, J. P. 2002. *The Columns of Egypt*. Manchester.

Poiron, P. 2022. "Colour Methodology: Interim report on the joint University of Memphis & the Université du Québec à Montréal Epigraphic Mission at Karnak" (provisional title; manuscript in preparation).

Prévôt, N. 2013. "The Digital Puzzle of the Talatat from Karnak: A Tool for the Three-Dimensional Reconstruction of Theban Buildings from the Reign of Amenhotep IV." In *Texts, Languages and Information Technology in Egyptology*, edited by S. Polis and J. Winand, 129–138. AegLeo 9. Liège.

Revez, J., T. Tidafi, C. Parisel, E. Meyer, N. Charbonneau, and A. Semlali. 2007. "Méthodes informatisées de relevés et de reconstitution archéologique: Le cas du temple d'Amon à Karnak." In *Proceedings of the Ninth International Congress of Egyptologists—Actes du neuvième congrès international des égyptologues. Grenoble, 6–12 septembre 2004*, edited by J.-C. Goyon and C. Cardin, 1599–1610. OLA 150. Louvain.

Revez, J., and P. J. Brand. 2012. "Le programme décoratif des colonnes de la grande salle hypostyle de Karnak: Bilan de la mission canado-américaine de 2011." *BSFE* 183:10–38.

Revez, J., and P. J. Brand. 2015. "The Notion of Prime Space in the Layout of the Column Decoration in the Great Hypostyle Hall at Karnak." *KARNAK* 15:253–310.

Rondot, V., and J.-C. Golvin. 1989. "Restaurations antiques à l'entrée de la salle hypostyle ramesside du temple d'Amon-Rê à Karnak." *MDAIK* 45:249–259.

Sullivan, E. A. 2012. "Visualizing the Size and Movement of the Portable Festival Barks at Karnak Temple." *BMSAES* 19:1–37.

AN ASSESSMENT OF DIGITAL EPIGRAPHY AND RELATED TECHNOLOGIES

PETER DER MANUELIAN

IT is ironic that Egyptological epigraphy, an altruistic endeavor aimed at preserving the ancient record for posterity, is often practiced today using commercial tools with intentionally built-in obsolescence. While pencil, pen, tracing paper, plastic mylars, and other "basic" tools may always have a role to play in the field (see chapters by Traunecker, Schenck), Egyptologists are increasingly reliant on digital tools over whose life-spans, preferred formats, and sustainability they have little or no control. Introductions to several of these exciting new methods are provided in other chapters in this section (see chapters by Wendrich, Vértes, Revez, Gaber). Since we now appear to be at a technological crossroads—where the hardware and software tools are changing faster than we and our budgets can keep up with them—it is perhaps time to step back and attempt a brief assessment of the state of the art and to reexamine whether some of our basic research and documentation goals and methodologies are still valid.

EVOLUTION OF SCIENTIFIC ILLUSTRATION: THE PATH TO "TRAINED JUDGMENT"

This book is primarily concerned with why we record, what we record, how we record, and finally, how best to disseminate the results. Epigraphy as defined by Egyptology— the facsimile recording of scenes and inscriptions on stone, wood, and other media— differs from definitions found in neighboring disciplines. Classics and Northwest Semitic studies, for example, lay more emphasis on a philological/palaeographical approach to epigraphy (www.digitalepigraphy.org; Bruun and Edmondson 2014;

www.brown.edu/Research/CoDE/; Parker and Rollston 2016), while Egyptology, in the best cases, reproduces the ancient Egyptians' intertwining of text and figural representation. How did our techniques evolve to their current state, and what is the epistemology behind these techniques? Where do the humanities and the sciences intersect over epigraphy, and how do we balance the technical precision possible with today's digital tools with the human element in creating reliable documentation? In an effort to provide some intellectual historical background, I would like to adopt terminology regarding three somewhat sequential phases of scientific illustration, the third of which informs, or should inform, our approach today: "truth-to-nature," "mechanical objectivity," and "trained judgment" (Daston and Galison 2010).

Fundamentals of scientific documentation in the eighteenth century focused on truth-to-nature, particularly in the representation of nature in encyclopedic atlases presenting the world's phenomena. Here, the intent was to portray the generic, the ideal, not the specific item at hand; hence a flower or a snowflake illustration presented the amalgamated composite of dozens of images, the universally perfect snowflake. We find this approach in use even today, where flora and fauna are drawn in a lifelike manner, even though the individual specimen represented never actually existed.

From the first half of the nineteenth century, scientists became aware of the problems with truth-to-nature representation, for the latter obscured the reality of objects. The real world, they perceived, was much messier, and less regular. Ideal shapes were far too removed from nature to be reliable. Scientists now preferred to represent not the subjective, idealized truth-to-nature version, but the objective and specific item, warts and all. Real, imperfect snowflakes began to creep into scientific atlases, replacing their earlier, perfectly symmetrical, universalist counterparts. To quote Daston and Galison, being objective meant to "aspire to knowledge that bears no trace of the knower—knowledge unmarked by prejudice or skill, fantasy or judgment, wishing or striving" (Daston and Galison 2010, 17).

As a banal Egyptological example, we might consider a sun disk (Gardiner Sign List N5) or semicircular bread loaf hieroglyph (X1). The truth-to-nature approach would represent a perfect circle (N5) or semicircle (X1). The same representation based instead on mechanical objectivity would appreciate the imperfections and asymmetry of the specific signs on a specific wall, for there is no absolutely perfect sun disk on any Egyptian inscription, and the rendering would portray all of these individualized flaws accounted for. Another example of the early truth-to-nature approach lies in hieroglyphic printing press fonts and their current-day digital equivalents (Gardiner 1928). As Gardiner and Norman and Nina de Garis Davies designed the hieroglyphs used in Gardiner's *Egyptian Grammar* (Gardiner 1927, xv) based on Eighteenth Dynasty forms, generic, repeatable standards of the signs were of course wanted. Such fonts are indispensable today for typesetting edited hieroglyphic inscriptions, but who among us has not suffered the frustration of their generic nature failing to accurately represent the idiosyncrasies of a specific sign needed (a missing royal beard here or custom-shaped crown there).

As the nineteenth century gave way to the twentieth, problems with mechanical objectivity began to arise. Such overspecificity was blurring the boundaries between what was normal and what was atypical. How could scholars determine if they had produced a rendering that fell within established parameters for "normal" or that represented something truly unique? "Slowly at first and then more frequently, twentieth-century scientists stressed the necessity of seeing scientifically through an interpretive eye; they were after an *interpreted image* that became, at the very least, a necessary addition to the perceived inadequacy of the mechanical one" (Daston and Galison 2010, 311). It is this *interpreted* image that underlies our current approach to Egyptian epigraphy; otherwise, we would be striving to reproduce every chip, stain, and mark on the ancient wall surface to the detriment of the overall product. We may temporarily delude ourselves that we are dispassionately documenting with mechanical objectivity, creating knowledge that leaves "no trace of the knower," but such is an unattainable goal. And the human element, this *trained judgment*, is actually desirable, for it will help us decide which features to include or omit, which to highlight or de-emphasize, as we strive to create a record of ancient Egypt for scholarly research and future generations.

We might apply the three concepts briefly summarized above to Egyptian epigraphy, to demonstrate how we got from there to here, from then to now. Take, for example, the Champollion rendering in the Ramesseum of the siege of a Hittite fortress (Commission 1821–1822, 2: pl. 31), from the 1790s. Although the temple scene is, of course, specific, there is nevertheless a generic, universally representative quality to the rendering, as if it could apply to almost any ancient culture (truth to nature). Comparing this drawing to one of the same scene, a half-century later by Lepsius's artists, reveals a very different result (Lepsius 1849–1859, 3: pl. 166). In the latter case, the Lepsius artists were clearly pursuing their version of mechanical objectivity, even including block lines and damage in many of their drawings. Or let us compare another Champollion drawing, a chariot scene from the Battle Reliefs of Seti I at Karnak (Commission 1821–1822, 3: pl. 38) with its much more recent counterpart (Epigraphic Survey 1986, pl. 28). In the earlier French version, note the "western European" style representation of the torsos on the two largest male figures, shown fully frontal, while the Chicago House version follows the ancient Egyptian mode of representation. That drawing, with all of its interpreted decisions regarding block and architectural lines, damage, the delineation of sunk relief, and modern concrete fill, is an excellent example of trained judgment in epigraphy, "judgment-inflected vision as a goal for scientific sight" (Daston and Galison 2010, 311). James H. Breasted argued similarly, though in simpler terms, in early writings on the epigraphic practice (Breasted 1906, 5).

METHODOLOGY

If trained judgment is our modus operandi today, are our more modern methods holding true to the original philosophy and approach that once only featured tracing paper, plastic or vellum, and pencils and pens? No matter what medium we choose, we still have to interpret the data, make informed decisions about representation and publication, and work in the hope that others will not have to return to the same monument—which may by then display far worse preservation—and repeat/improve on our results.

One immediate advantage of working digitally lies in avoiding any direct contact with the ancient wall surface, with adhesives or other fixatives, something that is unavoidable with direct tracing methods. There are times when contact is necessary, such as when dealing with decorated blocks in reused contexts that are difficult to access (Vértes 2014, 18–19) or working with curved surfaces such as columns, although these can now be digitally "unrolled," but in general, methods are preferable that do not rely on equipment or humans touching decorated surfaces. Moreover, clearer visibility of the ancient surface results where film or other tracing papers, however transparent, do not cover it. The use of photographs as surrogates for the ancient surface allows for work at reduced scale, a critical feature when dealing with temple walls containing hundreds of meters of decoration.

Most digital epigraphy methods, stretching back to the early 1990s (Manuelian 1998b), revolve around modified versions of the Chicago House method (Johnson 2012), where scaled photographs form the template or base from which the artist works. As described earlier in this volume (see chapter by McClain), and therefore just briefly summarized here, photographs—either printed or digital—are "traced" in either preliminary ("pencil version") or final phase on screen. If physical photographs are pencil-traced in the field, the photographs may be subsequently scanned and further processed digitally on-screen. If the workflow is digital from the outset, then on-screen photographs form the base or template for digital "penciling" and "inking." Collations and corrections then follow, preferably in teams, until the drawing is finalized and approved for publication.

Among the advantages of digital epigraphy over traditional methods are ease of editing, scale alteration, merging of individual drawings into a composite, and repurposing for other uses (collation sheets, paleographies, 3D applications). Paper-based drawings using pen and ink only allow for a limited number of changes, since scraping away excess ink with a blade inevitably damages the paper's fibers. On-screen, there is a difference between bitmap and vector lines, which is discussed in what follows, but in both cases the editing of individual lines is easier and the number of "fixes" unlimited. Similarly, the scale of line weights and of final publication size sometimes change over the course of a project; the ramifications here could be serious for pen-and-ink drawings, but less so for digital ones. Large-scale scenes that are composed of many individual drawings are likewise much easier to manipulate on-screen by scaling, rotating, and even changing line weights to match across drawings produced at different times or by different artists. A single final result may be presented in multiples at different scales, from small "key plans" providing an overview of the entire scene, to individual larger-scale details of individual sections, all without the expensive photographic printing costs of bygone eras.

Regardless of whether one works digitally or not, there remain basic conventions of fundamental importance to creating clear, scientifically accurate, and aesthetically pleasing illustrations. Among them are the need to avoid leaving unaccounted for empty space, such as carved leg lines or hieroglyphs that suddenly stop with no explanation. Conventions for damage, plaster, recarving (D'Auria, Lacovara, and Roehrig 1988, 122, cat. 49, recarved rightmost figure), and so forth, are available and should always be used. White space should indicate a pristine, uncarved surface (Manuelian 2002, 790; 2009, 302–303) or an area of modern cement fill. Nor should damage outlines mirror carved or painted lines in style and line weight such that it is difficult to determine which is which, especially in areas of close contact. Conventions and standards are likewise necessary for incorporating data from other sources, such as earlier photographs or drawings that can be distinguished from the rest of the current epigrapher's work. And finally, sun and shadow lines are preferable to single line weights (see what follows).

Pixels versus Vectors

Perhaps the biggest change of mindset required in shifting from analog to digital methods of epigraphic work concerns the use of layers. It is of tremendous advantage to be able to isolate specific elements on their own layers in a digital drawing. Toggling a layer on and off, temporarily shifting an object's opacity for better visibility, color-coding the lines on a specific layer, stacking progressive layers containing elements such as block lines, edges of surface decoration, carved lines, graffiti, paint, and modern wall alterations (e.g., cement fills), all enhance the drawing process and streamline the workflow (Manuelian 1998b, 109). Even further, these layers aid, after the completion of the drawing, in research, teaching, and presentation of the scene or text in question, for one can "peel away" individual items to reveal and focus on others, such as palimpsests, without requiring additional labor (Manuelian 1998a). One can even introduce temporary or hypothetical restorations as "added value" to the finished product.

Layers play a less critical role for drawings that use only a single line weight to represent all the carved elements. This was the method preferred by scholars such as Henry G. Fischer, whose delicate line quality did the ancient monuments great justice, but nevertheless did not capture the sense of topography, of raised or sunk relief (Fischer 1996). I would argue that the inclusion of sun and shadow lines, now fairly well established as a standard convention in Egyptian epigraphy (for a recent exception: Herzberg 2016), adds fundamental value to the documentation, and wherever possible should always be preferred. Differing line weights communicate immediately to the reader whether the decoration is in raised or sunk relief; they lend a sense of three-dimensionality to the artwork, and help distinguish between what can otherwise be very confusing tangles of overlapping offerings, human arms, legs, or other elements (Manuelian 1998b, 106–107). Once we have opted for using differing line weights, then the use of layers can have an even larger role to play in the composition of a drawing.

The use of layers in digital drawing also differs, often drastically, depending on whether one works with pixels (bitmaps or raster images) or vectors (see what follows). This is perhaps the most fundamental decision the artist must make in choosing a digital epigraphic workflow today. Each method has its advantages and disadvantages; the comments that follow center around two current popular and platform-independent drawing applications, Adobe Photoshop (bitmap) and Adobe Illustrator (vector), although these are by no means the only options available. In both cases, the use of a digital drawing tablet and stylus, to replace a trackpad or computer mouse, is the preferred input device. Tablets produced by Wacom seem to represent the input device of choice at this writing, but personal tablet devices are acquiring ever more features and sophistication.

Epigraphic work with bitmaps uses lines and shapes consisting of individual pixels (small squares filled with color, usually percentages of black in our epigraphic usage). Otherwise known as raster images, these square pixels are dependent on the image's resolution to hold their quality. In other words, changing their scale can often produce unwanted results or a loss of sharpness. Drawing or painting with bitmap pixels is probably the more natural and intuitive of our two methods, most akin to analog drawing procedures. The artist can focus on the hieroglyph or figural element at hand, without too much concern about whether it overlaps with other elements; lines are editable by simply adding more pixels inside or outside the line, and using basic eraser tools or other customized shapes to remove unwarranted pixels.

By contrast, vector objects consist of mathematically computed lines occurring between "anchor points" set by the artist. These objects are resolution-independent; relying on Bezier curves, they present the flexibility of editing entire shapes or curves as discrete elements. While applications such as Photoshop seem exclusively bitmap- or raster-based, and Illustrator vector-based, there is in fact some overlap to the workflows between these two approaches. In Photoshop, the freehand brush is certainly one tool for tracing ancient Egyptian carved or painted lines. But for the smoothest fidelity to the ancient Egyptian carving, a better method actually imitates the vector drawing technique of Illustrator. By using the Photoshop pen tool, one can define a path first, and then "stroke" that path of lines or curves with any desired line weight. The result is not a vector line, but a smoothly calculated path of individual pixels. Before deleting the path, one can move it and/or restroke it with another line weight. In this way one can add digital ink to the outside or the inside of an existing line of pixels to create smooth transitions from sun to shadow lines. A similar process can be used to remove pixels for the transition between sun and shadow lines. The line with its sun/shadow transition resides completely on the same drawing layer in this case, and Adobe Photoshop could be said to combine the best of both worlds, smooth vector-based drawing that results in a bitmapped line or shape (Vértes 2014, 131–133).

Pure vector-based drawing operates somewhat differently. The paths are created the same way, but the resulting line or shape is mathematically connected. Changing the curve of one arm, enlarging an offering loaf hieroglyph, or thinning out a nose requires merely adjusting (nonprinting) anchor points by their handles. This flexibility is not possible with (unconnected) bitmap lines and shapes (although a Photoshop feature called "puppet warp" approximates this process). What is less intuitive, however, is that with vector lines often the artist now has to think in terms of closed paths, and the path can be difficult to close when objects break off due to damage at the edge of a block, or

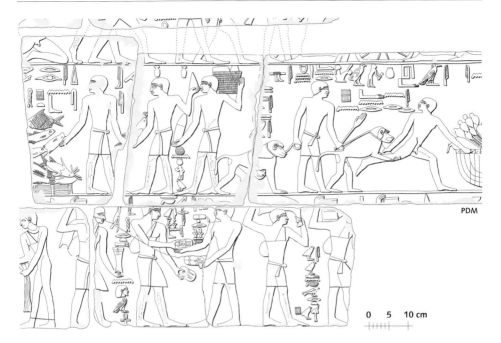

FIGURE III.9.1. Detail from the east wall corridor of the Saqqara mastaba of Tepemankh, demonstrating the difficulties of drawing vector objects across separate limestone blocks; including portions of Brussels E 7297, Cairo CG 1556, Moscow I.1.a.5566, and University College London 14310. Drawing by the author.

continue from one block onto another (Figure III.9.1). Creative solutions to close paths, where undesired lines are hidden beneath other layers, are frequently required.

Two methods are available for creating sun-to-shadow line transitions with vectors. The first uses layers, or at least "send to front" and "send to back" options. The object shape, such as a sun disk hieroglyph, is filled with white, and then duplicated. The duplicated sun disk is then filled with black, and sent behind, or put on a layer underneath the white-filled sun disk. Next, by offsetting the black sun disk (down and to the right for raised relief, up and to the left for sunk relief), one creates a smooth transition of sun and shadow lines using two distinct objects. Editing the thickness of a shadow line is thus far simpler with vectors than with bitmaps.

The second vector method for sun and shadow transitions is a feature peculiar to Adobe Illustrator: the variable line weight tool. In earlier iterations of this application, a line was "stroked" with one, and only one, line weight, such as .25, or 1.0. But the variable line weight tool allows for the same vector line to be thickened or thinned at any point along its path, either manually, or with values typed into a dialog box at each designated point. Using this tool systematically and successfully could eliminate the need for "sun objects" and "shadow objects" altogether, reducing the number of layers necessary, and solving some of the problems of incomplete or unclosed vector paths. To my knowledge, Egyptologists have yet to explore this tool more thoroughly.

It is gratifying to see the amount of digital epigraphy expand in recent years, at Luxor (Epigraphic Survey, Krisztián Vértes, and www.digital-epigraphy.com), Abydos (Sameh Iskander and Ogden Goelet; see what follows), Karnak (Christophe Thiers, temple of Ptah; René Preys at the Second Pylon), Deir el-Bersha (Marleen De Meyer), and Abusir (Jolana Malatkova), just to name a few projects. As noted earlier, each digital epigrapher has a range of options open and must choose the method best suited to the task at hand: bitmaps versus vectors, sun and shadow lines, portable versus studio-bound devices, the need for flexible editing, for repurposing the drawing for other uses, and so forth. My own experience in the past led me to favor vector drawing and Adobe Illustrator, but there are now arguably conclusive arguments to be made for bitmap drawing and Photoshop. The drawing in Figure III.9.2 is a vector drawing. A recent publication, created with a vector drawing workflow (Iskander and Goelet 2015), adopts a landscape format to better accommodate the drawings. While this might make for unwieldy book-shelf storage (for an older and smaller landscape example, see Manuelian 2003), it does great justice to the quality of the digital artwork and allows for reproduction at a suitable scale for viewing details.

Colleagues have often asked whether auto-tracing tools might enhance and speed up the process of digital epigraphy. I have yet to see an application that can produce artwork to meet all Egyptological expectations. Absent, too, would be the "trained judgment" referred to earlier. But perhaps the same technological developments that are carrying face-recognition software to new heights may one day allow us to revisit auto-tracing. One thing is clear: we are not keeping pace in our epigraphic output with the deterioration of the monuments. Whether this means that "crowd-sourcing" and a certain deprofes-sionalization of our workflow (that is, less Egyptology, more digital technology) is the answer, is difficult to assess at present.

Studio and Field Work

In 1998, I speculated that portable devices might one day allow for digital work right at the ancient monument, either in the field or in a museum (Manuelian 1998b, 113). That day has now arrived with a host of drawing tablets, and the range of options will no doubt have expanded more by the time these words appear in print. While tablets have been available for many years, it is only more recently that they possess the processing power to contain full computer operating systems, removing the need to attach them to a laptop and allowing for powerful, full-version drawing applications such as Photoshop and Illustrator to run natively on them (some current examples: Wacom Cintiq Companion 2; Microsoft Surface Pro; and eventually Apple's iPad). Even in those cases where operating systems do not (yet) allow for full drawing applications, there is still great potential for drawing in the field with these devices. There will always be chal-lenges to working with these devices in the field, from issues with battery longevity, to screen glare and refresh rates, ability to handle large photographs as drawing template layers, available Internet connections with sufficient bandwidth, convenience of file

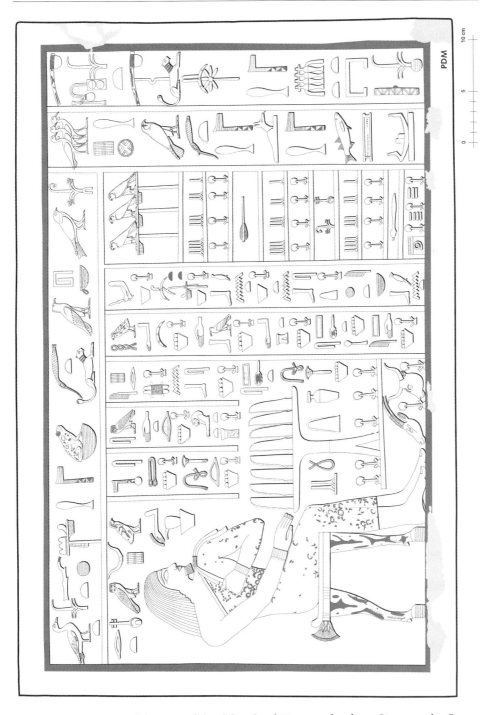

FIGURE III.9.2. Digital drawing of the slab stela of Wepemnefret from Giza mastaba G 1201; Phoebe A. Hearst Museum of Anthropology, Berkeley, 6–19825. Red color (gray in print versions) represents elements painted but not carved. Drawing by the author.

format and file export options, and even protection from dust and sand. The ergonomics of the devices, their weight and ease of use in the often less-than-ideal field conditions, must also be considered. But development is moving in the right direction, and on-site digital epigraphy has become easier, not harder, over time, moving us ever closer to an all-digital workflow, collation sheets included. Powerful drawing tablets are just one of many devices in the archaeologist's toolkit that are currently revolutionizing the immediacy with which we can process archaeological data on-site.

The Third Dimension

Up to this point we have discussed some of the digital tools that assist the Egyptologist/artist in applying trained judgment to the epigraphic process. New visualization technologies are on the horizon, just now reaching critical mass, and these may fundamentally alter our workflow (Factum Arte et al. 2012; Reeves 2015). Chief among them is 3D, and "objectivity" becomes much more complex when one moves from 2D to 3D (see chapter by Wendrich). Virtual reality, augmented reality, and their shrinking costs—while reducing physical size of the devices, from CAVEs (Cave Automatic Virtual Environment) and visualization labs to stereo handsets and smartphones—all give us an immersive experience with the ancient material record. Distinguishing between video games, educational experiences, and 3D research tools with proper source documentation of an archival quality is no mean task; and for purposes of epigraphy, examples of the latter category are few and far between. The admirable Aegaron project, for example, a joint initiative between UCLA and the German Archaeological Institute (http://dai.aegaron.ucla.edu) aims to gather high quality, academically accurate architectural plans of Egyptian monuments online. But no attempt is made at photorealistic reconstructions or epigraphic treatment of decorated wall surfaces; these are essentially wireframe renderings. Digital Karnak, also hosted by UCLA (http://dlib.etc.ucla.edu/projects/Karnak/), moves closer to reality in its architectural renderings, but here too the goal stops short of Egyptian epigraphy. A new project initiated by Elaine Sullivan aims at a comprehensive approach to the monuments of "3D Saqqara," but the focus here is on the sacred landscape rather than individual tomb or temple wall decoration. Ramadan Hussein and colleagues have initiated an all-digital workflow for the Saite tombs at Saqqara (Lang, Hussein, Glissmann, and Kluge, forthcoming).

Photogrammetry, 3D scanning, RTI (reflectance transformation imaging), and other topographically oriented capture methods now have the ability to produce extremely high resolution facsimiles of ancient wall surfaces and other objects. By lighting the same surface from multiple directions and then blending the resulting images together, RTI allows for interactive control of the light source, as well as many specular enhancement tools (e.g., http://culturalheritageimaging.org/Technologies/RTI/). This is optimal for epigraphic work, as it mimics the epigrapher's own predilection for illuminating the wall surface from different angles to confirm where the carved lines are. A more basic substitute for RTI in epigraphy consists of simply layering differently lit images of the same surface area within Photoshop or Illustrator, and toggling these layers on or off as needed for optimal viewing prior to tracing. A more interactive interface, combining RTI with digital epigraphy in a single application, would be a significant advance in our workflow, if it has not already become available by the time this volume appears.

Our own experience at Harvard University with 3D visualization at Giza has only recently begun to integrate traditional archaeological documentation with 3D visualization in a comprehensive manner. Including high-quality epigraphy in this formula is possible but must overcome issues of bandwidth and format standardization, not to mention the collaboration between colleagues with vastly differing skill sets. The painted and carved subterranean chapel of Meresankh III (G 7530-sub) is one of the experiments the Giza Project has undertaken in recent years. Here, the epigraphy from the original Giza Mastabas volume by Dows Dunham and William Kelly Simpson (Dunham and Simpson 1974) was "repurposed," that is, texture-mapped onto a 3D model of the tomb chapel and then colorized based on surviving pigments in the mastaba (Figure III.9.3). We learned much from creating this interactive model, and the immersive experience is a useful teaching tool, but not necessarily a replacement or improvement on the epigraphic record, nor does it contain the type of orthorectified data necessary for a truly archival product; it is more of teaching tool. To begin with, for practical reasons the original Harvard University–Boston Museum of Fine Arts Expedition-era drawings were used as the underlying epigraphic template for the 3D reconstruction. These drawings, prepared in the late 1920s with some additions and

FIGURE III.9.3. 3D visualization of the west wall of the subterranean chapel of Queen Meresankh III, Giza mastaba G 7530-sub, based on HU-MFA Expedition epigraphy from the 1920s. 3D model by David Hopkins and the Giza Project, Harvard University.

corrections by W. S. Smith in the early 1950s and by other Museum of Fine Arts staff in the early 1970s, hardly conform to some of the more rigorous epigraphic conventions of today. Second, the resolution of our locally hosted 3D model of the tomb is quite high, but to load the tomb model on the Internet requires a lower-count polygon model, and thus some of the resolution and quality are lost. (Presumably, these limitations will disappear with time). The model presents some interesting architectural study opportunities and has already provided new research questions for us, but these are more related to the three-dimensional space and orientation of the structure than to the details embedded in the epigraphy.

How these tools and projects will alter our objectivity and our trained judgment remains to be determined. There have been valuable attempts to bring some standardizations and definitions of best practices to our efforts (for example, Denard 2009). Some are skeptical, asserting that archaeologists have often tended to "*apply* VR techniques first and *think* about them later" (Gillings 2005, 224). The notion that we are "bringing the past back to life" is also a myth; as Gillings writes, "rather than treating VR models as wholly objective simulations that should always aim to replicate some source reality as faithfully as possible, VR models should instead be seen as constructs which can never be wholly authentic" (Gillings 2005, 230). Or, to put it even more harshly: "Even if you follow the rules, the only certain thing about any reconstruction drawing is that it is wrong. The only real question is, how wrong is it?" (James 1997, 25). A recent volume on computer-generated archaeological visualizations even has the intriguing subtitle "Between Added Value and Deception" (Wittur 2013).

With these objections to virtual reality, coupled with powerful tools such as photogrammetry and RTI lighting and spectral imaging effects, we might be tempted to ask the question: Should we keep drawing in faithful adherence to our traditional Egyptological approach? I would argue in the affirmative, for none of these techniques quite replaces the "trained judgment," the value added to the interpretation of the ancient record by the eye of the Egyptologist. To those who might argue that we have lost the human element in our rush to adopt digital tools (see the hypothetical reactions quoted by Rick 2012, 443), one has only to look at examples in the manual of digital epigraphy by Krisztián Vértes (2014) or its online companion, digital-epigraphy.com. These examples faithfully—and digitally—reproduce the Chicago House method, down to the accurate reproduction of damage, stippling/modeling, and even fragmentary traces of color. Most readers today would be unable to distinguish these digital drawings from traditional pen-and-ink Chicago House epigraphy. In fact, these methods are taking us into the realm of reproducing paint traces on decorated wall surfaces; with today's on-demand printing and online dissemination potential, we have the ability to take traditional Egyptological epigraphy into territory that earlier publication methods could not have enabled.

The reproduction of color and recording of painted wall surfaces that are *not* carved, have in the past been seen as the Achilles heel of the digital approach. Painted lines, being of variable and varying width, were deemed too irregular to reproduce with digital tools. But we have seen above that both bitmap and vector drawing tools have the ability to reproduce lines of any style and fluctuation. Digital drawings also allow for color-coding of selected areas. In the recent publication of the Theban tomb of Menna, black indicates decoration at time of recording by Melinda Hartwig's team. Green shows the original decoration when Robert Mond's photographs documented the tomb, and blue lines show the first phase of (ancient Egyptian) decoration on the Valley Festival Wall. Artist Pieter Collet traced digital photos that were stitched together (Hartwig 2013, xvi, 22, 48–49, fig. 2.8b). An early, analog example of such color-coded hieroglyphs is the hand copy of the decree of Horemheb (Kruchten 1981, foldout plate). Hartwig's volume extends its analysis far beyond digital drawing to include a wide variety of archaeological science applications, such as analysis of the chemical composition of the pigments used on the different walls of the tomb.

It is hoped that eventually 3D immersive visualizations will also include the option to experience Egyptian wall decoration at the same quality levels that we currently enjoy studying a drawing by the Epigraphic Survey, or the Czech Expedition to Abusir, or the Franco-Egyptian Center at Karnak. Perhaps properly prepared vector drawings might better assist in the conversion effort than bitmap drawings, as they can be more easily resized for 3D mapping purposes. Vector lines can always be exported and converted to raster, but the conversion in the opposite direction is more problematic, auto-trace applications notwithstanding.

Challenges

Keeping pace with technological change is an obvious challenge to digital epigraphy. This writer has already experienced the termination of his once favorite vector drawing application, and despite the porting of hundreds of drawings over to different software, even the common EPS (Encapsulated Postscript) format failed to preserve many elements painstakingly added. Formats and standards are still in flux. Beyond these questions, however, lurks the larger one of data management plans. Safe storage of paper-inked drawings represents the familiar analog challenge; the digital challenge is even greater, for even despite the integrity of file formats and data, the hardware readers and players will continue to evolve, eventually rendering old files unreadable. Cloud storage represents an admirable solution, provided there are enough mirror sites and backups to assure longevity. A suitable system of metadata for version control is likewise key, so that loss of a digital artist to employment elsewhere does not render entire file structures and storage locations inaccessible. A host of new sustainability obligations, including future format conversion, must be built into the workflow, as the digital life-span of epigraphic artwork requires maintenance like any other source of valuable electronic data. With careful planning, the trained judgment applied to the epigraphic process can also survive via the potentially long-term sustainability of digital recordings, one of the most mission-critical aspects of Egyptological primary source documentation.

BIBLIOGRAPHY

Breasted, J. H. 1906. "First Preliminary Report of the Egyptian Expedition." *AJSL* 23 (1):1–64.

Bruun, C., and J. Edmondson. 2014. *The Oxford Handbook of Roman Epigraphy.* Oxford.

Commission des sciences et arts d'Egypte (Commission). 1821–1822. *Description de l'Egypte, ou, Recueil des observations et des recherches qui ont été faites en Égypte pendant l'éxpédition de l'armée française,* Antiquités, vols. 2–3. 2nd ed. Paris.

Daston, L., and P. Galison. 2010. *Objectivity.* New York.

D'Auria, S., P. Lacovara, and C. H. Roehrig. 1988. *Mummies and Magic: The Funerary Arts of Ancient Egypt.* Boston.

Denard, H., ed. 2009. "The London Charter (for the Computer-Based Visualization of Cultural Heritage)." http://www.londoncharter.org.

Digital-Epigraphy. http://www.digital-epigraphy.com/

Dunham, D., and W. K. Simpson. 1974. *The Mastaba of Queen Mersyankh III G 7530–7540.* Boston.

Epigraphic Survey, The. 1986. *Reliefs and Inscriptions at Karnak* III: *The Battle Reliefs of King Sety I.* OIP 107. Chicago.

Factum Arte, The Society for the Friends of the Royal Tombs of Egypt, The Factum Foundation for Digital Technology in Conservation, and the University of Basel. 2012. *The Authorized Facsimile of the Burial Chamber of Tutankhamun with Sarcophagus, Sarcophagus Lid and the Missing Fragment from the South Wall.* With texts by A. Lowe and J. Macmillan Scott. [Madrid?]

Fischer, H. G. 1996. *Varia Nova.* New York.

Gardiner, A. H. 1927. *Egyptian Grammar: Being an Introduction to the Study of Hieroglyphs.* Oxford.

Gardiner, A. H. 1928. *Catalogue of Egyptian Hieroglyphic Printing Type.* London.

Gillings, M. 2005. "The Real, the Virtually Real and the Hyperreal: The Role of VR in Archaeology." In *Envisioning the Past: Archaeology and the Image,* edited by S. Smiles and S. Moser. 223–239. Oxford.

Hartwig, M., ed. 2013. *The Tomb Chapel of Menna (TT 69): The Art, Culture, and Science of Painting in an Egyptian Tomb.* Cairo.

Herzberg A. 2016. "Zu den memphitischen Grabreliefs in der Sammlung des Ägyptischen Museums–Georg Steindorff–der Universität Leipzig." *ZÄS* 143 (1):34–59.

Iskander, S., and O. Goelet. 2015. *The Temple of Ramesses II in Abydos.* 2 vols. Atlanta.

James, S. 1997. "Drawing Inferences: Visual Reconstructions in Theory and Practice," in *The Cultural Life of Images: Visual Representation in Archaeology,* edited by B. L. Molyneaux, 22–48. London.

Johnson, W. R. 2012. "The Epigraphic Survey and the 'Chicago Method.'" In *Picturing the Past: Imaging and Imagining the Ancient Middle East,* edited by J. Green, E. Teeter, and J. A. Larson, 31–38. OIMP 34. Chicago.

Kruchten, J.-M. 1981. *Le décret d'Horemheb: Traduction, commentaire épigraphique, philologique et institutionnel.* Brussels.

Lang, M., R. Hussein, B. Glissmann, and P. Kluge. "Digital Documentation of the Saite Tombs at Saqqara." *Studies in Digital Heritage,* forthcoming.

Lepsius, C. R. 1849–1859. *Denkmäler aus Ägypten und Äthiopien.* 6 vols. Berlin.

Manuelian, P. Der. 1998a. "A Case of Prefabrication at Giza? The False Door of Inti." *JARCE* 35:115–127.

Manuelian, P. Der. 1998b. "Digital Epigraphy: An Approach to Streamlining Egyptological Epigraphic Method." *JARCE* 35:97–113.

Manuelian, P. Der. 2019. "The 2D/3D conundrum: An epigraphic experiment from the early days of digital epigraphy." http://www.digital-epigraphy.com/projects/the-2d-3d-conundrum-an-epigraphic-experiment-from-the-early-days-of-digital-epigraphy

Manuelian, P. Der. 2002. "Unfinished Business: The Giza Tablet of Tjenti (JE 72135)." In *Egyptian Museum Collections around the World: Studies for the Centennial of the Egyptian Museum, Cairo*, edited by M. Eldamaty and M. Trad, 777–790. Cairo.

Manuelian, P. Der. 2003. *Slab Stelae of the Giza Necropolis.* PPYE 7. New Haven.

Parker, H. D. D., and C. A. Rollston. 2016. "The Epigraphic Digital Lab: Teaching Epigraphy in the Twenty-First Century. *NEA* 79 (1):44–56.

Reeves, N. 2015. "The Burial of Nefertiti?" *ARTP. Valley of the Kings. Occasional Paper* 1:1–16.

Rick, J. 2012. "Realizing the Illustration Potential of Digital Models and Images: Beyond Visualization." In *Past Presented: Archaeological Illustration and the Ancient Americas*, edited by J. Pillsbury, 413–446. Washington, DC.

Vértes, K. 2014. *Digital Epigraphy.* Chicago. Retrieved from https://oi.uchicago.edu/research/publications/misc/digital-epigraphy.

Wittur, J. 2013. *Computer-Generated 3D-Visualisations in Archaeology: Between Added Value and Deception.* Oxford.

....

PRACTICAL ISSUES CONCERNING EPIGRAPHIC WORK IN TOMBS AND TEMPLES

....

HANANE GABER

BECAUSE epigraphy has often been undeservedly overlooked, it was described as the "Cinderella of the Egyptological science" (Faulkner 1945, 115). It is not, however, implemented as an end in itself, since it produces primary data for the study of different aspects of Egyptian culture (Bell 1996, 97). Epigraphy, as an auxiliary science of history, focuses on the investigation of monumental decoration. It includes the documentation, translation, interpretation, and publication of texts and related figures (Traunecker 1987, 262–263; Dorman 2001, 471–472). Recording monuments is a priority, especially at those sites that are endangered and rapidly disintegrating (Caminos 1987, 57; Bell 1987, 43–44, pls. 1–2; Manuelian 1998, 97–98).

As a first step of epigraphy, the recording of texts and scenes should be accurate and reliable (Bell 1996, 97). The amount and accuracy of information has not been the same in all periods due to epigraphers' technical tools, knowledge, and standards. Some of the first freehand copies made for the *Description de l'Égypte* and produced by other Egyptologists in the nineteenth century were of excellent quality (Caminos 1976, 3–7; Dorman 2001, 472–474). Interesting discrepancies can be seen, however, when a text and scene have been reproduced by different groups, such as, for example, the battle reliefs of Seti I at Karnak (Champollion [1845] 1969, 294–294(a); Rosellini [1832] 1977, pls. 60–61; The Epigraphic Survey 1986, 15–16). Despite their differences, the earlier records are very important because the inscriptions have suffered damage since that time. Other recording methods, such as photography and tracing, were established later. The technological tools currently available provide new ways to approach epigraphic work.

The epigrapher can now select from new and traditional epigraphic techniques. Many factors should be taken in consideration in order to choose the most appropriate method: the work season, the available equipment, the number of members taking part in the mission, the kind of material that should be copied, and the degree of the completeness of the record (Caminos 1976, 19–20; Traunecker 1987, 263–264; Dorman 2001, 475). The present contribution aims to outline how the practical issues of working in tombs and temples often dictate the choice of epigraphic system, how epigraphers have previously dealt with the particular challenges of working in each place, and how new technologies help to solve epigraphic problems, taking into account my recent work in tombs and temples.

THE TOMBS

The conservation status of a tomb or other monument should be examined before starting an epigraphic project in order to choose the most suitable technical way to study its texts and figures. The walls of burial chambers are sometimes covered in a layer of dirt caused by the accumulation of dust or smoke. Ideally, a conservator would remove this layer before epigraphic work begins, as happened in the chapel of Sennefer (TT 96A) (Tavier 2007). An interesting case is the tomb of Seti I, which has suffered not only from the ravages of time but also from modern travelers and early epigraphers. The Theban Mapping Project then removed sections of graffiti dated from the nineteenth and twentieth centuries and sent them to museums around the world, and cleaned from the walls the traces of wax and vegetable fiber that G. B. Belzoni had applied in order to carry out the oldest tracings (Lowe 2016, 540–541).

When I worked for my doctoral thesis in the tombs of Amennakht, Nebenmaat, and Khameteri (TT 218, TT 219, TT 220) with the IFAO French Mission in Deir el-Medina, it was difficult to ask to clean some parts of the tombs, as the Supreme Council of Antiquities had restored them in the mid-1990s (Gaber 2002a; Gaber 2002b; Gaber 2004). In order to see more details, I used different types of artificial light in the burial chambers and sunlight when it illuminated the south parts of the chapels TT 218 and TT 219 in the morning and their north parts in the afternoon.

Tombs are often characterized by their small and dark areas. The small amount of available light that penetrates chapels, mastaba rooms, and other tiny areas has typically ruled out photography as a viable method of recording wall scenes (Caminos 1976, 16). The Oriental Institute, however, recorded the mastaba of Mereruka at Saqqara with photographs and with facsimile drawings (The Sakkarah Expedition 1938). The first epigraphers used not only mirrors but also many silver-papered reflectors to conduct light to remote underground rooms (Wilkinson and Hill 1983, 19–20). New technologies, particularly digital photography, help facilitate the taking of photographs in difficult light conditions. In one of the Deir el-Medina chapels, natural sunlight, diffused evenly in the space through a light piece of cloth that was hung in the entrance, was enough to make photogrammetric measurements and a 3D model (Onézime and Pollin 2014, 388).

But to photograph other scenes, continuous artificial lighting or camera flashes are currently necessary (Onézime and Pollin 2014, 379–380; Lowe 2016, 539).

Because of photography problems, especially in the past, tracing is one of the oldest methods for studying inscriptions and reliefs in small and poorly lighted chapels (Traunecker 1987, 279–281). The epigrapher copies the surfaces to be recorded on a transparent film. This task is not one of mechanical drawing, but of objective drawing. The epigrapher should avoid all personal artistic tendencies and try to imitate the original tracings of the ancient artist. This work requires intense concentration and constant analysis and interpretation. When the traced lines are collated (i.e., compared and analyzed with the original), the hieroglyphs and the figures are penciled or crayoned before being reduced for publication (Traunecker 1987, 269–270, 279–281; Bell 1987, 50–51; Caminos 1976, 23–24). This is the method used by Norman de Garis Davies to copy many Theban tombs in Luxor and Memphis with excellent results (e.g., Davies 1920; Caminos 1976, 11). Other epigraphers have followed his example (e.g., Polz 1997). To achieve their work, modern copyists need much more natural or artificial light than did the ancient artist because they aim to match their drawings with the tomb inscriptions and figures (Wilkinson and Hill 1983, 18–22).

When the scene is damaged, the epigrapher can combine epigraphic methods. S/he might prepare a direct tracing. The second technique is photographing with different lights to get the best shots. Recent improvements in digital imagery would help the epigrapher to review the completeness of drawings and to make a "subjective" decision about how to do it. The Chicago House method faithfully records all significant details (Bell 1987, 47). A similar point of view considers a drawn copy as communicating the current state of the wall, called "strata," which include all details of texts and figures, including damage and additions that have affected the wall up to the present time (Polz 1987, 134–135).

Another complication besides damage to a scene is difficult breathing conditions and high temperatures caused by artificial light sources and other factors that could prevent and discourage staying a long time in a burial chamber to carry out a one-to-one tracing. The large number of representations and texts in numerous decorated rooms has also prompted epigraphers today to prepare tracings from digital photographs, as in Saite tombs (e.g., Régen, forthcoming). Otherwise, direct tracings would need very long periods of continuous work on site, which is not possible for most Egyptologists, aside from large epigraphic missions.

Two new technologies have resolved the difficulty in taking photographs in narrow areas. The first one is the 3D laser scanner. This expensive tool has been used in a few projects, such as the tombs of Seti I and Tutankhamun and some of Abusir tombs (Lowe 2016, 535–540; Malatkova 2011, 195–199). The second solution is photogrammetry as a 3D digitizing technique (Onézime and Pollin 2014, 378–379; see chapter by Revez).

Most tombs have beautifully colored inscriptions and figures. The accurate recording of colors was very problematic in the past for technical reasons: the inability of cameras to accurately capture colors as the eye sees them, the expensive cost of printing color photographs, the soil and debris on the walls that obscured paint colors, and the lighting problems mentioned above (Caminos 1976, 22–23; Traunecker 1987, 275; Bell 1987, 49, 53; Le Saout 1982, 89; Wilkinson and Hill 1983, 22–23). The description of pictorial shades using Munsell Soil Color Charts allowed readers to recognize exact colors and their variants (Alzogaray and Vera 2012, 117–126).

If the cost of producing colored plates is still quite high, the faithfulness of their reproductions is more secure through new technological tools, such as digital photography and 3D laser scanning. Through this last technique, colors in high resolution were recorded in the tombs of Seti I and Tutankhamun (Lowe 2016, 536).

In the tombs TT 218–TT 220, I combined many epigraphic approaches according to the conservation status of the monument and tiny areas. Because the burial chambers are well conserved, their decoration was recorded in digital images and old black-and-white photographs that have more details than recent ones. I did a freehand, autographic version of the texts, taking into account the relative proportions between signs and also between columns in a scene (Traunecker 1987, 283–285; Pantalacci and Traunecker 1990, 14–15). I later replaced the manual copy of inscriptions by typographic characters (JSesh) to prepare the final publication according to the edition standards. I have also carried out tracings from photographs of characteristic hieroglyphs to comment on their palaeography. Combining old and recent photographs, typographic characters, and drawings of many hieroglyphic signs was less time-consuming than tracing the whole very long set of inscriptions in the burial chambers that are mainly composed of solar hymns and Book of the Dead chapters.

However, complete direct tracings were essential, as photographs were not enough to record the tiny entrance corridor leading to the burial chambers and chapels of TT 218, TT 219, and TT 220. As high-quality digital photographs of the tombs of Amennakht and his sons (TT 218–TT 220) had been made, I decided to record only the major broken areas when they intrude on the ancient carved and painted lines. Combining digital imagery and drawings to include a minimum of damaged parts reduced the amount of time spent drawing a scene and made its reading clear.

Major epigraphic progress due to new technologies has been made between the starting of the study of these graves and its present final edition that will be submitted soon for publication to the IFAO. When I started the work in these tombs, photographs of the tiny entrance corridor were not taken perpendicularly to its walls, but from the end of the corridor, as there was not enough room. Applied recently to TT 218–TT 220, photogrammetry provided orthorectified photographs for the tiny entrance corridor that will be presented with the direct tracings of this area in the next publication of these graves.

In the chapel of Amennakht (TT 218), many personal names and titles mentioned in the excavations report are no longer visible (Bruyère 1928, 55–68). Direct tracings recorded the actual status of the wall, but restitutions of damaged texts were made in the transliteration and the translation of hieroglyphic inscriptions. In this case, when some remains of hieroglyphic signs that are only flakes of paint became invisible, new technologies are extremely helpful. When digital photographs or 3D models are inserted into specified software programs, such as DStrech, the epigrapher can see details that are not visible to the naked eye (Onézime and Pollin 2014, 388). Applied to Amennakht's chapel (TT 218), this approach enables one to see inscriptions that then are added to the tracings.

The Temples

Initially, one might not realize that the epigrapher has to face similar problems in a tomb as in a temple, but there are some common practical issues between both types of monuments.

A common trait shared between both cultic spaces is the darkness. Some temple walls are currently not lit because they are behind other recent buildings or columns (Vértes 2014, 18). Some rooms also are completely dark because of their ancient function as storage areas and crypts. In temples dating to the Greco-Roman era, these rooms are often richly decorated. Parts of temples like these ones share certain characteristics with tombs and, likewise, also share the same epigraphic solutions that were mentioned earlier.

As in tombs, if some parts of the inscriptions and scenes have disappeared, in particular the upper registers in temples, the epigrapher could combine many recording procedures. A direct tracing could be drawn with a vector-based software and enhanced with preserved details from old photographs in order to reconstitute the damaged texts and figures, as was done for the Saite chapels of Ayn el-Muftella in Bahariya and Debod Temple (Labrique 2014a, 163–164; Díaz-Iglesias Llanos and Méndez Rodríguez 2014).

Many *dipinti* and graffiti that are on temple walls and in tombs need to be studied. Sometimes, they could not be noticed for some generations as their rough outlines were obscured under a layer of soot. The traditional way to record them is by photographing and direct drawing, when the area in which they are situated is cleaned (Kurth, Waitkus, and Effland, 2010, 1–2). Modern technologies make possible an association of two kinds of photographs that benefit from computer aid. The first one is an interactive reflectance transformation imaging (RTI) image, which combines a set of shots taken in the same circumstances. The location of the camera should be fixed during the whole work with the only variable being light. The second photograph results from the insertion of the RTI image in ImageJ and DStretch software (Witkowski, Chyla, and Ejsmond 2016).

Despite these common issues, some differences distinguish a tomb's structure and its work conditions from those of a temple: open areas, numerous separated blocks in some cases, large number of hieroglyphs in the Greco-Roman temples, and the great heights of walls and carved surfaces.

In temples, many halls and rooms are large and partially or completely illuminated by the sunlight. These conditions, combined with the generally good state of preservation in temples, favor the use of direct tracings, as is used by the Franco-Egyptian mission in Karnak Temple (Pécoil 2000, 31; see chapter by Thiers). This method is more appropriate for stones, such as sandstone and granite, because photographs of these stones are often not legible enough to serve as a basis for drawings.

The open areas of many rooms in a temple and their access to sunlight also favor digital photography. To capture wall scenes under optimum light, the epigrapher should choose the best time in the daily course of the sun when a wall of a court or other open room is well lit (Thiers and Abdel Aziz 2016, 35). In other cases, however, the sunlight makes the photography as well as the reading of the inscriptions quite difficult. For example, when epigraphic work is carried out in a hypostyle hall, openings in the ceiling pose an obstacle for the photographer trying to shoot all the walls with the same light. The openings were thus obscured during the photography of the hypostyle hall of Sokar and Nefertem in the temple of Seti I in Abydos (Gaber 2010). The epigraphic team might also work sometimes in the night with artificial light if the daylight makes the inscriptions invisible, as happened in the Hathor Temple in Serabit el-Khadim (Leclant and Clerc 1995, 253).

The remains of a temple are sometimes reduced to separate blocks. These can be recorded by photography and by direct tracings, as in the case of Montu Temple in Tod and Bastet Temple at Tell Basta (Thiers 2003; Brandl 2003). The photographing of certain blocks is particularly problematic as they can be very heavy, unstable, and difficult to move when they are not in their original places (e.g., blocks of a destroyed wall or reused stones), and their bright granite material inhibits the camera's ability to capture their reliefs in photographs. The photographer might use a tent, a mirror, and a small structure to fix a camera on telescopic beams and to move it easily in parallel to the photographed block (Wenzel and Beyer 2003). This fixed system makes it possible to take a series of shots of each stone without moving the position of the whole equipment for each shot, which saves time and effort. The epigraphy of other blocks, such as the *talatats* that were found in the ninth pylon in Karnak, is more problematic. Their large number, totaling around six thousand stones, and the absence of a direct visual connection between them presents difficulties to their recording and study. Epigraphers have not only used photography and direct tracings to document them but also inventoried and indexed them, and entered that information into a database. The latter enables research by many criteria corresponding to indexed iconographic topics and makes it possible to reassemble photographs of the blocks and insert line drawings into the missing areas between them (Vergnieux 1999, 57–92; Lauffray 1980; Bell 1996, 104).

Temples from the Greco-Roman era have a unique feature: the large number of hieroglyphs as compared with earlier eras and their numerous variants, as is found in the temples at Esna, Deir Chelouit, and el-Qal'a. This phenomenon should be considered when choosing an epigraphic method for sites dated to this era. The difficulties created by the many and diverse hieroglyphs found in these texts will often complicate the ability to copy them in tracing in the temple. On the one hand, the simple identification of the sign variants is very difficult, and on the other, the Ptolemaic text edition must be interpreted in order to be accessible to the reader (Sauneron 1959, 159–160; Zivie 1982, xiii; Pantalacci and Traunecker 1990, 15). Epigraphers resolved this problem in the past with two solutions. The first one was a freehand-drawn copy of the texts, which could take into account the relative proportions between signs and also between columns in a scene (Traunecker 1987, 283–285; Pantalacci and Traunecker 1990, 14–15). The second possibility was choosing typographic characters to transcribe the inscriptions, as in the Esna temple publications (Sauneron 1963, vii–viii; Sauneron 1959, 159–160). Despite the relative ease and the speed of the autographic versus the typographic transcription of texts, the latter method does not communicate the original shapes of the signs (Traunecker 1987, 282). Some epigraphers combine the typographic transcription of texts with tracings of representative group of signs in order to comment on their paleographic forms. Other epigraphers, however, prefer to prepare complete tracings from photographs, as was done at the temple at Athribis (Leitz, Mendel, and El-Masry 2010). This task can now be realized through digital epigraphy (see what follows). In addition to the lines drawn by vector software, there is another epigraphic technique that would be faster. The digital photographs, the hieroglyphic signs, and the bonding of stones (i.e., the spaces between the stone blocks) are drawn by means of Bezier curves in the software Autocad. Despite the fact that this method has been only applied to Karnak Temple, it could be adapted to other temples for its simple and flexible use (Meyer et al. 2006).

One should find an epigraphic system adapted to the great height of the walls and the carved architectural elements in temples dated from New Kingdom and Greco-Roman eras. In order to deal mainly with these both difficulties, digital epigraphy was chosen to record the complex of Sokar and Nefertem in Seti I's temple at Abydos (Gaber 2010). The methodological principles are the same as those established by the Oriental Institute, and it offers the epigrapher the benefits of having computer aid (see chapters by McClain, Vértes). The process of digital epigraphy includes two main steps (Manuelian 1998). The first step is to provide an image that will be imported into a vector drawing program. The image could be a scanned facsimile drawing reduced to a scale of 1:1, an old slide that has been digitally scanned, a digital photograph, or a photograph produced by photogrammetry or by 3D scanner. The second step is the drawing of the texts and scenes from the image with a vector-based software and digitizing tablet (Vértes 2014, 14–15; Manuelian 1998, 102). Thanks to the support of the *Seminar für Ägyptologie* in Cologne and the German Archaeological Institute (DAI) in Cairo, students in Cologne University and employees in the former Supreme Council of Antiquities had the chance to learn these digital tracing techniques (Gaber 2010; Gaber 2013).

The advantages to the digital methods are numerous: the ease of corrections, the fast process of copying drawn hieroglyphic signs, the easy addition of variants to the corpus, and the comparison of the hieroglyphs' palaeography. The difference between digital and traditional epigraphy is comparable to producing a text with word processing software or with a typewriter (Manuelian 1998, 108–110; Malatkova 2011, 192).

Despite the advantages of digital epigraphy, it is not an easy task to get good undistorted photographs of texts and scenes located high on such temple walls or on carved architectural elements. It is, however, an essential step as it forms the basis of the whole epigraphic work (Malatkova 2011; see chapter by Kurth).

Epigraphic work done at great heights on a temple wall requires the use of ladders or scaffolds to be positioned in front of and parallel to the photographed scene to avoid distortion (Vértes 2014, 14). New technologies now make digital photography easier.

Photogrammetry associates the topographical survey of the architecture of a monument to its decoration. In some cases, this procedure saves the effort of using ladders or scaffolds that require a long time to be set into place (Onézime and Pollin 2014, 381). If for some reason an epigraphic mission could not use this new technology, cameras fixed on telescopic beams enable epigraphers to take photographs of elevated texts and figures without building scaffolding. The missions of Edfu and Kom Ombo have recently used this system (Labrique 2014b, 165).

The first step of digital epigraphy, which is photography of high parts of walls and carved architectural elements, was one of the big challenges for the studying project of the Sokar and Nefertem complex. Photogrammetry and cameras fixed on telescopic beams were not available during the missions at the Abydos temple, as their use was developed later. Ladders and scaffolds have been used in successive missions. When the photographer stood on a ladder, he tried different kind of lights to get a clearer and sharper image, but the camera position was not consistent every time. It was then very difficult to gather two shots of the same scene in a computer program to draw complementary details. Thanks to the American mission at Shunet el-Zebib, which lent scaffolds for the work in the Sokar and Nefertem complex, and due to its well-trained workmen, the photography of the elevated scenes and texts was successful (Gaber 2010; Gaber 2013).

The carved scenes and texts on a cylindrical column or on a vaulted ceiling in the complex of Sokar and Nefertem are naturally distorted on photographs (Figure III.10.1). In the past, epigraphers solved this problem by using rubbing, squeezes, or direct tracings. Rubbing was used to reproduce the decorated columns of Seti I's temple in Abydos (Calverley and Broome 1938, viii, pl. 19–26; Caminos 1976, 15–18; Le Saout 1982, 88; Traunecker 1987, 267–269; Dorman 2001, 474–475). Direct tracing of the text is one of the most commonly employed methods of copying curved surfaces. A member of the French mission bought to Luxor nylon sheets that were used to copy the columns of Esna Temple (Dorman 2001, 474; Pécoil 2000, 31; Le Saout 1982, 88). Facsimiles are usually used by the Epigraphic Survey to copy columns, while flat surfaces are copied from photographs (Dorman 1998, xx–xxi; Vértes 2014, 40). Again, new technologies provide some appropriate solutions for the difficulty of recording curved areas. With photogrammetry and 3D computer modeling, the epigrapher produces images that overlap with one another. The images can be gathered in the form of a plane surface, thus enabling epigraphers to draw inscriptions from photographs with the help of vector software (Meyer et al. 2006, 8–9; Chandelier et al. 2009, 38–39).

It was not possible to carry out direct tracings of the three columns of the hypostyle hall of Sokar and Nefertem and the vaulted ceiling of the chapel of Nefertem because the Egyptian Ministry of State for Antiquities has forbidden this method in Seti I's temple in Abydos. Digital photography of the columns and the vaulted ceiling served then as basis for the tracings. However, obtaining undistorted photographs was not easy, especially before the development of the photogrammetry procedure. One of the principles of this method has been followed during the digital photography of the curved areas. It means that the photographer had a great deal of overlap between individual photographs of one column scene to gather them as plane surface with a computer software

FIGURE III.10.1. Photograph of Sokar hypostyle hall, west column, north scene: original image. © Mission Abydos-Cologne.

(Adobe Photoshop). This procedure enables the epigrapher to do tracings of the whole scene from one plane photograph through vector software (Adobe Illustrator). Two kinds of processes were used in digital photography. When two or three shots of one scene on a column (i.e., a quarter of one column) were taken, their rectifying and gathering as a plane surface through specialized software was difficult and needed careful checking. This procedure consisted of comparing dimensions of the original photograph with the orthorectified one (i.e., stretched in order to simulate that the photograph was taken perpendicularly to the wall) to avoid as much distortion as possible. When the overlap between the individual photographs of one representation was bigger, meaning that one column scene was recorded by nine shots, they were put together and more easily rectified using computer software (Figures III.10.2 and III.10.3).

During the work in the Sokar and Nefertem complex, whose decoration was unfinished and left unpainted, another technical problem was the difference in colors in photographs that were taken with different lights. In order to resolve this difficulty, the photographer placed a fixed colorimetric scale on the photographed surface to guarantee the accuracy of the colors. This procedure allows the viewer to calibrate the colors of the scale in comparison with those of the walls (Figure III.10.1; Gaber 2013, 182–183, figs. 1–2).

FIGURE III.10.2. Sokar hypostyle hall, center column, north scene: orthorectified image.
© Mission Abydos-Cologne.

Conclusion

The same recording solutions could be appropriate in similar circumstances in tombs and temples. Both places have dark rooms and graffiti or other invisible or erased paintings. However, other practical issues are different when working in different places. In tombs, the epigrapher should find the best epigraphic method to record decorated small and dark areas in tombs. Potentially problematic issues when doing epigraphy in temples include texts and scenes located on high walls, decorated carved columns or vaulted ceilings, and the difficulty in interpreting the large corpus of hieroglyphic signs in Greco-Roman temples. The work condition sometimes dictates the epigraphic method. For example, photography should be used instead of direct tracing to record decorated high walls.

In TT 218, TT 219, and TT 220 of Deir el-Medina, the problems that I faced were related to the tiny areas and damaged walls, for which direct tracings have been prepared. New technologies have helped to resolve some epigraphic problems by using photogrammetry for the whole tomb, including tiny places, and software that helps to

FIGURE III.10.3. Sokar hypostyle hall, center column, north scene. Drawing by Johanna Schmitz. © Mission Abydos-Cologne.

see details that are not visible to the naked eye. During the work in the complex of Sokar and Nefertem of Seti I's temple, other practical issues were problematic, mainly the height of walls and carved columns. Digital epigraphy was the most appropriate way to deal with both issues.

Whether traditional tracings or digital epigraphy is used, the epigrapher could get the best epigraphic results when taking into consideration the work circumstances of each site, and also the preferred method of recording. The accuracy of epigraphy is certainly improved by the enhancement of computer tools and software. However, this new technology could not be the major factor for excellence in recording Egyptian monuments. Quality in epigraphy finally lies in the best use of work circumstances, the appropriate choice of epigraphic technique, and numerous collations.

ACKNOWLEDGMENTS

I thank Laurent Bavay, Françoise Labrique, Sandra Lippert, Olivier Onézime, Isabelle Régen, Christophe Thiers, and Thierry Van Compernolle for the discussions we had about this topic.

BIBLIOGRAPHY

Alzogaray, N. C., and M. S. Vera. 2012. "Las variables del color en la tumba de Neferhotep (TT49)." In *Novos trabalhos de Egiptologia Ibérica: IV Congresso Ibérico de Egiptologia—IV Congreso Ibérico de Egiptología*, vol. 1, edited by L. M. de Araújo and J. das Candeias Sales, 117–126. Lisbon.

Bell, L. 1987. "The Epigraphic Survey: The Philosophy of Egyptian Epigraphy and Sixty Years' Practical Experience." In *Problems and Priorities in Egyptian Archaeology*, edited by J. Assmann, G. Burkard, and V. Davies, 43–55. London.

Bell, L. 1996. "New Kingdom Epigraphy." In *The American Discovery of Ancient Egypt: Essays*, edited by N. Thomas, 97–109. Los Angeles.

Brandl, H. 2003. "Die epigraphische Reliefaufname." In *Rekonstruktion und Restaurierung in Tell Basta*, edited by C. Tietze, 138–145. Arcus 6. Potsdam.

Bruyère, B. 1928. "Rapport sur les fouilles de Deir el Médineh (1927)." *FIFAO* 5:53–91.

Calverley, A. M., and M. F. Broome. 1938. *The Temple of King Sethos I at Abydos, Volume 3: The Osiris Complex*. Edited by A. H. Gardiner. London.

Caminos, R. A. 1976. "The Recording of Inscriptions and Scenes in Tombs and Temples." In *Ancient Egyptian Epigraphy and Paleography*, 3–25. New York.

Caminos, R. A. 1987. "Epigraphy in the Field." In *Problems and Priorities in Egyptian Archaeology*, edited by J. Assmann, G. Burkard, and V. Davies, 57–67. London.

Champollion, J.-F. (1845) 1969. *Monuments de l'Égypte et de la Nubie*, III. Paris. Reprint, Geneva.

Chandelier, L., B. Chazaly, Y. Egels, E. Laroze, and D. Schelstraete. 2009. "Numérisation 3D et déroulé photographique des 134 colonnes de la Grande Salle Hypostyle de Karnak." *Revue XYZ* 120:33–39.

Davies, N. de G. 1920. *The Tomb of Antefoker, Vizier of Sesostris I and His Wife, Senet (No. 60)*. TTS 2. London.

Díaz-Iglesias Llanos, L. E., and D. M. Méndez Rodríguez. 2014. "Digital Epigraphy of the Temple of Debod." *EA* 45:39–41.

Dorman, P. F. 2001. "Epigraphy." In *Oxford Encyclopedia of Ancient Egypt*, edited by D. B. Redford, 471–477. New York.

Dorman, P. F. 1998. "Preface." In *Reliefs and Inscriptions at Luxor Temple, Volume 2: The Facade, Portals, Upper Register Scenes, Columns, Marginalia, and Statuary in the Colonnade Hall*, by The Epigraphic Survey. OIP 116. Chicago.

Epigraphic Survey, The. 1986. *Reliefs and Inscriptions at Karnak, Volume 4: The Battle Reliefs of King Sety I*. OIP 107. Chicago.

Faulkner, R. O. 1945. "Review of N. de G. Davies, The Tomb of Rekh-mi-Re at Thebes. Publications of the Egyptian Expedition XI. New York, 1944." *JEA* 31:115.

Gaber, H. 2002a. "L'au-delà selon les artisans: Le décor des sépultures d'Amennakht, de Nebenmaat et de Khameteri (tombes thébaines n° 218, 219, 220)." *Les Dossiers d'Archéologie* 272:38–47.

Gaber, H. 2002b. "Différences thématiques dans la décoration des tombes thébaines polychromes et monochromes de Deir al-Médîna." *BIFAO* 102:211–230.

Gaber, H. 2004. "L'orientation des défunts dans les 'caveaux–sarcophages' à Deir el-Médina." *BIFAO* 104:215–228.

Gaber, H. 2010. "Le complexe de Sokar et de Nefertoum dans le temple de Séthi I à Abydos." *Dialogues d'Histoire Ancienne* 36(1):187–194.

Gaber, H. 2013. "La chapelle de Nefertoum dans le temple de Séthi I à Abydos." *Dialogues d'Histoire Ancienne* 39(1):180–183.

Kurth, D., W. Waitkus, and A. Effland. 2010. *Edfu: Neue Graffiti und Ritualszenen des Tempels von Edfu*. Die Inschriften des Tempels von Edfu, Abteilung 2, Dokumentationen 2. Gladbeck.

Labrique, F. 2014a. "Ayn el-Mouftella." *Dialogues d'Histoire Ancienne* 40(1): 163–164.

Labrique, F. 2014b. "Kom Ombo." *Dialogues d'Histoire Ancienne* 40(1): 165–166.

Lauffray, J. 1980. "Les 'talatats' du IXe pylône et le *Teny-menou* (assemblage et première reconstruction d'une paroi du temple d'Aton dans le musée de Louqsor)." *Karnak* 6:67–89.

Leclant, J., and G. Clerc. 1995. "Fouilles et travaux en Égypte et au Soudan, 1993–1994." *Orientalia* 64(3): 225–355.

Leitz, C., D. Mendel, and Y. El-Masry. 2010. *Athribis II: Der Tempel Ptolemaios XII. Die Inschriften und Reliefs der Opfersäle, des Umgangs und der Sanktuarräume*. 3 vols. Cairo.

Lowe, A. 2016. "Tomb Recording: Epigraphy, Photography, Digital Imaging, and 3D Surveys." In *The Oxford Handbook of the Valley of the Kings*, edited by R. H. Wilkinson and K. Weeks, 528–543. Oxford.

Malatkova, J. 2011. "Searching for an Undistorted Template (Digital Epigraphy in Action)." In *Old Kingdom, New Perspectives: Egyptian Art and Archaeology 2750–2150 bc*, edited by N. Strudwick and H. Strudwick, 192–199. Oxford.

Manuelian, P. Der. 1998. "Digital Epigraphy: An Approach to Streamlining Egyptological Epigraphic Method." *JARCE* 35:97–113.

Meyer, É., P. Grussenmeyer, C. Parisel, J. Revez, and T. Tidafi. 2006. "A computerized solution for the epigraphic survey in Egyptian Temples." *JAS* 11:1605–1616.

Onézime, O., and G. Pollin. 2014. "La place de la photogrammétrie en égyptologie et en archéologie égyptienne: Réflexions méthodologiques et premiers résultats sur les chantiers de l'IFAO." *BIFAO* 114:375–396.

Pantalacci, L., and C. Traunecker. 1990. *Le temple d'el-Qal'a. I: Relevés des scènes et des textes. Sanctuaire central, sanctuaire nord, salle des offrandes 1 à 112.* Cairo.

Pécoil, J.-F. 2000. *L'Akh-menou de Thoutmosis III à Karnak: La Heret-ib et les chapelles attenantes. Relevés épigraphiques.* Paris.

Polz, D. 1987. "Excavation and Recording of a Theban Tomb: Some Remarks on Recording Methods." In *Problems and Priorities in Egyptian Archaeology*, edited by J. Assmann, G. Burkard, and V. Davies, 119–140. London.

Polz, D. 1997. *Das Grab des Hui und des Kel: Theben Nr. 54.* AVDAIK 74. Mainz.

Régen, I. Forthcoming. "Tombe de Padiaménopé (TT 33), (1er–15 novembre 2015)." In *Rapport d'activité. Supplément au BIFAO* 116:254–259.

Rosellini, I. (1832) 1977. *I monumenti dell'Egitto e della Nubia. Parte Prima. Monumenti Storici.* Pisa. Reprint, Geneva.

The Sakkarah Expedition. 1938. *The Mastaba of Mereruka, Part I.* OIP 31. Chicago.

Saout, F. Le 1982. "Les techniques de relevés épigraphiques." *Dossiers Histoire et Archéologie* 61:88–91.

Sauneron, S. 1959. *Quatre campagnes à Esna.* Esna I. Cairo.

Sauneron, S. 1963. *Le Temple d'Esna.* Esna II. Cairo.

Tavier, H. 2007. "*Materiam superabat opus*: La conservation-restauration de la chapelle de Sennefer (TT 96A)." *EAO* 45:33–42.

Thiers, C. 2003. *Tôd: Les inscriptions du temple ptolémaïque et romain, II. Textes et scènes nos 173–329.* FIFAO 18. Cairo.

Thiers, C., and M. Abdel Aziz. 2016. *French-Egyptian Centre for the Study of the Temples of Karnak. MoA-CNRS USR 3172, Activity Report 2015.* Luxor.

Traunecker, C. 1987. "Les techniques d'épigraphie de terrain: principes et pratique." In *Problems and Priorities in Egyptian Archaeology*, edited by J. Assmann, G. Burkard, and V. Davies, 261–298. London.

Vergnieux, R. 1999. *Recherches sur les monuments thébains d'Amenhotep IV à l'aide d'outils informatiques: Méthodes et résultats.* 2 vols. CSEG 4. Genève.

Vértes, K. 2014. *Digital Epigraphy.* Chicago. Retrieved from https://oi.uchicago.edu/research/publications/misc/digital-epigraphy.

Wenzel, G., and H.-D. Beyer. 2003. "Die photographische Reliefaufnahme." In *Rekonstruktion und Restaurierung in Tell Basta*, edited by C. Tietze, 153–156. Arcus 6. Potsdam.

Wilkinson, C. K., and M. Hill. 1983. *Egyptian Wall Paintings: The Metropolitan Museum of Art's Collection of Facsimiles.* New York.

Witkowski, P., J. M. Chyla, and W. Ejsmond. 2016. "Combination of RTI and Decorrelation: An Approach to the Examination of Badly Preserved Rock Inscriptions and Rock Art at Gebelein (Egypt)." In *CAA2015. Keep the Revolution Going: Proceedings of the 43rd Annual Conference on Computer Applications and Quantitative Methods in Archaeology. Volume 1*, edited by S. Campana, R. Scopigno, G. Carpentiero, and M. Cirillo, 939–944. 2 vols. Oxford.

Zivie, C. M. 1982. *Le Temple de Deir Chelouit: 1–55, Inscriptions du propylône et de la porte du temple.* Cairo.

CHAPTER III.11

···

GRAFFITI

···

CHIARA SALVADOR

In a volume dedicated to epigraphy and palaeography of ancient Egypt, graffiti can be regarded as "an integral part of Egyptian writing practice and of official culture" (Parkinson 1999, 92), and as such, they are treated here as a category in its own right. The word "graffiti" (plural of graffito) comes from the Italian verb *graffiare* (to scratch), which derives from *graphium* (Greek γραφιον), the Latin word for a stylus, the pointed rod or metal tool used as writing implement on waxed tablets (Lewis and Short 1900, 824).

Graffiti reflect a widespread writing practice that is attested in Egypt and throughout the ancient world (Baird and Taylor 2011; Ragazzoli et al., 2018). Defining this category of evidence, however, is complicated by its huge diversity. Graffiti consist of texts (often in a mix of scripts), individual signs, and drawings, including geometric and abstract images. Textual and pictorial graffiti are occasionally combined so as to form more or less elaborate and formal scenes. Graffiti are often perceived as being extremely rough, hastily scribbled, and/or lacking any previous planning. This may be true in some instances, but graffiti can also be carefully thought through and skillfully executed by scribes and/or artists either for themselves or on commission. Their size, visibility, and the techniques used to make them vary considerably. Graffiti can be very small and hidden in dark, inaccessible areas or very large and displayed prominently. The better surviving examples are carved. These include graffiti that have been finely incised with a sharp tool and others that have been crudely hammered out. Graffiti can also be painted, and these tend to survive only in interior spaces, which accounts for why they are mostly preserved in tombs. More elaborate examples are incised, plastered, and painted. The finest ones can be inlaid, of which only hollowed surfaces usually survive (e.g., Frood 2016, 321, fig. 2).

In Egypt, graffiti were left virtually everywhere and throughout all periods, from prehistory (rock art) to the end of the pharaonic era and up to the present. They are found in natural landscapes, such as along desert roads, and on man-made surfaces, mostly tombs and temples; domestic structures might have been inscribed with graffiti as well, but archaeological evidence is too scant to prove it. Some graffiti appear isolated, though others often cluster and "dialogue" with one another. Caution is required when referring to graffiti as "informal" and "unofficial." Such definitions depend on context and are never synonyms of something "illicit." Although one cannot exclude that some graffiti were illicit, their widespread preservation in active sacred contexts (e.g., Salvador 2016) demonstrates that they were commonly accepted. Their nature is so diverse that any attempt to define more precisely this category of evidence has so far been frustrated by counterexamples (e.g., Navrátilová 2010, 309–310). As of now, there is no general agreement as to whether pottery and masons' marks should be included in this category. The same applies to terminology. Some scholars focus on technique and adopt the distinction between "graffiti" (incised) and "*dipinti*" (painted). Others focus more on context and distinguish "graffiti" (on man-made surfaces) from "rock inscriptions" (on natural surfaces). Such terminology is convenient when dealing with a fairly homogeneous corpus of graffiti, yet it appears insufficient to designate this fuzzy category as a whole. For convenience, this chapter adopts the all-encompassing term "graffiti" to indicate all those texts, signs, marks, and drawings that have been deliberately marked on a surface that was not designed to receive them (Dijkstra 2012, 19; Frood 2013, 286).

History of Graffiti Recording

The word "graffito" was first introduced to Egyptology by Auguste Mariette in 1850 during his fieldwork season at the Serapeum (Desroches Noblecourt 1973, 154), even though copies of some graffiti in the temple of Philae have been produced as early as 1799 (e.g., Commission 1822, pl. 55). Despite travelers' and scholars' early interest in graffiti, these have hardly been the object of systematic research. For a long time, archaeologists and epigraphers working in Egypt, as elsewhere, have failed to acknowledge graffiti as a distinct epigraphic category. Textual graffiti have often been examined only for their content, but their usual brevity, as opposed to most monumental inscriptions, often disappointed scholars seeking new historical data. This is exemplified by Gardiner, who contributed a chapter on graffiti in Davies's publication of the Twelfth Dynasty Theban Tomb 60, but commented, "there is but little information beyond a few proper names to be gleaned from these fortuitous scribblings" (Davies 1920, 27). As Ragazzoli (2013, 273) points out, Egyptologists' initial approach to these texts was inevitably influenced by a generally dismissive attitude of scholars, exemplified in opinions about graffiti in Pompeii, even though these included hundreds of literary texts. These had been considered "examples of distortion which affects 'real' literature as it passes into the popular imagination, where it is consumed and reproduced by those not fully competent to understand it" (Milnor 2014, viii). Such an approach led scholars of both disciplines to dismiss graffiti as "low" cultural products that could hardly provide any relevant information (Baird and Taylor 2011, 1–2).

One exception to this prevalent attitude is represented by the pioneering work of Spiegelberg (1921), who in 1895–1896 conducted a systematic epigraphic mission in the

Theban necropolis to record graffiti of the workmen of Deir el-Medina and visitors of the royal tombs. His work on the graffiti of the Theban mountain was later continued by Černý and his team, resulting in a monumental work of four volumes that is still considered a milestone in graffiti research (Černý et al. 1969–1983). Other scholars have dealt with graffiti, but mostly within broader studies (for overviews, Desroches Noblecourt 1973; Navrátilová 2015, 15–26; on an overview of published textual graffiti, see Peden 2001).

Over the past two decades, however, an ever-growing attention toward this category of evidence has emerged. An increasing effort is put into recording them systematically and studying their implications within well-defined contexts (e.g., Di Cerbo and Jasnow 2011; Dijkstra 2012; Frood 2010, 2013; Navrátilová 2015; Pelt and Staring, in press; Ragazzoli 2013; Staring 2011; Tallet 2012). This reflects an interest in more interpretative and sociological analyses of monuments that take into account their "use-life," that is, the ways in which monuments are modified and appropriated through time, sometimes acquiring new meanings (van Walsem 2006, 112). Graffiti are now commonly recognized as adding layers of historical and cultural data to the surface in which they are inscribed (Staring 2011, 145), and their presence reveals people's attitudes toward a monument or an environment at the time when they were produced (see chapter by Navratilova). As such, they are valuable sources to access aspects of Egyptian society usually unattested in other inscriptions and scenes.

Documenting Graffiti

This section outlines some documentation issues that are peculiar to graffiti. Given the variety of this discrete, yet loosely defined category, some of the points that follow may partially duplicate those treated in other contributions to this volume.

Documenting a corpus of graffiti can be described as a four-step process comprising (1) a preliminary survey, (2) recording, (3) collation, and (4) a post-recording process. This is inevitably a schematic overview that seeks to highlight the main stages of the process as they seem in 2016. Despite being presented as clear-cut, each of these four phases is inherently interlaced with the next, but for clarity's sake they are discussed separately.

Survey

"Survey" here is intended as the process of locating graffiti and does not include recording, which for convenience is treated as a distinct phase. The aim of a graffiti survey is to examine and record the position of each individual drawing, mark, and inscription present in an area, so that it can be easily retrieved and recorded at a second stage. This is an essential step toward a preliminary assessment of a graffiti corpus. However, identification and location of the material to be recorded can be challenging, and one of the peculiarities of graffiti is that they are often very difficult to detect. This is due to two main factors. First, unlike most scenes and texts carved and/or painted in funerary and temple contexts (which are arranged on walls according to well-defined criteria), graffiti can be inscribed on any surface, increasing exponentially the areas in which they can be found. This need not, however, imply that graffiti were left in random places (on graffiti patterns at different periods, see Rutherford 2003, 182–185). Second, graffiti can be chameleonic and very hard to spot even under close examination. Painted graffiti tend to fade and become almost invisible, being easily mistaken for stains on the wall. In some cases, photography, together with digital enhancement, can help detect some graffiti otherwise invisible to the human eye or, in the case with old archival photos of faint painted graffiti, help improve their reading (e.g., Di Cerbo and Jasnow 2011, 46–47). This can be attained by altering the light and color adjustments on Photoshop or through other image processing programs, such as the open-source Image-J (http://rsb.info. nih.gov/ij/). In particular, the D-stretch plug-in to Image-J (http://www.dstretch. com), acquirable online through a donation, has proven extremely effective with faint red-ink inscriptions, as demonstrated by Roland Enmarch in his epigraphic project in Quarry P at Hatnub (conference paper, "Scribbling through History," Oxford, September 25, 2013).

Carved graffiti, on the other hand, can be incised very lightly on the surface and be virtually invisible even from a close distance, unless viewed in a raking light. Natural erosion, deliberate erasure, and palimpsests can further complicate their visibility. Therefore, it is highly advisable to survey a place several times and at different hours of the day, to examine all surfaces under different light conditions. In reality, this is not always possible: some areas, due to their location, are never hit by a natural raking light, or only over a short period of the year, which may not correspond to the epigraphers' field season. Some places may be too remote to be visited more than once. In such cases, a mirror can help redirect sunbeams so as to create a raking light and reveal the presence of possible graffiti, and in dark places, a torch or a cost-efficient portable LED lamp can be used instead.

Surveying may pose different challenges with respect to the scale and accessibility of the area of inquiry. According to whether this is part of a built or natural environment, the plans and elevations of a structure or topographical maps can be used to plot detected graffiti: the more detailed the initial drawing, the more accurate the resulting graffiti map is going to be. The latter allows a preliminary assessment of the size of the corpus and its overall density, which may highlight clusters and/or isolated graffiti.

Survey techniques vary according to the size and nature of the investigated area as well as the equipment at one's disposal. Graffiti in a temple wall, for instance, can be anchored to preexisting features in the elevation, such as block lines or other scenes, or directly onto photographs of the wall (Figure III.11.1). Mapping graffiti in a desert though may pose more of a challenge. When Černý and his team surveyed graffiti on the Theban mountain in 1966, they used 1:2000 stereo-photogrammetric maps with contour lines, indicating altitudes and depressions, every two meters. These had been produced for the project from stereoscopic aerial photographs by the National Geographic Institute of Paris (IGN) in 1965–1966 (Černý et al. 1969–1983, I.1:iii–iv, viii). Graffiti were

FIGURE III.11.1. Examples of graffiti (within circles) plotted on features of the elevation and digitally labeled. Detail of the west wall of the court of the seventh pylon, temple of Amun, Karnak. © CNRS-CFEETK.

then plotted on enlargements of individual sections of cliffs that had been drawn by the surveyors of the IGN (Černý et al. 1969–1983, II.1:i–ii).

Technological progress has made this process easier and more reliable. Contemporary desert graffiti surveys can benefit from satellite images and employ Global Positioning System (GPS) to acquire the absolute position of a graffitied area (e.g., Tallet 2012). This instrument has the advantage of being extremely precise and portable. However, a GPS alone is not sufficient to pinpoint the relative position of each graffito in the case of a complex cluster. For the latter, a precise drawing of the whole surface is needed. This can be obtained using a traditional (manual) topographical drawing, or with the aid of a total station, or else capturing the whole surface with a 3D laser scanner. Although very accurate, both devices are extremely expensive and heavy to carry around. A cost-effective substitute for this technology is offered by the employment of a simple digital camera and Agisoft PhotoScan software, which generates 3D surfaces from digital photographs (http://www.agisoft.com).

Plotting graffiti on a plan or map is essential, but hardly sufficient to locate and record graffiti at a later stage, when they can easily escape sight under altered light conditions. It is good practice to keep a diary in which to annotate the position and to give a brief

FIGURE III.11.2. Recording graffiti (labeled on paper tape) on an outcrop in cemetery D, Amara West, Sudan. Photo by Paolo Del Vesco.

description and a sketch of the graffiti. This information should be complemented with photographs, ideally with a scale and a reference to the north. In the case of clusters, temporary labels made of paper tape can be employed to further ease their identification (Figure III.11.2). These however can be easily removed by hot and sandy wind. Labels can be added digitally onto the photograph of a cluster, thus avoiding any alteration to the surface; this proves particularly effective when graffiti cluster on decorated surfaces that should not be affected in any way (Figure III.11.1).

The survey is important not only as a preparatory step to plan recording, but also at a later phase of analysis. A detailed graffiti map allows an assessment (and interpretation) of graffiti with respect to their relationship with one another and their surrounding landscape. Such a map may highlight some graffiti hotspots in geologically meaningful areas, such as graffiti carved in the Theban royal necropolis next to rock cracks (e.g., Dorn 2014, 65), or in accessible parts of a structure, such as visitors' graffiti left in tomb chapels (e.g., Navrátilová 2015; Ragazzoli 2013), or it may reveal clusters in cool, shady areas, such as the unfinished tomb MMA 504 that overlooks the temples of Deir el-Bahri (Ragazzoli and Frood 2013, 32).

Recording

As with "formal" inscriptions and scenes, recording graffiti is in the first place a means of preservation. Graffiti, like all other evidence, are destined to disappear with the passage of time, due to a combination of natural and anthropic factors (e.g., Di Cerbo and Jasnow 2011, 49). Thanks to published and unpublished documentation produced by epigraphers, it is today possible to retrace graffiti that were investigated earlier, assess their current state of preservation, integrate them with newly discovered ones, and sometimes ascertain that some recorded graffiti are no longer extant. Detailed and faithful documentation is therefore of paramount importance to guarantee, or at least attempt, the preservation of this category of evidence and to enable research and analysis, especially since in many cases epigraphic records may eventually turn out to be the only surviving data.

Some recording methods can be more objective than others, but are not necessarily the best. A method used to produce highly accurate records of incised graffiti is that of squeezes, employed at least since the time of Spiegelberg, in the late nineteenth century, until more recently (e.g., photographs of some squeezes produced by Traunecker in the 1970s in his unpublished archive of Karnak graffiti, housed at the Griffith Institute, Oxford). Squeezes were usually obtained by pressing wet paper against an incised surface with the help of a flat brush and then letting it dry before removing it (McLean 2002, 67). This produced an impression of the incised graffito that was economic, portable and, if well executed, extremely accurate. Archival squeezes, also from very early expeditions, remain a valuable research tool to check hardly accessible or worn inscriptions, which at times may provide new readings of published material (e.g., current research by Charlotte Booth, *A Study of the Egyptian Squeezes in Small UK Collections*). This is the case with an oracle inscription (Sinai 13), which was collated with archival squeezes in the British Museum and published in a corrected edition by Baines and Parkinson (1997). Nevertheless, this technique has some limitations. First, squeezes are not effective with very shallow or painted graffiti. Second, their production process is nonselective, and the incised graffito is recorded along with its visual background noise—gouges, scratches, surface porosity, and asperities—not facilitating readability. But most importantly, squeezes are destructive and no longer acceptable on conservation grounds. When detached, the paper cast removes part of the incised surface, including also plaster and pigments, damaging it irreversibly.

In contrast, a nondestructive and sustainable technique, employed since its invention, is photography. Digital photography in particular has the advantage of producing high-resolution records, virtually as many as one desires, at a very low cost. Photographs can provide information about a graffitied surface, including possible traces of color, as well as about its overall context, complementing any other recording method. In addition, digital photographs can be easily manipulated using Photoshop or similar software for enhanced legibility. Nevertheless, photography alone is not enough to record graffiti, especially incised ones, as their legibility can vary considerably according to the light and the angle from which they have been taken (McLean 2002, 68). Further, as a noninterpretative method, photography does not distinguish what has been carved and/or painted intentionally from other surface alterations. This is why traditional epigraphy, in its various styles, such as the CFEETK and Chicago House methods (see chapters by Thiers, McClain), is still often regarded as the most effective way to produce a clear and detailed record.

Traditional epigraphy consists of tracing with a thin permanent marker on a transparent film adhering to the graffitied surface, thus producing a 1:1 record. Since transparent films are electrostatic, the surface to be recorded needs to be gently cleaned with a brush to prevent the film from attracting too much dust, which would prevent the epigrapher from seeing what is underneath. The transparent film should be secured with some kind of adhesive, making sure not to damage the original surface. Last, after careful observation and with the aid of a mirror to guarantee a strong raking light, one should proceed with the tracing, following the edges of each figure and sign.

This process may sound straightforward, and probably every epigrapher has been approached at least once by a tourist who has dismissed their work as requiring no skills or effort. In fact, the production of an accurate epigraphic record involves specific skills and training. Unlike squeezes and photography, epigraphy involves a level of interpretation that aims to establish what to trace as part of the graffito and what to mark as unintentional scratches or deliberate erasures. In other words, epigraphy is a constant *decision*-making exercise, in which there is a tension between precision and objectivity, on the one hand, and on the other, a necessity to minimize visual background noise so as to produce an informative and readable drawing. Essential requirements for an epigrapher are well-developed observation skills and some knowledge of the object to be recorded, be that its iconography or palaeography. Specific epigraphic conventions are also applied. For instance, to minimize distortions due to marker thickness, painted graffiti are traced using as a guide the inner side of the edge of each sign, employing a method similar to that applied to ostraca (Ragazzoli, pers. comm., August 12, 2016). As for carved graffiti, these are usually marked with a double line, following the inner and outer line of every incision composing the sign, rather than tracing a single line at the center of the inci-sion. When interplay between graffiti and "formal" scenes occurs, the former are usually traced with a thinner line, while dotted lines usually indicate gouges and scratches. Finally, elements traced in a different color or a differently dotted line may indicate palimpsests.

Compared to photography this method is time-consuming. Yet, while photography is the starting point for advancing hypotheses of readings that need to be checked onsite, epigraphy is the result of these two activities combined. In this respect, epigraphy is much more than a recording technique; it is also an analytical tool in itself that very often provides an interpretation to otherwise obscure graffiti.[1]

Variations of this method include tracing graffiti on a transparent film over a printed downscaled photograph or drawing them digitally, on a drawing tablet or on a com-puter, from high-resolution rectified photographs (see Di Cerbo and Jasnow 2011, 35; see chapters by Thiers, McClain, Vértes). The latter has the great advantage of allowing remote work, which is essential when time in the field is not sufficient to record every-thing manually. As discussed later, no drawings thus produced can be deemed reliable unless verified against the original.

Current technological advances are expanding possibilities to record and clarify readings of previously unclear graffiti. Alongside digital enhancement mentioned previously, reflectance transformation imaging (RTI) is proving very effective on incised

---

[1] In 2017 Egyptian authorities issued a ban on traditional epigraphic recording, so this technique is no longer permitted in Egypt, but is still allowed in the Sudan.

palimpsest and partially erased graffiti, such as those carved on the temple of Ptah at Karnak (Frood and Howley 2014). The method is affordable and consists of taking a number of high-resolution photographs of a graffito along with a reflecting sphere; keeping the camera firmly in the same position, each photograph is taken with an external light positioned at slightly different angles, until a rotation of 360° is completed. All photographs (between thirty and seventy) are then processed through RTI software. This produces a highly detailed image of the graffito whose light can be manipulated in every direction, sometimes clarifying readings and processes of carving. Thus, RTI can be considered the advanced version of a squeeze, with the advantage that it produces more reliable and readable images without damaging the original surface. A limit of this technique, however, is that it is harder to apply on graffiti carved high up on a surface, for which large and stable scaffoldings are necessary to position the camera on a tripod while being able to move the light source around the graffito at each shot. Another downside of RTI is that the final image results in a large file that can be consulted only in its digital format. Paper publications can only provide single shots of the image, losing the possibility for the reader to control the light and double-check readings. Recently, 3-D modeling and orthophotography are proving reliable and more flexible techniques to produce high-resolution facsimiles of graffitied surfaces (Urcia, Darnell, and Darnell 2018).

In conclusion, recording strategies vary considerably in relation to a number of factors, including the type and context of graffiti to be recorded as well as the resources and time at the epigrapher's disposal. Sophisticated equipment and lengthy field seasons are ideal, but good results can be obtained even with limited means and time. Flexibility and creativity are important skills in the field, especially when an unplanned opportunity to record a graffito presents itself, as in 2014, when I was working as a find registrar in Amara West, Sudan. Having learned that a desert outcrop in cemetery D was covered in graffiti, I offered to document them. Due to the tight schedule, I suggested that I record them photographically and produce the drawing of only the most complex one. In the dig house, I found a roll of transparent sheet, which was perfect for epigraphy, but there was no fine marker, no self-standing mirror with which I usually work, nor any marker remover to erase and correct my drawing. A thick permanent marker and the small hand-mirror from my bedroom, which I could hold with my teeth while lying on the sand, were used to produce an informative and accurate drawing. And the jungle-formula repellent in which we were "bathing" every day proved more effective in removing parts of my tracings than in keeping insects away (Figure III.11.2).

Collation

All epigraphic records, whether realized on a transparent film on the graffitied surface, on a scaled photograph, or produced digitally, always need to be checked against their original source. In epigraphy, this procedure is called collation and is an essential step in the documentation process, not only with graffiti, but with every epigraphic record.

Although an integral part of recording, collation is here briefly treated separately to emphasize its importance as a key stage of documentation.

Graffiti need to be checked with fresh eyes, that is, not immediately after producing a drawing. Whenever possible, this should be done under optimal light conditions so as to catch any possible inaccuracy or slip. In order to limit possible biased readings, collation is best done by a person other than the one who produced the drawing, although this is not always possible. As the subtlest variations of light can suggest a different reading, it is fairly common to integrate small amendments to the first drawing. In particular, signs that at a first view appear to be intentional may later appear to be part of the surface roughness, or vice versa.

Post-Recording Process

Once information has been acquired through different techniques—squeezes, traditional epigraphy, or high-resolution rectified photographs—the image has to be processed in order to be suitable for publication and for being securely archived.

The three-dimensionality of squeezes makes them particularly challenging to process, store, and preserve in the long term. Squeezes are made of layers of paper; with time, these tend to exfoliate and crumple due to their storage conditions. Conservators can stabilize old squeezes, slowing down this deterioration process, but the best way to preserve and store them is with digitization (McLean 2002, 73). This can be done by photographing paper casts with a raking light in order to capture the topography of the surface. Smaller squeezes can also be scanned, though images tend to be rather flat due to the even light source, with the risk of losing detail. The process of digitization is extremely useful not only for conservation and storage, but also for publication in two dimensions.

Photographic images can be used to produce epigraphic drawings of the incision, either on a transparent film over the photo or digitally through drawing software. As with traditional epigraphy, all drawings traced on a transparent film have to be inked to be ready for publication. Until a few years ago inking was done manually, directly over the original drawing (see chapter by McClain), but now this method has often been replaced by digital inking on layer-based graphics editors, such as Photoshop and Illustrator. The first step of this process is the digitization of the epigraphic drawing through a scanner or rectified photographs. In this way, the drawing produced on site can be imported into the preferred program, where it can be traced over according to established conventions. Both Photoshop and Illustrator have the great advantage of allowing infinite modifications to the digital drawing, which can be saved and/or exported in several different formats. In addition, drawing can be done on different layers, and each individual layer can be visualized or concealed according to need. This is particularly useful with palimpsest graffiti that can be visualized in isolation from the inscriptions on top or underneath them, revealing different production phases. A major difference between Photoshop and Illustrator is that the first is a raster program that basically implies drawing freehand, whereas the second is a vector-based program, which is computer-assisted drawing that uses paths based on anchor points (Vértes 2014, 58–59). More developed artistic skills are required to produce a good image in Photoshop, but these images are often more "natural looking" compared with those realized in Illustrator, which tend to be slightly schematized. Illustrator, however, produces images that can be enlarged or shrunk infinite times without affecting image resolution, making it an extremely versatile tool with regard to publication. In this respect, an important consideration when producing a digital drawing is its final destination. To ensure the published image is informative and readable, conventions should match the format, size, and aim of the publication. A drawing of a palimpsest graffito, for instance, should be printed in such a way so as to allow the reader to appreciate different phases of carving, using different line-thicknesses and colors or gray tones. However, if the drawing needs to be printed at a reduced scale, as is often the case, it must be simplified, as too many details would make it illegible. When publishing a drawing, a scale must always be included (Figure III.11.3). In addition, a photograph of the graffitied surface next to the drawing will provide a sense of the materiality of the graffito and its context and will enable a check on the quality of the epigraphy.

FIGURE III.11.3. Detail of an *ankh* sign belonging to the marginal inscription of Ramesses IV carved next to the graffito of a vulture and on top of a damaged hieratic inscription. West wall of the court of the seventh pylon, temple of Amun, Karnak. Drawing by the author. © CNRS-CFEETK/Chiara Salvador.

CONCLUSIONS

The increase in graffiti publications in the last decade has advanced research in this field considerably, making new corpora of graffiti accessible to scholars. This has allowed comparative studies, highlighting recurring patterns in similar contexts. A case in point are the New Kingdom visitors' graffiti left in tomb chapels of the necropoleis of Upper and Lower Egypt, which reflect a widespread pious attitude toward the sacredness of the tomb (e.g., Navrátilová 2015; van Pelt and Staring, forthcoming; Ragazzoli 2013). Likewise, publications of corpora of inscribed graffiti provide a new base for palaeographic studies, which are crucial for a better understanding of different forms of writing and literacy (e.g., Ali 2002).

More generally, the growing attention to graffiti has allowed scholars to step back from a biased perspective, which views graffiti as an act of defacement, and to restore them to their sociocultural milieu. As a result, it is now widely acknowledged that graffiti are not mere self-indulgent scribbles left by people who were bored or who aimed to subvert the rules of their culture/society, but meaningful marks left by people who interacted with a particular environment and wanted to leave ephemeral or permanent marks of themselves.

ACKNOWLEDGMENTS

This contribution is dedicated to Elizabeth Frood, who has taught me everything I know about epigraphy and graffiti. I am deeply indebted to Chloé Ragazzoli for her valuable comments. I am very grateful to Richard Parkinson for our fruitful discussions. Many thanks to Paolo Del Vesco for his help and patience. I thank Pauline Calassou for teaching me the basics of Illustrator and Tina Di Cerbo and Krisztián Vértes for showing me their method. Last, I wish to express my gratitude to the editors for taking me on board this project and improving an early draft of my paper.

BIBLIOGRAPHY

Ali, M.-S. 2002. *Hieratische Ritzinschriften aus Theben: Paläographie der Graffiti und Steinbruchinschriften*. GOF 34. Wiesbaden.

Baines, J., and R. Parkinson. 1997. "An Old Kingdom record of an oracle? Sinai Inscription 13." In *Essays on Ancient Egypt in Honour of Herman te Velde*, edited by J. van Dijk, 9–27. EM 1. Groningen.

Baird, J., and C. Taylor, eds. 2011. *Ancient Graffiti in Context*. RSAH 2. New York.

Commission des sciences et arts d'Egypte (Commission). 1822. *Description de l'Égypte, ou, Recueil des observations et des recherches qui ont été faites en Égypte pendant l'expédition de l'armée française*. Antiquités, vol. 5. 2nd ed. Paris.

Černý, J., C. Desroches Noblecourt, M. Kurz, et al. 1969–1983. *Graffiti de la montagne thébaine*. 4 vols. Cairo.

Davies, N. de Garis. 1920. *The Tomb of Antefoḳer, Vizier of Sesostris I, and of His Wife, Senet (no. 60)*. TTS 2. London.

Desroches Noblecourt, C. 1973. "La quête des graffiti." In *Textes et langages de l'Égypte pharaonique: Cent cinquante années de recherches 1822–1972. Hommage à Jean-François Champollion 2*, edited by S. Sauneron, 151–183. Cairo.

Di Cerbo, C., and R. Jasnow. 2011. "Recent Documentation of Medinet Habu Graffiti by the Epigraphic Survey." In *Perspectives on Ptolemaic Thebes: Papers from the Theban Workshop 2006*, edited by P. Dorman and B. Bryan, 35–51. SAOC 65. Chicago.

Dijkstra, J. H. F. 2012. *Syene I: The Figural and Textual Graffiti from the Temple of Isis at Aswan*. BBf 18. Darmstadt.

Dorn, A. 2014. "Von Graffiti und Königsgräbern des Neuen Reiches." In *The Workman's Progress: Studies in the Village of Deir el-Medina and Other Documents from Western Thebes in Honour of Rob Demarée*, edited by B. Haring, O. Kaper, and R. van Walsem, 57–71. EU 28. Leiden.

Frood, E. 2010. "Horkhebi's Decree and the Development of Priestly Inscriptional Practices in Karnak." In *Egypt in Transition: Social and Religious Development of Egypt in the First Millennium BCE. Proceedings of an International Conference, Prague, September 1–4, 2009*, edited by L. Bareš, F. Coppens, and K. Smoláriková, 103–128. Prague.

Frood, E. 2013. "Egyptian Temple Graffiti and the Gods: Appropriation and Ritualization in Karnak and Luxor." In *Heaven on Earth: Temples, Ritual, and Cosmic Symbolism in the Ancient World*, edited by D. Ragavan, 285–318. Chicago.

Frood, E. 2016. "Temple Lives: Devotion, Piety, and the Divine." In *Egypt: Millenary Splendour; The Leiden Collection in Bologna*, edited by P. Giovetti and D. Picchi, 316–323. Milano.

Frood, E., and K. Howley. 2014. "Applications of Reflectance Transformation Imaging (RTI) in the Study of Temple Graffiti." In *Thebes in the First Millennium BC*, edited by E. Pischikova, J. Budka, and K. Griffin, 625–638. Newcastle.

Lewis, C., and C. Short. 1900. *A Latin Dictionary*. Oxford.

McLean, B. 2002. *An Introduction to Greek Epigraphy of the Hellenistic and Roman Periods from Alexander the Great Down to the Reign of Constantine (323 BC–AD 337)*. Ann Arbor.

Milnor, K. 2014. *Graffiti and the Literary Landscape in Roman Pompeii*. Oxford.

Navrátilová, H. 2010. "Graffiti Spaces." In *Egypt in Transition: Social and Religious Development of Egypt in the First Millennium BCE. Proceedings of an International Conference, Prague, September 1–4, 2009*, edited by L. Bareš, F. Coppens, and K. Smoláriká, 305–332. Prague.

Navrátilová, H. 2015. *Visitors' Graffiti of Dynasties 18 and 19 in Abusir and Northern Saqqara: With a Survey of the Graffiti at Giza, Southern Saqqara, Dahshur and Maidum*. 2nd ed. Wallasey.

Parkinson, R. 1999. *Cracking Codes: The Rosetta Stone and Decipherment*. London.

Peden, A. 2001. *The Graffiti of Pharaonic Egypt: Scope and Roles of Informal Writings (c. 3100–332 BC)*. PdÄ 17. Leiden.

Pelt, W. van, and N. Staring. In press. "Interpreting Graffiti in the Saqqara New Kingdom Necropolis as Expressions of Popular Customs and Beliefs." *Rivista del Museo Egizio 3*.

Ragazzoli, C. 2013. "The Social Creation of a Scribal Place: The Visitors' Inscriptions in the Tomb Attributed to Antefiqer (TT 60) (with newly recorded graffiti)." *SAK* 42:269–323.

Ragazzoli, C. and E. Frood. 2013. "Writing on the Wall: Two Graffiti Projects in Luxor." *EA* 42: 30–33.

Ragazzoli, C., Ö. Harmanşah, C. Salvador, and E. Frood, eds. 2018. *Scribbling through History: Graffiti, Places and People from Antiquity to Modernity*. London.

Rutherford, I. 2003. "Pilgrimage in Greco-Roman Egypt: New Perspectives on Graffiti from the Memnonion at Abydos." In *Ancient Perspectives on Egypt*, edited by R. Matthews and C. Roemer, 171–190. Encounters with Ancient Egypt. London.

Salvador, C. 2016. "Graffiti and Sacred Space: New Kingdom Expressions of Individuality in the Court of the Seventh Pylon at Karnak." In *10. Ägyptologische Tempeltagung: Ägyptische Tempel zwischen Normierung und Individualität. München, 29.–31. August 2014*, edited by M. Ullmann, 111–128. KSGH 3, 5. Wiesbaden.

Spiegelberg, W. 1921. *Ägyptische und andere Graffiti (Inschriften und Zeichnungen) aus der thebanischen Nekropolis*. Heidelberg.

Staring, N. 2011. "Interpreting Figural Graffiti: Case Studies from a Funerary Context." In *Current Research in Egyptology 2010: Proceedings of the Eleventh Annual Symposium, Leiden University 2010*, edited by M. Horn, J. Kramer, R. Mairs, et al., 145–156. Oxford.

Tallet, P. 2012. *La zone minière pharaonique du Sud-Sinaï I: Catalogue complémentaire des inscriptions du Sinaï*. MIFAO 130. Cairo.

Vértes, K. 2014. *Digital Epigraphy*. Chicago. Retrieved from https://oi.uchicago.edu/research/publications/misc/digital-epigraphy.

Walsem, R. van. 2006. "'Meaningful Places': Pragmatics from Ancient Egypt to Modern Times. A Diachronic and Cross-Cultural Approach." In *Site-Seeing: Places in Culture, Time and Space*, edited by K. Zijlmans, 111–146. Leiden.

Urcia, A., J. C. Darnell, C. M. Darnell, and S. E. Zaia. 2018. "From Plastic Sheets to Tablet PCs: A Digital Epigraphic Method for Recording Egyptian Rock Art and Inscriptions." *African Archaeological Review* 35 (2): 169–189. https://doi.org/10.1007/s10437-018-9297-z

PRACTICAL ISSUES WITH THE EPIGRAPHIC RESTORATION OF A BIOGRAPHICAL INSCRIPTION IN THE TOMB OF DJEHUTY (TT 11), DRA ABU EL-NAGA

ANDRÉS DIEGO ESPINEL

"…This wall, rust-stained
and covered with moss, has seen one kingdom after another,
stood in the storm, steep and tall, then tumbled."

"The Ruin" (Anglo-Saxon poem; translation by R. Liuzza)

INTRODUCTION

THE past is a heap of ruins. Despite the great number of decorated Egyptian monuments that have survived to this day, few of them are completely intact and fully legible. Consequently, while reading an ancient text, it is common to come across lacunae and sequences of illegible signs that, in many instances, seem vital for its complete understanding. Without some phrases, a word, or even a single sign (i.e., a semagram or numeral), epigraphers are deprived of information that can be critical for understanding and interpreting past events. Conversely, in some instances, only a few inscribed blocks from a larger text can be placed or rearranged and used to argue for the reconstruction of an entire text, thus, consequently, creating a false sense of the text's completeness. That is the case, for example, with the different restorations of the Old Kingdom annals that were made by guessing the arrangement of the fragments of the Palermo Stone (Hornung, Krauss, and Warburton 2006, 21–25; Hsu 2010, 80–81) and the restoration from a few fragmentary blocks of a *Weihinschrift* (votive inscription) in Niuserre's sun temple at Abu Gurob (Helck 1977).

In some instances, researchers have opted to fill in the small gaps with restorations inferred by the general context, by well-known formulae and expressions, or by iterations in other sections of the preserved text or in similar texts. The same line of reasoning has been applied to restoring larger lacunae of texts from smaller preserved fragments. These practices are attested, for instance, in frequently consulted and referenced works, such as Sethe and Helck's (1906–1958) *Urkunden*, and prove the linguistic and epigraphic proficiency of their authors. However, these brilliant exercises of erudition can lead to unexpected consequences. Sometimes the texts are taken as correct and decisive readings by other researchers or especially by the general public who, when reading translations derived from those texts, do not recognize editors' marks signaling the Egyptologists' restorations. Consequently, these provisional additions become inserted in the interpretative discourse of Egyptian history, creating the impression that the text is more complete than it is and even leading to inaccurate interpretations.

Restoring a fragmentary text must involve less enthusiastic practices. Such a restoration should be based not only on the text's content but also on other factors that, sometimes, are as decisive and informative as the text, such as the support materials—the material on which the text is inscribed or painted—the epigraphic features of the text, or the various states of preservation of its fragments. Epigraphy is not only the study of carved and painted decoration, but also the analysis of the interaction between the decoration and its support. As sides of the same coin, both sets of elements intermingle, shaping and displaying a common message. Therefore, as stated in what follows, any epigraphic restoration involves both texts and their inherent materialities. Like a message in a bottle recovered from the sea, the information contained in epigraphic texts has been retrieved by the very fact that the texts were intentionally put on a precise material and in a precise place.

This chapter[1] deals with "bottles" rather than with "messages," even though both are closely connected. In the following pages, practical considerations related to the material restoration of ancient Egyptian epigraphic texts are presented, taking as a case study the author's experience on the restoration of an inscription, the so-called "red stela"

[1] I thank José Manuel Galán (CSIC), director of the Spanish mission at Dra Abu el-Naga, for allowing me to participate in his project as epigrapher for more than ten years, for his assistance regarding the images in this article and other information from the excavation, and for his suggestions after reading a draft of this chapter. Thanks are also extended to all the Egyptologists, archaeologists, restorers, geologists, and Egyptian workers who have contributed to the restoration of the "red stela." I am also indebted to the volume editors, Vanessa Davies and Dimitri Laboury, for their invitation and comments, and for improving greatly my English.

or second biographical inscription in the tomb of Djehuty (Galán 2014a, 252 and fig. 11.1, no. 22). Research on the history of the stela and its fragments, as well as the problems and applied solutions derived from its physical reconstruction are discussed in order to serve, hopefully, as a piece of advice for the study and restoration of similar monuments.

TT 11: General Features

The tomb of Djehuty (TT 11), Hatshepsut's overseer of the treasury (c. 1470 BCE), is located in the central area of Dra Abu el-Naga (Galán 2014a, 247–252). Contrary to the rest of the key officials of Hatshepsut's court, who were buried at Sheikh Abd el-Qurna, Assasif, and el-Khokha, Djehuty chose a different area: an already overbuilt landscape occupied by different kinds of tombs dating back to the First Intermediate Period. Djehuty's reasons or circumstances for building his tomb in such an atavistic place are not clear (Diego Espinel 2014, 299; Galán 2014b, 8). Whatever they were, they decisively shaped the later history and subsequent deterioration of the monument.

First, the chapel was hewn into a series of four narrow strata of limestone of the "Thebes geological formation" (Cuezva et al. 2016). In that precise area, these beds are frail and contain many natural cracks and fissures (Galán 2014b, 4). Consequently, carefully cut blocks were frequently fixed with mortar by the stoneworkers and carvers in the spaces where original degraded limestone pieces previously fell down, and minor breaks were plastered with gypsum that, when necessary, were painted, carved, or modeled. Moreover, the limestone there is porous and very sensitive to changes caused by salt crystallization (i.e., the flowing of internal salts toward the rock surface due to the nature of the substrate, to salt-system features, or to changes in humidity and temperature) (Galán 2014b, 13). In many instances, this feature and some events connected to it have seriously affected, as stated later, the legibility and preservation of the tomb decoration.

Second, Djehuty's tomb is located next to other earlier and later chapels and shafts. Because of the tombs' proximity to one another, stoneworkers cutting later tombs often opened holes into earlier tombs and created stairs carved into the stone or made with mudbricks in order to communicate between the tombs. Many of these entrances could have been hewn intentionally in the Third Intermediate Period (Galán 2014a, 247n3), or even earlier, when the workers cutting a tomb accidentally ran into older ones, as is evident in Djehuty's shrine (Galán 2014a, 252–253). Subsequently, these interconnected spaces were enlarged and readapted not later than the second century BCE to create a series of subterranean galleries or "catacombs" devoted to the burial of animal mummies (Galán 2014b, 13–14). Actually, the wall containing the inscription under study was cut to connect TT 11 with Kampp's tomb, numbered—399—(Kampp 1996, 190–192, 769). As part of a bigger complex, not yet delimited or fully understood, Djehuty's chapel also suffered from the site's later abandonment at an unknown date. The history and rambling arrangement of the subterranean galleries played a role in a sequence of different human and natural events that transformed them. For instance, on the walls of TT 11, there are attestations of Djehuty's and Amun's *damnatio memoriae*, marks of water that ran through breaks in the rock, and evidence of intense fires possibly connected to the cremation of mummies or human remains, intense air currents, or the tomb's later religious reuse (Galán 2014b, 13). All of these processes, the sequence and impact of which are not yet completely understood or ordered chronologically (team geologist S. Sánchez-Moral pers. comm.), led to several erosive processes related to the aforementioned porosity of the local limestone. These circumstances contributed to an irregular state of conservation of the decoration and inscriptions of TT 11 that, apparently, did not suffer any other significant damages after the Roman Period (Galán 2014b, 14). From that moment on, the most noteworthy alterations are several attempts, some of them successful, to cut out reliefs during the past century. The evidence of these attempts is found in a few parts of the corridor and shrine (Serrano 2014, 283, fig. 12.8, at the left).

As a result of their storied geology and history, the walls of TT 11 constitute a lavish catalog of epigraphic and preservation problems, such as blank areas, faded texts, salt-crusted or mud-covered surfaces awaiting cleaning, burned surfaces, Demotic texts traced over the reliefs, and well-preserved fragments recovered mainly from the debris outside the tomb.

Restoring the "Red Stela"

Many of the aforementioned features are visible on the "red stela," which is one of the four big stelae carved on the walls of Djehuty's tomb. Two of the stelae are at either ends of the façade of TT 11, forming a monumental entrance along with two life-size statues and a carved sidewall (Diego Espinel 2014, 299–303; Galán 2015, 184, fig. 1). At the north is the so-called Northampton stela or first biographical inscription (Spiegelberg 1900), and at the south is a stela with a hymn to Amun-Re (Galán 2015, 185–192). Two other stelae were carved at both ends of the transverse hall (see e.g., Galán 2009, 162–163). Because of the color in which their carved hieroglyphs were painted, these two stelae have been conventionally called the "blue stela" or third biographical inscription, located at the southern end of the transverse hall, and the "red stela" or second biographical inscription, which stands opposite it, at the northern end of the same room (Figure III.12.1a). Both stelae have suffered extensive damage.

The "blue stela" sustained damage long ago, possibly even before the fires and floods that destroyed the chapel at some point during the late New Kingdom and the Ptolemaic Period. Nowadays there are no remains in situ of the original inscription that was written in lines from right to left. Its general content can only be guessed, despite the recovery of approximately 280 fragments inside and outside of the chapel. Many of the fragments are small and contain only a few hieroglyphs in any single line. Around fifty were retrieved during the excavations of the area by P. E. Newberry and

FIGURES III.12.1A–B. The "red stela" in 2002 and at the completion of the restoration work (photographs courtesy of J. M. Galán).

W. Spiegelberg in 1898 and 1899 under the auspices of the Marquis of Northampton (Northampton, Spiegelberg, and Newberry 1908), but those were only partially placed by Sethe (*Urk.* IV 441.15–444.8). More than half of them, aside from portions of other ones, are currently lost. Although the stela has not yet been studied, its fragments suggest that the original inscription contained an apparently formulaic biographical text, a list of offerings to and feasts of various deities, and different religious expressions. Because only small and extremely fragmentary sections of the text have been recovered, it is possible that the text might contain additional biographical information about Djehuty.

The "red stela" inscription was also carved from right to left. It is an important document because it offers new insights on Djehuty's life and works that complement the information given by the "Northampton stela." The wall on which it was carved was opened in order to connect the corridors of Djehuty's chapel and Kampp's tomb—399—at some point in the New Kingdom or early Third Intermediate Period. The big hole destroyed a large portion of the right part of the stela. Fortunately, part of the original inscription remained in place. As with many other parts of the tomb decoration, however, it subsequently suffered different erosive processes because of water, fire, and eolic action. As stated in what follows, these processes, and others, are important factors in determining the original location of the fragments, since direct work with blocks at the site of the stela is essential in order to better understand their material characteristics and avoid false assumptions concerning possible locations of the blocks.

Evidence both in the remaining parts of the stela and in their fragments suggests at least eleven different events that changed the stela's original state:

1. Embedding of blocks—at least one—with mortar in wall spaces where the original limestone fell down. This repair happened while carving the inscription or preparing the stela's stone surface.

2. On least in three occasions, the carvers corrected the text, recarving new signs over older ones. At that time, the surface of the stela had already many cracks, as evidenced by the fact that red paint had dripped into them. Some crevices were possibly plastered with gypsum, as is attested in other parts of the tomb.

3. Systematic *damnatio memoriae* of the name of Djehuty and his parents—mainly his father—shortly after the tomb was finished (Galán 2014, 252, fig. 11.3). The *damnatio* also affected the name of the god Thot.

4. *Damnatio memoriae* of Hatshepsut's royal cartouches both in the lunette and in the main text a few decades after the tomb was completed, possibly at the end of the reign of Thutmose III (Dorman 2005; Roth 2005). Again, the *damnatio* was exhaustive throughout the tomb.

5. Atonist iconoclasm of Amun's name is attested in the façade and courtyard. In some instances, the attacks show evidence of the semiliteracy of the Atonist agents. For instance, they attacked the word "*mnḫ*" because of its visual and audial similarity to the deity's name *Imn* (Manuelian 1999). Regarding the "red

stela," Sethe (*Urk.* IV 433nd) cautiously suggested that the destruction of Gardiner's sign S28 (fringed cloth) occurred as a result of Amun's proscription because of the visual similarity between that sign and game board sign (Y5) in the name of Amun. However, this idea should be discarded, as the name of the god was not canceled in other parts of the inscription. Amun's name in the *ḥtp di ny-swt* formula at the beginning of the stela is destroyed, but due to the poor preservation of the text, it is impossible to discern whether or not this damage was intentional. Actually, there is no evidence of Atonist iconoclasm of Amun's name in the internal decoration of TT 11.

6. Accidental fall of blocks caused by the frailty of the stone. The reliefs on these blocks are well preserved, still retaining red paint and, in some instances, red guidelines. These "fresh" features indicate that this event occurred soon after the completion of the stela, but, at least in one instance, after Djehuty's *damnatio*.

7. A hole was cut in the wall when both relief and painting were relatively well preserved, long before the reuse of the tomb as part of the Ptolemaic galleries. The aggressors probably took advantage of a shallow rectangular-shaped depression carved on the floor at the bottom of the left side of the stela (Figure III.12.1b). The depression may have been intended for a shaft. If so, it was abandoned soon after its initial cutting. It is not possible to know whether the depression formed part of the original plan of Djehuty's tomb or whether it was carved later, as a mirror shaft to a smaller and square-plan shaft (1 × 1.2 m) cut at the other side of the transverse hall during the Saite Dynasty (Galán 2010).

8. Remnants of an intense fire that obscured the surface of the stela and, in some instances, cracked part of it, mainly in the lower left border. The burned surface did not suffer any other alterations probably because it was partially covered by debris.

9. Highly "washed out" surfaces in the upper half of the stela due to the combination of fire, water, and wind. All signs are legible, but with no side-lighting reading is difficult. In other parts of the tomb, such erosive process happened before the second century BCE, since Demotic graffiti were painted on the already worn walls (Galán 2014b, 14). The borders of the shallow shaft at the foot of the stela also suffered such erosion.

10. Carving of some steps in the shallow shaft and in the hole on the stela during the Ptolemaic Period.

11. Subsequent fall of fragments—generally small—from the worn surfaces and the lower right border of the stela. Small sections of the text recorded in situ by Sethe (Northampton, Spiegelberg, and Newberry 1908, pl. 34) are currently missing, indicating that those blocks fell down in the last century.

This sequence of events had different effects on different parts of the stela and its blocks. One hundred twenty-five fragments have been retrieved so far. Five of them cannot be ascribed to the stela with complete certainty. Thirty-four fragments were discovered by Newberry and Spiegelberg and were subsequently studied and published by Sethe (*Urk.* IV 431.15–444.8).[2] Moreover, Sethe's restoration of the inscription was included in a plate of the final report of Northampton's excavations (Northampton, Spiegelberg, and Newberry 1908, 1*, pl. 34; Figure III.12.2). When the German scholar visited the tomb in 1905, fourteen blocks were already missing, and he had to rely on Spiegelberg's notes and drawings to study the inscription (Galán 2009, 162–163). During the cleaning and excavation of the chapel, courtyard, and other surrounding areas by the Spanish mission at Dra Abu el-Naga since 2002, all but twelve of the missing blocks have been rediscovered—some only partially—along with many previously undiscovered ones (Figure III.12.3). Seventy-two fragments have been placed in their original spots on the wall (Figure III.12.1b, 4–5).

Both the remaining text of the stela in situ and the recovered fragments show very different states of preservation (Figure III.12.4). For instance, a large part of the stela and some of the fragments are badly weathered, according to which of the aforementioned events they were subjected to, as well as various other episodes they "lived" later. Some fragments seem brand new, while others are severely worn or are damaged by salts, soot, or smoke. The diversity of their current conditions is also related to the different places from which the blocks have been recovered (Figure III.12.3). All these elements are meaningful. They suggest that every fragment essentially had a different history before it was deposited in the many layers of debris that accumulated over several thousand years in the neighboring areas of the tomb. With this in mind, it is important to state that, for the sake of better epigraphic study and restoration, it is necessary to consider both the original epigraphic support and the fragments as artifacts in their own right.

Historical information about Djehuty's "red stela" is rich and interesting despite its fragmentary state, and a philological study of this document is currently in progress by J. M. Galán. The themes of the different sections help guide a relocation of many fragments. The "red stela" begins with an initial dedicatory inscription—a *ḥtp dì ny-swt* formula—related to different gods (lines 1–5) and a series of conventional epithets of Djehuty (lines 5–14). The rest of the inscription is a biographical text dealing with different building and reckoning activities by Djehuty during the joint reign of Thutmose III and Hatshepsut and more conventional biographical phrases (lines 14–25). The final lines contain an appeal to the living (lines 25–30).

Relying exclusively on the contents of the text, however, can lead to incorrect interpretations. Sethe's restoration of the "red stela" is surprisingly accurate (Northampton, Spiegelberg, and Newberry 1908, pl. 34; *Urk.* IV 431.6–441.13), considering the few blocks he had to work with (Figure III.12.2). Apparently, he worked directly with some of the blocks recovered during Northampton's excavations when he visited the tomb in 1905 (Diego Espinel 2014, 303). His study was also informed by notes and drawings, now lost, that were given to him by Spiegelberg and perhaps also by Newberry (see, for

---

[2] Some blocks discovered inside the tomb from Northampton's excavation and one other, at least, that was not recorded by Spiegelberg have barely legible numerals painted on their backs with a luminous green pencil. Unfortunately, it has not been determined whether they were painted by Spiegelberg, Sethe, or someone else.

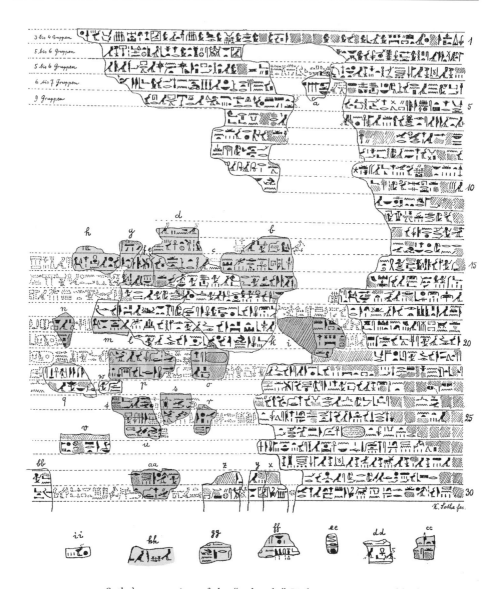

FIGURE III.12.2. Sethe's restoration of the "red stela." Light gray areas are blocks currently lost. Dark gray areas are misplaced fragments (after Sethe in Northampton, Spiegelberg, and Newberry 1908, pl. 35).

instance, *Urk*. IV 436nna–b.). Despite having a limited number of blocks to work with, Sethe matched different blocks to one another and correctly placed many of them in their original positions. Even with his mastery and skill, some fragments were placed in the correct register, but in the wrong location, and the position of others is completely incorrect. Moreover, the width of the stela in his restoration drawing is considerably narrower than the stela's actual width.

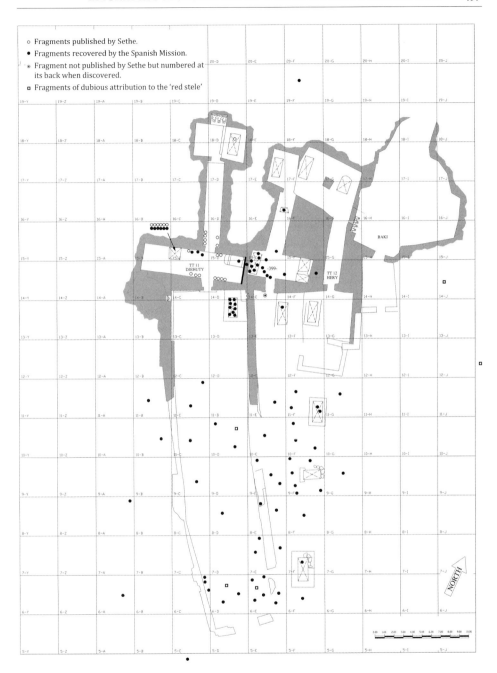

FIGURE III.12.3. Dispersion of fragments of the "red stela." The stela is marked as a bold black line at the right end of the transverse hall of TT 11 (original map by C. Cabrera and J. Ivars, courtesy of J. M. Galán). This map does not include two fragments of the inscription with no clear provenance.

Working from the texts of the fragments, Sethe's restored inscription is, in many instances, far from close to the original one. His experience serves as a good piece of advice for avoiding long textual restorations. The best technique is to follow the preserved text and the way the fragments physically fit with each other. Personal experience has demonstrated that any textual restoration, even one based on remaining traces or similar parallels, can lead to wrong readings and conclusions (see, e.g., Diego Espinel 2013, 28nh).

Aside from their epigraphic contents, the stela fragments have a series of physical features that have been shaped by their depositional lives and are connected to the events mentioned above. Together with their texts, they permit one, in many instances, to locate the blocks on the wall or, on the contrary, to help to dismiss them from certain parts of the stela. Such features, of course, interact and cannot be ordered in an unambiguous hierarchical order since any of them can be decisive—either alone or in connection with other ones—for locating single fragments or small groups. There are, at least, five physical features to be considered:

1. The condition of the surface of the inscription in situ is relevant. Keeping in mind the various episodes of the progressive degradation of the stela, the blocks' different states of preservation have been of great help for placing fragments back on the wall. For instance, many "washed out" fragments come undoubtedly from the upper half of the stela that lost a considerable part of its text after the erosive process that began possibly after the Ptolemaic Period. Consequently, according to the moment when the reliefs fell down, the breaks on the wall appear as either worn cuts or clean and fresh negative scars. More precisely, the emplacement of the worn blocks may even be more exact due to their different color: grayish-colored blocks come from the upper half of the stela, and yellowish- or ochre-colored fragments come from the lower right half.

2. The shape and size of the fragments is also important. Based on their contents alone, some blocks could be ascribed to precise lines. However, when they were placed in their alleged original positions, they did not fit with other fragments whose position was totally clear or with the remaining traces on the stela. Consequently, the initial presumed location had to be discarded. For example, Sethe had placed block "i" close to the remaining text of the stela, in lines 19 to 21 (Northampton, Spiegelberg, and Newberry 1908, pl. 35, fig. 2). When physically placed in this spot, this block turned out to be too thick. It was eventually placed at the end of lines 18 to 20. Moreover, the lower border of block "i" had been recarved, indicating that this part of the wall had been reworked in order to insert a limestone block that, happily, was also recovered.

3. The aforementioned example introduces a third element of epigraphic study: the importance of studying the blocks and inscriptions directly. The size and color of the fragments and the kind of erosion they experienced, for instance, is necessary information that can only be obtained by directly studying the blocks. Relying solely on a virtual restoration on paper or on the computer can lead to mistakes. No doubt, Sethe's study of the blocks was basically made in this virtual way despite his visit to the tomb. In spite of his ability to match fragments from paper notes, Sethe would have better

approximated the original location of the blocks if he had had the chance to work leisurely with them in situ. As has already been mentioned, his restoration relied on the presumption that the stela was narrower than it really is.

A wooden sandbox of approximately 2.50 × 1.75 × 0.30 m has been a critical tool for directly studying the blocks of the "red stela" and for confirming or discarding matches and restorations. It was placed in the courtyard of TT 11, not far from Djehuty's transversal corridor, where the fragments were stored in plastic boxes just beside the "red stela." The close proximity of the sandbox, the fragments stored in boxes, and the stela were essential for a comfortable and efficient restoration.

4. Changes in the *ductus*—the writing and carving characteristics of a particular inscription—are another element to keep in mind when restoring texts. Virtually all of the scenes carved on the walls of TT 11 have their own features. The different kinds of carving, dimensions of signs, and even colors of the limestone become essential for identifying the provenance of many blocks. The same can be said about the ductus. Different artists' hands have not yet been identified on the "red stela." Such a task is hindered by the worn state of many parts of the stela. But the arrangement of the text and the way the signs were carved occasionally permit one to better define a fragment's possible location. This is especially evident in the lower lines of text. There, the hieroglyphic signs are slightly bigger, not as carefully carved, and spaced farther apart from one another. Being so close to the ground, the stonecutters probably had to adopt unsuitable postures for carving the lowest lines and so had difficulty executing carvings as precise as those found elsewhere on the stela.

5. The preservation of the blocks and other physical features, such as darkened surfaces because of fire or the presence of *damnatio* erasures, can offer clues about the fragments' locations or, conversely, mislead the restorer about a possible relocation. For instance, some of the fragments with fresher colors fell down from the stela before the text was completed (Figure III.12.4). Some of the fragments still have horizontal guidelines painted in red that marked where the tops and bottoms of the hieroglyphs should be carved or show fresh signs of the erasure of Djehuty's name and his filiation. These early fragments did not face the same fate as the fragments that fell off of the wall later, some of which are damaged on the surface that had been placed on the wall with mortar. The hieroglyphs on one fragment are well preserved, but they are completely darkened by a grayish layer of smoke, suggesting that the fragment was subjected to fire. Moreover, a fragment that matches it is even darker, but fits perfectly with another block that preserves the red paint.

Time is another important factor when facing this kind of restoration. The excavation and restoration of Djehuty's tomb and neighboring tombs started in 2002 and is still ongoing. Contrary to Sethe's brief visit to TT 11 in 1905, the annual dig seasons for over a decade have permitted a continuous study of the fragments and, therefore, a better understanding of the inscription. Moreover, new blocks from TT 11 and other tombs are

FIGURE III.12.4. Different states of preservation: a well-preserved block fitted into the worn inscription of the wall (photograph by the author).

discovered every season, and they help us to understand the text and relocate previously discovered fragments. Therefore, the current restoration of the stela should be taken as a final version . . . in progress.

PUTTING FRAGMENTS IN PLACE

Sometimes, after a virtual restoration of the stela on paper or in the sandbox, it is possible to attempt an actual reconstruction of the inscription by putting the fragments back in their original places. In the case of the "red stela," such an initiative was a rather problematic affair, since it implied an important change to Djehuty's tomb in relation to connected structures. The decision to put—or not—the blocks of the stela back on the wall spurred a long negotiation among different agents. Director, restorers, epigraphers, archaeologists, architects, antiquities inspectors, *reis*, workers, and even occasional visitors provided different insights and opinions—sometimes completely opposed to one another. Any possible intervention was constrained by material considerations, such as the number, size, and condition of the located relief fragments. Since any decision would be controversial, the debate for choosing the best solution was lengthy. On the one hand, restoring the blocks meant, for instance, closing a side entrance to another tomb and altering the nature of the tomb in its final form when it was part of a complex catacomb integrated by a system of older interconnected chapels, burial shafts, and galleries during the Ptolemaic Period. Moreover, the restoration could make it more difficult to relocate blocks that might be discovered in future seasons. On the other hand, a restoration would consolidate an extremely damaged wall to prevent future collapses and degradations. Additionally, a restoration would delimit the initial extent of Djehuty's chapel and would enable us to dispose of several boxes of stones stored inside the tomb. After a long debate and many different assessments, the second option was finally chosen mainly because it would enhance the conservation and stability of the wall.[3] This solution was agreed on providing that the new wall would be built in such a way that parts of it could be easily removed in order to add new fragments to it.

Initially, a cleaning and consolidation was made in the dirtiest and most friable areas of the preserved parts of the stela in situ. When completed, a restoration of the rest of the stela started. It followed four separate steps (restorer M. A. Navarro, pers. comm.). First, the original shape of the stela was projected by means of vertical and horizontal threads. Since the left side was completely lost, the limit was estimated by studying and measuring the right side. Second, the hole of the wall was closed with bricks and cemented up to the level in which the fragments with texts would be placed. The third step was to place the fragments with the help of hydraulic lime mortar (1 part lime, 3 parts sharp—i.e., gritty—sand), bricks—some of them scored—and small limestone pieces. At the same time that the restoration was in progress, a solid brick wall was built at the stela's back, from Kampp's tomb —399—, in order to reinforce the common wall between both tombs. The surface of the front of the stela was then covered with a layer of mortar so that the fragments stood out from the wall by about 1.5 cm. Finally, the fill was covered with another fine layer (c. 1 cm) of nonhydraulic lime mortar colored with mineral pigments to be lighter than the original wall. The restoration took three seasons (2011–2013), and it was not easy. The fragments had suffered different erosions and damages, and the rock walls of the tomb had shifted over time. Consequently, blocks sometimes did not fit perfectly on the wall. Fortunately, however, such problems did not stop the completion of the restoration (Figure III.12.1b).

The possibility of painting on the wall the texts of six placed fragments that are currently lost but had been recorded by Spiegelberg and Sethe (Figure III.12.3) is still being considered. Sethe's copies are far from meticulous, but the inclusion of the texts that they contained would be of great help since they would render the stela more complete and more understandable for visitors and, moreover, they would draw attention to the existence of the unrecovered blocks.

---

[3] Cleaning, consolidation, and restoration of the walls was done by Pía Rodríguez, Nieves López, and Miguel Ángel Navarro, following the criteria suggested by Leandro de la Vega(†). Joan Ivars and the bricklayer Ahmed el-Tuamy also took part in the restoration.

This case study and the practical issues derived from it should be taken as pieces of advice rather than precise guidelines. As Caminos stressed (1976, 14–15), every wall has its own epigraphic difficulties and circumstances, and every epigrapher has to face them not with just one set of solutions, but by using, among other things, common sense, imagination, and skill.

Bibliography

Caminos, R. A. 1976. "The Recording of Inscriptions and Scenes in Tombs and Temples." In *Ancient Egyptian Epigraphy and Palaeography*, 1–25. New York.

Cuezva, S., J. García-Guinea, A. Fernández-Cortés, D. Benavente, J. Ivars, J. M. Galán, and S. Sánchez-Moral. 2016. "Composition, Uses, Provenance and Stability of Rocks and Ancient Mortars in a Theban Tomb in Luxor (Egypt)." *Materials and Structures* 49:941–960. doi:10.1617/s11527-015-0550-5.

Diego Espinel, A. 2013. "A Newly Identified Old Kingdom Execration Text." In *Decorum and Experience: Essays in Ancient Culture for John Baines*, edited by E. Frood and A. McDonald, 26–33. Oxford.

Diego Espinel, A. 2014. "Play and Display in Egyptian High Culture: The Cryptographic Texts of Djehuty (TT 11) and Their Sociocultural Contexts." In *Creativity and Innovation in the Reign of Hatshepsut: Papers from the Theban Workshop 2010*, edited by J. M. Galán, B. M. Bryan, and P. F. Dorman, 297–335. SAOC 69. Chicago.

Dorman, P. F. 2005. "The Proscription of Hatshepsut." In *Hatshepsut: From Queen to Pharaoh*, edited by C. H. Roehrig, R. Dreyfus, and C. A. Keller, 267–269. New York.

Galán, J. M. 2009. "Early Investigations in the Tomb-Chapel of Djehuty (TT 11)." In *Sitting beside Lepsius: Studies in Honour of Jaromir Malek at the Griffith Institute*, edited by D. Magee, J. Bourriau and S. Quirke, 155–181. OLA 185. Leuven.

Galán, J. M. 2010. "Campaign 2010: Campaign Summary." http://www.excavacionegipto.com/el_proyecto/campaigns.php?year=2010&option=summary.

Galán, J. M. 2014a. "The Inscribed Burial Chamber of Djehuty (TT 11)." In *Creativity and Innovation in the Reign of Hatshepsut: Papers from the Theban Workshop 2010*, edited by J. M. Galán, B. M. Bryan, and P. F. Dorman, 247–272. SAOC 69. Chicago.

Galán, J. M. 2014b. "The Rock-Cut Tomb-Chapels of Hery and Djehuty on the West Bank of Luxor: History, Environment and Conservation." In *The Conservation of Subterranean Cultural Heritage*, edited by C. Sáiz-Jiménez, 3–16. Boca Ratón.

Galán, J. M. 2015. "Hymns to Amun-Ra and Amun in the Tomb Chapel of Djehuty (TT 11)." In *Joyful in Thebes: Egyptological Studies in Honor of Betsy M. Bryan*, edited by R. Jasnow and K. M. Cooney, 183–196. MVCAE 1. London.

Helck, W. 1977. "Die 'Weihinschrift' aus dem Taltempel des Sonnenheiligtums des Königs Neuserre bei Abu Gurob." *SAK* 5:47–77.

Hornung, E., R. Krauss, and D. A. Warburton. 2006. "Royal Annals." In *Ancient Egyptian Chronology*, edited by E. Hornung, R. Krauss, and D. A. Warburton, 19–25. HdO 83. Leiden.

Hsu, S.-W. 2010. "The Palermo Stone: The Earliest Royal Inscription from Ancient Egypt." *AoF* 37: 68–89. doi: 10.1524/aofo.2010.0006.

Kampp, F. 1996. *Die thebanische Nekropole: Zum Wandel des Grabgedankens von der XVIII. bis zur XX. Dynastie*. 2 vols. Theben 13. Mainz.

Manuelian, P. Der. 1999. "Semi-Literacy in Egypt: Some Erasures from the Amarna Period." In *Gold of Praise: Studies on Ancient Egypt in Honor of Edward F. Wente*, edited by E. Teeter and J. A. Larson, 285–298. SAOC 58. Chicago.

Northampton, W. C., Marquis of, W. Spiegelberg, and P. E. Newberry. 1908. *Report on Some Excavations in the Theban Necropolis during the Winter of 1898–9*. London.

Roth, A. M. 2005. "Erasing a Reign." In *Hatshepsut: From Queen to Pharaoh*, edited by C. H. Roehrig, R. Dreyfus, and C. A. Keller, 277–283. New York.

Serrano, J. M. 2014. "The Composition of the Opening of the Mouth in the Tomb-Chapel of Djehuty (TT 11)." In *Creativity and Innovation in the Reign of Hatshepsut: Papers from the Theban Workshop 2010*, edited by J. M. Galán, B. M. Bryan, and P. F. Dorman, 273–295. SAOC 69. Chicago.

Sethe, K., and W. Helck. 1906–1958. *Urkunden der 18. Dynastie*. 22 vols. Urk 4. Leipzig.

Spiegelberg, W. 1900. "Die Northampton Stele." *RT* 22:115–125.

......

PALAEOGRAPHIC INTERPRETATION IN THE WAKE OF A *LOGIC OF WRITING-IMAGERY* AS APPLIED TO THE FORMATIVE PHASE OF WRITING IN THE PRE- AND EARLY DYNASTIC PERIODS

......

LUDWIG MORENZ

He who writes with the chisel,
has no handwriting

Heiner Müller, "Mommsen's Block"

PALAEOGRAPHY BETWEEN NORMALIZATION, STANDARDIZATION, AND STYLIZATION VERSUS FORMAL PLASTICITY AND OPENNESS

By its very nature as a phonographic notation system, writing requires, more than traditional imagery, the formation of a coherent system, therefore, a certain conventionalization, normalization, and standardization of the cultural technique of writing (on "cultural technique(s)," see Kassung and Macho 2013, especially 17–18 for the three highlighted aspects: self-referential, context-neutral, and media-based). At the same time, there was a remarkably high degree of tolerance in the Egyptian writing system in several areas (from sign forms to orthography). For a successful crossing over, written communication, however, must have a reasonably clearly defined scope and rules for the actors, but with such requirements, a more specific capability of freedom in ways of expression was obtained at a higher level in this cultural context (Selz 2007). This area is a central research field of palaeographic interpretation.

During the fourth and early third millennium BCE, in the arena of a comprehensive sociocultural development, there developed a community of writers and readers in the Nile Valley, a group that likely constituted barely one percent of the total population (accurate estimates are problematic and, of course, hypothetical: Baines 2007; no reliable data is available for the Pre- and Early Dynastic Periods). In this formative phase of the development of the first known territorial state in world history, an area of over eight hundred kilometers north to south was in play socioeconomically and culturally, and written texts should be able to speak "for themselves" under these conditions of the "extended communication situation" (i.e., oral and written, K. Ehlich 2007). As the basis, over five thousand years ago, of the newly developed form of communication, writing had certain codes and rules that must be learned by the user and that required a certain professionalization (so a teaching body, sometimes without the school institution) (Baines 2004; Morenz 2004a, 2013, 239–276; Stauder 2010; Vernus 2012, 2016). At the same time, a dedicated openness and plasticity in sign forms and sign use existed in the phono-semantic hybrid of Egyptian writing. This fundamental openness of the system affected both orthography and palaeography, the latter being what interests us here, while at the same time thinking about and considering the other. The fourth and early third millennium was a period of transition from initially anarchic inventions to regulatory control and unification and thus a real system of writing. Regarding the actors, we can describe this in terms of a sociology of knowledge as a development from speculators in writing to rentiers (i.e., those who dabble and innovate in writing and those who work with writing that is already developed).

Already from the fourth millennium BCE on, we find in the Nile Valley more monumental and also clearly cursive sign forms. While it has been shown that papyrus was used since the First Dynasty as a writing material (Morenz 2011, 23–24), the oldest preserved inscribed papyri, date from the time of King Khufu (Fourth Dynasty) (Tallet 2014). However relevant this differentiation in writing was from earlier times—particularly regarding ink markings on vessels from Tomb U-j at Abydos (Dreyer 1998)—it will, in the following, not be considered (see chapter by Ali).

For Egyptian writing, the following function as important factors: iconicity (inner form) and figurativity (outer form) of the signs (Vernus 2012, 2016), it being understood that for the palaeographic point of view, of course, the figurative design is central. For palaeographic interpretation, we know various relevant and more or less self-evident factors, such as shape, color (Staehelin 2000), material (Regulski 2010, 16–46), and context (which determines the particular individual signs) (Verhoeven 2015b).

The earliest known written documents from the Nile Valley, such as the labels attached to supplies of goods from the ruler's tomb U-j in Abydos, show great variation in the figurativity (i.e., figurative rendering) of the hieroglyphs (Dreyer 1998; Stauder 2010; Vernus 2016). Yet, a clearly developed system already appeared in the iconicity in particular. A typical example is the variants in the reproduction of the sign group Plant + Jackal in the labels for goods in U-j 74–77 (Table III.13.1).

Despite the significant formal differences, the same two hieroglyphs are obviously always meant in these cases with such different forms, and the tolerance for variation with respect to hypothetical basic types was particularly high. The U-j 74 label has a different size than U-j 75–77, and indeed the variation of that label is clearly more prominent in comparison with the sign forms of the other labels. Perhaps this difference can be explained by another scribal hand or scribal tradition. Similar observations can also be made for multiple documented sign combinations.

Most notably, in the third millennium in the framework of the development of writing, sign forms were also more normalized. This normalization development corresponds with the question about conscious writing reform in the Nile Valley, such as the so-called Hierakonpolis reform at the end of the fourth millennium BCE (on early writing reforms, see Morenz 2011). The fundamental question of tolerance of variation at different levels applies especially in palaeographic terms, such as:

1. Culture as a whole
2. Region
3. Time
4. Social conditions
5. Material conditions
   etc.

Although we do not have any particular specific ancient Egyptian word for the concept of palaeography, in the wider sphere, it belongs with epithets about scribal competency, like *jqr dbs.w* ("excellent of fingers;" a rather rare epithet of scribes, used for the literary figure Neferti too). Although the self-referential ancient Egyptian statements on this topic are scarce, nevertheless, we can draw some conclusions from material practices. Palaeography probably belongs for the Egyptians in the category of *nfr*, in the sense of "beautiful," which at the same time comprises eugraphy (i.e., the beauty of the act of writing; Vernus 1982) and orthography. A sense of style is assumed at least partially for the epigraphic side. Specifically, this is comprehensible for us in an archaizing style (Manuelian 1994) that hearkens back to a distant past, as in a Late Period stela from the Serapeum (possibly from the Twenty-sixth Dynasty) with a hieroglyphic column that in form recalls the time of Djoser, approximately two millennia prior (Schäfer 1933, 2, fig. 1; Malinine, Posener, and Vercoutter 1968; Wildung 1969).

Not only did the stela of Padibastet adopt King Djoser's titulary, but in fact it even imitated the writing style of the Third Dynasty (Malinine, Posener, and Vercoutter 1968,

Table III.13.1. Inscriptions from the Predynastic Period and the First Dynasty. All photographs taken by the University of Bonn Archaeological Mission to the Sinai. All line drawings made by Susanne Kroschel.

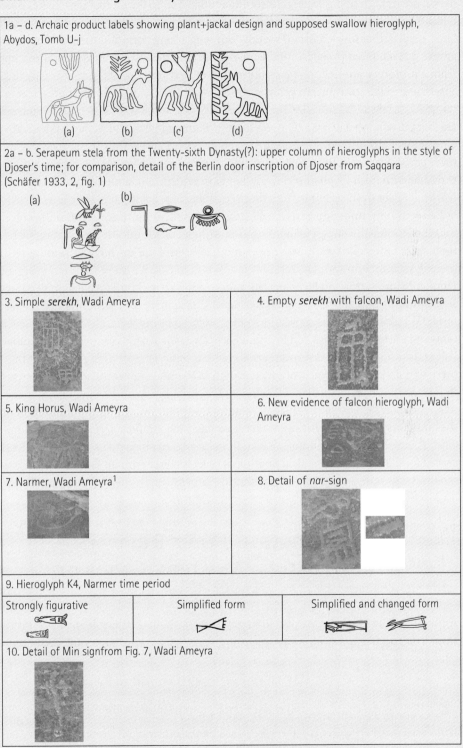

1a – d. Archaic product labels showing plant+jackal design and supposed swallow hieroglyph, Abydos, Tomb U-j

(a) (b) (c) (d)

2a – b. Serapeum stela from the Twenty-sixth Dynasty(?): upper column of hieroglyphs in the style of Djoser's time; for comparison, detail of the Berlin door inscription of Djoser from Saqqara (Schäfer 1933, 2, fig. 1)

(a) (b)

3. Simple *serekh*, Wadi Ameyra

4. Empty *serekh* with falcon, Wadi Ameyra

5. King Horus, Wadi Ameyra

6. New evidence of falcon hieroglyph, Wadi Ameyra

7. Narmer, Wadi Ameyra[1]

8. Detail of *nar*-sign

9. Hieroglyph K4, Narmer time period

Strongly figurative	Simplified form	Simplified and changed form

10. Detail of Min signfrom Fig. 7, Wadi Ameyra

[1] This reading is plausible because of the second sign. The *mr*-chisel, nevertheless, is also quite different. See Regulski 658–659. In addition, the rotation of 90 degrees should be noted.

93–94, no. 117).[1] In doing so, it is clearly differentiated from the hieroglyphs in the register beneath, and this difference impressively shows a consciousness of style in epigraphy. Such a stylistic, cultivated use of writing, bridging a long period of time, was in no way always or even often practiced in the Nile Valley, and here, we can expect a direct copy from a prototype about 2000 years older. In fact, texts that are strikingly archaizing in speech and spelling are often epigraphically not really old looking. This becomes clear in as impressive a text as the so-called Famine Stela of Sehel, which was written in the Ptolemaic era, but purports to date from Djoser's time (Wildung 1969; Goedicke 1994; Quack 2013). One reason for this form of graphic design could be that at that time in the area of Aswan, there probably was no Djoser-era inscription available as a prototype. (Although there is early evidence from Elephantine, we do not have evidence for a monumental script from Djoser's era; for the inscription from the time of Unas, see Seidlmayer 2005.)

Palaeography, understood as a collection of sign forms in space and time, is of technical benefit for the concrete identification of signs or for questions of dating (Möller 1909–1912; Goedicke 1988). More research has been done on hieratic as opposed to hieroglyphs (for the former, Verhoeven 2015a). First of all, more than ten years ago, Dimitri Meeks (2004, preface) started a project for hieroglyphic palaeography, intensively working on specific case studies (such as Collombert 2010). There is also the work of H. G. Fischer's various scholarly studies (1976, 1986, 1996) and N. Beaux's several essays on the Old Kingdom and Pre- and Early Dynastic Periods (2009a, 2009b, 2009c). I. Regulski has published a monograph on the topic (2010). The great potential of hieroglyphic-palaeographic work was recognized decades ago and also partially treated in a large sign list (particularly Petrie 1927). Epigraphic work in Egyptology focused temporally on the end of the third millennium BCE with its strong regionalization and the questions of regional writing systems and the palaeographic *period eye* (i.e., the specific viewing habits of a cultural zone and a cultural time; Baxandall 1972). These works served for dating and regional attribution of objects (Fischer 1968; Brovarski 1989), and the studies were also combined with cultural-historical questions (Fischer 1962).

PALAEOGRAPHICALLY RELEVANT DICHOTOMIES: AN OPEN CATALOG

An approach to the field of palaeography from a media-archaeological perspective would be to offer a list of what are to me some of the most relevant dichotomies

---

[1] The writing style is not mentioned there, but A. Mariette hypothesized a model from the area around Djoser. This is plausible, but given the brevity of the inscription, it is questionable how confidently an object like the Berlin door inscription can be identified as a concrete example (Wildung 1969, 76). Why was there was a reference to Djoser here? Among other possible explanations (Wildung), we can speculate whether Djoser's name "Divine in Body" (*Ntrj H̱.t*) was based on the Apis.

(Table III.13.2) to mark out the playing field of the use of scripts in the realm of the writing-image (i.e., *Schrift-Bild*). These dichotomies are, in part, self-explanatory, but can also guide a research program on image-literacy and writing-imagery (i.e., *Schrift-Bildlichkeit* and *Bild-Schriftlichkeit*).

Also in view of the development of the character set and of the scribal techniques, questions arise regarding revolution, reform, partial modernization, *visible* and *invisible hands*, and the so-called "phenomenon of the third kind" (i.e., human made, but in the absence of human planning; Keller 1990). Following the sources, concrete personalizations of developments, such as the question of the role of the "overseer of the royal scribes" (*mdḥ.w sš.w nsw.t*), as potential catalysts of graphic traditions are very uncertain (Kahl 1994; Morenz 2004a). Even if we cannot concretely identify them, it should be noted that the development of writing was brought about by concrete actors while at the same time the cultural technique of writing itself implied a certain agency (i.e., a disciplinary effect of writing on thought: Goody 1977; contributions in Ernst and Kittler 2006).

How far was the development of palaeography simply under the rubric of a general development of writing, and how far can we recognize it as specifically, uniquely palaeographic? The Pre- and Early Dynastic Periods under consideration here are particularly interesting as the formative phase of Egyptian culture (Morenz and Kuhn 2011) specifically of writing (Schott 1950; Kahl 1994) and even more specifically of palaeography. Here, in particular, a new work by Regulski (2010) has been published in which a lot of material was treated. Scharff's work (1942) is particularly interesting in terms of palaeographic interpretation. Although the conclusions drawn here are at least partially outdated by new material (in particular the main argument, based on an analysis of signs, that the development of writing occurred in the area of Lower Egypt), but the approach and method remain instructive and interesting.

REGIONAL CASE STUDY: A PRE- AND EARLY DYNASTIC TABLEAU OF INSCRIPTIONS FROM THE SINAI

Among the sensational new discoveries in the history of writing of recent years belongs the tableau of inscriptions from Wadi Ameyra in the southwest Sinai (Tallet and Laisney 2012) because local inscriptions from the third and fourth millennia BCE are witnesses of early Egyptian expeditions in the Sinai and their directing monumentality at cultural memory is not only extremely important historically, but is also the main source for our understanding of the history of media and especially of palaeography in the Pre- and Early Dynastic Periods.[2] Far removed from the royal capital, inscriptions were placed by

---

[2] I am very grateful to our host, Sheikh Rabia Barakat, for leading us to this place during an excursion in the fall of 2012.

Table III.13.2. Some Dichotomies That Mark Out the Playing Field of the Use of Scripts in the Realm of the Writing-Image (i.e., *Schrift–Bild*)

Normalization/standardization	Tolerance of variation
(Separability of the community of writer and reader)	(in Egyptian writing very high)
Material conditions	Idea[1]
Monumental writing	Cursive writing
(The Egyptian writing system was basically bigraphical (i.e., bigraphisch), but also hybrid (Ali 2002) and with permeable boundaries; also, transposition errors from cursive to monumental (compare Kahl 1994, 15).)	
Iconic sign status	Figurative sign status
(Permeable boundaries between image and writing; see Vernus by chapter.)	
Hieroglyph	Symbologramm (i.e., complex signs with multiple functions from the time of the late fourth and early third millennium BCE: Morenz 2008, 61–65)
Character	Image (In Egyptian graphic communication, images can be understood as *large characters* and hieroglyphs as *small images*.)
Cultural rules	Individual creations (i.e., special hieroglyphs: e.g., Morenz 2008, 141–145)
Interest in design	Recognizability through conciseness of form[2]
Appropriateness of place and subject	Individual scribal competence (i.e., deviations upwards and downwards)
Tradition	Innovation
(Problem: scholastic institute, i.e., family system versus "academy")	(Specific contemporary needs and competencies) Variable by: region, social conditions, type of text
Texts left unfinished, high variation in the figurative quality of the characters	Perfection of writing–image in longer inscriptions
Single sign	Entire text

[1] In the field of art history, this difference between work and imagination is referred to in Lessing's famous formulation of "Raphael without hands."

[2] *Zeitschrift für Semiotik* 31:1–2 (2009): Prägnanter Inhalt – prägnante Form; for the concise form, a greater design effort can be required. In this context is the question of to what extent economic thinking was operative in Egyptian writing history and how much writers wanted to save expenses.

Egyptian expeditions in the southwest Sinai from Predynastic times—typified by the empty *serekh* sign both with and without falcons above it (Hendrickx, Friedman, and Eyckerman 2011, 141–144)—to the time of King Nebre of the Second Dynasty (Tallet and Laisney 2012, document 6 and fig. 12) (Table III.13.1.2–1.3).[3] In particular, the royal title and name were recorded and inscribed multiple times in a boat (Table III.13.1.4, 1.6).

Judging by its size, the boat is more of an image than a character (in Regulski (2010, 578–579), such boats are listed as characters), but we can interpret the overall composition as a complex symbologramm in the sense of *Expedition (=Boat) of the King NN (=Name and Title)*. The monogram-like association between boat and *serekh* in the example of Narmer (Table III.13.1.6) speaks also to this specific interpretation. The representation of the boat varies considerably, and there are even different boat types represented (Table III.13.1.4, 1.6).

The significant ruptures of the stone on the lines of the characters present a technical difficulty for rendering the hieroglyphic character set. The question arises in regard to palaeographic understanding whether in such cases it should be sketched exactly according to archaeology or whether the presumed intended shape should be taken into consideration more. The material conditions lead to variations of the actually intended form, and depending on the issue, both can be interesting. In fact, an exact reproduction of the outlines sometimes alters the image too much and in any case, creates such an impression visually (Raggazoli 2013).

The Narmer period inscription deserves a closer examination in the context of the name spellings (Table III.13.1.6–1.7). We know the *serekh* representations of Narmer both by curved as well as—as here—with a straight upper line. In fact, there existed in the catfish hieroglyph great variance in Narmer's time from highly pictorial to extremely simple, whereby we, large scaled, distinguish approximately three basic variants of differing figurativity (Regulski 2010, 474; Table III.13.1.8). The *nˁr*-catfish (Regulski hieroglyph K4) in the rock inscription from Wadi Ameyra falls in the category of the greatly simplified figurative sign forms.

In the case of some Nar(-mer) spellings, one actually wonders whether it was really always "written." In fact, we can, in certain cases, also count on the possibility of the imitation of writing in so far as the writing-image could have been mimicked (especially with regard to objects with the *nˁr*-inscription from places like Tell el-Erani; Morenz 2004b).

Above the Narmer scene at Wadi Ameyra appears an additional hieroglyph (not listed in Tallet and Laisney 2012, 387, document 4; Table III.13.1.9), which we can identify as an approximate parallel to the inscriptions on the famous Min statues from Coptos. We can also assume that this expedition of Narmer's was made to the southwest Sinai under the patronage of the god Min as a deity associated with foreign regions (e.g., a route with stations at Coptos, the Eastern Desert (possibly near wadis like Wadi Hammamat and Wadi Qash), and then to Wadi Ameyra).

---

[3] The use of writing was initially located in the vicinity of the royal area, but came to be used in remarkably different locales. This applies particularly to the distribution of a remarkable number of documents with the inscribed name of Narmer in the Nile Valley and the Levant.

PALAEOGRAPHIC INTERPRETATION
OF TWO ROYAL HIEROGLYPHS

In the following, the developments and problems of early epigraphy and palaeography are presented and rehearsed in two specific case studies.

Why Did Just the Bee Function as a Graphic Royal Symbol?

Some small animals, such as bees and spiders, are strikingly fertile for the production of myths. In many cultures, they were and are symbolically charged with meaning because their shape, behavior, and/or products fascinate(d) people. Besides their dreaded poison, spiders are especially associated with the elaborate webs they weave (so thus their association with weaving, etc.), while bees are chiefly known for honey, their sting, bee states, and bee dances. The aspects of kingship and state, honey and sting, are, for example, conceptually linked in the *Hieroglyphica* of Horapollo (1.62), an author of the fifth century CE (Thissen 2001, 39; for the laconic statement "for the king, a bee," see van der Horst 1984, frag. 12). The earliest use of the bee as a character comes from the ancient Egyptian culture, where the hieroglyph (Gardiner sign list L2) has appeared since the First Dynasty (i.e., from the early third millennium BCE) (Kahl 2002–2004, I:138–139; Regulski 2010, 476–478). Here, it has the reading *bj.t*, and the fixing of the royal title *bj.tj* was the earliest written use of the sign (Kahl 2008; Feierabend 2009, 62–63). Besides the phonetic meaning, one may well think of a particular iconic and symbolic significance to the bee-sign here (on the uncertain etymological link with *bt^c* "strong man," see Schneider 1993). Using a collection of early records, which were significant in content and quite fragile, Jochem Kahl (2008) suggested that the *bj.tj* title was a reference to the king's aspect as a "collector." Now the original reasons for the word and the character selection of hieroglyphs are certainly not to be figured out at such a great temporal divide, but this aspect seems at any rate to have become particularly important over the course of history. While it is far from easy to accurately define the conceptual world and associations of the bee in the mentality of Pre- and Early Dynastic Egyptian history, the analogy of the bee is obvious in certain aspects of the concept of royalty. In addition to the prominent position of collecting marked by Kahl (2008) as a central aspect of legitimate rule in the Nile Valley—that is, welfare and social protection—the aspect of valor—embodied in the stinger—also applies in the case of the bee in addition to its honey collecting. In this sense, we can point out that in the hieroglyphic sign forms of the First Dynasty, the stinger is clearly marked in the hieroglyphic image of the bee (Regulski 2010, 476).

Social protection and the valor-welfare combination are two central aspects of the ancient Egyptian rhetoric of kingship, and as other associations, we can also consider order and hierarchy—that is, state formation and (especially due to their size) the emphasized queen bee (perhaps not understood as "queen," as also in Horapollo)—and perhaps even bee dances (possibly understood with a sacred dimension?). In mythical-metaphorical imagination, the bee is, in any case, excellent as a metaphorical embodiment of the concept of king. Although because of insufficient evidence we cannot say with absolute certainty whether the word (*bj.tj*) and especially the choice of the character was actually thought of along these lines, it is at least plausible that this assumption relates to both the concept of king as a thought pattern and the principles of character selection in the script of the Nile Valley during the late fourth and early third millennium BCE (Vernus and Yoyotte 2005; Feierabend 2009; Evans 2010). In this case, in terms of palaeographic interpretation, it is remarkable that the bee stinger is clearly highlighted especially in the early sign forms. It is notable that it forms a characteristic in the scene and encourages reflection. Thus, it is at least plausible that first, with the bee, the royal aggression-potential was expressed and second, this was also expressed in a specific figurative sense by the hieroglyph in the scene.

Swallow versus Falcon: Palaeography and Early Royal Ideology in the Nile Valley

The last centuries of the fourth millennium BCE may be taken by analogy with Mesopotamia as a period of city-states in the Nile Valley, where several contemporary rulers of that time were called by the title *wr* ("great one"). This title appeared to be written with the swallow hieroglyph (G36), and indeed, from a palaeographic inspection of the hieroglyph variants on archaic labels from Tomb U-j at Abydos, it is clear from the beak that a song bird is meant with this sign form, not a bird of prey (Morenz 2004a).

One caveat, however, is how great an importance one could ascribe to the difference between a falcon's beak versus a songbird's beak for this early phase of the hieroglyphic script. No later than the time of the Predynastic King "Arms" (*sḫn*, or *k3*, or other possibilities; our phonetic reading remains highly hypothetical), a distinct falcon's beak appears (Table III.13.1.5), but one must also take into account that some later falcon representations show no clear falcon beak (Regulski 2010, 418–430). Although ultimately there can be no certainty in this case, I would like to assign to the bird sign in question from the label from Abydos Tomb U-j the both palaeographically and historically plausible reading of *wr*.

In contrast, the rulers of the newly created territory-states of the late fourth and early third millennium BCE were no longer "just" *wr* ("great"), but upgraded sacredly once more as *Ḥr*—(the deity) Horus. Horus not only was one of the great deities of Egypt but also functioned since the late fourth millennium in the Nile Valley as a central title of the king. Thus, King Narmer was spoken of as "Horus(-King) Narmer," and during the following decades and centuries, the Horus title was an essential element of pharaonic titulary (Beckerath 1984). In the early Egyptian Nile Valley, the Horus-centered concept of kingship implied an idea of the double Horus, namely,

1. Horus-king in human form
2. Solar Horus-deity in falcon form.

A witness of this is the magnificent palette of Narmer because there, the Horus-king Narmer is shown interacting with the solar Horus deity in falcon form, and the Horus-king is placed in the scene as a kind of human incarnation of the deity Horus (Morenz 2014). Horus was the chief deity of the archaic capital with the later Greek name Hierakonpolis ("Falcon city"), while the ancient Egyptian place name *nḥn* can be explained as *n/m-ḥn* ("place of alighting") (Morenz 2004a, 76, 100–105). The place name could be specifically related to this alighting of the Horus falcon (Hendrickx, Friedman, and Eyckerman 2011). How far can we understand the striking ambivalence of "Horus" as a chief solar deity and at the same time as Horus-king as a product, which was charged with sacred meaning, of the Hierakonpolitan royal ideology of the late fourth millennium BCE and perhaps was even understood as their most momentous contribution to *Pharaoh Fashioning*? In addition, we can expect and assume that these media developments left their mark in the script.

On the monuments of Narmer, the idea of the double Horus was already distinctly elaborated. This does not have completely clear-cut boundaries, but according to the epigraphic evidence, the development from *wr* to *Ḥr* occurred historically somewhat before King Narmer (Regulski 2010).

An obvious falcon's beak can be identified in some documents of King "Arms" (*sḥn/k3/*...), while some evidence for the so-called *'Irj-Ḥr* (or perhaps better simply *Ḥr*) show the falcon's beak and another, the songbird's beak (Table III.13.1.4–1.5). The evidence from Ameyra most likely belongs in the group of birds with the songbird beak, while the Narmer falcon from Ameyra (Table III.13.1.6) clearly has a falcon's beak. A falcon can also be seen on the empty *serekh* at Ameyra (Table III.13.1.3).

Here, however, there is the problem of accurate dating, because we cannot necessarily assume that the empty *serekh* could not have been made, for example, by semiliterate people who simply did not write the corresponding king's name in the palace façade. In this respect, approaches to dating remain hypothetical with this argument.

Perhaps the transition from swallow to falcon was done in the time of the so-called *'Ir j-ḥr*, and this assumption would correspond with the use of both the "old" and the "new" sign form in precisely this period. Perhaps here was, at first, a proper name "(deity) Horus," which then in the subsequent Egyptian tradition was reinterpreted as a royal title (as we know from the intercultural word chain: Caesar, Kaiser, Czar).

The path from *wr* ("great one") to *Ḥr* ("Horus") took place before King Narmer, but after the time of the ruler's tomb U-j at Abydos. We can observe a gradual development in the royal *mise-en-scène*, but also see at the same time a media quantum leap in Pharaoh Fashioning with Narmer—the alleged first ruler and founder of the territorial state (Wilkinson 2000). In the realm of the falcon, we can see how important palaeographic analysis can be for our understanding of royal ideology and history.

PROSPECTUS

In respect to palaeography, Heiner Müller's pithy statement could be problematized, but it was part of his "Mommsen's Block," which at that time was concerned with the difference between "hard" historical writing and "soft" literature. Nevertheless, it remains an interesting question how far we can differentiate traditions of particular times, regional writing schools, or individual scribal hands. From the beginning of Egyptian writing with the archaic label inscriptions from Abydos to differently constructed sign forms like the plant on the label Abydos U-j 74–77 (Table III.13.1.1), this material indicates different scribal hands, but a specific media-sociological localization remains a task for future research. However, it suffers from the problem of limited data and, of course, the accident of preservation.

The connection discussed here in a few examples of general palaeographic issues with regard to specific individual cases seems to me to be particularly productive. It shows the multilayered nature of the development of writing. Palaeography was a factor in the history of writing, which appears to be an interaction with many other aspects. When considered in terms of the history of writing, it is clear that the formative phase of Egyptian culture was a remarkable time for the development of writing and also especially for writing-images.

BIBLIOGRAPHY

Baines, J. 2004. "The Earliest Egyptian Writing: Development, Context, Purpose." In *The First Writing: Script Invention as History and Process*, edited by S. D. Houston, 150–189. Cambridge.

Baines, J. 2007. *Visual and Written Culture in Ancient Egypt*. Oxford.

Baxandall, M. 1972. *Painting and Experience in Fifteenth-Century Italy: A Primer in the Social History of Pictorial Style*. Oxford.

Beaux, N. 2009a. "Écriture egyptienne l'image du signe." In *Image et conception du monde dans les écritures figuratives. Actes du Colloque Collège de France-Académie des Inscriptions et Belles-Lettres, Paris, 24–25 janvier 2008*, edited by N. Beaux, B. Pottier, and N. Grimal, 242–287. Paris.

Beaux, N. 2009b. "Étude de quelques hieroglyphs égyptiens." In *Image et conception du monde dans les écritures figuratives. Actes du Colloque Collège de France-Académie des Inscriptions et Belles-Lettres, Paris, 24–25 janvier 2008*, edited by N. Beaux, B. Pottier, and N. Grimal, 288–313. Paris.

Beaux, N. 2009c. "Le signe figurative égyptien: Types de (sur-)motivation." In *Image et conception du monde dans les écritures figuratives. Actes du Colloque Collège de France-Académie des Inscriptions et Belles-Lettres, Paris, 24–25 janvier 2008*, edited by N. Beaux, B. Pottier, and N. Grimal, 364–371. Paris.

Beckerath, J. von. 1984. *Handbuch der ägyptischen Königsnamen*. MÄS 20. Berlin.

Brovarski, E. 1989. "The Inscribed Material of the First Intermediate Period from Naga-ed-Dêr." PhD diss., University of Chicago.

Collombert, P. 2010. *Le tombeau de Mérérouka*. PH 4. Cairo.

Dreyer, G. 1998. *Umm el-Qaab I: Das prädynastische Königsgrab U-j und seine frühen Schriftzeugnisse*. AVDAIK 86. Mainz.

Ehlich, K. 2007. "Textualität und Schriftlichkeit." In *Was ist ein Text? Alttestamentliche, ägyptologische und altorientalistische Perspektiven*, edited by L. Morenz and S. Schorch, 3–17. BZAW 362. Berlin.

Ernst, W., and F. Kittler, eds. 2006. *Die Geburt des Vokalalphabets aus dem Geist der Poesie. Schrift, Zahl und Ton im Medienverbund*. Munich.

Evans, L. 2010. *Animal Behaviour in Egyptian Art: Representations of the Natural World in Memphite Tomb Scenes*. SACE 9. Oxford.

Feierabend, B. 2009. "Honig und Biene im pharaonsischen Ägypten: Eine Studie anhand schriftlicher und bildlicher Quellen." PhD diss., Johannes Gutenberg University Mainz. Retrieved from ubm.opus.hbz-nrw.de/volltexte/2014/3643/pdf/doc.pdf.

Fischer, H. G. 1962. "The Archer as Represented in the First Intermediate Period." *JNES* 21:50–52.

Fischer, H. G. 1968. *Dendera in the Third Millennium B.C. Down to the Theban Domination of Upper Egypt*. New York.

Fischer, H. G. 1976. *Varia*. New York.

Fischer, H. G. 1986. *L'écriture et l'art de l'Égypte ancienne*. Paris.

Fischer, H. G. 1996. *Varia Nova*. New York.

Goedicke, H. 1988. *Old Hieratic Paleography*. Baltimore.

Goedicke, H. 1994. *Comments on the "Famine Stela."* Varia Aegyptiaca Supplement 5. San Antonio.

Goody, J. 1977. *The Domestication of the Savage Mind*. Cambridge.

Hendrickx, S., R. Friedman, and M. Eyckerman. 2011. "Early Falcons." In *Vorspann oder formative Phase? Ägypten und der Vordere Orient 3500–2700 v. Chr.*, edited by L. D. Morenz and R. Kuhn, 129–162. Philippika 48. Wiesbaden.

Horst, P. W. Van der. 1984. *Chairemon: Egyptian Priest and Stoic Philosopher*. EPRO 101. Leiden.

Kahl, J. 1994. *Das System der ägyptischen Hieroglyphenschrift in der 0.–3. Dynastie*. GOF 29. Wiesbaden.

Kahl, J. 2002–2004. *Frühägyptisches Wörterbuch*. 3 vols. Wiesbaden

Kahl, J. 2008. "*nsw* und *bit*: Die Anfänge." In *Zeichen aus dem Sand: Streiflichter aus Ägyptens Geschichte zu Ehren von Günter Dreyer*, edited by E-M. Engel, V. Müller, and U. Hartung, 307–351. Wiesbaden.

Kassung, C., and T. Macho, eds. 2013. *Kulturtechniken der Synchronisation*. Paderborn.

Keller, R. 1990. *Sprachwandel: Von der unsichtbaren Hand in der Sprache*. Tübingen.

Malinine, M., G. Posener, and J. Vercoutter. 1968. *Catalogue des stèles du Sérapéum de Memphis: Tome Premier*. Paris.

Manuelian, P. Der. 1994. *Living in the Past: Studies in Archaism of the Egyptian Twenty-Sixth Dynasty*. London.

Meeks, D. 2004. *Les architraves du temple d'Esna: Paléographie*. PH 1. Cairo.

Möller, G. 1909–1912. *Hieratische Paläographie*. 3 vols. Leipzig.

Morenz, L. D. 2004a. *Bild-Buchstaben und symbolische Zeichen: Die Herausbildung der Schrift in der hohen Kultur Altägyptens*. OBO 205. Fribourg.

Morenz, L. D. 2004b. "Hieroglyphen im frühbronzezeitlichen Südpalästina." *ZDPV* 120:1–12.

Morenz, L. D. 2011. "Die Systematisierung der ägyptischen Schrift im frühen 3. Jahrtausend v.Chr.: Eine kultur- und schriftgeschichtliche Rekonstruktion." In *Vorspann oder formative Phase? Ägypten und der Vordere Orient 3500–2700 v. Chr.*, edited by L. D. Morenz and R. Kuhn, 19–47. Philippika 48. Wiesbaden.

Morenz, L. D. 2013. *Kultur- und mediengeschichtliche Essays zu einer Archäologie der Schrift: Von den frühneolithischen Zeichensystemen bis zu den frühen Schriftsystemen in Ägypten und dem Vorderen Orient.* Thot. Beiträge zur historischen Epistemologie und Medienarchäologie 4. Berlin.

Morenz, L. D. 2014. *Anfänge der ägyptischen Kunst: Eine problemgeschichtliche Einführung in ägyptologische Bild-Anthropologie.* OBO 264. Fribourg.

Morenz, L. D., and R. Kuhn, eds. 2011. *Vorspann oder formative Phase? Ägypten und der Vordere Orient 3500–2700 v. Chr.* Philippika 48. Wiesbaden.

Petrie, H. 1927. *Egyptian Hieroglyphs of the First and Second Dynasties.* London.

Raggazoli, C. 2013. "The Social Creation of a Scribal Place: The Visitors' Inscriptions in the Tomb Attributed to Antefiqer (TT 60) (with newly recorded graffiti)." *SAK* 42:269–323.

Regulski, I. 2010. *A Palaeographic Study of Early Writing in Egypt.* OLA 195. Leuven.

Quack, J. 2013. "Hungersnotstele." Retrieved from https://www.bibelwissenschaft.de/stichwort/21646/.

Schäfer, H. 1933. "Der Reliefschmuck der Berliner Tür aus der Stufenpyramide und der Königstitel Ḥr-nb ." *MDAIK* 4:1–17.

Scharff, A. 1942. *Archäologische Beiträge zur Frage der Entstehung der Hieroglyphenschrift.* Munich.

Schneider, T. 1993. "Zur Etymologie der Bezeichnung 'König von Ober- und Unterägypten.'" *ZÄS* 120:166–181.

Schott, S. 1950. *Hieroglyphen: Untersuchungen zum Ursprung der Schrift.* Wiesbaden.

Seidlmayer, S. 2005. "Bemerkungen zu den Felsinschriften auf Elephantine." In *Texte und Denkmäler des ägyptischen Alten Reiches*, edited by S. Seidlmayer, 287–308. TLA 3. Berlin.

Selz, G. J. 2007. "Offene und geschlossene Texte im frühen Mesopotamien: Zu einer Text-Hermeneutik zwischen Individualisierung und Universalisierung." In *Was ist ein Text? Alttestamentliche, ägyptologische und altorientalistische Perspektiven*, edited by L. Morenz and S. Schorch, 64–92. BZAW 362. Berlin.

Staehelin, E. 2000. *Von der Farbigkeit Ägyptens.* Leipzig.

Stauder, A. 2010. "The Earliest Egyptian Writing." In *Visible Language: Inventions of Writing in the Ancient Middle East and Beyond*, edited by C. Woods, 137–147. OIP 32. Chicago.

Tallet, P. 2014. "Des papyrus du temps de Chéops au ouadi el-Jarf (golfe du Suez)." *BSFÉ* 188:25–49.

Tallet, P., and D. Laisney. 2012. "Iry-Hor et Narmer au Sud-Sinaï (Ouadi 'Ameyra): Un complément à la chronologie des expéditions minières égyptiennes." *BIFAO* 112:381–398.

Thissen, H. J. 2001. *Des Niloten Horapollon Hieroglyphenbuch, I: Text und Übersetzung.* AfP 6. Munich.

Vernus, P. 1982. "Espace et idéologie dans l'écriture égyptienne." In *Le sycomore*, edited by A. L. Christin, 101–114. Paris.

Vernus, P. 2012. "Les origines de l'écriture hieroglyphique de l'Égypte ancienne." In *Les origines de l'écriture*, 113–166. Paris.

Vernus, P. 2016. "La naissance de l'écriture dans l'Égypte pharaonique: Une problématique revisitée." *Archéo-Nil* 26:105–134.

Vernus, P., and J. Yoyotte. 2005. *Bestiaire des pharaons.* Paris.

Verhoeven, U., ed. 2015a. *Ägyptologische "Binsen"-Weisheiten I–II. Neue Forschungen und Methoden der Hieratistik. Akten zweier Tagungen in Mainz im April 2011 und März 2013.* AAWLM 14. Stuttgart.

Verhoeven, U. 2015b. "Stand und Aufgaben der Erforschung des Hieratischen und der Kursivhieroglyphen." In *Ägyptologische "Binsen"-Weisheiten I–II. Neue Forschungen und Methoden der Hieratistik. Akten zweier Tagungen in Mainz im April 2011 und März 2013*, edited by U. Verhoeven, 23–63. AAWLM 14. Stuttgart.

Wildung, D. 1969. *Die Rolle ägyptischer Könige im Bewusstsein ihrer Nachwelt. Teil I: posthume Quellen über die Könige der ersten vier Dynastien*. MÄS 17. Berlin.

Wilkinson, T.A.H. 2000. "What a King Is This: Narmer and the Concept of the Ruler." *JEA* 86:23–32.

....

READING, EDITING, AND APPRECIATING THE TEXTS OF GRECO-ROMAN TEMPLES

....

LAURE PANTALACCI

To the layperson, the Greco-Roman temples of Upper Egypt are among the most impressive memories to keep from a trip in Egypt. For Egyptologists as well, these huge monuments are of prime import, as first-rank sources of knowledge on post-pharaonic—and pharaonic as well—religion. Nevertheless, their study is considered as a special field of Egyptological studies. The word "Ptolemaic," derived from the name of the Hellenistic rulers following Alexander's conquest, is often and will be here applied as a loose designation to post-pharaonic monuments (Quack 2010) roughly between the late fourth century BCE and the early third century CE. Here only the temples are discussed, excluding private monuments like statues and stelae, which, though using the same language and graphic system and being composed by the same authors, are considered to belong to a different genre. The next pages are intended both as a basic description of Ptolemaic epigraphy for specialists of other fields or beginners in Egyptology, and as a reflection on the practices of editors and readers of Greco-Roman temples.

Because of their good preservation and their mass of decoration, these monuments have attracted much attention since the earliest days of the rediscovery of Egypt. Parts of their architecture and decoration were already documented by the scholars of the Napoleonic *Expédition d'Égypte* between 1798 and 1801 (see chapter by Gady). Soon after the decipherment of the hieroglyphic script by Champollion in 1822, the first Egyptologists visiting Egypt copied selected scenes and texts in the major temples of Philae, Kom Ombo, Dendera, and Edfu, and in many small or large sanctuaries now vanished. In 1870, the first volume of the publication of Dendera temple by Mariette appeared. In those early days, Ptolemaic epigraphy was part of the common Egyptological practice. Mariette also encouraged Rochemonteix to publish Edfu extensively, a project finally carried out by Émile Chassinat between 1892 and 1934 (see chapter by Kurth). These pioneering undertakings, on a truly monumental scale, laid the principles for analyzing and editing Ptolemaic temple decoration for several generations to come.

PICTURES AND ICONIC TEXTS

Compared to "classical" Pharaonic monuments, Ptolemaic temple walls were practically blanketed with pictorial scenes and/or columns of texts. Because of the outsized dimensions of the monuments, they display a variety of offering scenes unknown before. The number of horizontal registers increases up to three or four. The scenes also bring to light a number of individual gods or divine companies rarely heard of before, borrowed from old religious *corpora* or more recently created. Processions of divine beings occupying registers along the length of walls are frequent, especially in the *soubassement* and the upper frieze, but the scene or tableau remains the basic decorative unit, showing a real or symbolic ritual episode. Whereas the New Kingdom scenes were practically silent, each Ptolemaic picture is provided with a relatively long text. The hieroglyphic comments specify the title of the rite, the identity of the king and the god(s), the dialogue between them, and, in some cases, additional strings of divine or royal epithets in the *Randzeilen* or marginal columns. So interpreting a scene requires full understanding of the accompanying captions, and not infrequently, fragments of original information—related or not to the nearby picture—can be extracted from the texts, in spite of their formulaic nature.

The representation itself may underline the unrealistic, symbolic character of the rite: for example, in scenes of killing of the enemies or of wild animals, the sacrificed victims are often represented on a minuscule scale (Derchain 1966). During the past decades, a number of studies have been devoted to specific ritual scenes in Ptolemaic temples: offering the lotus, the mirrors, the country, slaughtering the oryx, to mention but a few. These detailed studies resulted in evidencing both local and "national" beliefs, specificities and generalities, and the balance between them. Obviously, the small scale of studies concentrated on a single type of scene is restrictive. Consequently, such thematic studies, useful as they are, can only superficially deal with the network of correspondences and echoes that the Egyptian scribes built between the different elements of the decoration. While the depictions are mostly standard, variations appear regularly in accompanying texts, graphemes and/or vocabulary being carefully chosen to refer to the particular context (see *infra*). Additionally, new offerings, specific to single deities, appear at that time, for example, the offering of dates to Osiris. Dates were a basic staple in Egypt and were offered to the dead since the dawn of Egyptian history. More specifically, in this context, they are supposed to help with curing and reassembling the dismembered body of the god (Cauville 1980). This is the kind of theological innovation that the epigrapher has to account for without much help from older parallels.

While the scenes have often been categorized according to their typology, editors of Ptolemaic monuments usually pay little attention to art historical or purely iconographic aspects. Conversely, scholars interested in visual studies (e.g., Vassilika 1989) may overlook the texts, despite the strong iconic value of Ptolemaic hieroglyphs. Obviously, the balance between text (and its translation) and pictures is difficult to keep, and the publications have been biased since early on. At the end of the nineteenth century, the early and quick development of hieroglyphic fonts was a decisive step for Egyptological publications in general. For Ptolemaic temples in particular, the role of Émile Chassinat, editor of Edfu and of a great part of Dendera texts, was crucial. Trained as a printer before becoming an Egyptologist, while directing the Institut français d'archéologie orientale, he was keen to create a new printing-house in Cairo, both to avoid the cumbersome process of printing hieroglyphic texts in Europe and to create print characters as close as possible to the original Ptolemaic signs. Indeed, in the post-pharaonic period, many variants of common hieroglyphs were in use, be they signs newly created or reactivated from past periods. To account for these variations, printing was—and still is today—felt to allow the most accurate rendering. Replacing the hand-drawn volumes of Mariette or Brugsch, where figures and texts were published together on the same plate, the volumes issued from the IFAO press definitely resulted in the physical division between pictures and texts, giving the hieroglyphic texts a strong priority over the pictorial information. Whereas all the texts are edited in the same way, whatever their content may be, in some volumes of Edfu or Dendera, it happens that the scale of some drawings, for scenes reputedly less informative, is quite small, and their details hardly legible.

As a result, the academic knowledge of the major Greco-Roman temples is mostly textual, while the pictorial data are frequently neglected. A basic exercise for training the beginner Ptolemaicist consists in reconnecting the texts of Edfu or Dendera with the corresponding plate, to reconstruct the integral scene. In recent publications like Esna (Sauneron) or Athribis (Leitz), texts and images usually closely follow one another, but remain dissociated all the same. And despite the rapid technological evolution of drawing and printing technologies, the hieroglyphs, carved most frequently on columns and on temple walls, are still arranged into lines and systematically oriented from left to right. As a result, the text often loses its original orientation and its proximity with the figures, so that the visual co-text and context of the signs become difficult to grasp. Only for smaller Ptolemaic monuments (precinct gates, mammisi, etc.), a few scholars have taken the step of abandoning the print characters and reverting to nineteenth-century epigraphic methods, by publishing complete copies of the scenes in line drawing, figures, and texts on the same plate (e.g., Clère 1961; Junker 1958; Junker and Winter 1965; Leitz 2014). In recent publications, much of the line drawing for scenes is done digitally on a photograph. Whenever the epigraphic quality and the preservation of the monument are satisfactory, it would be suitable and sufficient to apply the same treatment to the text, following the classical Chicago epigraphic methods (see chapter by McClain) as being the closest rendering of the original.

Photographs of individual scenes are an excellent medium for direct study and have been part of temple publications for a long time. Chassinat edited the first series of photographs for Edfu as early as 1929 and a whole volume of photos in 1933 (*Edfou XI*). Nevertheless, until quite recent times, only a limited number of photo plates appeared in print; so older publications leave most of the scenes incompletely documented. Whenever possible, collating the plates with the printed text generally improves the understanding of a scene. Nowadays, the use of digital shots allows extensive publication of the photographic documentation either on paper alone (Cauville 1997b; Leitz 2014; Biston-Moulin and Thiers 2016) or both on paper and in electronic format (Leitz, Mendel, and El-Masry 2010). This medium will certainly develop even more in the near future; and it will certainly renew and enrich the approach of Ptolemaic studies by providing at once full access to all data for each scene.

Some parts of temples, such as doorframes, friezes, and specialized chapels, are mostly or exclusively carved with texts. Many of these texts are directly connected with practical purposes: they may be litanies and hymns recited during daily or festive rituals, performative texts directed at priests or believers, and so on. Not infrequently, they are repeated in several locations in the same temple or appear in different temples when they happen to reflect a "national" tradition (e.g., the *snḏ*-hymns calling believers to respect and fear the local god: Rüter 2009). The quest for parallels, through Ptolemaic and/or older *corpora* of texts, is of prime importance for any epigrapher, but even more for Ptolemaicists. The comparison between parallel texts shows the skills of priests, who manage to tailor their sources to the available space or to merge "national" and local traditions. Well beyond the literal decipherment of Greco-Roman sources inside or outside a temple, the epigrapher needs a substantial diachronic knowledge of pharaonic religious-funerary tradition. Identifying sources is not always easy: graphic updates and changes, principally cuts and interpolations, sometimes make older texts hardly recognizable. Ptolemaic priests were in antiquity, and still are, admired and praised for their deep knowledge, culture, and interest in their heritage. They benefited from the rich book stocks of their temple library, known to us both through some of the original papyri that were once part of such collections (Osing 1999) or only through the book titles, often referring to age-old rituals (Thiers 2004). It is a real challenge for the modern scholar to measure up to their excellence.

In addition to this reference to Pharaonic religious heritage, the Greco-Roman Period also witnessed an intense creativity, attributed by some specialists to the extended and intimate contacts of Egypt with Mediterranean culture at large (Derchain 2000). Be that as it may, many Ptolemaic texts appear to us as new, unique compositions, remaining unparalleled—at least in the current state of our knowledge. Derchain has actively argued for the concept of authorship for smaller, remarkable Ptolemaic monuments, such as the doorway of Ptolemy Euergetes in Karnak (Derchain 1996; Derchain 2000). Specific scenes and hymns were composed and carved even for the smallest sanctuaries. At el-Qal'a, a much corrupted text, probably a royal hymn, remains nearly illegible— partly for lack of parallels (Pantalacci and Traunecker 1998, 157; see chapter by Traunecker). It seems the scribe copying the text from a papyrus in hieratic (or Demotic?) script misread many signs (for comparable analyses, see Kurth 1999), unintentionally producing a cryptographic text.

The term "cryptography" is sometimes applied to Ptolemaic texts as a whole. Though it has been loosely used by earlier scholars, it is clear that texts meeting the literal sense of this word, that is, written exclusively with unusual graphemes aiming to hide their meaning from the reader, are uncommon. Nevertheless, the word "cryptographic" generated the *communis opinio* that reading Ptolemaic texts was difficult, whereas most Ptolemaic "running" texts, after a little training, become easily legible to readers of classical Middle Egyptian. Indeed, many signs with "Ptolemaic" phonetic values were already used the same way in Late Period private inscriptions (Quack 2010, 75–76). Recent publications of important collections of statuary from the Third Intermediate and Late Periods should contribute, in the near future, to improving the knowledge of the graphic system in use during the last millennium BCE. Only a negligible percentage of Greco-Roman texts, mainly specific compositions, such as dedicatory inscriptions or hymns, use a special set of rare "cryptographic" hieroglyphs. Those generally combine several signs in a single grapheme and tend to include representations of living beings. Their use increases significantly in the Roman Period (Klotz 2012, 567–571)—maybe to meet or pique the interest of Greek or Roman aficionados or nationalistic priestly scholars? This trend is particularly obvious in Esna (Sauneron 1959, 51–52). A well-known example from this monument is the double frieze composed of a long series of identical signs, rams for one, crocodiles for the other (Leitz 2001b). However, the phraseology of "cryptographic" texts—in Esna, hymns to the local god; in Dendera, dedication texts or royal titularies—is so conventional that with the help of the complementary signs, even uncommon phonetic values can be established with a reasonable degree of certainty.

More generally, striking features of Ptolemaic and Roman texts are the large stock of signs and the systematic preference for visually suggestive graphemes, to add a pictorial or symbolic meaning to the literal one. This has been emphasized by the first scholars studying late temples (Junker 1903), and it holds true especially for texts carved in remarkable locations like friezes or crypts (Cauville 2002). For instance, at the angles of Dendera temple, special use was made of the divine figures of Re and Osiris to write the words *nḥḥ* and *ḏ.t*, their alternating figures expressing the rising and setting of the sun on the east and west corners of the temple, embodying the twin conceptions of eternity (Cauville 2001, 4). The use of hieroglyphs as icons or ideograms is far from new; but there, it is brought into play to an extent never met before. Current editing methods, though frequently including detailed comments on paleography, hardly succeed in taking into account all these subtleties.

"Grammaire du temple" and Other Decorative Patterns

When elaborating the decoration program of a temple, the Egyptians constantly kept in mind the global architectural setting of decoration, be it doorframe, wall, column, chapel, hall, and so forth. This concern about the wide architectural context has been described as a system, in particular by Philippe Derchain, who in the early 1960s coined the phrase "grammaire du temple" (Derchain 1962). The basic principle is the symmetry of scenes and texts on both sides of the spatial axis. Again, this is not a novelty, since it has been the rule for decorating Egyptian monuments presumably since the first dynasties. But the majestic scale of the Ptolemaic temples and their excellent preservation gives an exceptionally acute vision of this principle. A wide range of ritual themes and combinations was available, and the task of the scribes in arranging the symmetrical program of the two halves of architectural elements or spaces, like pylons, courts, or halls, must have been relatively easy. The correspondence between the pairs of scenes is rarely the sheer repetition of the same offering. More often, a parallel is established between two rites of comparable meaning (for example, wild animals and human foes of the god as identically chaotic forces: Derchain 1966).

Following this principle, the editor of a Ptolemaic monument usually splits the decoration in symmetrical halves, reading alternatively first the left, then the right corresponding registers. This apparent symmetry can conceal essential differences of meaning. For instance, though the processions and lists of toponyms on the soubassement of the girdle wall in Edfu look symmetrically arranged on its external and internal walls, a thorough examination shows that the decoration particularly emphasizes the defensive action of the god Horus in the external scenes, while the internal sides mostly refer to the traditional repertoire of cultic scenes (Jambon 2014).

In addition to the horizontal connections between paired registers, there exist also vertical links between scenes. A recent study on the decoration of external walls of the naos of Dendera concluded that in this case, though the usual horizontal symmetry does exist, the scenes are primarily designed to be read in vertical sequences (Leitz 2001a, 230–248). A degree of continuity exists between lower, middle, and upper scenes, showing a thematic identity or proximity, like successive episodes of the offering of myrrh or of the myth of the "distant Goddess." Additionally, a limited horizontal symmetry between the east and west walls of the *couloir mystérieux*, the girdle corridor around the naos, is also visible. Here the principle of the "multiplicity of approaches" fully applies. These "mysterious" corridors are complex spaces, since their internal wall belongs to the sanctuary, while their external wall is pierced by the doors of the girdling chapels. So no continuous visual symmetry could be achieved anyway. Rochemonteix gave priority to the logic of spatial contiguity, when he included the façades of the girdle chapels in the *couloir mystérieux* at Edfu. This course of action resulted in a somewhat incoherent sequence of publication, and later editors rather published together the texts of façade and doorjambs with the inner walls of the secondary chapels. Moreover, the theological influence of such chapels is sometimes also felt in the outside decoration surrounding its door, interrupting the decorative pattern of the corridor proper. The seventy-seven protecting divinities of Pharbaitos proceeding on five registers (instead of two for the rest of the wall) to surround the door of Sokar-Osiris Chapel in Dendera are a case in point (Chassinat 1934, 5–6 and pl. 88; Goyon 1985, 224–226, 256–259). Such a complexity does not occur only in corridors. Every space with multiple doorways poses similar problems. A miniature example is the offering hall in the temple of el-Qal'a, at the cross of two cultic axes, which measures roughly 7 × 4 m and is pierced by no less than six doors. This layout leaves very little space available for decoration properly related to the specific function of the room.

Well beyond the mechanical principle of visual symmetry, a more subtle manner of connecting together scenes from different registers of the same wall consists in building textual echoes between two scenes, for instance by using homographs, homophones, homonyms, or a common semantic or visual field (Labrique 1992, 298–302; Leitz 2001a, 169–172, 325–326). On the southern jamb, western wall of the gate of Euergetes in Karnak (Clère 1961, pl. 40:11–13), a picturesque passage, attributed to Ahmose son of Smendes (Derchain 1996, 90–91), describes a young bull in the marshes "who drinks water, a lily to his nose and a lotus around his neck" (Derchain 1995, 2). These poetic words, included in a scene showing twice the run of the sacred bull of Khonsu in front of the god, are hardly understandable in their immediate context. Actually, the description rather applies to the figure of the bulls in the offering procession of the lower register just below (Clère 1961, pls. 36–37). It thus forms a subtle link between text and picture, between this specific scene dedicated to Khonsu and the conventional sequence of fecundity figures under it. So, far from being a purely dichotomous montage, the decoration program rather forms a complex network, both vertical and horizontal, of images and meaning in each space, and sometimes also on the larger scale. The Ptolemaic Osirian complexes on the terrace of Dendera show an exceptional skill in combining original ritual scenes with the long texts about Khoiak celebrations, chapters from the Book of the Dead, geographical and divine processions, scenes from the Osirian ritual, and so forth, divided between the "East" and "West" complexes of rooms (Cauville 1997a, 209–214). The metaphor of knitting or weaving seems quite appropriate here to describe the structure of this decoration program, interweaving textual and pictorial material from a large, heterogeneous stock relating to the Osirian rites.

FOLLOWING REAL OR VIRTUAL ORIENTATIONS

The connection of distant chapels with a remote or purely virtual pole may result in apparently incongruous orientations of scenes or texts, thus becoming a source of perplexity for scholars. Virtual orientations had long existed in Egyptian monuments (Traunecker, 2020), but during the Ptolemaic Period their number increased. Since local topography did not always meet the theological ideal, in reality the orientation of monuments is often symbolic, as for example in Dendera, where the temple opens actually to the North, when it should symbolically open due East (Mariette 1875, 39–41). These kinds of problems—and their solutions—are more conspicuous in the Greco-Roman Period because temples are better preserved and also because highly specialized spaces, with specific theology and rites, multiply inside the temple itself or in its *temenos*. Lastly, the growing importance of astronomical science and beliefs in religious practice might have reinforced this priestly concern for orientation.

A well-known case is the mammisi, a modest building where the sun was annually (re)born as a child-king. So it should open to the East; on the other hand, normally the axis of a mammisi had to run perpendicular to the axis of the main temple (Kockelman 2011, 1). In Coptos, the main temple, dedicated to Min and Isis, opens to the West: hence the perpendicular, South–North orientation of the mammisi. But the solar theology supposed an East–West orientation, and this was achieved virtually through the reliefs. As a result, the western half of the sanctuary was decorated as if it was the South, that is, Upper Egypt, while the "North" was to the magnetic East (Pantalacci 2014).

This concern for orientation sometimes induces discrepancies in the decoration program. A well-known case is the famous zodiacal ceiling in the Osirian chapel of Dendera, oriented on the true cardinal points, unlike the wall decoration (Cauville 1997a, 79). Another puzzling practice is the use of retrograde writing. It can apply to very limited sections of scenes or texts, such as the divine name, so that the god receiving offerings and the hieroglyphs noting his name always face the same direction, looking from inside the naos outward. In other cases, whole texts (of friezes, lintels, etc.) are written in retrograde orientation. In Edfu, for instance, the orientation of the lintels of the eastern chapels happens to be identical to the corresponding western ones, instead of being symmetrically reversed. The reasons for such inversions in some rooms, and not in others, have yet to be found (Cauville 1983, 83–84).

Tracing the Logic and the Dynamics of the Decoration

As mentioned already several times, the *raisons d'être* of a number of features still escape us. Why did priests decide to copy on stone some old reference texts (such as hymns or rituals), apparently directly borrowed from the temple library, in certain locations? For lack of experience, the first Ptolemaicists did not always recognize them as units nor pay attention to their layout: so Chassinat edited in reverse order the famous donations texts of Edfu (Meeks 1972, x). In some cases, the Egyptian scribes themselves were confused when partitioning a long text between several walls or columns. A case in point are the long hymns engraved on several columns of the hypostyle hall in Esna. They do not follow at all what is considered elsewhere—for example in the hypostyle hall of Dendera—to be the logical architectural order. Sauneron relates vividly his efforts to reconstruct the thread of the textual sequences (Sauneron 1959, 75–140 and pl. 18). In addition to long texts split between several columns, fragments of hymns and calendars are squeezed in the free spaces, without apparent order. So the decoration pattern of the columns remains partly unexplained.

A possible factor of disruption in the temple decoration scheme is the diachronic dimension. The decoration of huge monuments was a long process, carried out over decades by successive teams. Contrary to popular opinion, Egyptian religion was not immutable and especially during the last centuries of its history, was strongly exposed to rapid moves and changes. Temples were erected on an unprecedented scale and at a hectic pace. Even on small-scale projects like el-Qal'a, the evolution in the theological program is blatant (Pantalacci and Traunecker 1998, 2–4). In major temples, such changes also existed, but detecting them requires an in-depth study of the monument (Cauville 1983, 60). Does it mean the beliefs and cults actually evolved? Is it only a different visual elaboration by new teams of priests? The idea of "wall theology" proposed by Traunecker (1991) should induce the epigrapher to apply different grids to the scenes and texts in different spaces of a temple, contributing to a diachronic approach not only of the writing system (like Cauville 2001), but also of the theological elaboration.

Sauneron (1959) has advocated a better interaction between architectural and epigraphic studies. To this effect, he introduced in the publication of Esna the small-scale diagrams of walls for each scene in order to locate it more easily. This practice is now widespread among editors of Ptolemaic temples. Though undoubtedly improving our perception of scenes in their context, it necessarily reduces this context to a single wall, separated from the architectural unit to which it belongs.

Egyptian priests certainly had a different, more limited, but also more personal and physical experience and knowledge of temple decoration. A special category of reliefs has been termed "cultic" because of their location in spaces open to nonpriestly believers (Gutbub 1984). In Dendera, Kom Ombo, and elsewhere, representations of the main deity on the rear exterior wall allowed those to "see the god" and establish a direct visual contact with the divine outside the naos. Like other scenes of exterior walls since Pharaonic times, the carving was supplemented with fittings of wood, (precious) stones, and metals. Presumably, such reliefs were of interest mainly to occasional visitors or pilgrims, as a summary of the main theological data of the place. Here, the visibility of the scenes is an essential feature, achieved both by their special layout (huge size, deeper carving, etc.), their adornment, and the direct lighting of these walls by sunlight. Reading temple decoration also means stressing the importance of such images, though the accompanying texts are generally limited in length and content.

Inside the temple as well, the study of lighting is an essential tool to better evaluate the importance of the space and its decoration. The major part of the walls, either because of the dim light or because of their height, remained invisible. The best-lighted parts were doorways and lower registers (Zignani 2008, 117–119). Here, the correspondences are neither vertical nor horizontal, but follow the course of temple users inside the sacred space. Hence, the exclusive choice of well-lighted locations for important texts, hymns or monographs, various sacred lists, and instructions for priests, obviously intended to be seen and read, or even memorized, perhaps used for didactic purposes, when training the priestly staff (Gutbub 1973, 182–183).

This dynamic dimension of temple decoration also appears in particular inscriptions possibly related to a visit to, or tour of, the temple, either by members of the staff or by external visitors. Let us consider the location of the so-called monographs, exposing the fundaments of local theology and mythology (von Lieven 2014). The format of these didactic notes is sometimes limited to a short mention of the name of the chapel or door (Traunecker 1992, 162–166, no. 29–30). Whatever their length, their location in the inner temple suggests that they were intended to be actually visible, mostly for the local priests (Recklingshausen 2014), and maybe used as manuals for priestly education. Similarly, it is generally admitted that some hymns are specifically linked with processions—often pictured in their vicinity (Kockelmann 2014, 541–542). They should help us visualize strongly differentiated zones inside the temple. For example, the *snḏ*-hymns, urging believers to fear and respect the divinity, are always located at the periphery of the temple (Rüter 2009, 77), sometimes even on the outer façade or in the passage of a monumental gate, a space probably accessible also to laypersons. As for the so-called Instructions to the Priests, the jambs of side doors are their favorite location. They appear along the main temple axis or in service entrances, in the stairways, or even in the *wabet* complex. Describing the behavior appropriate for clergymen while inside the temple (Traunecker 1992, 205–210), these texts follow their path inside the monument.

Recently, attention has been drawn to the decoration patterns of the soubassements (Rickert and Ventker 2014). A papyrus preserving a number of designs for soubassement frieze, published by Quack (2014), shows that although without texts, this part of the decoration was a strong visual code mastered by the Ptolemaic decorators. The surviving section of the papyrus offers a wide variety of standardized motifs, but actually many more are attested from the extant temples (Dils 2014). These collections of patterns encourage epigraphers to pay attention not only to the texts but also to the anepigraphic elements. A case in point comes from the southern precinct of Coptos, where the lower register of doorjambs is repeatedly decorated by tableaux of lions armed with knives (Traunecker 1992, 211–212). While transposing in two dimensions the classical leonine statues protecting a temple, they also represent Shu and Tefnut, who received a cult in this precinct. Their location, on the west or north face of doorways, follow the priestly path leading from the main temple through the Osirian complex to the Southern Cemeteries (Pantalacci, forthcoming). While fulfilling their traditional role as guardians, they also provide a dynamic link between local theology and rites performed for the dead in the necropolis.

Regarding the textual data, Ptolemaicists can already rely on a wide range of specialized tools: extensive publications of main and secondary temples, lexicographical and bibliographical tools, elements of paleography, architectural studies, and monographs about specific chapels or buildings, specific scenes, and specific texts. The next step could be to better take into account the physical spatiality of the monuments, inasmuch as it can be observed or reconstructed with certainty. The current development of architectural studies and the growing number of tools for three-dimensional models can become a valuable help to visualize the interplay between related elements of the decoration. Furthermore, systematically reconnecting the temple data with their wide context (particularly, contemporary private stelae and statues), could contribute significantly to both our understanding of the texts and our knowledge of the priestly elite in Ptolemaic and Roman times.

BIBLIOGRAPHY

Biston-Moulin, S., and C. Thiers. 2016. *Le temple de Ptah à Karnak*. BiGen 49. Cairo.

Cauville, S. 1980. "Une offrande spécifique d'Osiris: Le récipient de dattes." *RdE* 32:47–64.

Cauville, S. 1983. "Une règle de la 'grammaire' du temple." *BIFAO* 83:51–84.

Cauville, S. 1997a. *Le temple de Dendara: Les chapelles osiriennes, Vol. II: Commentaire*. BdE 118. Cairo.

Cauville, S. 1997b. *Le temple de Dendara X: Les chapelles osiriennes*. 2 vols. Cairo.

Cauville, S. 2001. *Dendara: Le fonds hiéroglyphique au temps de Cléopâtre*. Paris.

Cauville, S. 2002. "Entre exigence décorative et significations multiples: Les graphies suggestives du temple d'Hathor à Dendara." *BIFAO* 102:91–135.

Chassinat, É. 1934. *Le temple de Dendara: Tome deuxième*. Cairo.

Clère, P. 1961. *La porte d'Évergète à Karnak*. MIFAO 84. Cairo.

Derchain, P. 1962. "Un manuel de géographie liturgique à Edfou." *CdE* 37 (73):31–65.

Derchain, P. 1966. "Réflexion sur la décoration des pylônes." *BSFE* 46:17–24.

Derchain, P. 1995. "La justice à la porte d'Évergète." In *3. Ägyptologische Tempeltagung. Hamburg, 1.5. Juni 1994. Systeme und Programme der ägyptischen Tempeldekoration*, edited by D. Kurth, 1–12. ÄAT 33/1. Wiesbaden.

Derchain, P. 1996. "Auteur et Société." In *Ancient Egyptian Literature: History and Forms*, edited by A. Loprieno, 83–94. PdÄ 10. Leiden.

Derchain, P. 2000. *Les impondérables de l'hellénisation: Littérature d'hiérogrammates*. MRE 7. Brussels.

Dils, P. 2014. "Die Ornamentdecoration auf dem Mauerfuss der Tempel der griechisch-römischen Zeit. Ein Überblick über die Soubassements 'ohne Text.'" In *Altägyptische Enzyklopädien: Die Soubassements in den Tempeln der griechisch-römischen Zeit. Soubassementstudien I*. 2 vols., edited by A. Rickert and B. Ventker, 877–963. SSR 7. Wiesbaden.

Goyon, J.-C. 1985. *Les dieux-gardiens et la genèse des temples (d'après les textes égyptiens de l'époque gréco-romaine). Les soixante d'Edfou et les soixante-dix-sept de Pharbaethos*. 2 vols. BdE 93. Cairo.

Gutbub, A. 1973. *Textes fondamentaux de la théologie de Kom Ombo*. 2 vols. BdE 47. Cairo.

Gutbub, A. 1984. "Kom Ombo et son relief culturel." *BSFE* 101:21–45.

Jambon, E. 2014. "Les soubassements de l'intérieur du mur d'enceinte d'Edfou." In *Altägyptische Enzyklopädien: Die Soubassements in den Tempeln der griechisch-römischen Zeit. Soubassementstudien I*. 2 vols., edited by A. Rickert and B. Ventker, 793–818. SSR 7. Wiesbaden.

Junker, H. 1903. *Grammatik der Dendaratexte*. Vienna.

Junker, H. 1958. *Der große Pylon des Tempels der Isis in Philä*. DÖAW Sonderband. Vienna.

Junker, H., and Winter, E. 1965. *Das Geburtshaus des Tempels der Isis in Philä*. DÖAW Sonderband. Vienna.

Klotz, D. 2012. "Egyptian Hieroglyphs." In *The Oxford Handbook of Roman Egypt*, edited by C. Riggs, 563–580. Oxford.

Kockelmann, H. 2011. "Mammisi (Birth House)." In *UCLA Encyclopedia of Egyptology*, edited by W. Wendrich. Los Angeles. http://digital2.library.ucla.edu/viewItem.do?ark=21198/zz0026wfgr.

Kockelmann, H. 2014. "Das Soubassement der griechisch-römischen Tempel als Ort hymnischer Rede. Ein Überblick." In *Altägyptische Enzyklopädien: Die Soubassements in den Tempeln der griechisch-römischen Zeit. Soubassementstudien I.* 2 vols., edited by A. Rickert and B. Ventker, 301–320. SSR 7. Wiesbaden.

Kurth, D. 1999. "Der Einfluß der Kursive auf die Inschriften des Tempels von Edfu." In *Edfu: Bericht über drei Surveys; Materialien und Studien*, 69–96. ITE, Begleitheft 5. Wiesbaden.

Labrique, F. 1992. *Stylistique et théologie à Edfou: Le rituel de l'offrande de la campagne: Étude de la composition.* OLA 51. Leuven.

Leitz, C. 2001a. *Die Außenwand des Sanktuars in Dendara: Untersuchungen zur Dekorationssystematik.* MÄS 50. Mainz.

Leitz, C. 2001b. "Die beiden kryptographischen Inschriften aus Esna mit den Widdern und Krokodilen." *SAK* 29:251–276.

Leitz, C. 2014. *Die Gaumonographien in Edfu und ihre Papyrusvarianten: Ein überregionaler Kanon kultischen Wissens im spätzeitlichen Ägypten.* 2 vols. SSR 9. Wiesbaden.

Leitz, C., D. Mendel, and Y. El-Masry. 2010. *Athribis II: Der Tempel Ptolemaios XII.: Die Inschriften und Reliefs der Opfersäle, des Umgangs und der Sanktuarräume.* 3 vols. Cairo.

Lieven A. von. 2014. "Mythologie and Lokaltheologie in Soubassements. Das Beispiel Kom Ombo." In *Altägyptische Enzyklopädien: Die Soubassements in den Tempeln der griechisch-römischen Zeit. Soubassementstudien I.* 2 vols., edited by A. Rickert and B. Ventker, 51–67. SSR 7. Wiesbaden.

Mariette, A. 1875. *Dendérah: Description générale du grand temple de cette ville.* Vol. 6. Paris.

Meeks, D. 1972. *Le grand texte des donations au temple d'Edfou.* BdE 59. Cairo.

Osing, J. 1999. "La science sacerdotale." In *Le décret de Memphis: Colloque de la Fondation Singer-Polignac*, edited by D. Valbelle and J. Leclant, 127–140. Paris.

Pantalacci, L., and C. Traunecker. 1998. *Le temple d'el-Qal'a, II: Relevés des scènes et des textes. Couloir mystérieux, cour du "Nouvel An," Ouabet, Per-nou, Per-our, Petit vestibule. Nos 113–294.* Cairo.

Pantalacci, L. 2014. "Les sept Hathors, leurs bas et Ptolémée IV Philopator au mammisi de Coptos." *BIFAO* 114:397–418.

Pantalacci, L. Forthcoming. "Les deux lions de Coptos." In *Mélanges May Trad.* Cairo.

Quack, J. 2010. "Was ist das 'Ptolemäische'?" *WdO* 40/1: 70–92.

Quack, J. 2014. "Die theoretische Normierung der Soubassement-Dekoration: Erste Ergebnisse der Arbeit an der karbonisierten Handschrift von Tanis." In *Altägyptische Enzyklopädien: Die Soubassements in den Tempeln der griechisch-römischen Zeit. Soubassementstudien I.* 2 vols., edited by A. Rickert and B. Ventker, 17–27. SSR 7. Wiesbaden.

Recklingshausen, D. von. 2014. "Monographien in den Soubassement." In *Altägyptische Enzyklopädien: Die Soubassements in den Tempeln der griechisch-römischen Zeit. Soubassementstudien I.* 2 vols., edited by A. Rickert and B. Ventker, 29–50. SSR 7. Wiesbaden.

Rickert, A., and B. Ventker, ed. 2014. *Altägyptische Enzyklopädien:. Die Soubassements in den Tempeln der griechisch-römischen Zeit. Soubassementstudien I.* 2 vols. SSR 7. Wiesbaden.

Rüter, S. 2009. *Edfu: Habt Ehrfurcht vor der Gottheit NN. Die snḏ-n-Hymnen in den ägyptischen Tempeln der griechisch-römischen Zeit.* ITE 2. Gladbeck.

Sauneron, S. 1959. *Quatre campagnes à Esna.* Esna I. Cairo.

Thiers C. 2004. "Fragments de théologies thébaines: La bibliothèque du temple de Tôd." *BIFAO* 104: 553–572.

Traunecker, C. 1991. "De l'hiérophanie au temple: Quelques réflexions…." In *Religion und Philosophie im Alten Ägypten: Festgabe für Philippe Derchain zu seinem 65. Geburtstag am 24. Juli 1991*, edited by U. Verhoeven and E. Graefe, 303–317. OLA 39. Leuven.

Traunecker, C. 1992. *Coptos: Hommes et dieux sur le parvis de Geb*. OLA 43. Leuven.

Traunecker, C. 2020. "Orientations réelles et imaginaires dans l'architecture égyptienne." In *Mélanges Michel Azim*, Cahiers de Karnak 17. Cairo.

Vassilika, E. 1989. *Ptolemaic Philae*. OLA 34. Leuven.

Zignani, P. 2008. *Enseignement d'un temple égyptien: Conception architectonique du temple d'Hathor à Dendara*. Lausanne.

....

HISTORY OF RECORDING DEMOTIC EPIGRAPHY

....

JAN MOJE

THE largest and most exhaustively examined corpora of written sources from ancient Egypt are those of papyri and ostraca in their several attested languages and scripts, including Demotic. In contrast, Demotic epigraphic (abbreviated in what follows as "DE") sources are scarcely taken into account, maybe also due to their comparatively small quantity and their long-lasting status as an "unloved child" (Spiegelberg 1924).

"Demotic" is called the last but one phase of the Egyptian language as well as the script in which it was written, used since the Saite Dynasty (from about 664 BCE). It was primarily intended for papyri (cf. also Hoffmann 2000, 24), but already in the Late Period, inscriptions in Demotic were written on other materials as well. Nevertheless, those sources remain in the minority. They are the topic of this comprehensive look into the history of recording DE sources. Thus, the general development shall be outlined, focusing on important and epoch-making steps and editions, not mentioning every single publication of DE texts.

"Epigraphic texts" in this chapter refers to those texts that are engraved or inked onto solid but movable text carriers, such as coffins, stelae, and so forth, being in direct connection with the text on them, but also having their own independent function, as given in the list that follows (Table III.15.1). As such, excluded from this study are graffiti/mason's marks, ostraca, mummy labels, leather, and tablets/writing boards, as well as, for example, letters to the dead on vessels or school exercises. (For an overview concerning Demotic mummy labels, see Vleeming 2011, ostraca Zauzich 1986, graffiti Moje 2010 and what follows.)

As of December 2019, the database "www.Trismegistos.org" lists a total of merely 1,878 DE objects as thus defined—a rather small number when taken into consideration with the total of 18,600 published Demotic sources listed there in general.

Table III.15.1 Overview of attested DE sources. Credit: J. Moje, after www.trismegistos.org, 12/2019.

object	stone	wood	pottery	metal	faience	clay, linen, cartonnage
Amulets					1	
Architectural building inscriptions etc. [exception, not movable, but not graffiti]	37					
Clothes (linen, sandals)						5
Coffins (human/animal)	37	53	29	14		31
Funerary furniture (boxes, censer, stands, shrines, naoi)	2	11		10		
Mummy bandages						115
Music instruments (flute, bells, tongs, sistra)				5		
Offering tables	40					
Pebbles, polyhedron	16					
Statues and statuettes	54	17	1	9		
Stelae	717	2				
Tools (stoppers, cubits, mirrors, torches, weight, stamps, slingshot projectile)	3		4	4		1
Vessels	9		588	44	3	
Unclear DE objects (unpublished, fragmentary, unidentified)	16					

A Short Overview of the Development of Demotic Epigraphy since the Late Period

Originally, Demotic was intended for papyrus documents. DE sources are first attested from the Late Period, but still rarely. For Upper Egypt, *Trismegistos* mentions nine documents only, which are mainly from the religious centers Thebes and Abydos. In contrast, there are many more Memphite DE sources.

The peak in the number of datable sources from the Ptolemaic Period can be considered around the reigns of Ptolemy II Philadelphos and Ptolemy III Euergetes. Afterward, the quantity of attested sources fluctuates on a slightly lower level. Approximately 80 percent of the datable Ptolemaic DE sources are written in stone, followed by wooden coffins and statues, as well as metal vessels and ritual equipment, such as offering stands, statuettes, sistra, or bells. Remarkable is the dominance of monolingual DE sources, constituting about 75 percent of the entire corpus. Among the bilinguals, the largest quantities are those combining Demotic with the other Egyptian scripts hieroglyphic or hieratic. The use of the language of the new government, Greek, was then still very rare in bilingual epigraphic sources with a Demotic part. This is not astonishing given that Greek was at first mainly used for administrative documents on papyrus.

During the Roman Period, the situation changed. The use of DE text carriers increases only in the beginning of the new era. The Augustan reign can be considered as both the beginning and the maximum extent of Roman DE sources. After 14 CE, the number of sources declines rather rapidly. The last DE documents, which are coffins, date to the reign of Severus Alexander.

THE NINETEENTH CENTURY

The Beginnings: Initial Recording of DE Sources

The beginning of academic research on the Demotic script is not connected with a papyrus, but with one of the most famous epigraphic records containing Demotic: the engraved trilingue from Rosetta with identical texts in hieroglyphs, Demotic, and Greek, the so-called Rosetta stone (see chapter by Regulski). The stone was found by a French officer of Napoleon's army during the first expedition to explore Egypt and its cultural heritage in 1798. In the famous *Description de l'Égypte* (Commission 1823, 5:pl. 55; see chapter by Grimm), only the Rosettana itself is presented, besides some Demotic graffiti and a copy of a Demotic Book of the Dead. Twenty years before the decipherment of the "hieroglyphic language" by Jean-Francois Champollion (1790–1832), the Swedish orientalist Johan David Åkerblad (1763–1819) was already able to publish (1802) identified personal names and phonetic unilateral signs within the Demotic part of the Rosettana. He presented these in a table with handwritten corresponding signs, drawn schematically rather than as facsimiles.

Another scholar, the German archaeologist and philologist, Friedrich von Schlichtegroll (1765–1822), also engaged with the Rosettana (1818). He reproduced a detailed facsimile of all three scripts made earlier in London, even though for today's needs, it is partly insufficient. In his work, he did not focus on the Demotic itself.

Champollion himself also incorporated the Demotic script into his grammar and decipherment studies. His publications include several handwritten Demotic signs, but they do not cite the objects from which these sign (forms) were taken. Beyond that, he mainly used excerpts of several texts and hardly ever reproduced one complete inscription, a fact that was often criticized by scholars throughout the nineteenth century, explicitly formulated in Brugsch (1850). In his *Notices descriptives*, the only Demotic texts that Champollion gives attention to are some graffiti.

These early scholars were not engaged with DE records in detail, due to the fact that in their time not much more than the Rosetta stone—or only squeezes and drawings of it—was available for study. In addition, these early scholars were primarily interested in deciphering the scripts themselves rather than turning their attention to publishing a single object or larger object corpora. This meant that they used DE material without differentiations concerning the materiality of the text carrier. Over the course of the following years, this started to change.

Johann Heinrich Karl Menu Freiherr von Minutoli (1772–1846), a Prussian officer who led the second official expedition to Egypt from 1820 until 1821 by order of the Prussian government, described his discoveries extensively (1825). His collection formed part of the core of the future Egyptian section of the museum (*Aegyptische Abtheilung der Königlichen Museen zu Berlin*). Even though he was unable to read hieroglyphs or Demotic, he published the first private DE object (aside from the Rosettana), seeing it as an entire source—the object together with its inscriptions. It is a wooden snake coffin (Berlin ÄM 7232, see Figure III.15.1A+B).

The quality of his "facsimile" is rather poor, but from a scientific point of view, he can be considered more as an interested collector than a philologist or demotist. Minutoli described the *dipinto* as "*in enchorischen Charakteren*," which indeed means "Demotic." Additionally, he reasoned from the appearance of this script that it must be written from right to left. A translation is not provided. It took about 100 years before the first correct translation was published by Wilhelm Spiegelberg (1927). Note that the head of the snake on the lid, still visible in the old facsimile, is already lost in the 1927 photo. From the "income" of Minutoli's expedition, the first academic publication of a Demotic non-papyrological document was presented to the public in 1836, as to be shown later.

The English physician Thomas Young (1773–1829) published two volumes of draw-ings of inscriptions with their surrounding scenes, but without any commentary (1823, 1828). Young also included hieratic and Demotic texts, the latter on papyrus and stone. Under the term "Hieroglyphics," he subsumed not only the figurative signs but also all other ancient Egyptian scripts, such as hieratic and Demotic. His hieroglyphs differ from the appearance of the originals, and the same can be stated for his Demotic drawings.

For DE sources, we can refer—besides the ubiquitous Rosetta inscription in his first volume—to five private Demotic stelae in the possession of the British Museum (EA 184, 188, 375, 387, and 392). Interestingly, most of them are bilingual hieroglyphic-Demotic and therefore represent the first epigraphic bilinguals with Demotic ever published.

Note the numbers and letters at the edges of the right drawing (Figure III.15.2b), which remind one of modern maps but are totally unusual for publishing Egyptian stelae. Line numbering had not been established in Egyptology at that time.

Since 1828, the Italian former horse trader and private excavator Giuseppe Passalacqua (1797–1865) was the first director of the newly established Egyptian collection in Berlin, which was formed mainly from his own and Minutoli's collections. Repudiated within the Egyptological community as an amateur and "quirky" Egyptologist with a dubious smattering of knowledge, Passalacqua presented the first academic and high-quality publication of a Demotic document other than a papyrus. For this reason, his contribution

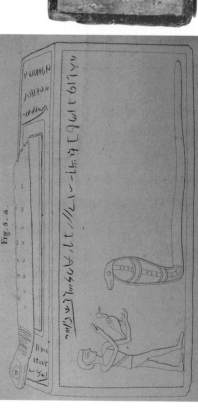

FIGURE III.15.1A+B. The first private DE source brought to public: Snake coffin Berlin ÄM 7232 (left side), missing since 1945.

Facsimile: Minutoli 1825, pl. 34; Photo: © Staatliche Museen zu Berlin—Ägyptisches Museum & Papyrussammlung ÄM 7232, Archiv (1927).

FIGURE III.15.2A+B. The first published Demotic/bilingual stelae by Thomas Young (= London, British Museum EA 387, 392).

Facsimiles: Young 1828, pls. 48, 51. Not to scale.

shall be mentioned here even though his article was about an ostracon from Minutoli's contribution to the Berlin Egyptian Collection (today, Ostr Berlin P. 890). This first "modern" object edition was published with an excellent facsimile—and the first analysis of such a private Demotic source in a wider context (Passalacqua 1836). This forgotten *editio princeps* was brought to light again by Karl-Theodor Zauzich (1986), one hundred fifty years after its publication.

Unlike modern editors, Passalacqua not only numbered the lines but also grouped the texts' signs ("*Gruppen*") into a word or a component of a word. Then he tried to read one group after another. After his philological analysis, he provided an attempt at an interpretation of its cultural context based on content and dating.

The Italian Egyptologist and orientalist Ippolito Rosellini (1800–1843) accompanied Champollion on the Franco-Tuscan expedition to Egypt from 1828–1829 (see chapter by Manniche), the third great survey through the country. After the death of his French colleague, Rosellini was responsible for editing the results of this expedition in nine folio volumes, appearing between 1832 and 1844, but interestingly not a single DE source was included here.

The fourth official expedition to Egypt was that of the venture on behalf of the Prussian king Friedrich Wilhelm IV under the leadership of Karl Richard Lepsius

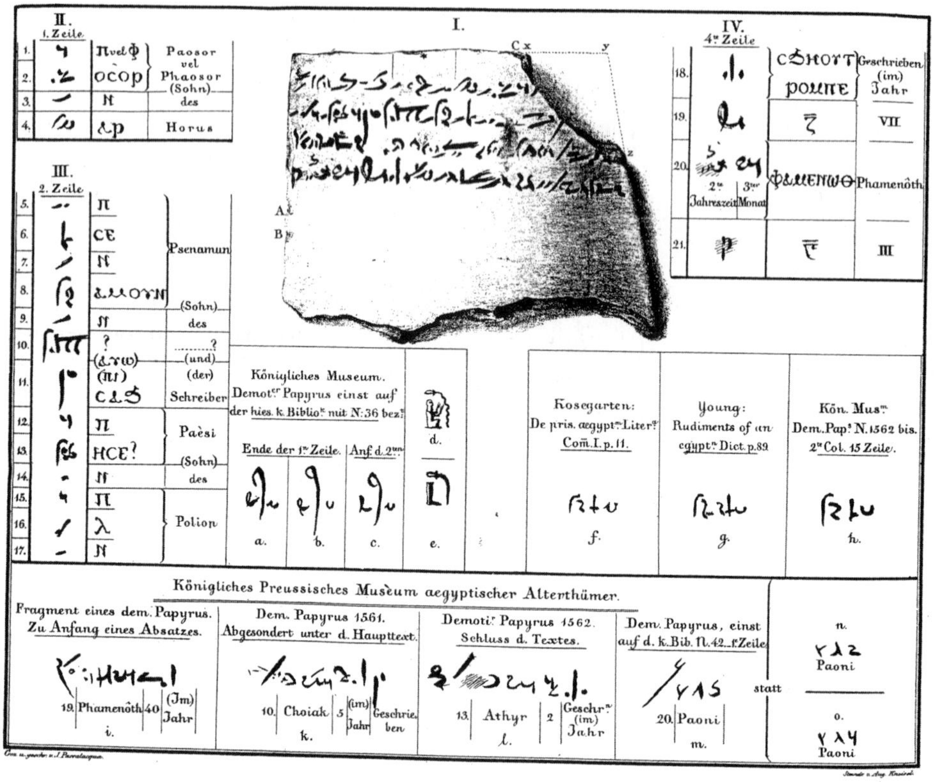

FIGURE III.15.3. The first scientific analysis of a Demotic ostracon, made by Joseph Passalaqua in 1836 (= Ostr. Berlin P. 890).

From *Hallesche Literaturzeitung* Junius 1836:593–601.

(1810–1884) (see chapter by Loeben). The results of this great expedition were published in several folio volumes with detailed drawings of objects, inscriptions, landscape sceneries, and very accurate plans. The final(!) "plates volume" (Lepsius 1859) contains inscriptions in several languages and scripts apart from hieroglyphs, named "Inschriften mit Ausschluß der Hieroglyphischen." Here again at the very end, within *Abtheilung VI Blatt 24–74*, several Demotic inscriptions were published. These facsimiles can be considered the first editions of engraved Demotic texts in high quality, meaning that they closely correspond to the appearance of the originals. Only parts of the Demotic-Greek so-called "Moschion stela," which is now stored in the Ägyptisches Museum Berlin (ÄM 2135), are given by Lepsius in facsimile. Remarkably, this is the one and only DE source appearing within this huge and important edition series.

The First Attempts at Scientific Recordings of DE Sources

The first German Demotist was Heinrich Brugsch. After a long absence of more than two decades, he again started turning Egyptology's attention toward DE sources.

Educated in Berlin, he was a protégé of Alexander von Humboldt, a situation that was not approved of by Richard Lepsius. While still a schoolboy, Brugsch studied the Egyptian language and scripts. He wrote the first draft of a Demotic grammar as early as 1845, most of which does not need modification even today and can be considered as the starting point of scientific Demotic studies. Five years later, he edited a DE corpus (Brugsch 1850). From the long title, it is clear that here also the Rosettana was still the starting point for research on DE texts. In his preface, Brugsch points out that the up until then completely neglected hieroglyphic-Demotic bilinguals will be of the greatest value for the decipherment of the Demotic script and language. His collection of bilinguals, which contained hand-drawn facsimiles with first attempts of translation and commentary, was intended for such further studies. Besides some papyri and the Rosetta inscription, two funerary stelae (Paris, Musée du Louvre C119 and 678) are also edited. Those stelae were the first ones published after Thomas Young's facsimiles edition in 1828. Additionally, the only two known examples of a trilingual offering table and a trilingual coffin (Berlin, Ägyptisches Museum ÄM 2304 and ÄM 504) are presented. It took more than 150 years before a new summarizing study combining the three text parts was edited (Moje 2013). Heinrich Brugsch's book can therefore be considered as the first scientific edition dedicated to (bilingual) DE objects.

Samuel Sharpe (1799–1881), a British Bible scholar, banker, and Egyptologist, published three volumes of inscriptions (1837–1855). In the final volume, he also presented, unfortunately without any commentary or translation, mediocre drawings of four Demotic and one Greek-Demotic stelae (Sharpe 1855, pls. 64, 70, 71 = Berlin ÄM 2125, 2130, 2132, BM EA 837, 838).

Later the already mentioned Heinrich Brugsch also edited the six volumes of his huge *Thesaurus Inscriptionum Aegyptiacarum*. The volumes 5 (*Historische Inschriften*) and 6 (*Bautexte und Inschriften verschiedenen Inhalts*) (1891) are dedicated to inscriptions of all Egyptian periods. A large part of these volumes are occupied by DE texts and bilinguals presented in his own hand copies often together with their German translations.

Brugsch sorted the texts according to their content, "*nach dem Grundsatz divide et impera sollte man das inhaltlich Zusammengehörige nicht voneinander trennen*" ("in accord with the principle *divide et impera*, contents belonging together should not be separated"; Brugsch 1891, 5:VII). This is one of the main, but from a current point of view rather "hidden," merits of the *Thesaurus*. For DE sources, this is the very first attempt to use a comprehensive DE corpus for analyses. In this case, his methodology is due to historical and chronological interests, as Brugsch himself points out in the foreword of volume 6.

Volume 5 groups together all of the texts known at that time belonging to the high priests of Memphis, as well as sources concerning the Apis cult. Both of these groups contain hieroglyphic, Demotic, and hieroglyphic-Demotic inscriptions. Volume 6 contains the first synopsis of a hieroglyphic-Demotic text, the Tanis stela, and a version of the Canopus sacerdotal decree.

Afterward, the number of available Demotic papyri increased rapidly. The main interest of Demotic text editions studies now shifted from stelae to papyri. The number of publications of DE stelae, statues, and so forth, and their analyses, were greatly limited.

The Twentieth Century

The Second Step in Recording DE Sources Systematically: Corpus Editions

In the beginning of the twentieth century, Demotic studies are primarily associated with Wilhelm Spiegelberg (1870–1930), the second important German Demotist after Heinrich Brugsch. He undertook the first efforts of exploring DE sources systematically. For this purpose, the second step in the development of recording DE sources was his three-volume publication of the Demotic inscriptions on text carriers other than papyri from the Egyptian Museum Cairo in the framework of the *Catalogue Général* (CG) project (Spiegelberg 1904, 1906–1908, 1932). In the introduction to volume 1, Spiegelberg reflects on the classification of those texts and their text carriers for the first time. His catalog presented to contemporary scholars a larger corpus of DE material including high quality photos and/or facsimiles. Given that at that time only a very limited number of Egyptologists were able to read Demotic, this was of particular importance. Spiegelberg provided his own translations and comments, deviating from the regular structure of the CG volumes. The translations contain some minor inaccuracies, and his datings are sometimes slightly too late, but at that time, no preparatory work existed to enable more precise dates. "*Die demotische Epigraphik steckt ja noch in den Kinderschuhen*" ("DE is still stuck in its infancy"), as Spiegelberg states in the preface to his first 1904 edition. Therefore, his pioneering work cannot be overestimated. Besides those catalogs, he edited several DE texts in various articles (compiled by Farid 1995, 334–335).

In the period after Spiegelberg, research on DE sources declined again. Publications concerning single DE texts are scattered only (compare Farid 1995, 313–338), whereas comprehensive and systematic analyses are still lacking. The main focus of demotists' research was still set on the nonepigraphic texts preserved by papyri and secondarily, ostraca, because only these sources were available in larger quantities.

Primarily topographically based collections and publications of relevant DE texts began rather late. To be mentioned first, after Brugsch's *Thesaurus* 5 (1891), is Reymond's study (1981) of a particular family's records. For the Demotic parts only, hand drawings are given, which are not of palaeographical value, but this study was aimed at the Memphite priestly institutions and not specifically at Memphite DE sources themselves. A new edition of this corpus was recently published (Panov 2015). Other studies of particular groups of sources are only partially dedicated to DE sources, but mainly to Greek respectively Hieroglyphic stelae (Abd el-ʾAl, Grenier, and Wagner 1985; Abdalla 1992).

The large corpus of the stone and pottery coffins of the sacred ibises from the Ibiotapheion at Tuna el-Gebel has been a topic of published research since Heinz Josef Thissen edited a first overview on the Demotic inscriptions on these objects (1991). The final publication is planned for the near future, with two large corpora edited respectively by the late Thissen and Jan Moje and by Mahmoud Ebeid. The latter has already edited several small texts from this necropolis.

The Third Step in Recording DE Sources Systematically: Collecting Metadata

The third main step relating to a systematic and comprehensive exploitation of DE material was undertaken by Adel Farid when he published his PhD thesis (1995). The bibliography especially for the DE sources contains at least 122 pages, followed by a bibliography listing alphabetically all editors of DE sources. For the first time, all known DE inscriptions were compiled and sorted by content and materiality. Afterward, Farid published several DE sources (e.g., Farid 1999).

THE TWENTY-FIRST CENTURY

Increasing Research on DE Sources

Sven P. Vleeming's first Demotic *Sammelbuch* (2001) was inspired by the *Sammelbuch Griechischer Urkunden aus Ägypten* begun by Friedrich Preisigke. This collection contains a multiplicity of published DE objects in mainly stone, metal, and wood. The texts are of dedicatory and ritual content. Funerary inscriptions are excluded. Corresponding to the basic idea of a *Sammelbuch*, the focus is mainly on the Demotic texts or text parts themselves and not on full publications of the entire DE objects. Additionally, the volume contains bibliographical references and all metadata. Important are the black handcopies accompanying nearly every text, partly drawn anew for this publication. All texts are made accessible together with transcriptions, translations, and elaborated indices. This can be considered as the first entire and comprehensive collection of metal DE sources ever published. A fourth volume, *Demotische Denkmäler* of the *Catalogue Général*, is in preparation, where all published DE inscriptions from the Cairo museum shall be collected (Farid 2002).

A list of corrections, the two-volume *Demotische Berichtigungsliste* with annual *addenda*, represents another important tool for epigraphic research (Den Brinker, Muhs, and Vleeming 2005), especially the second volume, which is dedicated to ostraca and various other publications, including DE sources. Therein, corrections and additions to Demotic text editions are collected, as well as new readings and comments, sorted by the original publications.

Corpora of solely DE sources concentrating on one place only have been examined (Moje 2008a, 2008b, 2011). The objects received commentary and tentative palaeographical remarks. Another work (Devauchelle and Widmer 2011) treats Demotic funerary stelae from the East Delta in their cultural context, focusing on objects mentioning females. Devauchelle shall also be mentioned as author of several recent articles on DE sources and graffiti.

Vleeming's second Demotic *Sammelbuch* (2011) contains DE sources as coffins and sarcophagi for humans respectively animals and mummy linen next to the labels.

Another geographically focused edition of DE documents (Smith, Andrews, and Davies 2011), collects all stelae from the mother cows inked—and less often carved—with Demotic inscriptions and presents a full catalog with translations, photos, and, to some extent, facsimiles as well as commentaries.

The next corpus of already published DE objects compiled for a reason other than an *editio princeps* was composed of twenty-five newly translated votive inscriptions with commentary (Vittmann 2012).

Perspective: Future Research Possibilities in Recording DE Sources

Additional larger—not only bibliographical—collections of DE sources have not occurred so far, besides future, planned volumes of the *Demotisches Sammelbuch*. This gap is being filled by the database www.Trismegistos.org, which was begun by the Cologne/Leuven project *Multilingualism and Multiculturalism in Graeco-Roman Egypt* under the auspices of Mark Depauw in 2005 and is henceforth continuously added to and updated. In this database, all Egyptian textual sources from about 800 BCE onward are collected with their metadata. All published DE sources and all other Demotic sources can be researched.

Palaeographical research on DE texts, comparable to the work of Ola el-Aguizy (1998) and the Heidelberg project of Claudia Maderna-Sieben, Jannik Korte, and Fabian Wespi for Demotic papyri (see chapter by Quack et al.), did not occur in the past, apart from sporadic remarks on single signs and writing within other studies. Wilhelm Spiegelberg already noted in his article on status and future duties of Demotic studies (1924) that next to a palaeography of Demotic papyri, "*ein besonderer Band... den demotischen Steininschriften vorbehalten bleiben (müsse), weil sie mit dem Grabstichel auf Stein gemeißelt ihren eigenen Schriftcharakter entwickelt haben*" ("a special volume should be reserved for Demotic stone inscriptions because due to them being carved in stone, they have developed their own sign shapes"). This desideratum will be met in the future with the author's ongoing project "Palaeography of Demotic Epigraphy" (Moje 2012–2013), which focuses on Demotic, engraved stone and wood objects.

Summary

The beginning of research on DE sources dates to the early nineteenth century with translation attempts on the famous trilingual sacerdotal decree found in Rosetta in 1798. Afterward, scattered publications of hand-drawn pseudo-facsimiles were made by researchers from England, France, and Germany, but those drawings still did not totally match the look of the original. Those publications contain no translations or analyses. Their aim was only to present new material for the decipherment of Egyptian texts, but they lack both a special interest specifically in Demotic and in reproductions of the original shape of the single signs. On the other hand, these scholars saw "Egyptian texts" as including hieroglyphics, hieratic, and Demotic signs, not separating the latter as belonging to a unique science.

Although Giuseppe Passalacqua presented the very first scientific research on a Demotic ostracon in 1836, it was not until 1850 that Heinrich Brugsch edited drawings and synoptic translations of hieroglyphic/Demotic bilinguals written on stone and wood. As one of the first scholars, he had the "fresh" awareness of their value for the future understanding of Demotic as its own language and an independent script. In his *Thesaurus* 5, Brugsch (1891, 1040) states for the first time in Egyptology that the Demotic script engraved in stone shows a *ductus* different from that written on papyrus, even if he himself never undertook palaeographical research in DE. This scholar also published the first geographically focused DE corpus.

The second milestone in scientific and comprehensive DE research is represented by the *Catalogue Général* volumes of Wilhelm Spiegelberg on the Cairo museum DE sources at the beginning of the twentieth century (1904–1932). At that point publications of DE sources moved beyond the level of submitting mere hand-drawn "facsimile" material for future research and included more and more comprehensive studies of those long-neglected documents, seeing them on the same level as, for example, hieroglyphic stelae. This century saw more and more published adequate facsimiles of DE made directly from the object itself, mainly in minor studies. As a third step, Adel Farid (1995) published his important first bibliography on those sources together with an initial metadata collection of all objects known to him at that time.

Since the twenty-first century, DE sources have come into focus more intensively. Here, Sven Vleeming's ongoing *Sammelbuch* series (e.g., 2005) must be mentioned as the fourth important work, which was a mark of true progress in that it enables scholars to deal more comfortably with DE objects. A palaeography of the DE corpus with engraved texts, which was demanded by Spiegelberg in 1924, is in preparation by the present author. For the future, the online database www.Trismegistos.org will provide Egyptologists with easy access to all metadata concerning texts from Egypt, including DE sources being equitable to all other written sources.

REQUIREMENTS CONCERNING THE PUBLICATION OF DEMOTIC EPIGRAPHIC OBJECTS

As the first publications were handmade pictures without any claim to palaeographical accuracy, it was a long time until DE objects were published appropriately, considering all relevant aspects. A modern DE edition should contain all metadata, detailed descriptions of the object, and full transcriptions and translations. Important are high-quality

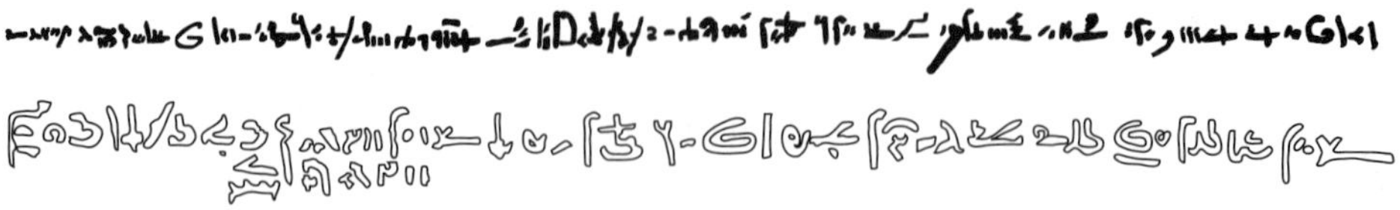

[Demotic script facsimile lines]

FIGURE III.15.4. Facsimiles of inked vs. engraved Demotic.

Facsimiles J. Moje. Coffin Berlin ÄM 504, and offering table Berlin ÄM 2304
[only Demotic parts]. Not to scale.

photos with suitable lighting, accompanied by facsimiles of the inscriptions as vector graphics, including remarks as to whether they are made directly from the original via writable transparent film or 3D laser scanning, from a photo or from a squeeze. Palaeographic tables containing all words of the inscriptions should be given, with differentiations whether the Demotic script was painted or engraved on the object. In the first case, the Demotic should be given with filled black lines, in the latter with double outlines only (cf. Figure III.15.4). Also, damage to the surface in the vicinity of the text as well as broken parts should be indicated by different types of lines (e.g., dotted or dashed). At the best, the single facsimiles should be divided into entire words, because the Demotic script consists more of (ligature) group writings than of separate single signs (aside from pure alphabetical writing, of course), which often cannot be transcribed in a one-to-one hieroglyphic version. Last but not least, the DE source should be analyzed concerning sociocultural, historical, and archaeological contextualization.

ADDENDUM: SHORT OVERVIEW OF RECORDING DEMOTIC GRAFFITI (DG)

Besides papyri and ostraca, DG form one of the largest corpora of Demotic texts. Recording these texts began as early as that of the DE, in comparable quantities. Some of the early scholars dealing with DG were often the same who paid also attention to DE sources.

Already in the famous *Description de l'Égypte* (Commission 1823, 5:pl. 55), some DG from Philae and Medinet Habu are published in facsimiles.

Five years later, Thomas Young (1828) edited in his publication some copies of Demotic graffiti from Massara quarry based on drawings by Sir John Gardner Wilkinson.

The final volume of Lepsius's expedition publication (1859) contains, besides the aforementioned Moschion stela, several graffiti found at Nubian temples, which were not edited in translation until about ninety years later in a monumental work by Francis Llewellyn Griffith. Also, these facsimiles are the first high-quality ones of DG and represent the first large corpus of such texts.

The next publication dedicated partly to DE was Brugsch's *Thesaurus* volumes 5–6 (1891). Here, DG, ostraca, and some papyri are presented. It took several decades until

DG came in to Egyptologists' focus again: Francis Ll. Griffith (1862–1834) edited a huge volume (1935–1937) on nearly all known DG from the Dodekaschoinos, providing facsimiles, translations, and commentary, partly expanded by Bresciani (1969). William F. Edgerton (1893–1970) published contemporaneously (1937) facsimiles of DG from the mortuary temple of Ramesses III in Medinet Habu, but without analysis. This desideratum was much later met by Thissen (1989), and an expanded project introduced by Di Cerbo and Jasnow (2011).

In the aftermath, smaller geographically focused DG corpora (Wadi Hammamat, Western Thebes) were brought to the public by H. J. Thissen (1979), R. Jasnow (1984), and J. K. Winnicki (1987).

One of the main recent scholars dealing with DG was E. Cruz-Uribe, who presented several DG corpora (1995, 2001, 2008, 2016), and S. Vleeming's third Demotic *Sammelbuch* (2015) is dedicated mainly to DG.

BIBLIOGRAPHY

Abd el-'Al, 'A el-H., J.-C. Grenier, and G. Wagner. 1985. *Stèles funéraires de Kom Abu Bellou*. Paris.

Abdalla, A. 1992. *Graeco-Roman Funerary Stelae from Upper Egypt*. Liverpool.

Aguizy, O. el-. 1998. *A Palaeographical Study of Demotic Papyri in the Cairo Museum from the Reign of King Taharqa to the End of the Ptolemaic Period (684–30 B.C.)*. MIFAO 113. Cairo.

Åkerblad, J. D. 1802. *Lettre sur l'inscription égyptienne de Rosette, adressée au citoyen Silvestre de Sacy*. Strasburg.

Bresciani, E. 1969. *Graffiti démotiques du Dodecaschoene: Qertassi—Kalabcha—Dendour—Dakka—Maharraqa*. CS. Cairo.

Brugsch, H. 1850. *Die Inschrift von Rosette: Nach ihrem ägyptisch-demotischen Texte sprachlich und sachlich erklärt*. Berlin.

Brugsch, H. 1891. *Thesaurus inscriptionum Aegyptiacarum: Altägyptische Inschriften*. Vols. 5–6. Leipzig.

Commission des sciences et arts d'Egypte (Commission). 1823. *Description de l'Egypte, ou, Recueil des observations et des recherches qui ont été faites en Égypte pendant l'expédition de l'armée française*. Antiquités Vol. 5. 2nd ed. Paris.

Cruz-Uribe, E. 1995. *Hibis Temple Project. II; The Demotic Graffiti of Gebel Teir*. San Antonio.

Cruz-Uribe, E. 2001. "Demotic Graffiti from the Wadi Hammamat." *JSSEA* 28:26–54.

Cruz-Uribe, E. 2008. *Hibis Temple Project 3: The Graffiti from the Temple Precinct*. San Antonio.

Cruz-Uribe, E. 2016. *The Demotic Graffiti from the Temple of Isis on Philae Island*. Atlanta.

Den Brinker, A. A., B. P. Muhs, and S. P. Vleeming. 2005. *A Berichtigungsliste of Demotic Documents*. 2 vols. StudDem 7. Leuven.

Devauchelle, D., and G. Widmer. 2011. "Des stèles et des femmes dans le delta oriental: À propos de quelques stèles démotiques funéraires." In *Aegyptiaca et Coptiaca: Studi in onore di Sergio Pernigotti*, edited by P. Buzi, 155–167. Oxford.

Di Cerbo, C., and R. Jasnow. 2011. "Recent Documentation of Medinet Habu Graffiti by the Epigraphic Survey." In *Perspectives on Ptolemaic Thebes: Papers from the Theban Workshop 2006*, edited by P. F. Dorman and B. M. Bryan, 35–51. SAOC 65. Chicago.

Edgerton, W. F. 1937. *Medinet Habu Graffiti: Facsimiles*. OIP 36. Chicago.

Farid, A. 1995. *Fünf demotische Stelen aus Berlin, Chicago, Durham, London und Oxford mit zwei demotischen Türinschriften aus Paris und einer Bibliographie der demotischen Inschriften.* Berlin.

Farid, A. 1999. "Eine demotische Stele im Übersee-Museum Bremen." *MDAIK* 55:7–12.

Farid, A. 2002. "A Forthcoming Fourth Volume of Die Demotischen Denkmäler IV, Die Demotischen Inschriften, Catalogue Général des Antiquités Égyptiennes du Musée du Caire." In *Egyptian Museum Collections around the World*, vol. 1, edited by M. Eldamaty and M. Trad, 345–350. 2 vols. Cairo.

Griffith, F. L. 1935–1937. *Catalogue of the Demotic Graffiti of the Dodecaschoenus.* TemplImm 19. 2 vols. Oxford.

Hoffmann, F. 2000. *Ägypten: Kultur und Lebenswelt in griechisch-römischer Zeit. Eine Darstellung nach den demotischen Quellen.* Berlin.

Jasnow, R. 1984. "Demotic Graffiti from Western Thebes." In *Grammata Demotica: Festschrift für Erich Lüddeckens zum 15. Juni 1983*, edited by H. J. Thissen, K.-Th. Zauzich, 87–105. Würzburg.

Lepsius, C. R. 1859. *Denkmäler aus Ägypten und Äthiopien.* vol. 6. Berlin.

Minutoli, H. von. 1825. *Reise zum Tempel des Jupiter Ammon in der Libyschen Wüste und nach Ober-Aegypten in den Jahren 1820 und 1821.* Berlin.

Moje, J. 2008a. *Demotische Epigraphik aus Dandara: Die demotischen Grabstelen.* IBAES 9. London. http://www2.hu-berlin.de/nilus/net-publications/ibaes9/index.html.

Moje, J. 2008b. "Die demotischen Stelen aus Hussaniya/Tell Nebesheh." *JEA* 94:183–208.

Moje, J. 2010. "Entwicklung der bilinguen und monolinguen demotischen Graffiti im Ägypten des ersten Jahrtausends v. Chr." In *Egypt in Transition: Social and Religious Development of Egypt in the First Millennium BCE. Proceedings of an International Conference, Prague, September 1–4, 2009*, edited by L. Bareš, F. Coppens, and K. Smoláriková, 286–304. Prague.

Moje, J. 2011. "Weitere demotische und bilingue Stelen aus Tell Nebesheh und Kom el-Hisn." *JEA* 97:167–194.

Moje, J. 2012–2013. "Projektvorstellung: Eine Paläographie der demotischen Epigraphik (PDE)." *Enchoria* 33:91–103.

Moje, J. 2013. "Die hieroglyphisch/demotische Stele Louvre E 13074: synoptische Untersuchung der bilinguen Inschriften." *SAK* 42:233–249.

Panov, M. V. 2015. *Istochniki po istorii zhrecheskikh semei Memfisa i Letopolia v pozdnii period* [Documents on the history of the priestly families from Memphis and Letopolis in the Late Period]. 2 vols. Novosibirsk.

Passalacqua, J. 1836. "Brief an S. Excellenz den Herrn General von Minutoli über eine demotische Scherbenschrift." *Intelligenzblatt der Allgemeinen Literatur-Zeitung* Dezember:593–600.

Reymond, E. A. E. 1981. *From the Records of a Priestly Family from Memphis I.* ÄA 38. Wiesbaden.

Schlichtegroll, F. von. 1818. *Ueber die bey Rosette in Aegypten gefundene dreyfache Inschrift.* Munich.

Sharpe, S. 1837–1855. *Egyptian Inscriptions from the British Museum and Other Sources.* 2 vols. London.

Smith, H. S., C. A. R. Andrews, and S. Davies. 2011. *The Sacred Animal Necropolis at North Saqqara: The Mother of Apis Inscriptions.* Texts from Excavations 14. London.

Spiegelberg, W. 1904. *Die Demotischen Denkmäler, 30601–31166, I: Die demotischen Inschriften.* CGC. Leipzig.

Spiegelberg, W. 1906–1908. *Die demotischen Denkmäler, 30601–31270, 50001–50022, II: Die demotischen Papyrus*. 2 vols. CGC. Strassburg.

Spiegelberg, W. 1924. "Der gegenwärtige Stand und die nächsten Aufgaben der demotischen Forschung." *ZÄS* 59:131–140.

Spiegelberg, W. 1927. "Der Schlangengott *Pe-Neb-onch*." *ZÄS* 62:37–38.

Spiegelberg, W. 1932. *Die demotischen Denkmäler III: Demotische Inschriften und Papyri (Fortsetzung), 50023–50165*. CGC. Berlin.

Thissen, H. J. 1979. "Demotische Graffiti des Paneions im Wadi Hammamat." *Enchoria* 9: 63–92.

Thissen, H. J. 1989. *Die demotischen Graffiti von Medinet Habu. Zeugnisse zu Tempel und Kult im Ptolemäischen Ägypten. Transkription, Übersetzung und Kommentar*, DemStud 10. Sommerhausen.

Thissen, H. J. 1991. "Demotische Inschriften aus den Ibisgalerien in Tuna el-Gebel: Ein Vorbericht." *Enchoria* 18:107–113.

Vittmann, G. 2012. "Demotische Weiheinschriften." In *Grab-, Sarg-, Bau- und Votivinschriften*, edited by B. Janowski and D. Schwemer, 129–144. TUAT.NF 6. Gütersloh.

Vleeming, S. P. 2001. *Some Coins of Artaxerxes and Other Short Texts in the Demotic Script Found on Various Objects and Gathered from Many Publications*. StudDem 5. Leuven.

Vleeming, S. P. 2011. *Demotic and Greek-Demotic Mummy Labels and Other Short Texts Gathered from Many Publications: Short Texts II:278–1200*. StudDem 9. Leuven.

Vleeming, S. P. 2015. *Demotic Graffiti and Other Short Texts Collected from Many Publications: Short Texts III 1201–2350*. StudDem 12. Leuven.

Winnicki, J. K. 1987. "Vier demotische Graffiti in den Königsgräbern in Theben." *Enchoria* 15:163–168.

Young, T. 1823. *Hieroglyphics, collected by The Egyptian Society*. vol. 1. London.

Young, T. 1828. *Hieroglyphics, continued by the Royal Society of Literature*. vol. 2. London.

Zauzich, K.-T. 1986. "150 Jahre Erforschung demotischer Ostraka." *Enchoria* 14:129–134.

....

ASPECTS OF THE RELATIONSHIPS BETWEEN THE COMMUNITY OF SHEIKH ABD AL-QURNA AND ANCIENT EGYPTIAN MONUMENTS

....

ANDREW BEDNARSKI AND
GEMMA TULLY

As demonstrated throughout this book, epigraphers must navigate a host of complex relationships both on and off site. Another relationship, mentioned thus far largely in passing, exists when working on a site with a living population. This chapter explores the multifaceted nature of local Egyptian peoples' relationships with nearby monuments through the lens of a single case study: the site of Sheikh Abd al-Qurna and its local population.

THE QURNAWI AND THE WEST

....

Until recently, the local people of Sheikh Abd al-Qurna, known in English as the Qurnawi, lived in houses built on and around ancient Egyptian tombs on Luxor's West Bank. The tombs within Qurna form one part of what is known as the Valley of the Nobles, which, in turn, is part of a much larger ancient desert necropolis. The area has been a site of human habitation, use, and reuse, for many millennia, long before the oldest Pharaonic tombs had been built. During the Pharaonic period, nonroyal elites carved and decorated hundreds of tombs in this sacred landscape. In the Greek and then Roman periods of Egyptian history, new burials were dug alongside their more ancient counterparts, and existing tombs were incorporated into new practices. By late antiquity, in the Coptic Period, some of Qurna's tombs were used as dwellings and structures for local monastic communities. It has been suggested that by the early sixteenth century, these tombs may have been reused once again: as shelter for Bedouin and Arab peoples who had settled in the area earlier.[1] It might have been the descendants of this last group who eventually built the shrine to Sheikh Abd al-Qurna, which lends the area its name, atop the mountain range overlooking the site. The complexity of the reuse and renegotiation of Qurna reflects the organic nature of cultural landscapes in general, as they are constantly reshaped and incorporated into different communities over time (Figure III.16.1). In keeping with this fluid state, it is important to remember that the

FIGURE III.16.1. A view of the Sennefer Hotel, in the hamlets of Sheikh Abd al-Qurna, prior to demolition. Credit: Gemma Tully 2008.

---

[1] Kees van der Spek (2011, 57–78) proposes a possible settlement date of the sixteenth century. Recent archaeological work, however, calls this hypothesis into question (Bednarski, forthcoming).

meanings ascribed to such landscapes also change over time and from people to people. We will return to this topic shortly.

Western Interest in Qurna

The tombs of Sheikh Abd al-Qurna may have been connected to the countries of Europe long before Europeans began systematically to research and collect the material culture of ancient Egypt. Mummies from Egypt, after all, were sought-after commodities in Europe from the Middle Ages through the early modern period, and Qurna certainly had an enormous collection of them. This incredible store of human artifacts, a prized ingredient in European medicines and artists' paints, may have linked the two regions during this period (van der Spek 2011, 75–78). Yet it was Napoleon Bonaparte's catastrophic 1798 invasion of Egypt that focused European interest on Egypt. The aftermath of this invasion opened the country to foreign exploration of Egypt in general and Qurna in particular. By the early nineteenth century, a number of European explorers had made their way across huge swaths of the country, and in collaboration with various levels of the Egyptian government, antiquities were pilfered and collected on a grand scale. Artifacts taken from Qurna's tombs constituted some of the historically important collections of this period, such as those amassed by Frédéric Cailliaud (Bednarski 2014, 3–29; Mainterot 2011). Cailliaud, in fact, recognized that Qurna's tombs could provide more than physical objects for study back in Europe. He, along with a small number of early nineteenth-century European explorers, sought to copy methodically many of the scenes and texts found on the tombs' walls. Like his more famous contemporary, John Gardner Wilkinson, Cailliaud believed that by copying these texts and scenes, the subject matter of which is markedly different than what is found in the country's royal burials and temples, he could create an historical record of the everyday lives of the ancient Egyptians. Wilkinson's own recording efforts, generously illustrated by Joseph Bonomi, resulted in a bestseller back in Europe: his *Manners and Customs of the Ancient Egyptians* (1847; see chapters by Manniche, Emery). This early epigraphic work was a fundamental source of information throughout the nineteenth century for anyone interested in, or intending to study, ancient Egypt. The abundance of perceived practical information on the daily lives of the ancient Egyptians that the Qurna tombs contained, and their incorporation into important early works on Egyptian civilization, may have lent the tombs a disciplinary centrality that continues to this day. Early copyists and epigraphers made the tombs' wall scenes accessible to the Western reading public and, in so doing, made them famous. Reproductions of the tombs' decorated walls, in the form of drawings, facsimiles, and photographs, are now fundamental building blocks for undergraduate instruction in Egyptology. In addition, the tombs' relative ease of access, due to their proximity to the city of Luxor, makes them important destinations for both group and independent study tours. This accessibility stands in stark contrast with that of historically important, nonroyal tombs in other parts of the country, such as those in Middle

Egypt. It is perhaps the ease with which foreign Egyptologists might access the Qurna tombs, the ease with which one might continuously provision a scholarly mission in Qurna, and the acknowledged historical and archaeological importance of the area that has resulted in the near continuous exploration of this part of the Theban necropolis for the past two hundred years. Given the abundance of textual information that the tombs contain and given the strong and traditional philological grounding of the majority of Egyptologists, it should come as no surprise that epigraphic efforts continue to be at the heart of Qurna's exploration.

A Deeper Understanding
of Qurna and Its People

The Qurnawi lived in Qurna as a robust community until 2006, when, over a period of several years, they were evicted and systematically relocated to another portion of Luxor's West Bank, and their traditional homes atop the ancient tombs were demolished.

From the early nineteenth century, when Europeans first began exploring Qurna in earnest, up until 2010, the Qurnawi played an important role in foreign epigraphic and archaeological projects at the site. Such work was traditionally facilitated through the hospitality the Qurnawi showed to foreigners and through the services that they provided during fieldwork. Yet despite the continuous and impactful presence of the Qurnawi on efforts to record the site's ancient past, the importance of their contributions to scholarship has been overlooked, and they have largely been omitted from narratives of Qurna (on the exclusion of the Qurnawi from the historical record of Qurna, see van der Spek 2011, 20–38). The past two hundred years of scholarly and popular publications on Qurna have overwhelmingly focused on the excavation and recording of its ancient tombs, and sparse attention has been devoted to the people who lived atop and around the tombs in which scholars toiled or to the modern structures that directly impacted on the ancient tombs. In recent years, however, a corpus of work has emerged that highlights the interaction of the Qurnawi with the site and begins to create a place for them in existing narratives (aside from van der Spek 2011, see Simpson 2003, 2010; Gamblin 2004; Duggan 2012; Tully and Hanna 2013; Strong and Bednarski 2016; Bednarski 2017). In so doing, this avenue of research demonstrates fundamental links between the archaeological site of Qurna and the Qurnawi's former way of life.

The history of the Qurnawi, both above and below ground, over the course of many generations, made Qurnawi culture and its communal relationships with the landscape unique from other populations on the West Bank. The integration of the ancient tombs into modern domestic architecture and the resulting blending of layers of use, history, and meaning were at the very heart of Qurna's communal identity. This blend provided a draw for tourists and the occasional researcher, seeking a landscape to reconcile powerful Orientalist perceptions of Egypt as a modern country living in and among the remnants of its glorious past. The Valley of the Nobles achieved this in its contemporary life. Children played among the monuments, and donkeys fed under rudimentary shelters. There were tea shops, colorful *hajj* paintings, mosques, local *mulids* (festivals), mudbrick extensions to brightly painted intergenerational family homes, and the sale of replica antiques as tourist items. All of this took place alongside, and some activities even took place within, the ancient tombs, many of which coincidentally depict scenes of Pharaonic "daily life." During Tully's first visit to Qurna to conduct doctoral research, she met a Qurnawi who worked as a guard at one of the nearby monuments. As he explained to her, from his perspective, "the tombs and the modern life are entwined" and, while he acknowledged that many things have changed over the millennia, "much of what you see our ancestors doing on the tomb walls is not so different to our lives now" (Anonymous, in discussion with Tully, 2008).[2] According to Tully, this interpretation of the relationship between the nearby monuments and the resident local population was reiterated many times over the course of her fieldwork, both by the Qurnawi she met and by tourists who perceived a special connection between the accessible ancient tomb's imagery, some of which depict families and celebrations, and the modern locals' hospitality: food, family, friendship, music, and dancing—the essence of a community. In addition, the fact that the tombs were part of people's homes imbued them with a centrality to the Qurnawi's private and public lives. These tombs had become places where the living slept to keep cool in the summer months, where they stored food, where they kept animals, and where guests were welcomed. These perceptions, including the impact of this distinctive sociocultural and landscape setting on those visiting for pleasure, business, or research and on those residing in the area, were explored by Tully during a further anthropological survey in the winter of 2011–2012. This survey comprised interviews with a range of stakeholders in Qurna and throughout the Theban necropolis to explore how people used and valued the area (Tully and Hanna 2013).[3] The survey documented that prior to the hamlets' removal, and in keeping with many of Tully's first impressions, of equal allure for many Egyptologists and epigraphers was the seeming connectivity between the natural landscape, the archaeological site, and the living population (Figure III.16.2). To this group, Qurna provided an impression of interchange between past and present, natural and man-made, death and daily life; an impression that, to them, appeared to be unique to the area of Qurna and the wider Valley of the Nobles. This perspective manifested itself in comments made by archaeologists, epigraphers, and other Egyptologists, from students visiting for the first time, to field directors who had spent half a lifetime working in the landscape.

Other studies of Qurna offer further insight into some of these perceived connections, including how Qurnawi men and women interacted with the ancient material culture that used to surround them. Such interactions went beyond the archaeological

---

[2] All interviewees asked to remain anonymous. Their names, therefore, have been withheld by mutual agreement.

[3] Special thanks to Professor Dr. Claudia Näser for her help in facilitating and guiding this research.

FIGURE III.16.2. A view, looking west, of a portion of the hamlets of Sheikh Abd al-Qurna in the midst of demolition. Credit: Gemma Tully 2008.

work that the Qurnawi were employed to do. It is a common belief in Upper Egyptian communities, for example, that ancient artifacts and monuments can have magical properties, and that this magic can be harnessed in a positive manner. The Qurnawi believed that the power of many of their local monuments could be used to increase women's fertility (van der Spek 2011, 294–302; Blackman [1927] 1968, 98–99). Interviews conducted with Qurnawi confirmed the perception that visits to certain monuments, such as the tomb of Rekhmire, or that of Nakht, could help a woman to conceive. It is easy to understand the reasoning behind such a belief, that tombs might improve a person's fertility and domestic prosperity, given the longevity of the tombs and their many depictions of children, animals, food, family life, and agricultural production. Such a belief, however, was not limited to the private tombs of Qurna's ancient elite. The scenes in the "birth colonnade" of Hatshepsut's enormous mortuary temple, Deir el-Bahri, for example, were also identified by Qurnawi as possessing a similarly beneficial power, and an analogous rationale was offered for this belief (van der Spek 2011, 299–300).

Yet many Qurnawi believed that the supernatural properties of the site's monuments could affect them negatively. Like other Egyptians, they believed in 'afrit and jinn, powerful spirits recognized to a certain extent in orthodox Islam. The Qurnawi also believed in a terrifying phenomenon they called qabus. The definition of qabus ranged from nightmares to dangerous physical confrontations with monsters, and many believed that it was the direct adverse result of living in a necropolis.[4] Similarly, they believed that the *jinn* who resided in Qurna could stop people who searched for antiquities in the houses built atop the ancient tombs or in the tombs themselves. *Jinn* might even exact revenge on families that had grown rich from the sale of such ill-gotten illicit antiquities (van der Spek 2011, 308–318). These beliefs can be viewed as reinforcing the notion that the interpretation of, and interactions with, archaeological sites is often the result of one's experiences. The Qurnawi's belief in *jinn* and *qabus* might be partially explained by aspects of anthropological and heritage theory that suggest that individuals and communities view their experiences of "home" and "locale" as crucial aids to remembering the past, enforcing social order, and passing on communal identity (Bernbeck and Pollock 1996, 138; Harrison 1994, 135). The Qurnawi's daily practices, or "habitus" (Bourdieu 1985; Hillier and Rooksby 2005), were partly shaped through a local sense of place and through the impact of their local history, both of which were powerfully reinforced by the nearby physical remains of material culture, such as ancient tombs, generations of extensions to mudbrick houses, and the painted histories of intergenerational *hajj* pilgrimages. These daily visual reminders of identity and tradition may have been enhanced by less tangible cultural elements, such as festivals, which further entwined concepts of ancient and contemporary community and reinforced unspoken "laws" that guided Qurnawi life, cemented differences between Qurna and other West Bank communities, and, ultimately, resulted in the Qurnawi understanding and experience of the site/landscape, their home, in a uniquely "local" way.

Evidence of the impact that Qurna's ancient material culture had on the Qurnawi was sometimes plain to see. This material surrounded them, they worked extensively with it through excavation, and they guarded it as official stewards of the area's monuments. Scenes from local ancient tombs, for example, could be found in some of the *hajj* paintings, visual recounting of family members' pilgrimages to Mecca, that adorned their modern houses (see Figure III.16.1). The inclusion of these scenes, such as those from the tomb of Sennefer, personalized these paintings and made it clear that the individual who undertook the depicted pilgrimage could only have come from Qurna.[5] Prior to the Qurnawi's relocation, the production of ancient replicas also formed an important part of the community's economy (Figure III.16.3). These objects, produced using ancient material as their inspiration, were sold to visiting tourists, sometimes with the understanding that they were reproductions and sometimes under the veil that they were authentic antiquities. Skilled craftsmen in Qurna could produce such objects in many forms. Over the course of the American Research Center in Egypt's (ARCE) Qurna Site Improvement (QSI) project, for example, two subtly carved figures on a piece

---

[4]   Tully did not encounter mention of *'afrit* during her fieldwork. This might be due to the fact that much of her research was done post-demolition. It is possible that, at that point, perceived negative implications of living in Qurna were less actively discussed.

[5]   As these paintings were copied, in part, from ancient tomb scenes, they can be viewed as examples of modern epigraphy, undertaken by the Qurnawi. Thanks to Meghan E. Strong for this suggested perspective.

FIGURE III.16.3. A view of the new settlement, looking West, to which the Qurnawi were relocated. Credit: Claudia Näser 2012.

of limestone, clearly rendered to look like images from the tomb of Ramose, were recorded, as were an abundance of modern shabtis (Bednarski 2017, fig. 3; American Research Center in Egypt 2013a, 2013b). These contemporary objects are clearly based on ancient equivalents, and some of the steps needed in their production mirrored ancient techniques. On the topic of making such items, however, it is important to note that there is no direct tradition of production linking the material culture of the ancient Egyptians and the "tourist" items created by the Qurnawi. Instead, such objects were the result of a combination of motifs familiar to the Qurnawi and an international demand for particular items and designs (van der Spek 2011, 254, 258). Nonetheless, according to Tully during her 2011–2012 fieldwork, the Qurnawi regularly conveyed unprompted pride in being skilled craftspeople with regard to ceramic production, stone carving, alabaster carving, and traditional weaving, and they believed, at least in part, that they were maintaining ancient traditions. This perspective was also asserted by several Western artists interviewed by Tully and Hannah, and such assertions supported feelings of affinity about the quality and authenticity of the art that, as outsiders, they were inspired to produce.

The Qurnawi's intimate, complex, and long-standing relationship with Qurna and its monuments has, on some occasions, prompted them to put themselves in harm's way. Such was the case during the 1997 Luxor massacre at Hatshepsut's mortuary temple (for the latest discussion of the massacre, see van der Spek 2011, 18, 402n2–3). This was also the case during the 2011 Egyptian Revolution. With regard to the latter event, on January 28, many of the relocated Qurnawi traveled to Qurna with locals who lived near the Ramesseum and those from Naga al-Sawalem.[6] Bearing rifles and sticks, they amassed at the site in response to news that the government prison in Armant, south of Luxor, had been opened, many prisoners had been released, and the police tasked with protecting Qurna had been withdrawn. Fearing for the integrity of the site, this ad hoc group largely remained at Qurna for eighteen days, claiming that it was under their protection, before dispersing. This event demonstrated that the Qurnawi's affinity for the site persisted even after their removal from Qurna, the destruction of their traditional homes, and the apparent lack of support from local authorities in a time of crisis. Such a response challenges the historical stereotype of the Qurnawi as only interested in the site as a source from which antiquities might be illicitly obtained and sold (for a discussion of this stereotype, see van der Spek 2011, 20–28). Such actions, in fact, appear to stand in contrast to incidents of mass looting in the Memphite necropolis at about the same point in time. After security forces withdrew from the area of Memphis on January 28, as they did in Qurna, evidence suggests that entire local villages partook in looting archaeological sites. In the villages near Abusir, Saqqara, and Dahshur, for example, people were observed using megaphones to encourage mass digging (Hanna 2015).[7]

THE QURNAWI AND EGYPTOLOGY

As this cursory introduction implies, conducting epigraphic work at an Egyptian site that is inhabited by people brings with it challenges and opportunities for research that might not be encountered during work at a site devoid of a living population. In the case of Qurna, foreign missions had to navigate a relationship not only with the local branch of the Egyptian government but also with the Qurnawi, who were heavily invested stakeholders. Such missions, though, have always benefited from the Qurnawi's local knowledge of the site. Early explorers relied on this knowledge to navigate the landscape in order to find and access tombs. More recently, as ARCE's QSI project progressed, this knowledge provided clues to the modern uses to which many of the tombs that formed part of the demolished houses were put. As an archaeologist, Bednarski was used to excavating rooms within ancient structures and then formulating hypotheses to explain the uses for such rooms and the possible actors that had impacted on them. While he oversaw the recording of the remains of portions of the modern hamlets, however, he and his team of archaeologists were able to talk directly with those people who had either lived in the structures they were documenting or who knew the people who had lived in those structures. As a result, and in stark contrast with his

---

[6] Many thanks to Dr. Monica Hannah for the following account of these events and their impact on nearby archaeological sites. Personal correspondence with Tully, 2017.

[7] At the time of writing, the contrasting states of preservation of the archaeological sites of Memphis and Qurna are evident through satellite imagery, with Memphis having fared far worse after the 2011 Revolution.

experiences excavating ancient buildings, it was possible to learn about the people who had used the building, sometimes for generations, as well as their activities inside them. In addition to knowledge of the site, the Qurnawi continue to provide a local network from which to organize logistical support for scholarly work. Lastly, as noted earlier, the site's ancient material culture has formed an integral part of Qurnawi culture and identity. Their very lives atop the tombs imbued the monuments and their associated remains with new meaning and transformed the ways in which visitors interacted with this material.

Not surprisingly, after nearly two hundred years of foreigners working in Qurna, competing national, regional, professional, and interpersonal politics have resulted in a long and complicated relationship between the Qurnawi and Egyptology. This relationship is, in part, colored by the disciplinary limitations of Egyptology. The field did not develop with a view toward incorporating the stories and histories of local populations, and from the personal experiences of the authors, there remains considerable resistance on the part of some professionals to consider doing so. Such resistance may be a result of the fact that Qurna has not historically attracted the interests of contemporary anthropologists and ethnographers, making it somewhat easier for Egyptologists working in the area to gloss over questions and issues often addressed by such professionals. More broadly, as van der Spek posits, "Given its certain 'classical' philological focus, and despite its associations with archaeological anthropology, Egyptology has had a somewhat uncomfortable relationship with other social sciences, preferring to concern itself with its immediate—ancient—focus rather than adding measurably to and engaging itself actively with an understanding of self in the contemporary world" (van der Spek 2011, 338). Numerous pressures, including those of a logistical, financial, cultural, and geopolitical nature, can make conducting fieldwork in Egypt difficult. It is perhaps because of such pressures that both authors have noted the preference of certain mission directors to err on the side of political caution when framing their research questions and conducting their fieldwork. Van der Spek goes one step further in his general analysis of Egyptological fieldwork, suggesting a disciplinary bent within Egyptology to avoid difficult questions of local identity if they interfere with work. To him, Egyptology appears "more concerned with self-preservation than with frank and fearless debate and the exploration of ideas that may range beyond the immediate boundaries of its own discipline" (van der Spek 2011, 338).

If this is true, historically, it would not have been difficult for scholars new to Qurna to focus their recording efforts on subjects other than the Qurnawi. Dominant nineteenth- and twentieth-century Western perceptions prioritized the site's ancient monuments to the exclusion of its living population, who were often stereotyped as tomb robbers (van der Spek 2011, 23–28; Desroches-Noblecourt 1963, 55–57). Such a perception was not counteracted by the Qurnawi's active and positive role in the legitimate exploration of the Theban necropolis. This was partly because work that was undertaken in Qurna, and more broadly throughout Egypt, has not traditionally credited the roles played by locals. There is indication, however, that Egyptologists are beginning to recognize such historical omissions of local populations, and their contributions to work, and that they are taking steps to address this lacuna. Both the Petrie Museum and the Garstang Museum now credit the workers of past excavations on the artifact labels that they exhibit. This, at the very least, inserts Egyptians into the excavation and post-excavation histories of objects. Similarly, it is now accepted practice in European and American dig diaries, professional presentations, and other types of publications, to credit the appropriate *reis* (foreman) with archaeological finds or leadership roles within work. In recent years, some publications have also devoted considerable attention to reconstructing and positing the contributions of local workers into the record of fieldwork (Quirke 2007). In a similar vein, there have been foreign efforts in Qurna (Simpson 2017), as at other Egyptian sites, to engage peoples in their local histories (Tully 2016; Moser et al. 2002; Hanna, Keshk, and Aboubakr 2012; Heliopolis Heritage Initiative 2017; Abdel-Qadar, Kosc, and Barnard 2012). There is also a concerted effort on the part of foreign Egyptologists to provide not only jobs but also training to local people through fieldwork. These piecemeal efforts stem generally from a recognition that Egyptians need to be included more fully into the process of Egyptian archaeology. To this end, between 2011 and 2014, ARCE ran two archaeological field schools, as well as other capacity building initiatives in Qurna, in tandem with its QSI Project. In addition, ARCE has recently administered an epigraphy field school in Qurna (see chapter by Schenck).

Such disciplinary steps, however, appear to have come too late to impact positively on the dialogue regarding the removal of the Qurnawi. The traditional omission of the Qurnawi from Qurna's historical record appears to have lent justification to local plans to remove them from the site in the early years of this century. Such plans were far from new, having found purchase in the early twentieth century (for the history of plans to relocate the Qurnawi, see van der Spek 2011, 435n9). The 2000 United Nations and Egyptian government's Luxor 2030 Heritage Plan (Barsoum 2000), which sought to remove and relocate the Qurnawi, appears based on the perspective that the people of Qurna were detrimental to the security and maintenance of what was ultimately defined as a touristic landscape (Bednarski 2017; Strong and Bednarski 2016, 126–143; van der Spek 2011). While the process by which the Qurnawi were removed and their homes destroyed is now generally understood, the influence of professional Egyptology, long dependent on the Qurnawi, in the justification of their removal has not yet been explored. The work of archaeologists and epigraphers frequently plays a significant, if often unrecognized, role in the arbitration of local peoples' identity politics. Issues of legitimacy are integral to heritage debate and can be manipulated by those in positions of power to shape claims of ownership to the past. Heritage is both a resource in, and a process of, negotiation in the cultural politics of identity. "Archaeologists and other 'experts' are therefore required to make conscious and informed choices in the ways in which they define and engage with heritage, and those communities who have a stake in heritage management" (Smith 2010, 159). Certain truths about the way in which a community is represented are more easily subsumed into political and heritage decision-making than others (Smith 2010, 161). Despite all of the complications listed here, personal and professional relations between the Qurnawi and foreign expeditions in general remain strong. Outside of work, foreign professionals are still readily offered the hospitality that is now a defining characteristic of the Qurnawi. Invitations for tea, dinners, and weddings continue, and the presence of foreigners at the funerals of local colleagues remains welcome.

Moving Forward

The number of attempts to broaden our understanding of Qurna's past, beyond the Pharaonic phase of the site's history, has been increasing this century. Such efforts have occurred parallel to more comprehensive studies of other sites (Redmount 2003; Tokuse and Oka 2014) and to more nuanced explorations of the history of Egyptology (Reid 2001; Colla 2007; Carruthers 2015) and modern Egyptian society (Wendrich 1999, 2013). From a disciplinary point of view, these new and complementary investigations might be reflective of larger shifts within the field of Egyptology toward a broader conceptualization of sites than has traditionally prevailed and in favor of incorporating methodologies found within the study of cultural landscapes and social history. If such changes, either short or long term, are occurring within the discipline, they are most likely informing, and being informed by, the many, mainly younger, Egyptians taking action through social media to protect what is perceived to be "local heritage" (Egypt's Heritage Taskforce 2017; Save Alex 2017). It is perhaps not too optimistic to believe that an increasing social awareness and desire for social action on the part of both foreign professionals and local activists are blending to push the discipline of Egyptology in new and positive directions.

Bibliography

Abdel-Qadar, M. W., Z. Kosc, and H. Barnard. 2012. "Giving Voice to the Ababda." In *The History of the Peoples of the Eastern Desert*, edited by H. Barnard and K. Duistermaat, 399–416. Los Angeles.

American Research Center in Egypt. 2013a. "Qurna Site Improvement Project, Q08." http://archive.arce.org/conservation/Qurna/q/q08.

American Research Center in Egypt. 2013b. "Qurna Site Improvement Project, Q14." http://www.arce.org/conservation/Qurna/q/q14.

Barsoum, L. K., ed. 2000. *The Comprehensive Development for the City of Luxor Project* (CDCL). Sponsored by the Ministry of Housing, Utilities and Urban Communities (MHUUC) and The United Nations Development Program (UNDP). Cairo.

Bednarski, A. 2014. *The Lost Manuscript of Frédéric Cailliaud: Arts and Crafts of the Ancient Egyptians, Nubians, and Ethiopians*. Cairo.

Bednarski, A. 2017. "The Ruined Hamlets of the Theban Hills: ARCE's Record of the Latest Stratigraphic Layers of Sheikh Abd el Qurna and El Khokha." In *Now Behold My Spacious Kingdom. Studies Presented to Zoltán Imre Fábián On the Occasion of His 63rd Birthday*, edited by Bori Németh. Budapest. 127–141

Bernbeck, R., and S. Pollock. 1996. "Ayodhya, Archaeology, and Identity." *Current Anthropology* 37(1): 138–142.

Blackman, W. (1927) 1968. *The Fellahin of Upper Egypt*. Reprint. London.

Bourdieu, P. 1985. "The Genesis of the Concepts of Habitus and of Field." *Sociocriticism* 2:11–24.

Carruthers, W., ed. 2015. *Histories of Egyptology: Interdisciplinary Measures*. New York.

Colla, E. 2007. *Conflicted Antiquities: Egyptology, Egyptomania, Egyptian Modernity*. Durham.

Desroches-Noblecourt, C. 1963. *Tutankhamen: Life and Death of a Pharaoh*. London.

Duggan, P. D. 2012. *Villager Participation in the Relocation of El Gourna, Egypt*. Royal Institution of Chartered Surveyors research report. London.

Egypt's Heritage Taskforce. 2017. Facebook page. Accessed April 2017. https://www.facebook.com/EgyptsHeritageTaskForce.

Gamblin, S. 2004. "Luxor: A Tale of Two Cities." In *Upper Egypt: Identity and Change*, edited by N. Hopkins and R. Saad, 267–284. Cairo.

Hanna, M. 2015. "Documenting Looting Activities in Post-2011 Egypt." In *Countering Illicit Traffic in Cultural Goods: The Global Challenge of Protecting the World's Heritage*, 47–63. Paris.

Hanna, M., F. Keshk, and S. Aboubakr. 2012. "The Documentation of the Cultural Heritage of the Bedouin of South Sinai: A Pilot Study in Serabit al-Khadim." In *The History of the Peoples of the Eastern Desert*, edited by H. Barnard and K. Duistermaat, 358–368. Los Angeles.

Harrison, S. 1994. "Forgetful and Memorious Landscapes." *Social Anthropology* 12:135–151.

Heliopolis Heritage Initiative. 2017. Facebook page. Accessed April 2017. https://www.facebook.com/HeliopolisHeritageInitiative.

Hillier, J., and E. Rooksby. 2005. *Habitus: A Sense of Place*. Aldershot.

Mainterot, P. 2011. *Aux origines de l'égyptologie: Voyages et collections de Frédéric Cailliaud, (1787–1869)*. Rennes.

Moser, S., D. Glazier, J. E. Philips, L. Nasser El Nemer, M. S. Mousa, et al. 2002. "Transforming Archaeology through Practice: Strategies for Collaborative Archaeology and the Community Archaeology Project at Quseir, Egypt." *World Archaeology* 34 (2): 220–248.

Quirke, S. 2007. *Hidden Hands: Egyptian Workforces in Petrie's Excavation Archives 1880–1924*. London.

Redmount, C. 2003. "The Egyptian Modern Pottery Project: Pilot Phase Findings." In *Egyptian Pottery: Proceedings of the 1990 Pottery Symposium at the University of California Berkeley*, 153–322. Berkeley.

Reid, D. M. 2001. *Whose Pharaohs? Archaeology, Museums, and Egyptian National Identity from Napoleon to World War I*. Berkeley.

Save Alex. 2017. Facebook page. Accessed April 2017. https://www.facebook.com/save.alex.9?fref=ts.

Simpson, C. 2017. Qurnae History Project. Accessed April 2017. http://www.qurna.org/discovery.html.

Simpson, C. 2003. "Modern Qurna: Pieces of an Historical Jigsaw." In *The Theban Necropolis. Past, Present and Future*, edited by N. J. Strudwick and J. H. Taylor, 244–249. London.

Simpson, C. 2010. "Qurna: More Pieces of an Unfinished History." In *Thebes and Beyond: Studies in Honour of Kent R. Weeks*, edited by Z. Hawass and S. Ikram, 197–218. Cairo.

Smith, L. 2010. "Empty Gestures? Heritage and the Politics of Recognition." In *Cultural Heritage and Human Rights*, edited by H. Silberman and D. F. Ruggles. New York.

Spek, K. van der. 2011. *The Modern Neighbours of Tutankhamun: History, Life and Work in the Villages of the Theban West Bank*. Cairo.

Strong, M. E., and A. Bednarski. 2016. "Living in the Shadow of the Beautiful West: Contested Space in Sheikh Abd al Qurna." *In the Trenches, Archaeological Review from Cambridge*, 31 (1):126–143.

Tokuse, T., and E. Oka. 2014. "Life in Archaeological Sites and Settlements in Asuka Village as a Model Case for Managing Settlements Adjacent to Archaeological Sites: A Proposal for the Future of Saqqara." *JCHC* 2:5–37.

Tully, G. 2016. "From Community Archaeology to Civilian Activism: The Journey of Cultural Resources Management through Heritage Dialogue in Egypt." In *Collaborative Heritage Management*, edited by G. Tully and M. Ridges, 181–208. Piscataway

Tully, G., and M. Hanna. 2013. "One Landscape Many Tenants: Uncovering Multiple Claims, Visions and Meanings on the Theban Necropolis." *Archaeologies* 9(3): 362–397.

Wendrich, W. 1999. *The World According to Basketry*. Los Angeles.

Wendrich, W. 2013. "The Relevance of Ethnoarchaeology: An Egyptian Perspective." In *Contesting Ethnoarchaeologies: Traditions, Theories, Prospects*, edited by A. Marciniak and N. Yalman, 191–209. New York.

Wilkinson, J. G. 1847. *The Manners and Customs of the Ancient Egyptians*. 5 vols. 3rd ed. London.

PART IV

....

ISSUES IN PALAEOGRAPHY

....

CHAPTER IV.1

....

THE SIGNIFICANCE
OF MEDIUM IN
PALAEOGRAPHIC STUDY

....

DIMITRI MEEKS

IT should first be noted that the word "medium" is ambiguous. It implies both the mechanisms of a process and the environmental context in which the latter develops. It falls within a chain of transmission where historical-cultural heritage, the mastery of knowledge, mechanisms to produce and transmit, and the actor(s) play a major role. In Egyptology, we speak of media rather than medium, as there are many filters, constraints, and obstacles between the object taken into consideration and its final transmission to a targeted audience. Between a document, a given monument, and a completed palaeographic study, different actors and different tools intervene, governed by strategies both scholarly and intellectual, which themselves are governed, almost always unconsciously, by the nature of the subject matter, but also by the history of the discipline. The subject matter is perceived as a function of a given culture that generates assumptions that will incidentally develop over time. The very notion of palaeography, in the general sense, is primarily governed by its origins. As a discipline, it emerged mainly in the West in the seventeenth century and was first concerned with ancient handwriting, Greek, Latin, and medieval. It was only interested in alphabetical cursive scripts, which excluded carved or incised monumental writings that fall within the bounds of epigraphy and, at the time, nonalphabetic scripts. It is this dichotomy that until very recently, governed palaeographic studies of ancient Egypt scripts. From the beginning of Egyptology, the more a script required effort to read and decipher it, the more it entailed the need for palaeographic studies without this need always being quickly recognized and found over time, thus a response gradually adapted to develop-ments in the discipline. In this respect, the cursive scripts and hieroglyphs experience different paths. The very nature of these scripts previously dictated the methods of recording and transmission, which are certainly similar in the initial phase of treatment of texts, but quite different in the production of an end result. The fact that the number of characters is limited in cursive scripts, but is very high in hieroglyphs, has greatly facilitated the task of hieraticists and complicated that of epigraphers. Yet, again unconsciously, the responses associated with the palaeography of alphabetic scripts somehow infiltrated the palaeographic approach to Egyptian scripts.

The final medium, namely, the table summarizing the different forms of all the letters of an alphabet, is relatively simple, but this simplicity is difficult to apply as such to Egyptian scripts. We have chosen, thus far, to organize this kind of tabulation according to the order in which the hieroglyphs are classified in the catalogs of printing fonts, metallic or digital. These catalogs, however, do not provide valid palaeographic forms, and the equivalences that one is obliged to seek there are not satisfactory, nor are the ordering methods that they offer. Making a correspondence between hieratic characters and these typographic forms is now considered obsolete and must be stopped; it appears more and more as a total impasse regarding hieroglyphs. To sidestep this incongruity, we can say today that only results obtained, or sadly, still to come, from palaeographic studies provide or will provide true correspondences of hieratic signs and a viable method of classification for both hieratic and hieroglyphs.

The first medium is, of course, the researcher him/herself faced with what s/he has to study, publish, and transmit as knowledge. Whether a flimsy writing surface (papyrus, leather, parchment, paper) or a more durable one (stone, metal, wood, bone, etc.), one has, in both cases, manuscripts in the most concrete sense of term; only the intermediate tool, the original medium, between the human hand and the writing surface changes: brush or reed pen in the first case, chisel or any tip capable of cutting into a hard surface and leaving a lasting trace there in the second. But cursive scripts can be traced in ink on durable writing surfaces (ostraca and walls of monuments, for example) or engraved and incised in stone (stelae and rock walls). In turn, hieroglyphs can be traced, especially as seen in late documents, in ink on papyrus (Beinlich 1991; Herbin 2008). All of this also applies to cursive hieroglyphs, whose nature seems clearly defined, but which is hardly so today. Between the quasi-hieroglyphs of the first hieratic texts of the Fourth Dynasty (Tallet 2015), the simplified hieroglyphs of the Coffin Texts (Terrace 1968), the classic cursive hieroglyphs of the New Kingdom funerary texts (Lapp 1997), and the simplified hieroglyphs of the Late Period funerary and religious texts (Vandier 1962, Clère 1987, Beinlich 2000)—to mention only a few—they represent a body which has not yet been explored in full, the research being, to date, mostly concentrated on the classical forms of the New Kingdom. Moreover, they present for the palaeographer the sometimes delicate matter of drawing boundaries between different categories, boundaries that are not always strictly chronological. An approach that is at once synchronic, diachronic, and typological will require an enormous effort of counting and cataloging that has barely begun.

The interchangeability between type of scripts, writing method, and writing surface had, for palaeography, various consequences regarding working methods implemented as much from the point of view of history as from Egyptology. This art of the hand that is ancient writing, a consequence of a living knowledge in its time, will be taken over and worked by another art of the hand, this one of the researcher, a consequence of knowledge acquired and inevitably imperfect. The means of the researcher are also different—photography, handcopy, the range of signs, cataloging, and possibly commentary—and depends only very little on the nature of the original writing surface. But if the ancient scribe or carver works for the most part on blank and prepared surfaces, the palaeographer must accept every document in its condition, as it has been handed down to him/her by the vagaries of history. One of the main constraints of palaeography is that it can only take into account well-preserved signs showing all the details without which palaeographic study would be superficial or impossible. Now the documents that have delivered ancient Egypt to us are often in poor or partially preserved condition. Damaged examples and partial signs can be retained only if they are considered to be unique specimens or *hapaxes*. Their inclusion is useful only with the expectation of a new occurrence of better quality that would complement the existing occurrence and confirm it. The chain of media leading to the final stage of palaeography is complex; it can also be interrupted by factors that the researcher does not control, particularly the filter constituted by the previous publications of documents or monuments s/he wants to study. In any case, if the photograph and the handcopy are essential starting points for palaeographic study, documents or monuments published in these forms result only rarely in a detailed palaeography. In addition, older publications seldom correspond to current requirements of reproduction and are not useful for palaeography.

The difficulties encountered today when producing palaeographic studies, regardless of the writing surface, are related to the history of Egyptology. If we want to understand why these studies have developed slowly in the case of cursive scripts and practically not at all until recently in the case of hieroglyphs, we cannot avoid reflecting on history. Hieratic has a long palaeographic tradition because it is a freely handwritten script, where the forms of signs vary greatly and depend as much on the writer as on the era in which they were written. As it is, they must be deciphered whenever a new document is edited. The editor's attention falls as much on the individual sign as on the group in which it is placed. Hieroglyphs give, to some extent, the illusion of changing only relatively little over time. Their pictographic character has often suggested that the being, the thing that they represent, had only a secondary interest in relation to their role in combination with all the other hieroglyphs in the same text, that is, their semantic role in the broad sense. The hieroglyph is considered individually only because it must be copied, and not to recognize it, as with a hieratic sign. It quickly merges into a group at the very moment when it is read. From such a perspective, palaeography has no compelling, binding interest. Hieratic palaeography, until recently, was mainly an aid for reading the original; reading hieroglyphs did not require such a tool.

The need to quickly make available to researchers a large number of texts brought about the use of simple freehand copy of texts. In the early days of Egyptology, researchers and archaeologists were generally good draftsmen and could copy texts in a manner that was elegant and easily readable. At that time, they sought to create hieroglyphic fonts in order to enable the rapid and thorough publishing of texts (Smitskamp 1979). Three of them were in use until the advent of digital fonts for computers: the Theinhardt font, the font called Gardiner, and that of the Institut français d'archéologie orientale du Caire.

However, because of structural costs, only the last was used on a massive scale to publish entire monuments, especially the Late Period temples of Edfu, Dendera, and Esna. For a very long time, handwritten copies and typography also made the published texts inaccessible to all palaeographic study since many of these publications are accompanied only by a small number of photographs, often barely legible, or none at all. Pierre Lacau, because he was also trained as an epigrapher, is the only one who attempted a—quite brilliant, as it happens—analysis of the hieroglyphic system using typeset texts, which can still serve as inspiration (Lacau 1954). These publications, which are also a medium for the transmission of texts, as well as the handwritten publications, are dead ends for palaeography. They stand between the original and the work of the palaeographer and present several problems of choice: Should one ignore a very good publication, generally considered to be definitive, and redo the work based on the original monument? Should one use it as a base and collate what has been published on the original? The answer lies as much in the technical aspects—will one use the same means as those enjoyed by one's predecessors?—as the practical—is it helpful to redo a work already done, and can funding be arranged for such an undertaking? It is, of course, more useful to study an unpublished monument or one whose publication should be completely redone, but this brings us back to site excavation; a site that is interesting for this type of monument should automatically include palaeography in its work plan, which is very rarely the case. Contrary to what one might think, the palaeography of cursive texts on papyrus faces, more often than we believe, a similar problem.

In the beginning was the facsimile. This medium, acceptable for carved hieroglyphs and for cursive on papyrus, was systematically used by scholars on the Egyptian expedition led by Bonaparte. It is worth recalling that Jacques-Joseph Champollion-Figeac, the brother of the founder of Egyptology, was the first to make extensive use of this method for Latin palaeography, among others, while a professor at l'École des Chartes in Paris (Champollion-Figeac 1835–1841). At a time when photography was in its infancy, the handcopy was the only means of making known a greater number of ancient documents. The fact that it is a substitute for the original could, in some circumstances, make it exceedingly precious as evidenced by the misadventures of one of the basic manuscripts of the Instructions of Amenemhat: Papyrus Millingen. The original had been seen in Italy by Amédée Peyron, who made a facsimile in 1843; it was then given to Emmanuel de Rougé and, at his death, to Gaston Maspero, who in turn made a rather rough facsimile that he published (Maspero 1880). The original manuscript was never rediscovered, and for more than eighty years, Egyptologists worked from the facsimile of Peyron's facsimile. By chance, the latter was rediscovered in 1962 between the pages of a book in the Egyptology library of the Collège de France in Paris and was quickly published (Lopez 1963).

Photography, for its part, as soon as its use spread, was soon considered the most objective possible reproduction of texts. The publication of cursive texts, especially, benefits from this because a papyrus is more easily photographed than a tomb or temple wall and uses fewer resources. But the quality of the printed reproduction of photographs on paper is largely dependent on the technique used. The most successful, and also the most expensive, were often replaced by simpler techniques, but these were of little use to palaeography. Whatever the quality of the original photographs, their reproduction on paper always made them lose a significant part of their legibility. A palaeography showing signs in photographs, and not in handcopy, can exhibit crosshatching that masks the finer details (Backes 2016).

The palaeographer wishing to make the most of the documentation must scan these pages and rework them using image processing software. Even palaeographies whose paper reproductions are of a high quality can fall victim to this defect (Manuelian 2003). Only electronic media—a DVD, for example—allows photographs to retain the best definition. But as it has been pointed out, a palaeography on such a material is usually possible only for a perfectly preserved monument and where the epigraphy has a certain elegance (Beaux 2015). Palaeographies of this type are few, but they help to reinforce the idea among epigraphers that it is mainly the beautiful hieroglyphs that merit interest.

Whether the secondary textual source, after the original, is the facsimile or the photograph, the palaeographies of cursive and hieroglyphic texts have followed different paths under the influence of the constraints and habits mentioned earlier.

Very early, Egyptology had available a first big corpus of papyri—those of Turin published in facsimile (Pleyte and Rossi 1869–1876). The first hieratic palaeography was published shortly afterward (Levi 1880) based on a number of manuscripts in Turin, London, Paris, and Leiden. Due to their age, hieratic palaeographic studies have gone through several stages that have led them to the verge of a complete replacement of their methods and perspectives. After the palaeography of Levi, the three volumes of Georg Möller (1927–1936) provided a high-quality working tool that allowed the development of hieratic studies and ultimately a familiarization of all Egyptological professionals with this type of writing. Cursive documents often present difficulties in reading and interpretation, and it was necessary to find a way to make them easily understandable to the greatest number of people even before translating them. Hieratic is transcribed into hieroglyphs, mostly handwritten according to the rules fixed at the end of the first third of the twentieth century (Gardiner 1929; Faulkner 1935), and Demotic simply into conventional transliteration in Latin characters. There is a hesitation regarding the earliest periods of Demotic. Cursive hieratic texts are usually transcribed into hieroglyphs, while those in archaic Demotic are not. Here, in fact, the line between what can be transcribed and what cannot separates what is only in the domain of hieratic what is in the domain of Demotic, what can have an exact correspondence in the hieroglyphic system and what no longer has that. Demotic signs are no longer more or less simplified substitutes for hieroglyphs, and this writing system develops independently of the others, although interferences may occur. It is, of course, always possible to transcribe a Demotic text in hieroglyphs, but it is a task that proved the rather artificial usage and is essentially reserved only for learning and teaching (Depauw 1997). Unfortunately, hieratic transcriptions have been used for grammatological studies when they have no palaeographic value, helping to reinforce the idea that the study of Egyptian writing can do without originals and can be worked from Egyptologists' hieroglyphs. The particular situation of hieratic studies was finally able to achieve a new vision, a promising future, materialized in the palaeography of late hieratic texts prepared by Ursula Verhoeven (2001). This work proposed not only a new method of dating manuscripts, since widely adopted, but also novel options for the future of hieratic studies. Today, these have materialized as a vast collective research program under the responsibility of its initiator and supported by the Academy of Sciences and Literature Mainz (Verhoeven 2015; see chapter by Gülden et al.).

Besides the use of typography, hieroglyphic texts were first published in the form of handwritten copies rarely respecting the detail and finesse of the signs. A palaeography was hardly considered, the hieroglyphs being first considered according to aesthetics, what was pleasing to the eye, and preferably elegantly colored. The seminal work of Griffith (1898), although it represents the first attempt to describe and analyze the signs themselves, is mostly a beautiful album that still today is browsed with pleasure, like also that of Nina Davies (1958). These are not palaeographies, but collections of images. Griffith's publication seems to have been inspired by a remark by Petrie, with whom he had worked: "epigraphy should not be merely a study of arbitrary signs, but also of the greatest interest as throwing a light on the civilization" (Petrie 1892). This succinctly describes what a hieroglyphic palaeography must be: the prerequisite, well documented, for a discipline that emerges now with some difficulty, Egyptian grammatology. Regarding hieroglyphs, there has not been a strong palaeographic tradition until recently. The only exception is the small, but very useful, diachronic palaeography of Francoise Le Saout (1981). After listing the many challenges facing the palaeographer, Fischer concluded, "it must appear obvious that hieroglyphic palaeography is a much less straightforward matter than hieratic, and that a simple chronological exposition of this subject, analogous to Georg Möller's tabulation in his *Hieratische Paläographie* is virtually impossible unless some features are ignored in order to facilitate the comparison of other features" (Fischer 1976a, 44). The most recent publications combine the publication of texts in facsimile and in photography accompanied by a typographical transcription. The presence of the latter, if it is explained by the need to make damaged or corrupt passages legible and if in these cases, it provides well-founded restorations based on parallels, reveals the distance that is often created in the eyes of some Egyptologists between Egyptian hieroglyphs and the hieroglyphs that are most familiar to them: typeset or handwritten. Palaeography, in the best situations, is postponed. These publications may, for some, remain simple intermediaries where the palaeographer will randomly meet her/his needs. This feature does not fail to influence, quite unconsciously, rendering texts in facsimile. Every epigrapher is not necessarily a palaeographer. The latter must have not only a knowledge of forms, like an epigrapher, but also experience that spans the history of the script, of the most minute details and their possible significance. Hieroglyphs are drawings, and an important part of the work increasingly falls to professional artists having Egyptological training. To achieve the most reliable final publication, epigraphers often work today in teams, each one having some responsibility for copying and checking. This practice was brought to its highest point of perfection in Luxor by Chicago House, which now uses the best digital technology to arrive at still unmatched results (Vértes 2014; see chapters by McClain, Vértes).

The published volumes, if they represent a source of great palaeographic wealth, have not produced palaeographies yet dedicated to them. However, this approach is now considered for the volumes to come (Davies 2017).

Henry G. Fischer (1976b, 1977a, 1977b, 1996) devoted his work to show what the palaeographic and grammatologic study of hieroglyphs, even poorly engraved, could bring to our knowledge of Egyptian writing, of the significance of the sometimes smallest details, and also of the language. Yet if he greatly influenced the practices of philology, if his palaeographic studies have been extensively used, he has hardly been followed with regard to palaeographic drawing. Even for small monuments—stelae, statues—few Egyptologists accompany those that they publish with a facsimile and almost never with a palaeographic review. This is due to the fact that few of them have mastered drawing and even when they are practiced, some facsimiles are only good approximations if one looks at the details. In the *Corpus Antiquitatum Aegyptiacarum*, among others, certain volumes devoted to the Kunsthistoriches Museum Wien offer small palaeographies of remarkable hieroglyphic forms for each monument where it is deemed useful. It would be desirable to see this method become widespread. A large number of such lists would eventually allow syntheses of document types or chronological periods. All that has been described falls under occasional experiences for the most accomplished work, but is usually a scattering without coordination.

In following the paths traced by Fischer and taking into account the different gaps and constraints, a hieroglyphic palaeography program was created in 2002 at the Institut français d'archéologie orientale du Caire (IFAO; Meeks 2004). The goal is, by selecting one or some monuments representative of an era, to gradually cover the entire history of hieroglyphic writing. It was originally envisaged, for reasons of economy, to work on already published monuments whose drawings, done from photographs, could be collated against the originals except in cases where the available handcopies are considered sufficient, especially in the case of monuments that are difficult to access and require significant logistics. The volumes provide not only plates, where all important variants of all signs used in a monument are included, but also a commentary, as detailed as possible, specifying the identity of what each sign represents as a pictogram, describing how the sign or its variants differ or not from a form generally considered as a standard outside of the studied monument, and listing the uses of each sign in the texts of the studied monument. The time was ripe for the creation of this program, as evidenced by the publications of major palaeographic work that soon followed (Hannig 2006; Moje 2007; Regulski 2010). Whether the program of the IFAO or the other projects, all worked on facsimiles, except for Hannig, who chose photographic reproduction, with the disadvantages that have been mentioned. For now, research in hieroglyphic palaeography is disorganized and follows different approaches and methods. For most of this work, the concerns are more or less those that have dominated hieratic studies: to date text, if possible with sufficient accuracy; to recognize the schools of carvers; and to see specific hands. Hieroglyphs, however, do not readily adapt to such inquiries. These are possible only in quite specific cases. An era like the First Intermediate Period, with its very typical epigraphy, is instantly recognizable and allows chronogeographic analyses (Callender

2019). The workshops and hands can be differentiated only in some textual corpora well circumscribed in time and space. Studies in hieroglyphic palaeography are still only emerging, but have in the future opportunities that go far beyond simple morphological considerations.

The advent of the computer age and the emergence of personal computers, digital photography, and especially in the mid-1980s, vector graphic design software using Bézier curves has completely changed the way of reading, copying, and disseminating texts and has led to a drastic reconsideration of the entirety of epigraphic and palaeographic work in its practices and its aims, and has also led to a consideration of new practices and new horizons, still unexplored, of which this tool gives a glimpse. The first concern relates to the technical nature of this new medium. Egyptologists are generally slow to adopt technological breakthroughs. When the typewriter, which gradually developed during the second half of the nineteenth century, went into commercial use, researchers continued until at least the early twentieth century to provide publishers with handwritten texts, leaving it to them to produce a printed book complying with the author's choice. With the digital, this relationship was reversed. The epigrapher and palaeographer must provide the publisher with a final result for which they do not always control the chain of production. If the division of labor between graphic designers and Egyptologists is essential, their coordination is not always obvious. If this is clear in major projects such as Chicago House, already mentioned (Vértes 2014), it is much less so for many other projects. The respective roles of the graphic designer and the Egyptological check are not always obvious. The less the epigrapher her/himself controls digital vectorization, the less s/he will be able to effectively check the drawing of the graphic designer, especially if s/he does not have in sight the publication of a palaeography of the monument that s/he wants to edit. The digital medium risks robbing the Egyptologist, if s/he is not careful, of the final result of a work that s/he will have validated. Here, the concurrent publication of high-definition photographs in digital form is indispensable to avoid questions about the nature of the final result. The hierarchy of functions is desirable; its dilution is not.

Here again the hieraticist and the epigrapher-palaeographer follow different paths. With their past experience, hieraticists have taken over the future of their discipline. The Mainz program (Verhoeven 2015) abandoned the idea of a simple update of Möller's work (1927–1936). The latter was based on a very limited number of sources. The digital tool can expand research to all that is known. The program is part of an ambitious perspective made possible with long-term support and funding. Digital recording allows the consideration of an archived corpus of documents, as complete as possible, gradually leading to a catalog of signs both synchronic and diachronic. Vectorized drawings will consider how each sign has been drawn according to a method already used (Allen 2002), as well as the environment in which each sign is located, quadrats, ligatures, or its frequency. This palaeography will also be open to various approaches: chronological or geographic, according to the nature of the texts. It will therefore lead to a reassessment of our knowledge in this particular field of Egyptian writing. The undertaking boasts a fortunate circumstance that makes the task easier. If the basic textual corpus is immense, the number of signs used throughout the entire history of hieratic is very small—about six hundred. In addition, over time, the body of evidence has remained relatively stable, each historical period bringing only a few truly specific signs. Recording and treatment strategies are accordingly made easier.

Hieroglyphic palaeography must also cope with the enormity of the textual corpus that it cannot easily gather in a global digital archive. Earlier publications of monuments, many of which will not be republished in a useful way for a very long time, whose photographic coverage still poses complex logistical problems, continue to be an obstacle to a program similar to that of hieratic. Digital photo archives now available online, either of institutions or museums, were not made from a palaeographic perspective; their definition is almost always insufficient and makes them unsuitable for a study of this type. DVDs containing high-definition photographs remain the exception. The enormity, also, of the corpus of signs, for which no catalog exists at all, does not facilitate the task of the palaeographer. The digital tool, however, opened up the possibility of gaining ground and spurred an initial awareness, still insufficient, of the need to study hieroglyphic writing, the very basis of Egyptology, from all original monuments. The delay, despite what already exists, allows only slow progress. It is already possible, however, to use palaeographic material for accurate grammatological analyses where putting it in diachronic perspective highlights aspects of the history and psychology of writing that could not be otherwise shown (Meeks 2007, 2010). Not to mention that this material will provide the necessary basis for the development of a totally new classification system of hieroglyphs finally independent from catalogs of typographic fonts (Meeks 2013). This development of hieroglyphic palaeography is being structured through the digital medium.

Egyptian written culture was bi-, even multiscriptal (Lieven and Lippert 2016), simultaneously using, according to the era, hieratic and hieroglyphs or Demotic, hieratic, and hieroglyphs. The different digital corpora of hieratic, hieroglyphs, cursive hieroglyphs, but also in a much longer term abnormal hieratic and Demotic (Donker van Heel 2015), when they will happen, based on the same or similar standards, will be called one day to communicate and to join forces so that we can finally study the world of ancient Egypt scripts in all its diversity and recognize all correspondences. The digital tool is not only a medium, but also a nexus.

BIBLIOGRAPHY

Allen, J. P. 2002. *The Heqanakhte Papyri*. PMMA 27. New York.

Backes, B. 2016. *Der "Papyrus Schmitt" (Berlin P. 3057): Ein funeräres Ritualbuch der ägyptischen Spätzeit*. 2 vols. ÄOP 4. Berlin.

Beaux, N. 2015. "Une chapelle de Sésostris Ier à Karnak Paléographie." In *Une chapelle de Sésostris Ier à Karnak*, edited by A. Arnaudiès, N. Beaux, and A. Chéné. EdE 13. Paris.

Beinlich, H. 1991. *Das Buch vom Fayum: Zum religiösen Eigenverständnis einer ägyptischen Landschaft*. ÄA 51. Wiesbaden.

Beinlich, H. 2000. *Das Buch vom Ba*. SAT 4. Wiesbaden.

Callender, V. G. 2019. *El Hawawish. Tombs, Sarcophagi, Stelae: A Palaeography.* PH 8. Cairo.

Champollion-Figeac, J.-J. 1835–1841. *Chartes et manuscrits sur papyrus de la Bibliothèque royale: Collection de fac-simile accompagnés de notices historiques et paléographiques et publiés pour l'École royale des chartes.* Paris.

Clère, J. J. 1987. *Le papyrus de Nesmin: Un Livre des Morts hiéroglyphique de l'époque ptolémaïque.* BG 10. Cairo.

Davies, N. M. 1958. *Picture Writing in Ancient Egypt.* Oxford.

Davies, V. 2017. "Complications in the Stylistic Analysis of Egyptian Art: A Look at the Small Temple of Medinet Habu." In *(Re)productive Traditions in Ancient Egypt*, edited by T. Gillen, 203–228. AegLeo 10. Liège.

Depauw, M. 1997. *A Companion to Demotic Studies.* PapBrux 20. Brussels.

Donker van Heel, K. 2015. "Abnormal Hieratic Is Not Dead; It Just Smells Funny." In *Ägyptologische "Binsen"-Weisheiten I–II. Neue Forschungen und Methoden der Hieratistik. Akten zweier Tagungen in Mainz im April 2011 und März 2013*, edited by U. Verhoeven, 371–381. AAWLM 14. Stuttgart.

Faulkner, R. O. 1935. "Some Further Remarks on the Transcription of Late Hieratic." *JEA* 21:49–51.

Fischer, H. G. 1976a. "Archaeological Aspects of Epigraphy and Palaeography." In *Ancient Egyptian Epigraphy and Paleography*, 29–50. New York.

Fischer, H. G. 1976b. *Varia.* Egyptian Studies 1. New York.

Fischer, H. G. 1977a. "The Evolution of Composite Hieroglyphs in Ancient Egypt." *MMJ* 12:5–19.

Fischer, H. G. 1977b. *The Orientation of Hieroglyphs, Part I: Reversals.* Egyptian Studies 2. New York.

Fischer, H. G. 1996. *Varia Nova.* Egyptian Studies 3. New York.

Gardiner, A. H. 1929. "The Transcription of New Kingdom Hieratic." *JEA* 15:48–55.

Griffith, F. Ll. 1898. *A Collection of Hieroglyphs: A Contribution to the History of Egyptian Writing.* London.

Hannig, R. 2006. *Zur Paläographie der Särge aus Assiut.* HÄB 47. Hildesheim.

Herbin, F.-R. 2008. "Trois papyrus hiéroglyphiques d'époque romaine." *RdE* 59:125–146.

Lacau, P. 1954. *Sur le système hiéroglyphique.* BdE 25. Cairo.

Lapp, G. 1997. *The Papyrus of Nu (BM EA 10477).* London.

Le Saout, F. 1981. "Étude de paléographie hiéroglyphique." In *La chapelle d'Achôris à Karnak II*, edited by C. Traunecker, F. Le Saout, and O. Masson, 149–249. 2 vols. Paris.

Levi, S. 1880. *Raccolta dei segni ieratici egizi nelle diverse epoche con i corrispondenti geroglifici ed i loro differenti valori fonetici.* Turin.

Lieven, A. von, and S. Lippert. 2016. "Egyptian (3000 BCE to ca. 400 CE)." In *Biscriptality: A Sociolinguistic Typology*, edited by D. Bunčić, S. L. Lippert, and A. Rabus, 256–276. Heidelberg.

Lopez, J. 1963. "Le papyrus Millingen." *RdE* 15:29–33.

Manuelian, P. Der. 2003. *Slab Stelae of the Giza Necropolis.* PPYE 7. New Haven.

Maspero, G. 1880. "Le papyrus Millingen." *RT* 2:70.

Meeks, D. 2004. *Les architraves du temple d'Esna: Paléographie.* PH 1. Cairo.

Meeks, D. 2007. "La paléographie hiéroglyphique: Une discipline nouvelle." *EAO* 46:3–14.

Meeks, D. 2010. "De quelques 'insectes' égyptiens: Entre lexique et paléographie." *Perspectives on Ancient Egypt: Studies in Honor of Edward Brovarski*, edited by Z. A. Hawass, P. Der Manuelian, and R. B. Hussein, 273–304. Cairo.

Meeks, D. 2013. "Dictionnaire hiéroglyphique, inventaire des hiéroglyphes et Unicode." *Document numérique* (RSTI série DN) 16 (3):31–44.

Möller, G. (1909–1912) 1927–1936. *Hieratische Paläographie: Die Aegyptische Buchschrift in ihrer Entwicklung von der fünften Dynastie bis zur Römischen Kaiserzeit.* 3 vols. Reprint, Leipzig.

Moje, J. 2007. *Untersuchungen zur Hieroglyphischen Paläographie und Klassifizierung der Privatstelen der 19. Dynastie.* ÄAT 67. Wiesbaden.

Petrie, W. M. F. 1892. *Medum.* London.

Pleyte, W., and F. Rossi. 1868–1876. *Papyrus de Turin.* 2 vols. Leiden.

Regulski, I. 2010. *A Palaeographic Study of Early Writing in Egypt.* OLA 195. Leuven.

Smitskamp, R. 1979. "Typographia Hieroglyphica." *Quaerendo* 9: 309–336.

Tallet, P. 2015. "Ouadi el-Jarf." In *Rapport d'activité 2014–2015,* 42–49. BIFAO 115 Suppl. Cairo.

Terrace, E. L. B. 1968. *Egyptian Paintings of the Middle Kingdom: The Tomb of Djehuty-nakht.* London.

Vandier, J. 1962. *Le papyrus Jumilhac.* Paris.

Verhoeven, U. 2001. *Untersuchungen zur späthieratischen Buchschrift.* OLA 99. Leuven.

Verhoeven, U. 2015. "Stand und Aufgaben der Erforschung des Hieratischen und der Kursivhieroglyphen." In *Ägyptologische "Binsen"-Weisheiten I–II, Neue Forschungen und Methoden der Hieratistik. Akten zweier Tagungen in Mainz im April 2011 und März 2013,* edited by U. Verhoeven, 23–63. AAWLM 14. Stuttgart.

Vértes, K. 2014. *Digital Epigraphy.* Chicago.

CHAPTER IV.2

···

HIEROGLYPHIC PALAEOGRAPHY

···

FRÉDÉRIC SERVAJEAN

IT may seem curious that hieroglyphic palaeography has, apart from some limited cases, never been made the subject of systematic studies until recently, unlike hieratic palaeography, which now regularly produces extensive studies (Möller 1909–1936; Verhoeven 2001), complemented by philological analysis (Meeks 2006, 315–365) or even exclusively based on the palaeographic dimension of a manuscript (Gasse 2002). As for Demotic palaeography, although it has been slower to develop, for reasons specific to the discipline on which there is no need to dwell here, its works are more advanced than those of hieroglyphic palaeography (El-Aguizy 1998).

It is difficult to find logical reasons for this state of affairs; maybe it is due to the large number of monumental inscriptions in raised and sunken relief, or painted with care on the walls of temples, tombs, sarcophagi, and so forth—which J. Assmann (2000, 13) calls "monumental discourse"—that fixes the forms of signs and erases all evidence of the process of "manufacture." This set of signs is a figurative script that was hardly changed with regard to its core principles throughout Pharaonic history. Luc Delvaux perfectly describes this state of affairs:

> The Egyptian term to designate the draughtsman, "scribe of outlines," perfectly summarizes the permanent proximity of image and writing and even the absence of any clear demarcation in Pharaonic civilization between these two systems of representation, which are traditionally distinct in Western thought. Through the similarity of the processes they implement, both applying the same aspective rules, which were applicable without fundamental changes over the course of the three thousand years of Egyptian history, the scribe draws the writing, and the draughtsman writes the image. Egyptian writing, in contrast with that of other Mediterranean cultures, did not experience a development towards abstraction.   (Delvaux 2013, 68)

This analysis is widely accepted by the community of researchers (Winand 2006, 146). By "Egyptian writing," L. Delvaux means "the hieroglyphic script," because hieratic and

Demotic writings demonstrate a trend toward abstraction. On the other hand, what is characteristic of Egyptian writing is that this development is in no way accompanied by a disappearance of the first purely figurative writing—hieroglyphs. All coexisted with a functional specialization, hieroglyphs restricted mainly, but not exclusively, to texts that we can qualify—in order to simplify things—as religious (Servajean 2016, 22–23).

In addition, the analysis of L. Delvaux aims to present things in a synthetic manner, which is why it does not consider an aspect of the hieroglyphic script that is always absent from analyses relating to hieroglyphs and the various attempts at palaeography that have emerged: cursive hieroglyphs. Because the latter, while retaining their figurative dimension, move away from drawing, approaching the hieratic to which they gave rise. As discussed in what follows, before starting to "draw"—on the various writing surfaces that received hieroglyphic inscriptions—the scribe begins first by writing, in the full sense of the term, using these cursives.

Palaeography is the science of ancient writing. But as Jean Mallon wrote in 1952, in a fundamental work related to Roman palaeography, this definition must be clarified and expanded:

> Palaeography aims to study not only writings, but the entirety of the external characteristics of all monuments, without exception, that bear texts, inscriptions of all kinds, papyrus, parchment, wax tablets, etc., a study that should not refrain from the secondary use, and in every useful measure, of data provided by internal characteristics. Palaeography, in short, must deal with graphic monuments of every type and, in each case, in a complete manner. The most diverse types of graphic monuments are represented among those of the Roman era that have come into our hands, especially in the last eighty or so years, the material existing for a study, coherent and without artificial barriers, of their external characteristics.   (Mallon 1952, 11)

This definition refers, of course, to Roman palaeography, but it is equally valid for hieroglyphic palaeography, performing, of course, the necessary corrections.

We establish, in what follows, the history of the latter and the state of the topic; we then address the problem of cursive hieroglyphs and their relationship with the monumental hieroglyphic script.

FROM DRAWN HIEROGLYPH TO WRITTEN HIEROGLYPH

Even if, for a long time, there has not been a real hieroglyphic palaeography, as was pointed out earlier, there are nevertheless some pioneering works. It is thus possible to mention the work of F. Ll. Griffith (1898), in which the author assembles a very limited set of beautiful hieroglyphics, dating from the Middle and New Kingdoms and from multiple sites (Deir el-Bahri, el-Kab, el-Bersheh), drawn and painted in

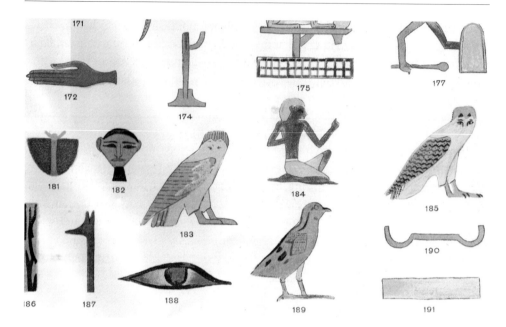

FIGURE IV.2.1. Detail of Griffith 1898, pl. 9.

color (Figure IV.2.1). Emphasizing the beauty of the signs chosen by Griffith is not insignificant because, it should not be forgotten, the hieroglyphic script is a figurative script, each sign being also, beyond its graphic dimension, the drawing in miniature of an element of the universe created by the deities in all of its diversity: divinities themselves, sky, earth, humans, animals, plants, artifacts, imaginary beings, and so forth.

This collection brings together 193 signs. It is very far from what can be assumed to be the total (approximate) number of inventoried signs. In the first part, Griffith begins by describing these hieroglyphs, while stressing the existence of certain variations in drawing and then their connection with the language of the ancient Egyptians.

Griffith implemented the same method in the work of N. de G. Davies (1900, pls. 4–18). 411 hieroglyphs are inventoried on the same principle, in the form of black and white copies; fourteen are featured in color (Davies 1900, pl. 18). In this work, Griffith tries to systematize his approach, considering also some signs that were less aesthetically striking and coupling it with a commentary, but less extensive than that of the previous volume.

This close association that hieroglyphs have with drawing is found elsewhere, for example, in the three volumes by N. M. Davies (1936), in collaboration with A. H. Gardiner. The author reproduced there many paintings of the Old, Middle, and New Kingdoms. Certainly, the hieroglyphs—thirteen in number and also accompanied by a brief commentary (Davies 1936, 3:16–17)—occupy a more modest place, but their presence in the work shows that despite their graphic dimension, they were also considered an artistic production (Davies 1936, 1:pl. 6). But it is probably with her book *Picture Writing in Ancient Egypt* (Davies 1958) that this type of work reached its peak: 112 signs drawn and painted in watercolor are listed there with a table of correspondence referring to Gardiner's sign list (Davies 1958, vii–viii). Once again, the selection criterion for the signs is aesthetic, and hence, the precision with which they are depicted, "the selected signs illustrated here have been chosen from those where the painted detail shows most variation" (Davies 1958, 27).

Despite the interest in these works, it was difficult to establish a true palaeography based on them, that is to say, without systematic study of all the signs recorded in the monuments examined by these authors. One reason—certainly not mentioned, but nevertheless happily real—that prevented the birth of a true hieroglyphic palaeography is the problem of the number of signs: how many hieroglyphic characters does this script have available? No exhaustive list exists simply because it is almost impossible to realize (Collombert 2007, 15–28). Each scribe was able, if he desired, to change a sign or create a new one. In addition, these signs can present significant differences (Collombert 2007, 20–21): at what point should we consider that we are dealing with a variant? How to define the concept of variation? In short, so many difficulties have delayed the birth of this discipline. That is why, when there was a question about carrying out (falsely) comprehensive studies, authors based them on existing lists of typographic signs, mainly that of Gardiner (1927, 438–548). Beyond the remarkable character of the latter, in particular the classification of signs and the quality of the remarks that relate to it, the approach is misleading because it includes no "real" signs, but typographic characters, that is to say, Egyptological creations that only imperfectly reproduce the original Egyptian signs.

The first work documenting a thorough analysis of these characters is the book of P. Lacau (1954); the whole thing was augmented in the first few pages with a reflection on the nature of hieroglyphs. Certainly, Lacau relies mainly on typographic signs, but he happens to introduce handcopies to support his thoughts. However, the desire for some comprehensiveness can only limit the possibility of the development of this type of work. Lacau himself points out: "As for the analysis of the diverse forms that each sign could take in writing over the centuries, it is useless to insist all the time that it will be necessary to put in order the elements of so superabundant a written material [. . .]. One must study the lives of some seven hundred signs for more than three thousand years, through uninterrupted documentation. There is guaranteed work for the coming generation" (Lacau 1954, 136).

Serge Sauneron is, apparently, the first to have had the sense of the methodology on which to base a true palaeography of the hieroglyphic script. In fact, he writes in 1971 about work done by H. Wild in the mastaba of Ti: "This work [initiated on the advice of Sauneron himself] should lead to the development of a collection of forms of signs, recorded in a given monument at a given time, a preliminary step essential for a more general study of Egyptian epigraphy [. . .]" (Sauneron 1971, 299). It is from this perspective, as shown in the epigraph to her work that reproduces, among others, this remark of Serge Sauneron's, that Françoise Le Saout (Traunecker, Le Saout, and Masson 1981, 1:149–249, 2:pl. 1–13) published the palaeography of the Hakor Chapel at Karnak. All signs were listed there—multiple copies per sign being retained—reproduced in handcopy, described, and commented on. This systematic analysis allowed Le Saout to emphasize "a great graphic freedom," probably due to what she calls the "spirit of play" resulting from a great "diversity in rendering the same sign"; thus, for example, the tadpole sign (Gardiner I8) that eventually transforms into a frog "or even the intervention of fashion with the various forms of sandals" (Traunecker, Le Saout, and Masson 1981, 1:205).

The figurative dimension also requires—and it is from this perspective that the first palaeographic analyses were made—an examination of what the scribes represented and how they represented it; all of these signs, the *mdw nṯr*, "words of the deity," as referred to in the Egyptian, form a kind of transposition in miniature of the universe created by the deities. The analysis of each of these signs—for example, those that represent artifacts—allows a better understanding of the world in which the ancient Egyptians lived and especially how they conceived of it. It is in this perspective that Henry George Fischer directed his research, that is to say, considering the sign—the Egyptian sign, copied by hand, and therefore not typographic—in relation to what it symbolized. The ethnographic dimension of this work is evident and extremely fruitful (Fischer 1976a, 1976b, 1977, 1996, 1999). In addition, this method must take into account certain data: the geographical context of the inscription's production, its architectural context, that of the owner of the monument (i.e., a tomb), social context, manufacturing context, immediate context (i.e., its relationship to the entire group of images and texts surrounding the monument), and the choice of materials (Fischer 1976a, 30–39). One cannot underestimate the magnitude of the epistemological break that these works involved. It is no longer possible today to design a palaeography that departs from them.

The first systematic program of hieroglyphic palaeography was launched by Dimitri Meeks in 2004. It is based on this double dimension: the combination of a monument by monument work, as Serge Sauneron proposed, without neglecting the ethnographic approach of H. G. Fischer. According to Meeks:

> All signs from the same monument retained for the palaeography are drawn to the same scale and keep their size relative to each other. In the final plates, each type of sign is numbered in sequential order. Under this paragraph number are grouped all variants of the same type of sign. [...] It is hoped that the commentary will be developed as possible. Its organizational scheme is simple. It is divided into paragraphs, each paragraph number referring to paragraph number on the plates. At the head of each of them is placed a vignette that illustrates the most representative type of each sign studied [...]. The form of each paragraph is divided into three parts. Section (a) specifies what the sign represents as a pictogram [...]. Section (b) describes how a sign or its variants diverge or not from a general form considered as a standard [...]. Section (c) lists the uses of each sign in the contexts where it is used on the monument studied.   (Meeks 2004, xxii, xxiii; see Figure IV.2.2)

The first volume of the collection was dedicated to the architraves of Esna Temple (Meeks 2004), and six others followed (Haring 2006; El-Enany 2007; Collombert 2010; Servajean 2011; Engsheden 2014; Lenzo 2016). The works of Dimitri Meeks, which combine palaeography, lexicography, and ethnography—diachronic and synchronic—show how fruitful his method is. Just refer to the examples given in the introduction to his

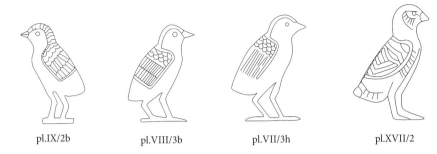

pl.IX/2b   pl.VIII/3b   pl.VII/3h   pl.XVII/2

FIGURE IV.2.2. Detail of §249 of Meeks (2004, 282), depicting several variations of the quail chick sign in the architraves of Esna Temple.

palaeography of the architraves of Esna temple, as well as to other works on specific palaeographic points (Meeks 2004, 2007, 3–14; 2010, 273–304).

The hieroglyphic script, it has been said, is first and foremost a figurative script, unlike other Mediterranean scripts. What the signs represent—and the details are important—allows the writer to marshal a supply of additional information of a semiotic type. These have produced work on hieroglyphic semiotics, very focused on theory, and which are based primarily on the study of typographic hieroglyphs. However, one hieroglyphic sign is not necessarily identical to its peer, and the scribe did not refrain from, if needed, changing it. These differences, intended or unintended, are absent from iconic, typographical signs, the many variants being erased in favor of a single sign. In working on the iconic sign, the researcher denies, obviously, information of the highest importance (Goldwasser 1995, 2002).

Despite the obvious progress in recent years, there is an area that, for now, escapes paleographers interested in hieroglyphs: cursive hieroglyphs. *Cursive writing* refers to *writing whose handwritten signs result from the simplification of signs engraved with care.* Note that this terminology could be a problem. Indeed, for what Gardiner calls cursive writing (Gardiner 1927, frontispiece, legend of the bottom photograph), some authors prefer the "designation of *semi-cursive* writing" (Fischer 1976a, 40), a classification perhaps owing to the fact that this script is intermediary between monumental noncursive writing and cursive hieratic. It is nevertheless noted that the problem of cursive hieroglyphs is beginning to be considered in certain works (Verhoeven 2015, 23–64; Lücher 2015, 85–118; Graefe 2015, 119–142), and that this gap will likely be filled in the coming years; a long-term program—twenty-three years—of a systematic inventory of cursive hieratic signs *but also hieroglyphic* has just been launched at the University of Mainz by Professor Ursula Verhoeven-van Elsbergen (Johannes Gutenberg Universität Mainz 2014).

These cursive hieroglyphs, mostly recorded on papyrus, but which can be found elsewhere, for example, on ostraca, have never been fully studied. When we accept the idea that their palaeographic treatment is as necessary as that of hieroglyphic noncursive writing, we immediately raise a similar—and necessary—distinction to the one that Roman palaeography made about documents written at "a single time" (i.e., a papyrus) and those "developed over time" (i.e., an inscription engraved on a temple wall).

As written by J. Mallon, "The criterion of the process, distinguishing monuments written all at once from those developed over time, is obviously fundamental when one seeks to know the mechanism of ancient writing" (Mallon 1961, 555). Slightly before that, he wrote in this regard, "All writing was an arrangement of lines, made according to a mechanism determined by the hand under the control of the eye that could, fixing a given form, arrange a new *ductus*, a new mode of line arrangement. The bare line arrangement is seen in the graphic monuments executed all at once that are written or inked on papyrus, parchment, marble, or wood, for example, or drypointed on wax, clay, lead, plaster, slate, or stone. But a line arrangement was fixed exactly, and the mechanism of its ductus was not necessarily camouflaged in some other graphic monuments where it was covered by a stroke of the chisel or brush, or in a mosaic; these last monuments were developed through a process over time" (Mallon 1961, 554–555). This analysis holds true for hieroglyphic palaeography. Gardiner distinguished in this respect several types of monuments and writings (I have numbered the quoted text): "At the outset hieroglyphic was used for all purposes; on stelae [1] of stone and the like the signs are incised, or more rarely in raised relief, without interior markings; in temples and tombs [2] where their decorative effect was of account the hieroglyphs were often executed with the most elaborate detail and beautifully colored; upon papyrus [3] the outlines were, on the other hand, abbreviated to a very considerable extent" (Gardiner 1927, 9, § 8). Incidentally, he offers a range of these three possible uses of writing in the photographs in the frontispiece of his *Egyptian Grammar*. In reality, these three categories can be reduced to the two categories of J. Mallon:

- Inscriptions made all at once = Type 3 Gardiner;
- Inscriptions developed over time = Types 1 and 2 of Gardiner.

Note that Fischer splits the third type in two (Fischer 1976a, 40, fig 4; 40–44), which excludes, we will see in the following paragraph, the *signs traced all at once with a simple ductus* (3b of Fischer) and *signs traced all at once with a complex ductus* (3a of Fischer).

It should be noted that in Dimitri Meeks's program of hieroglyphic palaeography, two very special monuments seem to fall in the category of monuments written all at once: the paleographic study of the tomb of Sennedjem at Deir el-Medina and that of the tomb Nakhtamun at the same site (Haring 2006; Servajean 2011), while all other work on hieroglyphic palaeography, even the oldest, have always focused on signs developed over time.

From Cursive Sign to Hieroglyphic Image of a World in Miniature

Hieroglyphs are figurative signs that precisely represent the elements of the universe created by deities in all of its diversity. When it comes to drawing these monumental hieroglyphs, one might think that the problem of the ductus does not arise; the word ductus designates "the order of succession in which the scribe has executed the lines, and the direction in which he makes each of them (from left to right, from top to bottom, etc.)" (Mallon 1952, 22 [3]). According to Mallon, it should also be considered as part of a comprehensive study of signs of "the following concepts: forms, writing angle, *ductus*, module, 'weight' of writing, and finally, subject matter, without neglecting the internal characteristics and in particular the nature of the text" (Mallon 1952, 22).

The word "ductus" is attested for the first time in connection with writing in Quintilian (*Institution Oratoire* I, 1:25; Blanchard 1999, 5): "I do not approve at all, in fact, what I see done in many cases: teaching young children the name and the succession of letters before their forms (*forma*). With this practice, it is difficult for them to recognize letters, and consequently, children are not applying their attention itself to the drawing (*ductus*) since they follow their memory, which goes faster" (Cousin 2003, 62).

Any written marks, all signs of writing present on a writing surface involve a ductus, that is to say, a regular manner of producing a form, if not identical, at least in a manner sufficiently recognizable as to be "readable." This implies, each time, a series of identical gestures to obtain an almost uniform and always identifiable drawing. But only approximately, because each sign originating from the same hand will present minor differences in the same monument, which will grow as soon as it is no longer the same writer.

Consider the sign depicting a quail chick (Gardiner G43). Examples can be found in the papyrus of Ani (P. BM EA 10470, Nineteenth Dynasty); in the lines that follow, there is much talk of the papyrus of Ani.

Knowing the drawing of a sign is primarily—but not exclusively—from top to bottom and from the beginning of the inscription toward the end, here is how the ductus breaks down (P. Ani 7, 32).

- Step 1: The reed pen first outlines the beak, then the curve of the head and the front part of the animal to the top of the foreleg;
- Step 2: The scribe lifts the reed;
- Step 3: The scribe puts the reed at the base of the neck, draws the back of the animal to the rump, then returns to join the bottom of the foreleg;
- Step 4: The scribe lifts the reed;
- Step 5: The scribe puts the reed to the right of where the line of Step 1 had stopped, draws the foreleg, then the line on the ground;
- Step 6: The scribe lifts the reed;
- Step 7: The scribe draws the hind leg and the line on the ground that joins with that of Step 5.

A quick survey shows that this ductus changes little over time, and even if there are some variations, they do not truly change the morphology of the sign. We must therefore emphasize the great stability of cursive hieroglyphs over several millennia. In reality, it is not in the history of cursive hieroglyphs that one looks for changes in the ductus, but in the passage, early on, from this to hieratic. This passage did not cause the disappearance of the first figurative signs, unlike the same process in other early writing systems, but on the contrary, their preservation. This leads to the coexistence of two scripts: hieroglyphic and hieratic, with, for each, a functional specialization, as we have seen. Any changes in the ductus relating to hieroglyphic signs would have resulted in a distortion of the "object" represented and the gradual disappearance of the figurative nature of the sign. This is a paradox particular to *Egyptian writings*: on one hand, the acceptance of a change in ductus resulting in hieratic, with the corollary of an obvious reduction in the figurative nature, which disappears completely with Demotic over the course of the first millennium BCE; on the other hand, the desire, for scribes composing "religious" texts, to preserve a "stable" writing (hieroglyphs) without changing the ductus.

To return to Papyrus Ani, one will see that in some cases the signs may be more detailed, approaching what might be called "drawn hieroglyphs." One finds them in a modified ductus at the beginning and end of the *volumen* inevitably more carefully drawn (P. Ani 1, 19).

The ductus of this sign is more difficult to establish, but examining the series recorded in Papyrus Ani, it is possible to tease it out without too much difficulty. It is also easy to observe that it differs from the former in several respects, probably because the outline is closer to a drawing. Somehow, this type of sign is similar to those drawn on the walls of monuments, temples, tombs, and so forth, without being identical to the latter. We consider that the first type discussed above uses a *simple ductus* and the second a *complex ductus*.

An examination of outlines of the same sign, or better, of all in the same monument allows us, in some cases, to get a very precise idea of the development of a manuscript. The method is obvious and relatively simple to implement for texts written all at once, but more complex for those written over time.

Writing Signs All at Once

The study of palaeography that follows concerns cursive hieroglyphs on papyrus. We focus again on the sign of the quail chick in Papyrus Ani. The results discussed here are obviously incomplete because a palaeographic study entails the examination of all signs recorded in the text studied. Despite this, it will show what a quick palaeographic review of a single sign can bring to the study of a single manuscript.

Table IV.2.1 lists all types of the quail chick sign (Gardiner G43) recorded in Papyrus Ani. In the images on the papyrus, it can be seen that the latter consists of several successive segments, each written by a specific scribe. The study of these segments can distinguish the "steps" of writing in different texts, recorded in this *volumen*, which is twenty-three meters long. Each of the resulting types will be described to identify morphological differences in each one, which is the only way to determine the number of scribes who participated in writing the texts recorded in the manuscript.

It seems that Papyrus Ani consists of ten segments corresponding to the ten types highlighted at the beginning of this analysis (Table IV.2.1). These segments, probably initially made separately from one other, were combined in a second phase to form the

Table IV.2.1. The quail chick sign (Gardiner G43) in the papyrus of Ani (P. BM EA 10470)

The first number accompanying the vignettes corresponds to the sheet, the second to the column, the numbering being from left to right.

1. Sheets 1–4	
1, 19	4, 7
2. Sheets 5–9 (up to column 32)	
5, 8	9, 13
3. Sheets 9 (cols. 33–34)–10 (first 8 columns)	
9, 33	10, 3 10, 5
4. Sheets 10 (cols. 9–40)–12 (first 25 columns)	
10, 11	11, 31 (bottom)
5. Sheets 12 (cols. 26–32)–14	
13, 1	13, 20
6. Sheets 15–19 (first 22 columns)	
15, 28	18, 21
7. Sheets 19 (cols. 23–37)–22	
20, 4	22, 14
8. Sheets 23–29 (first 26 columns)	
24, 21	28, 16
9. Sheets 29 (cols. 27–36)–35	
30, 3	34, 20
10. Sheet 36–37	
36, 18	

manuscript in its current form. The description of types also indicated that there were, in fact, five scribes, some of whom had worked on multiple segments (Table IV.2.2.A–B). By comparison, for E. A. W. Budge ([1895] 1967, cxliii), the manuscript "was written by three or more scribes," and for O. Goelet (Von Dassow 1994, 142), "the papyrus consists of the work of no fewer than three scribes/artists."

The segmentation of the manuscript also yields results similar to those arrived at by B. Leach and R. B. Parkinson (2010) in their study of the borders of Papyrus Ani. It is clear, therefore, all the interest there is to lay the foundations for a palaeography of cursive hieroglyphic inscriptions, that is to say, those made all at once.

Writing Signs in Multiple Stages

Paleographic analyses performed to date fall, for the most part, in this category. They were never interested in the problem of ductus. The reason for this is probably because a reconstruction of it seems difficult, the figurative signs resembling drawing more than the writing of abstract signs, like Greek and Latin letters. Is it possible, in these circumstances, to recover the ductus of hieroglyphs made over time?

Table IV.2.2. Description of different types of quail chick hieroglyphs from P. Ani

Scribe	Signs and Segments	Description
1	See Table 1 1, 19 Segment 1	The bird's beak, very short, is well drawn by a line that then forms the curve of the head and continues to the lower back. The front and back of the body are equally well marked by a line that, however, does not join the lower part of the beak. A small dot represents the eye. At the front of the body, a line runs near the back and another in dots portrays the usually speckled aspect of the bird's feathers. The legs are represented almost vertically with the ground line very pronounced towards the front. The line weight is heavier on the lower back and legs.
2	See Table 1 36, 18 Segment 10	The beak, longer than the previous type, is straight and well defined by a line that then forms the curve of the head (less pronounced than the previous) and continues to the lower back. The front and back of the body are also well marked. A small dot represents the eye. At the front of the the body, two lines portray the usually speckled aspect of the bird's feathers. The legs, thinner than those of the former, are represented slightly slanted with a ground line very pronounced towards the front. The line weight is heavy on the back and light on the legs (unlike the previous sign).
3	See Table 1 9, 13 Segments 2, 4, 6, and 9	The bird's beak is well marked, strongly emphasized and curved downward. The body is sharply inclined. The lines representing the front and back parts join only very imprecisely between the legs. The latter are represented almost vertically with a ground line very pronounced towards the front. The line weight is heavier on the head, rump, and legs.
4	See Table 1 13, 20 Segments 3, 5, and 8	The beak, very strong and curved, is less elongated than the previous type. In some cases, it is difficult to distinguish the neck, which forms with it a simple inkblot. The lines representing the front and back parts of the body (straighter and longer than the previous type) do not come close to joining in the lower part of it. The legs, slightly oblique and with a ground line very marked towards the front, has been represented without touching the rest of the body. The line weight is heavy on the head and back.
5	See Table 1 22, 14 Segment 7	If the head and the body resemble those of Scribe 3, the lines of the legs, by contrast, are different: at ground level, they exhibit a slight bend, and the ground line is systematically absent.

Some monuments allow a study from this perspective. To consider only one example, the tomb of Horemheb in the Valley of the Kings (KV 57) lends itself particularly well to a work of this type because in the process of being decorated, many walls have been left as is (Hornung 1971). A review of the latter allows us to distinguish four steps in the "manufacture" of a monumental text:

1. The space reserved for text is "filled" with red signs, divided in the most balanced way possible. This first step is to assess whether the space reserved for a given text is sufficient and whether it allows the signs to be laid out regularly (Hornung 1971, 44, upper). To do this, the scribe recorded the required signs at the desired scale,

with the chosen orientation. The ductus of these signs is simple and, at least for the quail chick sign (G43), identical to the texts discussed previously (Hornung 1971, 59 [a]).

2. These texts are reworked, probably by another scribe, who corrects them, modifying the arrangement or the orientation of signs (Hornung 1971, 58 [b]), enriching them with further details, moving them, or changing the inscription (Hornung 1971, 58 [b]). The ink used for this step is black. The signs are already more elaborate, and the ductus complex.

3. The signs are worked in raised or sunk relief.

4. The signs are painted, the scribe still adding a few details (Hornung 1971, 58 [b]).

It therefore seems necessary to proceed to the paleographic study of these two cursive hieroglyphs (to the simple and complex ductus), when it is possible to distinguish them on the same graphic monument made over time. A study of the work done by scribes over the course of these four steps allows us to follow the development of the sign's morphology step by step and to lay the foundation for thinking about not only the process used to produce—transform—a hieroglyph, but also the reasons for such a transformation. Similarly, and beyond what the philological analysis offers, it will also be possible to better understand the work of the scribe from a graphic, and also a semantic and semiotic, point of view.

If for a long time the work of hieroglyphic palaeography remained in a rudimentary stage, research has taken a new direction since the 1970s, thanks to the work of H. G. Fischer and D. Meeks; there is no need to return to the remarkable results that these researchers achieved. Nevertheless, it seems necessary to also add to them executing a palaeography of signs drawn all at once and simple or complex ductus. Indeed, to better distinguish the nature of the latter, as well as the writing habits of scribes, it will be difficult to avoid a successful completion of paleographic work on graphic monuments completed all at once, papyrus, ostraca, and so forth, knowing that the signs of simple ductus are the foundation of every hieroglyphic inscription, whether made all at once or over time. It is over them that the modified signs will be placed, enriched with additional details, and engraved and painted with care when found on graphic monuments made over time. Furthermore, only the emphasis and analysis of the different steps that governed the creation of a monumental inscription will allow one to know in detail and in concrete terms, the methods of scribes, who too often are reduced to mere shadows that, with difficulty, are perceived behind the texts studied by epigrapher and philologist. Only in these conditions will hieroglyphic palaeography be in a position to make up lost time, the significance of which some researchers have obviously already grasped (Davies 2017).

BIBLIOGRAPHY

Aguizy, O. el-. 1998. *A Palaeographical Study of Demotic Papyri in the Cairo Museum from the Reign of King Taharqa to the End of the Ptolemaic Period (684–30 b.c.).* MIFAO 113. Cairo.

Assmann, J. 2000. *Images et rites de la mort dans l'Égyte ancienne: L'apport des liturgies funéraires. Quatre séminaires à l'École Pratique des Hautes Études.* Paris.

Blanchard, A. 1999. "L'hypothèse de l'unité du *ductus* en paléographie papyrologique." *Scrittura e Civiltà* 23:5–27.

Budge, E. A. W. (1895) 1967. *The Egyptian Book of the Dead (the Papyrus of Ani) Egyptian text: Transliteration and Translation*. London.

Collombert, P. 2007. "Combien y avait-il de hiéroglyphes?" *EAO* 46:15–28.

Collombert, P. 2010. *Le tombeau de Mérérouka: Paléographie*. PH 4. Cairo.

Cousin, J. 2003. *Quintilien, Institution Oratoire*. Paris.

Davies, N. de G. 1900. *The Mastaba of Ptahhetep and Akhethotep at Saqqareh, I: The Chapel of Ptahhetep and the hieroglyphs*. ASE 8. London.

Davies, N. M. 1936. *Ancient Egyptian Paintings*. 3 vols. Chicago.

Davies, N. M. 1958. *Picture Writing in Ancient Egypt*. Oxford.

Davies, V. 2017. "Complications in the Stylistic Analysis of Egyptian Art: A Look at the Small Temple of Medinet Habu." In *(Re)productive Traditions in Ancient Egypt*, edited by T. Gillen. AegLeo. Liège.

Delvaux, L. 2013. "Écriture et dessin." In *L'art du contour: Le dessin dans l'Égypte ancienne*, edited by G. Andreu-Lanoë, 68–73. Paris.

Enany, Khaled el-. 2007. *Le petit temple d'Abou Simbel: Paléographie*. PH 3. Cairo.

Engsheden, Å. 2014. *Le naos de Sopdou à Saft el-Henneh (CG 70021): Paléographie*. PH 6. Cairo.

Fischer, H. G. 1976a. "Archaeological Aspects of Epigraphy in Palaeography." In *Ancient Egyptian Epigraphy and Palaeography*, 1–25. New York.

Fischer, H. G. 1976b. *Varia*. Egyptian Studies 1. New York.

Fischer, H. G. 1977. *The Orientation of Hieroglyphs: Part I. Reversals*. Egyptian Studies 3. New York.

Fischer, H. G. 1996. *Varia Nova*. Egyptian Studies 3. New York.

Fischer, H. G. 1999. *Ancient Egyptian Calligraphy: A Beginner's Guide to Writing Hieroglyphs*. New York.

Gardiner, A. H. 1927. *Egyptian Grammar*. Oxford.

Gasse, A. 2002. *Un papyrus et son scribe (le* Livre des Morts Vatican*—Museo Gregoriano Egizio 48832)*. Paris.

Goldwasser, O. 1995. *From Icon to Metaphor: Studies in the Semiotics of Hieroglyphs*. OBO 142. Freiburg.

Goldwasser, O. 2002. *Prophets, Lovers and Giraffes: Wor(l)d Classification in Ancient Egypt*. GOF 38. Wiesbaden.

Graefe, E. 2015. Über den parallelen Gebrauch von hieroglyphischen, kursivhieroglyphischen und hieratischen Schriftzeichen in Totentexten." In *Ägyptologische "Binsen"-Weisheiten I–II. Neue Forschungen und Methoden der Hieratistik. Akten zweier Tagungen in Mainz im April 2011 und März 2013*, edited by U. Verhoeven, 119–142. AAWLM 14. Stuttgart.

Griffith, F. Ll. 1898. *A Collection of Hieroglyphs: A Contribution to the History of Egyptian Writing*. London.

Haring, B. J. J. 2006. *The Tomb of Sennedjem (TT1) in Deir el-Medina: Palaeography*. PH 2. Cairo.

Hornung, E. 1971. *Das Grab des Haremhab im Tal der Könige*. Bern.

Johannes Gutenberg Universität Mainz. 2014. "Egyptologist of Mainz University Receives Approval for Long-Term Project through the 2015 German Academies' Program to Study Ancient Egyptian Cursive Scripts." Press and Public Relations. December 3, 2014. https://www.uni-mainz.de/presse/17777_ENG_HTML.php.

Lacau, P. 1954. *Sur le système hiéroglyphique*. BdE 25. Cairo.

Leach, B., and R. B. Parkinson. 2010. "Creating Borders: New Insights into Making the Papyrus of Ani." *BMSAES* 15:35–62.

Lenzo, G. 2016. *Les stèles de Taharqa à Kawa: Paléographie*. PH 7. Cairo.

Lücher, B. 2015. "Kursivhieroglyphischen Ostraka als Textvorlagen: Der (Glücks-) Fall TT 87." In *Ägyptologische "Binsen"-Weisheiten I–II. Neue Forschungen und Methoden der Hieratistik. Akten zweier Tagungen in Mainz im April 2011 und März 2013*, edited by U. Verhoeven , 85–118. AAWLM 14. Stuttgart.

Mallon, J. 1952. *Paléographie romaine*. Scripturae Monumenta et Studia 3. Madrid.

Mallon, J. 1961. "Paléographie romaine." In *L'histoire et ses méthodes*, edited by C. Samaran, 553–584. Encyclopédie de la Pléiade 11. Paris.

Meeks, D. 2004. *Les architraves du temple d'Esna: Paléographie*. PH 1. Cairo.

Meeks, D. 2006. *Mythes et légendes du Delta d'après le papyrus Brooklyn 47.218.84*. MIFAO 125. Cairo.

Meeks, D. 2007. "La paléographie hiéroglyphique: Une discipline nouvelle." *EAO* 46:3–14.

Meeks, D. 2010. "De quelques 'insectes' égyptiens: Entre lexique et paléographie." Perspectives on Ancient Egypt: Studies in Honor of Edward Brovarski, edited by Z. A. Hawass, P. Der Manuelian, and R. B. Hussein, 273–304. Cairo.

Möller, G. 1909–1936. *Hieratische Paläographie*. 3 vols. Leipzig.

Sauneron, S. 1971. "Les travaux de l'Institut français d'archéologie orientale en 1969–1970." *BIFAO* 69:283–306.

Servajean, F. 2011. *Le tombeau de Nakhtamon (TT 335) à Deir al-Medina: Paléographie*. PH 5. Cairo.

Servajean, F. 2016. "Hiéroglyphes: Quelques réflexions sur l'écriture des Anciens Égyptiens." In *À l'école des scribes: Les écritures de l'Égypte ancienne*, edited by L. Bazin Rizzo, A. Gasse, and F. Servajean, 19–45. Milan.

Traunecker, C., F. Le Saout, and O. Masson. 1981. *La chapelle d'Achôris à Karnak II*. 2 vols. Paris.

Verhoeven, U. 2001. *Untersuchungen zur späthieratischen Buchschrift*. OLA 99. Leuven.

Verhoeven, U. 2015. "Stand und Aufgaben der und der Erforschung of Hieratischen Kursivhieroglyphen." In *Ägyptologische "Binsen"-Weisheiten I–II. Neue Forschungen und Methoden der Hieratistik. Akten zweier Tagungen in Mainz im April 2011 und März 2013*, edited by U. Verhoeven 23–63. AAWLM 14. Stuttgart.

Von Dassow, E., ed. 1994. *The Egyptian Book of the Dead: The Book of Going Forth by Day, being the Papyrus of Ani (Royal Scribe of Divine Offerings), written and illustrated circa 1250 bce, by scribes and artists unknown, including the balance of chapters of the Book of the Dead known as the Theban recension, compiled from ancient texts, dating back to the roorts of Egyptian civilization*. Translated by R. O. Faulkner and O. Goelet Jr. San Francisco.

Winand, J. 2006. "L'image dans le texte ou le texte dans l'image? Le cas de l'Égypte ancienne." *Visible* 2 (2):143–161.

CHAPTER IV.3

···

METHODS, TOOLS, AND PERSPECTIVES OF HIERATIC PALAEOGRAPHY

···

STÉPHANE POLIS

HIERATIC is the name given to one of the cursive scripts of ancient Egypt. It is the tachygraphy related to the Egyptian hieroglyphic script (see chapter by Vernus), both of which are realizations of a single original writing system that arose independently in Egypt around 3200 BCE. On a continuum of figurativity that ranges from greater iconicity to greater abstraction, hieroglyphs are characterized by their high degree of iconicity, while hieratic graphemes are more abstract. On the correlated axis of visual appearance, the hieroglyphic script is intrinsically spatial, with depictive graphemes displaying pictorial qualities, while hieratic signs are characterized by the linearity of their shape resulting from their cursive realization. Figure IV.3.1 encapsulates how the five main native Egyptian scripts—namely, the hieroglyphic (see chapter by Servajean), cursive hieroglyphic (see chapters by Ali, Lucarelli), hieratic (see chapters by Gülden et al., Fischer-Elfert), abnormal hieratic (see chapter by Donker van Heel), and Demotic scripts (see chapters by Moje, Quack)—are distributed along these two correlated dimensions.

From a diachronic point of view, hieratic is best not seen as a descendant of the hieroglyphic script (Goedicke 1988, vii–viii). During the formative period of the writing system, the degree of figurativity of the pictorial signs could vary significantly according to the writing surfaces and modes of inscription, but remained high overall. As such, a distinction between different scripts does not make much sense for the earliest times. The extension of writing to different functional settings, however, quickly led to specific scribal practices and conventions (Regulski 2010, 2016).

The monumental hieroglyphic script is characterized by highly iconic graphemes, while cursive forms are usually executed with rush brush and ink. The first documents that display the simplifications and abbreviations characteristic of later hieratic inscriptions

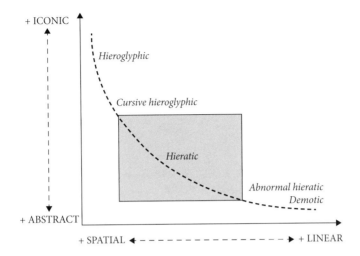

FIGURE IV.3.1. The five main native Egyptian scripts.

date to the Second Dynasty (Regulski 2009) and can be labeled "proto-hieratic." Among the longhands, there is no clear-cut distinction between the so-called cursive hieroglyphic (see chapter by Ali) and hieratic scripts before the end of the Old Kingdom. The cursiveness of signs is variable, but two different scribal traditions can only be witnessed from the First Intermediate Period (c. 2100 BCE). From then on, cursive hieroglyphs maintained a strong link with the figurative realm throughout ancient Egyptian history—and correspondingly have been used mostly in sacralized contexts (Vernus 1990)—while the hieratic signary evolved progressively toward more abstract and linear shapes. Hieratic, however, never lost its link with the iconic domain. Whereas the degree of cursiveness typical of abnormal hieratic and Demotic scripts led to a gradual loss of connection with the figurative sphere, the hieratic signs—even though frequently characterized by ligatures, abbreviations, and diacritics—kept an actual link with their representational origin (see "Systemic Variation" section, later). (Note that diacritics may appear to distinguish between specific values of polyfunctional signs. A famous example is the Eighteenth Dynasty addition of a stroke to the bovine ear (Gardiner F21) so as to visually hint at the roots *sḏm* "hear" (with one stroke) and *jdn* "ear" (with two strokes).)

Figure IV.3.2 visualizes the diachronic developments of ancient Egyptian scripts (for a detailed discussion, see Verhoeven 2015, 39–48); because each script has a separate and distinct tradition (Fischer 1976, 43), Egyptian written culture can be characterized as intrinsically "multiscriptic." Specifically, it shows that the hieratic longhand—originally used mostly as a notation script on jars and vessels before becoming the regular cursive for most of ancient Egyptian history—was progressively limited to its book-hand style after the Ramesside period. Hence, a correlation develops during the late periods between this script and priestly writing, which accounts for the name γράμματα ἱερατικά (*grámmata hieraticá*) that Clement of Alexandria (second century CE) coined to refer to this script (*Stromata*, V, 4,20–21) and from which modern labels such as "hieratic," "hiératique," and "hieratisch" derive (see chapter by Winand).

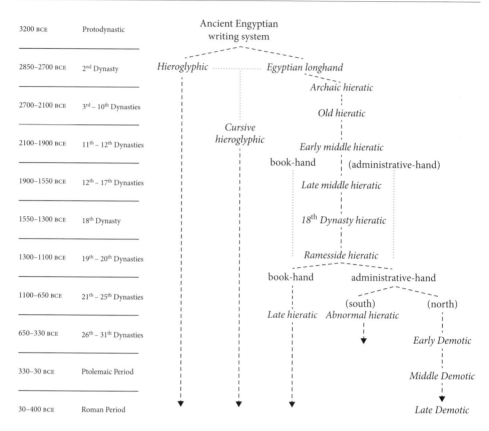

FIGURE IV.3.2. Historical development of the ancient Egyptian scripts.

Excellent introductions to the history of hieratic, and to material and methodological questions pertaining to the study of this cursive script, are readily available (Gasse 2016; Verhoeven 2015; Wente 2001). This chapter focuses on complementary aspects and addresses two main questions. First, what tools are available for studying hieratic texts, and what directions will future research on this script take? Second, what are the fields of application of hieratic palaeography? Hieratic palaeography is indeed at the crossroads of many areas of research that are outlined in the second section of this chapter.

Hieratic Palaeographies: Studying Written Variation

The first hieratic palaeography is the work of Champollion himself (1821, pls. III–VI) in an early attempt to demonstrate the systematic equivalences between hieroglyphic and hieratic signs and groups. This investigation led him to the famous statement that "les principes généraux de l'écriture hiératique sont absolument les mêmes que ceux qui régissent l'écriture hiéroglyphique pure et linéaire" (1824, 353, §114, with pls. A–K), thereby acknowledging the fact that the hieroglyphic and hieratic scripts are two realizations of one single writing system, with graphemes that can fulfill both semographic and phonographic functions (Polis and Rosmorduc 2015). As a result, Champollion's grammar not only abounds in hieratic examples and spellings but also provides synoptic tables with the correspondences between hieroglyphic and hieratic signs (1836, 35–46, 535–548).

While Champollion's approach can be characterized as panchronic, a proper diachronic investigation of the hieratic script started with Erman (1890, II:32–56), who compared seventy signs coming from seventeen different manuscripts (Twelfth–Twenty-second Dynasties), and identified a regular opposition between the "*Unciale*," or book hand, and the "*Cursive*," or administrative hand (compare Figure IV.3.2). He further described patterns of evolution between older and newer forms of the same signs, opening up the possibility of dating manuscripts, thanks to palaeography.

This diachronic approach culminated in the admirable (and still unsurpassed) work of Möller ([1909–1912] 1927–1936). The three volumes of his *Hieratische Paläographie* (with the *Hieratische Lesestücke* I–II of 1927) indeed remain an indispensable tool for both learning hieratic and studying hieratic texts. Besides the insightful introductory remarks, palaeographic tables covering thirty-two sources (mostly book hands), ranging from the Fifth Dynasty to the Roman Period, provide the hieratic shapes corresponding to more than seven hundred individual hieroglyphic signs (including numbers and measurement units) and seventy groups and ligatures.

Specific palaeographies have most often accompanied the edition of new hieratic documents—overviews are provided by Posener (1973) and Wimmer (1995, 3–5)—but only a handful of comparative studies have been published since Möller's pioneering work: Goedicke (1988) for old hieratic, Wimmer (1995) for administrative Ramesside hieratic, and Verhoeven (2001) for the late hieratic book hands. They focus on more restricted periods, but include a diachronic dimension (which is even central to the latter two studies that are successful in suggesting more accurate dating based on the hieratic script).

The steady publication of new hieratic sources, without making these studies obsolete, constantly brings in new hieratic signs, shapes, and ligatures that are likely to refine or modify our understanding of the ancient Egyptian hieratic cursive. The sources recently made (or about to be) available for old hieratic, for instance, include the Fourth Dynasty papyri of Wadi el-Jarf (Tallet 2017), the Gebelein papyri (Posener-Kriéger 2004), the Abusir papyrus archive (Posener-Kriéger, Verner, and Vymazalová 2006), and the hieratic inscriptions on the clay tablets from Balat (e.g., Soukiassian, Wuttmann, and Pantalacci 2002, 331–384) to name a few. The same trend is observed for later periods and is certainly not about to decrease. As an illustration, many papyri (Töpfer 2018) and thousands of Ramesside hieratic ostraca from Deir el-Medina (see chapter by Fischer-Elfert) still await proper publication. Consequently, it seems reasonable to assert that a "New Möller" (Posener 1973, 29) can nowadays only be conceived as digital palaeography, which would have the advantages of being both expandable and searchable according to several criteria, and which is the avenue chosen by the long-term (Mainz-based) project *AKU—Altägyptische Kursivschriften* (see chapter by Gülden et al.).

In the next sections, future perspectives for hieratic studies are outlined, adopting a variationist approach that envisions the written continuum as a structured heterogeneity. Following this line of thought, both diachronic and synchronic variations can appear at three different levels. First, variation may be systemic, namely, it can result from the potentialities of the ancient Egyptian writing system as a whole, which is flexible as regards the repertoire of signs and their syntax. Second, variation can be contextually driven, that is, linked to particular norms that govern the use of a script in a given context and lead to specific handwriting styles and formats. Third, variation can result from the actual written performance, which is connected to the capabilities of individual scribes and to the medium and writing tools that he uses (see chapter by Meeks).

Systemic Variation: The Hieratic Signary and Its Syntax

Belonging to a single writing system, hieroglyphic and hieratic scripts share features that have not yet been thoroughly explored. I first discuss essential characteristics of the hieratic graphemic stock, and then turn to the syntax of these minimal units.

Just like the hieroglyphic signary (Vernus 1982, 101–105), the repertoire of hieratic signs is characterized by its *extendability*: hieratic never lost its figurative potential— even within the most abstract and linear administrative hand styles—which implies that scribes could relatively freely enrich the repertoire with new semograms (pictograms, logograms, and classifiers alike) that do not necessarily have hieroglyphic equivalents (e.g., Pantalacci 2005, 276–278). As an illustration, one can consider some classifiers used in the Ramesside "letter to the king relating to the foundation of a statue" of P. Turin Cat. 1879, v° (Hovestreydt 1997). While describing the statue (*KRI* VI, 335:5–15), the scribe used four hieratic signs that are not completely exceptional, but failed so far to be recorded in the palaeographic tools: the *shendyt*-kilt, the *khepresh*-crown, the *mekes*-scepter, and the curved horns.

Although the basic hieratic signary is certainly more limited than the hieroglyphic one (Collombert 2007), with approximately five hundred different signs shared across periods (Verhoeven 2015, 34), the complete inventory of hieratic signs is still to be established (and regularly updated based on the publication of new material). Correspondingly, the abstract hieratic shapes directly interact with the figurative hieroglyphs. This phenomenon, which is attested for all periods, has long been noted, but has not yet been systematically studied. It includes (1) the influence of hieratic shapes on hieroglyphic ones, (2) the creation of hieroglyphic signs (or variants thereof) that are modeled on hieratic ones, (3) the hieroglyphic signs that inherit functions from others because of their similar hieratic shapes, and (4) the confusion between hieroglyphic signs due to the similarity between the equivalent hieratic signs (Lenzo 2015, 279–285). Linked to this last point is the question of hieratic drafts for (and copies of) hieroglyphic texts. Although the use of cursive hieroglyphs as an intermediate script for executing monumental inscriptions is well attested (Lüscher 2013), the existence of direct hieratic *Vorlage* of hieroglyphic texts is still disputed (Haring 2015).

In terms of (topo)syntax, the hieroglyphic and hieratic scripts originally shared the same plasticity as regards the general layout, with two possible organizations: texts could be written in vertical columns or in horizontal lines. However, the hieratic script quickly developed specific norms, which underwent a long-term diachronic evolution. Throughout the Old Kingdom and during the first part of the Twelfth Dynasty, the unmarked layout was vertical, while the horizontal lines were meaningfully exploited as formatting devices, for example, for headings or for signaling a shift of genre, such as the copy of the decree brought to Sinuhe that is marked by a change from columns to lines. (For a detailed analysis, including the fact that the scribe did not go back to the column layout afterward, see Parkinson (2009, 93–96).) In the course of the Twelfth Dynasty, however, the horizontal layout becomes increasingly frequent and is regular during the reign of Amenemhat III. The marked-unmarked opposition is then reversed, as can be observed for instance in the Lahun papyri (Collier and Quirke 2002), and the vertical layout, which is subsequently abandoned for hieratic texts, became associated with religious and sacralized texts written in cursive hieroglyphs. (Exceptions to this principle, such as the vertical protasis in the *Dream Book* of P. Chester Beatty III (Gardiner 1935, II, 5–8a), are certainly to be envisioned as isolated creative practices.) The arguments that have been proposed to account for this change are mostly practical and common-sense ones (Wente 2001, 206–207): preventing the scribe's hand from smudging lines previously penned; forming pages on the papyrus scroll that are easier to consult and process; increasing the speed of writing; adopting a layout that necessitates less space. However, the process as a whole has not yet been described thoroughly and requires detailed studies.

As regards text orientation, hieratic is a right-to-left script only—with signs facing right—which is the preferred reading order for hieroglyphs. It is also important to stress that hieratic developed an independent tradition as regards the organization of the graphemes within a line. While the syntax of the hieroglyphic graphemes is essentially spatial and flexible (Polis 2018), the hieratic script leans toward a more linear and rigid organization of the signs. Quadrat arrangement is not mandatory, graphemes can combine in (complex) ligatures (within which the signs are not neatly individualized), and interlines are exploited by some signs. Consequently, the calligraphic principles of the hieratic script differ significantly from those of the hieroglyphic script, and orthographic variation is much less pervasive in hieratic texts, which favor fixed spellings for groups of hieratic signs. The availability of electronic corpora that integrate the graphemic level, such as *Ramses Online* (ramses.ulg.ac.be), should facilitate future research in this promising field.

Normative Variation: About Styles and Visual Formats

In parallel with the extension of hieratic scripts to various functional spheres (Gasse 2016, 63–68)—from labels and administrative texts, to literary, scientific, and religious compositions—specific norms developed regarding the handwriting styles and formats linked to particular scribal practices.

Regarding handwriting styles, clear differences in abstraction and linearity appear already during the Old Kingdom. The execration texts of the end of this period (e.g., Abu Bakr and Osing 1973; Osing 1976) and of the First Intermediate Period (e.g., Posener and Osing 2013), for instance, already display the kind of cursiveness that will become characteristic of the administrative-hand style that is juxtaposed with the uncial (also called literary or book-hand) style from the Twelfth Dynasty. Studies about the administrative-hand style of particular (post-)Ramesside documents are available (e.g., Gasse 1988, 237–244, pls. I–XIX; von Bomhard 1998) and allow one to conceive of how the more cursive styles developed into abnormal hieratic (Upper Egypt) and (to a lesser extent) Demotic (Lower Egypt; compare Figure IV.3.1). Complementarily, Verhoeven's (2001) detailed study of the late hieratic book-hand style significantly advanced our understanding of late developments of the uncial and its relationships to the styles of earlier times. However, much remains to be done both in order to fulfill Möller's projects of investigating the history of individual styles and to describe the uses of different styles in individual texts. In this respect, it is rather self-evident that a simple dichotomy between book- and administrative-hand styles is not adequate for describing the variety of graphic registers encountered in the documents and that the history of these styles is not linear: in the extant material, some periods (e.g., the Ramesside period) display much more stylistic variation than others (e.g., the Second Intermediate Period).

Furthermore, specific norms developed locally. A canonical example, already studied by Erman and Möller, is the clustering of the four hands of P. Harris I in two groups. The hands of so-called Theban scribes "A" and "B" and the ones of the Heliopolitan and Memphite scribes "C" and "D" display regularities that suggest the existence of two different schools, respectively southern and northern, at the end of the New Kingdom (Grandet 1994, I, 23–26, despite the pessimistic view of Megally [1971, 21–22]). Research about regional norms, which would include the (cursive) hieratic Coffin Texts, is still a desideratum in the field (Posener 1973, 30).

Visual formatting of hieratic texts is also subject to regular variations depending on a variety of factors, which are primarily related to the text function and context of use. Eyre (2013, 41–54) provided an overview of the main formatting devices on papyrus, and his approach can be fruitfully extended to other media (see "Performative Variation"). Besides the (vertical versus horizontal) text organization discussed earlier (see "Systemic Variation"), the following strategies can be investigated in relation to the basic *scriptio continua*: (1) the ruling lines used to create full tables (a common Old Kingdom practice), to separate different sections of a text (as in the Rhind mathematical papyrus), to divide a text in columns or lines (a late development, see Quack 2015, 445–450), or to demarcate the text from images (Rößler-Köhler 1990); (2) the text layout, with specific arrangements, such as the use of line breaks (e.g., in lists or literary compositions), paragraphs, indentations, and *vacat* (or blank spaces, see Rößler-Köhler 1984); and (3) the structuration devices, such as punctuation marks (Tacke 2001), rubrics (or more broadly the alternation between black and red ink;

compare Posener 1951), or sections markers (like *ḥw.t* or *grḥ*). Finally, paratextual elements—such as numbering of lines and pages, marginal annotations, or emendations and corrections of the text—although not strictly genre dependent, are often indicative of the function of texts and linked to specific practices that still await detailed treatment. Practically, a diplomatic approach to ancient Egyptian hieratic documents would certainly unveil regularities regarding the correlation between the aforementioned strategies, as well as their diachronic evolutions.

Performative Variation: Scribal Hands and Materiality of Writing

If the specific purpose of hieratic texts called for particular handwriting styles and visual formatting devices, variation of the cursive is not only a matter of norms perpetuated through teaching and tradition—with occasional reforms of the system, for instance, with a return toward more iconic hieratic shapes during the early Eighteenth Dynasty (Megally 1971, 1–11; Parkinson and Quirke 1995, 27–28). Indeed, the long-term diachronic changes studied by most hieratic palaeographies are rooted in synchronic variation, which can be observed in individual scribal performances. Megally (1971) has been an early advocate of the synchronic approach to variation. He showed that different forms of the same hieratic signs regularly occur in a single text and observed that there is a general tendency toward greater linearity and abstraction as the text unfolds (e.g., Janssen 2000, 52; Dorn and Polis 2016, 67–69). As such, various degrees of iconicity of the same hieratic sign (see already Champollion 1836, 15–17) coexist in a single hieratic text.

In order to study this aspect, Allen (2002, 76–78, 193–226) showed that it is important not to limit the investigation to the general shape of hieratic signs, but to explore the *ductus* and to determine the number and the order of the strokes in the drawing of individual signs. In his palaeographic sign-list (Figure IV.3.3), he reproduced the signs in outline so that the arrangement of overlapping strokes can be seen.

This method has been fruitfully used for identifying scribe-specific habits within and across documents (Ragazzoli 2012, 229–230), and paves the way for a detailed analysis of the "stratigraphy of writing" (Parkinson 2009, 90–112), which implies tracking the scribe's hand from the closest possible vantage point. What are his habits in terms of ductus? When is he changing, sharpening, and refilling his pen, reinking signs made at the end of a previous dip, smudging, erasing, and correcting signs, or adapting the layout of the text to physical features of the medium? All of these "operations" that affect the shapes and organization of hieratic signs are traces of the scribes' agency and habitus and give us access to the cognitive processes at work when writing a hieratic text.

The physicality of writing is of primary significance here. The study of hieratic cannot do without envisioning writing as a material practice (Piquette and Whitehouse 2013, Piquette 2018). The media (Eyre 2013, 22–41) are not simply given, but created or chosen by human agents, with purposefully prepared and delimited surfaces. Together with the writing tools, they profoundly impact the forms of hieratic signs. However, the variety of hieratic shapes and ductuses that results from the use of different writing media and tools has not yet been studied in a comparative perspective.

Two modes of inscription are attested for the hieratic script: writing by addition, which implies the use of ink, and writing by subtraction, which entails some sort of carving. The combination of subtraction and addition, which is common for hieroglyphic inscriptions that are often both carved and painted (see chapter by Laboury), is exceptional for hieratic documents. (See, for instance, McDowell (1995) for an ostracon, which was probably erected as a stela in the hut of its owner, with the hieratic text deeply incised and filled with blue frit.)

Writing by addition is by far the most common. The scribe is then drawing signs with pen and ink, which originally gave the hieratic script its cursive aspect. During the pharaonic era, scribes used a thin pen made of rush (about 0.15 cm in diameter), held about 3–6 cm away from its writing end. It is only around 100 BCE that the Greek-origin sharpened reed pen (*Phragmites communis*) was progressively adopted for hieratic texts (Quack 2015, 444–445), which led to significant palaeographic changes. There is virtually no limitation to the kinds of media that could be inscribed with inked hieratic texts. Although papyrus is the writing surface par excellence, vessels and wooden tags, ostraca flakes of (lime)stone or potsherds, wooden boards and tablets (regularly covered in stucco), leather rolls, linen and coffins, as well as walls (*dipinti*) are common media.

Writing hieratic by subtraction, on the other hand, corresponds to specific practices—like the expedition inscriptions or graffiti in the mountains (e.g., see chapter by Ali) or some magical bricks (e.g., Silverman 1996)—to particular locations—for instance, the clay tablets of the Dakhla Oasis written with a pen in bone (e.g., Soukiassian, Wuttmann, and Pantalacci 2002, 331–384)—and to given periods—one can think of the post-Ramesside (particularly of the Libyan period) incised hieratic inscriptions on walls and stelae (Lenzo 2015; for a good illustration of hieroglyphic and hieratic scripts intertwined on such monuments, see Popko 2016). The ductus of the lapidary and incised hieratic inscription can only approximate the smooth ductus of free-flowing ink from a rush pen.

Applying Hieratic Palaeography

As we have just seen, the study of hieratic cursive provides heaps of information about the scribal norms and practices of different places and periods, but the use of palaeographic tools is most often motivated by a specific practical need. When studying hieratic originals, scholars have to check their readings against a repertoire of written forms that have been duly identified in order to ascertain the validity of their transcription into standardized hieroglyphs. The next section describes the main steps of this process, from the decipherment of the text to its normalized hieroglyphic transcription and dating based on the shapes observed in the reference tools. In the last section, a developing field of hieratic palaeography is introduced, namely, the identification and clustering of particular hands both within and across documents. Recent studies and promising avenues for future applications in this domain are discussed.

Reading, Publishing, and Dating Hieratic Texts

Although museums around the world are still filled with unpublished hieratic material, it is fair to say that the better-preserved documents have naturally been favored by previous generations of hieraticists. The help of a magnifying glass is accordingly not always sufficient in order to make sense of the faint traces of ink on the writing surface. Digital microscopes are nowadays both affordable and user-friendly (e.g., the Dino-Lite solutions), and they conveniently replace the old-school lenses. In this domain, digital imaging also helps significantly in two respects (Grandet 2017). First, photographs can be taken in wavelengths that range beyond visible light (Reggiani 2017, 141–145) so as to reveal texts that cannot be seen with the naked eye. Infrared imaging, in particular, has proven to be efficient (Bülow-Jacobsen 2008), especially in case of lack of contrast between the background and the carbon-based ink. Experiments with multispectral imaging have also been conducted, with promising preliminary results for hieratic texts, such as the ones found on execration figurines (van der Perre 2017). Second, even with regular digital photographs, the use of raster graphic software, such as Gimp or Adobe Photoshop, is very often helpful. Especially impressive are the results produced by the DStrech plugin for ImageJ by Harman (www.dstretch.com) (see chapter by Wendrich). Initially developed for digital enhancement of rock pictographs, its performances on hieratic inscriptions are admirable.

Having deciphered what one can, the next step is normally to prepare a facsimile that will document what the editor's eye could perceive, which is not necessarily visible on the photograph. Ostracon BTdK 640 illustrates this point (Dorn 2011, III, 514–516). The accuracy of the hieroglyphic transcription of the beginning of the first three lines could indeed not be assessed without the facsimile. In practice, facsimiles are mostly used for the media whose surface is not flat since it allows the flattening of the shape of signs that the photograph of a three-dimensional object necessarily

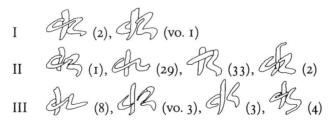

I   ✎ (2), ✎ (vo. 1)

II ✎ (1), ✎ (29), ✎ (33), ✎ (2)

III ✎ (8), ✎ (vo. 3), ✎ (3), ✎ (4)

FIGURE IV.3.3. The ductus of Gardiner A1 in the Heqanakhte papers, between two and four strokes (Allen 2002, 193).

distorts. Facsimiles are consequently not included in the publications of hieratic papyri (since photographs became affordable). Traditionally, facsimiles are realized with a pencil and drafting paper ("*kodatrace*") put directly on the surface of writing. When done carefully, the facsimile process may stop there, and a scan of the drafting paper shall produce an acceptable result. However, a second step is often taken. The tracing is inked manually, or scanned and retraced, using vector-drawing software, such as Inkscape or Adobe Illustrator. An advantage of the second method is that it allows the visualization of the order of brush strokes (e.g., Navrátilová 2015). Nowadays, some scholars skip the first step involving the drafting paper altogether and produce facsimiles directly on computer, while checking their drawing against the original. This method is recommended in the case of fragile documents, but produces inaccurate results if the writing surface is curved (as with ceramic ostraca), since the starting point is a photograph that flattens the three dimensions and distorts the writing surface. It should be stressed that facsimiles are interpretations and, as such, supplement the picture, but cannot substitute for it (Burkard, Goecke-Bauer, and Wimmer 2002).

Unlike facsimiles, hieroglyphic transcriptions are necessarily included in the publication of hieratic texts. Scholars considered creating a standardized hieratic font for transcribing hieratic texts. This idea goes back as far as Pleyte (1865) and regularly resurfaces. However, given the significant evolution of this script through time, as well as the great variety of hieratic styles on the one hand, and because of the transposability between the hieratic and hieroglyphic scripts on the other hand, such a project does not make much sense from a scholarly point of view. As argued by Gardiner (1929), a hieroglyphic transcription of the original should be provided, as it constitutes an interpretation of the cursive accessible to any trained Egyptologist, and—provided that it respects certain (arbitrary) principles—enables the reader to form a fairly good idea of what the manuscript looks like. (Note that the publication of hieratic texts includes more and more frequently a transliteration and a translation, which appreciably helps the reader, but is demanding for the editor. The evolution of the publishing practices for the ostraca of the IFAO, between Černý and Posener's minimalist editions and the full publications by Grandet and Gasse, is illustrative of this trend.)

Finally, the editors of hieratic documents have to suggest a date for the material being published. Among other criteria—such as prosopographical and grammatical features or information about provenance—palaeographic arguments are often resorted to (and are sometimes the only ones on which one can rely). Several diachronic approaches to hieratic palaeography prove to be especially useful in this respect—from Erman (1890, II:32–56) and Möller ([1909–1912] 1927–1936, 1920) to Wimmer (1995, 1998, 2001) and Verhoeven (2001)—and comparisons with other documents of a specific period help to significantly narrow down the period of composition (and sometimes to redate certain manuscripts). Because of the high degree of synchronic variation for individual signs, Janssen (1984, 305; 1987, 161; 1997) has been skeptical about the possibility of using palaeography for dating purposes. Although his argument applies to a certain extent to the Deir el-Medina hieratic material of the Ramesside period (where one tries to specify the precise date of composition within the Ramesside period), an approximation with a margin of less than one hundred years can be attained in the vast majority of the cases.

Identifying, Clustering, and Individualizing Hands

One thing is to identify several hands within a single document (e.g., von Bomhard 1998; Verhoeven 2001, 29–60), yet another is to track a single hand across several texts. In the first case, one is generally dealing with one handwriting style in synchrony (or short-term diachrony), and significant differences between hands are usually sufficient to hypothesize that several scribes were at work. In order to track a single handwriting from one text to another, one has to evaluate how great the degree of variation can be within one person's handwriting according to the circumstances of production (Sweeney 1998) and how this handwriting evolved through time (Dorn 2015).

Janssen (1987, 2000) was the first to suggest a proper methodology for tackling this issue. He stressed the importance of considering groups—rather than isolated signs—and distinguished between "principal variations" (i.e., completely different ways of shaping a sign) and "incidental variations" that are characterized by their irregular occurrences in a manuscript. One step further, van den Berg and Donker van Heel (2000) demonstrated that larger units, such as proper names or entire words, are more likely to reveal individual scribal habits than smaller ones. Within a set of documents that share the same provenance, they showed that hands can be clustered with a fair degree of certainty based on such a palaeographic approach.

The general appearance of handwriting is also crucial (Gasse 1992). As it turns out, it can indeed be more regular and telling than the shape of isolated signs or even groups (Dorn and Polis 2016, 67–73). This field is still in its infancy, and four main domains have to be investigated simultaneously: (1) the habits that relate to the size of the brush, to the density of ink, and to the number of dips; (2) the regularities in terms of ductus, with the types of pen pressure (ranging from full to loose), the spacing of signs, and the movement, rhythm, and speed of the hand; (3) the general features of signs, including their size and width-height ratio, their slant (rightward, upright, or leftward), as well as their curved versus angular aspect; (4) and the format of the text, especially regarding the baseline (rigid, bouncy, or wavy) and its orientation (straight, ascending, descending, or curved), as well as leading (i.e., the distance between baselines).

Finally, individualizing the hands, namely, attaching the name of a scribe to a particular handwriting is only possible in favorable conditions, such as the presence of colophons at the end of manuscripts (e.g., Ragazzoli 2012), as well as with "signed" scribal exercises (McDowell 1996) and texts (Dorn 2017; Polis 2017). The specific sociocultural setting of Deir el-Medina during the Ramesside period, where a vast quantity of information about the scribes is available, constitutes an especially promising area of research in this domain. However, the words of Černý (1973, 222–223) are to a large extent still accurate more than forty years later: "whether, and how far it will be possible to classify the variety of hands appearing in the documents of the Tomb, and to link the handwritings to individual scribes, are questions which must (…) be left to future research."

Bibliography

Abu Bakr, A. M., and J. Osing. 1973. "Ächtungstexte aus dem Alten Reich." *MDAIK* 29:97–133.

Allen, J. P. 2002. *The Heqanakht Papyri*. PMMA 27. New York.

Berg, H. van den, and K. Donker van Heel. 2000. "A Scribe's Cache from the Valley of Queens? The Palaeography of Documents from Deir el-Medina: Some Remarks." In *Deir el-Medina in the Third Millennium AD: A Tribute to Jac. J. Janssen*, edited by R. J. Demarée and A. Egberts, 9–49. EU 14. Leiden.

Bomhard, A. S. von. 1998. *Paléographie du Papyrus Wilbour: L'écriture hiératique cursive dans les papyri documentaires*. Paris.

Bülow-Jacobsen, A. 2008. "Infra-Red Photography of Ostraca and Papyri." *ZPE* 165:175–185.

Burkard, G., M. Goecke-Bauer, and S. Wimmer. 2002. "Editing Hieratic Ostraca: Some Remarks for the New Centennium." In *Egyptian Museum Collections around the World*, vol. 1, edited by M. Eldamaty and M. Trad, 197–206. Cairo.

Černý, J. 1973. *A Community of Workmen at Thebes in the Ramesside Period*. BdE 50. Cairo.

Champollion, J.-F. 1821. *De l'écriture hiératique des anciens égyptiens*. Grenoble.

Champollion, J.-F. 1824. *Précis du système hiéroglyphique des anciens Égyptiens, ou recherches sur les élémens premiers de cette écriture sacrée, sur leurs diverses combinaisons, et sur les rapports de ce système avec les autres méthodes graphiques Égyptiennes*. 2 vols. Paris.

Champollion, J.-F. 1836. *Grammaire égyptienne: Ou, principes généraux de l'écriture sacrée égyptienne appliquée à la représentation de la langue parlée*. Paris.

Collier, M., and S. Quirke. 2002. *The UCL Lahun Papyri: Letters*. Oxford.

Collombert, P. 2007. "Combien y avait-il de hiéroglyphes?" *EAO* 46:15–28.

Dorn, A. 2011. *Arbeiterhütten im Tal der Könige: Ein Beitrag zur altägyptischen Sozialgeschichte aufgrund von neuem Quellenmaterial aus der Mitte der 20. Dynastie (ca. 1150 v. Chr.)*. 3 vols. AH 23. Basel.

Dorn, A. 2015. "Diachrone Veränderungen der Handschrift des Nekropolenschreibers Amunnacht, Sohn des Ipu." In *Ägyptologische "Binsen"-Weisheiten I–II. Neue Forschungen und Methoden der Hieratistik. Akten zweier Tagungen in Mainz im April 2011 und März 2013*, edited by U. Verhoeven, 175–218. AAWLM 14. Stuttgart. http://aku.uni-mainz.de/hieratic-studies-online/.

Dorn, A. 2017. "The *iri.n* Personal-Name-Formula in Non-Royal Texts of the New Kingdom: A Donation Mark or a Means of Self-Presentation?" In *(Re)productive Traditions in Ancient Egypt: Proceedings of the Conference Held at the University of Liège, 6th–8th February 2013*, edited by Todd Gillen, 593–621. AegLeo 10. Liège.

Dorn, A., and S. Polis. 2016. "Nouveaux textes littéraires du scribe Amennakhte (et autres ostraca relatifs au scribe de la Tombe)." *BIFAO* 116:57–96.

Erman, A. 1890. *Die Märchen des Papyrus Westcar*. 2 vols. Berlin.

Eyre, C. 2013. *The Use of Documents in Pharaonic Egypt*. Oxford.

Fischer, H. G. 1976. "Archaeological Aspects of Epigraphy and Palaeography." In *Ancient Egyptian Epigraphy and Palaeography*. New York.

Gardiner, A. H. 1929. "The Transcription of New Kingdom Hieratic." *JEA* 15:48–55.

Gardiner, A. H. 1935. *Hieratic Papyri in the British Museum. Third Series: Chester Beatty Gift.* 2 vols. London.

Gasse, A. 1988. *Données nouvelles administratives et sacerdotales sur l'organisation du domaine d'Amon: XXᵉ–XXIᵉ dynasties, à la lumière des papyrus Prachov, Reinhardt et Grundbuch (avec édition princeps des papyrus Louvre AF 6345 et 6346–7).* 2 vols. BdE 104. Cairo.

Gasse, A. 1992. "Les ostraca hiératiques littéraires de Deir el-Medina: Nouvelles orientations de la publication." In *Village Voices: Proceedings of the Symposium "Texts from Deir el-Medîna and Their Interpretation," Leiden, May 31–June 1, 1991,* edited by R. J. Demarée and A. Egberts, 51–70. Leiden.

Gasse, A. 2016. "Une caverne d'Ali Baba, la documentation hiératique des anciens Égyptiens." In *À l'école des scribes: Les écritures de l'Égypte Ancienne,* edited by L. Bazin Rizzo, A. Gasse, and F. Servajean, 61–71. CENiM 15. Milan.

Goedicke, H. 1988. *Old Hieratic Paleography.* Baltimore.

Grandet, P. 1994. *Le Papyrus Harris I (BM 9999).* 2 vols. BdE 109. Cairo.

Grandet, P. 2017. *Catalogue des ostraca hiératiques non littéraires de Deîr El-Médîneh. Tome XII, nos 10276–10405.* DFIFAO 50. Cairo.

Haring, B. J. J. 2015. "Hieratic Drafts for Hieroglyphic Texts?" In *Ägyptologische "Binsen"-Weisheiten I–II. Neue Forschungen und Methoden der Hieratistik. Akten zweier Tagungen in Mainz im April 2011 und März 2013,* edited by U. Verhoeven, 67–84. AAWLM 14. Stuttgart. http://aku.uni-mainz.de/hieratic-studies-online/.

Hovestreydt, W. 1997. "A Letter to the King Relating to the Foundation of a Statue (P.Turin 1879 Vso.)." *LingAeg* 5:107–121.

Janssen, J. J. 1984. "A Curious Error (O. IFAO. 1254)." *BIFAO* 84:303–306.

Janssen, J. J. 1987. "On Style in Egyptian Handwriting." *JEA* 73:161–167.

Janssen, J. J. 1997. "Review of: Stephan Wimmer, *Hieratische Paläographie der nicht-literarischen Ostraka der 19. und 20. Dynastie,* 2 Vol., Wiesbaden: Harrassowitz, 1995." *BiOr* 54:338–345.

Janssen, J. J. 2000. "Idiosyncrasies in Late Ramesside Hieratic Writing." *JEA* 86:51–56.

Lenzo, G. 2015. "L'écriture hiératique en épigraphie à l'époque napatéenne." In *Ägyptologische "Binsen"-Weisheiten I–II. Neue Forschungen und Methoden der Hieratistik. Akten zweier Tagungen in Mainz im April 2011 und März 2013,* edited by U. Verhoeven, 271–295. AAWLM 14. Stuttgart. http://aku.uni-mainz.de/hieratic-studies-online/.

Lüscher, B. 2013. *Die Vorlagen-Ostraka aus dem Grab des Nachtmin (TT 87).* BAÄ 4. Basel.

McDowell, A. G. 1995. "An Incised Hieratic Ostracon (Ashmolean HO 655)." *JEA* 81:221–225.

McDowell, A. G. 1996. "Student Exercises from Deir El-Medina: The Dates." In *Studies in Honor of William Kelly Simpson* 2, edited by P. Der Manuelian, 601–608. Boston.

Megally, M. 1971. *Considérations sur les variations et la transformation des formes hiératiques du Papyrus E 3236 du Louvre.* BdE 49. Cairo.

Möller, G. (1909–1912) 1927–1936. *Hieratische Paläographie: Die Aegyptische Buchschrift in ihrer Entwicklung von der fünften Dynastie bis zur Römischen Kaiserzeit.* 3 vols. Reprint, Leipzig.

Möller, G. 1920. "Zur Datierung literarischer Handschriften aus der ersten Hälfte des Neuen Reichs." *ZÄS* 56:34–43.

Navrátilová, H. 2015. "Records of Hieratic Graffiti in Dahshur and the Use of Graffiti in the Study of New Kingdom Hieratic." In *Ägyptologische "Binsen"-Weisheiten I–II. Neue Forschungen und Methoden der Hieratistik. Akten zweier Tagungen in Mainz im April 2011 und März 2013,* edited by U. Verhoeven, 249–270. AAWLM 14. Stuttgart. http://aku.uni-mainz.de/hieratic-studies-online/.

Osing, J. 1976. "Ächtungstexte aus dem Alten Reich (2)." *MDAIK* 32:133–185.

Pantalacci, L. 2005. "Nouveautés graphiques et lexicales dans le corpus des textes de Balat." In *Texte und Denkmäler des ägyptischen Alten Reiches*, edited by S. J. Seidlmayer, 275–285. TLA 3. Berlin.

Parkinson, R. 2009. *Reading Ancient Egyptian Poetry: Among Other Histories*. Chichester.

Parkinson, R., and S. Quirke. 1995. *Papyrus*. London.

Perre, A. van der. 2017. "The Egyptian Execration Statuettes (EES) Project." In *Proceedings of the XI International Congress of Egyptologists, Florence Egyptian Museum, Florence, 23–30 August 2015*, edited by M. C. Guidotti and G. Rosati, 667–670. Oxford.

Piquette, K. E. 2018. *An Archaeology of Art and Writing: Early Egyptian Labels in Context*. Cologne.

Piquette, K. E., and R. D. Whitehouse. 2013. *Writing as Material Practice: Substance, Surface and Medium*. London.

Pleyte, W. 1865. *Catalogue raisonné de types égyptiens hiératiques de la fonderie de N. Tetterode, à Amsterdam*. Leiden.

Polis, S. 2017. "The Scribal Repertoire of Amennakhte Son of Ipuy: Describing Variation across Late Egyptian Registers." In *Scribal Repertoires in Egypt from the New Kingdom to the Early Islamic Period*, edited by J. Cromwell and E. Grossman, 89–126. Oxford.

Polis, S. 2018. "The Functions and Toposyntax of Ancient Egyptian Hieroglyphs: Exploring the Iconicity and Spatiality of Pictorial Graphemes." *Signata: Annales des seìmiotiques / Annals of Semiotics* 9, 291–363.

Polis, S., and S. Rosmorduc. 2015. "The Hieroglyphic Sign Functions: Suggestions for a Revised Taxonomy." In *Fuzzy Boundaries: Festschrift Für Antonio Loprieno*, edited by M. Müller, S. Uljas, A. Dorn, H. Amstutz, and M. Ronsdorf, 1:149–74. Hamburg.

Popko, L. 2016. "Die hieratische Stele MAA 1939.552 aus Amara West: Ein neuer Feldzug gegen die Philister." *ZÄS* 143:214–233.

Posener, G. 1951. "Sur l'emploi de l'encre rouge dans les manuscrits égyptiens." *JEA* 37:75–80.

Posener, G. 1973. "L'écriture hiératique." In *Textes et langages de l'Egypte pharaonique, cent cinquante années de recherches, 1822–1972*, vol. 1, edited by S. Sauneron, 25–30. BdE 64. Cairo.

Posener, G., and J. Osing. 2013. "Tablettes-figurines de prisonniers." *RdE* 64:135–175.

Posener-Kriéger, P. 2004. *I papiri di Gebelein: Scavi G. Farina 1935*. Turin.

Posener-Kriéger, P., M. Verner, and H. Vymazalová. 2006. *Abusir X: The Pyramid Complex of Raneferef. The Papyrus Archive*. Prague.

Quack, J. F. 2015. "Rohrfedertorheiten? Bemerkungen zum römerzeitlichen hieratisch." In *Ägyptologische "Binsen"-Weisheiten I–II. Neue Forschungen und Methoden der Hieratistik. Akten zweier Tagungen in Mainz im April 2011 und März 2013*, edited by U. Verhoeven, 435–468. AAWLM 14. Stuttgart. http://aku.uni-mainz.de/hieratic-studies-online/.

Ragazzoli, C. 2012. "Un nouveau manuscrit du scribe Inéna? Le recueil de miscellanées du Papyrus Koller (Pap. Berlin P. 3043)." In *Forschung in der Papyrussammlung: Eine Festgabe für das Neue Museum*, edited by V. M. Lepper, 207–239. Berlin.

Reggiani, N. 2017. *Digital Papyrology, I: Methods, Tools and Trends*. Berlin.

Regulski, I. 2009. "The Beginning of Hieratic Writing in Egypt." *SAK* 38:259–274.

Regulski, I. 2010. *A Palaeographic Study of Early Writing in Egypt*. Orientalia Lovaniensia Analecta 195. Leuven.

Regulski, I. 2016. 'The Origins and Early Development of Writing in Egypt'. *Oxford Handbooks Online* 2016 (May). DOI: 10.1093/oxfordhb/9780199935413.013.61.

Rößler-Köhler, U. 1984. "Zum Problem der Spatien in Altägyptischen Texten: Versuch einer Systematik von Spatientypen." *ASAE* 70:383–408.

Rößler-Köhler, U. 1990. "Die formale Aufteilung des Papyrus Jumilhac (Louvre E.17110)." *CdE* 65:21–40.

Silverman, D. P. 1996. "Magical bricks of Hunuro." In *Studies in honor of William Kelly Simpson 2*, edited by P. Der Manuelian, 725–741. Boston.

Soukiassian, G., M. Wuttmann, and L. Pantalacci. 2002. *Balat VI: Le palais des gouverneurs de l'époque de Pépy II. Les sanctuaires de ka et leurs dépendences.* FIFAO 46. Cairo.

Sweeney, D. 1998. "Friendship and Frustration: A Study in Papyri Deir El-Medina IV–VI." *JEA* 84:101–122.

Tacke, N. 2001. *Verspunkte als Gliederungsmittel in ramessidischen Handschriften.* SAGA 22. Heidelberg.

Tallet, P. 2017. *Les papyrus de la mer Rouge, I: Le "journal de Merer" (Papyrus Jarf A et B).* MIFAO 136. Cairo.

Töpfer, S. 2018. "The Turin Papyrus Online Platform (TPOP): An Introduction." *Rivista del Museo Egizio* 2. https://rivista.museoegizio.it/article/the-turin-papyrus-online-platform-tpop-an-introduction/

Verhoeven, U. 2001. *Untersuchungen zur späthieratischen Buchschrift.* OLA 99. Leuven.

Verhoeven, U. 2015. "Stand und Aufgaben der Erforschung des Hieratischen und der Kursivhieroglyphen." In *Ägyptologische "Binsen"-Weisheiten I–II. Neue Forschungen und Methoden der Hieratistik. Akten zweier Tagungen in Mainz im April 2011 und März 2013*, edited by U. Verhoeven, 23–63. AAWLM 14. Stuttgart. http://aku.uni-mainz.de/hieratic-studies-online/.

Vernus, P. 1982. "Espace et idéologie dans l'écriture égyptienne." In *Le sycomore*, edited by A. L. Christin, 101–114. Paris.

Vernus, P. 1990. "Les espaces de l'écrit dans l'Égypte pharaonique." *BSFE* 119:35–56.

Wente, E. F. 2001. "Scripts: Hieratic." In *The Oxford Encyclopedia of Ancient Egypt*, edited by D. B. Redford. Oxford.

Wimmer, S. J. 1995. *Hieratische Paläographie der nicht-literarischen Ostraka der 19. und 20. Dynastie.* 2 vols. ÄAT 28. Wiesbaden.

Wimmer, S. J. 1998. "Hieratische Paläographie: zur Datierung der nicht-literarischen Ostraka." In *Proceedings of the Seventh International Congress of Egyptologists, Cambridge, 3–9 September 1995*, edited by C. Eyre, 1227–1233. OLA 82. Leuven.

Wimmer, S. J. 2001. "Palaeography and the Dating of Ramesside Ost raca." In *Structuring Egyptian Syntax: A Tribute to Sarah Israelit-Groll*, edited by O. Goldwasser and D. Sweeney, 285–292. LingAeg 9. Göttingen.

CHAPTER IV.4

....

CARVED HYBRID SCRIPT

....

MOHAMED SHERIF ALI

INSCRIPTIONS in ancient Egypt were executed until the Late Period in two main scripts: hieroglyphic and hieratic. From the very beginning, hieroglyphs were mainly carved or painted on stelae and on the walls of temples and tombs and were often executed with elaborate details so as to catch the eye of visitors or passers-by. Hieratic was normally written with brush and ink on papyri, ostraca, or other surfaces for the purpose of practical, daily life writing. Both scripts could be incised in stone or painted with ink (Junge and Behlmer 2001, 260–261).

Since the Old Kingdom, hieroglyphic inscriptions carved in stone show different standards of execution, which can be easily recognized over time (for example, CG 1615, 1622, and 1624; Borchardt 1937–1964, 2:86, 92–93, 95, pls. 82, 84). Most of the inscriptions of the category quarry texts and graffiti were left by the members of quarrying expeditions (Eichler 1993; Seyfried 1981; Hikade 2001). They were usually executed in a manner different from the embellished standard forms found in temples, tombs, and other locations. We can define three cases of these inscriptions, as follows (Ali 2002, 12–35):

1. Inscriptions made in perfectly executed (i.e., canonical) hieroglyphs or, at least, successful attempts to do so
2. Inscriptions made in purely hieratic characters
3. Inscriptions that have a mixture of hieroglyphic and hieratic signs or that have signs of a "middle form" between hieroglyphic and hieratic (i.e., the hybrid script)

Although the phenomenon of hybrid texts came into existence in the Old Kingdom, it became very clear and regular in the texts of the Middle Kingdom, and it can be traced through the end of the New Kingdom and later.

CLARIFICATION OF THE PHENOMENON "HYBRID SCRIPT"

Checking the Middle Kingdom's inscriptions of this kind in several sites in Egypt in order to pursue this phenomenon can lead to significant results. This study begins with the Middle Kingdom examples because texts of this kind are very frequent in this period. Such inscriptions are frequent and common in quarries, either on the rocks of the site or on separate stones or stelae there. The stelae in such sites were official documents that attested to royal or authoritarian existence. Very interesting examples can be presented.

MIDDLE KINGDOM

At the site of Wadi el-Hudi, located thirty-five kilometers southeast of Aswan, where the ancient Egyptians extracted gold and amethyst (Simpson 1986, 1113–1114), several texts from the Middle Kingdom provide excellent examples of this phenomenon. For example, the text Wadi el-Hudi 11, which dates to the reign of the Senowsret I, depicts the head of an expedition to that place (Fakhry 1952, 29, fig. 24, pl. 12). Although the style of the hieroglyphs is not optimal, the hieroglyphic appearance of the signs is quite clear. This indicates that the writer of the text was keen to use conventional hieroglyphic forms. The same observation can be made about stelae found at the site, such as text number 16 (Fakhry 1952, 35, fig. 28, pl. 14; Sadek 1980–1985, 37, pl. 7.). This stela belongs to Intefiqer and dates to the reign of Senwosret III. Although the signs of the text mostly appear in perfect hieroglyphic forms, the hieratic form can be found in line 8 (see Table IV.4.1.1; but compare Seyfried 1981, 44). Other texts from Wadi el-Hudi are completely inscribed in hieratic, such as the texts of Wadi el-Hudi 30 and 35, where this hieratic character is obviously dominant (Fakhry 1952, pl. 19; Sadek 1980–1985, 56, 59, pls. 14, 17).

In Wadi el-Hudi, we also find the third category of texts, where the signs are executed in both hieroglyphic and hieratic forms together or in a middle form, a hybrid script between the hieroglyphic and the hieratic scripts. This type of sign's execution is frequent in Wadi el-Hudi. The best example is text number 6, where we can see this mixture of different forms of scripts (Fakhry 1952, 23–24, fig. 20, pl. 9; Sadek 1980–1985, 16–19, pl. 3; Seyfried 1981, 11–16).

The text carved on black granite stela-like rock begins with the date and the name of Senwosret I written in three horizontal lines in quasi-hieroglyphic forms. Below, there are two vertical lines with the name and the titles of the official sent to the quarry and the reason for his trip to that place. On the left of these two vertical lines, there is a block of

Table IV.4.1. Comparison of Standard Forms of Hieroglyphs with Carved Signs

	Gardiner number	Hieroglyph	Reference
1	D41		Wadi el-Hudi 16:8
2	V31		Wadi el-Hudi 6:4; Möller 1909, 511
3	A1		Wadi el-Hudi 6:4; Möller 1909, 33
4	Q1		Wadi el-Hudi 6:4; Möller 1909, 383
5	D21		Wadi el-Hudi 6:4; Möller 1909, 91
6	X1		Wadi el-Hudi 6:4; Möller 1909, 575
7	Y5		Wadi el-Hudi 6:5; Möller 1909, 540
8	A50		Wadi el-Hudi 6:5; Möller 1909, 26
9	T18		Wadi el-Hudi 6:6; Möller 1909, 443
10	W25		Wadi el-Hudi 6:7; Möller 1909, 496
11	A2		Wadi el-Hudi 6:8; Seyfried 1981, 11; Möller 1909, 35
12	Q3		Wadi el-Hudi 6:9, 13; Möller 1909, 388
13	A24		Wadi el-Hudi 6:10–11; Möller 1909, 15
14	V1		Wadi el-Hudi 6:10; Möller 1909, 833
15	M17		Wadi el-Hudi 6:11; Möller 1909, 282
16	V1		Wadi el-Hudi 6:11; Möller 1909, 632
17	O29		Wadi el-Hudi 6:12; Möller 1909, 363b
18	W9		Wadi el-Hudi 6:12; Möller 1909, 508
19	N23		Wadi el-Hudi 6:14; Möller 1909, 324
20	Y1		Wadi el-Hudi 6:4; Möller 1909, 538b
21	G29		Wadi el-Hudi 6:4; Möller 1909, 208
22	U28		Wadi el-Hudi 6:7; Möller 1909, 391
23	M3		Wadi el-Hudi 6:8; Möller 1909, 682
24	D34		Wadi el-Hudi 6:10–11; Möller 1909, 113
25	M24		Wadi el-Hudi 6:14; Möller 1909, 290
26	D21		Wadi el-Hudi 6:4–5; Möller 1909, 682
27	G7		Wadi el-Hudi 6:5
28	Y5		Wadi el-Hudi 6:5–6

29	X1	⌢	Wadi el-Hudi 6:4, 6
30	N25	⏝⏝⏝	Wadi el-Hudi 14:9, 12–13
31	M16	🌱	Wadi el-Hudi 14:12
32	G29	🦩	Wadi el-Hudi 14:17
33	G1	🦅	Wadi el-Hudi 14:17
34	G41	🦆	Wadi el-Hudi 14:18
35	G39	🦆	Wadi Hammamat 82
36	I5A	⬠	Wadi Hammamat 82
37	A1	𓀀	Wadi Hammamat 82
38	N23	⚏	Wadi Hammamat 64
39	G29	🦩	Wadi Hammamat 64
40	M12	𓆸	Wadi Hammamat 64
41	M36	🪮	Wadi Hammamat 64
42	Y3	𓏞	Lower Nubia 92
43	A1	𓀀	Lower Nubia 92
44	M17, G1, A1	𓀀🦅𓏏	Lower Nubia 94
45	G43	🦅	Wadi Allaqi 46
46	D36	▙▃	Wadi Allaqi 46
47	D40	◻⏌	Wadi Allaqi 46
48	Z4	//	Wadi Allaqi 46
49	A1	𓀀	Wadi Allaqi 46

Note: For Wadi el-Hudi 6, see Fakhry 1952, 23–24, fig. 20, pl. 9; Sadek 1980, 16–19, pl. 3; Seyfried 1981, 11–16. For Wadi el-Hudi 14, see Fakhry 1952, 33–34, fig. 27, pl. 13a; Sadek 1980–1985, 33, pl. 7. For Wadi Hammamat 82, see Goyon 1957, 98, pl. 19. For Wadi Hammamat 64, see Goyon 1957, 86–88, pl. 21; Couyat and Montet 1912–1913, 85, no. 123. For Lower Nubia 92, see Žába 1974, 129–131, fig. 194, pl. 111. For Lower Nubia 94, see Žába 1974, 131, fig. 196, pl. 112. For Wadi Allaqi 46, see Piotrovsky 1983, 49, pl. 147.

text including nine horizontal lines written in a frame with separation lines. It is worth mentioning that Fakhry (1952, 24) considered the two vertical columns as "work of another hand" different from the writing in the frame. The scribe intentionally gave the first three lines an official appearance through his attempt to execute the hieroglyphic signs in the ideal forms. The following lines, however, are different, as we find so many signs in their hieratic forms (Table IV.4.1.2–19). On the other hand, there are also signs that have a middle form between hieroglyphic and hieratic (Table IV.4.1.20–25).

Beside the hieroglyphic forms, which are also present in the text, we find that some signs appear more than once in the text, written in both the hieratic and the hieroglyphic or the "middle form" (Table IV.4.1.26–29). The forms of the sign Gardiner A1 represent a very special case in that text, as this sign was incised in several forms ranging from pseudo-hieroglyphic to pure hieratic (Ali 2002, 15, Abb. 4).

The same mixture of hieroglyphic, hieratic, and hybrid signs can be found in other Wadi el-Hudi texts, such as Texts 13, 14, 29, 34, 59, 93, and others (Fakhry 1952, pls. 11b, 13a, 18b, 21b, 33a, 24a–25a; Sadek 1980–1985, pls. 6–7, 14, 16). In the text Wadi el-Hudi 14, for example, we find within the hieroglyphic text many hieratic signs. The sign Gardiner N25 occurs many times in a similar form (Table IV.4.1.30), and Gardiner M16 occurs in a hieratic form (Table IV.4.1.31), while we have some other signs that have hybrid forms, such as the bird signs Gardiner G29, G1, and G41 (Table IV.4.1.32–34).

Likewise, at Wadi Hammamat, we find many inscriptions were made in this hybrid character apart from the texts executed there in a standard hieroglyphic or hieratic script. In the short text number 82, which was carved on the rock walls of the site, we find within the hieroglyphs of the personal name *Jrw sꜣ Sbk-ḥtp* the sign Gardiner G39 written in hieratic (Table IV.4.1.35), while the hybrid forms of the signs Gardiner I5A and A1 also appear (Table IV.4.1.36–37). In Wadi Hammamat text number 64, which was partially written in hieroglyphs, we find among the recognizable signs the hieratic form of Gardiner N23 (Table IV.4.1.38), whereas we can recognize the hybrid forms for the signs Gardiner G29, M12 (in the number 5,000), and M36 (Table IV.4.1.39–41).

The Middle Kingdom texts of the Sinai show us some cases in which the hybrid appearance is evident. Despite the difficulty interpreting text number 168, its incision is obviously a hybrid one (Gardiner, Peet, and Černý 1952–1955, 148, pl. 55). We can also observe the same thing in the Middle Kingdom in other sites like Nubia and Thebes (Žába 1974; Spiegelberg 1921, no. 924, 969; pls. 103, 107.).

New Kingdom

In spite of the existence of this phenomenon in the New Kingdom, it occurs in considerably fewer examples. We meet some examples of this kind at sites in Lower Nubia, for example, where we can trace this phenomenon. In text 92, the sign Gardiner Y3 occurs in its hieratic form (Table IV.4.1.42), and the sign Gardiner A1 occurs in its hybrid form (Table IV.4.1.43), while the other signs are written in their hieroglyphic forms. The text number 94 of Lower Nubia shows likewise the same thing, as we see the signs Gardiner M17, G1, and A1 in their hieratic forms (Table IV.4.1.44)

This way of writing is also evident in the New Kingdom texts of Wadi Allaqi, which is located approximately 180 kilometers south of Aswan in the Eastern Desert (Černý 1947, 52–53; Gundlach 1986). In text number 46 of Wadi Allaqi, the sign Gardiner G43 occurs two times in both of its hieratic forms and another time in the hieroglyphic form (Table IV.4.1.45). Moreover, the signs Gardiner D36, D40, Z4, and A1 occur in their hieratic forms (Table IV.4.1.46–49). The other signs in the text have a hieroglyphic character.

STATISTICAL STUDY

This hybrid way of writing texts was very remarkable with both its interesting mixture of hieroglyphic and hieratic signs and the use of a middle form between hieroglyphic and hieratic. What was also remarkable was the decline in this way of writing in the New Kingdom versus the abundance of such texts in the Middle Kingdom. In a study published in 2002 (Ali 2002, 12–35), the phenomenon of hybrid texts was analyzed, as texts from different sites containing graffiti and quarry inscriptions were examined and statistically assessed. Among these sites were places in which both Middle Kingdom and New Kingdom texts exist. The inscriptions considered in that study were those of the sites Wadi el-Hudi, Lower Nubia, Thebes, Wadi Hammamat, and the Sinai in the Middle Kingdom, whereas inscriptions of the sites Lower Nubia, Wadi Allaqi, Wadi Hammamat, and the Sinai constituted the material of the New Kingdom. Thebes was excluded from the statistical evaluation of New Kingdom texts because the number of the hieratic inscriptions from that site is sufficiently high to negatively affect the other values.

There was a problem with the definition of a hybrid text, especially when just one hieratic or hybrid sign occurs in a hieroglyphic text. As mentioned earlier, graffiti and inscriptions at quarry sites were typically executed according to noncanonical standards. Hieroglyphic texts at such sites, which with their official appearance represent the reigning institution that was in charge of sending the expedition to the site, should not be considered as hybrid texts even if, as is the case with the inscription Wadi el-Hudi number 16 mentioned earlier, one or more hieratic or hybrid signs intrude into the text (Fischer 1976, 43–44). This situation is little a bit different from the phenomenon of hybrid texts, and the use of one or two such signs in hieroglyphic texts is the subject of another study now being conducted (Ali, forthcoming a). The examination of different texts from the aforementioned sites has revealed certain results.

From these statistics, it is obvious that the hybrid way of writing reached a peak during the Middle Kingdom, while its usage became considerably restricted in the New Kingdom. Moreover, if we assume the region of Wadi Hammamat to be the only representative of hybrid texts in the Late Period, as this is the only place containing such texts from that time, we can recognize that the frequency of the hybrid script became very rare in the Late Period. Corresponding with the decrease in texts written in a hybrid script, there is a marked increase in the use of the hieratic script in New Kingdom graffiti and quarry inscriptions. In two of the three areas containing inscriptions from both the Middle and the New Kingdom, we can easily notice the expansion in the number of hieratic texts. These two areas are Nubia and Wadi Hammamat, while the third area, the Sinai, shows almost no difference between the Middle and the New Kingdom (Ali 2002, 27, Abb. 28).

Since that last study (Ali 2002) was done, some new materials from other sites have been published, such as graffiti inscriptions on the Western Desert road between Thebes and Hou, south of Nag Hammadi (including the inscriptions of Gebel Tjauty, Wadi el-Ḥôl, and the Western Hinterland of Qamûla, Darnell 2002, 2012); some inscriptions from the Sinai, at Serabit el-Khadim (Tallet 2012); and inscriptions found in the vicinity or on the western side in Ain Sukhna (Abd el-Raziq et al. 2002, 2011).

In the inscriptions on the Western Desert road north of Thebes, we are still able to identify examples of the phenomenon of hybrid script, such as text 17 from Gebel Tjauti from the Middle Kingdom (Darnell 2002, 59–61, pl. 34) and the New Kingdom text Matna el-Barqa No 1 (Darnell 2012, 135, pl. 175). In the Sinai, examples from the Middle Kingdom can be quoted, such as text number 20 in Wadi Umm Themaim, southwest of Serabit el-Khadim and west of Wadi Maghara (Tallet 2012, 44, pl. 15; Tallet 2002, 378–379) and text number 103 from Serabit el-Khadim (Tallet 2012 95, pl. 62).

Although each of these two groups of texts has its own peculiarities, they follow the same pattern already set out regarding hybrid texts. Middle Kingdom inscriptions from the Western Desert road sites and the vicinity executed in a hybrid script constitute about 37.25 percent (19 texts) of the total number of texts (51), whereas the texts of the same script in the New Kingdom make up only 17.8 percent (5 texts out of a total of 28). It is also important to note, however, that the number of hieratic texts in this group decreased during the New Kingdom (45.1 percent in the Middle Kingdom versus 36.7 percent in the New Kingdom). This trend is the reverse of what was seen at the sites treated earlier in the first study.

The recently published group of texts from the Sinai does not deviate from the previous conclusion. In accord with the previous results, which show a general reduction in the number of hybrid texts in the New Kingdom, the hybrid texts of the newly published Sinai group are 40 percent of the total number of Middle Kingdom texts (20 texts out of a total of 50), whereas there are no texts of this kind dating to the New Kingdom. If we consider the total number of texts in the Sinai, that is, the texts published by Gardiner, Peet, and Černý (1952–1955), plus the texts more recently published by Tallet (2012), we have for the hybrid type of inscription a ratio of about 24.7 percent of Middle Kingdom inscriptions (60 texts out of a total of 243) and 6 percent of the New Kingdom (12 texts out of a total of 200). These ratios correspond to the general trend seen in the hybrid kind of texts between the Middle and the New Kingdoms. The statistical evaluation of the whole group of texts from the Sinai is, however, so interesting that further study should be dedicated to it, not only for the hybrid texts, but also for the other kinds of inscriptions (Ali, forthcoming b). Sinai represents doubtless a special case in this context. As a peripheral region, its proximity to West Asia and the Levant, its demographic of nomads, the occurrence there of a new alphabet, which might have been the origin of all other alphabets in the ancient world and above all as a region, where the mining of turquoise and copper was done, it should have a peculiar position and special conditions, which of course led to this different case from the other sites (Morenz 2011, 59–102; 2012, 239–251; 2014, 31–32).

The Relationship of the Hybrid Characters to the Other Egyptian Scripts

The existence of the hybrid way of writing is evident in the Middle and New Kingdoms. Although the number of attestations of this text decline in the New Kingdom, we can still find examples of it until the Late Period (i.e., Couyat and Montet 1912–1913, 61, 64, Nos. 70, 83, pls. 17, 19). Moreover, a few examples of hybrid scripts date from the Old Kingdom, as we will see later. In order to understand this way of writing and the reasons for its use, one has to recall the history of Egyptian writing and the phases of its development in order to investigate the possible roots of hybrid writing and how it changed over time.

The characteristic features of the hybrid way of writing correspond with those of cursive hieroglyphs. That script, which is also called the "script of the Book of the Dead," is first attested in the Twelfth Dynasty (Möller 1909, 3n1; Brunner 1973, 46; see chapter by Lucarelli). It was used from that time on for religious and medical texts and took its forms from archaic hieratic writings (Schlott 1989, 82; Ali 2001, 30–31; Brunner 1973, 46). Like the carved hybrid script, the script of cursive hieroglyphs, which is executed in paint, is also characterized by signs that have "middle forms," (i.e., the forms lie somewhere between hieroglyphic and hieratic signs) and by using a mixture of hieroglyphic and hieratic signs. Unlike cursive hieroglyphs, however, hybrid signs that have the middle forms are not always consistently executed.

The hybrid script can be better understood by looking at H. Fischer's (1976) discussion of writing styles. Fischer (1976, 39–40) first laid out the traditional theory formulated by Sir Alan Gardiner. In his grammar, Gardiner (1957, sec. 8; the sequence used there is a bit different) distinguished three styles of hieroglyphs, presumably with reference to the Middle Kingdom and later: (1) the hieroglyphs of temples and tombs that were often executed with the most elaborate detail and beautifully colored; (2) the hieroglyphs incised on stelae of stone and the like without interior markings;(3) the hieroglyphs used on papyri, where the outlines were abbreviated to a very considerable extent. Then Fischer added (1976, 40–42), "This last category, sometimes known as 'semi-cursive' or 'book-writing'…became still more cursive in ink inscriptions during the Middle Kingdom; those of the Twelfth Dynasty and later may appropriately be called 3b [Fischer 1976, 41, Fig. 4; Figure IV.4.1], while the older style, which persisted in inscriptions incised on metal and wood may be called 3a. The latter was also used, with scarcely any modification, in the early Eighteenth Dynasty, down to the Amarna Period, after which it seems to have been somewhat less frequent."

This seems to be a good starting point to understand this hybrid way of writing. In this context, we are most interested in Fischer's styles 3a and 3b. The signs' executions in both styles seems to be a kind of simplification of styles 1 and 2 in Fischer's figure, that is, of hieroglyphic forms, either with or without internal detail. Simplification of this type was probably used when the writer could not or did not need to expend much time and effort or when the writer was not in the position to execute detailed or ornate hieroglyphs. One can expect this was certainly the case with the persons who executed graffiti and quarry inscriptions. Moreover, as Fischer stated, his style 3a was incised on metal and wood and was known from the Old Kingdom (Fischer 1976, 42). Style 3b or the cursive hieroglyphs, which is also a simplification of the hieroglyphic form, seems to be a modification of style 3a and bears a great similarity to hieratic writing. This similarity is certainly due to the technique of writing with ink and brush on papyrus, which is identical to the scribal method of hieratic writing. Furthermore, cursive hieroglyphs may have been used for the same practical reasons that hieratic writing was used.

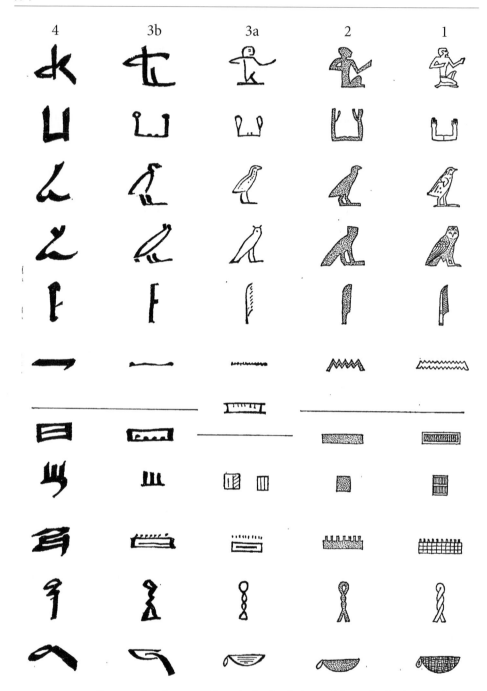

FIGURE IV.4.1. Less cursive forms of hieroglyphs (1–2), incised hieroglyphs (3a), and more cursive forms (3b–4). Created by: H. G. Fischer (1976, Fig. 4). Credit: The Metropolitan Museum of Art.

The similarity of cursive hieroglyphs to hybrid inscriptions is also evident (Ali 2002, 29–30, Abb. 30). That means we have now three similar ways of writing: semi-cursive (Fischer 3a), cursive hieroglyphs (Fischer 3b), and our hybrid script. The common feature among the three ways of writing is the middle form or the mixture of hieroglyphic-hieratic signs. Because style 3a is evident in the Old Kingdom (Fischer 1976, 40) and because some hybrid quarry inscriptions could also be dated to the Old Kingdom and shortly afterward in the Sinai (Doc. No. 5, 13, 15; see Tallet 2012, 27, 32, 50, pls. 8, 12) and in the Nile Valley (Gebel Tjauti text no. 5, Wadi el-Ḥôl text no. 13 [First Intermediate Period]; see Darnell 2002, 28–29, 123, pls. 18, 93) and in light of the fact that the script of cursive hieroglyphs had taken its forms from archaic hieratic, one can propose that a simple method of writing (the cursive way) arose some time after the Archaic Period, and the forms of the signs in this cursive method of writing were inspired from archaic hieratic.

Although the use of cursive writing was somewhat rare in the Archaic Period, this way of writing more fully developed during the Old Kingdom. Cursive writing was then used for some texts written on papyrus or on walls (Fischer 1976, 40; Fischer's examples are: Posener-Kriéger and de Cenival 1968, pls. 1–3, 20–22; Junker 1940, pls. 3–5, 7–9). At other times, cursive writing was incised in stone (CG 1305, Borchardt 1937–1964, 1:5, pl. 1), including in quarry inscriptions (Fischer 1976, 40; Doc. No. 5, 13, 15 in Tallet 2012, 27, 32, 50, pls. 8, 12). This cursive way of writing was presumably easier for persons who could write, but who were not artists or who perhaps could not execute the standard hiero-glyphic forms or their elaborate details. The cursive way of writing changed again at the beginning of the Twelfth Dynasty with the beginning of the classical language and writ-ing stage (Loprieno 1995, 5–8; Junge and Behlmer 2001, 264–265). At that time, cursive hieroglyphs appeared in their standard form, which seemed rightly—according to com-mon theory (Möller 1909, 3n1; Brunner 1973, 46; Schlott 1989, 82; Ali 2001, 30-31)—to have derived its forms from archaic hieratic. Two scripts were in use during the Twelfth Dynasty: the semi-cursive 3a and the cursive hieroglyphs 3b, beside the hybrid way of writing in graffiti and in quarry inscriptions. That type of writing was just another form of the two previously mentioned cursive styles. The use of semi-cursive hieroglyphs 3a decreased beginning in the New Kingdom, as evidenced by the very few examples from that time, and this decline continued in the Late Period (Fischer 1976, 42), which corre-sponds to the trends in the use of the hybrid script in the New Kingdom and the Late Period, as outlined earlier.

BIBLIOGRAPHY

Abd el-Raziq, M., G. Castel, P. Tallet, and V. Ghica. 2002. *Les inscriptions d'Ayn Soukhna*. MIFAO 122. Cairo.

Abd el-Raziq, M., G. Castel, P. Tallet, and P. Fluzin. 2011. *Ayn Soukhna II: Les ateliers métal-lurgiques du Moyen Empire*. FIFAO 66. Cairo.

Ali, M.-S. 2001. "Die Kursivhieroglyphen: Eine paläographische Betrachtung." *GM* 180:9–21.

Ali, M.-S. 2002. *Hieratische Ritzinschriften aus Theben: Paläographie der Graffiti und Steinbruchinschriften*. GOF IV/34. Wiesbaden.

Ali, M.-S. Forthcoming a. *Die hieratischen Zeichen innerhalb der hieroglyphischen Texte*. Thot, Beiträge zur historischen Epistemologie und Medienarchäologie. Berlin.

Ali, M.-S. Forthcoming b. *Die hybride Schrift in Sinai im Lichte des neuen Materials*. Studia Sinaitica. Berlin.

Borchardt, L. 1937–1964. *Denkmäler des Alten Reichs (ausser den Statuen) im Museum zu Kairo*. 2 vols. CGC. Berlin.

Brunner, H. 1973. "Hieratisch." In *Ägyptologie: Ägyptische Schrift und Sprache*, edited by H. Kees, 40–47. 2nd ed. HdO 1. Leiden.

Černý, J. 1947. "Graffiti at the Wādi el-'Allāḳi." *JEA* 33:52–57.

Couyat, J., and P. Montet. 1912–1913. *Les inscriptions hiéroglyphiques et hiératiques du Ouâdi Hammâmât*. MIFAO 34. Cairo.

Darnell, J. C. 2002. *Theban Desert Road Survey in the Egyptian Western Desert. Volume 1: Gebek Tjauti Rock Inscriptions 1–45 and Wadi el-Ḥôl Rock Inscriptions 1–45*. With the assistance of D. Darnell and contributions by D. Darnell, R. Friedman, and S. Hendrickx. OIP 119. Chicago.

Darnell, J. C. 2012. *Theban Desert Road Survey II: The Rock Shrine of Paḥu, Gebel Akhenaton, and Other Rock Inscriptions from the Western Hinterland of Qamûla*. New Haven.

Eichler, E. 1993. *Untersuchungen zum Expeditionswesen des ägyptischen Alten Reiches*. GOF IV/26. Wiesbaden.

Fakhry, A. 1952. *The Inscriptions of the Amethyst Quarries at Wadi el-Hudi*. Cairo.

Fischer, H. G. 1976. "Archaeological Aspects of Epigraphy and Palaeography." In *Ancient Egyptian Epigraphy and Palaeography*, 27–50. New York.

Gardiner, A. 1957. *Egyptian Grammar*. 3rd rev. ed. London.

Gardiner, A., E. Peet, and J. Černý. 1952–1955. *The Inscriptions of Sinai*. 2 vols. MEEF [36]. London.

Gundlach, R. 1986. "Wadi Allaqi." In *Lexikon der Ägyptologie*, edited by W. Helck and W. Westendorf, 6:1095–1096. Wiesbaden.

Hikade, T. 2001. *Das Expeditionswesen im ägyptischen Neuen Reich: Ein Beitrage zu Rohstoffversorgung und Aussenhandel*. SAGA 21. Heidelberg.

Junge, F., with H. Behlmer. 2001. "Language." In *The Oxford Encyclopedia of Ancient Egypt*, edited by D. Redford, 2:258–267. New York.

Junker, H. 1940. *Gîza IV: Bericht über die von der Akademie der Wissenschaften in Wien auf gemeinsame Kosten mit Dr. Wilhelm Pelizaeus unternommen Grabungen auf dem Friedhof des Alten Reichs bei den Pyramiden von Gîza. Die Maṣṭaba des kAjmanx (Kai-em-anch)*. DÖAW 71(1). Vienna.

Loprieno, A. 1995. *Ancient Egyptian: A Linguistic Introduction*. Cambridge.

Möller, G. 1909. *Hieratische Paläographie: Die ägyptische Buchschrift in ihrer Entwicklung von der fünften Dynastie bis zur römischen Kaiserzeit*. Vol. I, *Bis zum Beginn der achtzehnten Dynastie*. Leipzig.

Morenz, L. D. 2011. *Die Genese der Alphabetschrift: Ein Markstein ägyptisch-kanaanäischer Kulturkontakte*. WSA 3. Würzburg.

Morenz, L. D. 2012. "Die Alphabetschrift: Eine kulturgeschichtliche Skizze ihrer Genese." In *Sign Culture—Zeichen Kultur*, edited by E. W. B. Hess-Lüttich, 239–251. Würzburg.

Morenz, L. D. 2014. *Das Hochplateau von Serabit el-Chadim: Landschaftarchäologie und Kulturpoetik*. Studia Sinaitica 1. Berlin.

Posener-Kriéger, P., and J. L. de Cenival. 1968. *Hieratic Papyri in the British Museum. Fifth Series: The Abu Sir Papyri*. London.

Sadek, A. I. 1980–1985. *The Amethyst Mining Inscriptions of Wadi el-Hudi.* 2 vols. Warminster.

Schlott, A. 1989. *Schrift und Schreiber im Alten Ägypten.* Munich.

Seyfried, K.-J. 1981. *Beiträge zu den Expeditionen des Mittleren Reiches in die Ost-Wüste.* HÄB 15. Hildesheim.

Simpson, W. K. 1986. "Wadi el Hudi." In *Lexikon der Ägyptologie,* edited by W. Helck and W. Westendorf, 6:1113–1114. Wiesbaden.

Spiegelberg, W. 1921. *Ägyptische und andere Graffiti (Inschriften und Zeichnungen) aus der thebanischen Nekropolis.* 2 vols. Heidelberg.

Tallet, P. 2002. "Notes sur le ouadi Maghara et sa région au Moyen Empire." *BIFAO* 102:371–387.

Tallet, P. 2012. *La zone minière pharaonique du Sud-Sinaï.* 2 vols. MIFAO 130. Cairo.

Žába, Z. 1974. *The Rock Inscriptions of Lower Nubia.* Prague.

CURSIVE HIEROGLYPHS IN THE BOOK OF THE DEAD

RITA LUCARELLI

ONE of the most characteristic features of the Book of the Dead scrolls of the early New Kingdom is their script, which is generally named "Book of the Dead cursive," or *Totenbuch-Kursive* in German (Schlott 1989, 82). The German spelling started to be used in the 1950s in studies on ancient Egyptian script variants and on the Book of the Dead papyri. Its English equivalent, "Book of the Dead cursive," may have originated from that. In earlier publications, the script used for the Book of the Dead manuscripts and other magical texts was variously named. While editing the first Book of the Dead sources, Lepsius (1867, 11) used the term *Buchhieroglyphen*, "book-hieroglyphs," while almost two decades later, in his synoptic edition of the Book of the Dead papyri of the New Kingdom, Naville (1886, 32) only differentiated between "hieroglyphic" and "hieratic" manuscripts, although mentioning that a *Mittelschrift*, "middle script," was recognizable in those papyri where "certain signs had almost a hieratic form while others remained discernible figures."

In any case, the commonly used *Totenbuch-Kursive*/"Book of the Dead cursive" refers to a more accentuated cursive and linear character of writing as compared to the hieroglyphs on monumental inscriptions, but it cannot clearly be distinguished from other kinds of cursive hieroglyphs used in non–Book of the Dead sources (Ali 2001, 9). Therefore, *Totenbuch-Kursive* can be employed as a conventional term, but it should be clear that we are not dealing with a specific variant of cursive at all (contra Zauzich 2002; see Verhoeven 2015, 41). We could instead include the Book of the Dead cursive within the more general definition of "linear script," which has been proposed as a denomination for cursive variants of the hieroglyphic script used mainly for religious, magical, medico-magical, and ritual texts of the Middle Kingdom in order to distinguish them from literary texts written in hieratic (Verhoven 2015, 25).

ORIGINS AND USAGE

The *Totenbuch-Kursive* employed in papyri of the New Kingdom did not begin a new writing tradition, limited only to Book of the Dead texts, but it stemmed from earlier copying practices and from a traceable and progressive development of writing with a reed-pen and ink mainly on pottery and hard stone vessels (Regulski 2016, 16). Different theories exist as to the origin of cursive hieroglyphs, for example, as originally a local script variant from Middle Egypt or as parallel to but independent from hieratic, similar to the cryptographic script employed especially in royal tombs of the New Kingdom (Allam 2009, 33–37; Verhoeven 2015, 46).

In some cases, the richness in detail of cursive hieroglyphs, for instance, in central compositions in scrolls, such as the final judgment of the dead, would raise the question if, in many cases, the *Totenbuch-Kursive* should not just be considered a form of monumental hieroglyphs, only painted with a reed pen instead of carved or painted on the wall and with a more or less frequent insertion of hieratic signs.[1]

It seems that at least since the Middle Kingdom, cursive hieroglyphs were preferred to hieratic when decorating monuments and large funerary objects, such as coffins, with texts of a magical character. The Twelfth Dynasty coffin of Seni from el-Bersheh shows how cursive hieroglyphs could be adapted to different writing frames and mixed with monumental hieroglyphs. In the interior of the coffin (BM EA 30842; Taylor 2010, 65), the decoration consists of a row of detailed hieroglyphs with the offering formula (ḥtp-dỉ-ny-sw.t), followed by a *frise d'objets* surmounted by a line of cursive hieroglyphs. One of the objects in the frieze depicts a white papyrus sheet with cursive hieroglyphs written in a column and in retrograde writing, the same kind of writing occurring in the register below with the proper Coffin Texts spells. The alternating occurrence of fully painted and colored hieroglyphs and cursive hieroglyphs embedded in one of the commodities depicted in the frieze, followed by the proper spells in cursive hieroglyphs is a clear evidence of how, already in the Middle Kingdom, this script was central in the funerary culture and art of ancient Egypt. Similarly, an inscribed papyrus sheet or scribal tablet, containing a spell of the Coffin Texts, is depicted among a series of tomb offerings on a Middle Kingdom coffin (CG 28092; Lüscher 2015, 91).

Rarely, the Coffin Texts occur also in hieratic while cursive hieroglyphs are occasionally employed for texts painted on tomb walls of the Middle Kingdom. For example, it seems that on the eastern wall of the burial chamber of a Twelfth Dynasty tomb (TT 60) a sort of "papyrus-facsimile" with columns of cursive hieroglyphs between the images has been reproduced. Particularly interesting are the titles of funerary texts copied in the tomb, which occur in horizontal lines, as if imitating the layout of the ritual and funerary papyri (Morenz 1996, 62–74). Also at Beni Hasan, cursive hieroglyphs and hieratic occur in tombs no. 2 and 3, where the decorative program includes scenes of

---

[1] This consideration came after discussing the character of monumental versus cursive hieroglyphs with Ogden Goelet, whom I wish to thank for having shared his ideas on this matter.

scribes inspecting and listing goods and compiling documents written in cursive scripts, which have been called "cartellini," intended as small inscribed cards (Donnat 2012; Ragazzoli 2017, sec. 6.1.1).[2] That use of cursive hieroglyphs and hieratic shows an attention to what has been brilliantly defined by Ragazzoli as "anthropologie de l'écriture"; through the recorded form of writing, one can distinguish which scenes in the tomb's decorative program indicate practices related to daily life and administration (represented by cursive scripts) in contrast to the sacral environment of ritual activities, mainly represented by monumental hieroglyphic writing.

A certain palaeographic resemblance can be noted also among cursive hieroglyphs and hybrid scripts, in between hieroglyphs and hieratic, used for graffiti and rock inscriptions (see Ali chapter). However, we cannot assume a close relationship among the two cursive forms (Book of the Dead cursive and hybrid scripts) because of a few main different features of the graffiti and rock inscriptions: the writing material first of all (stone and other hard materials), a more variegated audience and a non-strictly ritual or magical function of the texts. What instead cursive hieroglyphs of the Book of the Dead and hybrid scripts seem to have in common is the will, on behalf of the scribe, to function as an alternative to the prestigious monumental hieroglyphs in different writing contexts, namely quarries and rock walls of various places in one case and wooden coffins, papyri, or tomb walls (among the main writing surfaces of the *Totenbuch-Kursive*) for the other. A certain type of graffiti, which occur in tombs with inscriptions addressed to tomb visitors, are clearly written in cursive scripts, mainly in hieratic, but with occasional cursive hieroglyphs embedded in the inscription, as in the case of a peculiar "graffito-stela" found in a tomb at Deir el-Bahri (MMA 504, E.2.14; Ragazzoli 2017, 212–220). This graffito reports an extensive text in hieratic, whose first line, which includes an offering formula, is written in a cursive script; the whole text is moreover inscribed in a stela-like frame with a rounded top, as for indicating its official and monumental character. In the same tomb, cursive hieroglyphs have been interestingly used to record scribes' signatures, as to express a certain monumental decorum; similar "monumentalized signatures" have been found in graffiti of the Theban area and in the Sinai, also dating to the New Kingdom (Ragazzoli, forthcoming, 131).

Cursive Hieroglyphs in the Book of the Dead versus Cursive Hieroglyphs Everywhere Else

As mentioned previously, the distinction between a "Book of the Dead cursive" and other kinds of cursive hieroglyphic writings could be justified only as a convention. Without a detailed palaeographic study, which could illustrate differences between

---

[2] I thank Chloe Ragazzoli for kindly providing a copy of her unpublished publications.

cursive scripts, we cannot truly define the *Totenbuch-Kursive* as a self-standing form of script. A palaeography of cursive forms has been a desideratum for decades, and only recently it has been undertaken by the Mainz-based project "Altägyptische Kursivschriften" (see chapter by Gülden et al.). Up until now, there have been only a few isolated attempts to produce a paleographic study of cursive hieroglyphic script in all its variants and not only limited to Book of the Dead sources (Ali 2001).

As for the Book of the Dead cursive, there are only a few studies, focused on individual documents (e.g., Milde 1991, 17–18) or on groups of papyri produced in the same period (Munro 1988, 193–197; Niwiński 1989, 91–92 and Table VII a–c), which have attempted a basic and still limited palaeographic comparative analysis of cursive hieroglyphs as specifically occurring in Book of the Dead papyri. This kind of study is made difficult because of the static character of cursive hieroglyphs, which seem resistant to consistent changes of forms through time, although handwritings may vary (Haring 2006, 8n6; Verhoeven 2015, 38). The resistance to palaeographic change is also accompanied by a tendency to archaization especially in papyri and coffins of the end of the New Kingdom and the beginning of the Third Intermediate Period, whose cursive hieroglyphs clearly imitate Ramesside models and consequently make it difficult to date them on a palaeographic basis (Niwiński 1989, 92). Moreover, the palaeographic study of cursive hieroglyphs of the Book of the Dead is complicated by the hieratic signs and the fully detailed hieroglyphs mixed with the cursive forms, as well as by the variety of individual scribes' hands; it was indeed a not uncommon practice, within Book of the Dead workshops, to have more than one scribe working on the same scroll, especially when dealing with particularly long papyri. The papyrus of Ani is an example of at least two scribes compiling the manuscript (Goelet 2010, 129). In other cases, though, it has been possible to match two different fragments to one Book of the Dead scroll by detecting the same handwriting in cursive hieroglyphs (Milde 1991).

CURSIVE HIEROGLYPHS VERSUS HIERATIC

A main, basic difference can be individuated between cursive hieroglyphs and hieratic, namely the lack of ligatures between signs in the cursive script, which instead characterize hieratic. Moreover, while the Book of the Dead cursive on papyrus is written in vertical columns and can face either right or left, hieratic texts are almost always copied in horizontal lines, and the signs face right, as in Book of the Dead papyri produced especially in the Twenty-first Dynasty, whose hieratic seems to have developed from literary texts of the Ramesside Period. Moreover, certain hieratic individual signs can be found inserted in columnar texts written in cursive hieroglyphs as well. A few hieratic Book of the Dead on papyrus, dated to the Eighteenth Dynasty and written in columns, exist as well (Munro 1988, 190–191). More rarely, Book of the Dead texts on linen, with columnar format and hieratic script may be found, such as for three fragments kept in Cairo and dated also to the early Eighteenth Dynasty (Cairo JE 96804; Munro 1994, 47–48).

Finally, even a leather fragment is attested, dated to the Eighteenth Dynasty, where the text is in hieratic, although not in columnar format (BM 10281; Shorter 1934). This peculiar specimen may have been used as model papyrus first and then adapted as part of the funerary equipment of the deceased, since the owner's name seems to have been added only secondarily in place of the impersonal term *s(j)*, "man." Most of the papyri produced at Thebes in the early New Kingdom are, however, in cursive hieroglyphs with insertions of isolated hieratic signs.

Although, when looking at the form of individual signs, cursive hieroglyphs seem to be more similar to monumental hieroglyphs than to hieratic, the influence of the latter cannot be denied (Haring 2015, 71). Moreover, cursive hieroglyphs almost always keep part of the pictographic character of monumental hieroglyphs and, similar to the latter and in particular in the Book of the Dead papyri, they can be occasionally painted with attention to detail and color, as in the judgment scene of the papyrus of Ani (BM EA 14070; Parkinson and Quirke 1995, 24, fig. 1).

While the hieratic script undergoes an evident evolution and changes forms through-out time so that we can distinguish an archaic, old, middle, and late forms of hieratic, such a distinction is more difficult to make for cursive hieroglyphs, which, as already mentioned and similar to cryptographic script, are more static or tend to follow the archaization occurring in funerary art and literature during the New Kingdom and Third Intermediate Period.

The influence of the hieratic script, with hieratic signs inserted into texts written in cursive hieroglyphs, can be noted also on the earliest examples of Book of the Dead texts, dated to the Eighteenth Dynasty (Munro 1988, 254–257). For instance, in the Eighteenth Dynasty papyrus of the royal scribe *Nḫt-'Imn* (P. Berlin P. 3002; Naville's Ba), hieratic signs seem to have been used for space saving at the end of a few columns, and other hieratic signs can be found scattered within the other columns too (Munro 1997, 4). While in certain papyri, the number of inserted hieratic signs is consistent, in other documents, it is very limited; in the so-called Papyrus Brocklehurst of the period of Amenhotep II, only ten hieratic signs have been detected within the cursive hiero-glyphic text, four of which are signs for birds (Munro 1995, 3). It is especially interesting to note how one sign can occur in hieratic as well as in cursive hieroglyphics within the same papyrus, showing a high degree of variation in scribal practices.

SOURCES

In general, most of the documents written in cursive hieroglyphs are of religious or magi-cal character; medical treatises could also be written in cursive hieroglyphs in columnar format and retrograde writing, similar to religious and magical texts, from the Middle Kingdom, as attested by Ramesseum Papyrus V (Gardiner 1955, Tables XV–XVII).

While the earliest homogeneous corpus of texts written in cursive hieroglyphs are the so-called Coffin Texts, the earliest examples of which date to the First Intermediate

Period, similar "linear" hieroglyphs seem to have developed as early as the Second Dynasty, contemporaneously to hieratic and monumental hieroglyphic. A mix of cursive hieroglyphs and hieratic signs is attested also in texts produced at the time of Cheops, as well as the so-called Abusir papyri. In the latter, cursive script was chosen for headings and labels, while the main text is written in hieratic; this feature is reminiscent of the use of less cursive script, imitating the monumental hieroglyphs, employed in the opening scene (the so-called etiquette) of hieratic Book of the Dead papyri of the Third Intermediate Period, where they functioned as image captions to indicate especially the owner's name and titles or short invocations or declarations pronounced by deities (Lenzo Marchese 2004). In a Sixth-Dynasty tomb in the cemetery at Giza, cursive hieroglyphs have been chosen to decorate a few sections of the burial chamber where, in place of monumental hieroglyphs used elsewhere in the tomb, short textual columns describe a colloquial speech of individuals represented on boats and list clothes, boat parts, and equipment (Schlott 1989, 175–176). Therefore, we may conclude that the cursive script is characterized, since its first occurrences, by being mixed and alternated with other types of scripts (from monumental hieroglyphs to hieratic) within the same context and source, from papyrus to tomb walls. Moreover, the main users of cursive hieroglyphs, in these early, Old Kingdom attestations, are nonroyal persons, namely elite officials who were gaining privileges and governing decentralized regions in a period of weakening royal power at the end of the Old Kingdom (Schlott 1989, 182).

To the end of the Middle Kingdom are dated two papyrus fragments containing copies of spells of the Pyramid Texts, found in the archive of the funerary temple of Pepy I (Sixth Dynasty) in Saqqara. The two fragments constitute recto and verso of one piece; they were originally part of two different papyri, which were later collated together. The script used on this artifact is a cursive form close to hieratic on what looks like the oldest side and a more elegant, still cursive hieroglyph (with retrograde writing) on the other side (Berger el-Naggar 2004). Most probably, these fragments functioned as model papyri for copying the spells on monuments or to archive them; instead of the personal name of the beneficiary of the spell, they present the formula *Wsir mn pn*, "the Osiris so-and-so," which is found in other model papyri as well (Lüscher 2015, 90–91).

Semi-cursive forms of hieroglyphs occur also in the Ramesside tombs of Deir el-Medina, where a selection of texts from the Book of the Dead were copied on the walls, very probably from model papyri written in cursive hieroglyphs. These painted copies of monumental hieroglyphs are not of a very elaborate type, since generally they lack most of the interior details except when those details are necessary to recognize one sign from another, as in the tomb of Sennedjem at Deir el-Medina (TT 1). The latter, which is decorated mainly with texts and vignettes of the Book of the Dead, provides a good example of cursive hieroglyphs in a tomb that, although classified as monumental hieroglyphs because of the presence of inner details, present clear influences of both hieratic and cursive hieroglyphs. Similar to the Middle Kingdom tomb mentioned before (TT 60), also in this case we have evidence, in one section of the tomb, of the use of retrograde writing for imitating the layout of a funerary papyrus of the Book of the Dead type and, as a matter of fact, the spell recorded in that section is part of the Book of the Dead corpus (Haring 2006, 7–10).

Besides papyri, earlier examples of Book of the Dead texts in cursive hieroglyphs occur on funerary shrouds and linen from Thebes. Among others, a few funerary shrouds kept in Turin and Uppsala, belonging to a female *Tḥ-ms* (*sꜣt ny-swt*, "princess") and to a male *Tḥ-ms* (*sꜣ Nb-sw*, "son of Nebsu"), dated to the end of the Seventeenth/beginning of the Eighteenth Dynasty (reign of Ahmose I), present a handwriting and layout closely resembling that of papyri of the same period (Ronsecco 1996). As in the papyrus examples, hieratic signs can be inserted in texts on linen, as in a fragment of linen kept in Boston, dated to the first half of the Eighteenth Dynasty on a palaeographic basis only, thanks to those hieratic signs inserted in the cursive hieroglyphs (McDonald 1981). However, with the exception of a few specimens like the linen fragment in Boston, the hieratic signs occurring in these documents are not helpful for dating purposes since they do not seem to have been realized by scribes who were fluent in hieratic and also because not enough signs are attested for an exhaustive palaeographic analysis (Munro 1988, 193).

The Book of the Dead manuscripts in cursive hieroglyphs of the Eighteenth Dynasty, which start to be produced from the reign of Thutmose III, are much more numerous than those in hieratic, which makes it clear that cursive was the most popular and standardized form of script in the New Kingdom for the Book of the Dead genre. According to Naville (1886, 33–34), starting from the Nineteenth Dynasty, cursive hieroglyphs were replaced by monumental hieroglyphs in the illustrated Book of the Dead scrolls. However, I. Munro (1988, 195) has shown that also after the Eighteenth Dynasty, monumental hieroglyphs were mostly used for the opening vignette and for hymns included in the papyri, while the main text was still mainly written in cursive hieroglyphs. Moreover, on the basis of the papyri of the Book of the Dead produced during the New Kingdom, I. Munro (1988, 193–197) has individuated a group of documents written in "standardized" cursive hieroglyph (*Norm-Kursivhieroglyphe*), and she has attempted to use the cursive script as a dating method for the manuscripts. Among the signs found in this group of papyri, which show a more homogeneous form, are the hieroglyphs for *m* (Gardiner G17), *ꜣ* (G1), and *w* (G43), as well as the determinative of male personal names (A1) (Munro 1988, 194, 196, and 257, List 20). Particularly interesting is the case of the latter, namely, the hieroglyph of the seated man, which seems to occur in the Book of the Dead cursive in three different forms, with the arm pointing down, up, or horizontally; however, it has been noted how within the same document, one can find more than one variant, written by the same hand, therefore not being indicative of a specific period of production (Lüscher 2015, 100).

Totenbuch-Kursive occurs also on coffins of the priests of Montu from the Twenty-first to the Twenty-sixth Dynasty that are decorated with variants of Book of the Dead spells (Gauthier 1913). Moreover, in the Eighteenth Dynasty, in particular in the tombs of Thutmose III and Amenhotep II, cursive hieroglyphs are employed for the texts of the Amduat, while monumental hieroglyphs are used from Tutankhamun onward (Warburton 2007, 7–9). Cursive hieroglyphs in columnar format and written in retrograde were used also when extracts of the Amduat were copied on papyrus in the Twenty-first Dynasty and when a second funerary scroll accompanied the Book of the Dead papyrus (Sadek 1985).

The Third Intermediate Period and in particular the Twenty-first Dynasty is a crucial moment for scribal techniques and the textual tradition of the Book of the Dead. Beside continuing the earlier custom of writing Book of the Dead spells in columns of cursive hieroglyphs and with retrograde writing, hieratic is introduced as well, probably as a consequence of the more common practice of employing hieratic for copying texts of daily magic. While, as mentioned earlier, in the early New Kingdom, only a few papyri of the Book of the Dead were written in hieratic or included longer hieratic sections within a main text written in cursive hieroglyphs (Munro 1988, 190–192), the consistent number of Book of the Dead scrolls written in hieratic at Thebes especially during the Twenty-first Dynasty clearly shows the existence of specialized local workshops, where the High Priests of Amun and their family members could commission different kinds of magical papyri for protecting their journey in the netherworld. It is noteworthy that, in this period, the Book of the Dead scroll was often accompanied by a second funerary papyrus of the Amduat, or Litany of Re–type, or by another funerary composition, including the Book of the Dead. The most pictographic ones among these peculiar scrolls were called "mythological papyri" when first published, although they are just a different typology of funerary papyri of that period. Although images outnumber the text in this kind of papyri, when texts do occur, they are written also in the columnar format and in cursive hieroglyphs, more or less defined with interior details. Similar to the papyri of the Book of the Dead genre, the hieroglyphs of these mainly pictographic documents were painted more or less rapidly according to the major or minor length of the text so that the short hieroglyphic captions of figures are generally less cursive than those employed for incantations. Among these additional scrolls that accompanied the Book of the Dead papyri for the burial of the Theban priests of the Third Intermediate Period, only a few have been inscribed with hieratic texts, namely, a papyrus for queen Nedjemet (BM 10490; Lenzo 2010) and a papyrus kept in Turin (Turin 1789; Niwiński 1989, 209–210). This kind of evidence shows that, at least in the Theban region, the use of cursive hieroglyphs for funerary texts was not restricted to Book of the Dead scrolls only, but that it was employed for mortuary texts at large, while the hieratic script, when employed, is mostly found in scrolls of the Book of the Dead genre.

Also in the mortuary papyri of the first millennium BCE, it is clear that the scribes, similar to those of the New Kingdom, were attempting to imitate monumental script by enriching many hieroglyphs with internal details. An example of this practice is a Book of the Dead papyrus dated to the Twenty-fifth Dynasty, whose script has been defined as "linear hieroglyphs" (Munro and Taylor 2009, 6), since many signs are sketched with interior details. However, this kind of writing, where certain hieroglyphs, such as the owl hieroglyph (G17), are always cursive, is similar to that of many other earlier funerary scrolls and can be considered a form of Book of the Dead cursive hieroglyphs as well.

Scribal Training and Copying Practices

The cursive script was very probably also part of the scribal training although, since it required superior writing skills, it was introduced to practicing scribes only after they could master the relatively easier and more abstract hieratic script. It is, however, interesting how some of the hieratic texts clearly employed as school exercises recall features that are typical of cursive hieroglyphs of the Book of the Dead and of cursive hieroglyphs in general, such as the columnar format, the absence of ligatures between signs, and the very recognizable form of each hieroglyph. This is the case with Kemyt, a Middle Egyptian text copied extensively on ostraca, writing boards, and papyri of the New Kingdom, most of which have been found in Deir el-Medina; the typical script of the Kemyt is indeed a very archaizing hieratic in columns, similar to what is called "Old Hieratic" (Möller 1909, 3), whose copying practice was probably aimed at providing scribes with the expertise for copying funerary and magical texts in tombs and on funerary objects, including the papyri of the Book of the Dead (Goelet 2010). We do not have clear evidence of Book of the Dead texts used for didactic purposes; their sacrality and divine origin did not lend itself to such a purpose. However, other kinds of texts of religious and magical character were included in miscellanies for didactic exercises, and in a few cases, excerpts of the Book of the Dead have been found on ostraca too (e.g., BM EA 29511; Demarée 2002, 25, Table 74). The Book of the Dead extracts on ostraca were anyway much less common than those occurring on papyrus, and it is difficult to say whether these specimens should be considered preliminary drafts employed as models in order to copy the final versions on tomb walls or whether they were used just for scribal exercises. A clear example of ostraca used as model texts for a tomb are those of TT 87 of the Eighteenth Dynasty, whose text sequence, written in non-retrograde columns of cursive hieroglyphs, is the same as that found on the walls of the tomb itself and includes funerary spells of the Coffin Texts and Book of the Dead corpus (Lüscher 2015). In this specific case, Lüscher was referring to *Zwischen-Vorlage*, namely, an intermediate textual model between those kept in the archive or library of the temple and the final version of the text as found in the tomb. It is therefore interesting to note how cursive hieroglyphs were used both for the master copy and for the final version of the text on tomb walls. This is, however, not the case for other tombs whose walls were painted with monumental hieroglyphs, where it is less probable that these *Zwischen-Vorlagen* were written in cursive hieroglyphs or hieratic and then transformed into full hieroglyphs, which would have been rather complicated for copyists. Probably, master-copies in full hieroglyphs existed as well, although they have not been found; many figurative and textual ostraca found in tombs seem instead to have served as secondary copies, studies, or exercises made on the basis of already existing tomb paintings and decorations (Haring 2015).

CONCLUSIONS

Even when agreeing in interpreting *Totenbuch-Kursive* as not different from the cursive hieroglyphic writing attested in non–Book of the Dead sources, one still needs to deal with its interrelationship with hieratic and monumental hieroglyphs in order to understand whether it develops from one or from the other. In a recent article, E. Graefe (2015, 123) has proposed to consider cursive hieroglyphs as "abbreviated forms of hieroglyphs, which stand independently from hieratic" (*Abkürzungsformen von Hieroglyphen, die unabhängig vom Hieratischen entstanden*). This would imply, as Graefe also writes, that Book of the Dead texts were originally written in hieroglyphs and that the cursive script is a consequence of the difficulty of drawing, with a pen and ink, detailed monumental hieroglyphs on papyrus. Moreover, texts in cursive script could derive only from master copies written either in full or cursive hieroglyphs. According to this theory, cursive hieroglyphs should be considered as a simplification of full hieroglyphs more than as a less cursive variant of them, if compared to hieratic. Many cursive hieroglyphic signs representing humans and animals, such as the eagle for ꜣ (G1), sꜣ- and bꜣ-birds (G39, G29), the seated man (A1), and king (A41), are much more similar to full hieroglyphs than to hieratic. On the other hand, a number of cursive signs are instead much closer to hieratic (for instance, the pꜣ-bird (G40); Graefe 2015, 123) so that it is difficult to define which one of the two scripts, monumental hieroglyphs or hieratic, had the bigger influence on the cursive hieroglyphs employed also for Book of the Dead texts. Similar evidence comes from an already mentioned study of the cursive hieroglyphs (Ali 2001), where a few Book of the Dead papyri have been selected to produce a sample of a paleography of cursive hieroglyphs; the high number of variants of one sign within the same papyrus, as one can note in the comparative table at the end of the article (Ali 2001, 15–19), shows not only the high occurrence of hieratic mixed with cursive hieroglyphs but also how different scribes were working on the same papyrus. In particular, the seated man (A1) mostly occurs in cursive forms, while the jar stand (W11) and the man with stick (A24) are attested only in hieratic in the Book of the Dead papyri used in the table (Ali 2001, 14, 20). Ali individuates at least two hieroglyphs—*p* (Q3) and *k* (V31)—for distinguishing cursive hieroglyphs from hieratic scripts, since in the former they appear as full hieroglyphs.

My impression is that the same high degree of variation that we find in the layout, spell selection, vignettes, and length of the Book of the Dead tradition on papyrus is mirrored also in the so-called *Totenbuch-Kursive* script. For this reason, it is difficult to establish a category of papyri of the Book of the Dead written in "pure" *Totenbuch-Kursive,* as also pointed out in a previous study (Graefe 2015, 122–123).

Totenbuch-Kursive basically represents *one* of the many occurrences of a more cursive variant of monumental hieroglyphs, which is attested since at least the Middle Kingdom, and that the static character of this script does not allow much variation of forms in relation to time or local traditions, except for individual scribal hands and archaizing features of certain signs. The fact that Book of the Dead papyri written in cursive hieroglyphs almost always also include hieratic signs as well as painted variants of monumental hieroglyphs shows that probably *Totenbuch-Kursive* was a very fluid variant of monumental hieroglyphs and that scribes working on those documents possessed high skills and self-confidence in deciding which hieroglyphs and in which parts of the text to write more or less cursive variants compared to the "standard" cursive forms probably found on the model papyri, which were written either in monumental or cursive hieroglyphs as well as in hieratic.

BIBLIOGRAPHY

Allam, M. 2009. "Die Kursivhierolyphen: Sind sie Hieroglyphen oder Hieratisch? Zur Stellung der Kursivhieroglyphen innerhalb der ägyptischen Schriftgeschichte." *ASAE* 81:33–37.

Ali, M.-S. 2001. "Die Kursivhieroglyphen: eine paläographische Betrachtung." *GM* 180:9–21.

Berger el-Naggar, C. 2004. "Des Textes des Pyramides sur papyrus dans les archives du temple funéraire de Pépy Ier." In *D'un monde à l'autre: Textes des Pyramides et Textes des Sarcophages*, edited by S. Bickel and B. Mathieu, 85–90. BdE 139. Cairo.

Demarée, R. J. 2002. *Ramesside Ostraca*. London.

Donnat, S. 2012. "Donner à voir la différence: Détail et singularité dans la chapelle de Khnoumhotep II à Béni Hassan (XIXe siècle av.n.è., Égypte)." *Ktèma* 37:145–159.

Gardiner, A. H. 1955. *The Ramesseum Papyri*. Oxford.

Gauthier, H. 1913. *Cercueils anthropoïdes des prêtres de Montou*. 2 vols. Cairo.

Graefe, E. 2015. "Über den parallelen Gebrauch von hieroglyphischen, kursivhieroglyphischen und hieratischen Schriftzeichen in Totentexten." In *Ägyptologische "Binsen"-Weisheiten I–II. Neue Forschungen und Methoden der Hieratistik. Akten zweier Tagungen in Mainz im April 2011 und März 2013*, edited by U. Verhoeven, 119–142. AAWLM 14. Stuttgart. http://aku.uni-mainz.de/hieratic-studies-online/.

Goelet, O., Jr. 2010. "Observations on Copying and the Hieroglyphic Tradition in the Production of the Book of the Dead." In *Offerings to the Discerning Eye: An Egyptological Medley in Honor of Jack A. Josephson*, edited by S. H. D'Auria, 121–132. Leiden.

Haring, B. J. J. 2006. *The Tomb of Sennedjem (TT1) in Deir el-Medina: Palaeography*. PH 2. Cairo.

Haring, B. J. J. 2015. "Hieratic drafts for hieroglyphic texts?" In *Ägyptologische "Binsen"-Weisheiten I–II. Neue Forschungen und Methoden der Hieratistik. Akten zweier Tagungen in Mainz im April 2011 und März 2013*, edited by U. Verhoeven, 67–84. AAWLM 14. Stuttgart. http://aku.uni-mainz.de/hieratic-studies-online/.

Lenzo Marchese, G. 2004. "La vignette initiale dans les papyrus funéraires de la Troisième Période intermédiaire." *BSEG* 26:43–62.

Lenzo, G. 2010. "The Two Funerary Papyri of Queen Nedjmet (P. BM EA 10490 and P. BM EA 10541 + Louvre E. 6258)." *BMSAES* 15:63–83.

Lepsius, C. R. 1867. *Älteste Texte des Todtenbuchs nach Sarkophagen des altägyptischen Reichs im Berliner Museum*. Berlin.

Lüscher, B. 2015. "Kursivhieroglyphische Ostraka als Textvorlagen: der (Glücks-)Fall TT 87." In *Ägyptologische "Binsen"-Weisheiten I–II. Neue Forschungen und Methoden der Hieratistik. Akten zweier Tagungen in Mainz im April 2011 und März 2013*, edited by U. Verhoeven, 85–117. AAWLM 14. Stuttgart. http://aku.uni-mainz.de/hieratic-studies-online/.

McDonald, J. 1981. "An Eighteenth-Dynasty Linen in the Museum of Fine Arts, Boston." *JEA* 67:56–60.

Milde, H. 1991. *The Vignettes in the Book of the Dead of Neferrenpet.* EU 7. Leiden.

Möller, G. 1909. *Hieratische Paläographie: die ägyptische Buchschrift in ihrer Entwicklung von der fünften Dynastie bis zur römischen Kaiserzeit.* Vol. 1. Leipzig.

Morenz, L. D. 1996. *Beiträge zur Schriftlichkeitskultur im Mittleren Reich und in der 2. Zwischenzeit.* ÄAT 29. Wiesbaden.

Munro, I. 1988. *Untersuchungen zu den Totenbuch-Papyri der 18. Dynastie.* London.

Munro, I. 1994. *Die Totenbuchhandschriften der 18. Dynastie im Ägyptischen Museum Cairo.* ÄA 54. Wiesbaden.

Munro, I. 1995. *Das Totenbuch des Bak-su (pKM 1970.37/pBrocklehurst) aus der Zeit Amenophis' II.* HÄT 2. Wiesbaden.

Munro, I. 1997. *Das Totenbuch des Nacht-Amun aus der Ramessidenzeit (pBerlin P. 3002).* HÄT 4. Wiesbaden.

Munro, I., and J. Taylor. 2009. *Der Totenbuch-Papyrus der Ta-shep-en-Chonsu aus der spiten 25. Dynastie: (pMoskau Puschkin-Museum I, 1b, 121).* HÄT 10. Wiesbaden.

Naville, É. 1886. *Das ägyptische Todtenbuch der XVIII. bis XX. Dynastie.* Berlin.

Niwiński, A. 1989. *Studies on the Illustrated Theban Funerary Papyri of the 11th and 10th centuries B.C.* OBO 86. Freiburg.

Parkinson, R. B., and S. Quirke. 1995. *Papyrus.* London.

Ragazzoli, C. Forthcoming. *L'épigraphie secondaire dans les tombes thébaines.* Paris.

Ragazzoli, C. 2017. *La grotte des scribes à Deir el-Bahari: La tombe MMA 504 et ses graffiti.* MIFAO 135. Cairo.

Regulski, I. 2016. "The Origins and Early Development of Writing in Egypt." Retrieved from www.oxfordhandbooks.com/view/10.1093/oxfordhb/9780199935413.001.0001/oxfordhb-9780199935413-e-61

Ronsecco, P. 1996. *Due Libri dei Morti del principio del Nuovo Regno: Il lenzuolo funerario della principessa Ahmosi e le tele del Sa-Nesu Ahmosi.* CMET 1:7. Turin.

Sadek, A.-A. F. 1985. *Contribution à l'étude de l'Amdouat: Les variantes tardives du Livre de l'Amdouat dans les papyrus du Musée du Caire.* OBO 65. Freiburg.

Schlott, A. 1989. *Schrift und Schreiber im Alten Ägypten.* Munich.

Shorter, A. W. 1934. "A Leather Manuscript of the Book of the Dead in the British Museum." *JEA* 20:33–40.

Taylor, J. H., ed. 2010. *Journey through the Afterlife: Ancient Egyptian Book of the Dead.* London.

Verhoeven, U. 2015. "Stand und Aufgaben der Erforschung des Hieratischen und der Kursivhieroglyphen." In *Ägyptologische "Binsen"-Weisheiten I–II. Neue Forschungen und Methoden der Hieratistik. Akten zweier Tagungen in Mainz im April 2011 und März 2013,* edited by U. Verhoeven, 23–63. AAWLM 14. Stuttgart. http://aku.uni-mainz.de/hieratic-studies-online/.

Warburton, D. 2007. *The Egyptian Amduat: The Book of the Hidden Chamber.* Zurich.

Zauzich, K.-T. 2002. "Demotische Musterbriefe." In *Acts of the Seventh International Conference of Demotic Studies: Copenhagen, 23–27 August 1999,* edited by K. Ryholt, 395–401. Copenhagen.

CHAPTER IV.6

SOME ISSUES IN AND PERHAPS A NEW METHODOLOGY FOR ABNORMAL HIERATIC

KOENRAAD DONKER VAN HEEL

THE term "abnormal hieratic" was first coined by Francis Llewellyn Griffith (1909, 3:11). This may perhaps be the most apt description ever, although not all authors are equally happy with it, preferring terms such as "late cursive hieratic" (Martin 2007, 26) or "Kursivhieratisch" (Vittmann 2015). The problem with terms such as these, however, is that "hieratic" already implies a degree of cursiveness, and this was the exact reason why the Egyptians started using it. They wanted to write their documents more quickly than before, so they resorted to more cursive forms, which we call "hieratic."

Abnormal hieratic is the ultimate, highly abbreviated administrative hieratic writing used in the south of Egypt during the Twenty-fifth and Twenty-sixth Dynasties. The language used—and especially the legal phrases—strongly reminds one of the language we know from New Kingdom Deir el-Medina. Griffith was the first to note that it was clearly not Demotic and therefore had to stem from a different scribal tradition. He also perceived that texts written in abnormal hieratic were actually already known from the Twenty-second Dynasty and even earlier (e.g., Möller 1921). Until recently, the general view was that this script was confined to the Theban area, meaning that texts have sometimes been provenanced to Thebes even if no provenance was known (e.g., P. BM EA 10906 and 10907; for references to these and other inventory numbers mentioned in this study, see the Leuven DAHT database at trismegistos.org or Vittmann 2015). However, abnormal hieratic texts—or some of its precursors—have now been found in Thebes, Abydos, el-Hibeh, Elephantine, the Dakhla Oasis, Qasr Ibrim, Heracleopolis, and perhaps even the Fayyum. One other notion that has recently been abandoned is that abnormal hieratic was used exclusively for administrative purposes. The discovery of P. Queen's College (in 1997), which will be published in the foreseeable future by

Hans-Werner Fischer-Elfert (large literary text from the reign of Piye or Taharqa) and Günter Vittmann (large account from the reign of Taharqa), has actually raised the number of literary abnormal hieratic texts to two. The overall number of known abnormal hieratic texts has also risen considerably. Comparing an earlier list provided by Vittmann (1982) with the recent chronological list provided by the same author (Vittmann 2015, 411–421), the number rises from a mere thirty-seven items to well over two hundred, and many, many more if all the material from, for example, the Dakhla Oasis and el-Hibeh becomes available. If we then also include, for example, fragments published by Spiegelberg (1898, pls. 39–41 (ostraca) and 46 (papyrus fragments)), as well as the enigmatic O. MMA 19.3.24 (Donker van Heel 2016) and P. Louis de Vaucelles, the number rises once again (Figure IV.6.1). The latter papyrus was sold at auction by Sotheby's London only in November 2015. It is an account from years 12 and 13 in the reign of Taharqa, comprising fourteen sheets that are mostly written on both sides.

Much has already been done in this domain in the past hundred and so years, but listing these achievements would take up too much space. For previous work by, for example, Georg Möller, Francis Griffith, Jaroslav Černý, I. E. S. Edwards, Richard Parker, and especially Michel Malinine, whose brilliant analysis was carried on by Sven Vleeming, Annie Gasse, Bernadette Menu, Günter Vittmann, and Koenraad Donker van Heel, to name some of the most prolific authors, the reader is referred to the excellent overview provided by Vittmann (2015). At present, however, there are only two authors engaged in the systematic publication of abnormal hieratic texts, namely Günter Vittmann and Koenraad Donker van Heel, suggesting that a lack of manpower is actually one of the most serious issues in this domain. As was proposed earlier by Donker van Heel (2015a), authors working with abnormal hieratic material have a real responsibility to train a new generation. In Leiden, this ambition is taking shape. Two students, to wit, Steffie van Gompel and Petra Hoogenboom, have been studying abnormal hieratic for the past four years and are now both working on their own publications (P. Louvre E 7849 + 7857 A–B and P. Louvre E 7859 and a study on (the roots of) abnormal hieratic). They will also assist Donker van Heel in the publication of P. Louis de Vaucelles, together with Robert Kade (Heidelberg), Vincent Morel (Geneva), Guy Nicholls (Liverpool), and Cary Martin (London). But clearly much more needs to be done to keep abnormal hieratic studies afloat. Although more initiatives are underway, such as, for example, the publication of P. Prachov by Malthe Römer (2016), the abnormal hieratic Turin papyri by Sven Vleeming, and the texts from el-Hibeh by Matthias Müller (2009), some of these projects were initiated decades ago, without any tangible results to date. In the meantime, much of this material is not readily available to other authors. In the case of the material from el-Hibeh, a delay is quite understandable, however, given the many hundreds of fragments and texts contained in the archive. In view of the difficulty of some of the above texts, hieraticists can, of course, hardly be expected to publish their results within five years, but ten years should be the maximum individual authors should be allowed to hold exclusive publication rights. One obvious solution would be for the collections housing these texts to make them available online in high-resolution color

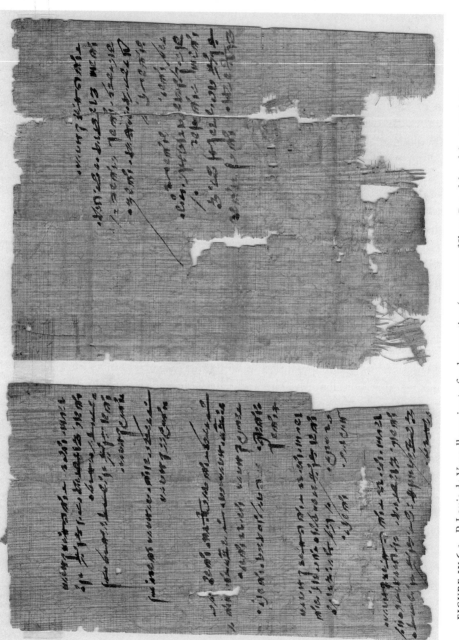

FIGURE IV.6.1. P. Louis de Vaucelles prior to final mounting (courtesy of Ilona Regulski of the British Museum).

photographs and to invite authors to contribute through what one might call *open invitation expert sourcing*. This would require a new approach to publishing papyri—in other words, a novel methodology—but some of the issues in abnormal hieratic are clearly too complicated to be solved by individual authors on their own.

Before going into some of the other issues in this domain, of which there are many, this chapter first takes a closer look at what makes abnormal hieratic so different from early Demotic. It then investigates what happened when these scribal traditions were used side by side in Thebes, ultimately leading to the demise of abnormal hieratic during the reign of Ahmose II. This was most probably the result of a conscious administrative reform, as was convincingly argued by Martin (2007).

Once it establishes a notion of what abnormal hieratic really is and why it is so important that Egyptologists should work with this material, the chapter addresses some of the issues described earlier (Donker van Heel 2015a). To conclude, it outlines an ambition for the future, namely, the design of a Leiden-based abnormal hieratic database that should include all published sources, as well as multiple educational features to facilitate the study of abnormal hieratic for students from all over the world. Although some learning tools have been online for some time now (such as the freely available online Donker van Heel 2013), technology can help us to take bolder steps than envisaged a mere twenty years ago.

ABNORMAL HIERATIC VERSUS EARLY DEMOTIC

Much has already been written about the rise of Demotic—presumably in Sais in the Delta—where in the eighth and seventh centuries, it developed out of the late cursive hieratic used in the north, while scribes in the south of Egypt still wrote abnormal hieratic. Whether this northern hieratic that gave birth to early Demotic was highly cursive (Malinine 1953–1983, 1:vii–xxi.) or slightly less cursive (el-Aguizy 1992, 94) is not investigated here. The only thing that is relevant at this point is that from the reign of Psammetichus I onward, Demotic texts appear to journey southward, for example, P. Rylands 1 and 2 from year 21 of Psammetichus I (644 BCE). These papyri were found in el-Hibeh and were published by Griffith (1909). Until recently, these were believed to be the oldest early Demotic papyri known at present (although they still contain an oath, which is an abnormal hieratic feature), but this honor now belongs to a papyrus from year 16 found at el-Lahun (Vittmann 2015, 383n3). The oldest document showing clear early Demotic influences is Stela Louvre C 101, however, from regnal year 8 of Psammetichus I (Malinine 1975). It was found at Saqqara.

Under the Twenty-sixth (Saite) Dynasty, much was happening in Egypt in the administrative, political, legal and military domains. After subduing all the local potentates in the Delta with the help of foreign (Greek) mercenaries, Psammetichus I still faced the problem of conquering the south of the country and building a kingdom from what had been a fragmented state for centuries on end. For that, he would need an efficient administration based on a uniform legal system. Through diplomacy rather than battle, he managed to install his daughter Nitocris in Thebes as the next in line to the very influential position of Divine Adoratress of Amun. Thus, he effectively gained control over Theban politics, although he probably could never have achieved this without the help of local strongmen, such as Montuemhat (Martin 2007, 25). The most revealing early Demotic source describing this period is P. Rylands 9 (Griffith 1909; but see now Vittmann 1998). Although the text was written under Darius I, it describes the fortunes and especially the misfortunes of a once powerful priestly family from the reign of Psammetichus I onward. But it also provides an insightful account into some of the reforms carried out under the Saite kings. The implementation of early Demotic across all of Egypt would—even if we do not know exactly how this was achieved in the end— seem to fit seamlessly into this pattern of Saite reforms, which would be brought to an effective conclusion by Ahmose II, under whose reign abnormal hieratic documents were phased out of use. He could have simply issued a decree stating that from a specific date onward, abnormal hieratic legal documents would no longer be admissible as evidence in a court of law.

However, as was seen above, while early Demotic Papyrus Rylands 1 and 2 and Stela Louvre C 101 were making their appearance on the legal language stage, scribes in Thebes were still using their own cursive administrative script, abnormal hieratic. In its most extreme form, this may actually have become so cursive that reading it would have been cumbersome even for half-trained Theban scribes, but almost certainly for scribes in the Delta. Still, abnormal hieratic is an entirely logical and organic development out of Ramesside administrative hieratic, via later texts, such as the Oracular Decrees (which are literary rather than administrative), P. Reinhardt, and P. Prachov. It is just that somewhere along the way, the southern administrative hieratic took the wrong turn. What is, however, very important to remember is that with this southern scribal tradition there also came a purely southern legal tradition, defined by the manner in which the scribes would formulate legal terminology. In short: scribes from the north had an entirely different way of phrasing their legal formulae than scribes from the south. Thus, it is actually very easy to discern between, for example, abnormal hieratic and early Demotic marital property arrangements, sales, or land leases (see what follows), simply because the northern and southern approach to legal formulae differed so much. In general, however, one can say that the early Demotic clauses are often more precise and also more flexible. However, Martin (2007, 28) noted that many abnormal hieratic legal documents were phrased precisely enough to suit their purpose. On the other hand, an antiquated clause saying that one would not listen to any claimant's statement (*bn sḏm=tw rꜣ=f*) in the scribal office, which is known from abnormal hieratic—and was shown to be derived from Ramesside administrative hieratic by Černý (1945, 41ne)—never occurs in early Demotic texts.

The first author to give a very clear-cut—and brilliant—overview of what exactly is the difference between abnormal hieratic and early Demotic was Sven Vleeming.

In a seminal article (Vleeming 1981), he investigated both scribal traditions from different perspectives, for example, layout and placement of the witness subscriptions. Although his article has now been superseded by new findings (see, e.g., Donker van Heel 1995, 48–62, and the insightful comments of Martin 2007, 33–34n40, on the layout of a document probably being one of the least suitable criterions to discern between early Demotic and abnormal hieratic), it remains mandatory reading for anyone aspiring to work in this domain. The best way to illustrate—and understand—the difference between abnormal hieratic and early Demotic, however, may be by simply looking at the level of standardization in both scribal traditions. And here we see that early Demotic—or Demotic in general—seems much more advanced, which to the mind of this author suggests that whereas abnormal hieratic was the result of an organic development, Demotic actually may have been subjected to a conscious design—or standardization—process. This standardization extends not just to the legal formulary (more precise in Demotic) but also to the number of ways in which a word or sign could be written. Take, for instance, the writing of 'Imn "Amun." Right from the start, the early Demotic scribes had settled for one uniform writing (Table IV.6.1.1). By contrast, the abnormal hieratic

Table IV.6.1. List of Early Demotic (1.1) and Abnormal Hieratic (1.2–1.9) Signs. (Note that 1.4 is damaged at the left.)

scribes could more or less make their own choice, because there were six different ways to write *ʾImn* (Table IV.6.1.2–1.7).

If we look at the legal formulary, the same occurs. To denote a land lease, the early Demotic scribes used the verb *shn* "to commission, entrust," which quickly acquired the meaning "to lease" (or at least has done so for Demotists), but the strange thing is actually that *shn* was still widely used in New Kingdom Deir el-Medina—in Ramesside administrative hieratic, being the direct precursor to abnormal hieratic—for "to commission, entrust," but apparently never found its way into abnormal hieratic legal formulary. This may, however, also be due to the relative paucity of the sources.

In the abnormal hieratic land leases published so far, such as P. Louvre E 7851 recto, we see that scribes again had an ample selection, namely *rdi i sk3* "give to plow," *rdi* "give," *šp i sk3* "receive to plow," and *šp* "receive" (Figure IV.6.2). Some of these terms are very imprecise from a legal point of view, but again both *rdi i sk3* (O. DeM 958) and *šp* (LRL 36 = P. BM EA 10412) in the context of leasing can be traced back to Ramesside administrative hieratic from Deir el-Medina.

If we look at documents pertaining to sales (for the difference between the abnormal hieratic and early Demotic sales, see Menu 1988), we will quickly see that the early Demotic sales clause is clear-cut: *di=k mtr ḥ3t.ṱ=i n p3 ḥḏ n (object sold)* "You have

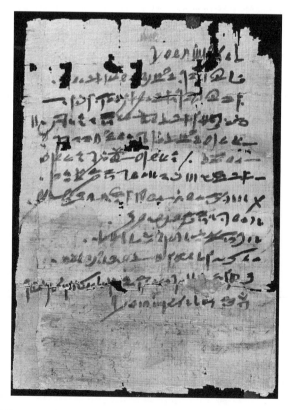

FIGURE IV.6.2. P. Louvre E 7851 recto (courtesy of Geneviève Pierrat-Bonnefois of the Louvre).

satisfied my heart with the silver for (object sold)," without mentioning the price. Abnormal hieratic sales always mention the price, or, to quote Martin (2007, 29): "So, in other words, the document ceases to be a record of an actual 'transaction' as such, i.e. the handing over of a sum of money, and becomes the record of a legal procedure, the transfer of ownership and of legal title. There has been [in Demotic] a conceptual step-up in the underlying principle." In the satisfaction clause of sales, the abnormal hieratic scribes also refer to the heart being satisfied, although they phrase it slightly differently, namely *m ib hr(=i)* "me being satisfied of heart." The reason for adding the suffix *=i* in this clause is that when the same clause is used for several persons acting as a single legal party, it is clearly written *m ib hr=n* even if one would seem more comfortable with *m ib(=i) hr* and *m ib=n hr*. However, the combination of *ḥ3t* and *mtr* that would become part of the standard early Demotic sales clause was, in fact, also used side by side by the abnormal hieratic scribes, which again illustrates the lack of standardization in this script. For instance, in P. Louvre E 3228 etiq. F carton B line 7 (year 5 of Taharqa), the declaring party states: *iw mtr ḥ3t(=i)* "whereas my heart is satisfied" where one would have expected *m ib hr(=i)*. Note, however, that this text is a receipt rather than a sale. The inventory number Louvre E 3228 actually covers eight abnormal hieratic papyri, two of which have never been published since they were purchased for the Louvre in the nineteenth century (Donker van Heel 2015b).

So did the abnormal hieratic scribes wholly refrain from trying to standardize their script? In fact, it appears they did not, but one has the impression that whenever they did, this may have been the result of an organic, natural development rather than conscious choice, which seems like another nice way to describe abnormal hieratic as a script. There are two signs that, as far as this author's knowledge goes, could perhaps qualify as examples of standardization in abnormal hieratic. The first is the so-called multifunctional sign, which apparently had never solicited any comments before it was first described (Donker van Heel 2013, 2015a). It looks deceivingly simple (Table IV.6.1.8), but it served a large number of purposes: the *t* + the *sp* sign in *ḥ3.t-sp*, the abbreviated quail chick (Gardiner Z7), *t* + *3* (feminine article), the aleph *3*, the seated man + duck for *s3* "son," the second part of *p3* (masculine article), the *t* + egg as the female divine determinative, *'Imn*, the tusk (Gardiner F18), the phonetic complement of *šp* "receive," *qt* "kite," and the seated man in *rmṯ* "man," and no doubt other uses of this sign that will surface in the future. The similarity of this sign to the early Demotic masculine article *p3*—and its possible implications—raises another of the many issues in this domain: has the difficulty of the script discouraged mainstream Egyptology from venturing into thinking about questions such as these? In the present situation, only a few authors are facing far too many issues in palaeography, lexicography, and prosopography (compare Vittmann 2013).

The same applies to one of the simplest abnormal hieratic signs (Table IV.6.1.9). It was used to write the book roll determinative, the walking legs determinative, the flesh determinative, sometimes even for a *p*, the noble seated on a chair with flagellum (Gardiner A51), the seated man determinative, and *sp-sn* "twice." Just like the multifunctional sign, this rather looks like an organic development rather than conscious choice,

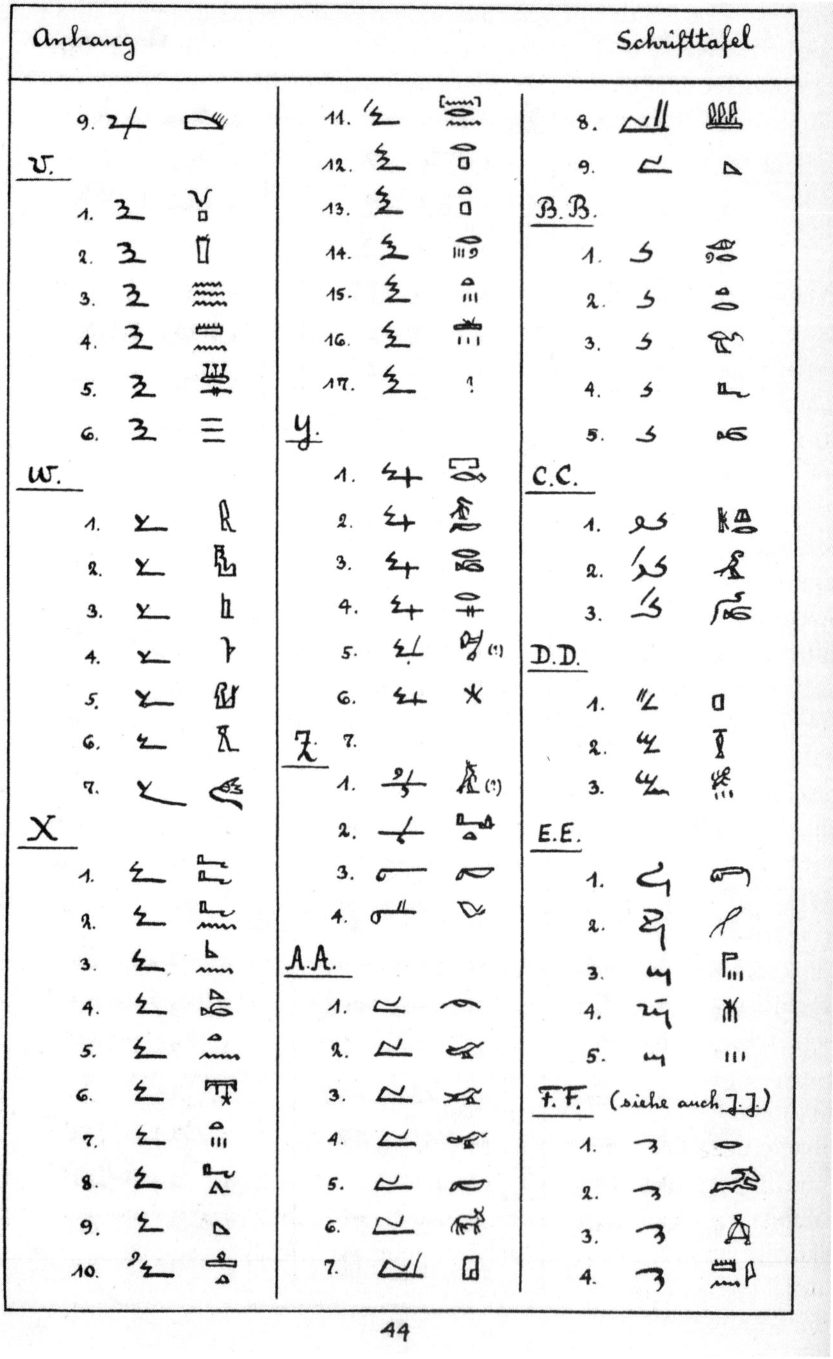

FIGURE IV.6.3. A page from Erichsen's (1937) *Schrifttafel* showing the standardization of signs by early Demotic scribes.

although we have no way of knowing. But this is where the abnormal hieratic scribes stopped, whereas the (early) Demotic scribes took standardization to the extreme, as can be taken from Erichsen (1937, 44; Figure IV.6.3). The ligatures and signs that would acquire an entirely different look in abnormal hieratic seem to have been rigorously brought under a single header in (early) Demotic.

The Interaction of Abnormal Hieratic and Early Demotic in Thebes

We do not know how exactly early Demotic was implemented in Thebes. We only know that it was and that the last line of abnormal hieratic occurs in the witness list of the early Demotic land lease P. Louvre E 7837, which was written in 535 BCE. What we can say is that for some decades, both scribal systems were used side by side in Thebes and that they influenced each other, although this influence was mostly exerted by early Demotic on abnormal hieratic rather than vice versa. This suggests that even if there never was a decree by Ahmose II to ban abnormal hieratic documents as valid legal documents in a court of law from a specific date onward, early Demotic could in specific cases have more or less imposed itself on individual scribes, for which there is some evidence (see what follows), simply because it was more efficient. Maybe also clients would be increasingly more likely to be asking the Theban scribes for a legal document after the latest fashion. One has the feeling that the human tendency for going with the latest trends may have played a role here as well, even if we cannot prove it. Thus unfolded a three-stage process by which abnormal hieratic was supplanted by early Demotic, which has been well described by Martin (2007, 30). We can actually see Theban abnormal hieratic scribes trying to cope with the new trend in writing.

For instance, in the abnormal hieratic marital property arrangement P. Louvre E 7849 + 7857 A–B (590 BCE), the scribe used the first line exclusively for the dating formula, as was the custom in abnormal hieratic (Vleeming 1981, 39; compare, however, Donker van Heel 1995, 55–56). The son of this scribe wrote a marital property arrangement in 549 BCE (he clearly learned the trade in his father's office), the writing of which is stunningly similar to the writing in the document written years before by his father, except that the son continued with the text in the first line directly after the dating formula, which was the early Demotic custom. Should one ascribe this to the growing influence of early Demotic, or is it just a fluke?

Some scribes, however, appear to have made a conscious switch from the old tradition to the new, only betraying their roots through minor slips of the pen. P. Louvre E 7844 is an early Demotic land lease from 555 BCE. The layout selected for this text—the so-called narrow type—came from the abnormal hieratic tradition (Vleeming 1981, 37; but compare Martin 2007, 33–34n40), which is also suggested by the fact that the first line was reserved for the dating formula only. The subscriptions of the witnesses were written directly below the main text, which is another abnormal hieratic characteristic. The text itself is in perfect early Demotic, but in line 7 the scribe suddenly writes *rn* "name" in a curious mix of both abnormal hieratic (*rn* ligature) and early Demotic (seated man with hand to mouth determinative). A telling fact or a curious coincidence? Note, however, that what we believe to be the early Demotic seated man with hand to mouth determinative actually already occurs, for example, in the hieratic P. Abbott from the reign of Ramesses IX (Möller 1927, 3).

P. Louvre 7845 A, a land lease from 554 BCE, seems to be a certain case of an abnormal hieratic scribe who embraced the new scribal tradition. The text is of the so-called wide type—which may or may not be an early Demotic feature—and it is written in early Demotic, although specific words are in perfect abnormal hieratic (Donker van Heel 1995, 256). In the clause about the division of the harvest between the landlord and the lessee, the scribe even used the term *wḏꜣ.t* "remainder," which never occurs in early Demotic land leases, but is common in their abnormal hieratic counterparts (Donker van Heel 2016, 107–109). To this author, the fact that the scribe of P. Louvre E 7845 A wrote what is probably the most clumsy harvest division clause ever is, in fact, relevant, because it shows that even if the Theban scribes worked with early Demotic templates, which would have been the most sensible thing to do (as suggested by Martin [2007, 30]), he clearly had not brought it with him when he wrote this text, reverting to what he remembered from abnormal hieratic, but not getting it exactly right.

Two Theban scribes from an important scribal family symbolize how early Demotic managed to impose itself on their local writing tradition. In the family tree (Table IV.6.2), we see five scribes from two generations. The first thing that strikes one is that two of the sons of Petehorresen were trained in abnormal hieratic and two—probably younger brothers—wrote early Demotic. Just imagine the interesting conversations these men must have had together! Of these five men, Petehorresen and his son Peteamunip are by far the most intriguing because the documents they wrote clearly show how early Demotic—slowly but inevitably—made its mark on them.

Although this unique case has been investigated before (Donker van Heel 1994; summarized by Martin 2007, 28–29), this study cannot be complete without them. As just

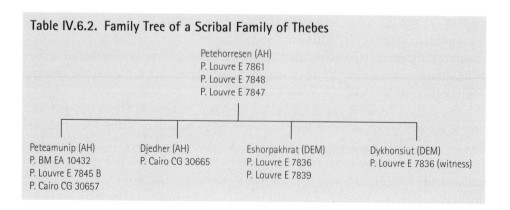

Table IV.6.2. Family Tree of a Scribal Family of Thebes

Petehorresen (AH)
P. Louvre E 7861
P. Louvre E 7848
P. Louvre E 7847

Peteamunip (AH)	Djedher (AH)	Eshorpakhrat (DEM)	Dykhonsiut (DEM)
P. BM EA 10432	P. Cairo CG 30665	P. Louvre E 7836	P. Louvre E 7836 (witness)
P. Louvre E 7845 B		P. Louvre E 7839	
P. Cairo CG 30657			

seen, the father, Petehorresen, wrote three abnormal hieratic texts: P. Louvre E 7861 (568 BCE), 7848 (559 BCE), and 7847 (552 BCE). P. Louvre E 7861 is of the narrow type, but the witness list is placed on the verso of the papyrus, almost directly behind *ḏd* "has said" on the recto, which is a regular feature in early Demotic, but otherwise unknown in abnormal hieratic, except in the case of the abnormal hieratic P. BM EA 10113 (570 BCE); the placement of the witness list is another example of the rising influence of early Demotic (Vleeming 1981, 43–44). Note, however, that the vertical stroke immediately following the initial *ḏd* at the beginning of line 2—an abnormal hieratic feature, which is not written in early Demotic—is missing in P. Louvre E 7861, while being present in 7848 line 1 and 7847 line 2. His decision to lay out P. Louvre E 7848 in a wide format may also be due to early Demotic influence, as is his writing of the initial *ḏd* immediately following the dating formula in line 1. Note, by contrast, that both P. Louvre E 7861 and 7847 show the expected abnormal hieratic narrow type layout, reserving line 1 for the dating, line 2 starting with the initial *ḏd*. One certain influence of early Demotic is in the way this scribe writes the name *'Imn* in all three texts: P. Louvre E 7861 line 11, 7848 lines 2 (twice) and 8, and 7847 lines 2 and 9 (in the name of his own father). But in the latter text, the same scribe also writes *Imn* once in abnormal hieratic (line 3), neatly conveying some of the confusion he must have felt at times. His son Peteamunip, who worked in his father's office, signs P. Louvre E 7847 as a witness, but he writes *'Imn* in his own name again in abnormal hieratic.

By far the most interesting early Demotic influence is Petehorresen's creative use of the early Demotic sales clause *dỉ=k mtr ḥꜣt.ṱ=ỉ n* "You have satisfied my heart with" in both P. Louvre E 7861 and 7847, albeit adapted to the legal situation. This ability to adapt is precisely what made early Demotic such an effective writing system.

As has been suggested earlier, his son Peteamunip wrote the abnormal hieratic land lease P. BM EA 10432 in 556/555 BCE, although his name is lost in the lacuna (Donker van Heel 1994, 122; the same happened with the name of his father in P. Louvre E 7861, but see Donker van Heel 1995, 243). In this text, he sometimes writes *'Imn* in abnormal hieratic (line 7) and sometimes in early Demotic (lines 3 and 7), just as his father did in P. Louvre E 7847. But apparently Peteamunip (or his father) had been watching his early Demotic colleagues closely, because Peteamunip also uses the verb *sḥn* "to commission, entrust" in line 9, which is not known from the abnormal hieratic land leases, but is a standard feature in their early Demotic counterparts.

P. Louvre E 7845 B, which was written after 554 BCE, is a mere fragment in abnormal hieratic. Again, Peteamunip's name is in the lacuna, save for a trace and his father's name, rendering the identification certain. But when he writes *'Imn* in line 4, it is in early Demotic. The spelling of the word *ḫpr* "to become" in the harvest clause in line 7, however, is still purely abnormal hieratic, namely *ḫpryꜣ*, which also occurs in P. BM EA 10432 line 11 (damaged, but sufficient traces left).

But Peteamunip's *piece de résistance* is undoubtedly P. Cairo CG 30657, written in 547 BCE. Here, we see how in the years after he wrote P. BM EA 10432 and P. Louvre E 7845 B, he had been studying really hard to learn how to write early Demotic. The result is a perfect hybrid between the two writing traditions. Note, for instance, how this scribe makes a very creative use of the early Demotic sales clause *dỉ=k mtr ḥȝt.ṱ=ỉ n*, a trick he obviously had learned in his father's office. The mix of abnormal hieratic and early Demotic in this text is such that authors have always had great trouble assigning it to either scribal tradition, but it is simply a hybrid (Donker van Heel 1994) written by a scribe intent on mastering the new scribal tradition. So was the demise of abnormal hieratic in the south of Egypt simply the result of individual scribes converting to the new trend? Only future research can tell.

AMBITION FOR THE FUTURE

Although the issues in abnormal hieratic are vast and not just confined to palaeography (see also Vittmann 2013)—at present, we still lack a dictionary and a *Namenbuch*, for example, and until very recently there were no learning tools at all—modern technology (digitization) allows us to open up new ways to approach the problem. The learning tools that are now freely available to the interested student (Donker van Heel and Golverdingen 2013a, 2013b, 2014; Donker van Heel 2013) were designed from the start as interim solutions. The palaeography (fascicles IV and V) also made available online—as are all the other online tools—is still awaiting corrections. But this is yesterday's technology.

At Leiden University, we are now in the design stage of a website plus database that should ultimately contain all published abnormal hieratic texts in high-resolution color photographs. By tagging all individual words and personal names, it will be possible to click on any single word to see its transcription, transliteration, and translation, including a link to a database containing all other occurrences of this word in other abnormal hieratic texts, thus creating an eternally extendable dictionary and *Namenbuch* in one (compare Vittmann 1987). During the second *Binsenweisheiten* conference in Mainz (2013), Erhart Graefe demonstrated the feasibility of such a tagging system, which has everything one could hope to expect from a great learning tool. Other features that will be included on this website are instructional videos on the basics of deciphering abnormal hieratic, all the relevant literature (requiring an open source policy in all of academia), the possibility of interacting with students, and an online flashcard system for learning individual signs and sign groups. A very promising prototype of the latter has recently been designed by Kaan Eraslan from the EPHE Paris. Both Graefe's and Eraslan's solutions will, however, require the help of a digital jack-of-all-trades, the necessary funding, and the cooperation of all collections housing abnormal hieratic papyri and ostraca. But ultimately, this website should become the platform for the future, containing everything students would want to know about abnormal hieratic. And more.

Postscript: To date, the *Very Easy Crash Course in Abnormal Hieratic* (see Donker van Heel 2013, 2015a) has been taught in Munich, Mainz, Heidelberg, Leipzig, and Los Angeles, but there is now a very promising follow-up initiative from Germany. Hans-Werner Fischer-Elfert from Leipzig University has informed this author that he intends to design a course of his own. This author is also grateful to Cary Martin for a critical appraisal of (the language of) this study.

BIBLIOGRAPHY

Aguizy, O. el-. 1992. "About the Origins of Early Demotic in Lower Egypt." In *Life in a Multi-Cultural Society: Egypt from Cambyses to Constantine and Beyond*, edited by J. H. Johnson, 91–102. SAOC 51. Chicago.

Černý, J. 1945. "The Will of Naunakhte and the Related Documents." *JEA* 31:29–53.

Donker van Heel, K. 1994. "The Lost Battle of Peteamonip Son of Petehorresne." In *Acta Demotica. Acts of the Fifth International Conference for Demotists. Pisa, 4th–8th September 1993*, edited by E. Bresciani, 115–124. EVO 17. Pisa.

Donker van Heel, K. 1995. "Abnormal Hieratic and Early Demotic Texts Collected by the Theban Choachytes in the Reign of Amasis: Papyri from the Louvre Eisenlohr Lot." 3 vols. PhD diss., Leiden.

Donker van Heel, K. 2013. *A Very Easy Crash Course in Abnormal Hieratic: Being a Step by Step Introduction to the Least Accessible of All Ancient Egyptian Scripts*. Leiden.

Donker van Heel, K. 2015a. "Abnormal Hieratic Is Not Dead; It Just Smells Funny." In *Ägyptologische "Binsen"-Weisheiten I–II. Neue Forschungen und Methoden der Hieratistik. Akten zweier Tagungen in Mainz im April 2011 und März 2013*, edited by U. Verhoeven, 371–381. AAWLM 14. Stuttgart. http://aku.uni-mainz.de/hieratic-studies-online/.

Donker van Heel, K. 2015b. "P. Louvre E 3228: Some Late Cursive Hieratic Gems from the Louvre." *JEA* 101:320–325.

Donker van Heel, K. 2016. "An Enigmatic Ostracon from the Metropolitan Museum of Art and Some Other Things." In *Sapientia Felicitas: Festschrift für Günter Vittmann zum 29. Februar 2016*, edited by S. L. Lippert, M. Schentuleit, and M.A . Stadler, 107–121. CENiM 14. Montpellier.

Donker van Heel, K., and J. Golverdingen. 2013a. *An Abnormal Hieratic Reading Book, with a Palaeography of Abnormal Hieratic Signs and Sign Groups, Vol. I: Papyri from London, Brooklyn, Cairo and Leiden*. Leiden.

Donker van Heel, K., and J. Golverdingen. 2013b. *An Abnormal Hieratic Reading Book, with a Palaeography of Abnormal Hieratic Signs and Sign Groups, Vol. II: Papyri from Paris*. Leiden.

Donker van Heel, K., and J. Golverdingen. 2014. *An Abnormal Hieratic Reading Book, with a Palaeography of Abnormal Hieratic Signs and Sign Groups, Vol. III: Papyri from Oxford, Turin, Vienna and Tablets from Egypt and Leiden*. Leiden.

Erichsen, W. 1937. *Demotische Lesestücke, I: Literarische Texte mit Glossar und Schrifttafel, 3. Heft, Schrifttafel*. Leipzig.

Griffith, F. Ll. 1909. *Catalogue of the Demotic Papyri in the John Rylands Library Manchester*. 3 vols. London.

Malinine, M. 1953–1983. *Choix de textes juridiques en hiératique "anormal" et en démotique*. 2 vols. BEHE SHP 300; RAPH 18. Paris.

Malinine, M. 1975. "Vente de tombes à l'époque Saïte." *RdE* 27:164–174.

Martin, C. J. 2007. "The Saite 'Demoticisation' of Southern Egypt." In *Literacy and the State in the Ancient Mediterranean*, edited by K. Lomas, R. D. Whitehouse, and J. B. Wilkins, 25–38. Specialist Studies on the Mediterranean 7. London.

Menu, B. 1988. "Les actes de vente en Égypte ancienne, particulièrement sous les rois Kouchites et Saïtes." *JEA* 74:165–181.

Möller, G. 1921. "Ein ägyptischer Schuldschein der zweiundzwanzigsten Dynastie." *SPAW* 15:298–304.

Möller, G. 1927. *Hieratische Paläographie: Die ägyptische Buchschrift in ihrer Entwicklung von der fünften Dynastie bis zur römischen Kaiserzeit. Zweiter Band: Von der Zeit Thutmosis' III. bis zum Ende der einundzwanzigsten Dynastie.* Leipzig.

Müller, M. 2009. "The 'el-Hibeh' Archive: Introduction and Preliminary Information." In *The Libyan Period in Egypt: Historical and Cultural Studies into the 21st–24th Dynasties, Proceedings of a Conference at Leiden University, 25–27 October 2007*, edited by G. P. F. Broekman, R. J. Demarée, and O. E. Kaper, 251–264. Leiden.

Römer, M. 2016. "Die Datierung des Papyrus Prachov und andere Merkwürdigkeiten desselben." *GM* 248:111–122.

Spiegelberg, W. 1898. *Hieratic Ostraka and Papyri Found by J. E. Quibbell in the Ramesseum, 1895–6.* BSAE/ERA 2* [extra volume]. London.

Vittmann, G. 1982. "Papyri, kursivhieratische." In *Lexikon der Ägyptologie* IV, edited by W. Helck and W. Westendorf, 748–750. Wiesbaden.

Vittmann, G. 1987. "Ein kursivhieratisches Wörterbuch." In *Aspects of Demotic Lexicography. Acts of the Second International Conference for Demotic Studies, Leiden, 19–21 September 1984*, edited by S. P. Vleeming, 149–151. StudDem 1. Leuven.

Vittmann, G. 1998. *Der demotische Papyrus Rylands 9.* 2 vols. ÄAT 38. Wiesbaden.

Vittmann, G. 2013. "Kursivhieratische Texte aus sprachlicher und onomastischer Sicht." In *Perspektiven einer corpusbasierten historischen Linguistik und Philologie. Internationale Tagung des Akademienvorhabens "Altägyptisches Wörterbuch" an der Berlin-Brandenburgischen Akademie der Wissenschaften, 12.–13. Dezember 2011*, edited by I. Hafemann, 269–281. Berlin.

Vittmann, G. 2015. "Der Stand der Erforschung des Kursivhieratischen (und neue Texte)." In *Ägyptologische "Binsen"-Weisheiten I–II. Neue Forschungen und Methoden der Hieratistik. Akten zweier Tagungen in Mainz im April 2011 und März 2013*, edited by U. Verhoeven, 383–433. AAWLM 14. Stuttgart. http://aku.uni-mainz.de/hieratic-studies-online/.

Vleeming, S. P. 1981. "La phase initiale du démotique ancien." *CdE* 56:31–48.

DEMOTIC PALAEOGRAPHY

JOACHIM QUACK, JANNIK KORTE, FABIAN WESPI, AND CLAUDIA MADERNA-SIEBEN

RESEARCH HISTORY AND TOOLS

As regards the history of palaeographic research in Demotic studies, the list of noteworthy approaches is quite short. The problem is not that palaeography has not been recognized as a major task, but most scholars have limited their palaeographic analyses to single texts or rather small corpora. A number of scholars have expressed the desire to have an available palaeography to work with (Spiegelberg 1924, 132–133; Lüddeckens 1978, 15–16, 22; Depauw 1997, 57).

The reason for the lack of a comprehensive Demotic palaeography lies not only in the fact that composing it requires a considerable amount of effort and time but also in that the necessary groundwork has not been laid. Many texts have been published without palaeographic analyses (see Lüddeckens 1978, 16). In addition, the Demotic script, with its higher number of ligatures and abbreviated spellings, creates specific challenges when it comes to organizing a palaeography.

Despite these problems, a number of publications addressing Demotic palaeography are worth mentioning. Griffith (1909, 3:323–467) already provided a glossary of different word spellings found in the Rylands papyri, sorted chronologically. While these spellings were given as handcopies only, they were precise enough to enable estimations as to what a sign looked like at a certain period in time within the material, an approach that was later adopted on a much wider scale by Erichsen (1954) in one of the still most important reference works on Demotic language and script, although now partly outdated and not focused on palaeography. A number of text editions include similar glossaries, nowadays usually giving facsimiles or photographs rather than handcopies of word spellings, thus providing researchers with quality images. Therefore, projects with no special interest in palaeography, such as Lüddeckens et al. (2000) or Johnson (2001), offer images that can to a certain extent be used for palaeographic comparisons.

While some editions also include analyses of palaeographic features of the respective texts, more comprehensive studies are very rare. Exceptions are the editions of two Early Demotic archives / dossiers (Vleeming 1991, Pestman 1994). Here, the sign repertoires of the respective texts are analyzed thoroughly in respect of their hieroglyphic and hieratic predecessors, thus creating highly useful palaeographic tools for the research and comparison of Early Demotic signs, even beyond the limitations of the respective localities. A different approach was chosen by Zauzich (1968, 166–228), who analyzed the palaeographic characteristics of contracts of sale from the Ptolemaic Period. He concentrated on a small number of word writings and compared these for different scribes, arriving at a number of peculiarities that he could assign to specific times and/or places. Furthermore, he pointed out the value of measures and positioning of signs.

The most comprehensive palaeographic study so far has been published by el-Aguizy (1998). This publication provides attestations of many Demotic signs including their abnormal hieratic counterparts. The signs cover the Late and Ptolemaic Periods, a geographical space from Memphis to Upper Egypt, and different text types. Unfortunately, the publication is not unproblematic concerning the limited corpus of analyzed texts and repertoire of signs, and the disregard for the Roman Period entirely (for a more detailed discussion of the publication, see Vittmann 2000). In many cases, the number of sign attestations is too low for a detailed study, as in reality even one single text can contain different representations of a single sign. Also, the chosen chronological and topographical frames are too broad to allow detailed analyses.

A palaeography of all Demotic epigraphic sources has been conceptualized by Moje (see chapter by Moje). This publication will not be organized according to signs and groups but to entire words. A digital approach to a comprehensive Demotic palaeography that will analyze complete texts down to the level of the individual signs and groups, which then can be compared with those of other texts, is the Demotic Palaeographical Database Project (DPDP) being developed by the authors of this article.

METHODOLOGY

The main aim of palaeographic analyses is to compare and group scribal hands and to date and place hands and texts. The basic steps in any palaeographic analysis, regardless of the script, can be described as follows:

1. Decipherment of the signs or words in question
2. Analysis of the peculiarities of the hand
3. Comparison of the analyzed signs or words with their attestations in other hands and texts
4. Assignation of the analyzed hand to a certain time, place, text type and/or scribe and school

Decipherment

One Demotic sign can represent numerous different phonetic or semantic values, as exemplified by ⟍, which can stand for the phonetic values mšo, wo, ꜣbd, ḥn, mn, p, =n, .w, in, or hn (or parts of these) and as a determinative for ⟨img⟩, ⟨img⟩, or ⟨img⟩, depending on its context and scribe. Additionally, one functional sign can appear in different representations, depending on where, when, and in what type of text it was written. The sign with the phonetic value on thus can look like ⟨img⟩, ⟨img⟩, ⟨img⟩, or ⟨img⟩ in different hands. As the Demotic script was in use for over a thousand years, many signs underwent a development that must be taken into consideration. While these problems make it considerably more difficult to decipher texts, especially when they are fragmentary and offer only minimal context, they also leave the researcher and editor with the problem of how to organize a palaeographic table and make signs or groups searchable. In most text volumes, these tables are more or less arranged after Gardiner's hieroglyphic sign list (1957), usually with an extra section for group writings, and so looking up Demotic signs requires knowledge of the underlying hieroglyphs. A partial solution to this problem was given by Erichsen (1937, vol. 3), who published a list arranged by the actual Demotic sign shape.

Analysis

The main problem of any palaeographic analysis is the subjectivity of the scholar. While after dealing with texts thoroughly, scholars can assign certain general features to a hand, such as a cursive or uncial tendency, describing a hand's peculiarities on the sign level can be particularly difficult. In comparison with hieratic, the problem is increased in Demotic texts, where signs are further removed from their hieroglyphic origins and thus show less distinctive features. This can be demonstrated by the writing of the Egyptian article ⟨img⟩, pꜣ, "the," written like ⟨img⟩ in late hieratic and ⟨img⟩ in Demotic. To compensate for these circumstances, a systematic approach can be chosen, which should include precise measurements and descriptions as, for example, provided by computer-based algorithms. The need to do this meticulous work results from the fact that it objectifies the results and helps one understand the scholar's conclusions.

Comparison

In order to compare hands with each other, a clear definition of the compared parameters is necessary. A substantial problem is the question of what exactly qualifies as a Demotic sign (Quack 2014a, 214–215). For example, the typical appearance of the word onḫ, "to live," usually is ⟨img⟩ and can be traced back to hieroglyphic ⟨img⟩. The question is how, or even if, this word spelling can be subdivided into single signs. While the decision to treat the uniconsonantal ⟨img⟩ as one sign can hardly be questioned, even though it is composed of two strokes that originate from three hieroglyphic signs, the rest of the word offers more of a challenge. Should **I** count as a single sign even though it never occurs without the next one? Can **☾**, which originates from two hieroglyphic signs, which probably should not be split up within the Demotic sign, stand independently or only together with **I**? What if in some scribes' hands ⬚ looks like **☾**? Would this classify as one sign even though both strokes appear separately with the same hieroglyphic and phonetic values in other words, such as ⟨⸗⟩, ⬚, *ḫft*, "enemy" or ⟨⟩, ⬚, *nm*, "who?"? These questions are not easy to answer, which becomes a serious problem when comparing signs to each other. It also explains why a standard sign definition for the Demotic script has never been realized, maybe apart from lists such as Erichsen's (1937, vol. 3) and du Bourguet's (1976, 79–87), which in many cases do not give answers to these questions, in some cases taking apart Demotic signs in hardly acceptable ways (see Quack 2014a, 214–215, who also gives a possible solution to the problem by proposing a division into uniconsonantal signs, historical groups, and determinatives). A method that avoids this problem entirely is organizing a palaeography by complete words and not individual signs and groups (see chapter by Moje). While it is probably true that Egyptian scribes did not usually separate single units within one word and the analysis of complete word writings can be a fruitful approach, the problem of this method is that the reader cannot easily compare single signs within the corpus if he/she wants to. The search for a sign within complete words requires profound knowledge of word spellings and takes a much longer time than when signs are listed individually.

Assignation

A similar problem as with the analysis exists with the assignation of a hand to a certain place, time, and/or text type. It is almost impossible for the reader of a palaeographic assessment to evaluate its outcomes if the underlying criteria are not explained in detail. This becomes highly problematic when subsequent studies are based on these assessments. In this matter, it would be most helpful to have a discussion about which parts of individual signs show differences and which do not. Only clear definitions based on exact observations will be apt to set the basis for more systematic evaluations. Nevertheless, uncertainties cannot be eliminated entirely. Therefore, the above-described steps should be enhanced by nonpalaeographic data. Thorough palaeographic analyses should not ignore content, language, layout, and material of the medium and therefore should include linguistic, prosopographical, formal, technical, material, or contextual data. This information can help question and evaluate the palaeographic results.

CLASSIFYING DEMOTIC HANDS

Since Brugsch (1855), it is a commonplace to distinguish between three palaeographic stages of the Demotic script, which are referred to as Early Demotic, Middle or Ptolemaic Demotic, and Late or Roman Demotic. Each of these stages relates primarily to palaeography (in the strict sense, dealing with sign shapes) and not to orthography (dealing with word spellings) or language, although changes can also be observed in Demotic orthography and Demotic language.

The names of the alleged palaeographic stages imply certain developments and substantial shifts that are supposed to be contemporary to the major changes in the political history of late Ancient Egypt (Figure IV.7.1). This raises the question about the reason for and the manner of this palaeographic development. However, explicit descriptions of these palaeographic changes are rare. Brugsch described the first stage as containing the detachment of Demotic from hieratic signs ("commencements," 665–305 BCE according to his classification), which was followed by a self-contained writing system with its own aesthetics during the Ptolemaic Period ("époque du bon style"), and then resulted in a slender and rather cursive script in Roman times ("époque du gouvernement romain"). Another description of the major palaeographic stages of Demotic is found in Depauw (1997, 22–26), who describes the characteristic criteria of the first stage as the use of bold signs, close to their (not hieratic but) hieroglyphic origin, while a smaller and more stylized script characterizes the second stage (already beginning in the early fourth century BCE) and evolves into a "spidery" script with an even width of strokes in the third and final palaeographic stage. Thus, according to both descriptions, the main characteristic of the first transition seems to be the abstraction of the Demotic signs, while the second transition is characterized by the emergence of a more slender script.

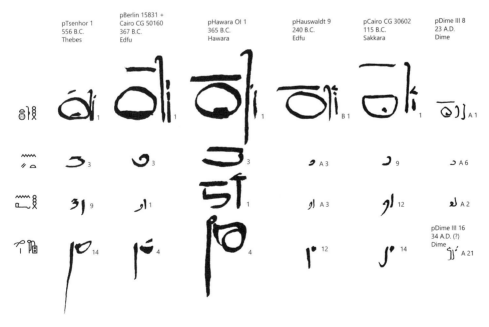

FIGURE IV.7.1. Some Demotic signs featuring a considerable palaeographic development, as well as differences in the palaeographic "registers." (Note the uncial character of pHawara OI 1 in comparison to the more cursive one of pBerlin 15831+Cairo CG 50160.)

As to the date of these palaeographic changes, opinions differ. Brugsch set the date of the first transition at 305 BCE and the second one at around 30 BCE. Spiegelberg (1899, 18–19; 1903, 12n3), however, pointed out that the script of what he then called the "transitional period" (Dynasties 25–30) changed into "proper" Demotic at the beginning of the fourth century BCE. Most Demotists have agreed with this, even though the line between Early and Ptolemaic Demotic is drawn at 332 BCE, for example, by el-Aguizy (1998, 3). Her classification aims, however, at the proper dating of sources rather than at palaeographic styles and modes of writing. Thus, "Ptolemaic Demotic" in this sense means belonging to the Ptolemaic Period and does not define a clearly distinguished palaeographic phase.

The second palaeographic transition should also be set earlier than the term "Roman Demotic" might suggest, if one takes the slender script and the even stroke-width as its characteristic features. These result primarily from the use of the Greek reed pen as a writing tool, which produced a thinner stroke with an even width and enabled smaller writings. The Greek reed pen, however, was already used during the late second century BCE in Demotic papyri (Tait 1988; Quack 2015, 444–445). Therefore, the change in writing tool rather separates the first and the second phase of Middle Demotic, a distinction proposed by Spiegelberg on the basis of the use of certain formulae common since the reign of Ptolemy V Epiphanes (Spiegelberg 1908, x). The significant shift between Late Ptolemaic and Roman Demotic, on the other hand, might primarily have been of orthographic and not of palaeographic nature.

In either case, it remains doubtful whether palaeographic developments of the Demotic script were really marked by clear-cut breaks, or if the changes in fact had the nature of transitional and overlapping phases. Especially the diachronic distinction between the "commencements" and the "bon style" of Demotic script is sometimes rather a synchronous one between different "registers" of writing, as a scribe could use uncial and cursive signs even in one and the same text (Martin 2013, 44). Furthermore, the impression of palaeographic breaks may essentially be influenced by major gaps in the transmission of Demotic texts, which coincide roughly with the political changes in the history of late Ancient Egypt. There are four major phases with an ample amount of Demotic sources (see Depauw et al. 2007, xiii; Hoffmann 2000, 26). A first rise in the documentation of Demotic texts begins with the reign of Psammetichus I, peaks during the reign of Darius I, and declines during the reign of Xerxes I. Two more phases can be identified between Alexander the Great, Ptolemy V Epiphanes, and Cleopatra VII Philopator, and a last phase afterward. Thus, each of these political periods can be aligned with one of the alleged palaeographic stages. Times of political change might indeed have influenced the palaeographic development of Demotic script to some extent. But evidence of a clear-cut break in palaeographic terms seems not to exist at any specific place.

Besides, it is only natural to assume that the palaeographic development was mainly characterized by gradual transitions, if one considers how palaeographic knowledge of the Demotic script was acquired by Egyptian scribes. There was no single university instructing all the scribes of Egypt, but evidence about scribal families (e.g., Pestman 1994, 155–163) indicates that scribes taught their sons. Furthermore, there were local writing schools at temples (although these may have focused more on the hieratic and hieroglyphic scripts, at least in earlier times), where also the notary's office seems to have been located at (Vleeming 1994). Thus, it is reasonable to assume that palaeographic knowledge (i.e., the primarily unconsciously applied idea of sign shapes) did not travel very far, and it seems likely that the overall palaeographic development of the Demotic script is to be explained by the emergence of local writing styles that spread out gradually rather than by centralized and binding revisions or reforms of the writing system (Quack 2018). However, the situation was probably different with regard to the origin of the Demotic script, as the newly invented writing system seems to have become compulsive in Egypt during the reign of Psammetichus I.

As the model of scribal education just mentioned suggests that palaeographic developments were mainly linked to certain localities, Demotic handwritings are nowadays not only grouped chronologically but also occasionally separated into manuscripts from Lower, Middle, and Upper Egypt. Regarding the ranges of these palaeographic areas, the terms mentioned might again be misleading to a nonadept, who, for example, has to know that the Delta is mostly uncharted territory in regard to Demotic palaeography (due to the lack of sources from this area). The expression "Lower Egypt" is in fact primarily related to Demotic handwritings from Memphis and may also include texts from the Fayyum, while "Upper Egypt" labels manuscripts predominantly from Thebes. In el-Aguizy (1998), "Middle Egypt" covers the Fayyum and the Nile Valley up to Asyut.

Particular statements about palaeographic differences between the alleged geographically determined classes of manuscripts are rarely found in Egyptological literature. Manuscripts from Memphis and the Fayyum show an uncial tendency reminiscent of Early Demotic according to Depauw (1997, 26; see also Martin 2013, 44). Zauzich (1968, 225–226), on the other hand, pointed out that there seems to be a systematic palaeographic difference between Upper and Lower Egypt in the writing of *ḥsb.t* "regnal year" (the writings of Lower Egypt usually featuring a stroke inside the *sp*-sign that is often missing in the writings of Upper Egypt, at least in Middle Demotic). Apart from these observations, palaeographic differences between an Upper and Lower Egyptian tradition are hardly specified.

In general, one would assume that any palaeographically coherent area more or less corresponded with the boundaries of ancient living environments, due to the fact that palaeographic knowledge was transmitted mainly through local schools and traditions. The difference between a northern versus a southern palaeographic tradition of the Demotic script should therefore coincide with the social topography of the Nile Valley. During the times when Demotic was in use, the Hermopolis region was indeed conceived as a border zone between the lower and the upper Nile Valley. The classical geographers Agatharchides, Strabo, and Claudius Ptolemy speak of a spatial unity called the "Thebaïs" that was separated from the northern parts by the natural border of the Nile cutting the valley next to Asyut. At the same time, they mention two garrisons and passages along the river (called the Hermopolitic and the Thebaïc *phylakē*). A similar social topography can also be recognized in the distribution of the Coptic dialects, as the border between the closely related Akhmimic and Lycopolitan/Asyutic dialects on the one hand, and the Fayyumic and Mesokemic dialects on the other hand lies in the region north of Asyut as well (see Peust 2010). Considering the Demotic ḥsb.t-sign, it is striking that the mentioned difference in writing also divides the valley in Middle Egypt, north of Akoris (Zauzich 1968, 194–195). However, at the same time, local rather than regional palaeographic traditions also existed, as can be observed especially in the Roman Fayyum, where manuscripts from Tebtunis can clearly be distinguished from manuscripts from Soknopaiou Nesos in terms of their palaeography.

Palaeographic "Registers" and Demotic in Different Text Types

Demotic characters and word spellings can show differences depending on their use in specific text types, even if these can be assigned to the same place and time. One way in which a text type can have an influence on the specific appearance of Demotic script can be found in legal contracts at least from the third century BCE, mainly in Memphis and the Fayyum. These contracts can feature an uncial variety of script, resembling Early Demotic script, which at that time was already out of use in other text types. This palaeographic "register" seems to be abandoned in the first century BCE (Martin 2013).

Concerning the use of Demotic in different text types in general, the Demotic script was mainly used as a chancellery script to record administrative texts, legal documents, and letters in the early phase (c. 650–400 BCE; for a detailed discussion of the rise of the Early Demotic script and its delimitation to abnormal hieratic, see chapter by Donker van Heel). Religious, scientific, and literary texts in this period were mostly still written in late hieratic, although some in Demotic script date already to the sixth century BCE (Quack 2014b, 58–60; 2016). One example of such an early text is Papyrus Rylands 9, also known as the "Petition of Petese" (TM 47388, Vittmann 1998). Although this is in a strict sense a documentary text, it can be seen as an example of Early Demotic poetic narrative literature due to its detailed style and the final "songs of Amun."

From the Ptolemaic Period on, the Greek language and script were introduced to the Egyptian administration. Many administrative texts were now written bilingually in Greek and Demotic. A Demotic document could either bear a Greek translation of parts or even the entire text, or a Greek document could be annotated with Demotic notes or translations (e.g., Zenon Archive, TM Arch 256). Even after 146 BCE, when it was obligatory to register legal documents in the *Grapheion* and mark them with a Greek registry note, they were still written in Demotic. Only in the late Ptolemaic Period, Demotic legal texts were supplemented or replaced on a larger scale by Greek documents (Clarysse 2010). The Late Demotic ostraca from the Temple of Narmouthis (Medinet Madi), which date from the middle of the second to the beginning of the third century CE, represent the last attestations of administrative texts in Demotic script and language (Vandorpe and Verreth 2012).

While Demotic lost its significance in administrative texts due to its substitution by Greek, it was increasingly used for nonadministrative compositions, such as literary, scientific, magical, and religious texts, from the early fourth century BCE until the late second century CE (Hoffmann 2009, 369–371). Texts written in older stages of the Egyptian language and script still existed, but from the late Ptolemaic Period on and particularly in the Roman Period, these were sometimes annotated with Demotic glosses, which transmit the phonetic value of individual words or which comment on the meaning of a word (Quack 2017).

The relevance of Demotic within the sphere of the temples is illustrated especially by the large number of papyri from Tebtunis and Soknopaiou Nesos, which mainly date to the Roman Period (first to second century CE). These texts were rarely new compositions, but mostly copies of earlier religious, scientific, or literary texts, which were made by scribes for the respective temple libraries (Quack 2006, 192). The last substantial group of texts written in Demotic script are magical texts, where Demotic remained in use until the middle of the third century CE (Dieleman 2010). In some graffiti, specifically from the island of Philae, Demotic was used until 452 CE (see TM 50864).

DEMOTIC SIGN INVENTORY

As mentioned previously, a definition of the concept of a sign is necessary to conduct palaeographic comparisons. However, neither is the categorization of hieroglyphic signs into phonograms, ideograms, and determinatives entirely applicable to the Demotic sign system nor is there a comprehensive Demotic sign theory even today (Quack 2014a; Vleeming 2013; Tait 2013).

In detail, identifying uniconsonantal signs and determinatives seems to be relatively uncomplicated (Tait 2013, 134–143). Uniconsonantal signs can be divided into three subcategories, according to their hieroglyphic predecessors. The first one includes the traditional Egyptian uniconsonantal signs that were transferred into Demotic directly without phonetic changes. One example is the two hieroglyphic uniconsonantal signs for *s*, 𓋴 and ⎯⎯, with their Demotic descendants ꜣ and ╼. The second subcategory comprises uniconsonantal signs that originate from so-called Late Egyptian syllabic groups. This can be exemplified by the third Demotic sign with the phonetic value s, ⫫, which is a descendant of the hieroglyphic group ⌐⤳ with the phonetic value *sꜣ*, and is often used for spellings of words of non-Egyptian origins (see Clarysse 1987, 10–13). The third subcategory includes uniconsonantal signs that derive from older multiconsonantal signs corresponding to one single hieroglyph, for example, Demotic ꜥ, *w*, which corresponds to hieroglyphic 𓏺, *wꜣ*.

The use of Demotic determinatives is basically similar to that of the hieroglyphic script of the Late Period, and they are usually easy to identify. However, it becomes difficult if these form an inseparable unit with phonetic signs. For example, the hieroglyphic group 𓏏𓄑 for sḫꜣ, "to write," which can easily be divided into a phonogram and two determinatives, seems rather inseparable in its Demotic descendant ▐°.

Demotic multiconsonantal phonograms form the most problematic group of Demotic signs, as they cannot as easily be isolated as entities (see the example for ꜥnḫ above, under "Comparison"). Quack (2014a, 215) proposes to use the term "historical group" for "sämtliche Stricheinheiten, die keine Einkonsonantenzeichen sind, aber dennoch Angaben über den Lautkörper des Wortes machen." A similar problem is the increasing ligaturization of Demotic, as signs can merge so strongly that single characters can no longer be divided. For example the word ini, 𓏏, "to bring" usually looks like ➥ in Early Demotic and later merges into ➤.

On the other hand, the Demotic sign inventory underwent a number of changes as some signs disappeared and new ones were incorporated. An example of a sign being marginalized is the determinative of the striking man ❤, 𓀞, which is more extensively used in Early Demotic and in many instances replaced by the determinative of the striking arm ➤✚, ﹏ in later stages.

New Demotic signs could be generated by modifying already existing ones. For example, starting with the reign of Alexander IV, a distinction between ⟋, ⬀ and ✓, ⎮⬀ appears as a graphical representation of the already existing phonetical distinction between the two consonants r and l.

Incorporations into the Demotic sign inventory could include signs of hieroglyphic and hieratic due to the interactions of Demotic and these older Egyptian scripts. Demotic language could be recorded in hieroglyphic script in monumental inscriptions (Quack 1995) and in late hieratic script on papyri (Quack 2010). On the other hand, linguistically older compositions, mainly religious ones, could be transferred into Demotic script without being translated into the Demotic language (Quack 2012). The latter case especially can lead to the intrusion of hieroglyphic or hieratic signs into the Demotic writing system. An extreme case is represented by the so-called semi-Demotic texts that regularly alternate between hieroglyphic or hieratic and Demotic signs (e.g., P. Vindob. 3873, TM 56081).

DEMOTIC ORTHOGRAPHY

An aspect of the Demotic writing system that is closely related to palaeography is word spelling, that is orthography. Demotic words can basically be spelled either traditionally, using historical groups, or phonetically, using uniconsonantal signs. The latter was used to adopt Greek loanwords and names into Demotic (see Clarysse 2013), as these of course did not possess any traditional Egyptian orthographies. Egyptian words, on the other hand, could also change their orthography from historical to phonetical. For example, the word bꜣ.w, "(divine) wrath," written 𓊃𓏤𓏏𓃒 in P. Rylands 9, 24.17 (TM 47388), a direct descendant of hieroglyphic 𓇳𓅿𓃻, is later spelled phonetically

⟨ᴣᴵ⟜, 𓂦𓏏𓄿𓏏𓏲, *bwꜣ* (Quack 2012, 223). This phenomenon is more regularly encountered in the Roman Period.

A hybrid of historical and phonetical orthography is represented by spellings that make use of phonetic complements, that is, uniconsonantal signs used to clarify a word's actual pronunciation. Occasionally, these phonetic complements could also be used to differentiate between different meanings of words of the same root, similar to determinatives. For example, the stem *bꜣk* (𐤟, 𓃢) was left uncomplemented in the words *bꜣk*, "slave" and *bꜣk*, "document," while a complementary *b* (𐤟ᴵᴸ, 𓃢ᵧᴸ) was added in the words *bꜣk*, "work" and *bꜣk*, "tax" (Quack 2014a, 218–221, with more examples).

BIBLIOGRAPHY

Aguizy, O. el- 1998. *A Palaeographical Study of Demotic Papyri in the Cairo Museum from the Reign of King Taharka to the End of the Ptolemaic Period (684–30 BC)*. MIFAO 113. Cairo.

Bourguet, P. du. 1976. *Grammaire fonctionelle et progressive de l'Égyptien démotique*. Leuven.

Brugsch, H. 1855. *Grammaire Démotique contenant les Principes Généraux de la Langue et de l'Écriture Populaires des Anciens Égyptiens*. Berlin.

Clarysse, W. 1987. "Greek Loan-words in Demotic." In *Aspects of Demotic Lexicography: Acts of the Second International Conference for Demotic Studies, Leiden 19–21 September 1984*, edited by S. P. Vleeming, 9–33. StudDem 1. Leuven.

Clarysse, W. 2010. "Bilingual Papyrological Archives." In *The Multilingual Experience in Egypt from the Ptolemies to the Abbasids*, edited by A. Papaconstantinou, 47–72. Farnham.

Clarysse, W. 2013. "Determinatives in Greek Loan-Words and Proper Names." In *Aspects of Demotic Orthography: Acts of an International Colloquium Held in Trier, 8 November 2010*, edited by S. P. Vleeming , 1–24. StudDem 11. Leuven.

Depauw, M. 1997. *A Companion to Demotic Studies*. PapBrux 28. Brussels.

Depauw, M., C. Arlt, M. Elebaut, A. Georgila, S. Gülden, et al. 2007. *A Chronological Survey of Precisely Dated Demotic and Abnormal Hieratic Sources*. TOP 1. Cologne.

Dieleman, J. 2010. "What's in a Sign? Translating Filiation in the Demotic Magical Papyri." In *The Multilingual Experience in Egypt from the Ptolemies to the Abbasids*, edited by A. Papaconstantinou, 127–152. Farnham.

Erichsen, W. 1937. *Demotische Lesestücke I: Literarische Texte mit Glossar und Schrifttafel*. 3 vols. Leipzig.

Erichsen, W. 1954. *Demotisches Glossar*. Copenhagen.

Gardiner, A. H. 1957. *Egyptian Grammar*. 3rd ed. London.

Griffith, F. Ll. 1909. *Catalogue of the Demotic Papyri in the John Rylands Library Manchester*. 3 vols. Manchester.

Hoffmann, F. 2000. *Ägypten: Kultur und Lebenswelt in griechisch-römischer Zeit. Eine Darstellung nach den demotischen Quellen*. Studienbücher Geschichte und Kultur der Alten Welt. Berlin.

Hoffmann, F. 2009. "Die Entstehung der demotischen Erzählliteratur: Beobachtungen zum überlieferungsgeschichtlichen Kontext." In *Das Erzählen in frühen Hochkulturen*, I. *Der Fall Ägypten*, edited by H. Roeder, 351–384. Ägyptologie und Kulturwissenschaft 1. Munich.

Johnson, J. H., ed. 2001. *The Demotic Dictionary of the Oriental Institute of the University of Chicago*. Retrieved from https://oi.uchicago.edu/research/publications/demotic-dictionary-oriental-institute-university-chicago.

Lüddeckens, E. 1978. "Stand und Aufgaben der Demotistik." *Enchoria* 8 (Sonderband): 15–23.

Lüddeckens, E., et al. 2000. *Demotisches Namenbuch*. Wiesbaden.

Martin, C. J. 2013. "Memphite Palaeography: Some Observations on Texts from the Ptolemaic Period." In *Aspects of Demotic Orthography: Acts of an International Colloquium Held in Trier, 8 November 2010*, edited by S. P. Vleeming , 41–62. StudDem 11. Leuven.

Pestman, P. W. 1994. *Les Papyrus Démotiques de Tsenhor (P. Tsenhor): Les archives privées d'une femme égyptienne du temps de Darius Ier*. 2 vols. StudDem 4. Leuven.

Peust, C. 2010. "Koptische Dialektologie anhand ägyptisch-arabischer Ortsnamen." *GM* 226:77–90.

Quack, J. F. 1995. "Monumental-Demotisch." In *Per aspera ad astra: Wolfgang Schenkel zum neunundfünfzigsten Geburtstag*, edited by L. Gerstermann and H. Sternberg-el Hotabi, 107–121. Kassel.

Quack, J. F. 2006. "En route vers le copte: Notes sur l'évolution du démotique tardif." *FDL* 27 (Les langues chamito-sémitiques (afro-asiatique) 2): 191–216.

Quack, J. F. 2010. "Inhomogenität von ägyptischer Sprache und Schrift in Texten aus dem späten Ägypten." In *Tradition and Transformation: Egypt under Roman Rule*, edited by K. Lembke, M. Minas-Nerpel, and S. Pfeiffer, 313–341. CHANE 41. Leiden.

Quack, J. F. 2012. "Old Wine in New Wineskins? How to Write Classical Egyptian Rituals in More Modern Writing Systems." In *The Idea of Writing: Writing across Borders*, edited by A. de Voogt and J. F. Quack, 219–243. Leiden.

Quack, J. F. 2014a. "Bemerkungen zur Struktur der demotischen Schrift und zur Umschrift des Demotischen." In *Acts of the Tenth International Congress of Demotic Studies, Leuven, 26–30 August 2008*, edited by M. Depauw and Y. Broux, 207–242. OLA 231. Leuven.

Quack, J. F. 2014b. "Imhotep—der Weise, der zum Gott wurde." In *Persönlichkeiten aus dem Alten Ägypten im Neuen Museum*, edited by V. M. Lepper, 43–66. Petersberg.

Quack, J. F. 2015. "Rohrfedertorheiten? Bemerkungen zum römerzeitlichen Hieratisch." In *Ägyptologische "Binsen"-Weisheiten I-II: Neue Forschungen und Methoden der Hieratistik. Akten zweier Tagungen in Mainz im April 2011 und März 2013*, edited by U. Verhoeven, 435–468. AAWLM 14. Stuttgart.

Quack, J. F. 2016. "Papyrus Heidelberg dem. 679. Ein frühdemotischer (sub)literarischer Text?" In *Aere perennius: Mélanges égyptologiques en l'honneur de Pascal Vernus*, edited by P. Collombert, D. Lefèvre, S. Polis, and J. Winand, 593–610. OLA 242. Leuven.

Quack, J. F. 2017. "How the Coptic Script Came About." In *Greek Influence on Egyptian-Coptic: Contact-Induced Change in an Ancient African Language (DDGLC Working Papers 1)*, edited by E. Grossman, P. Dils, S. Richter, and W. Schenkel, 27–96. LingAeg-StudMon 17. Hamburg.

Quack, J. F. 2018. "On the Regionalisation of Roman Period Egyptian Hands." In *Scribal Repertoires in Egypt from the New Kingdom to the Early Islamic Period*, edited by J. Cromwell and E. Grossman, 184-210. Oxford.

Spiegelberg, W. 1899. "Demotische Miscellen." *ZÄS* 37:18–46.

Spiegelberg, W. 1903. "Demotische Miscellen." *RT* 9:6–15.

Spiegelberg, W. 1908. *Die demotischen Denkmäler II: Die demotischen Papyrus*. 2 vols. CGC. Strasbourg.

Spiegelberg, W. 1924. "Der gegenwärtige Stand und die nächsten Aufgaben der demotischen Forschung." *ZÄS* 59:131–140.

Tait, W. J. 1988. "Rush and Reed: The Pens of Egyptian and Greek Scribes." In *Proceedings of the XVIII International Congress of Papyrology: Athens 25–31 May 1986*, edited by B. G. Mandilaras, 477–481. 2 vols. Athens.

Tait, W. J. 2013. "Unconsonantal Signs and Patterns of Change: Exploring the Orthography of the Demotic Script." In *Aspects of Demotic Orthography: Acts of an International Colloquium Held in Trier, 8 November 2010*, edited by S. P. Vleeming, 127–143. StudDem 11. Leuven.

Vandorpe, K., and H. Verreth. 2012. *Temple of Narmouthis: House of the Ostraca, Leuven Homepage of Papyrus Archives, Arch 534.* Retrieved from http://www.trismegistos.org/arch/archives/pdf/534.pdf

Vittmann, G. 1998. *Der demotische Papyrus Rylands 9.* 2 vols. ÄAT 38. Wiesbaden.

Vittmann, G. 2000. "Rezension zu O. el-Aguizy, *A Palaeographical Study of Demotic Papyri in the Cairo Museum from the Reign of King Taharka to the End of the Ptolemaic Period (684–30 B.C.)*." *Enchoria* 26:189–192.

Vleeming, S. P. 1991. *The Gooseherds of Hou (Pap. Hou): A Dossier Relating to Various Agricultural Affairs from Provincial Egypt of the Early Fifth Century B.C.* StudDem 3. Leuven.

Vleeming, S. P. 1994. "Some Notes on Demotic Scribal Training in the Ptolemaic Period." In *Proceedings of the 20th International Congress of Papyrologists, Copenhagen, 23–29 August, 1992*, edited by A. Bülow-Jacobsen, 185–187. Copenhagen.

Vleeming, S. P. 2013. "Notes on Demotic Orthography." In *Aspects of Demotic Orthography: Acts of an International Colloquium Held in Trier, 8 November 2010*, edited by S. P. Vleeming, 145–161. StudDem 11. Leuven.

Zauzich, K.-Th. 1968. *Die ägyptische Schreibertradition in Aufbau, Sprache und Schrift der demotischen Kaufverträge aus ptolemäischer Zeit.* 2 vols. ÄA 19. Wiesbaden.

CHAPTER IV.8

....

ISSUES AND METHODOLOGIES IN COPTIC PALAEOGRAPHY

....

ANNE BOUD'HORS

At the end of the third century, notwithstanding the fact that the detailed circumstances of the process remain unknown, the first Coptic manuscripts are emerging. Their language, the last step of Egyptian, appears fully fixed, although with various dialectal varieties, and their graphic system is standardized, after hesitations visible in the different texts called "Old Coptic," which are mostly attempts to transcribe Egyptian in Greek letters (Quaegebeur 1982; Satzinger 1991). This system uses the twenty-four letters of the Greek alphabet supplemented on the one hand by six signs (or seven for some dialects) borrowed from Demotic and corresponding to sounds unknown in Greek (Figure IV.8.1): ⲱ /š/, ϥ /f/, ⳑ /h/, ⳉ /x/, ⳃ /x/, ϫ /č/, ϭ /ky/, ϯ /ti/, and on the other hand by a syllabic superlinear marking. A notable exception to this system is provided by the Papyrus Bodmer VI, a copy of the book of Proverbs written in a peculiar dialectal variety (dialect P), which uses several Demotic signs not included in the Coptic script, while the syntax is fully Coptic (Kasser 1960).

The production of texts written in Coptic extends from the end of the third century to the late nineteenth. Two categories are traditionally distinguished: (1) literary texts, Christian or para Christian in content, translated from Greek or composed in Coptic, transmitted through books copied in intellectual circles, mostly monastic; (2) nonliterary texts, or documents, copied for a single occasion on various materials (papyrus, parchment, and paper as well as shards of clay and limestone chips called "ostraca"): these are legal documents, accounts, letters. The period considered here will not exceed the twelfth century, which is roughly both when Coptic completely ceased to be used in documents, as the result of the Arabization that began in the late seventh century, and when the great monastic libraries started declining.

FIGURE IV.8.1. A limestone ostracon with a Coptic alphabet (Thebes, seventh to eighth century). The Greek letters are on the first four columns and the Egyptian ones on the fifth. O.Frange 480, TT 29 inv. 292414. © Université Libre de Bruxelles, Brussels.

Coptic manuscripts, however, are rarely associated with an archaeological context and are often deprived of absolute dating. Thus the main challenge of palaeography is to overcome this lack, trying to place in time and space a witness detached from its original environment (Kasser 1991b). It is a still underdeveloped and inexact discipline, the task being complicated by the fragmented state of the documentation, the diversity of textual genres and dialects, and the multiplicity of materials as well as the conservatism of the scribes and copyists. It can rely to some extent on the comparison with Greek manuscripts produced in Egypt, especially in the period before the Arab conquest. It also shares several issues with the study of Oriental manuscripts. Other important questions related to social phenomena are also at stake in Coptic palaeography, namely, the existence and organization of writing centers (scriptoria) or the modalities of learning.

TO DATE OR NOT TO DATE (?)

The vast majority of Coptic manuscripts are not dated in an absolute way. Literary manuscripts started bearing dates only from the ninth century onward, when the practice of adding a colophon at the end of a manuscript, that is, a set of indications about the copyist and his book, became usual. The oldest dated manuscript comes from the Fayyum: it is just prior to 823, the date of donation mentioned in the colophon (van Lantschoot 1929, n° I). Documentary texts are also rarely dated, except for certain legal texts. More often, they have a relative date, referring to tax unities of fifteen years called "indictions" (the date is given for the "*n* year of the indiction"). Therefore, the question of dating has mobilized scholars since the nineteenth century. A quick overview of the different methods and attitudes toward this problem is instructive.

The first catalog of manuscripts was compiled by the Danish scholar Georg Zoëga ([1810] 1973). Its aim was to describe and classify thousands of parchment sheets and fragments written in Sahidic Coptic. At that time, their origin was unknown, but at the end of the nineteenth century, they would prove to be remains of the great library of the so-called White Monastery or Monastery of Shenoute in Upper Egypt. Zoëga was able to distinguish nine types of writing (Latin *classes*), which he classified from I to IX in a chronological perspective without assigning dates for the different types, but giving copies at the end of the catalog. The principles of this work, pioneering in every respect (for a more detailed presentation, see Buzi 2015), were followed by all scholars working on the remains of the same library in the late nineteenth and early twentieth centuries.

The *Album de paléographie copte* by Henry Hyvernat ([1888] 1972) has met an enduring success. Although not accompanied by any analysis, it provides photographic reproductions and short notices of a large number of manuscripts dated or assigned to the sixth through eighteenth centuries. That it does not contain examples of manuscripts older than the sixth century is due to the fact that most of the ancient Coptic manuscripts have appeared in the second half of the twentieth century.

It is worth quoting in full the title of the book by Stegemann (1936): *Koptische Paläographie: 25 Tafeln zur Veranschaulichung der Schreibstile koptischer Schriftdenkmäler auf Papyrus, Pergament und Papier für die Zeit des III.–XIV. Jahrhunderts; Mit einem Versuch einer Stilgeschichte der koptischen Schrift* (*Coptic Palaeography: 25 Plates Illustrating the Writing Styles of Coptic Written Records on Papyrus, Parchment, and Paper for the Period of the III–XIV Centuries; With an attempt at a stylistic history of Coptic writing*). This programmatic title covers indeed the largest attempt in terms of history of writing (third through fourteenth centuries). Both literary (*Buchschrift*) and documentary handwritings (*Urkundenschrift*) are taken into account, according to well-defined periods. The study concerns both the individual shapes of the letters and the general appearance of the writing, thanks to hand copies, on the basis of the largest possible number of dated witnesses. This is the only book that had the ambition to handle all of the handwritten documentation. Nevertheless, the extreme "systematization" of the book, its austerity (German written in Gothic letters), and the small number of photographic plates, may have discouraged many researchers from making it their reference. Nowadays only a few scholars—mostly German—cite and use it, which is unfortunate because the materials gathered and the issues raised therein remain relevant.

The book titled *Koptische Paläographie* (Cramer 1964) is generally overlooked. It is based on an individual analysis of the shape of each letter through the centuries (fourth to sixteenth), without giving clear criteria for the proposed dates. However, the collection of reproductions it provides can be of some use.

It therefore appears that the attempts to build a reasoned Coptic palaeography have proved unsuccessful. Throughout the twentieth century, a skeptical attitude has prevailed. As a result, the descriptions of manuscripts are mostly devoid of dates. On the other hand, efforts have focused on the description of the scripts.

To Describe and to Date:
Between Types and Periods

Different Terminologies

The descriptive terminology of Coptic writings varies from one description to another, with significant differences in appreciation and dating. The system proposed by Layton (1987) mentions the degree of inclination of the writing, the presence of thick and thin strokes, and the characteristic shape of certain letters. These criteria are used to distinguish between two major types of upright scripts: one where all the letters have about the same frame, virtually fitting a sort of square, the other generally thin, where a contrast between wide and narrow letters can be observed. To these two types some scholars give the respective designations of "unimodular" and "bimodular," coined by G. Cavallo (Emmel 2004) as an alternative to traditional terminology inherited from the Greek paleography, where they are called "biblical majuscule" and "Alexandrian majuscule" (Cavallo 1967; Irigoin 1959). Around the time when Greek manuscripts of the Byzantine world started to be copied with a minuscule script (ninth to tenth centuries), Coptic copyists continued to use a majuscule, both unimodular and bimodular. As for the latter, they adopted specific features, including a certain flattening and stiffness of certain characters, as well as ink dots at the end of the letters. Table IV.8.1 tries to give an idea of the equivalences between the different terms in use.

Types and Periods

These types can be matched with periods of time as shown in Table IV.8.2, which is inspired by a recently proposed classification for "canonized" scripts in early Greek manuscripts (Orsini and Clarysse 2012). It should be added to the types mentioned earlier an upright and thin majuscule, only found in papyri of the earliest period. Such a periodization remains rough, as several types of writing are used at the same time, especially the biblical majuscule, which has a long history, and even within the same

Table IV.8.1.

Layton 1987	Emmel 2004	Traditional
Upright, thick-and-thin style, wide ε,ο,c, 3 or 4-stroke м	unimodular	Biblical majuscule
Upright, narrow ε,ο,c, 3-stroke м	bimodular	Alexandrian majuscule Coptic majuscule
(Right-)sloping majuscule		(Right-)sloping majuscule

Table IV.8.2.

Type	Period	Literary	Documentary
Upright and thin majuscule (severe style); papyrus	fourth	X	X
Biblical majuscule	fourth through tenth	X	Occasionally
Alexandrian majuscule	sixth through tenth	X	Occasionally
Coptic majuscule	ninth through twelfth	X	------
Sloping majuscule	fourth through twelfth	X, especially after the ninth century and as "distinctive" script	X

manuscript. This latter phenomenon is known as the use of "distinctive" scripts. For example, a manuscript copied in unimodular majuscule may include section titles in bimodular majuscule, while the final annotations of the copyist (colophons) are generally written in sloping majuscule (Figure IV.8.2.).

RESORTING TO CODICOLOGY

Paleography and Codicology: A Comprehensive Approach

From the 1980s, emphasis was placed on the necessity to take into account not only the writing of a manuscript but also all its material aspects, according to the habits of catalogs of Greek manuscripts (Layton 1985). Such aspects include the materials, dimensions, layout (text written in full page or in columns), and organization of the quires. These principles have been implemented in many catalogs (Layton 1987; Depuydt 1993; Emmel 2004). Moreover, reports on Coptic palaeography presented since then to the Coptic Studies Congress always consider palaeography and codicology together (Emmel 1993, 1999; Boud'hors 2006; Torallas Tovar 2016). Nevertheless, a handbook is still a desideratum.

This comprehensive approach allows us to propose three stages in the production of Coptic manuscripts, based on the tools and indications available.

Three Main Phases

In the ancient period (fourth to sixth century), the scripts are indeed already diverse. However, the comparison with the more or less contemporary Greek manuscripts is

FIGURE IV.8.2.   A leaf of a manuscript with a Coptic translation of the *Acta Conciliorum* (White Monastery, tenth to eleventh century). The text is copied in Coptic majuscule, while the introductive sections are in sloping majuscule. IFAO, Copte 067v. © Institut français d'archéologie orientale, Cairo.

suitable. Besides, codicological features such as relatively small dimensions, lack of ornamentation, and copy in full page form a relevant set of data. Dating is more or less precise depending on the case. For example, the Greek and Coptic writings from the collection called "Papyrus Bodmer," which includes manuscripts in both languages written on papyrus and parchment, most of them datable to the fourth century, have been used for refined typological and qualitative comparisons (Orsini 2015). Coptic books of papyrus containing Gnostic texts, discovered at Nag Hammadi (Upper Egypt), still have their bindings, which contain fragments of documentary texts from the mid-fourth century that were recycled as stuffing material. These documents confirm the dating of the manuscripts themselves to a slightly later period. Conversely, the manuscripts can be used as a reference for other manuscripts displaying the same kind of characteristics.

From the second half of the ninth century onward, the existence of colophons and dated manuscripts, even though they are not the majority, facilitates comparisons. The manuscripts usually have larger dimensions and are copied in two columns. They mostly come from two great monastic libraries, namely, the monastery of Shenoute in Upper Egypt and the monastery of Saint-Michael in Fayyum. The latter ones, discovered in 1910, have significantly enriched the documentation in comparison with the first *Album de paléographie* (Hyvernat [1888] 1972). As for the White Monastery, where the manuscripts were found in a very fragmentary state, it is not rare to find an isolated leaf bearing a colophon, without being able to relate it to a manuscript. Although much remains to be done in reconstructing the books and classifying the many scripts in use at this time, substantial progress is also being achieved, particularly in the identification of individual hands (Suciu 2011, 2014).

Between these two extremes lies a particularly vague period, when comparisons with the Greek witnesses are no longer relevant, while palaeographic and codicological indications are not sufficiently decisive. To control the great fantasy in the dating proposals for manuscripts from this period, or at least to reduce the margins of uncertainty, other approaches should be considered, the provenance of manuscripts being one of them.

PALEOGRAPHY AND DIALECTS: THE RELEVANCE OF THE DIACRITICAL SIGNS

Various Types of Signs

Among the codicological aspects mentioned thus far, the signs deserve special attention. Coptic manuscripts contain a variable amount of diacritics, which are described in more or less detail according to catalogs and text editors. Some are inherited from the practice of Greek manuscripts and concern the organization of the text, either as the equivalent of a logical punctuation (dot or set of dots) or as the marking of paragraphs or sections (*paragraphus, coronis, diple*) (Layton 1987), with a variously developed ornamentation (Jansma 1973). Others are a superlinear marking of the letters that is part of the graphic system of Coptic. This is a syllabic marking unparalleled in Greek, a language where every syllable is vocalized. In Coptic, where only the stressed syllables are vocalized, the superlinear marking is used to transcribe the vocalization (/e/) of an unstressed syllable. Its use is optional and rarely systematic. It can take various forms and positions, according to copyists and above all to dialects. Finally, other signs adopting various forms (dots, apostrophes), function as separators of syllables, grammatical elements, or accentual units. The use of the latter varies considerably from one manuscript to another and even within a manuscript.

Manuscripts and Dialects

Generally, palaeographic studies do not consider dialects and concern implicitly manuscripts and documents written in Sahidic (S), a neutral dialect that was from the fourth until around the eleventh century the main literary and common language of the Nile Valley. As the literature in this dialect is by far the most massive, it has monopolized the attention of scholars.

Bohairic, the other main literary Coptic dialect, was used in northern Egypt as early as the fourth century and became from the eleventh century the official language of the Coptic Church, still being its liturgical language nowadays. A few manuscripts in this dialect are generally included in the palaeographic albums. The majority of witnesses to the period between the ninth and thirteenth centuries are in fact written in biblical majuscule, with use of various distinctive scripts for paratextual information (titles, colophons), as in Sahidic manuscripts, the most visible difference being the use of an additional letter (ϩ) exclusive to this dialect. Thereafter, the writing of Bohairic manuscripts evolved, until the nineteenth century, toward more flexibility and differentiation in the module and the line of the letters. For this period, which is beyond the framework established for this article, there are no studies. On the other hand, several witnesses to the early period (fourth–fifth centuries) have appeared in the second half of the twentieth century, as well as a large number of seventh century epigraphic inscriptions from the Kellia, a monastic site in Lower Egypt. A general study of Bohairic paleography would be therefore desirable.

The only "minor" dialect that survived until the tenth century is the Fayyumic. Some literary witnesses to this dialect display peculiar shapes of certain letters borrowed from Demotic (ϣ, ⲍ, ϭ). Although not as spectacular as the peculiarities of P.Bodmer VI, these differences allow the careful observer to identify a Fayyumic manuscript (Andersen, Holmen, and Tait 1999). Conversely, in the rare cases where a witness of this dialect does not have these features, one can wonder whether it is the product of a particular scriptorium, where practices were different.

In the ancient period (fourth–sixth centuries), several other literary dialects were in use. There are only a few palaeographic differences to be observed from one dialect to another, except for the diacritic signs, which should thus not be neglected. Nevertheless, some scholars do not reproduce them at all in their editions, considering that the super-linear marking was used as a reading aid in a text written without word division (*scriptio continua*), but has no reason to be in a text where the words are separated. This is only acceptable if a description of the system is provided.

Superlinear Signs and Dialects

In the standard use of Sahidic manuscripts (Layton 2000, §38), a superlinear stroke is put above the consonants м, ꞏ, р either when they are grammatical elements (preposition, genitive marker, negation, and verb in the case of р) or at the beginning of a word before another consonant (ꞏⲧⲟⲕ, ꞏⲙⲟꞏ); it is placed above two consecutive consonants that form an unstressed syllable, as a "connective stroke" (ⲍꞏ, ꞏⲧⲕ, ⲧⲏⲣ̄ꞏ); in addition, it is often to be found on the syllable ꞏ, where it looks like a little curve, as well as on inter-rogative ⲟⲩ and the Greek particle ꞏ. A consonantal /i/ is usually marked by a diaeresis.

In Bohairic manuscripts, the superlinear mark is closer to a dot. It is called *djinkim*, a Coptic word that means a movable "vowel sign," coined by medieval Coptic grammars based on the categories of Arabic grammar. Two successive systems have been identified, of which only the first fits the period considered here: "The old-style system, which is thought to have prevailed until about 1400 CE, marks only (1) single vowels forming a syl-lable (ⲁꞏⲓ ⲉ̇ⲃⲟⲗ, ⲁ̇ⲛⲟⲙⲓⲁ̇) and (2) м̇ and ꞏ̇ as grammatical elements (prepositions, genitive marker, negation), and at the beginning of a word, before another consonant (ⲣⲉⲙꞏ̇ⲭⲏⲙⲓ, ⲙⲁꞏ̇ⲥⲱⲛⲍ, м̇ⲧⲟꞏ, ꞏ̇ⲟⲟⲕ)" (Polotsky 1949). The same type of system exists in manuscripts of the Middle Egyptian dialect (M; see the details of these systems in Kasser 1991a).

Practices seem to vary in the Fayyumic manuscripts, even though they have not been systematically studied. Some have no marking at all; others display a system similar to the Sahidic one, but with short strokes in place of diaeresis, whereas a third category has a sporadic marking, which borrows from several systems. Studying these markings could contribute to the identification of different copy centers.

Northern systems (B and M) were not without influence on Sahidic manuscripts. In the *scriptorium* of Touton, in the Fayyum, the superlinear marking of the manuscripts dated to the ninth and tenth centuries can be defined as a combination between the standard Sahidic system and the late Bohairic one (*djinkim* above a vowel forming a syl-lable, on the first of two consonants beginning a word, on the prefix of Present I, on the definite article, and on the monosyllabic verb ⲱ). As the manuscripts copied in this *scriptorium* were sent to various monasteries, including the White Monastery in Upper Egypt, the identification of such a superlinear system is valuable to define the origin and possible date of a fragment (Nakano 2006).

PROVENANCE AND DATE: THE CASE OF THE BIBLICAL MAJUSCULE

A recent comprehensive study can be seen as an attempt to return to a strict Coptic palaeography, exclusively considering the shape and thickness of the letters (Orsini 2008). In the line of the work on the biblical majuscule (Cavallo 1967), it follows a division into four major phases. The final phase, to which many Coptic manuscripts belong, extends from the sixth to the second half of the ninth century, a period of "decline" of this writing, with a gradual mannerism. According to the author, until the beginning of the sixth century, there would be no chronological discrepancy between Greek and Coptic manuscripts; only after this period would Coptic scripts have their own development. This study faces two important challenges. First, it sticks to biblical manuscripts, while this type of writing has been used for many other types of text, including the works of the great monastic writer Shenoute. Second, it takes no account of the dating issues related to the provenance of the manuscripts. For example, the vast majority of sheets and fragments from the White Monastery are generally thought to have been copied in a period between the ninth and twelfth centuries. This is certainly a too short period, as codicological characteristics of several fragments point to an earlier date. However, it is not reasonable to assign a White Monastery fragment, such as Louvre E 9985 (among others), to the late fifth century on the basis of the script, without going a little bit in this discussion about the library and without taking into account the size, diacritics, and decoration.

Considering the provenance of the manuscripts can also elucidate regional practices. This is well illustrated by the case of manuscripts copied in the Theban region (western bank of the Nile at Luxor; Boud'hors 2008). Almost all the witnesses of the book production there are written on papyrus, many of them in biblical majuscule. While the study of the writing itself would do little to refine dating, we know that the monastic institutions of the region were active from the very end of the sixth until the late eighth century. In the absence of further data, one must be content with this range. Moreover, codicological features of these manuscripts are fairly uniform and can help locate other fragments whose provenance is unknown. Finally, despite the lack of colophons, many copyists are known by their correspondence. The Theban region is the place par excellence where literary and documentary handwritings coexist.

DOCUMENTARY SCRIPTS

Description and Dating

The problems posed by Coptic documentary palaeography (about seven thousand texts) have been formulated by Alain Delattre (2007): on the one hand, there are too few dated texts, which makes it impossible to establish a chronology of writing types, and on the other hand, the variety of scripts at a given time is wide. Besides, specific tools, such as albums or registers, are lacking, photographs in publications, especially the oldest ones, are not always satisfactory, and access to digital images is not yet sufficient. Thus, the description and dating of Coptic documents is still largely left to the subjectivity of the publisher.

An important distinction in the field of documentary texts, as opposed to literary manuscripts, which are almost always written by professional copyists, can be established between professional hands (notaries, public writers, professors) and nonprofessional hands (semiliterate, students, casual writers), the latter, which occur mostly in the letters, being almost impossible to categorize and date.

Descriptive Criteria

Several criteria are taken into account in the description of documentary Coptic writings, namely, inclination (usually right), cursivity (the more cursive a writing is, the more ligatures there are between letters, on the model of Greek writings), and the rather

Inv.Sorb. 2606

FIGURE IV.8.3. A tax receipt (eighth century, Middle Egypt). The script is minuscule and cursive. Inv.Sorb. 2606. © Université Paris-Sorbonne–Institut de Papyrologie, Paris.

bilinear or quadrilinear aspect: a writing is termed bilinear when the letters are contained between two imaginary lines, so all letters being roughly the same size (as in a majuscule); it is called quadrilinear when the height of the letters is spread on four imaginary lines, vertical strokes of some letters rising or falling until the extreme lines (comparable to a minuscule) (Figure IV.8.3).

As for dating, the opposition between majuscule or bilinear and minuscule or quadrilinear is the most relevant. "Until the sixth century, all Coptic texts are written in 'majuscule,' more or less cursive. Then, in the seventh and eighth centuries, the two types of writing coexist. The 'minuscule' scripts are primarily attested in the eighth century. From the ninth century onwards, only a majuscule survives, as a bilinear calligraphy of the quadrilinear scripts" (Delattre 2007).

Some Steps in the Development of Coptic Documents

Coptic documents from the archaic period (fourth century) were relatively few before the excavation of the site of Kellis (Dakhla oasis) at the end of the twentieth century that provided the library and correspondence of a Manichean community. These letters expand the range of types of writing known to that time. They are indeed using a majuscule script, but with various degrees of inclination and cursivity (Gardner and Choat 2004). Moreover, there are several examples of one and the same hand used to write letters from different senders, which shows the possible existence of scribal workshops even then in the Nile Valley.

Another set of documents that can be assigned to a delimited period of time is the bilingual (Greek and Coptic) archive of Dioscorus, poet and notary in the village called Aphrodite (Upper Egypt) during the sixth century. Greek papyri from the archive, whose study began long ago, provide good support to contextualize and date the Coptic pieces, currently under study (Vanderheyden 2012). Here again, different types of majuscule scripts coexist. This period can be considered as a kind of transition, as some writings are still quite upright and archaic, while regularly right-sloping hands, including Dioscorus's hand itself, are already announcing types common in the seventh century (MacCoull 1997).

The seventh and eighth centuries are the most complex period, when the documents are the most numerous, since at that time Coptic began to compete with Greek in the administration, a development that would slowly be dried up by the Arabization subsequent to the conquest of 641. Archaeological or historical data are lacking most of the time. Indeed, the Theban region provides papyri and ostraca with typical handwritings, namely, regularly right-sloping majuscules, for which a point of origin around the beginning of the seventh century is guaranteed by the presence of a date, thanks to the mention of a sun eclipse assignable to 601 on one of the ostraca (Gilmore and Ray 2006). However, looking at the examples given in Table 11 of Stegemann (1936), it is clear that this type of writing is still attested in a document dated to 732, while another document, dated 709 and coming from Aphrodito, is written in a very cursive minuscule. In fact, the two documents come from quite different backgrounds, one being a donation made to a monastery, the other part of the local administrative archive, directly dependent on the central government. Again, social and regional considerations are proving important.

In the ninth century, there was a return to majuscule scripts, especially in documents from Middle Egypt and Fayyum. They differ from the previous by the presence of small strokes or dots at the ends of some letters, which gives them a mannered appearance. Finally, in the later period (ninth to tenth centuries), letters are written on papyrus and paper in very cursive writings, sometimes almost illegible (most of the texts are still unpublished; see Crum 1905, pl. 15, n° 1214).

Specificities of Documentary Palaeography

Hands and Styles

Professional scribes can vary their styles. What has been defined for literary manuscripts as the practice of distinctive scripts is also observable in the documents. Thus, parts of documents written in different scripts are not necessarily due to different hands (Fournet 2008). For example, in the will, which is dated to 634, of Victor, superior of monastery of St. Phoibammon in the Theban region, the body of the will is written with the sloping majuscule in use in the Coptic documents of the region, while the writing—by the same hand—of the sentence marking the completion of the act (name and position of the scribe, circumstances of the copy) is upright, cursive, and quadrilinear, rather close to that of some contemporary Greek documents (Garel, forthcoming). In the same region, the correspondence of a monk named Frange was discovered. Living in the first half of the eighth century, he was copying manuscripts as part of his activities. In his letters, his writing varies between a slightly sloping and cursive script and an upright one, with well separated letters and diacritical marks similar to those found in literary manuscripts (Boud'hors and Heurtel 2010; Boud'hors 2017). Frange, however, had not been trained to be a notary, since his hand never reaches the cursivity of some administrative documents, such as the ones written by his contemporary Aristophanes, a professional scribe of the neighboring village of Djeme (Cromwell 2010).

Insights on Learning

Direct information is rare on how scribes were trained and more generally on the learning process of reading and writing. The Theban region, however, provides some insights in this respect. The monk Frange used to call himself a "master." Many exercises written on ostraca found in his hermitage show that he probably taught the basics of writing to several disciples or pupils. Judging by the large number of them where the hand resembles his, even though more hesitant, imitation was the basis of learning. Besides, Frange himself seems to have forged his writing by imitating his predecessors in the hermitage (Boud'hors and Heurtel 2010). Things may have been different for professional scribes of the village of Djeme. If the trade often passed from father to son, the scripts of the younger generation often resemble each other, but differ from those of the fathers, which rather suggests the existence of schools (Cromwell 2012).

Between Literature and Document: The Sloping Majuscule of Liturgical Texts

The sloping majuscule is found in both literary manuscripts and documents. Nevertheless, in the former, it functions primarily as a distinctive script, to copy titles, annotations, and colophons, that is to say, what is not properly literary, but paratextual (Boud'hors 1997). This type of script is also used in the copy of liturgical texts, especially hymns. Since hymns were first copied onto single sheets before being grouped into collections and books, the use of such writing is indicative of their documentary status. A study has recently been conducted on the development of the sloping majuscule in the liturgical texts (Mihálykó 2019, chap. 3). The same kind of consideration could be applied to magical texts.

BIBLIOGRAPHY

Andersen, M., B. Holmen, and J. Tait. 1999. "Palaeographical and Codicological Notes to Supplement Erichsen's Edition of the Copenhagen Fayumic Manuscript of Agathonicus: P. Carlsberg 300." *Enchoria* 25:1–19.

Boud'hors, A. 1997. "L'onciale penchée en copte et sa survie jusqu'au XVᵉ siècle en Haute-Égypte." In *Scribes et manuscrits du Moyen-Orient*, edited by F. Déroche and F. Richard, 117–133. Paris.

Boud'hors, A. 2006. "Paléographie et codicologie coptes: Progrès et perspectives (1996–2004)." In *Huitième congrès international d'études coptes, Paris 2004, vol. 1: Bilans et perspectives 2000–2004*, edited by A. Boud'hors and D. Vaillancourt, 95–109. CBC 15. Paris.

Boud'hors, A. 2008. "Copie et circulation des livres dans la région thébaine (7ᵉ-8ᵉ siècles)." In *"Et maintenant ce ne sont plus que des villages ...": Thèbes et sa région aux époques hellénistique, romaine et byzantine*, edited by A. Delattre and P. Heilporn, 149–161. Brussels.

Boud'hors, A. 2017. "Copyist and Scribe: Two Professions for a Single Man? Palaeographical and Linguistic Observations on Some Practices of the Theban Region According to Coptic Texts from the 7th–8th Centuries." In *Scribal Repertoires in Egypt from the Old Kingdom to the Early Islamic Period*, edited by J. Cromwell and E. Grossman, 274–295. Oxford.

Boud'hors, A., and C. Heurtel. 2010. *Les ostraca coptes de la TT 29: Autour du moine Frangé*. Études d'archéologie thébaine 3. Brussels.

Buzi, P. 2015. "Coptic Palaeography." In *Comparative Oriental Manuscript Studies: An Introduction*, edited by A. Bausi, P. G. Borbone, F. Briquel-Chatonnet, P. Buzi, J. Gippert, et al., 283–286. Hamburg.

Cavallo, G. 1967. *Ricerche sulla maiuscola biblica*. Florence.

Cramer, M. 1964. *Koptische Paläographie*. Wiesbaden.

Cromwell, J. 2010. "Aristophanes son of Johannes: An Eighth-Century Bilingual Scribe? A Study of Graphic Bilingualism." In *The Multilingual Experience in Egypt, from the Ptolemies to the Abbasids*, edited by A. Papaconstantinou, 221–232. Farnham.

Cromwell, J. 2012. "Following in Father's Footsteps: The Question of Father-Son Scribal Training in Eighth Century Thebes." In *Actes du 26e Congrès international de papyrologie. Genève, 16–21 août 2010*, edited by P. Schubert, 149–157. Geneva.

Crum, W. E. 1905. *Catalogue of the Coptic Manuscripts in the British Museum*. London.

Delattre, A. 2007. *Papyrus coptes et grecs du monastère d'apa Apollô de Baouît conservés aux Musées royaux d'Art et d'Histoire de Bruxelles*. Brussels.

Depuydt, L. 1993. *Catalogue of Coptic Manuscripts in the Pierpont Morgan Library*. 2 vols. Leuven.

Emmel, S. 1993. "Recent Progress in Coptic Codicology and Paleography (1988–1992)." In *Acts of the Fifth International Congress of Coptic Studies, Washington, 12–15 August 1992, Volume 1: Reports on Recent Research*, edited by T. Orlandi, 33–50. Rome.

Emmel, S. 1999. "Recent Progress in Coptic Codicology and Palaeography (1992–1996)." In *Ägypten und Nubien in spätantiker und christlicher Zeit: Akten des 6. Internationalen Koptologenkongresses, Münster, 20–26. Juli 1996*, 2 vols., edited by S. Emmel, M. Krause, S. G. Richter, and S. Schaten, 65–78. SKCO 6. Wiesbaden.

Emmel, S. 2004. *Shenoute's Literary Corpus*. CSCO 599–600, Subsidia 111–112. Leuven.

Fournet, J.-L. 2008. "P.Stras. V 318 complété: La grande *philoponia* d'Héracléopolis et les protocoles en cursive inclinée." In *Sixty-Five Papyrological Texts Presented to Klaas A. Worp on the Occasion of his 65th Birthday*, edited by F. A. J. Hoogendijk and B. P. Muhs, 243–253. PLB 33. Leiden.

Gardner, I., and M. Choat. 2004. "Towards a Palaeography of Fourth Century Documentary Coptic." In *Coptic Studies on the Treshold of a New Millennium II: Proceedings of the Seventh International Congress of Coptic Studies, Leiden 2000*, edited by M. Immerzeel and J. van der Vliet, 495–503. OLA 133. Leuven.

Garel, E. Forthcoming. *Héritage et transmission dans le monachisme égyptien. Les testaments des supérieurs du* topos *de Saint-Phoibammon à Thèbes*. Cairo.

Gilmore, G., and J. Ray. 2006. "A Fixed Point in Coptic Chronology: The Solar Eclipse of 10 March 601." *ZPE* 158:190–192.

Hyvernat, H. (1888) 1972. *Album de paléographie copte pour servir à l'introduction paléographique des Actes des Martyrs de l'Égypte* Paris. Reprint, Osnabrück.

Irigoin, J. 1959. "L'onciale grecque de type copte." *JÖBG* 9:29–51.

Jansma, N. S. H. 1973. *Ornements des manuscrits coptes du Monastère Blanc*. Groningen.

Kasser, R. 1960. *Papyrus Bodmer VI: Livre des Proverbes*. CSCO 194–195. Leuven.

Kasser, R. 1991a. "Djinkim." In *Coptic Encyclopedia*, 8 vols., edited by A. S. Atiya, 8:111–112, New York.

Kasser, R. 1991b. "Paleography." In *Coptic Encyclopedia*, 8 vols., edited by A. S. Atiya, 8:175–184. New York.

Layton, B. 1985. "Towards a new Coptic Palaeography." In *Acts of the Second International Congress of Coptic Studies, Roma, 22–26 September 1980*, edited by T. Orlandi and F. Wisse, 149–158. Rome.

Layton, B. 1987. *Catalogue of Coptic Literary Manuscripts in the British Library Acquired since the Year 1906*. London.

Layton, B. 2000. *A Coptic Grammar*. Wiesbaden.

MacCoull, L. S. B. 1997. "Dated and Datable Coptic Documentary Hands before A.D. 700." *Le Muséon* 110:349–366.

Mihálykó, Á. T. 2019. *The Christian Liturgical Papyri: An Introduction*. Tübingen.

Nakano, C. 2006. "Indices d'une chronologie relative des manuscrits coptes copiés à Toutôn." *JCoptS* 8:147–159.

Orsini, P. 2008. "La maiuscola biblica copta." *Segno e testo* 6:121–150.

Orsini, P. 2015. "I papiri Bodmer: Scritture e libri." *Adamantius* 21:60–78.

Orsini, P., and W. Clarysse. 2012. "Early New Testament Manuscripts and Their Dates: A Critique of Theological Palaeography." *ETL* 88(4): 443–474.

Polotsky, H.-J. 1949. "Une question d'orthographe bohaïrique." *BSAC* 12:25–35.

Quaegebeur, J. 1982. "De la préhistoire de l'écriture copte." *OLP* 13:125–136.

Satzinger, H. 1991. "Old Coptic." In *Coptic Encyclopedia*, 8 vols., edited by A. S. Atiya, 8:169–175. New York.

Stegemann, V. 1936. *Koptische Paläographie: 25 Tafeln zur Veranschaulichung der Schreibstile koptischer Schriftdenkmäler auf Papyrus, Pergament und Papier für die Zeit des III.-XIV. Jahrhunderts. Mit einem Versuch einer Stilgeschichte der koptischen Schrift.* Heidelberg.

Suciu, A. 2011. "À propos de la datation du manuscrit contenant le Grand Euchologe du Monastère Blanc." *Vigiliae Christianae* 65:189–198.

Suciu, A. 2014. "Coptic Scribes and Manuscripts: Dated and Datable Codices from the Monastery of Apa Shenoute, I: The Codices Inscribed by Victor, Son of Shenoute (First Half of the 12th Century." *JCoptS* 16:195–215.

Torallas Tovar, S. 2016. "Progress in Coptic Palaeography and Codicology (2004–2012)." In *Coptic Society, Literature and Religion from Late Antiquity to Modern Times: Proceedings of the Tenth International Congress of Coptic Studies, Rome, September 17th–22th, 2012 and Plenary Reports of the Ninth International Congress of Coptic Studies, Cairo, September 15th–19th, 2008*, edited by P. Buzi, A. Camplani, and F. Contardi, 431–456. OLA 247. Leuven.

Vanderheyden, L. 2012. "Les lettres coptes des archives de Dioscore d'Aphrodité." In *Actes du 26e Congrès international de papyrologie, Genève, 16–21 août 2010*, edited by P. Schubert, 793–799. Geneva.

Van Lantschoot, A. 1929. *Recueil des manuscrits chrétiens d'Égypte, Tome I: Les colophons des manuscrits sahidiques.* Leuven.

Zoëga, G. (1810) 1973. *Catalogus codicum Copticorum manu scriptorum qui in Museo Borgiano Velitris adservantur.* Rome. Reprint avec une introduction historique et des notes bibliographiques par J.-M. Sauget. Hildesheim.

CHAPTER IV.9

....

DIGITAL PALAEOGRAPHY
OF HIERATIC

....

SVENJA A. GÜLDEN, CELIA KRAUSE,
AND URSULA VERHOEVEN

HISTORY AND PRESENT STATE OF
RESEARCH AND METHODOLOGY

ATTEMPTS to transfer the signs of hieratic handwriting to a modern medium in order to easily reproduce and edit them originated in 1835, when the first font for hieratic characters was developed at the type foundry of the "Friedrich Nies'sche Buchdruckerei." Thirty years later, an improved font set was produced based on copies by Pleyte (1865) (Lüscher 2014, 74–75). But it was only during the twentieth century that questions were posed about (1) collecting the hieratic repertoire and (2) studying it for various purposes. Möller viewed the first three volumes of his *Hieratische Paläographie* ([1909–1912] 1927–1936) as a first step toward further studies on hieratic writing and was aware that the palaeographic lists with his handcopied facsimiles of signs would have to be constantly expanded and updated. His source material essentially consisted of thirty-two hieratic sources in literary hands (*Buchschrift*) that span a period of almost three thousand years. He omitted the documentary hands, whose forms steadily became more cursive over time, because he had planned to treat them separately. (On *Buchschrift* [uncial] as an almost calligraphic writing found on papyri, wood panels, and stone shards, as opposed to the smaller, more curtailed, and less ornate cursive or documentary hands [*Geschäftsschrift*], see Verhoeven 2001, 2–3.) Möller, however, died before he could realize his plan, and so his *Hieratische Paläographie* has remained the standard work that is widely used today.

In 1973, Posener (1973, 25–30) outlined not only the early history of *Hieratistik* (the science of hieratic) since Champollion, whose first hieratic palaeography appeared in 1824, but he also laid out the tasks for a future exploration of the hieratic script. In addition to a history of hieratic writing, studies on the arrangement of signs and their development, comparisons between hieratic and hieroglyphic signs, ligatures, and studies on the use of diacritical dots and dashes—to name just a few points listed by him—he also demanded a "nouveau Möller." A key feature of this was to record a manuscript's complete array of forms by enumerating the signs' different shapes, which should be arranged from the most simple to the most complex. It is not surprising that in the face of such requirements, and due to the continued lack of practical alternatives in handcopying and in print (see Polis chapter), a "nouveau Möller" has not yet been tackled. Instead, many individual palaeographies have arisen for particular periods or groups of sources. To meet Posener's demands and new research questions regarding cursive handwriting, a palaeography can now avail itself of digital techniques from which emerge new opportunities and also methodological and hermeneutical challenges (Gülden 2016).

The end of the twentieth century saw the first attempts at digital processing and analysis of hieratic manuscripts or palaeographies. On the basis of a standardized stroke sequence, Gosline (1999) attempted to systematically order every possible hieratic sign, ligature, or group writing and presented his study as a "font manual." (For a criticism, see van den Berg and Donker van Heel 2000, 9n2.) At the same time, Graefe (1999) developed a "program for the semi-automatic conversion of hieratic texts into hieroglyphs" ("Programm zur teilautomatischen Umsetzung hieratisch geschriebener Texte in Standardhieroglyphen").

Van den Berg and Donker van Heel (2000) were the first to make basic observations about the ability to transfer digital epigraphy to a digital palaeography of manuscripts. They presented different filter settings of image processing programs, which were not yet well known at that time. As a starting point for digital processing, they recommended that a portable object, such as a papyrus or ostracon, should ideally be directly scanned. Failing this, digitally created photographs or scans of photographs would be appropriate. Furthermore, they explained how a facsimile could be created through digital image processing and discussed the advantages of a vector-based format over bitmapped images as the foundation of a digital palaeography (van den Berg and Donker van Heel 2000, 39–42).

At the beginning of the twenty-first century, Quirke observed the change in working methods and reported on a project in which "computer-aided palaeography" was applied to the numerous papyri from Lahun. The approach to work changed over time: "Computing capacity here shifts from auxiliary 'computer-aided' to 'computer-enabled palaeography,'" and there was "a renewed focus on the aspect of numeracy" (Quirke 2010, 290). In addition, he explained the opportunities and new questions that a quantitative analysis allows in sociocultural terms. Ideally, however, experts should cooperate on digital and philological aspects, as well as on handwriting analysis: "These three roles could create out of quantitative and qualitative results a new agenda for understanding major changes beyond individual or collective intention" (Quirke 2010, 291).

Navrátilová described at length the steps of manual and digital documentation of hieratic graffiti and *dipinti*, such as secondary carved inscriptions and texts written in ink (Navrátilová 2015a, 309–316; 2015b, 253–261). The volume (Navrátilová 2015a), however, lacks corresponding pictures that one could compare and check against the printed, mostly digitally generated facsimiles. A palaeographic analysis was not done.

In Japan, Nagai created a database that digitally edited Papyrus Abbott according to lexicographical and palaeographical concerns. This Hieratic Database Project, however, is not yet publicly available (https://wdb.jinsha.tsukuba.ac.jp/hdb/about [August 15, 2016]).

Since 2015, the Mainz Academy project Altägyptische Kursivschriften (AKU) has been working on a digital palaeography, which should provide the basis for a systematic analysis of the various aspects of hieratic and cursive hieroglyphic script (https://aku. uni-mainz.de [August 15, 2016]). The project takes an interdisciplinary approach involving the cooperation of Egyptology and computational linguistics over the course of a lengthy time frame of twenty years. This arrangement will allow new trends in the digital humanities to be adopted and even, should the occasion arise, to influence working methods. Indispensable for such a project is the international exchange of information by specialized Egyptologists (Verhoeven 2015a, 2015b), as well as global cooperation in the creation of editions of handwritten manuscripts, in the extraction of the repertoire of signs and in the creation of the necessary digital data (vector paths). A very useful tool is the interdisciplinary portal of papyrological and epigraphic resources called Trismegistos (http://www.trismegistos.org; Gülden 2008), which digitally provides in database form the metadata for cursive written texts from the period 800 BCE to 400 CE. The AKU project intends to gradually complement that data for the older texts following the same model.

Outside of Egyptology, digital palaeography has made greater strides, which is largely due to the fact that the writings studied have been primarily alphabetic, which are closed repertoires with a relatively small number of different signs, namely, letters. In particular, various projects intensively studied medieval manuscripts and codices. Ciula (2005) first coined and defined the concept of "digital palaeography." This community is also aware of the issues and importance of communication between computer scientists and humanities scholars, especially palaeographers (Hassner et al. 2013).

Among the "big questions" of digital palaeography, Stokes (2015) remarked that digital processing, for example, provides statistical support for the work on finding joins and for the question of the diachronic aspect of the evolution of manuscripts. On the other hand, he points out to the difficulty that the generated data must always be identifiable and verifiable to the user or reader. It follows then that the visualization and the interface design of databases and other digital formats is of particular importance. The current discussion and reports on ongoing projects in various disciplines has taken place since 2008 in the online series "Codicology and Palaeography in the Digital Age" of the Kölner Institut für Dokumentologie und Editorik (http://www.i-d-e.de [August 15, 2016]).

Needs and Goals of a Digital Palaeography

In palaeographic research, discussions center on what digital methods can contribute to the understanding of the text production of literate cultures of the past. Everyone agrees that digital collections of historical writing surfaces should not just provide readily available substitutes for the original documents. Instead, they should be semantically analyzed by machines and ideally emerge as components of a global web portal, which unites diverse functionalities for scientists who work in palaeography.

Palaeography in the broadest sense includes the study of all aspects of surviving handwritings: materiality; size (of the characters themselves, the text, and the writing surface); objects and writing surfaces; manufacture and trade of portable writing surfaces; the localities involved in manufacture and trade; writing instruments and ink; posture; techniques and habits of writing; calligraphic versus economic (abbreviated) writing; speed of writing; writers, readers, and their sociocultural background; the shape and development of scripts and of individual signs; the combination and reciprocal influence of scripts (hieratic, abnormal hieratic, Demotic); orthographies; layout using lines or columns; bustrophedic writing; stichic writing; spacing, headings, and punctuation; the use of recto and verso in writing and rotation of the writing surface; corrections and comments; paratextual signs; vignettes and text-image based combinations. Significant points of research include the fragmentation of manuscripts and their joins or reconstructions and the possibilities for identifying writing hands and for assigning a date and place of origin to written sources. An evaluation using digital technologies, especially if they can be combined with statistical methods, can ideally provide answers to all of these questions based on qualitative and quantitative analyses (Verhoeven 2015b, 48–54).

In its narrower sense, the term "palaeography" represents the analysis of the individual signs that are usually compared with one another in tables. With such lists, signs can be first identified and when compared with other documents, can be given a relative date and a possible place of origin. The capabilities of a digital palaeography—in the form of a database—exceed this scope of research. It should not only save and display the signs recorded in a digital repository, but also allow the digital analysis and statistical evaluation of the signs. In addition, the data should be processed so that the digital copies of signs enriched with metadata can also be analyzed using digital methods in other future contexts external to the database.

Such digital palaeography is therefore, on the one hand, a dynamic archive for the sign repertoires of different source groups, gradually covering different eras, genres, and regions, and it is expandable and flexible. On the other hand, it is a versatile research tool because of the description, classification, and encoding of signs. The advantages of digital over traditional or analog palaeography will be explained in what follows.

Representation of Signs

The manner in which the hieratogram (on this term, see Verhoeven 2001, 1) is represented in a digital palaeography is flexible. Side by side, one can use: (1) excerpts from a scan of the original text including surrounding signs and the surface of the writing material; (2) a facsimile of the sign completely filled in with black, as in most traditional palaeographies; and (3) a facsimile that outlines individual strokes to indicate the stroke order.

The forms of hieroglyphs that are juxtaposed with the hieratograms should not be limited to the standardized forms of Gardiner's sign list. Rather, the hieratograms should also be compared with contemporary examples of hieroglyphs to visualize the characteristics of the shape.

Description of Signs

The single sign itself can be fully described in a palaeography database in terms of the following parameters: materiality, size, color, arrangement, morphology, stroke order, usual form or variant, function, and context. For the signs' form description (i.e., shape and style; Stokes 2011), it is recommended that neutral terms, which can be structured hierarchically in the form of a thesaurus, and a standardized and controlled vocabulary be used.

Examples of generalized descriptions are terms like the ones that Gardiner used in his sign list (i.e., tall, narrow signs or low, broad signs). The detailed description should consist of at least two elements. The first element includes the sign orientation (horizontal, vertical, diagonal) and the organization of lines (simple, complex, parallel, crossed, etc.). Also, the characteristic form would be established (closed, open, jagged, etc.). The second element of the detailed description contains an addition to the characteristic form and indicates its position. This second element can be freely combined with the first element of description, and describes the sign in greater complexity and detail.

These sign descriptions allow an initial analysis of intact signs and also help the user to identify heavily damaged hieratograms. At the same time, the metadata about the written source (materiality, dating, origin, location, genre, writer, script and language used, state of preservation, design and layout features, etc.) can be directly linked with the individual signs.

Sign Lists and the Encoding of Signs

Earlier palaeographies were mainly structured so that each hieratogram was attributed to a particular hieroglyph, and the latter have been categorized and sorted according to the state of research on what they represent. Möller mostly arranged the hieroglyphs in his palaeography on the 1875 sign list published by Theinhardt, but made some adjustments (Möller [1909–1912] 1927–1936, 71–74). Today, palaeographies are generally based on the sign list that Gardiner created for the first time in 1927 (Gardiner 1973, 438–548). Not all hieratograms, however, find a hieroglyphic counterpart in Gardiner's sign list, and in more recently published palaeographies new individual numberings were assigned. A digital palaeography offers the advantage that all numbering systems are collected in a concordance. They can be expanded and are searchable according to the user's own requirements. In addition and in order to avoid discrepancies between hieroglyphic and hieratic, a new classification of signs should be developed that focuses specifically on the sign repertoire and the spectrum of shapes in hieratic, and it should be used in conjunction with other numbering systems. An encoding that is currently being developed by the project Altägyptische Kursivschriften (Akademie der Wissenschaften und der Literatur | Mainz) reflects the classification of a sign and consists of three elements that identify a form in ever greater degree:

- the main sign,
- the form class (full form or abbreviation, each with regular form or variant), and
- the use in a sign group or ligature.

Contextualization of Signs

A digital palaeography provides the critical function of documenting and visualizing the recorded sign in its context and position on the writing surface (Figure IV.9.1). The association of a sign to the digitized version of the writing surface can be easily set up so that views of the manuscript, the column, and the group, among other things are facilitated.

FIGURE IV.9.1. Digital photograph of dipinto TN18 from Tomb N13.1 in Asyut in Middle Egypt (© Fritz Barthel) with digital outline drawing as overlay (© Svenja A. Gülden; Ursula Verhoeven).

Search Options

Unlike a static, printed palaeography, a digital palaeography can very agilely collect, analyze, and then visualize data about signs according to an individual research question. The query options are numerous, and possible searches include sign lists that consider

- a very limited time frame, but different writing surfaces,
- a specific writing surface (of a certain material), which is attributable to a specific genre and covers a large timeframe,
- a particular sign over a long period of time regardless of writing surface and genre in order to track the range and development of the sign,
- the display of signs with a similar shape, for example, to make a detailed study of the range and development of shapes either independently of or dependent on their specific importance in the context of a word.

For a statistical analysis of palaeographic data, metrics are of primary interest. These include among other things number of columns, number of lines, number of signs per line, number of strokes per sign, the frequency of dipping by the writer, and sign frequency in the text. From the dimensions of the size of the sign, proportions are calculated, such as the ratio of the height and width of individual sign shapes ("*modulus*": Stokes 2009, 313). In this way, similarities and differences in handwritings can be measured and calculated.

For users who prefer the traditional display of palaeographic lists to an individual database query, partial palaeographies can be exported from the database by the use of prebuilt queries, for example, for a specific period, genre, or writing surface, and made available for download. With regular updates of the data, newly entered texts can be incorporated into the existing list.

Visualization Options

Due to the storage and management of big data, care must be given to how search results are visualized. The list form of traditional palaeographies will in principle be retained, but the arrangement of parameters may vary, or completely different schemes may be used. For instance, the regional and temporal development of signs can be displayed by using a geobrowser: an application that allows spatial visualization of the data in point size/point clouds or other formats. Also, the variance, size, shape, frequency, or morphology of hieratic signs can be displayed more interactively and flexibly in digital formats than in print media, for example, by network visualization and cluster analysis (e.g., a scatter diagram with a point cloud). Interestingly, the connection with the digital reproduction of the writing surface can also happen, for example, when displaying lettering sequences, writing layers, or spelling variations of different hands. Components of the text can be directly selected and highlighted in the digital copy. In addition, descriptive data can be displayed together with the writing elements. Data generated in the course of automatic character recognition (e.g., distances between the characteristic parameters of vectors) can, via visualizations of multidimensional matrices, inform about a change of hands within a text. Yet these are only some types of visual analysis that are possible with palaeographic data. In the future, these options are expected to grow exponentially.

Requirements for a Digital Analysis

The repertoire of signs and the metadata in a palaeographic database not only must be representative for certain periods, regions, genres, and so forth, but also must meet certain conditions in order to allow for meaningful analysis. Writing sources should be of different types and materials, so they should include papyri, linen, wood, stone, ceramics, and so on. They should comprise portable and fixed surfaces (e.g., ostraca versus graffiti or dipinti), and moreover should represent different genres. Particularly meaningful, of course, are written sources, which are dated precisely and independently of the manuscript. While these are requirements for all, including traditional, palaeographical works, digital and statistical analyses furthermore demand a unified data format. It is not yet clear which format is the most suitable because the methods for digital analysis of cursive signs are rapidly developing. It is therefore recommended that signs be digitized from the beginning in multiple file formats (vector- and pixel-based) in order to try out different techniques and programs and, if necessary, to change along with the technology. For example, vector images can be used in the future for the development of new digital techniques for automated similarity searches, while automated pattern recognition requires pixel-based formats.

If a written source has not yet been studied palaeographically, the optimal starting point is digitally drawn facsimiles based on high-resolution photos or scans of the original text in a 1:1 ratio. The signs can then be extracted from the facsimile as individual files and stored in different formats (e.g., as .eps, .svg, .tif, and .png). For a mathematical and technical analysis, vector illustrations (.eps and .svg) are particularly suitable because the vector paths in the XML code, which are stored for vector graphics (Figure IV.9.2), describe the outlines of the signs in a mathematically precise manner. Outwardly similar signs can be found in the database by comparing these paths. The height and width of the signs are recorded in the XML source code as well, and can be converted to millimeters via a formula. The measurements can then be immediately defined and saved when signs are imported into the database.

XML (Extensible Markup Language) is a formal markup language that is extensible at will, through which, for instance, text phenomena can be semantically described and made evaluable by a computer. Therefore, the source code can be enriched with other elements, such as the palaeographical phenomena described in the database. Since 1987, the Text Encoding Initiative (TEI) has made available guidelines for such coding

```xml
<?xml version="1.0" encoding="utf-8"?>
<!-- Generator: Adobe Illustrator 16.0.0, SVG Export Plug-In . SVG Version: 6.00 Build 0)  -->
<!DOCTYPE svg PUBLIC "-//W3C//DTD SVG 1.1//EN" "http://www.w3.org/Graphics/SVG/1.1/DTD/svg11.dtd">
<svg version="1.1" id="Ebene_1" xmlns:x="&ns_extend;" xmlns:i="&ns_ai;" xmlns:graph="&ns_graphs;"
	 xmlns="http://www.w3.org/2000/svg" xmlns:xlink="http://www.w3.org/1999/xlink" x="0px" y="0px"
	 width="50.043px" height="29.552px" viewBox="0 0 50.043 29.552" enable-background="new 0 0 50.043 29.552" xml:space="preserve">
<switch>
	<foreignObject requiredExtensions="&ns_ai;" x="0" y="0" width="1" height="1">
		<i:pgfRef xlink:href="#adobe_illustrator_pgf">
		</i:pgfRef>
	</foreignObject>
	<g i:extraneous="self">
		<path fill="#1E1E1C" stroke="#1B181C" stroke-width="0.15" d="M5.452,10.883c0.08-1.092,0.088-2.185-0.088-3.267
			C5.302,7.238,5.254,6.93,5.272,6.539c0.017-0.369,0.064-0.84-0.148-1.167c-0.326-0.501-1.46-0.708-1.979-0.542
			C2.303,5.1,1.714,5.811,1.721,6.678c0.005,0.511,0.1,0.021,0.1,1.532c0.764-0.084,1.502-0.083,2.256
			c0.001,0.741,0.057,1.512-0.019,2.248c-0.062,0.609-0.099,1.225-0.167,1.833c-0.044,0.39-0.001,0.787-0.068,1.173
			c-0.056,0.322-0.216,0.654-0.167,0.99c0.03,0.211,0.113,0.486,0.186,0.686c0.229,0.63,0.819,1.113,1.298,1.507
			c0.356,0.294,0.753,0.628,1.186,0.731c0.338,0.08,0.84-0.003,1.156-0.103c0.108-0.507-0.229-0.95-0.323-1.401
			c-0.126-0.602-0.015-1.463,0.082-2.061c0.038-0.234,0.129-0.395,0.17-0.623c0.041-0.231,0.066-0.479,0.086-0.713
			C5.165,13.465,5.358,12.174,5.452,10.883z"/>
		<path fill="..."/>
		<path fill="..."/>
		<path fill="..."/>

	</g>
</switch>
```

FIGURE IV.9.2. Digitalization of a hieratogram with attached XML code. © Svenja A. Gülden.

(http://www.tei-c.org/Guidelines/P5/ [August 15, 2016]). In particular, the TEI module "Characters, Glyphs, and Writing Modes" (http://www.tei-c.org/release/doc/tei-p5-doc/de/html/WD.html [August 15, 2016]) and the subset Epidoc created by epigraphers (http://www.stoa.org/epidoc/gl/latest/[August 15, 2016]) are worth considering for the phenomena of script and handwriting. These guidelines have been designed, however, for text encoding and still need to be developed for the description of nonalphabetical characters and systems.

Another method of digital analysis of hieratic could be the extraction of signs from a pixel-based digital copy. Unlike a vector image, the underlying sign is not mathematically described, and other techniques must be used for analysis. The so-called content-based image retrieval enables the user of a database to display synoptically several samples of similar looking signs by selecting one sign image (a so-called snippet). This has already been used for "Exploring, Analysing and Categorising" medieval manuscripts (Cloppet et al. 2012, sec. 25–26).

PERSPECTIVES

The automated locating and identifying of signs and sign sequences in handwritten texts correspond approximately to the decipherment done by palaeographers. The starting points of such processes are the digital images of writing surfaces that exist as raster graphics. The graphics must first be subjected to a complicated preprocessing, which generally involves calibrating the image's color and size, eliminating noise, and binarizing color values with subsequent segmentation, that is, separating the writing from the background, for example, in lines and single words. Then special algorithms that recognize patterns are developed for the feature extraction (Cloppet et al. 2012, sec. 5–10), where the recognizable shapes are compared with an inventory of signs. In image processing, the optical character recognition (OCR) method is the most advanced for printed works because the characters produced by printing types generally do not have great variance. Research into the recognition of letters in handwritten documents is still ongoing (e.g., Aparna and Muthumani 2014). Methods similar to those of OCR are now being used for the recognition of scribal hands in medieval manuscripts (Fecker, Märgner, and Schaßan 2015). With automated character recognition, it is generally a matter of matching prominent points (or patterns) of characters, such as key points, outlines/curves, and texture, in separate parts of the image scans against each other so that the computer can "read" this. The software used must be individually trained for the process with specimens of writing of the best possible quality. In this connection, so-called classifiers are usually used to summarize the characteristics of certain image features into categories. On hieratic papyri, handwriting recognition has so far been tested only sporadically (Quirke 2010, 289–290). The extraction and categorization of features is furthermore used for the identification and measurement of text and image fields in handwritten documents (the analysis of layout).

Another task would be the allocation of signs or entire manuscripts to individual scribal hands in ancient Egyptian handwritings. Niels (2010) already discussed handwriting recognition programs (especially DTW: Dynamic Time Warping) used in forensic science. The focus was on both the identification of a written character and in particular the unambiguous assignment of one or more documents to a person. Not only has he tested sources in the Latin alphabet (e.g., English) but also the program was used for other "pen-based" fonts, such as Chinese, Arabic, Tamil, and also symbols and pictograms.

Conclusion

The digitized version of a handwritten document forms, in all cases, the basis for software-based, automated systematic analyses. The capabilities of these methods have been growing, and the development of appropriate applications and tools is an ongoing process.

A digitally operated palaeography uses computer-based methods, which support the practiced eye of palaeographers and can make a meaningful addition to the detailed study of the physical writing surface. The great advantage of these quantitative methods is in quickly detecting signs and loading and analyzing large amounts of material. Results that were previously obtained from small self-contained source groups can be reexamined by processing a broader corpus. Also, a comparative approach can be taken, where one consults additional corpora to make further points of comparison.

Certain questions regarding the materiality of historical objects can still only be verified by the examination of the three-dimensional original. This is particularly true for studies of individual objects. Digital tools, however, can provide palaeographers with a way to ask structural questions about the material and to check established knowledge against a wider set of data.

Bibliography

Aparna, A., and I. Muthumani. 2014. "Optical Character Recognition for Handwritten Cursive English Characters." *IJCSIT* 5 (1):847–848.

Berg, H. van den, and K. Donker van Heel. 2000. "A Scribe's Cache from the Valley of the Queens? The Palaeography of Documents from Deir el-Medina: Some Remarks." In *Deir el-Medina in the Third Millenium A.D.*, edited by R. J. Demarée and A. Egberts, 9–49. EU 14. Leiden.

Ciula, A. 2005. "Digital Palaeography: Using the Digital Representation of Medieval Script to Support Palaeographic Analysis." *Digital Medievalist* 1. doi:10.16995/dm.4.

Cloppet, F., H. Daher, V. Églin, H. Emptoz, M. Exbrayat, et al. 2012. "New Tools for Exploring, Analysing and Categorising Medieval Scripts." *Digital Medievalist* 7. doi:10.16995/dm.44.

Fecker, D., V. Märgner, and T. Schaßan. 2015. "Vom Zeichen zur Schrift: Mit Mustererkennung zur automatisierten Schreiberhanderkennung in mittelalterlichen und frühneuzeitlichen Handschriften." In *Grenzen und Möglichkeiten der Digital Humanities*, edited by C. Baum and T. Stäcker. Sonderband der Zeitschrift für digitale Geisteswissenschaften, Wolfenbüttel₁. doi:10.17175/sb001_008.

Gardiner, A. H. 1973. *Egyptian Grammar*. 3rd ed. London.

Gosline, S. L. 1999. *Introductory Late Egyptian*. Hieratic Paleography 1. Warren Center, Pa.

Graefe, E. 1999. "Projekt eines Programms zur teilautomatischen Umsetzung Hieratisch geschriebener Texte in Standardhieroglyphen und Erfassung von Texten in Transkription inklusive Zeichencode." In *Textcorpus und Wörterbuch: Aspekte zur ägyptischen Lexikographie*, edited by S. Grunert and I. Hafemann, 229–234. PdÄ 14. Leiden.

Gülden, S. A. 2008. "*Trismegistos*: An Interdisciplinary Portal of Papyrological and Epigraphical Resources." In *Information Technology and Egyptology in 2008, Proceedings of the meeting of the Computer Working Group of the International Association of Egyptologists (Informatique et Egyptologie), Vienna, 8–11 July 2008*, edited by N. Strudwick, 17–28. Bible in Technology 2. Piscataway.

Gülden, S. A. 2016 "Ein 'nouveau Möller'? Grenzen und Möglichkeiten. Ein (working) paper zum gleichnamigen Vortrag." Hieratic Studies Online 1, Mainz. http://nbn-resolving.de/urn:nbn:de:hebis:77-publ-557584.

Hassner, T., M. Rehbein, P. A. Stokes, and L. Wolf. 2013. "Computation and Palaeography: Potentials and Limits (Dagstuhl Perspectives Workshop 12382)." *Dagstuhl Reports* 2 (9):184–199. doi:10.4230/DagRep.2.9.184.

Lüscher, B. 2014. *Auf den Spuren von Edouard Naville: Beiträge und Materialien zur Wissenschaftsgeschichte des Totenbuches*. TbT Supplementa 1. Basel.

Möller, G. (1909–1912) 1927–1936. *Hieratische Paläographie: Die Aegyptische Buchschrift in ihrer Entwicklung von der fünften Dynastie bis zur Römischen Kaiserzeit*. 3 vols. Reprint, Leipzig.

Navrátilová, H. 2015a. *Visitors' Graffiti of Dynasties 18 and 19 in Abusir and Northern Saqqara*. 2nd ed. Wallasey.

Navrátilová, H. 2015b. "Records of Hieratic Graffiti in Dahshur and the Use of Graffiti in the Study of New Kingdom Hieratic." In *Ägyptologische "Binsen"-Weisheiten I–II. Neue Forschungen und Methoden der Hieratistik. Akten zweier Tagungen in Mainz im April 2011 und März 2013*, edited by U. Verhoeven, 249–270. AAWLM 14. Stuttgart. http://nbn-resolving.de/urn:nbn:de:hebis:77-publ-547544

Niels, R. M. J. 2010. *Allograph Based Writer Identification, Handwriting Analysis and Character Recognition*. Enschede.

Pleyte, W. 1865. *Catalogue raisonné de types égyptiens hiératiques de la fonderie de N. Tetterode, à Amsterdam*. Leiden.

Posener, G. 1973. "L'écriture hiératique." In *Textes et langages de l'Egypte pharaonique, cent cinquante années de recherches, 1822–1972*, vol. 1, edited by S. Sauneron, 25–30. BdE 64. Cairo.

Quirke, S. 2010. "Agendas for Digital Palaeography in an Archaeological Context: Egypt 1800 BC." In *Kodikologie und Paläographie im digitalen Zeitalter*, vol. 2, edited by F. Fischer, C. Fritze, and G. Vogeler, 279–294. SIDE 3. Norderstedt.

Stokes, P. A. 2009. "Computer-Aided Palaeography, Present and Future." In *Kodikologie und Paläographie im digitalen Zeitalter*, edited by M. Rehbein, P. Sahle, and T. Schaßan, 310–388. SIDE 2. Norderstedt.

Stokes, P. A. 2011. *Describing Handwriting*. London. Working paper. http://www.digipal.eu/blog/describing-handwriting-part-i/.

Stokes, P. A. 2015. "Digital Approaches to Paleography and Book History: Some Challenges, Present and Future." *Frontiers in Digital Humanities* 2(5). doi:10.3389/fdigh.2015.00005.

Verhoeven, U. 2001. *Untersuchungen zur späthieratischen Buchschrift*. OLA 99. Leuven.

Verhoeven, U., ed. 2015a. *Ägyptologische "Binsen"-Weisheiten I–II. Neue Forschungen und Methoden der Hieratistik. Akten zweier Tagungen in Mainz im April 2011 und März 2013.* AAWLM 14. Stuttgart. http://nbn-resolving.de/urn:nbn:de:hebis:77-publ-547544.

Verhoeven, U. 2015. "Stand und Aufgaben der Erforschung des Hieratischen und der Kursivhieroglyphen." In *Ägyptologische "Binsen"-Weisheiten I–II. Neue Forschungen und Methoden der Hieratistik. Akten zweier Tagungen in Mainz im April 2011 und März 2013,* edited by U. Verhoeven, 23–63. AAWLM 14. Stuttgart. http://nbn-resolving.de/urn:nbn:de:hebis:77-publ-547544.

HIERATIC PALAEOGRAPHY IN LITERARY AND DOCUMENTARY TEXTS FROM DEIR EL-MEDINA

HANS-WERNER FISCHER-ELFERT

DEIR EL-MEDINA AS A HOT SPOT OF HIERATIC DOCUMENTATION IN THE LATE NEW KINGDOM

THE village of Deir el-Medina, founded by Thutmose I, is situated in a valley west of Gurnet Murai and south of the Valley of Deir el-Bahri. Its inhabitants were responsible for the construction of royal tombs in the Valleys of the Kings and Queens in the New Kingdom.

Famous for a large number of private tombs, chapels, small temples, and particularly for the settlement itself, Deir el-Medina is also best known for its unmatched amount of written documentation. Apart from hieroglyphic inscriptions particularly in its tombs and chapels, it is especially a huge number of hieratic documents on papyri, ostraca, and other writing materials that is of capital interest in this contribution. Ostraca on potsherds as well as on limestone flakes rank first in terms of their sheer number. The Institute français d'archéologie orientale alone hosts about 13,000 pieces of which 873 literary ones and 1,275 administrative items have been published since the beginning of French excavations on this spot in 1917, amounting to about 16 percent. Mention should also be made of 568 pieces in the Museo Egizio in Turin, deriving from

Ernesto Schiaparelli's excavations in the Valley of the Queens and Deir el-Medina in the early twentieth century. These ostraca have a more or less well-documented findspot, whereas many hundred other ones and published in different catalogs derive from the antiquities' market and private collections with no documentation of their provenance whatsoever. From this circumstance follows that there is quite a substantial number of hieratic ostraca of the late New Kingdom whose provenance is very likely to be Deir el-Medina or its neighborhood, but in which cases we have no means of ascertaining if this really was their findspot. With regard to hieratic papyri, we are lucky to know, for example, the precise ancient spot of the so-called Chester Beatty papyri. Taken as a whole, the corpus as established by now ranges from the Nineteenth to the early Twenty-first Dynasty, with the Eighteenth Dynasty remaining entirely a *terra incognita* in our documentation.

In terms of the history of academic research on any of these hieratic sources it is to be deplored that there is still no Deir el-Medina hieratic palaeography covering all different types of cursive as well as semi-cursive *ductus* (< Lat. *ducere*—"to guide"; Rollston 2009, 5: "number, order, and direction of strokes"). A ductus as part of the characteristics of individual handwriting can be described as "includ[ing] the direction, sequencing, and speed with which the strokes making up a character are drawn" (wikipedia.org, accessed August 16, 2016). Such a comprehensive palaeography would cover a substantial amount of hieratic material from just one particular place and its close neighborhood over a limited period of time, that is, from around the middle of the thirteenth to the eleventh century BCE.

Today, we are still working with Georg Möller's one-hundred-year-old *Hieratische Paläographie I–III* (1909–1912). Due to mere chance, the first edition of his work appeared in those very years when Möller started excavating in Deir el-Medina himself on behalf of the Berlin Ägyptisches Museum und Papyrussammlung (1911). He was "on the hunt" particularly for hieratic texts, which he eventually found in two different areas of the settlement, but whose palaeography could not yet find its way into the second volume of his *Hieratische Paläographie*. Most of the pieces found their way into the collection of the Berlin Museum, some were lost during World War II.

There is also a certain scholarly preference to be observed in dealing with Deir el-Medina hieratic texts when it comes to their palaeographical aspects. Administrative texts like letters, contracts, deliveries of rations, juridical statements, and so forth (see "Nature of the Evidence") are typically treated and have been the focus of looking for the individual scribe responsible for their inscription (see "Regional and Individual Styles"). This approach has never been applied to literary and religious specimens from the same area on a systematic basis. Chances may be quite high in this field too, since many a literary copy is "signed" with the name of the very scrivener who produced it. For that very reason, this chapter tries to confront both segments with one another in order to cover as much as possible of the palaeographic phenomenology of this place and period.

NATURE OF THE EVIDENCE

The range of genres written in hieratic and semi-hieratic at Deir el-Medina, the Valleys of the Kings and Queens, and, for example, the archive discovered in front of the *Deutsches Haus*, west of the Ramesseum, still remains unmatched compared to any other place dating from the New Kingdom. Memphis-Saqqara, Amarna, and Abydos, for example, have supplied similar evidence from roughly the same period, but none of these areas can compete with the Theban settlement in terms of number and scope of hieratic texts and writing styles. The documentary evidence has recently been analyzed by Donker van Heel and Haring (2003) and Eyre (2013, 233–252), and the literary plus religious corpus was scrutinized by Mathieu (2003).

As the term "hieratic" implies more cursive sign forms, derived from pictorial hieroglyphs, we encounter a broad range of abbreviations, reductions, and ligatures of separate signs as well as of combinations or, even better, fusions of signs into a single group of strokes. The Ramesside Period in general can be regarded as the second peak of extreme cursivization, next to many documents from Twelfth and Thirteenth Dynasty el-Lahun and some administrative documents from Second Intermediate Period Thebes, such as P. Boulaq XVIII.

This style of writing is limited to documentary texts, and it is very likely to assume an official license behind this habit: Scribes will have been allowed to write their documents that very way. This rule, on the other hand, does not apply to literary or, for example, magical texts, with many exceptions to the rule telling their own story (see "A Documentary Privilege?"). Genres like narratives, teachings, love songs, hymns and prayers, next to incantations, were usually inscribed in a much less abbreviated and ligatured ductus.

Returning to administrative documents composed outside Deir el-Medina like grain accounts listing harvest produced on royal or temple domains as, for example, plots endowed by god's wives (*dwȝ.t-nṯr*), field cadasters, and revenue texts, we encounter an interesting habit: Scribes writing the headlines of their entries, mentioning, for example, the royal founder of the domains in question, practice a rather calligraphic style of writing with signs significantly taller than the ones in the following account entries. An example gives the name of the domain in bold hieratic signs leaning to the left (line 8), followed by extremely cursive entries (lines 9–14) with signs leaning to the right (Table IV.10.1.1).

Apparently the degree of cursivization was dependent on the degree of sacredness of institutions when directly connected to, for example, kings, princes, and gods' wives mentioned by title and name in rather mundane or secular accounts with no religious content whatsoever. As soon as it comes to noting down plots themselves, their location, and the names of the cultivators in charge of them, for example, the scribes switch to their most extreme abbreviations. One way of accounting for this feature in transcription is, for example, Gardiner's different size of hieroglyphic signs in his transcriptions (1948):

Table IV.10.1. Some Examples of Hieratic Writing from Deir el-Medina

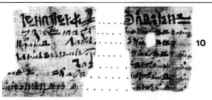

1. P. Louvre AF 6345 and Griffith Fragments recto. © Musée du Louvre/Christian Décamps

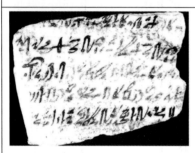

2. O.Nicholson Museum Sydney R. 97 (after Ray 2006, pl. 39; © Nicholson Museum Sydney)

3. O.Nicholson Museum Sydney R. 97, line5 © Nicholson Museum Sydney

4. O. Berlin P 14262 verso (after Burkard 2013, 69, fig. 5.1; © Ägyptisches Museum &
Papyrussammlung, Staatliche Museen zu Berlin, SPK. Photographer: Sandra Steiß)

5. Amennakht's signature in O. Berlin P.14262 verso (© Ägyptisches Museum &
Papyrussammlung, Staatliche Museen zu Berlin, SPK. Photographer: Sandra Steiß)

6. Part of a hymn from year 2 Ramesses V with Amennakht's signature in the antepenultimate line (O. Turin CG 57002 verso; © Museo Egizio di Torino)

7. Partial copy of *Satire on Trades* as copied by Neferhotep (II) (lines1–6 = P. Sallier II 11.1–5 and lines 8–12 = P. Sallier II 10.7–11.1 after Posener1934: O. DeM 1014 col. IIpl. 10a; col. I only in transcription; © IFAO)

8. Part of *Satire on Trades* as copied by Itnefer (P. Sallier II 6.1–3 after Posener1934, O. DeM 1022 col. II, pl. 14a; © IFAO)

9. Part of *Satire on Trades* as copied by Itnefer (P. Sallier II 4.4–6 after Posener 1936, O.DeM 1042 col. II, pl. 23*a*; © IFAO)

10. Beginning of the *Hymn to the Inundation* by Itnefer (after Posener 1934, O. DeM 1027 recto = outside & verso, pl. 16*a*; © IFAO)

11. Hymn and prayer as copied by the necropolis scribe Hori (O. Berlin P. 10844; © Ägyptisches Museum & Papyrussammlung, Staatliche Museen zu Berlin, SPK. Photographer: Sandra Steiß)

Signs done in calligraphic style are much taller, more vertical, and with less ligatures than the ones in the entries following their headlines. In Gardiner's transcription, their size is bigger than the ones in the entries attached to them respectively. In so doing, the modern reader of the sourcebook gets a rough idea of the innertextual graphemic divergence in terms of its two styles of hieratic used by one and the same scribe. It is absolutely unlikely to assume two individual scribes taking turns with every new section of such a document (for the switch from one scribe to another within one text column, see Janssen 2000, 55). Instead, this habit displays the fact that scribes destined to work as clerks, for instance, in the administration of grain accounts and field registers must have been trained to practice their hieratic in a twofold way: calligraphically and cursively. Calligraphy or the so-called *Kanzleischrift* ($\approx$ chancery script) has much in common with the average and contemporary literary style, a feature that would deserve more scholarly attention.

In contrast to representing different styles of hieratic in a single document by differentiating the size of signs in one's own transcription as done by Gardiner, ligatures have, to the best of the present writer's knowledge, never been highlighted in transcriptions in any way. Thus, by just looking at a transcription, without taking recourse to the original or to a high-resolution photograph, the modern interpreter lacks a significant pool of information on the material and aesthetic qualities of the manuscript in front of him/her. Highlighting even different shades of ink on the papyrus in a publication, next to counting individual strokes (= ductus) making up just one sign, locating the scribe's ink dippings, and so forth, belongs to the highest standards of modern edition techniques (Allen 2002, 81–85).

Ligatures and abbreviations quite frequently are problematic in terms of their precise transcriptions. Much is left to the individual scholar's personal experience and preferences. Some diagnostic problems were settled by Gardiner (1929). The problem remains always the same: How to transcribe a certain sign or sign-group according to what hieroglyphic equivalent? Do we have contemporary hieroglyphic equivalents in any single case, is hieratic advanced in its system of spellings and sign forms compared to its hieroglyphic pendant? Why does it use one pot as a determinative when another hieroglyph would be suitable? Is it more archaic or traditional as soon as applied to classical poems? This is but a small range of questions that have to be addressed in future studies on styles, ductus, and the overall palaeography of hieratic in general.

REGIONAL AND INDIVIDUAL STYLES

The Ramesside Period offers a sound basis for differentiating regional and individual styles of cursive writing. These differences may find their explanation in varying ways of teaching hieratic either at school or by private education. Egypt, at that period, is not very likely to have followed a nationwide curriculum.

Theban: Memphite Ductus

The palaeographic differentiation between an Upper and a Lower Egyptian style of hieratic in Ramesside times was discovered and first described by Samuel Birch (1876), followed in more detail by Adolf Erman (1903) and shortly after by Georg Möller (1909–1912, Vorwort, with further references). By looking at the texts on P. Harris I (BM EA 9999), Erman and Möller differentiated three different scribes, one originating from Heliopolis, the second from Memphis, and the final one displaying a Theban style. More recently, this approach was extended and refined by Pierre Grandet (1994, I:23–26). He also differentiates three individual scribes (see also von Bomhard 1998, 10–14, claiming four individual hands in P. Wilbour [reign Ramesses V]).

The general and methodological problem with this regional approach is the fact that most of the Ramesside hieratic papyri attributed a so-called Memphite or Lower Egyptian origin do not have any reliable archaeological provenance and documentation. Modern acquisition of hieratic manuscripts on the antiquities' market in or close to Memphis does not tell anything about their actual findspot, let alone about the exact place of their inscription, unless any internal evidence is available. The same rule applies to those assumed to display a Theban ductus without any archaeological record at hand.

Was There a Special Deir el-Medina Ductus?

Irrespective of these problems we have to ask if ever there was a specific Deir el-Medina style of hieratic writing. Since the settlement and its administration from the outside was part and parcel of the Theban nome in general and Karnak Temple administration in particular as well as Medinet Habu at the end of the Ramesside Period, it seems very unlikely to have developed such a local writing style. We have no means of telling precisely where any of the Deir el-Medina scribes were trained since there is no archaeological evidence of anything like a school building on this spot or in its immediate neighborhood (but see Gasse 2000). They may have been trained at the *école* discovered in the precinct of the Ramesseum by the French Mission (Leblanc 2004), but some, if not most, of them are very likely to have been educated by their own fathers or colleagues of their fathers instead. Amennakht (V), son of Ipuy, and his colleague Hori, scribe of the tomb, are a case in point as discovered by Bickel and Mathieu (1993), for which see the following section. They seem to have trained the sons of their peers crossways, perhaps expecting them to finish "one chapter a day" (Fischer-Elfert 1994).

Individual Hands

Identifying individual scribal hands is also closely connected to Deir el-Medina, and it is still being pursued on a broad scale. In stark contrast to older archives and libraries with hieratic texts of whatever genre, the Deir el-Medina-corpus in many cases offers the opportunity of attaching individual names to their scribblings.

A Documentary Privilege?

Subscriptions or colophons as they occur beneath the end of literary copies refer to only one single manuscript in every single case, and there is no way of attributing any other manuscript of the same period to the same scribe with 100 percent certainty (see, however, von Bomhard 1999). In Deir el-Medina, at least, we are on much safer ground, and in the meantime, we know quite a number of local scribes by their names and personal hands, in some cases even over a long period of time. Any of these identifications refer in the first instance to administrative, not to literary, manuscripts.

Before we take a brief look at such individual hands, mention should be made of the fact that theoretically there are two different kinds of identifying scribal idiosyncrasies:

1. There are those hands that may be attributed to scribes of the village known by their personal names and sometimes even by their filiation.
2. There are those hands that may be attributed anonymously only, without the possibility (yet) to precisely identify those scribes in our record.

Here is a—preliminary—list of those scribes that have either been identified by name as the copyist of certain texts (1) or to whom a number of copies can be attributed due to characteristic idiosyncrasies, but without accompanying personal signature (2):

(1):
Qenherkhepshef
Maanakhtef (iii and iv)
Amennakht (V)
Nakhtsobek
Djehutimose and Butehamun
(2):
Wennefer(?)
Late Nineteenth Dynasty ostraca from Siptah

Due to lack of space we cannot dedicate our attention to every single hand of this period that has been identified. Instead, we briefly consider only the case of Amennakht (V), son of Ipuy (*floruit* year 16 Ramesses III–year 4 Ramesses V), whose career is attested for about twenty-five years and whose hieratic displays some changes over this period of time (Dorn 2015). In addition to that, he is a splendid example of a scribe having been trained in practising at least three different types of contemporary hieratic, that is, the administrative, the *Kanzleischrift*, and the literary cursive.

The major difference between these three manifestations of hieratic may be described as follows:

- The administrative cursive is characterized by its rather small size of individual signs and ligatures, a high degree of abbreviation, the latter mainly concentrating on the "inner part" of words. Their initial as well as their final signs—determinatives in many cases—are kept more elaborate (e.g., the spelling of the word *hrw* "day" in P. DeM 34 V l. 15, Černý 1986, Pl. 24/*a*).

This habit may have been deemed necessary in order to facilitate separation and thus guarantee the identifiability of words while reading a text. Amennakht's copy (Table IV.10.1.2), which is a text about grain, and so forth, can be dated to the end of Ramesses III and early Ramesses IV. Dorn (2015, 194) would exclude it from his list of Amennakht's handcopies, which cannot be discussed here. A close-up shows his title plus name, albeit not his signature (Table IV.10.1.3).

- *Kanzleischrift* ≈ chancery script, characterized briefly in "Nature of the Evidence," earlier, may count as an offshoot of the literary style proper or as a subliterary style. In terms of its frequency, however, it does not carry too much weight.
- This rule does not apply to the literary cursive, as its signs on average are much taller, more calligraphic, less often ligatured, and in many cases much closer to their hieroglyphic correspondents. If done by a well-experienced hand, this habit helps modern readers in transcribing texts. An example is found in Amennakht's copy of a hitherto unknown religious composition as inscribed on O. Berlin P. 14262 verso (Table IV.10.1.4). This copy cannot be dated with any degree of certainty within this scribe's *floruit*. A close-up of his signature appears in the bottom line (Table IV.10.1.5). Dorn (2015) was able to discern a development of Amennakht's handwriting over the twenty-five years we can follow him in our documentation.

A general feature, not only of Amennakht's personal style, is the availability of different shapes of one and the same sign at the same time. Thus, a scribe may choose from this range of sign forms, and Dorn (2015, 181–185), for example, turns particular attention to two divergent forms of the *mn+n*-group in Amennakht's copies (Dorn 2015, 199 Abb. 9). This example represents an extremely cursive ligature of the group *mn+n*, which makes it look like a sign of its own.

A much more hieroglyphic and less ligatured form of the same group also practiced quite often by Amennakht (V) are the specimens culled from the recto and verso of O. Gardiner 25 and distributed over its two individual literary texts (Dorn 2015, 190 Tab. 1). In some places, our scribe prefers a ligature (recto 10 and perhaps in verso 8). Please mind the additional dot on top of the *mn*-sign in recto 1, which even adds to his choice or preference and for which there exists no diacritical need. In that case, it would have differentiated the group from a similar or even identical one. Diacritical traits like dots and hooks are quite common in hieratic, but do not come into general use until the Ramesside Period.

A feature displayed in O. Gardiner 25 may indicate the existence of different ways of teaching how to write and read hieratic properly in Ramesside Deir el-Medina, granting scribes at times a license to draw on whatever shape of sign or sign-group they would wish to produce. It will have to be tested, if this license applies to the copying process of literary texts as well, but with regard to administrative documents, Janssen's observations remain valid: "Obviously, the range of possibilities within the handwriting of an individual is fairly wide. Exactly how wide in a specific case can be determined only by looking at the way he usually formed his signs, for instance, whether he connected them by refraining from lifting his brush. But it is only the consistency of such a habit that is decisive: a single deviation proves nothing" (Janssen 2000, 156).

At this point, we should mention a very useful classification of different kinds of variation within the phenomenology and development or history of a personal handwriting as exemplified on a broad material basis by Berg and Donker van Heel (2000, 11–39, esp. 15), adapted from Janssen's approach (2000). A "free variation" (Eyre 1979, 86–87) or "incidental variation" (Janssen 2000, 52) may be identified within the body of writing of one and the same scribe, whereas a "principal variation" would point to a change of scribe within one and the same document. Janssen's test case (2004, with notes on 9–10) was the style and palaeography of the reunited P. Amiens+P. Baldwin from the second half of the Twentieth Dynasty. From a methodological point of view, he claims to identify diagnostic groups of signs or entire words, not just separate signs, occurring more than once in the text under study.

Along with the scope of variations, another important terminological aspect Janssen refers to is the change from a more "classical" style of hieratic to a more "cursive" one. It should be added that the classical style is phenomenologically closer to the contemporary literary style of hieratic, whereas a literary copy in a blunt administrative handwriting is difficult to identify. Administrative documents on the one hand and literary and religious texts on the other may have been attributed different degrees of sacredness, determining their style of writing. We will see that sometimes even palaeography in terms of the (alleged or real) age of the text copied determines the style of the Ramesside copyist. As always, exceptions to this rule are known, particularly from the field of magical incantations. A scribe writing a spell in a very cursive way may have been working under time constraints with the patient desperately waiting for the spell and ritual to be performed, and he may just as well have missed the proper attitude toward writing such a text in a more appropriate or "sacred" way.

Up to this point, we have only been discussing personal styles of Ramesside administrative hieratic from Deir el-Medina and beyond, trying to identify idiosyncrasies of scribes known by name or remaining anonymous due to lack of signatures below their copies. What is still missing is the palaeographic specificity of Deir el-Medina documents in terms of the overall place of this settlement's hieratic phenomenology between earlier New Kingdom and post–New Kingdom hieratic.

There exist only small samples of individual palaeographies of a limited number of documentary texts (one of the best is von Bomhard 1998 on P. Wilbour). The corpus of fifty-four late Ramesside letters and communications would be a representative and homogeneous assemblage of texts dating from roughly the same period and community of scribes.

Identifiable Hands in the Literary Corpus

There is no such palaeography of the Deir el-Medina literary corpus as published by now (Gasse 1992, 56–70; 2000), nor has any research on idiosyncrasies of individual, and at best identifiable, hands been done. This branch of hieratic studies is still in its infancy.

Once we extend the term "literary" to religious or magical texts, mention must be made of the palaeography by Giuseppina Lenzo of a corpus of Ramesside magical papyri, very likely to have come from somewhere in or around Deir el-Medina and preserved in the Museo Egizio in Turin, published in transcription and translation in Alessandro Roccati (2011, 195–251). Since this volume unfortunately does not include photographs, the palaeography cannot yet be checked against the originals.

The only corpus of visitors' *dipinti* supplied with a palaeography of its own still remains Megally's selection of 142 out of about 500 Ramesside hieratic inscriptions in black and blue(!) ink on the columns of the Thutmose III temple in Deir el-Bahri (Marciniak 1974, 173–266). With due respect to his quite voluminous palaeographic section, one may question the necessity of presenting every single reed leaf, owl, or water line. His transcriptions, however, are to be taken with caution and the attached photographs defy verification of his handcopies in many cases. What is needed is a diagnostic and representative selection of signs and sign-groups out of the overall phenomenology the corpus in question displays.

Literary texts in terms of narratives, teachings (in the Twentieth Dynasty also in letter form), hymns, prayers, and love songs, for example, usually display a nonadministrative style of hieratic. This means taller and on average clearly identifiable signs, a much lower degree of "cursivization", a tendency to avoiding ligatures of more than two signs wherever possible. Punctuation by means of usually placing red dots above the line at the end of metrical verses or parts of verses had become typical for literary copies since the end of the Twelfth Dynasty, without, however, ever becoming an absolute must. Exceptions to this rule are literary copies without any such dots or, on the other hand, administrative texts like official letters displaying them. In the latter case, those texts may have been used as epistolographic training for future scribes.

Copying literary texts along the lines of their appropriate hieratic style as characterized thus far is a trait of poems older than the Ramesside Period itself. "Classics" like the story of *Sinuhe*, teachings like those of king *Amenemhat I, Satire on Trades, Man for His Son*, and *Kairsu* rank highest on the Deir el-Medina "bestseller" list. *Ptahhotep* is represented by four manuscripts, three of which are potsherd ostraca with a more or less well-documented archaeological provenance plus three more or less joining papyrus fragments of a once perhaps complete copy of the teaching (Hagen 2012, 182–187).

McDowell (2000) lists fifteen literary ostraca with colophons having once named teacher and assistant, with some of the copyists' name now lost, four of which carry copies of the *Kemyt* in semi-hieratic or cursive-hieroglyphic. This offshoot of the Egyptian script displays the least similarity with cursive hieratic, and it is for this reason that these two styles cannot be compared with one another.

The time range for these kinds of literary copies in and around Deir el-Medina is "often difficult or impossible" to fix, but it "must fall within the main period of (literary) activity at that site, i.e. between the second half of the Nineteenth and the first half of the Twentieth Dynasty" (Hagen 2012, 72). In the Twentieth Dynasty, hieratic starts to be used for genuine compositions like the teachings of Amennakht (V), son of Ipuy, and his colleague Hori, scribe of the tomb, to name but these two examples. Both individuals are known from nonliterary sources, as we have seen earlier. The literary scene at Deir el-Medina is a mix of *re-productive* activity in terms of copying poems particularly from the Middle Kingdom, as it is *productive* in terms of new compositions created by some of its members trained and active in the scribal profession. The hieratic style of the copies of their own compositions differs in no way from that of the contemporary administrative cursive. A specimen of Amennakht's copy of a hymn with no classical precursor, most likely composed by the writer himself, has nothing particularly literary about the writing style (Table IV.10.1.6).

A typical literary hand is to be observed with O. DeM 1014 col. II (Table IV.10.1.7), representing a partial copy of *Satire on Trades*, dedicated by the apprentice scribe Neferhetep (II) to his master scribe/chief workman Nebnefer (I) (for both men and this dedication, see McDowell 2000, 226). Line 6–7 has the dedication styled in a rather clumsy, if not even archaizing, hieratic: *iw=s-pw• nfr <m>-ḥtp• [...] zḥꜣ Nb-nfr• ḥry-ꜥ=f Nfr-ḥtp•* "It has come well and <in> peace [...] scribe Nebnefer, his assistant Neferhetep." Fellow colleagues would have raised their eyebrows had they been sent a real missive letter by Neferhetep in this kind of cursive script.

Another scribe known from both documentary material (O. Cairo CG 25559 for which see Dorn 2011, 85) as well as copies of classical literary poems is Itnefer, son of Hor-[...], who had his *floruit* during the reigns of Ramesses IV–VI (McDowell 2000, 227–228; Dorn 2006, 78n34; 2011, 48–49, 85, 160, 162; O. 703, 704 [two exercises in the art of letter writing]). He copied stanzas of the *Hymn to Inundation* (O. DeM 1027) and two other ones from the *Satire on Trades* (O. DeM 1022, O. DeM 1042). Due to only one authentic administrative text signed by him, we can hardly compare his literary hieratic style with the one he practiced officially, as on O. Cairo CG 25559 (Černý 1935, pl. 29).

An example of a partial copy of the *Satire on Trades* by Itnefer (Table IV.10.1.8) displays a style of literary hieratic slightly different from the one on O. DeM 1042 done by the same scribe (Table IV.10.1.9), followed by his excerpt from the *Hymn to the Inundation* on O. DeM 1027 (Table IV.10.1.10).

The latest addition to this small corpus of Deir el-Medina scribes producing and copying literary compositions is O. Berlin P. 10844 by the hand of the necropolis scribe Hori (Burkard 2014). Due to a missing filiation, his precise identification remains problematic, but there is some likelihood to identify him with the individual acting as author of a brief teaching as preserved on O. Gardiner 2 rt. (Bickel and Mathieu 1993, 49–51). In that case, he would be the teacher of one of Amennakht's sons. Hori's *floruit* extended over the reigns of Ramesses III to number XI of that name (Donker van Heel and Haring 2003, 39–48; Table IV.10.1.11).

Even though the sheer volume of text is rather limited, the signs are executed very elegantly, attesting to a well-experienced scribe with a good sense of writing aesthetics. Hori did not copy this very personal hymn and prayer—Burkard (2014) can quote no parallel for the text as a whole—in the old-fashioned style like Neferhetep (II) did on O. DeM 1014 with his excerpt of the *Satire on Trades*. Instead, he concentrated on separate and elaborate sign forms.

As a rule, it seems quite likely that there was an unwritten rule in Deir el-Medina scribal training to make one's personal choice on four different hieratic palaeographies. He was expected to either draw on the palaeography typical of a classical poem (1.), a "modern" literary composition, (2.), a mundane or documentary text, (3.) or on a palaeography typical for entries or sections naming, for example, individuals of royal blood (4.):

1. In the first case, the copy would represent a more or less archaizing style of pre–New Kingdom hieratic (Table IV.10.1.7);
2. In the second case, it would look like Hori's hymn, Amennakht's teaching or hymns on kings, and so forth, with rather tall and elaborate signs and a limited number of ligatures and abbreviations (see also a partial copy of Amennakht's teaching by a student of his in Dorn 2011, No. 732, Taf. 637–638; see Table IV.10.1.11);
3. Administrative documents enjoyed a much higher degree of cursivization and speed in writing them down (e.g., Table IV.10.1.1, lines 9–14);
4. No. 3 was only to be circumvented when it came to taking down a royal protocol, the "royal" name of a plot of land, and so forth. In that case, scribes took recourse to the so-called *Kanzleischrift* or chancery style (Table IV.10.1.1, line 8).

The palaeography of Deir el-Medina hieratic—and certainly everywhere else in the country—demonstrates a broad gamut of styles dependent on what genre was to be put down into writing and who the addressee was.

Conclusion

Hieratic material from Ramesside Deir el-Medina proper, the Valleys of the Kings and Queens, and the Ramesseum is abundant, and thousands of texts still remain to be edited. In view of the ones that have been published and commented on already over the past one hundred years, it is to be noted that no comprehensive palaeography of the range of styles is yet available. Instead, scholars have focused very much on individual hands, and the reason for this is quite obvious. The spot is—next to el-Lahun of the Twelfth and Thirteenth Dynasties—the first one with such a high number of individuals known as active scribes in the administration of the Royal Tomb (*pȝ-ḫr*) from the Nineteenth to the early Twenty-first Dynasties, thus prior to the so-called Late Period. This very "personal"—if not even "private"—aspect attached to the hieratic corpus in its documentary as in its literary segments is, quite understandably, highly attractive for academic research. We will have to wait for another five hundred years until the Twenty-sixth Dynasty when entire families of Theban scribes writing first either abnormal hieratic and then switching to early Demotic from one generation to the next pop up in our documentation (see chapter by Gülden et al.).

BIBLIOGRAPHY

Allen, J. P. 2002. *The Heqanakht Papyri*. PMMA 27. New York.

Berg, H. van den, and K. Donker van Heel. 2000. "A Scribe's Cache from the Valley of Queens? The Palaeography of Documents from Deir el-Medina: Some Remarks." In *Deir el-Medina in the Third Millennium AD: A Tribute to Jac. J. Janssen*, edited by R. J. Demarée and A. Egberts, 9–49. EU 14. Leiden.

Bickel, S., and B. Mathieu. 1993. "L'écrivain Amennakht et son *Enseignement*." BIFAO 93:31–51.

Birch, S. 1876. *Facsimile of an Egyptian Hieratic Papyrus of the Reign of Rameses III, Now in the British Museum*. London.

Bomhard, A. S. von. 1998. *Paléographie du Papyrus Wilbour: L'écriture hiératique cursive dans les papyri documentaires*. Paris.

Burkard, G. 2013. "Amunnakht, Scribe and Poet of Deir el-Medina: A Study of Ostracon O Berlin P 14262." In *Ancient Egyptian Literature: Theory and Practice*, edited by R. Enmarch and V. M. Lepper, 65–82. Oxford.

Burkard, G. 2014. "Ostrakon Berlin P 10844: Hymnus und Gebet an Amun aus der Feder des Nekropolenschreibers Hori." In *"Vom Leben umfangen": Ägypten, das Alte Testament und das Gespräch der Religionen: Gedenkschrift für Manfred Görg*, edited by S. Wimmer and G. Gafus, 211–218. ÄAT 80. Münster.

Černý, J. 1935. *Ostraca hiératiques*. CG 25501–25,832. Cairo.

Černý, J. 1986. *Papyrus hiératiques de Deir el-Médineh, Tome II (nos XVIII–XXXIV])*. Edited by Y. Koenig. DFIFAO 22. Cairo.

Donker van Heel, K., and B. J. J. Haring. 2003. *Writing in a Workmens Village: Scribal Practice in Ramesside Deir el-Medina*. EU 16. Leiden.

Dorn, A. 2006. "MAA-nxt.w=f, ein (?) einfacher Arbeiter schreibt Briefe." *Living and Writing in Deir el-Medine: Socio-Historical Embodiment of Deir el-Medine Texts*, edited by A. Dorn and T. Hofmann, 67–85. AH 19. Basel.

Dorn, A. 2011. *Arbeiterhütten im Tal der Könige: ein Beitrag zur altägyptischen Sozialgeschichte aufgrund von neuem Quellenmaterial aus der Mitte der 20. Dynastie (ca. 1150 v. Chr.)*. 3 vols. AH 23. Basel.

Dorn, A. 2015. "Diachrone Veränderungen der Handschrift des Nekropolenschreibers Amunnacht, Sohn des Ipu." In *Ägyptologische "Binsen"-Weisheiten I–II. Neue Forschungen und Methoden der Hieratistik. Akten zweier Tagungen in Mainz im April 2011 und März 2013*, edited by U. Verhoeven, 175–218. AAWLM 14. Stuttgart.

Erman, A. 1903. "Zur Erklärung des Papyrus Harris." *SPAW* 21:456–474.

Eyre, C. J. 1979. "A 'strike' text from the Theban necropolis." In *Glimpses of Ancient Egypt: Studies in Honour of H. W. Fairman*, edited by J. Ruffle, 80–91. Warminster.

Eyre, C. J. 2013. *The Use of Documents in Pharaonic Egypt*. Oxford.

Fischer-Elfert, H.-W. 1994. "Vermischtes III." *GM* 143:41–49.

Gardiner, A. H. 1929. "The Transcription of New Kingdom Hieratic." *JEA* 15:48–55.

Gardiner, A. H. 1948. *Ramesside Administrative Documents*. Oxford.

Gasse, A. 1992. "Les ostraca hiératiques littéraires de Deir el-Medina: Nouvelles orientations de la publication." In *Village Voices: Proceedings of the Symposium "Texts from Deir el-Medina and Their Interpretation," Leiden, May 31–June 1, 1991*, edited by R. J. Demarée and A. Egberts, 51–70. Leiden.

Gasse, A. 2000. "Le K2, un cas d'école?" In *Deir el-Medina in the Third Millennium AD: A Tribute to Jac. J. Janssen*, edited by R. J. Demarée and A. Egberts, 9–49. EU 14. Leiden.

Grandet, P. 1994. *Le Papyrus Harris I (BM 9999)*. 2 vols. BdE 109. Cairo.

Hagen, F. 2012. *An Ancient Egyptian Literary Text in Context: The Instruction of Ptahhotep*. OLA 218. Leuven.

Janssen, J. J. 2000. "Idiosyncrasies in Late Ramesside Hieratic Writing." *JEA* 86:51–56.

Leblanc, C. 2004. "L'école du temple (ât-sebaït) et le *per-ankh* (maison de vie): À propos de récentes découvertes effectuées dans le contexte du Ramesseum." *Memnonia* 15:93–101.

Marciniak, M. 1974. *Deir el-Bahari I: Les inscriptions hiératiques du Temple de Thoutmosis III*. Warsaw.

Mathieu, B. 2003. "La littérature égyptienne sous les Ramsès d'après les ostraca littéraires de Deir el-Médineh." In *Deir el-Médineh et la Vallée des Rois: La vie en Egypte au temps des pharaons du Nouvel Empire: Actes du colloque organisé par le Musée du Louvre, les 3 et 4 mai 2002*, edited by G. Andreu, 117–137. Paris.

McDowell, A. 2000. "Teachers and Students at Deir el-Medina." In *Deir el-Medina in the Third Millennium AD: A Tribute to Jac. J. Janssen*, edited by R. J. Demarée and A. Egberts, 217–233. EU 14. Leiden.

Möller, G. 1909–1912. *Hieratische Paläographie: Die ägyptische Buchschrift in ihrer Entwicklung von der fünften Dynastie bis zur römischen Kaiserzeit*. 3 vols. Leipzig.

Ray, J. 2006. "Inscriptions and Ostraca in the Nicholson Museum: Hieroglyphic, Hieratic, Demotic and Carian." In *Egyptian Art in the Nicholson Museum, Sydney*, edited by K. N. Sowada and B. G. Ockinga, 211–224. Sydney.

Roccati, A. 2011. *Magica taurinensia: Il grande papiro magico di Torino e i suoi duplicati*. AnOr 56. Rome.

Rollston, C. 2009. *Writing and Literacy in the World of Ancient Israel: Epigraphic Evidence from the Iron Age*. ABS 11. Atlanta.

INDEX

....

Note: Tables and figures are indicated by an italic "*t*" and "*f*" following the page number.